THE COMPLETE
ILLUSTRATED
ENCYCLOPEDIA
of
PLANTS &
FLOWERS

THE COMPLETE ILLUSTRATED ENCYCLOPEDIA

of

PLANTS & FLOWERS

General Editor: David Joyce

EBURY PRESS
LONDON

Chief consultant	DAVID JOYCE
Consultants	SUE FISHER
	STIRLING MACOBOY
	ROGER MANN
	IAN PERCY
	TONY RODD

Writers

Text

Your Garden	Roger Mann
Annuals & Perennials	Dalys Newman
	Robin Simon
Shrubs	Peter Lavelle
	Dalys Newman
Trees	Henry Barrkman
	Heather Jackson
Bulbs, Corms & Tubers	Heather Jackson
	Julie Silk
Lawns, Ground Covers & Ornamental Grasses	Heather Jackson
	Robin Simon
Vegetables & Herbs	Gina Schien (*vegetables*)
	Denise Grieg (*herbs*)
	Heather Jackson
Fruit Trees, Nut Trees & Other Fruits	Heather Jackson
	Gina Schien
Indoor Plants	Heather Jackson
	Marnie Roper
Climbers & Creepers	Denise Grieg
	Heather Jackson
Chapter Introductions	Roger Mann
	Judy Moore

Field Trips
Andy Clements (*Dochu La*); John Forlonge (*Magallanes Region*); Maurie Kellett (*Fortin de las Flores*); John Manning (*Darling and Malmesbury*); Kristo Pienaar (*Cape Floral Kingdom*); Graeme Platt (*Coromandel Peninsula*); Julie Silk (*Blue Mountains, Mount Kinabalu, Norfolk Island*); Paul Sterry (*Grindelwald, Lundy*); Angus Stewart (*Guadalupe Mountains National Park*)

First published in 1994

1 3 5 7 9 10 8 6 4 2

Text copyright © Random House (Australia) Pty Ltd 1994, 1995

Photography copyright © with individual photographers as listed below 1994, 1995

First published in the United Kingdom in 1995 by Ebury Press, Random House, 20 Vauxhall Bridge Road, London SW1V 2SA

Random House Australia (Pty) Limited
20 Alfred Street, Milsons Point, Sydney,
New South Wales 2061, Australia

Random House New Zealand Limited
18 Poland Road, Glenfield,
Auckland 10, New Zealand

Random House South Africa (Pty) Limited
PO Box 337, Bergvlei, South Africa
Random House UK Reg. No. 954009

A CIP catalogue record for this book is available from the British Library.

ISBN 009 180957 6

General Editor: David Joyce

Managing Editors: Margaret Olds, Lisa Foulis

Senior Editor: Marie-Louise Taylor

Copy Editors: Deb Brown, Susan Page, Stephanie Campion, Kate Etherington, Margaret McAllister, Marnie Roper, Dawn Cockle, Heather Jackson, James Young

Art Director: Stan Lamond

Designer: Joy Eckermann

Maps: Stan Lamond

Typeset by Jan Greenville, Leonie Draper

Colour Separations by Pica Colour Separation Overseas Pte Ltd

Printed and Bound in Singapore by Tien Wah Press (Pte) Ltd

Photographers: Ardea (London), Tony Bomford, Geoff Bryant, Brinsley Burbidge, Claver Carroll, Andy Clements, Densey Clyne, Tony Curry, John Forlonge, Denise Grieg, Joanne Van Gruisen, Sarah Guesi, Ivy Hansen, Joy Harland, James Hyett (ARPS), Maurice Kellet, Stirling Macoboy, Brett McKay, Leo Meier, Geoff Moon, Kristo Pienaar, Gordon Roberts, Tony Rodd, Lorna Rose, Paul Sterry, Oliver Strewe, Ben Wallace, Gerry Whitmont, Brent Wilson, Australian Picture Library, Random House Picture Library

Page 1: Hanging baskets on lamp posts make a colourful display

Page 2: Rose bushes interplanted with columbines (*Aquilegia*) and other old-fashioned flowers

Page 5: The romance and beauty of old roses (Gil Hanly)

Pages 8–9: A lush, cool-climate garden (Gil Hanly)

Contents

CHAPTER 1

Your Garden

Everything You Need to Know to Plan,
Develop and Maintain Your Garden

We walk in a world of our own creation; and the pleasures of the gardens we create are many and lasting. True, the flower fades, the perfect tomato is brought to the table and is no more: but tomorrow there will be new flowers, other fruit; still the sunshine will sparkle on the lawn; the newly dug earth gives its sweet smell, rich with promise; and as the years and seasons pass, the garden matures in beauty. In our hectic and alienated times, what price an activity that brings us back in touch with the slow rhythms of nature?

But first we must begin its creation. A beautiful garden grows out of the interaction between the site, the climate, the soil, and the needs and desires of its owner; and there are as many ways to bring these together as there are gardeners. There is no 'right' way to make a garden—there is only the one that works best for you.

PLANNING THE GARDEN

Design for living

Most of us make our garden on the land about our house, and it augments the house's living space. Thinking about how you (and your family) want to live in your garden is as good a starting point for planning as any. Do you want a place for children to play, to sunbathe, to entertain friends at a barbecue, or to sit in the cool of a summer evening with a cool drink? Would you like a swimming pool? Do you need a place to wash the car, to hang out the washing, to hide the rubbish bin, or to make a compost heap? Do you want a place to grow vegetables and fruit or to produce a succession of flowers for cutting? Do you need a shed, or can tools, the lawnmower, portable garden furniture and what have you be kept in the garage? How important is privacy to you?

Think, if you like, in terms of 'garden rooms', remembering, however, that 'rooms' in a garden need not have the clearly defined functions that those in a house normally do. A sunny lawn can serve just as well for the children to throw a ball as it can for adults to relax; and if

you have a party, guests can wander out on to it and sit on the grass. On the other hand, the feet of chairs and tables tend to sink into grass if it is soggy from rain, and you may find yourself wishing for a paved area—a terrace, patio, call it what you will. Paving can get uncomfortably hot in summer, so this suggests the patio should be shaded: but you will probably want the winter sun, so you start thinking in terms of deciduous trees or of vines on pergolas. The patio probably should link up in some easy way with the living rooms, and in turn open out on to the lawn; perhaps it is the spot to display choice flowers or a piece of sculpture … or should the flowers or the sculpture go at the other side of the lawn to draw people out to admire them? Before you know it, a design for a garden room is taking shape …

Planning for the sun and shade

If you can arrange a balance of sun and shade, you have the option of sitting in either, and you gain a greater choice of plants you can grow. But shade doesn't stay in one place—the sun moves

Vine-covered arbors, favourite sitting places since the days of the Romans, are still an effective way to link house with garden.

around all the time. It moves daily from east to west of course; but it also shifts with the seasons, being higher in the sky in summer than in winter. So the pool of shade cast by a tree, for instance, is larger in winter than in summer—and a corner behind the shed may get sun in summer but not in winter.

It is a general rule that (in the northern hemisphere) the south side of the house is the sunny one, and the north is in the shade of the house itself. An area of garden with a south-facing aspect is an obvious choice for features that demand plenty of sun. It is the sort of place for a patio or terrace, although you may want to erect a lightly framed pergola so that you create sunny and shady areas. Full sun is what you need for a successful vegetable and fruit garden. Other features that are best in full sun are ornamental pools and swimming pools.

When you are planting consider the effect on the inside of the house as well as on the garden. Evergreen trees and large shrubs planted close to windows will cut out light all year round and may make rooms seem gloomy and dank. Even deciduous trees with heavy foliage can make rooms sombre during the summer months. In cool temperate regions it is probably wiser to rely on architectural features—such as cornices, eaves and verandahs—or curtains and shutters rather than plants to keep rooms cool during irregular periods of intense summer heat. Plants close to the house do help, though, to make the air seem fresh. For this purpose, you will find that climbers are among the most useful.

The garden's microclimate

One of the surprising discoveries made by many gardeners is that conditions in their own gardens can be markedly different from those of near neighbours. The microclimate takes time to assess and can be influenced by a wide range of factors. A relatively small difference in height above sea level can affect the length of the growing season, not to mention exposure to wind. On the other hand, a position in the lee of a small hill can be sheltered from prevailing winds, giving a garden an advantage over another close by. Differences in position on a slope can be critical. In a dip or in a position where a solid wall prevents cold air draining away there may be a frost pocket, resulting in a slow start to

A spot for outdoor living amidst lush greenery, the brightly painted walls adding colour.

growth in spring. A position under a sunny wall, however, is likely to provide much warmer conditions than can be found elsewhere in the garden, making it the best place for plants of marginal hardiness or for fruit that needs sun to ripen. The fact that you cannot appreciate the microclimate of your garden immediately is one very good reason for taking time when drawing up plans for its development.

Wind

Say 'windbreak' and most people immediately think of the rows of Lombardy poplars or pines that are used in open

Climbers can provide much-needed shade.

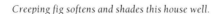

Creeping fig softens and shades this house well.

An inviting white summer house stands out against varied greens.

A modern interpretation of formal style.

ever you deal with the problem, the answer will be a compromise between view and shelter—but in gardening, as in life, compromises can often have the happiest results.

Privacy

How much privacy you need in the garden is a matter of temperament; some people like more seclusion than others. A new garden is apt to be dominated by fences and the neighbours' houses, but before you rush to surround yourself with dense growth like Sleeping Beauty in the fairy tale, take a careful look. Ignore the fence for a moment—you can mask it with creepers and shrubs—and concentrate on the neighbours' houses. If you arrange some trees or tall shrubs to mask these from your view, leaving the skyline open elsewhere, will that be sufficient?

It can be difficult to visualize how this is going to look; try taking some snapshots and sketching some foliage on them to get an idea how much cover you'll need. (This can be a good way of visualizing any changes you propose to the garden—and before-and-after pictures of the garden are well worth the effort of taking.)

Front gardens

The siting of a house on a plot of land generally creates two areas of garden: a relatively public area in front of the house, and a more private zone behind that is usually the centre of a family's outdoor activities. The front garden is basically a threshold to your property, a link between the street and the front door, and it is difficult, therefore, to make it intimate and private. It may be possible to screen a section using hedges or fences to make a front patio, at the same time blocking the view into front rooms from the street. However, there is still the need to have access to the house, and that really can't be forbidden to the person who comes to read the meters let alone your invited guests. You do need to have a clear path from the entrance to the front door, and to ensure it is well lit at night.

The front yard is the scene of the visitor's first and last impressions. Also it is neighbourly to have a garden that looks pleasing from the street and you will want to show off the architecture of the house to advantage. If you are a keen gardener, you may seize the opportunity

country. If you have a country garden you'll probably be thinking of belts of large trees. In the suburbs there is unlikely to be room for them, and so you'll be thinking of shrubs, small trees, and maybe fences and trellises. Nonetheless, you will want to screen the garden from the cold winds of winter and the desiccating winds of summer. Suitable shelter will make the garden a more pleasant place to be as well as reducing water loss and the risk of physical damage to plants. Trees and shrubs are more effective than structures for the purpose. If the wind hits a wall it just rebounds and comes down with renewed force, but foliage filters the wind and gives you shelter for a distance down-

wind about eight times the height of the planting. In a hot climate, you can use greenery as an air-conditioner simply by turning a sprinkler on it, converting a hot dry breeze into a gentle cool one.

Not all wind is undesirable. Light breezes are refreshing. Futhermore, a garden in which air circulates freely provides a healthier environment for plants than one where the air is still. Fungal diseases can present a serious problem where the air is stagnant. With a new garden observe wind patterns carefully before planting shelter belts and hedges or erecting fences and walls. The local geography can have surprising effects on prevailing winds. At the seaside, strong wind off the sea is a major factor in garden-making, but seaside gardens are a special case and we will look at them later.

Aligning a garden on a wonderful view can present a problem if it exposes it to the prevailing wind. Perhaps the best way to deal with it is to use fairly open-growing trees as light shelter that will help to break the wind without obscuring the view completely. Another solution is to group plants so that they frame segments of the view, the way a photographer arranges interesting things in the foreground of a picture. By using deciduous trees you will at least have the view in winter, although this may well be when winds are at their fiercest. How-

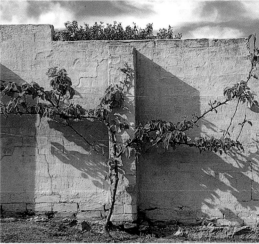

Detail counts: here, the fence and gate match the period colour scheme of the house, and the garden.

A cherry tree trained espalier to soften a wall.

Town gardens needn't be uninteresting.

to show off your skills. But on the other hand you may not want to spend a high proportion of your gardening time on an area you don't use much yourself and you may opt for a low maintenance design. It's up to you, but a word to the wise: in these days of high crime, it isn't a good idea to shroud the front of your house too much in greenery or with high fences. Burglars appreciate privacy too!

Town gardens

Town gardens have a unique charm. In a harsh, man-made environment they are a reminder, of the beauty of the natural world. More often than not they are miniscule, small pockets squeezed between buildings. However, their ornamental and restorative value is out of all proportion to their size. In a condensed form their colours, scents and sounds give many of the pleasures of a large garden, even though plants may often have to be grown in containers.

In some ways, a city garden is the ideal for busy people—there isn't room to overindulge in gardening! But a confined space does call for some editing of the wish list—you just can't include all the activities or all the plants you might want. The answer is to develop the garden as a living room; think of it as a courtyard and pave most of it—a garden that is all patio, in fact (the Spanish word

'patio' originally meant a paved court-yard garden just like this).

The walls and fences can be clad with climbing plants or with trained shrubs. If space allows, you might be able to contrive a pocket-handkerchief-sized lawn; but city conditions are against it. Surrounding buildings often block the sun, and few lawn grasses like shade. Chances are you'll wear the grass out underfoot anyway; and where are you going to store the lawnmower?

Creating a feeling of privacy is often the most difficult problem in town gardens, which will almost certainly be overlooked by neighbouring buildings. Like you, your neighbours will value some kind of screening. Extending walls and fences with trelliswork to support climbing plants is one solution. Pergolas carrying a drapery of plants can also be effective. Trees can also serve the same purpose but a specimen large enough to be useful will create a lot of shade, limiting the way the garden can be used as a leisure area and restricting the range of plants that can be grown satisfactorily in it. Furthermore, the roots of large trees can damage the foundations of a building or block drains.

Side gardens

An area at the side of a house can often be incorporated in the garden at the rear

by extending a screen (built or planted) from the front of the house to the boundary fence. Depending on aspect, this can be a nice place for a secluded patio, for the vegetable garden or for the compost heap. A planting of small trees and shrubs can provide an attractive frame for the house. Often, however, the space between house and boundary fence is simply a narrow strip. When this is the case the best couse is to treat it as a passageway, putting down a path and training plants on the fence and the house. Make the plants interesting enough to be worth visiting. Watering a long narrow area is difficult and tedious. Even if you elect to use hand-held hoses and movable sprinklers elsewhere in the garden, consider an in-ground system for the side garden.

Country gardens

A garden in the country sometimes offers more scope for ambitious schemes that can rarely be realized in town or suburb. However, cottage gardens of traditional style (idealized though this generally is) filled with old-fashioned flowers, herbs and vegetables can be created on quite a modest plot. Where there is plenty of ground the design can include sweeping driveways, vistas created by avenues of trees, and extensive views of countryside beyond the garden itself. In a grand country garden there is rarely a need to worry about the proximity of neighbours but you may well find that it is necessary to create extensive windbreaks.

How you decide to organise the space is very much a matter of taste. Many successful country gardens are based on a series of almost self-contained compartments divided by hedges, walls or fences. Although the plan may have a rather severe geometry, the impact this might make can be very much softened by loose planting within the various compartments. The appeal of this sort of garden lies in its rich variety, with contrasts between different sections, and the intricacy of the connections between components.

A much freer style more open to the surrounding country might, however, suit some sites better. The landscape approach can be based on broad, irregular expanses of lawn or rougher grass linking areas of woodland or less extensive plantings of trees and shrubs, perhaps featuring streams or stretches of still water. Grass right to the windows, in the manner of the eighteenth century, might seem to leave the house too unadorned. A conventional but attractive solution is to create a rather formal flower garden interposed between house and landscape.

Making a plan

The easiest way of developing a layout for the garden is to make a plan on paper. An empty piece of ground is apt to look larger than it is, and a plan can tell you whether you can in fact fit in all the things you want to accommodate. Start by making a plan showing the land as it exists. It doesn't have to be a work of art, but it is desirable that it be fairly accurately to scale, and that it shows the features that might influence your design. These include the boundaries and fences; any pavings, paths, driveways, immovable rocks and trees that might already be there; and, of course, the house itself, with its external doors and windows.

Don't forget to note desirable views that you will want to frame, undesirable ones that should be screened; the location of such nuisances as overhead wires or underground sewers and telephone lines; and the orientation of the site, from which you can work out exposure to sun. You may have builder's plans for the house that show many of these things, or you may need to spend a few hours with a long tape measure and paper to create the plan for yourself.

Then you can start to arrange your garden rooms—the patio near the living room, the vegetable patch in that sunny place near the kitchen door, the swimming pool, the path to the front door. Get them in the right places first, and then the decisions about what shapes they are to take, where the trees and shrubs are to go to frame them (and block out the view of that nosy neighbour), whether to give them floors of paving or grass, and what sort of plants to have can follow.

In a large garden, a variety of places to sit—and a whole succession of different pictures.

A formal vista like this needs a focal point—here, the comfortable white-painted seat.

Plan generously, allowing yourself room to move. If you make a lawn or terrace for sitting out, 3 sq m (about 32 sq ft) is about as small as you can get away with; paths less than about 1.5 m (about 4½ ft) wide are too narrow for two people to stroll along; a row of shrubs tall enough to give privacy will grow at least 2 m (about 6 ft) wide.

Remember that a plan is flat and very few sites are. A sketched cross-section is invaluable when it comes to laying out the garden. Changes of level, even if only a couple of steps leading up into the house, add greatly to the interest of a garden. Where there is very little variation in levels it may be worth contriving them to create a more dramatic design.

Two hints on plan making: Don't make your plans too big in scale or you'll spend an inordinate amount of time drawing on unmanageably large sheets of paper. A scale of 1:100 (used on most builders' drawings) is quite large enough. Do your basic 'as is' plan on good stout paper (graph paper makes setting out easier), and develop your ideas on tracing paper laid over it—this will save you having to redraw the house and fences all the time.

CHOOSING A STYLE

Don't worry that this care over the plan and layout will lead to a stereotyped garden. You can develop your ideas in any style you like, and clothe them with your favourites among the plants that your soil and climate allow. You might opt for a rigidly formal, symmetrical design, in the manner of old Italian, French and Dutch gardens, making much use of clipped hedges and statuary, with flowers used only as accents at key points. You might go to the opposite extreme and make flowers the theme, planting them in drifts and broad sweeps in classic herbaceous borders. The mixture of old-fashioned flowers and useful plants that characterizes the cottage garden can be adapted to many sites. Although picket fences and arches covered with climbing roses are very much a part of the cottage style, they are not obligatory. Taking your cue from the presence of a tree or several, you might decide on a woodland theme, treating your living spaces as woodland glades. You might aim to create a wild garden with native trees underplanted with wood anemones, snowdrops, bluebells, primroses and other spring flowers.

Brick steps, simply designed but generously proportioned.

The formal garden at its most magnificent: the garden of the Palace at Versailles.

Picket fences are traditionally white, but this dark-painted one emphasises both the pale house and the bright roses beyond.

Where the soil is acid another option is to plant a deciduous canopy under which shelter rhododendrons and azaleas (botanically all belonging to the genus *Rhododendron*) and camellias.

The different styles of gardening are more about the kinds of plants you choose and how you display them than about how you cultivate them. But, in deciding which you would like, do be realistic about the time you will be prepared to devote to your garden. If your present activities mean that you have little free time, will you be able to cope with extensive plantings of flowers or vegetables? Might you not be wiser to develop a love for low-maintenance trees, shrubs and perennials?

BUILDING THE GARDEN

Having made your plans for the garden, you can elect to have your designs carried out professionally, which may add to the value of your property. Or you can save money—and gain a great deal of personal satisfaction—by doing some or all of the work yourself. This will mean that you will have to make a considerable input in time and energy, so

it will save much frustration and back-tracking if you develop a game plan for doing the work in stages, perhaps over two or three years.

If you are impatient, remember that staging the work allows you time to ponder and to add the touches that lift a garden out of the ordinary. These can be difficult to anticipate on paper. They might be unusual and effective combinations of plants, pieces of furniture or sculpture, cleverly arranged lighting, even something as simple as laying a paving pattern in one way and not another—the sorts of inspirations that strike only while you are getting your hands dirty.

If you are starting from scratch, the best plan is the one that most landscape contractors follow. First, do any major reshaping of the ground which will need heavy equipment, build any retaining walls needed to hold the reshaped earth in place, and lay any soil drains needed. (All this is disruptive, messy work if you do it later.) Then you might lay your basic hard surfaces so that there is adequate access to the house, the garage and any outbuildings. If you can afford to lay paths and terraces at this stage do it, but if not you'll need to at least

provide some cover for the bare ground. This needn't be the final lawn; there is sense in growing a cover crop of clover to improve the soil—and this won't cause heartache if it gets dug up or torn around later.

Then, as early as possible, you should plant your most important trees: the earlier you get them in, the sooner you will be able to enjoy them as mature specimens. This might be enough for your energy and budget in the first year. If the garden looks a bit unfinished, plant annuals and other fast-growing plants to give you something to look at.

If you haven't laid your pavings already, they should be the big project for the second year, with the final grading and installation of the lawn to follow. However if your budget calls for it, you can sow the lawn now, leaving the future terraces simply in gravel or grass. Structures like pergolas might also form part of this second stage.

Stage three is the more detailed planting of things like shrubberies and ground covers. Stage four is the fine-tuning, the trying out of new plants, the adjusting of colour schemes, and so on. This can go on for as long as the garden is yours.

This sort of plan, whether carried out over two years, three or more, works for most people and situations, but don't treat it as obligatory. Use it as a basis for tailoring a strategy that will suit you.

Walls and fences

Walls and fences are worth spending time on, as they help to establish the style of the garden. You need them for privacy and to keep out intruders, but you want them to work for your design, not against you.

Walls are commonly built of brick or stone, although these materials are sometimes used only as the facing to others that are less expensive. Walls can make a handsome addition to a garden but cost usually limits their use to enclosing courtyards, where their style should closely match that of the house. Openings may be needed for access but a gate—or a window—should also frame a view and should be distinctively ornamental, like the moon gates inspired by Chinese gardens. Unless you really are skilled at building, leave masonry and its heavy foundations to the professional.

Wood in various forms is now the most widely used material for fencing, although other materials are sometimes employed. Wrought iron was popular in the nineteenth century but cost and the difficulty of finding skilled craftsmen to execute work of a high standard means that little new fencing is done today. Some wooden fences, like those of wrought iron, are open but can provide a visual and practical barrier. Post and rail fences may be appropriate in a rural setting. They will keep out large stock, but to stop sheep wandering in and to keep back dogs and children netting must be fitted from ground level to the bottom rail. Picket fences, consisting of regularly spaced wooden uprights on rails, can be seen through and are usually low enough to look over. There are many different patterns, the tops of the uprights being shaped in a variety of ways. The Japanese version in bamboo strikes a sophisticated note in modern gardens. The criss-cross square or diamond-shaped patterns of trellis also create open barriers. Trellis is generally bought in ready-made panels that need uprights to suppport them.

A close board fence is the most durable kind; it presents a solid surface. Upright posts support horizontal rails to which overlapping feather-edged boards

A beautifully detailed trellis fence.

Adding a panel of trellis at the top of the paling fence has gained greater privacy without making the whole thing too dominating.

are nailed. A capping rail runs along the top and a removable gravel board is attached at the bottom. This is the part of the fence most vulnerable to rotting; the board can be replaced without affecting the rest of the fence. Slatted fences have nearly the same solid effect as close board fences but the boards nailed to the horizontals are not feather-edged and gaps are usually left between them. An advantage of the slatted fence is that because some wind filters through the gaps the risk of turbulence on the lee side is reduced. The spacing between boards can be quite narrow and when clothed with climbers they are effective at creating privacy. Wattle hurdles make beautifully textured fences but a frame-work is needed to which the panels can be attached.

Most walls and fences look better when they are partly or completely covered by climbing plants and shrubs. Attach wires, trellis or netting to provide supports. When treating wood it is important to use a preservative that is not toxic to plants.

Walls and fences can be used like hedges to mark divisions within gardens as well as its boundaries. When enclosing garden rooms, their role is essentially visual; they do not have to provide secure physical barriers. They can be open, light and decorative in construction but unless well built they will soon be damaged by winds.

Retaining walls and steps

Retaining walls are heavy engineering rather than art, and you shouldn't attempt to design or build one more than about a metre (about 3 ft) high without the assistance of a professional. Lower walls are safer, provided you adhere to two rules.

First, the wall should be battered, that is leant back into the earth that it supports. The pressure of the earth is constantly trying to push the wall over, and once a vertical wall starts leaning outwards, it not only looks unstable, it is unstable. Second, water builds up behind the wall and, unless you give it some-where to go, its pressure will endanger the stability of the wall. You can lead it away by a drain behind the foot of the wall, or provide holes so that it can flow out through the wall face; either is effective.

With these two rules in mind, you can make your wall from a variety of materi-als—brick, stone, concrete blocks or

treated pine logs. All can look effective, and all can be clothed with plants to soften their appearance. Often, there is no need to make the wall in one lift; you can make it as a series of steps, with plants growing at each level—a terraced bank if you like. If you have the room to simply make a bank at a slope of 1:1 (no steeper), you can dispense with the wall altogether, using a dense ground cover to hold the bank against erosion. There will be run-off at the foot of any bank and you must ensure that the slope or a drain will carry the water away.

Whether you have retaining walls or banks, changes of level call for steps to get from one level to the other. They can be focal points in the garden design, but need to be planned with care if they are to be attractive and safe and comfortable to use. If you are going to use them at night, ensure they are well lit; but it is even more important that they should fit the feet of those who walk up and down them. The rule to ensure good, comfort-able steps is that twice the height of the step (the riser) plus its length (the tread), in centimetres, equals 66. The maximum height for a garden step is 16 cm (about 6½ in), but the ideal proportion is a riser of 12 cm (about 5 in) with a tread of 42 cm (about 17 in). Try to have an uneven number of steps, and to keep all in the same flight the same dimensions; if you must change the proportions to accom-modate a changing slope, separate the two lots with a landing.

The width of steps is a matter of proportion, though it is an accepted rule that the fewer you have, the wider they should be. The steps must not be slippery when wet; usually you can make them in any material suitable for paving. If they are wide enough, you could make the risers in brick or timber and the treads in grass—but that will involve you in some careful trimming. Whatever you make them of, ensure they are firm; a wobbly step is as dangerous as a slippery one.

Paths and paving

Grass provides a visually attractive and pleasantly soft surface for walking on that is suitable for large areas and also for paths where there is only light pedestrian traffic. In many parts of the garden, however, a firmer surface is needed. A wide range of materials is available and a choice can be made to suit most pockets that will be pleasing or at least satisfactory to look at. These materials fall into two main categories:

Spaced laths, painted white.

A cream picket fence hung with bougainvillea.

those that are laid as a continuous sheet, and those that are assembled from modules or blocks of irregular size.

Gravel, which creates the effect of a continuous sheet, in one of the cheapest materials to use and is suited to town or country gardens. It consists of smooth and water-washed small stones or crushed stone fragments that are more angular. There is a good colour range but this may not be reflected in local sup-plies. It is easily spread into awkward shapes and its soft, natural look flatters plants that are associated with it. Plants look attractive growing through gravel; an attractive way of using it is as an extensive mulch with paths laid through it. Among its disadvantages are its tendency to track through the house and onto the lawn, and on any but the very slightest of slopes it washes away. Herbicides may be needed to stop weeds growing through it and it is not comfort-able to walk on in bare feet. Gravel needs to be laid on a well-drained but firm base. Ideally this should consist of hardcore topped by coarse gravel over which is laid a layer of hoggin. This clay binder, over which the gravel is laid in a thin layer, helps prevent the gravel shifting. Each layer needs to be com-pacted by rolling.

Bark and wood chips laid over a firm base can be used in a similar way to gravel and look particularly attractive in paths through woodland gardens. A stepping-stone effect can be created using log sections, but unless these have wire netting laid over them they can be perilously slippery.

These materials are easily laid by the amateur gardener. Paving with concrete calls for greater practical skills and asphalt, probably only suitable for drives, needs to be laid by a professional. Concrete is a relatively inexpensive and hard-wearing material and can be laid to almost any shape. Large expanses of plain concrete can look dull, and colouring is rarely an improvement. Giving the surface a texture helps; a stiff broom worked over the newly laid concrete before it is completely dry is a simple method of creating a light texture. Exposed aggregate, produced by using a good quality gravel and gently hosing off the surface excess before the concrete is quite set, is even more attractive.

Concrete should be laid over compacted hardcore that is at least 10 cm (4 in) deep. Edging, such as laid bricks or timber boards, is essential. Concrete will crack if laid in wide seemless sheets even when it is reinforced. Lay it in panels not more than 3 m sq (10 ft sq) divided by expansion joints consisting of wood strips or courses of brick. You can buy the sand, cement and gravel and mix the concrete yourself or buy it ready mixed. If using ready-mixed concrete, make sure that everything is prepared for laying on delivery.

For the amateur gardener bricks are among the easiest materials to lay for paving. They are available in a wide range of colours and surface finishes but for paving the selection should be limited to those that will stand frost. Freezing conditions may cause softer bricks to flake and break up. In choosing a colour try to match existing brickwork.

Bricks should be laid on a base of compacted hardcore 7.5 cm (3 in) deep which is covered with a semi-dry mortar mix of approximately four parts sand to one part cement. Temporary edging of wood planking is needed while the bricks are being laid. Of the many patterns for laying basketweave is one of the easiest and most attractive, the bricks being laid flat in pairs or in threes on their side to form a square, the direction of the squares alternating. Stretcher bond, the kind that gives walls strength, uses half bricks at the end of a

course so that the joins of adjacent courses do not align. A diagonal herringbone is a strong and appealing pattern but many bricks will need to be cut to complete it. Start at one end and tap your bricks into place with a mallet, checking the levels at every stage. When the bricks are laid brush a dry mortar mix (use the same proportions of sand and cement as in the semi-dry mortar base) into all the joints and then water gently.

Several other materials should be laid in the same manner as bricks. These include setts, such as the superb granite

blocks that were once much used to pave roads, and various kinds of concrete block. Man-made materials can often be used very successfully in conjunction with stone and gravel.

The versatility of concrete is undeniable. It is available as precast slabs, usually about 6 cm (about 2½ in) thick and in a variety of sizes and shapes, which have been cast in steel moulds. Plain-surfaced slabs have the disadvantage of becoming slippery when wet. Textured surfaces give a better grip and of those, exposed aggregate is the most attractive finish. Slabs should be laid on

A rockery looks best planted so lavishly that the rocks are almost hidden.

A long flight of steps needs to be well lit for night-time safety and well upholstered with plants.

the same sort of hardcore that is used for brick with dabs of mortar or, where the wear is heavy, a continuous bed of mortar. Fill the joints with mortar before laying.

Stone is one of the best but also one of the most expensive paving materials. York stone, a natural sandstone, is the most widely used in Britain on account of its subtle graining and colouring. It is usually sold in rectangular slabs of varying sizes or as irregular shapes that can be used for crazy paving. Lay stone slabs in the same way as concrete slabs. Making the jigsaw patterns of crazy paving is time-consuming and some trimming is usually necessary to make the irregular shapes fit so that large amounts of mortar are not needed.

Slate, whose grey surface can be very sympathetic to plants, is a brittle stone that must be laid on a firm base. The same is true of marble—but if you can afford marble, the expense of having a marble mason lay it for you won't be a problem! Be careful of stone and brick in shaded places, as they can develop a surface growth of algae in hot weather. This is not only dirty looking and unsightly, but it makes the paving as slippery as glass. If it starts to develop, you should wash the paving down with either swimming pool chlorine or diluted

Paths and steps may be used to enhance the charm of your garden.

bleach, sweeping it on with a stiff broom to remove as much of the algae as possible. A pale blue solution of copper sulphate is even better, but neither treatment is permanent—in wet weather cleaning the pavement can be a regular chore. Concrete isn't so troubled by the problem.

Finally, no pavement except gravel should be perfectly level or there will be puddles everywhere when it rains. There should always be a fall, not less than about 1:200 (1:150 is better) to carry the water away—to a lawn, to planting beds, anywhere but towards the house.

Getting the soil in shape

If the builder has just left you with a brand new house, the first thing to do is to get rid of the inevitable heaps of rubbish. Call in a rubbish removal contractor, or get the builder to complete his work properly. The contract with him for the work should state that he will take up and reserve topsoil where he is to build. In theory the topsoil can subsequently be spread where you intend to make a garden. But before you can spread topsoil, you need to do some thorough cultivating. During construction work heavy equipment will have compacted the soil. Digging with a spade is hard work, though good exercise for the young and fit. You may prefer to hire a rotary hoe, complete with operator, for a day. This is the time to do the shaping of the ground, so that your lawns won't be full of bumps and hollows. It is also the time to get rid of perennial weeds. When these jobs are done you can spread your reserved topsoil. If you are in the position of having to buy in soil buy the best grade available, which should have a high humus content.

Those who acquire an established garden are often spared the work that a new garden presents but weed removal may still be a heavy chore and the garden may have suffered from a long period of neglect. Before you plant is the best time to improve soil in old garden beds, and the best way to do that is to dig by hand, to a spade's depth—as far, that is, as the blade of the spade will go. Turn the soil over and incorporate as much organic matter—manure, compost and the like—as you can lay your hands on. Leave it to settle for a few weeks. (More about soil and how to improve it can be found in the section 'Looking after the garden'.)

Low plantings on either side of this mellow brick path enhance the feeling of space.

A long flight of steps, but of such an easy grade that they aren't tiring. The material is bluestone.

An uncluttered lawn looks best; here, the mound of bright flowers sets off the perfect sward.

Installing the lawn

Most lawns are established at an early stage in the construction of a garden. The creation of a lawn at a later date is not something that is undertaken lightly. However, as a surface lawns are relatively inexpensive compared to paving and, although they require regular attention to look their best, they are extremely beautiful features in the garden.

Early autumn or late spring are the best times to put down a lawn. Warm conditions will encourage rapid germination of seed and at these times of the year there is less risk of young growth shrivelling because of lack of moisture. One option is to sow lawn seed. This is cheaper than the other option, laying turf, but it takes much longer to have a surface that will tolerate normal wear and tear. The range of grasses available in turf is sometimes limited, which may be a powerful reason for sowing your own selection. The choice you make depends very much on the kind of lawn you want. Seed for a top-quality lawn contains a high proportion of bents and fescues. They create a beautifully fine-leaved texture but only perform well if watered and mown regularly and not subjected to hard wear. The striped effect is achieved using a cylinder mower

fitted with a roller. For a family garden it is not worth establishing a fine lawn, which cannot be given a bowling-green finish when children use it as a play area. For a hard-wearing lawn that will tolerate a certain degree of neglect you need a mixture of tougher grasses. In these mixtures there is a high proportion of ryegrass and meadow grasses and a relatively low proportion of bents and fescues. A rotary mower gives a satisfactory finish to a general-purpose lawn. There are mixtures available for special conditions, including some that show fair tolerance to shade.

Ground that is to be laid to lawn should be prepared well in advance. Remove weeds, taking particular care to eradicate all perennials, and cultivate the ground before levelling it. This is time-consuming but will pay dividends later for bumps and hollows will cause problems when mowing. Once levelling has been completed, work the surface to a fine tilth and apply a general fertilizer a few days before sowing or laying turf. When sowing by hand it is best to distribute the recommended quantity of seed to a relatively small area at a time. You can mark out the surface, divided into equal areas, using string and pegs. Ensure an even spread by casting half the seed up and down and the other half across the plot. If you are sowing a large

area, it is worth hiring a machine that will distribute the seed evenly. Before sowing, shake the seed well to make sure that there is an even mixture of the different seed types. Water gently after sowing and subsequently as necessary. Grass seed will take seven to fourteen days to germinate. Do not cut new grass until it is about 5 cm (2 in) high. The first cuts should be made with the mower set high. Gradually reduce the height of the cut but only cut close when the lawn is well established. Young grass is easily damaged and a newly sown lawn will not take hard wear during its first growing season.

Laying turf may be a better solution to sowing if the lawn is small; at least you have the impression of an instant lawn. Even so, a newly laid lawn will not take heavy wear for about three months. There should be no delay in laying turfs so all preparatory work must be done before they are delivered. Prepare the ground as for sowing and lay the turfs in such a way that the joints do not align. In effect the turfs are laid in courses very much as bricks in a stretcher bond pattern. Lay the first row of turfs along a straight edge and leave shaping the edges until all the turf has been laid. To get the line of a curved edge lay a hose as guide; for a straight line stretch a string between pegs. Brush finely sieved loams into the joints, firm the turfs with the back of a rake and water. Unless turfs are watered thoroughly to keep them moist while grasses root into the prepared ground, it is quite possible they will shrink. Make the first cuts with the mower set high.

PLANT SELECTION

Choosing plants for the design

Half the art of successful planting design is learning to see plants as a whole. Don't just focus on the flowers, however gorgeous. Does the plant have attractive foliage, and what is more, is it attractive for a long time, even all year? If it isn't, is its moment of glory sufficient to keep you looking fondly at it during its off-days? Does it have an attractive habit, graceful and open, or neat, rounded and compact, boldly upright, cascading or whatever, or is it just a scruffy support for the flowers? What sort of texture does it suggest to the eye: fine, medium, coarse or bold, matt or glossy? Does it offer features other than flowers or fancy leaves—interesting bark or fruit perhaps, or fragrance? Is it easy to grow in your soil and climate, or will it be an unhappy invalid, needing constant attention? And, if your temperament suggests, does it carry pleasant associations, childhood memories perhaps? There are some plants that will seem to have that indefinable quality of distinction, that makes you say, 'Yes, I want to grow you!' and those are the ones you should plant.

The other half is learning to think of plants in terms of the role you want them to play in your garden design. This is particularly useful if you don't know everything there is to know about plants—and there are so many in the world that none of us can have even a nodding acquaintance with them all. It's much easier to talk to someone from a nursery or search through an illustrated book like this one if you have already focused your desires by thinking in terms of, say, a deciduous shrub, about 3 m (about 9 ft) tall, with yellow flowers, or an evergreen, cascading ground cover to trail over the retaining wall, than if you just ask 'What would look pretty?'

The art of all art is simplicity. Don't think you will be bored by having several plants of the one kind; it is much more effective to plant in groups than to weave an intricate tapestry composed of many individual specimens of different plants.

A word of warning. A common mistake in planting is to crowd plants too closely. Allow young plants room to grow, spacing them according to their ultimate spread so that they do not produce a tangled mass. Where we have given the width of a plant take note; where it isn't given, assume that it will spread to a width about two-thirds to three-quarters of its height, unless it is noted as 'spreading' or 'upright', in which case you can assume a greater or lesser figure.

Choosing plants for the conditions

For those who garden in temperate regions there is a vast range of plants to choose from, including introductions from many parts of the world and the results of centuries of selection and breeding. Success in growing plants depends on making choices that suit the growing conditions available. A major factor in success is a plant's hardiness, that is its tolerance of temperature range (this important topic is covered separately in the section 'Climate'), but there are other factors to take into account too.

Fortunately for the gardener not all plants are happy with the same levels of light. Some undoubtedly are only at their best in full sun and become drawn and sickly if planted in shade. This is true for most annuals and many other colourful garden plants. Other plants, among them natural woodlanders, relish cooler conditions. They are ideal for planting under trees and shrubs, especially in the shade cast by deciduous trees. Even in the really heavy shade that is cast by buildings or dense evergreens there are plants that will flourish, some, such as ferns, of exquisite beauty. There are, too, some very obliging plants that will do well in sun or shade. Plants such as lady's mantle (*Alchemilla mollis*) are invaluable in providing links between sunny and shady parts of the garden.

Another important contrast is be-

tween those plants that like moist, even boggy, conditions and those that must have free drainage and will even tolerate periods of drought. You are lucky if in the same garden you are able to offer a range of conditions from bog to a free-draining raised bed because this allows you to grow wonderfully lush and vigorous perennials that make astonishing growth in a single season as well as compact grey-leaved plants such as those that are found wild in rocky Mediterranean landscapes.

Tolerance of acidity or alkalinity in the soil is another major divide between plants. Some important ornamentals, notably camellias and rhododendrons, will only thrive in acid conditions. On

A well-planted garden.

A colourful display.

In a sloping garden, steps and paths of neatly tailored concrete pavers are softened by lavish plantings.

neutral to alkaline soils their leaves yellow and they sicken. There are, however, numerous plants that flourish on chalky alkaline soils, many of them, including mock oranges (*Philadelphus*), doing well over a wide range of soil types. The pH scale is used to measure the acidity or alkalinity of a soil. The scale measures from 1 to 14, pH7 being neutral; above 7 is alkaline and below 7 is acid. There are simple kits available that can be used to take a pH reading of the soil in your garden; these are based on the colour reaction of a sample that is mixed with an agent.

Trees

Trees are the most important plants in any garden—they grow bigger and live longer than any others, and they are the main creators of the form and structure of your garden. More than any other plants, they are the ones that enhance not only your garden but the entire street. They can provide, according to the type and how you place them, shade, shelter or privacy. Some give flowers in their season, and there is no better way of having the sensation of swimming in flowers than from a flowering tree. However flowers are not the prime consideration: elegant habit, attractive foliage and suitability for the position and use are more important.

Think of deciduous trees for summer shade and winter sun; of evergreens for screening and backdrops. Think too of trees that branch high enough to walk under, so that you can look up and see the sun shining through the branches as well as those that sweep the ground to be looked at from the outside as it were. Don't forget to think of the mature height and spread of your chosen tree, and how quickly it will reach full size. Scale is important: will it be too big for the garden, or just right? If you garden on a grand scale, you can think of forest giants; in small gardens, small trees are more appropriate.

Shrubs

Shrubs are the workhorses of the garden, filling in the structure at and below eye level. They can act as screens for privacy, soften the lines of the house, or be given starring roles by virtue of their flowers, fruit or handsome foliage. They provide detailed interest for less expense and work than any other plant. But don't forget to allow them room to

Trees provide shade, shelter and privacy.

do their job; most shrubs will grow nearly as tall as they are wide, and it would be a pity if you have to be constantly trimming to get past them.

Try to value shrubs as much for their habit and foliage as for their flowers. It can be very telling to place small, rounded shrubs in front of others that are tall and arching; to set dense foliage against shrubs which feature an open tracery of branches; to contrast an upright grower against one of spreading, prostrate habit.

And don't forget those shrubs which can be clipped to form hedges or topiary specimens, or those that lend themselves to training against a wall. Clipped and trained plants help to strike a note of formality in a garden.

Ground covers

Ground-cover plants are low-growing shrubs and perennials that form such dense growth that they suppress weeds. Some of the most useful are shade tolerant and are ideal for growing under trees and shrubs where few other plants will grow. Others are suitable for exposure to full sun and those that are

drought tolerant often provide the best solution to the problems posed by poor, dry soils. The flowers of ground-cover plants generally count for less than their foliage, which imposes a simple uniformity on selected areas of the garden. To be effective they need to be planted in colonies but attractive contrasts of foliage can be achieved when one colony lies adjacent to another. Weeding is necessary until they make a close cover.

Climbing plants

Do you have an unsightly fence or shed that you wish would vanish from your sight? Climbing plants to the rescue. Do you want to soften the lines of the house and make it blend with the garden? Try decorating the walls with a climber. Do you want shade in a hurry, and can't wait for a tree to grow? Build a pergola and grow a creeper over it. In two or three years you will have the shade, while a shade tree is still a sapling.

You can train some climbing plants to grow flat on the ground as ground covers—ivy is the classic example—or place them at the top of retaining walls to cascade down in a foam of greenery

Whether low or tall hedges introduce long horizontal lines to a garden and call for trees to balance them.

Seaside daisies set off the intricate patterns of tiled pavings. A mix of flowers would look restless here.

and flowers. Or, if you have a worthy but dull tree, try climbing a flowery climber into it to wreathe it in colour. This is one of the best ways of giving a new lease of life to an old fruit tree that no longer bears freely.

Climbers support themselves by twining, pulling themselves up using tendrils or attaching themselves to a surface by means of aerial roots or adhesive pads. It is important to provide a suitable support that is matched to the vigour of the climber.

Annuals and perennials

They don't have permanent woody stems, but annuals and perennials bear some of the brightest and most beautiful of all flowers, and no flower lover would be without them. The distinction according to the botanist is that annuals don't live to see their first birthday, ensuring their future by setting abundant seed; perennials live and flower for years. But matters in the garden are not as clear cut as that. There are many plants that are perennial in frost-free climates but always grown as annuals where winter cold cripples them—petunias, gazanias, scarlet salvias and the busy lizzie (*Impatiens wallerana*) for instance. Other plants that are perennial tend to lose their vigour after their first season. Delphiniums, for example, classics of the herbaceous border, give the best results from young plants that are propagated annually. Several important genera of ornamentals, among them gaillardias, pinks and rudbeckias, include annual and perennial species and hybrids. We have decided to list all our annual and perennial flowers together, and there is no reason other than horticultural convention why you shouldn't mix and match them in your plantings also.

Some gardeners are prejudiced against annuals, which only live for a few months and thus put their owners to the bother of replacing them when they die. But if annuals' lives are short, they are filled with gaiety; some of the world's best loved flowers are annuals—sweet peas, pot marigolds, poppies, larkspurs, everlasting daisies. Annual flowers are generous with their blooms, and they are a great boon to the owner of a new garden. They grow quickly and give you something to admire while your slower growing, permanent plants are developing. In an established garden, they provide continuity of flower while perennials and shrubs are coming into bloom and passing out again, and you can use them to draw attention to focal points in your design. Cluster them at the front door, around the patio, on either side of steps; they don't call for a permanent commitment, and you can change your colour schemes from year to year, even season to season. If you love novelty and variety, they are for you. Just don't make the mistake of building the garden around them—you do need those permanent plantings!

With the current fashion for cottage gardens, perennials are enjoying a great revival as these are a major feature of traditional gardens. Old-fashioned favourites and newer introductions are among the most useful and beautiful of all garden plants, coming up year after year. They deserve their place in the cottage garden but can also be displayed in grand herbaceous borders or, more

The unmatched brilliance of summer flowers—here zinnias, begonias and roses—calls for a simple green backdrop such as the leafy wisteria in this garden.

Daffodils can brighten a winter garden.

appropriately in the modern garden, in mixed borders with shrubs and bulbs. Many are grown mainly for their flowers but others have handsome leaves too, and some are providers of the boldest, most architectural foliage the garden contains. Use these in the way you use pictures and accessories and ornaments in a room; they draw the eye and provide the finishing themes. Perennials are so easy to propagate they allow you to expand your holdings year by year; and many a lifelong friendship has begun with the gift of a piece of some choice perennial flower.

Bulbs

If you want to initiate a friend into the joys of gardening, you could do worse than give him (or her) a packet of bulbs. If nature ever developed a foolproof way of packaging a plant it is this; just plant, add water, and before too long there will be flowers. We always associate bulbs with spring and with cool climates, but there are summer-flowering bulbs and bulbs for warm climates too. They all share a perfection of form and colour which is their own—but most only give a few flowers per plant each year. So plant them as generously as your purse will allow.

Bulbs can be grown in beds and borders and include some of the most effective plants for massed display in spring. Tulips and hyacinths are outstanding for this purpose. In mixed borders they can often be used to extend the shrub and perennial season.

For a more dreamy effect naturalize bulbs such as daffodils in grass under deciduous trees. They will flower year after year provided their leaves are allowed to die down before the grass is cut. Many bulbs make splendid container plants and are ideal for courtyard and terrace gardens.

Formal bedding needs to be on the grand scale of this bed of tulips and white daisies to look really stunning, and is most successful in public spaces.

Vegetables and herbs

Time was when it wasn't quite nice to admit you had a vegetable patch. The master and mistress of the house may have taken the keenest interest in the vegetable garden, but no visitor ever saw the vegetables growing. *They* only saw them after they had been harvested and the cook had had her way with them.

Nowadays, many of us take great pride in our vegetables, and for many people they are the most important part of the garden. If that includes you, why not display them with pride? Not in the front garden, perhaps (we don't want to place temptation in the way of light-fingered passers-by) but in a choice position in the back garden, where they get the sun they need and where you don't have to make a safari out to the back of the shed to admire their progress. Lay the plot out with care, casting an eye over the proportions of

Herbs lend themselves wonderfully to formal treatment as in this traditionally styled herb garden.

Even in the tiniest of ponds, you need to allow sufficient clear water to catch the light.

Water gardens can provide a serene blend of elegance and informality.

herbs in small formal gardens by themselves, and a small herb patch can be a pleasant accompaniment to a patio, but you needn't isolate them. Plant them as edgings to flowers, or set them among the blooms in a cottage garden mix. Their soft textures and varied greens will help stop a riot of colours turning violent with clashes—and their aromatic scents are a bonus.

Don't forget, too, that fruit trees can be outstandingly beautiful with a ravishing season of blossom followed by a display of ripening fruit. Let them take places of honour in your garden design.

Water gardens and water plants

In almost any garden water adds a special dimension of pleasure. It needn't take the form of the elaborate fountains that Italian and Islamic gardens specialize in; just a simple pond reflecting the sky and cradling a water lily or two can also bring great joy.

In designing a garden pond, the important thing to remember is that it is the water that is the purpose of the exercise. It is so easy to get excited by water lilies, Japanese irises and all the other water garden plants that the water vanishes in the greenery and you might as well have planted a regular flower bed. As a general rule, whether your pond be informal and naturalistic or frankly formal and artificial (and this is a matter of which will best suit the style of your garden as a whole), the water plants should cover no more than a third of the surface.

Various materials can be used to create a pool. One option is to use a rigid preformed fibreglass shape. Those looking like irregular puddles are often curiously conspicuous in the garden. A traditional method to create a water-holding basin is to line an excavated area with puddled clay. More straightforward is the use of concrete but even this calls for considerable practical skills. For the amateur gardener the easiest material to use in constructing a pool is a flexible liner made from plastic or butyl, a rubber laminate. The latter is particularly tough and long lasting.

Black is by far the wisest choice of colour. After excavating the pool, remove all stones and roots that might puncture the liner and then cover the base and sides of the hole with damp sand to form a cushion. The liner, layed

your beds and laying attractive paths between them (grass, brick and gravel all have their admirers) and giving them a flattering backdrop of shrubs or fruit trees, not just a bare fence or a shed.

The problem is that a vegetable bed is never full. Just as the plants are beginning to develop sufficient growth to be worth looking at, the cook descends on them and great gaps appear in your plantings. What to do? You could edge the beds with low-growing flowers (and why not include some annuals among the cabbages, to provide cut flowers for the house?) but it is even nicer to edge the bed with herbs. Most herbs are fairly low growing, and their scent is a pleasure as you plant and weed. Their varied greens and textures offer much scope for developing garden pictures. Think, for instance, of the grey-green of sage in front of the darker, matt green of cabbages or the brighter colour of lettuces …

There is an old tradition of growing

over the hole, will mould itself to the shape of the pool when filled with water. The best way to hide the edge of the liner is to tuck it under a coping of brick or stone. The lively sound and sight of moving water is very appealing. Electric pumps that recirculate water make it easy to install fountains, waterfalls and streams, which should be planned before the construction of a water feature.

In lined pools aquatics are usually planted in containers, wooden boxes being traditional. (You can't use plastic pots, which tend to float; it is a bit disconcerting to see a water iris topple over in full growth because its roots are trying to rise to the surface.) Give the plants rich soil and, at the point where the pond can overflow when it rains, plant some of the many desirable perennials that love wet feet. If the water garden bug really bites, you could make it the theme for the entire garden, taking your cue from some of the old gardens of China and Japan where the 'lake' occupies most of the garden and the viewers stroll around it.

Don't forget when you plant the pond to include as well as the water lilies some floating and submerged plants to oxygenate the water. These are essential if you aren't to have the pond all choked up with algae. Fish, which can be an additional beauty of a pool, need these plants too for cover and food. Goldfish in their various forms and varieties are the easiest to keep as well as the most decorative. There are, however, several diseases that affect ornamental fish; it pays to buy from a reputable supplier, who will be able to give advice on the size and number of fish suitable for your pool.

Hardiness

We have discussed the influence of climate on the design of the garden, but mainly from the point of view of the garden user's comfort. But your climate also determines, more than anything else, the selection of plants you can grow. The earth has many types of climate, from tropical to arctic, and nature has evolved plants to grow in all of them. When plants are taken from the wild and brought into cultivation, they will be happiest and easiest to grow where the climate matches that of their homeland. If it is markedly different, the plant will either not grow at all or it will lose its character. An extreme example is a tropical plant that perishes when

exposed to frost. Less familiar are cold-climate plants that need their winters to flourish and which make untypically lush growth, often prone to disease, when they are grown where the climate is mild. Alpines and bulbs from high altitudes often languish when grown in a gentle climate. Furthermore, the seed of many will not germinate unless subjected to a cold period.

The hardiness of a plant, its ability to survive climatic and environmental conditions and in particular its tolerance of temperature range, is part of its genetic make-up. In the United States, 'hardiness zones' have been worked out for the entire country (the most widely used system is that devised by the US Department of Agriculture), based on the average minimum temperatures expected and how long they occur. American gardeners have developed the habit of saying that a plant is hardy to zone 7 (or 3 or whatever) or 'suitable for zones 5 to 9'. The US zoning system has limited applicability to gardening in Europe but in broad terms the pattern is as follows: Zone 9 (-7 to -1 degrees C) includes the western coastal areas of the British Isles and Eire (where the climate is influenced by the Gulf Stream), western France and Portugal; Zone 8 (-12 to -7 degrees C) includes most of inland and eastern Britain, north-west Germany, Holland and mid- to eastern France; Zone 7 (-17 to -12 degrees C) includes the eastern Scottish Highlands, western and north-eastern Germany, the southern tip of Sweden, eastern France and the Massif Central.

LOOKING AFTER THE GARDEN

Preparing and cultivating the soil

Just what sort of soil you have doesn't influence the basic planning of the garden much as there are trees, ground covers and grasses suitable for just about any soil. But it does matter when it comes to choosing your plants, and then when you look after them. Geologists have developed many different classifications for soils, but for the gardener broad categories are more relevant. Garden soils are classed as light (or sandy), medium (or loam) and heavy (or clay), the terms referring to how easy they are to dig. (Sand is in fact weightier

than clay.) The depth of the topsoil overlaying less-fertile subsoil or even rock is also relevant, as is its acidity or alkalinity and its general fertility.

Strictly speaking, you should measure the average size of the rock particles that make up your soil to arrive at a scientific classification of it as sand, loam or clay. But these are measurements you can't make outside a laboratory. A simple but satisfactory test will allow you to make a useful assessment. Make a ball of slightly moist soil in your hand. Does it feel gritty and crumble as soon as you open your hand? Sand. Does it feel gritty, but hold its shape more or less? Sandy loam. Does it feel just slightly sticky and hold its shape but crumble if you poke it? Medium loam—count yourself lucky, because this is the sort of soil that gardeners' dreams are made of. Does it feel greasy, hold its shape and take a polish if you rub it with your fingers? Clay loam—heavy to work but not to worry; it will grow most things. Can you polish it and also mould it so that it holds a shape? Clay. Be prepared for hard work, but don't despair—clay soils are usually fertile. Away from the seaside pure sand is rare, and pure clay is not common either; most soils will fall in the range from sandy to heavy loam.

Below the topsoil you'll find the subsoil, which is usually, but not always, of the same type, but distinguished from it by a different colour, due to its lesser humus content. It is normally more tightly packed than the topsoil, so that plant roots don't penetrate it as easily. As it contains less humus, it is less fertile. You don't usually want to dig it up and mix it with the more fertile topsoil, but if a little of that happens, no great worry. Below the topsoil and subsoil you will eventually come across rock. Sometimes this is quite close to the surface, sometimes many metres down; but as long as you have about 30–50 cm (about 12–20 in) of topsoil before striking it (or a solid subsoil) you have sufficient depth to grow almost anything.

It is the subsoil that normally determines how well drained your soil is. This is perhaps the most important thing to know about your soil. While plant roots need water, they also need air; if the spaces between the soil particles remain clogged with water for too long, they suffocate. Test your drainage by digging a hole about 40 cm (about 16 in) deep, which is as deep as most of us can take a spade without strain, and fill it with water. Come back in 24 hours, and if it is

A display of annuals like these pansies and double daisies takes a lot from the soil, which you have to put back if you want to repeat it season after season.

quite empty, you have no worries about drainage. If there is still a puddle in the bottom, you will have to do something to improve it, unless you are content to specialize in wet ground plants. There are a lot of these; but, alas, many choice trees and shrubs, lawn grass, and most vegetables aren't included on the list.

There are two ways to improve drainage. If your garden design suits, you can make raised beds. These can be an advantage if you don't like bending. Hold the soil with a wall (brick, heavy timber or whatever) and you can sit down rather than crouch to garden. Or you can lay agricultural drain pipes, leading the excess water to a soakaway or a ditch. Thanks to the introduction of flexible plastic pipes, this isn't the difficult job it used to be, but it's still heavy work to dig a network of trenches to lay the pipes in. The usual arrangement is to lay branch lines across the slope, feeding to a main which should direct the water away from the house.

Poor drainage is generally a problem of low-lying land, especially where soil is a heavy clay. Generally, the sandier the soil, the better drained it will be—sometimes too well, so that you barely seem to have finished watering before you have to start again—and sloping sites are usually well drained too.

Mention has already been made of the pH scale that is used to measure the acidity or alkalinity of a soil and the simple testing kits that can be used to give a fairly accurate reading of a soil sample. Even without testing the soil you might be able to get a rough idea of its pH from knowledge of the local geology and by observing what grows well in local gardens. Hydrangeas are a good indicator; in acid soils their flowers are blue, while in alkaline soils they are pink. It is sometimes surprising, however, what variations in pH readings there can be over a relatively small distance. Samples from different parts of a garden can give acid or alkaline readings that vary

considerably in strength. Over a wider area you may find pockets of soil that in pH contrast sharply with the soil around them. There is no ideal pH reading for all plants but a slightly acid soil, with pH 6.8, allows a broad range to be grown satisfactorily.

The best advice to follow when you know the pH of your soil is to choose plants that like the growing conditions available (in the plant descriptions that follow, soil preferences are indicated). The pH level can be modified in the short term, but a long-term struggle against such a fundamental character of the soil is rarely justified by the results. The easiest adjustment is to make an acid soil more alkaline by adding pulverized limestone (calcium carbonate). Liming is hardly required for alkaline-loving ornamentals such as pinks (*Dianthus*) and bearded irises, which show a preference for alkaline soils but are fairly tolerant of mildly acid conditions. Liming the vegetable garden, however, may help to increase yields and will discourage clubroot, a disease affecting members of the cabbage family. Add lime well in advance of planting but not at the same time as manure, with which it may have a reaction that is detrimental to plants. Making an alkaline soil more acidic is possible with an application of sulphur, but it is a drastic measure that may cause more problems than it solves. If you must grow rhododendrons and other lime-haters but garden on an alkaline soil, use containers filled with an ericaceous compost, that is, one specially formulated for plants requiring acid growing conditions.

Finally, there is the big question: is the soil fertile? To an extent, this depends on its type. Sandy soils tend to be 'hungry', because the large spaces between their particles don't hold the water and the plant nutrients that it contains. Clay soils, with their smaller pores, hold the water and nutrients more readily and are often more fertile. Loam is the perfect balance. But fertility depends even more on the amount of humus the soil contains. This substance, the end-product of the rotting of the remains of plants and animals—organic matter for short— gives fertile soil its instantly recognizable dark colour. It provides the nourishment for all the microscopic life (bacteria, fungi, algae, tiny insects) which hold and release nutrients to the plants we grow. It also improves the soil texture, simultaneously aiding its water-holding capacity and its drainage.

If you want to improve the structure of your soil and maintain its fertility, the recipe is simple: add copious quantities of organic matter in the form of garden compost, well-rotted farmyard manure and leafmould. It is almost impossible to put too much of these materials into the garden.

It used to be said that double digging was necessary to prepare soil adequately for planting. This means cultivating the soil to the depth of two spade blades, sometimes expressed as two spits. It is now rather uncommon for this laborious form of cultivation to be carried out over extensive areas of the garden. Single digging, that is cultivation to a depth of one spade blade, is considered adequate for most purposes. If you have the time and the energy, the areas that benefit most from double digging are the vegetable garden and borders that are being created out of grassland. All digging is best done in the dormant season but not when the ground is wet,

The arum lily (Zantedeschia aethiopica)*, an obliging plant that actually loves wet, poorly drained soil.*

for you then run the risk of compacting it. Work compost in when you are digging and avoid mixing topsoil with subsoil.

Although a slightly acid, crumbly medium loam is the ideal soil, a beautiful and productive garden can be made with a much less promising growing medium. The frequent application of organic mulches to established beds and borders gives the best long-term chance of maintaining the soil in good heart.

Soil nutrients

The soil provides an anchor for plants and is also the source of nutrients that are essential for healthy growth. In the garden, where there may be heavy demands on the nutrient supplies, some form of additional feeding is generally necessary.

Most of a plant's substance is made up of hydrogen, carbon and oxygen, elements that it extracts from air and water by the process known as photosynthesis. As a by-product, green plants release oxygen into the air, thus making life possible for animals, including ourselves. The other elements that a plant needs are absorbed from the soil in very dilute solutions through its roots. Chief among these are nitrogen, phosphorus, potassium and calcium. Others, like magnesium, manganese, boron, iron and copper, are only wanted in tiny amounts and so are called trace elements.

Calcium is abundant in most soils, and on chalk, for example, can create very alkaline conditions. As we have seen, the addition of calcium, usually in the form of pulverized limestone, can be a way of reducing the acidity of a soil. It is most commonly applied on the vegetable garden, sometimes in the form of dolomite, which also contains magnesium, an element that is not normally in

Raised beds are a classic way to overcome less than perfect drainage—but they also are a great showcase for flowers.

Here a raised bed takes the place of a front fence. Scarlet cannas bring bright colour, contrasted with the soft blue of trailing Convolvulus sabatius.

short supply in soils but is a vital component of the green pigment chlorophyll.

Nitrogen is the major constituent of the air but in that form it is no use to plants. They need to absorb it in combination with oxygen (as nitrates) or with hydrogen (as ammonia). These come into the soil by several routes: they are formed by lightning in thunderstorms; they are released by the decay of once-living organisms; and they can be formed ('fixed') out of atmospheric nitrogen by certain bacteria that live in nodules on the roots of legumes, plants of the pea family. Nitrogen is a vital part of proteins, without which life can't exist. It is essential to plants if they are to grow and make abundant foliage. High-nitrogen fertilizers are commonly prescribed for lawns and for leafy crops like lettuces and cabbages. Nitrogen deficiency shows up in stunted growth and pale, wan-looking leaves, which usually drop prematurely. Sulphate of ammonia is the standard source of nitrogen in artificial fertilizers; blood and bone (which is mostly protein) is the richest organic source. Compost and manure also contain nitrogen in varying amounts depending, for example, on their origin and how old they are.

Phosphorus and potassium are needed for almost all life processes, but they play especially important roles in flowering and fruiting and in the creation of woody tissue. Consequently, plants that we grow for their flowers or which we want to make firm branches (trees and shrubs) need them in abundance. A fertilizer designed for them will be proportionately higher in these two elements than in nitrogen, too much of which can promote luxuriant leaves and few flowers.

Phosphorus doesn't occur pure in the soil, but in various salts. Most of these are very insoluble and it is something of a mystery how plants actually get hold of them, but it is thought that soil micro-oganisms play a role. Soluble or not, phosphorus eventually leaches from the soil and some soils are deficient in this element. This is so in Australia, which has some of the most ancient soils in the world. Its native plants have evolved for phosphorus-poor conditions and are sensitive to excess. Superphosphate is the standard inorganic phosphate fertilizer; the main organic sources of phosphorus are bone meal and blood and bone. Phosphorus deficiency creates stunted growth, with leaves showing odd russet tones.

Spring bulbs are ideal for the busy gardener; dormant in summer, they need no water when it is scarcest.

Potassium salts are highly soluble, and the element washes from the soil very easily. Fortunately, micro-organisms can fix it; but if you let a potassium-containing fertilizer get wet, you'll lose much of its nourishment. Various potassium salts are used in the making of inorganic fertilizers.

A ready home-made source of potassium is wood ash (not coal ash), which should always be kept under cover if it is not used immediately after burning. Seaweed is very rich in potash but salt must be washed off before it is added to a compost heap. Potassium deficiency shows first in yellowing of the tips and edges of older leaves, which eventually die.

The various trace elements each have their own functions, and each deficiency has its own symptoms (for example, the mottled yellow pallor of young leaves caused by iron deficiency, or the between-the-veins yellowing of older leaves associated with a lack of manganese). Deficiencies in trace elements are usually remedied by the application of a general fertilizer, which will contain a balanced mixture of them.

Compost

No garden should be without its compost heap. Compost is the most readily available source of organic matter, and it is free but for the labour in making it. That isn't all that great either. In a non-intensive way you can make compost by gathering together material such as fallen leaves and grass clippings, throwing them on a heap in an out-of-the-way corner and leaving it to break down. It may take several months or even a year, but sooner or later you'll find, under a skin of leaves and twigs that haven't completely rotted, a pile of the black, moist crumbly stuff that works such magic on any soil.

Compost purists will throw up their hands in horror at this casual approach. 'Compost making is a scientific process!' they'll say. 'A heap like that takes too long to rot, half the nitrogen will have evaporated as ammonia, and the compost won't be as rich as manure, as it would have been had it been made properly.' True; but compost isn't all that rich in N:P:K—that is not the point. Its main value is the humus it supplies to the soil, its direct value as fertilizer being only secondary. Let us look at the standard way of making compost which is not, however, an inflexible prescription.

First, you gather together roughly a cubic metre (1 cubic yard) of suitable material. This can be almost anything of organic origin, though the bulk will be plant matter. Meat and other scraps should not be added as these will attract rats and other vermin.

Ideally, you want a mix of coarse and fine material, so that the heap will be reasonably dense but not too packed, which will prevent air circulating. Suitable material includes thin layers of lawn clippings, shredded paper, pruning clippings (although woody stems need to be shredded) and annual weeds that have not yet set seed. Do not add perennial weeds; if they are not properly broken down, distributing compost will spread them throughout the garden. Avoid also diseased plants, which should be burned. Perfectionists build up collections of coarse and fine material separately so that they can put them in layers, like a layer cake.

You need to keep the heap compact. The best way to do this is to put it in a compost bin. Better yet, have two, side by side. Bins can be made of wood, bricks, or chicken wire stretched between four stakes, as you please and as your practical skills allow. (You can buy compost bin kits made from treated pine if you want to save head-scratching and trouble.) No need for a concrete floor; sitting the bin on the ground allows worms to enter the heap and assist with the rotting.

Into the bin, you throw about 20 cm (about 8 in) of stuff, and on that you sprinkle a nitrogen-rich 'starter', to encourage the bacteria and fungi that will do the rotting to begin their work.

Poultry manure or blood and bone will be just fine. You can buy compost starters that claim to contain cultures of the bacteria and fungi. No doubt they do, but it is a rare garden (a roof top in the city, perhaps) that doesn't already contain plenty of them blowing about in the air. To the mix, feel free to add left-over artificial fertilizer, manure (rotted or otherwise), ash and the like. They will all help enrich the compost.

Keep piling, in layers of stuff and starter, and when the bin is full, water it. Then you should cover it with a tarpaulin or old piece of carpet to keep the rain off. Almost at once there will be frantic activity from the bacteria and micro-organisms, the heap will start to get very hot in the middle, and there will be a smell of ammonia. No doubt this represents nitrogen being lost, but most of it will stay in the heap. The smell of rotten eggs indicates that not enough air is getting into the compost, which should be loosened with a fork. When the ammonia smell passes off (in a couple of weeks to a month) the heap is ready to be turned inside out, so that the bits on the outside get the benefit of the heat and activity of the middle. This is what the second bin is for—simply pitchfork everything into it, and the compost should be well turned. (Then you can start on making a new heap in the first bin.) Once again, the smell of ammonia; but this time when it fades there is no need to turn. That would disturb the worms, which will now come in and play their part in breaking down the compost. When most of them leave, it is ready to be shovelled out onto the garden. It will be black, crumbly and sweet-smelling and free from weeds and diseases, which will have been killed by the heat of fermentation.

The compost will keep for a while, but don't just sit and gloat over how gor-

geous it is. Compost is not an end in itself; it is meant to be put on the garden to improve the soil. The lazy gardener can make compost without even going to the trouble to make a heap. Just spread your suitable material straight on your beds as mulch, sprinkle it with a bit of blood and bone to ensure it doesn't take nitrogen from the soil as it starts to rot, and let it rot down in place. This has the fancy name of 'sheet composting'. There are neater mulches, more suitable for putting in the front garden where the neighbours might see them, but it's fine for the vegetable garden.

The makers of horticultural gadgetry have jumped on the compost band-wagon. In small gardens, the plastic compost bins are very useful; they take up less room than a full-sized bin and don't look quite so untidy. Some even come on a mount which enables you to turn them over and over, which the makers claim will accelerate the rotting process and give you compost in a couple of weeks. They don't hold much and are really only useful in a small garden or for the impatient. Shredders and chippers are useful if you have a lot of woody material such as prunings. The neat, same-sized pieces can be used for sheet composting. The mulch looks so much better than when it is thrown on as it came.

Animal manure

Until it has been mellowed by rotting, the dung of animals is too sharp and strong to put on the garden. It will burn plants it touches and the smell may be offensive. If you do acquire it fresh put it in a heap in an out-of-the-way place, or spread it on top of the compost heap and leave it to settle for six weeks or so, throwing an old tarpaulin or a piece of plastic sheet over it to keep rain from washing out the

A small compost heap held with bricks.

A plastic compost bin.

The traditional, triple compost heap.

soluble nitrogen and to discourage flies. It will not smell so strongly when it is ready to use.

Manure varies in richness and 'heat' according to the animal it comes from. Pig manure, not often seen for hygienic reasons, is the 'coldest', poultry manure the 'hottest'. Horse and cow manure fall somewhere in between. Stable manure, a mixture of horse dung and straw, is the most readily available form of animal manure. The Chinese have used 'night soil' for centuries and fertile stuff it is, but its use poses serious health risks. Treated sewage sludge is sometimes available and is safe to use.

Dig well-rotted manure into the beds you are preparing to plant, or spread it as a mulch. Or make liquid manure out of it; simply put some in a hessian bag and steep it in a garbage bin full of water like a tea bag. When the water is the colour of tea, it will be as rich in nitrogen as any artificial fertilizer. You can pour it around plants that need a quick boost, and throw the bag and its contents on the compost heap.

Old garden books, written when stable manure was readily available, recommend lavish applications of manure 15 or 20 cm (6 or 8 in) deep to be spread over beds and dug in, and this often twice a year. For the modern gardener limited supplies generally make use on this scale impossible but in principle it can be used generously alone or can be supplemented by garden compost. It adds nutrients to the soil but its role as a soil conditioner is just as valuable.

Treated animal manures, such as dehydrated and pelleted poultry manure, are available but their cost is generally high. They should be stored and used as recommended by the manufacturers.

Mulching

Mulches have become so much a part of gardening that it is hard to realize our parents found them a novelty. A mulch is a blanket you lay across the surface of bare soil to protect it against the crusting effect of rain and watering, to conserve moisture by blocking its evaporation from the surface, and to smother weed seedlings, and it can be of any of a wide variety of materials.

Cut-rate landscapers are fond of black plastic, which certainly holds moisture in and stops weeds; but it also blocks moisture getting in and eventually suffocates the soil. It is a fine way to kill

While bark chips are a favourite mulch, they rot very slowly and don't add much to the soil.

off weeds without digging or using weedkillers, but don't leave it on for more than six months or so. It is usually hidden beneath a layer of pebbles, which itself makes an effective mulch. Gravel and crushed rock or brick would serve too. These conserve a surprising amount of moisture, and by reflecting heat they keep the soil cool. Some stone mulches can be glary, but a subdued gravel provides a unifying texture to the surface of the garden that is sympathetic to plants.

Rocks don't add any fertility to the soil; organic mulches eventually rot down and add humus. There is an enormous variety you can use: grass clippings (don't pile these on more than a centimetre thick at a time, or they will clog into a thatch that suffocates the soil); fallen leaves; pine needles; compost; well-rotted manure; shredded prunings; straw; bark chips; old mushroom compost (careful, it tends to make the soil alkaline); and others which you'll find at the garden centre, the precise selection varying from place to place. Sawdust should be treated with caution; it takes a lot of nitrogen to start it rotting, and it is best heaped up with a bit of compost starter and left for a few months.

Which of these you choose depends on which is easy and cheap to get, and how you like the look of it. Some, like straw or bark chips, can look a bit raw when they are new, but once weathered

are inconspicuous. Unless the rotting process has already taken place, nitrogen will be taken out of the soil during the process of decay. To counteract this, sprinkle blood and bone over the mulch when you lay it.

How thick to apply mulch depends on how much you can afford, but the ideal with most materials is to have the mulch 3–4 cm (about 1½ in) thick, thinning it out a bit immediately around the stems of the plants. Less isn't so effective at smothering the weed seeds. Notice weed *seeds*; if weeds are already established, they will *benefit* from the mulch. Remove them first, and water the soil. Never, never, mulch dry soil—there has to be water to conserve! And a dry mulch will rob moisture from the soil beneath; water it after you spread it. The layer of mulch will thin out over time, as it is broken down. Topping up is best done as part of the spring routine but there's no need to use the same material year after year.

Planting

The act of planting only takes a few minutes, but how you do it is as important as anything else you ever do to a plant. Plant with care, and you get it off to a good start; do it carelessly and badly and you can cripple it for life. Most problems can be overcome by following a few simple guidelines.

Prepare the ground and allow it to

Planting seedlings into well-prepared soil.

Well-spaced plantings of ageratums.

settle in advance of planting. If you haven't been able to dig the whole bed, dig as much as you can. If you are planting a tree or a shrub in a lawn, remove turf to form a bed that is at least 1 m (3 ft) long and wide. This needs to be kept clear of grass for several years until the plant has had a chance to become established and in many cases it pays to keep the area at the base free of grass or weeds long term. The planting hole itself must be generous so that the plant will sit at the right depth and the roots will not be constricted.

When planting container-grown plants, disturb the roots as little as possible. Simply pulling on the plant is likely to damage it and leave roots behind. The right way is to tip the pot upside down, holding the plant in the fingers of one hand, and give the rim a sharp tap to release the pot from the root ball. It can then just be lifted off. If the pot is too big to do this, lie it on its side and tap; the plant should slide out sideways. Large specimens are some-times grown in large plastic bags. These are best cut away with scissors, and you can then lift the plant off the bottom (cradling the roots, not grabbing the stem and expecting it to take the weight of the soil).

If the plant is at all potbound and the roots are showing signs of going around in circles, gently release them and tease them out, or they will continue to circle forever and not break out into the

surrounding ground. Act quickly, so that the roots don't get a chance to dry out. The circling roots may need to be cut. This can be done by slashing the root ball in two or three places with a sharp knife; new, outward-going roots will grow where you cut.

Young bedding plants grown in trays should be tipped out gently. The easiest way to separate them is to cut their roots apart with a sharp knife. In pulling them apart you risk losing soil and bits of root.

Trees and shrubs are increasingly sold as container-grown specimens rather than 'balled and burlapped', with their roots bound in hessian or other material. If you acquire a root-balled tree or shrub, do not untie the wrapping until the plant is in its hole. Make sure that it is at the right depth and then untie the wrapping. Slide it out, tipping the plant backwards and forwards if necessary.

Fruit trees and roses are often sold bare-root, that is, without soil. These need care to ensure they don't dry out. Plan on planting them as soon as you get them home. If they cannot be planted immediately place them in a trench with the roots covered and, if the roots are dry when unwrapped, place them in a bucket of water. Before planting disen-tangle the roots, and trim any broken ones with sharp secateurs. Planting is simple enough: make your hole, spread the roots out over a small mound in the bottom, fill up with crumbly soil, firm and water well to settle the soil around

the roots. The greatest damage to plants going into the garden is caused by roots drying out. Have everything prepared in advance and work quickly.

As a general rule, set plants at their original depth. This is simple enough with container-grown plants, and a change of colour on the stems of root-balled and bare-rooted trees and shrubs usually indicates the depth at which they are grown. Add or take soil to adjust the hole's depth. With most plants, a slight difference will not make much difference but a frequent cause of failure is planting too deeply.

Grafted plants are normally set with the graft union just at soil level, though there are some exceptions. Some plants (for example citrus) are prone to collar rot if the graft is buried. In some cases planting so that the graft is below the surface is recommended to encourage plants such as lilacs to establish their own roots so that they take over from the rootstock. A much better course is to buy plants that are on their own roots in the first place.

Annuals can go in slightly deeper than they were in trays or pots, and most perennials are set with 5–8 cm (about 2–3 in) of soil above the crown. Bulbs, as a general rule, are set so they have as much soil over their noses as they are tall, though most won't mind if they are a bit shallower or deeper. Many have the remarkable ability to pull themselves down to where they feel comfortable.

Fill the hole in around the roots with soil, preferably mixed with organic material such as garden compost and, for woody plants and perennials, a slow-release fertilizer. Ensure that the soil is well firmed, so that the plant is stable. Staking of trees and shrubs may be necessary in exposed positions. The general view now is that low staking is preferable to the high staking that was previously standard practice, and that stakes should be removed after the second or third year. Water thoroughly so that soil settles around the roots. After watering apply a mulch around trees, shrubs and perennials.

The availability of container-grown plants means that planting can be carried out at almost any time of the year, even when plants are in active growth. The most consistent results are achieved by planting during dormancy, for even minimal disturbance to the roots will affect growing plants. However, if the choice is between planting and any risk of the plant drying out in its pot, plant. If

Nemesias, ideal for spring bedding.

Cinerarias, almost always sown in punnets (the seed is very small) and then planted out.

you do plant in the growing season, you will need to pay particular attention to watering, in the case of trees and shrubs for months. Shelter from wind and shade will all help to get plants established.

Looking after a lawn

Ask anyone who announces a dislike of gardening what they dislike about it, and chances are 'mowing the lawn' will be high on the list. This is understandable; it is a chore with little creativity about it. Yet it is the most important part of managing a lawn. Leave the grass unmown, and eventually it becomes a meadow—the grass gets long, and the weeds come in. How often and how short to mow depends on the type of grass and also, to an extent, on the season. Fine grasses like bents and fescues can take closer cropping than the coarser types like ryegrass, and in a dry summer it is wise to leave the grass a little longer than usual.

As with any plant, cutting back the foliage takes strength from it, and when it is growing slowly you shouldn't weaken it too much. As a general rule, the fine grasses can be cropped to 2 cm (about 1 in) or a shade more, the coarser ones to 3 cm (about 1½ in). Don't make the mistake of cutting as short as the mower will go in the hope of mowing less often. Scalping the grass only weakens it and allows weeds to get in—and then you'll be mowing more often, as the

weeds grow taller and faster than the grass and look dreadful.

The actual layout of the lawn can make mowing easier or more difficult. Don't clutter it with flower beds and specimen trees any more than you really have to; and avoid sharp corners and wriggly curves, which make it difficult to get the mower right to the edge without much backing off and returning. Ideally, no corner should be sharper than a right angle, no curve smaller than you can easily sweep the mower round. If you fancy grass paths, in the vegetable garden or in a formal rose garden for instance, don't make them narrower than the mower! It is easy to make them exactly the same width, and that way you only have to push the machine down them once; but in practice that requires such careful handling that you might as well have them wider and make two passes. The same applies to the space between two trees, should you plant a grove on the lawn. Here don't forget to allow for the eventual thickening of the trunks. A gentle slope is easy enough to mow, but anything steeper than about 1 in 4 is not only uncomfortable, but dangerous as well. Consider planting banks with no-mow ground covers rather than grass.

EDGES

Trimming edges is as time consuming a job as mowing. There is no real substitute for the old-fashioned edging shears

for this, though strimmers are adequate for the non-perfectionist. You can save a lot of work if you make your edges such that you can ride the mower over them. If you don't like the effect of brick, timber or concrete edging strips, at least keep the edges of your beds level with the grass and avoid the gutter so admired by municipal gardeners. And don't edge your plantings with fragile things like lobelias or wax begonias that can't take the odd bump from the mower wheels! Beware the junction of ground cover and grass. They will tend to invade each other and have you down on your hands and knees separating them. Mowing over the edge will make it look messy. If you can't make a mowing strip without introducing an unwanted element of formality, use ground covers or massed shrubs tall enough to have an overhang under which the mower can be tucked and which will hide the point where grass and planting meet.

GENERAL LAWN MAINTENANCE

Weeding can be another arduous aspect of weed control. It sounds like 'I told you so', but most sessions of hands-and-knees labour on the lawn could have been avoided, simply by starting with clean soil and keeping the grass growing strongly enough so that weeds don't get a chance to get in. If you do need to weed, it is often easier to cut the weeds out with a heavy kitchen knife than to use a trowel or hand fork, but make sure you get all the root. Or you can try painting the weed with a small brush dipped in a herbicide, relying on the vigour of your grass to cover the bare patch. (If you are unfortunate enough to inherit a lawn that is more than 35 per cent weeds, you might be better off ploughing the whole thing under and starting again.)

Is it possible to encourage the grass to grow strongly enough to be weed repellent? Yes, but first you need to water it: and here, more than ever, the golden rule of watering—infrequently but heavily—applies. A few minutes' sprinkling will revive the grass and have it looking fresh after a hot day, but grass roots are lazy, and this will only encourage them to stay close to the surface where they will suffer as soon as the surface soil dries out.

Thorough watering, sufficient to wet the soil down deep, and only repeating it when the surface soil has really dried, will force the roots deeper and you'll have a much more vigorous, drought-resistant lawn. Water properly and you shouldn't have to water more than once a week, even at the height of summer.

Fertilizing is easy. Choose a good brand of lawn fertilizer, and apply it according to the manufacturer's directions. Better yet, halve the quantity, and put it on in two lots a fortnight apart. Spring and autumn are the best times; and don't forget to water the fertilizer in thoroughly and at once, or you'll burn the grass. Organic fertilizers like animal manure and compost are too bulky to use on lawns.

Lawn pests include several grubs that live in the soil and eat the roots leaving dead, brown patches. Major infestations may need to be controlled by chemical means. Some gardeners also use chemical means to control worms, in themselves not harmful but, if their casts are not swept off promptly, these can give a foothold to weeds.

Moss often poses a problem on lawns and can be a symptom of poor drainage, low fertility or compaction. The application of a chemical lawn killer or lawn sand followed by scarification deals with moss but not the underlying problem. Several fungal diseases can attack lawns, causing them to wilt and leaving blank patches. They can be treated with fungicides but this is usually not necessary.

Constant pedestrian traffic and cars being driven onto the lawn can compact the soil so that it sets like cement and

One of the greatest joys of Camellia japonica *is that it needs so little pruning!*

water and air can't get in to the roots. The grass, no matter what you do, just doesn't grow vigorously. The easiest way to open up the soil is to use a powered or hand-operated aerator, a kind of spiked roller that makes holes in the surface of the lawn when run over it. Small areas can be aerated by spiking with a hand fork. The problem is worst on heavy soils, where it is a good idea to aerate every spring.

Pruning

Pruning is a frequently misunderstood gardening technique and yet the underlying principles are not complicated. The aim of cutting growth is to encourage a plant to realize its full ornamental potential or to yield good crops. The brutal containment that many plants suffer is a misuse of pruning techniques and is called for because of the bad planting of a tree or shrub being grown in a space that is inadequate for it. The need for drastic surgery can generally be avoided by using ornamentals of appropriate vigour and fruit trees on suitable rootstocks. Severe cutting back is in fact unlikely to provide a long-term solution to a plant that is too large for its space. Pruning, especially that carried out in winter, stimulates growth; hard cutting back of a tree or shrub is likely to initiate a cycle of vigorous growth checked by savage butchery.

A large number of plants require only minimal pruning. The essential minimal

programme consists of cutting out dead, damaged and diseased branches. This will improve the appearance of plants and help maintain them in good health. All cuts should be made back to sound wood and the prunings should be burned so that possible reservoirs of disease are destroyed.

Many plants that require little maintenance as mature specimens benefit from some initial pruning to form a well-balanced framework of branches. On trees it is generally enough to remove weak and badly placed growths. As a protection against infection woody plants compartmentalize wounds. It is now recognized that the practice formerly recommended when removing a branch completely of cutting it flush breaks the plant's own line of defence. Cuts to remove a branch should be made just outside the branch collar angled away slightly from the trunk.

The aim with shrubs (including roses) and trees with branched heads (as is the case with many fruit trees) should be to create an open-centred framework that allows free circulation of air and good light penetration. When shortening a branch it is important to make the pruning cut just above a bud or pair of buds that will grow in the right direction, usually out from the centre of the plant.

More rigorous early training is necessary to build up the framework of plants grown in restricted forms. A standard or pyramid of a fuchsia can be built up quite quickly but the growing points have to be pinched out frequently. A hedge or topiary specimen of a slow-growing plant such as yew may take more than ten years trimming before it attains its mature dense shape. The framework of an espaliered apple or pear is built up over a period of five to six years. At maturity restricted forms generally require regular pruning; hedges, for example, must be trimmed once, even several times, in the growing season and espaliered or cordon-grown fruit trees need annual summer pruning to keep them fruitful.

At maturity most fruit trees and soft fruits require some annual pruning to keep them productive, winter pruning concentrating on promoting the development of fruit buds as in the spur systems of apples. Some form of renewal pruning is also beneficial for a number of ornamentals. This pruning can take the form of a simple trim of plants such as lavendar that, if left unpruned, become straggly and bare at the base. Most roses benefit from annual pruning between autumn and spring; as a general rule they flower more freely on young wood. The highly bred modern roses, large-flowered (hybrid teas) and cluster-flowered (floribundas) benefit from more severe pruning than most categories of roses.

In the case of many shrubs, well-timed pruning that takes account of the age of wood that bears flowers can greatly enhance their ornamental effect. Many of the shrubs that bloom in spring flower on wood produced the previous year. To maintain a supply of vigorous stems such shrubs as forsythias are best pruned immediately after flowering so that young stems can develop and mature in the growing season that follows. Some shrubs, including the butterfly bush (*Buddleja davidii*) flower on wood produced in the current season, most of these blooming in mid- to late summer.

These are best pruned in spring, the stems of the previous season being cut back to a low framework of branches. Regular cutting back in spring is also necessary on shrubs such as *Cornus alba* 'Sibirica' that are grown for their colourful stems. It is the young wood that is the most highly coloured.

Whatever pruning is done should be carried out with sharp, clean tools. In a small garden a good pair of secateurs may be enough but a pair of long-handled loppers and a small pruning saw are invaluable in the larger garden. If the job calls for heavier equipment such as a chainsaw and the use of ladders it almost

Impatiens are easy to propagate—just pick a few stems and stand them in a glass of water to root.

certainly should not be carried out by the amateur gardener. The most serious injuries to gardeners result from the victim undertaking a job that should have been handled by a professionally qualified person.

Propagating

It is easy to buy plants but there is still satisfaction to be had in propagating your own and it is a relatively cheap way of building up stocks. The way most plants propagate themselves in the wild is from seed and this is the principal method used by gardeners. Seed-grown plants have the advantage that they start out life healthy—very few plant diseases are transmitted through the seed.

Some garden plants are sterile because of hybridity or doubling but most are capable of producing viable seed. However, many highly bred plants don't 'come true' from seed and in the uncontrolled breeding conditions of the garden related plants will often breed promiscuously. The seed sold by commercial suppliers is gathered from plants grown in specially controlled conditions to guarantee that they are true to type.

Vegetative methods of propagation—that is by division, from cuttings, or by layering or grafting—are used for many plants, including those that do not come true from seed as well as those that are slow to reach maturity, as are many trees and shrubs and to a lesser degree perennials. A new plant produced by

vegetative propagation is exactly the same as its parent. A group of plants propagated vegetatively from a single original is called a 'clone'. The named varieties of roses or fruit trees are examples.

GROWING SEEDS

Plants differ in the ease with which they can be raised from seed. Many familiar plants, especially annuals and biennials, germinate very readily, provided seed is fresh. Bought seed should give a good germination rate provided sowings are made by the date given and the seal of the packet has not been broken. It is usually not worth saving seed for the following year as the germination rate falls off markedly, although loss of viability is not a problem if you are saving seed for a second sowing in a few weeks, as is commonly the case with many vegetables. If you save your own seeds from the garden, make sure they are quite dry before you store them. The best place is in a sealed container in the vegetable drawer of the fridge. Remember, however, that not all plants will come true from seed. There is often some latitude in when to sow but for the best results follow the sowing times indicated on seed packets and in books such as this.

Seed can be sown where plants are to grow, in a seed bed outdoors, from which they will later be moved, or in trays and pots. Growing in containers allows plants to be started into growth early under glass. Whether you sow your seeds in their permanent position or in a seed bed, the ground should be well prepared in advance of sowing and all weeds removed and the surface worked to a fine tilth.

The addition of sand or vermiculite may help on heavy soils. For sowing in containers you need to use a proprietary seed compost. Before sowing water the seed bed thoroughly. The best way to water trays and pots is to stand them in a basin of water.

Most seeds should be sown thinly and covered by only a light layer of soil. Ordered sowings are best made in drills, the furrow being made with the corner of a rake or a pointed stick. Very fine seeds need only a light dusting of soil to cover them, and it can be easier to distribute them along the drill if you bulk them up with dry sand. Large seeds like those of nasturtiums and pumpkins can be placed individually; such plants are often sown where they are to spend their lives. Draw the soil over the drill and firm gently before watering with the finest spray your watering can or hose is able to deliver. Until the seeds have germinated, you need to keep them constantly, evenly moist, which will mean daily attention in warm weather.

Speed of germination varies from plant to plant and on temperature and humidity. In the right conditions most flowering annuals and vegetables appear in ten to twenty days, but perennials and shrubs can take much longer, some preferring to be sown in autumn and given a spell of cold before germinating in spring.

Even if seed has been sown thinly the seedlings will be too crowded to develop into strong plants. As soon as they are big enough to handle, when the first pair of true leaves has developed prick them off into another container or bed, where they can be grown on until transplanted to their final homes. If they are already in their permanent bed thin them out, leaving only the strongest at the required spacing.

The main cause of failure with young seedlings is damping off, a fungus that causes them to collapse. Poor drainage in the seed bed encourages it, and so does too close an atmosphere which you might get if you are sowing in a greenhouse or have enclosed the pots in plastic bags to keep them from drying out. Take the precaution of watering with a dilute fungicide as soon as you see signs of germination.

DIVISION

Division, the easiest method of propagating perennials and bulbs, is best done during the dormant season and is often carried out when beds and borders are being renovated. Use a fork to lift the clump of a perennial or bulb and shake off the excess soil. Sometimes the clump of a perennial will simply break up into pieces, but often you'll have to pull or cut it apart with a sharp knife or secateurs. Retain strong new sections with roots from the outside of the clump and discard the woody centre. The new plants can be set in position immediately or grown on in a nursery bed. In dividing bulbs such as daffodils, separate offsets from the parent bulb. This can usually be done by pulling gently. A few bulbs, especially snowdrops, are best divided while they are still in growth, immediately after flowering.

CUTTINGS

Stem cuttings are the standard means of propagating most woody plants. A stem cutting consists of a piece of stem about 15–20 cm (about 6–8 in) long, detached from the plant and put in a suitable medium in the expectation that it will make roots. Not all shrubs will strike from cuttings—eucalypts are impossible and rhododendrons and lilac recalcitrant—but most are easy enough. Cuttings are classed as follows: softwood or tip cuttings, taken from the ends of actively growing shoots in spring or summer (fuchsias, impatiens, lavender); semi-mature or half-ripe cuttings, taken after growth is complete but before it is quite ripe, usually about the middle of summer (camellias); and hardwood cuttings, taken in autumn or winter from wood which has fully matured and might even be dormant. Roses are the classic example of these.

All cuttings are prepared in much the same way. Take the piece of stem you want, allowing about 4 to 6 joints where the leaves arise, and trim the bottom end of the stem just below a leaf, using a razor sharp knife or blade so as not to bruise it. Cut off any leaves that will be buried, and trim the remainder in half to stop moisture loss. Then you simply insert your cutting in a very sandy soil, either in a pot or, in the case of hardwood cuttings, in a suitably sheltered bed, and keep it moist. Softwood and semi-mature cuttings are best kept in a humid atmosphere, the standard way being to enclose pot and all in a clear plastic bag. Nurseries now use misting

systems that keep the air of a greenhouse as humid as a Turkish bath, and these have allowed many plants to be propagated from cuttings that were previously regarded as difficult.

Dipping the end of the cutting in rooting hormone does help the 'take'. Rooting hormones are sometimes combined with a fungicide, which helps prevent infections getting in through the cut. Use only fresh rooting hormone, which has a short life.

The speed with which roots will form varies greatly. Be patient; as long as your cutting hasn't withered it will be trying to root. After a fortnight or so, you can tip the cuttings out of a pot to check on progress provided you don't disturb them. When you see roots growing, the plants can be potted on or transplanted, treating them as gently as seedlings.

LAYERING

Layering is a method of propagation used for shrubs that don't root easily from cuttings, but it is a useful way of increasing many shrubs when you only want a few new plants. Roots are encouraged to develop on a stem by covering them with soil while the stem is still attached to the parent plant. In autumn to spring bend down a young and vigorous flexible stem to soil level. Make a slanting cut on the underside of the stem where it is to be buried. Cover this with soil and turn the end of the stem upwards, tying it to a short stake. The application of rooting hormone to the cut will encourage rooting. By autumn it should be possible to cut the young plant from its parent but some layers may need to be left until the following year. Many sprawling or creeping plants—including hypericum, and ground-cover ivies—will layer themselves naturally, and they are the easiest of all plants to propagate. Rummage around the base of an old plant, and chances are you'll find new ones waiting for you.

AIR-LAYERING

If it isn't possible to bend a stem down to the ground for the purpose of layering, air-layering or marcottage is an option to consider. This always looks like magic, but it isn't difficult. Spring or early summer is usually the best time; select a vigorous young stem and trim off any leaves except for those at the end and cut a slit on the underside. If you are worried about the stem breaking, brace it with a stick for reinforcement. Pack moist sphagnum moss into and around

Ivy cuttings will often root in water, but ground-cover plantings usually layer themselves.

Controlling pests and diseases

A list of the pests and diseases that can attack plants and a description of the chemical arsenal available with them risks discouraging the inexperienced gardener completely. It can't be denied that there are destructive pests and diseases but the problems they pose must be kept in perspective. Vigorous plants that are grown in appropriate conditions often resist attack, especially from diseases. When they are attacked most plants are not immediately over-whelmed by hostile forces and there are generally warning signs that allow the gardener to take action before a problem becomes serious. In most gardens a moderate level of damage caused by pests and diseases can be tolerated without the appearance or usefulness of plants suffering catastrophically. Many problems are specific to certain plants

the cut before enclosing it in a sealed plastic sleeve. The moss must remain for rooting to take place. It may take up to two years before the layer can be detached and potted up.

GRAFTING

Grafting is a relatively specialized gardening technique and one that has a long history. Although it is carried out in a variety of ways, all methods involve uniting a budded stem from one plant to the roots of another. On the face of it this propagating technique, used mainly on wooded plants but also on a few perennials, seems unnecessarily compli-cated but it has the advantage of bringing together desirable characteristics from the plant providing the roots (the rootstock) and the plant grafted on it (the scion). You might want to give a cultivated plant the strength of wild roots, which is why roses are almost always grafted despite many of them doing quite well from cuttings. Con-versely, you might want to reduce the vigour of the scion. This is the often the case with fruit trees. An apple tree on its own roots will normally grow unmanageably tall. Graft it on to a less vigorous, 'dwarfing' rootstock and you produce a smaller (and often more fruitful) tree, although both plants keep their genetic identity.

Grafting needs to be done at the optimum time, between late winter and early spring when the cells of the

cambium, the band of green tissue just beneath the bark, are dividing actively. To make the union requires exquisite care in matching the cambium layers. Fail in this, and the graft won't take. This is delicate surgery, calling for sharp knives and a steady hand.

Budding, the method used for roses and fruit trees, is the simplest form of grafting, and the one you should start with before graduating to cleft grafting and veneer and approach grafting.

Snails.

Slugs.

Cabbage butterfly caterpillars love nasturtiums.

A 'snail trap'.

and unless you grow these you are unlikely to come up against the offending pest or disease. The most common problems are usually easy to diagnose so that appropriate action can be taken.

SNAILS AND SLUGS

Slugs and snails stand out as being among the most bothersome of all the common pests. They eat the leaves of many ornamentals and vegetables and have a particular fondness for tender foliage such as that of young seedlings. They will also eat flowers and some species of slug do damage to root crops, especially potatoes. The presence of silvery trails near plants that have holes in leaves and that may even be stripped to the stem is a sure indication that slugs or snails have been active, which is most likely at night and after rain. Collecting and squashing them provides a measure of control but calls for constant vigilance. A less time-consuming method of control is to scatter specially formulated slug pellets among plants. Those who object to the use of pellets on environmental grounds sometimes use beer as an attractant, pouring it into saucers or small dishes set up to their rims in soil; snails and slugs drown in it. Some protection can be given to choice plants by surrounding them with a circle of ash or sharp grit, which these pests will usually not cross.

CATERPILLARS

Caterpillars are the juvenile stages of moths and butterflies and some are voracious feeders on garden plants. Fortunately the caterpillars of some of the most attractive butterflies and moths do very little damage in the garden and are often very specific in the food plants they require. One of the chief pests among caterpillars is that of the cabbage white butterfly, which feeds not only on cabbages and related plants such as broccoli, cauliflowers, Brussels sprouts and the various Chinese cabbages but also on wallflowers, stocks, honesty and nasturtiums.

Other troublesome caterpillars include those of the tortrix moth, which attack the leaves of many plants and make their home by binding together leaves with silk-like threads. Squash leaves before opening or otherwise the caterpillar is likely to wriggle away. The caterpillars of the codling moth are a major pest of apples, pears and quinces. The moth lays its eggs on the developing fruit, which by the time it ripens is ruined

Codling moth damage.

by the little grubs that have established themselves inside. When the caterpillars are fully grown, they leave the fruit to pupate in crevices in the bark and in litter at the base of the tree. A reasonable measure of control can be achieved by hanging pheromone traps in trees between late spring and mid-summer. These attract and trap male moths with the result that egg fertilization is reduced.

Removing caterpillars by hand is in many cases the easiest means of control. Biological control with the bacterium *Bacillus thuringiensis* gives caterpillars a disease (milky spore disease) fatal to them but not to birds or animals; it can be highly effective in the greenhouse but is not practicable in the open garden.

EARWIGS AND BEETLES

Earwigs and the adults of several beetles do damage to plants by eating leaves. Earwigs are particularly active on dahlias and chrysanthemums. Vine weevils attack a wide range of shrubs, including rhododendrons and camellias, as well as grape vines and herbaceous plants. Several beetles are more specific. The red lily beetle, for example, attacks mainly bulbous plants, especially lilies and fritillaries.

Low levels of infestation of some of these pests can be tolerated, removal by hand providing a reasonably satisfactory measure of control. Earwigs can be tempted to lodge in inverted flowerpots loosely stuffed with straw and set on stakes among vulnerable plants. When they are inactive during the day the earwigs can be removed and destroyed. Chemical methods of control involve using sprays such as permethrin and pirimiphos-methyl.

GRUBS ACTIVE BELOW THE GROUND

Roots, bulbs and tubers are attacked by a number of grubs that live in the soil. The larvae of chafer beetles, for example, attack the roots and the stem base of many plants. They are cream-coloured,

Red spider mite damage.

Aphids on a rose bush.

plump and typically C-shaped. A similar range of plants is affected by leatherjackets, the larvae of daddy-long-legs. More specific are the maggot-like larvae of carrot flies (which also attack celery, parsley and parsnips) and onion flies which, as their name suggests, attack mainly onions. Some protection can be given to susceptible plants by watering them with pirimiphos-methyl. Ground that is affected can be treated with chlorpyrifos + diazinon.

APHIDS AND OTHER SAP-SUCKING PESTS

The big tribe of sap-sucking pests includes aphids (greenfly and blackfly), which are very common and are capable of increasing at a phenomenal rate in favourable conditions. The damage they cause is not dramatically obvious as is that done by leaf-eating pests, but they can severely stunt and distort the growth of plants and they spread virus diseases. Most sap-sucking pests can be controlled by a wide range of pesticides and it is advisable to spray before infestations become heavy. Pirimicarb has the advantage of being selective against aphids, leaving beneficial insects (but also other pests) unharmed. Systemic insecticides, the most important of which is dimethoate, are used extensively as a means of control. These are absorbed by the plant and render its sap poisonous to the pests. Systemic insecticides have several advantages. They are not washed off by rain, they protect the whole plant,

Mildew on a grape leaf.

Sooty mould.

Hollyhock rust.

even parts the spray has not reached, and they remain effective for several days. They should be used with care on vegetables and fruit. Do not eat crops that have been sprayed sooner than the safe period noted in the directions.

SCALE INSECTS

A wide range of plants, including trees and shrubs in the open garden and many conservatory and greenhouse plants, can be attacked by scale insects. There are several different kinds, usually showing as yellow, brown or white raised ovals or circles on the undersides of leaves. These are sap suckers that lead sedentary lives, secreting a carapace of wax to protect themselves. They are not easy pests to control. Deciduous fruit trees, which are often infested, can be sprayed with a tar oil wash in winter. A malathion spray can be used at other times and is most effective on outdoor plants when applied in early to mid-summer. If the plant or the infestation is small, you can brush methylated spirits on to the scales. An old toothbrush is ideal for this purpose and, if it scrubs the insects off, so much the better—they can't crawl back on.

EELWORMS

Nematodes or eelworms are microscopic worm-like creatures that live in the soil and attack the roots or bulbs of a range of plants. The destruction of the roots causes the plant to wilt and often die, and they cause bulbs to rot. They also transmit viruses. They are especially fond of tomato roots and daffodil bulbs. No chemical controls are available to the amateur gardener and affected plants should be dug up and burned. African and French marigolds are said to secrete substances into the soil that drive nematodes away, which is why they are

Black spot on a rose leaf.

often planted with tomatoes. Daffodil bulbs can be treated with hot water without damaging bulbs but killing the eelworms. Dormant bulbs immersed in water must be maintained at a constant temperature of 44 degrees C (112 degrees F) for a period of three hours, making this difficult treatment for the amateur gardener to carry out. In the vegetable garden crop rotation is the only real defence.

BACTERIA

The bacterial diseases are the rarest, which is just as well as they are difficult to treat. The most common bacterial diseases are those that cause cankers and galls on the stems and sometimes the leaves of stone fruit, tomatoes and oleanders. Here you can do little except remove and burn the affected parts in the hope of destroying all the bacteria, a course of action to follow too if you get bacterial leaf spots on ivy or geraniums. Gladiolus bulbs are sometimes affected by bacterial scab, which manifests itself

Mosaic virus on an apple tree.

in black, rooted areas. Burn any affected bulbs, and make sure you don't replant in the same place.

FUNGI

A wide range of fungi can attack garden plants, some being specific to particular plants. Many are conspicuous, visible as mildews, moulds and rusts on the leaves, flowers and stems of plants. Poor air circulation and crowding often encourage the development of fungi such as botrytis and plants that are excessively lush tend to be vulnerable. Good garden hygiene will reduce the risks of plants being affected. In some cases the risk of the problem can be reduced by choosing resistant plants. Antirrhinums, for example, tend to be prone to rust, but there are cultivars that show good resistance. One of the disappointing features of modern roses is that so many cultivars remain prone to black spot, powdery mildew and rust. Some of the old species and cultivars such as the Albas are on the whole much healthier plants. If susceptible cultivars are chosen there is little choice but to spray on a regular basis throughout the growing season.

Contact fungicides such as Bordeaux mixture, originally developed in the nineteenth century to protect the French vineyards against mildew, are of limited use in dealing with infections established in the tissue of plants. Systemic fungicides such as benomyl, on the other hand, attack fungi in the plant tissue itself. Fungi, however, sometimes develop resistance to a systemic fungicide that is used repeatedly and it may be necessary to change the compound from time to time.

Some soil-borne fungi can be devastating in their effect. The most dreaded is honey fungus (*Armillaria*). This can affect a wide range of trees, shrubs, climbers and also some perennials. It produces black fungal strands (rhizomorphs) like boot laces and the fruiting bodies are honey-scented mushrooms. Drenching the soil with fungicide is not an effective control and can wreak havoc on humus-producing micro-organisms. It can spread from the roots or stump of a dead tree to a live one. It is a wise precaution when taking out a tree or shrub to remove the stump and as much of the roots as possible, if necessary having a contractor chip or grind out the stump. Any affected plant should be taken out and burnt. When replanting an area that has been affected, avoid susceptible plants such as privets and rhododendrons. Some plants, yew and *Cornus* among them, have some resistance to the fungus.

Another serious soil-borne fungus is clubroot, which causes stunted growth in members of the cabbage family, including flowers such as stocks and weeds. The mould responsible is found in poorly drained acid soils. Improving the drainage, liming and crop rotation are the best means of control.

VIRUSES

The most serious diseases of plants are caused by viruses; all plants can be affected. There are many viruses, some with a wide range of hosts, and there is no way of treating affected plants. The principal symptoms are distortion of the leaves and flowers, weak growth and undersized plants and, in many cases, mottling of the foliage and streaking in the flowers. Sometimes the effect of viral attack is thought ornamental; it is a virus that breaks the colour of tulip blossoms into stripes. Even viruses that are tolerated reduce the vigour of plants and most plants that are affected by viruses should be lifted and burned as soon as possible. Viruses are transmitted by sap-sucking pests such as aphids and various soil-borne pests, including nematodes. They can also be transmitted by the exchange of plant fluids on secateurs and tools used in propagation. Control of pests and good garden hygiene will reduce the risk of viruses being spread.

Buy whenever possible certified virus-free stock. Do not propagate vegetatively from affected stock but, as few virus diseases are transmitted through seed, growing from seed is usually a satisfactory way of propagating those plants that will come true from seed.

Weeds

It is often said that a weed is simply a plant in the wrong place. Weeds are generally vigorous and fast-growing plants that compete with ornamentals and useful plants for light, nourishment and water. They are a feature of almost every garden and the chore of dealing with them is probably the least enjoyed of all gardening jobs. Two measures can greatly reduce the labour of weed control. Ground-cover plants that form a dense carpet of vegetation prevent the germination of weed seed. The ground cover can consist of a colony of a single plant but the same effect can be achieved by close planting of mixtures. Mulching also discourages the germination of weed seeds but compost and farmyard manure unless very well rotted are likely to contain seeds that may present a weed problem of their own. It is essential to clear ground of perennial weeds before planting ground-cover plants or applying mulches. The soft texture of mulches means that any weeds that do come up are usually easy to pull out.

Weeds can be annuals, perennials or even shrubs or trees. Annuals, such as groundsel and shepherd's purse, complete a whole life cycle, even several generations, in a single year. They are the most troublesome weeds in those parts of the garden, such as the vegetable plot, which are dug regularly. It is important to deal with these before they set seed, preferably at seedling stage. It is often difficult to use chemical controls where annuals weeds are growing among crops and ornamentals and the most effective method of dealing with them is by hand-weeding and hoeing. Provided that they have not set seed, annuals weeds can be put on the compost heap.

Perennials weeds persist from year to year. Many, including ground elder and stinging nettle, are herbaceous; some, such as bramble, are woody. Hand-weeding is often used to remove them and can be an effective means of control over relatively small areas but it is important to remove all fragments of root or rhizome and any bulbs. The ground needs to be checked again for any sign of regrowth a month or so after hand-weeding. Perennial weeds should not be put on the compost heap.

The availability of chemical controls has made perennial weeds much easier to deal with. There are several different categories of weedkiller. Those that work by direct contact, affecting foliage and stems, can be effective against annuals but do not destroy the roots of perennials weeds. Others, including glyphospate, act on the foliage but also move down to the roots and are among the most useful for controlling perennial weeds. It does not persist in the soil so new plants can be put in as soon as weeds are dead but, as it is not selective, killing garden plants as readily as weeds, it must be applied with care. In addition to these there are soil-acting weedkillers that are absorbed by the roots of growing plants. They are often applied to keep ground clear around the base of fruit trees and ornamentals. Dichlobenil is typical in being residual. It is essential to check the manufacturer's information concerning the period that must elapse before planting and sowing where these chemicals are used. Several selective weedkillers are also available. Most kill broad-leaved weeds but do not affect grasses and are therefore useful for treating weeds in lawns. Some kill only grasses and leave broad-leaved plants undamaged.

Weedkillers, like all garden chemicals, are potentially dangerous. Store them in a secure place out of the reach of children. Keep them in their original containers to avoid the risk of misuse. Take the greatest care in using them. Follow the manufacturer's instructions in mixing and applying. Wear gloves and protective clothing to keep chemicals off the skin. Do not spray in windy weather and avoid breathing in the fumes. Wash up thoroughly after using weedkiller and dispose carefully any surplus diluted solution.

One last thought on weeds: before

Couch escaping from the lawn.

The edible dandelion (Taraxacum officinale).

Creeping oxalis (Oxalis corniculata).

Yellow clover (Trifolium dubium).

you pull out a tiny seedling, do make sure it *is* a weed. Sometimes garden plants seed themselves, and you might be pulling out something choice by mistake. Give the suspect a chance to identify itself first; if it turns out to be a weed after all, no harm will be done unless you have waited so long that it has started to go to seed.

ORGANIC GARDENING

The interest in organic gardening has gone hand in hand with the growing awareness of the importance of conserving the environment. As individuals we may not be able to do much about saving the Amazon rainforests, but we can do something about the patch of land we have in our own stewardship, keeping it healthy and free from poisons, in harmony with nature.

Some see organic gardening as simply a nostalgic return to old-fashioned ways

before the rise of modern technology. However, the basic philosophy of organic gardening—returning what we can to the soil and avoiding chemicals that might damage the environment—is simply common sense. A fertile soil is one that contains a flourishing population of micro-organisms, and they cannot long endure without the constant replenishment of humus that comes from compost or manure. Chemical fertilizers don't help them and, what is more, fertilizers do leach from the soil to pollute waterways and other soils. Sprays, no matter how non-toxic their manufacturers hope them to be, should always be regarded as poisonous and dangerous to the environment until proved otherwise.

Many gardeners who really care about their soil and garden make compost; give preference to organic fertilizers rather than chemicals like superphosphate and sulphate of ammonia; and use chemical sprays only when absolutely necessary,

after less drastic controls of pests and diseases have failed. This position involves a degree of compromise that would be unacceptable to passionate organic gardeners. The claims some of them make that the result of strict organic gardening practices is more flavourful, more nutritious vegetables and prettier flowers are difficult to settle on a purely scientific basis.

GARDENING IN CONTAINERS

On the face of it growing plants in containers seems a perverse thing to do. Why imprison a plant in a pot where it is utterly dependent on you to water and fertilize it, and where it will need more care than it would if it were growing in the ground?

There are many reasons.

First, you can give a potted plant individual care, with a soil mix designed to suit it, watering or not just as it needs it, and a position in sun or shade as it requires. Some plants with specialized needs such as rhododendrons, which need an acid soil, are often grown as pot plants for this reason. Baby plants, whether grown from seeds or cuttings, are usually brought on in pots while they are too delicate to take their chances in the competition of the open garden. They will suffer less shock when they are transplanted than they would if they were lifted from the open ground; and most modern nurseries grow most of their plants in pots for this very reason. They can be planted at almost any time of the year with reasonable certainty of success.

Then, you might want to grow your plant on a paved terrace, on a verandah, even on a balcony or roof. Here, pots can make the difference between having some plants or having none at all. Or you might be renting your house on a short lease, and want to be able to take your plants with you when you go—plant them in the ground and you are making a present of them to your landlord.

Put a plant in a handsome container, and you give it importance that can be used effectively in the design of a garden. Container-grown plants can make arresting focal points at the end of a vista, provide accents at various points in the garden marking, for example, changes of level, and create formal display, for instance on a terrace patio.

Where potted plants are being massed like these regal pelargoniums, unattractive plastic pots will be largely hidden by foliage.

You can take advantage of the portability of containers to arrange a changing display, retiring one plant as its flowers fade and bringing in another that is just coming into bloom. In this way it is possible to maintain an interesting collection of container plants throughout the year.

Very many plants can be grown satisfactorily in containers, at least in the short term. Full-sized trees need large planters as are often used in civic schemes, although the amateur gardener may find planting on this scale too cumbersome. A half-barrel is itself a large container—and will need two people to shift it if it is already planted up—but it is quite big enough to grow a medium-sized shrub. Bearing in mind that a container plant like this draws the eye, choose one that looks good for as much of the year as possible. Think of long-flowering, handsome evergreens like camellias and *Pieris*.

Smaller pots offer their own possibili-

ties. Suitable ornamentals include annuals, spring bulbs (which can provide a display earlier than those in the open garden), perennials and ferns; even vegetables and climbing plants are possible. (Try training sweet peas up a tripod of tall stakes to make an eye-catching column of bloom.) A cluster of small or medium-sized pots has more impact than just one, and you can mix and match your plants just as the mood takes you.

Window boxes and hanging baskets are particularly useful for decorating buildings. Geraniums and petunias are much used in plantings because they flower over such a long period but there are many other plants to choose from, those of trailing habit looking very effective. Many need full sun, although ferns and fuchsias are among several good shade-tolerant plants. Edible herbs can be attractive and are ideal for a position outside the kitchen window. It pays to have windowboxes of generous

size—20 cm (about 8 in) is not too wide or deep. Ensure that all containers above ground level are firmly secured.

The containers themselves offer great choice. Plastic pots have been much improved in recent years, and there are more to choose from than just the plain ones, useful as they are as temporary homes for plants that are going to be planted out. The material doesn't age well, however. Furthermore its lightness, usually an asset, is a disadvantage when it is holding a tall plant.

Terracotta is the material with several thousand years' tradition behind it, and even in the plainest models its warm colour is flattering to almost any plant displayed in it. It has an advantage over plastic in that it is porous; it is harder to overwater a plant in terracotta. Salts from fertilizer tend to make a white bloom on the surface, which isn't pretty. It does wash off easily, but it can also be minimized by painting the inside of the pot with olive oil before you plant—a trick practised by the ancient Romans. As long as you don't have an accident, terracotta will last for hundreds of years, mellowing in beauty as it ages.

Glazed earthenware and porcelain pots can also be beautiful. They offer good accommodation for plants, with three caveats: they are sometimes rather fragile; the fancier ones are apt to distract from the plants they are supposed to be showing off; and most are not frost resistant.

Wood is traditional for containers too, whether in the form of cut-down barrels or in more elaborate designs like the Versailles tubs originally designed for the gardens of Louis XIV. Wood has the advantage of keeping the roots of plants cool in hot weather. Choose wooden containers as much for their durability as their looks. Teak, western red cedar and oak are the timbers of choice; treated pine is a reasonably economical alternative. All will last longer if they are treated or painted. Wood is the material of choice for window boxes.

Reinforced concrete, the material of the most daring modern architecture, was first developed to make flower pots nearly 200 years ago, and concrete pots have been with us ever since. Their walls

have to be thick; most concrete pots are tub-sized and heavy. The weight is a disadvantage; few concrete tubs are truly portable. So is the ease with which the material can take moulded decoration, usually with unhappy results. The most attractive concrete pots are simple in design, and these days are often coloured and finished to resemble stone. You can paint them, though moisture from inside usually causes the paint to flake off in a couple of years.

Splendidly carved urns and vases of stone and marble are sometimes available although they are expensive to buy.

Should you be fortunate enough to have one, you have a work of art which could be the focal point of the entire garden.

Whatever material a container is made of it must have adequate drainage holes; nothing will kill your plants faster than wet feet. For the same reason, it isn't wise to stand an outdoor pot in a saucer, which will stay full in wet weather. Only do this for real water lovers like arum lilies. Place crocks (pieces of broken pots) over the drainage holes to keep the soil from washing out. Metal gauze can be used as an alternative and this will help to keep out worms. Cover the base

Bring potted spring bulbs out to show them off, then retire them after they have finished flowering.

A collection of different terracotta pots, given unity by a common theme of grey foliage: catnip (Nepeta), lamb's ears (Stachys) and sun roses (Helianthemum).

A container need not sit in splendid isolation. This decorative urn filled with pansies adds a graceful note to a bed of flowers in fetching blue and yellow tones.

with a layer of gravel for drainage; and then add your potting compost and plant, ensuring a couple of centimetres between the finished level of the compost and the rim.

It is possible to make up your own potting compost but sterilization is difficult and for most gardeners it is better to use a proprietary mix. There are soil-based kinds, usually prepared according to the John Innes formulation (John Innes is not a brand name), and soil-less composts. John Innes No. 2 is suitable for a wide range of plants. Many of the soil-less composts are peat based. In recent years environmental concerns about the exploitation of peat reserves

has led to the use of peat alternatives such as coir fibre in these composts. Most composts include lime and are not suitable for rhododendrons and other plants that require an acid soil. For these it is necessary to use an ericaceous compost.

Plant more densely but otherwise follow the same method of planting as is used in the open garden. For a dense display of bulbs plant in two layers. The most important requirement for planted containers is regular watering. The addition to the compost of water-retaining granules will help prevent sudden water loss but even so watering must be frequent during hot and windy

weather. Dense planting makes heavy demands on nutrients, which are also leached out by frequent watering. Regular applications of soluble fertilizer throughout the growing season will help sustain display. Renew compost completely after a succession of spring and summer planting.

Annuals are simply discarded at the end of their season; most other plants can be top-dressed annually and repotted every two to three years. If a plant is not to be moved on to a large container it may be necessary to prune its roots. Tip the plant out of its container, shave a centimetre or so off the sides of the root ball with a sharp knife, and replant.

Right: A garden seat is the perfect place to sit and enjoy the fruits of your labour.

CHAPTER 2

Annuals &
Perennials

*A*nnuals and perennials, the mainstay of a garden, can provide year-round colour and interest. Horticulturally, annuals are those plants which complete their life cycle, from seed to seed, in a season, while perennials generally live for three years or more.

Within the vast group of perennials are evergreens, such as the hardy agapanthus and iris, which are ideally suited to temperate climates, and the herbaceous types, such as asters and gentians, which are able to cope with severe winters as they die back at the end of the summer and form new shoots after a dormant period.

Traditionally these plants were used for massed displays called carpet bedding, where plants were selected to form disciplined colour displays. Today this type of formal, high maintenance display is usually restricted to very large private gardens or parks for special events, while the keen gardener experi-

ments with plants to provide varied and interesting combinations.

Annuals are ideally suited to this experimentation as they are not permanent. One summer the garden could be a subtle combination of creams and soft blues of the newer viola hybrids, another season a completely different effect could be achieved by using bright blue salvias and bold yellow marigolds in the same position. In this way the novice gardener can decide which colour combination is the most pleasing and go on to repeat these colours in the permanent planting of a garden.

Planting Combinations

By combining perennials with annuals in a more informal manner the garden loses that 'all or nothing' effect which is so evident when a bed of annuals has 'finished' and is again planted out with tiny seedlings. By placing clumps of perennials besides drifts of annuals the eye is drawn from one accent to another, say from a group of low-growing

annuals in front to the taller perennial flower spikes behind. Annuals are marvellous for providing a festive welcome to an entrance or a splash of colour to a shrub border when the garden is to be used for a special event. For a continuous effect, group them with perennials, staggering the flowering times of the plants so that when a small pocket of annuals is nearly past its prime a perennial just behind is about to strut its stuff. This complementary display can take a few seasons to achieve as many perennials need two years to bloom, but don't give up as experimenting in this way is one of the most rewarding aspects of gardening.

Apart from colour combinations within a garden, try to tie in the house colour to that of a garden display so they complement one another—a red or red-orange toned house looks good surrounded by bright oranges/yellow/rusty reds and creams while a white or muted pastel painted house blends well with soft blue, mauve, pink and white flowers plus masses of silver foliage.

Chrysanthemums can provide a spectacular display of colour.

Just as important as linking the house to the garden, is the overall siting of the garden beds. Most annuals demand full sun to flower well so be sure to choose an aspect where the plants will receive as much light, particularly morning sun, as possible. Give them generously wide beds ensuring the colourful display will not be overwhelmed by shrub foliage or robbed of nutrients by the roots of nearby permanent plants.

Instant Colour Effects

One of the most welcome developments in recent years is the increase in the number of annuals and perennials available in 'instant colour' pots. Once red geraniums were the only available way to provide a splash of colour in early spring, now, right through the seasons a pot or tray of mature, flowering annuals can be purchased to add instant colour to a garden dead spot or patio. And don't overlook hanging baskets filled with annuals to highlight a garden colour scheme. If potting up seedlings to make your own instant colour, take care to choose plants that fall gracefully over the edge of the basket. Both upright and sprawling types can produce a very decorative display in large pots or tubs.

As discussed earlier, annuals, by their very nature, aim to set as many seeds as possible within a very short life span. Gardeners can extend the flowering period by cutting the blooms for indoor use or nipping off faded flowers before they set seed and so decide it's all over for another year. Remember, if you follow this procedure it is good practice to provide regular nourishment to the plants in the form of a quick-acting fertilizer designed to promote flowers, rather than foliage growth.

Soil Preparation and Planting

To ensure good strong growth and maximize flowering, prepare your garden beds soundly. If the area to be planted has not been dug over before, it is a good idea to double dig. This means that the topsoil, say a fork's depth, is weeded and put aside and the soil under this layer is dug over to the depth of a fork. Humus, such as well-rotted manure, or compost can be added to this layer to help break up heavy clay

With their large spikes of showy, pea flowers, Lupinus *species will enhance any garden.*

particles or to add moisture retentive qualities to sandy soils. This double digging is particularly beneficial to perennials which can be left in the same position for some years. Replace the top layer of soil and prepare this surface in accordance with your planting needs. If planting perennials, a dressing of well-rotted manure or compost or a complete fertilizer can be added while roughly digging the soil over, whereas if hardy annual seeds are to be sown directly into the soil in temperate areas this top layer needs to be well dug over to remove any clods, then raked evenly to ensure a smooth, even surface.

In many areas the local climate determines when and if seeds can be planted directly into the ground. A much greater success rate is ensured, should there be a possibility of a late frost, if seeds are sown in a greenhouse or on a warm, weather-proof veranda or

similar sheltered spot. This guarantees that the seedlings are ready to be transplanted as soon as weather permits.

Whereas annuals are grown from seed each season, perennials have various ways of being propagated. Most can be grown from seed, however this usually takes longer for blooms to form. If established crowns or rhizomes are divided, new plants, true to form, are generally established more quickly and often produce flowers the following season.

For gardeners in all climatic zones annuals provide welcome displays of colour, especially in the early spring, while perennials put on a colour parade once a year, often as a bonus to distinctive foliage. What's more, perennials pay handsome dividends, providing the gardener with a source of plant material with which to experiment with design and colour combinations each season.

Achillea filipendulina 'Gold Plate'

Achillea millefolium

Achillea 'Moonshine'

Acanthus spinosus

Aconitum napellus

Acaena 'Blue Haze'

Acanthus mollis

ACAENA

A small genus of plants, native to New Zealand, which make excellent ground cover, forming tight mats of attractive foliage that stays evergreen in all but the most severe winters. The more vigorous species are ideal to grow at the edge of the border and to soften the harsh edges of paving, while the more compact species are excellent for the rock garden. Their small, rounded heads of summer flowers are less ornamental than the coloured burs which follow in late summer and autumn. Acaenas do best in sun or partial shade and a well-drained soil. Propagate by division in spring.

A. 'Blue Haze'

A vigorous plant ideal for ground cover with finely cut steel-blue leaves that form a dense, evergreen carpet around 10 cm (about 4 in) high and attaining a spread of 75 cm (about 30 in). In summer bronze-red rounded flowerheads are produced, which develop into red, shiny burrs in autumn. Propagate by division in spring.

A. microphylla

This mat-forming, evergreen perennial has divided green leaves which are tinged with bronze when young. Reddish flowerheads develop into decorative burrs in autumn. This species has a neat, compact habit, with a height of 5 cm (about 2 in) and a spread of 15 cm (about 6 in).

ACANTHUS

BEAR'S BREECHES, OYSTER PLANT

These ancient Mediterranean perennials are grown mainly for their handsome leaves and curious spikes of flowers. They make spectacular feature plants and are useful for covering steep banks. They are fully hardy, doing best in sun but tolerating semi-shade. They need a rich, well-drained soil and are best suited to temperate gardens. Flowers appear in early summer, after which the plant dies back. Remove spent flowers, stems and dead leaves and propagate by division in autumn/fall or from seed sown in spring. Watch for snails and other insect pests and water well except when dormant.

They have deep roots and are therefore difficult to eradicate if incorrectly planted. This genus has been immortalized by the Greeks, who used the motif to decorate the capitals of their Corinthian columns.

A. mollis

This strong, upright-growing, semi-evergreen has large, deeply serrated and veined, bright green leaves. It produces tall spikes of funnel-shaped flowers, with purple calyces and whitish petals, in summer. It grows to 1 m (about 3 ft) high with a 45 cm (about 18 in) spread. It likes partial shade.

A. spinosus

This species has very large, deeply divided, arching dark green leaves with spiny points. In summer it bears bold spikes of white flowers tinted with purple. It grows to 1.2 m (about 3½ ft) high with a spread of 60 cm (about 24 in).

ACHILLEA

YARROW, MILFOIL

There are about 200 species of *Achillea*, most native to Europe, Asia and North America. Foliage is fern-like, and masses of large, flat heads of tiny daisy flowers are borne in summer in shades of white, yellow, pink and red. They are hardy perennials, easily grown and tolerant of poor soils, but doing best in sunny, well-drained sites in temperate climates. They multiply rapidly and are easily propagated by division in late winter or from softwood cuttings in early summer. Flowering stems may be cut when spent or left to die down naturally in winter,

when the clumps should be pruned to stimulate strong spring growth. Fertilize in spring. Achilleas are suitable for massed border planting and rockeries, and flowerheads can be dried—retaining their colour—for winter decoration. This genus is named after Achilles, who in Greek mythology used the plant to heal wounds. On St John's Eve, the Irish traditionally hang yarrow in the house to ward off evil.

A. filipendulina 'Gold Plate'

A strong-growing, erect cultivar reaching 1.2 m (about 3½ ft) or more with a spread of 60 cm (about 24 in). It has aromatic, bright green foliage, and in summer bears flat, rounded heads of golden-yellow flowers, 10–15 cm (about 4–6 in) wide. This species is a valuable border plant.

A. millefolium

A shrubby plant growing to 60 cm (about 24 in) tall with feathery, dark green foliage and crimson flowers in summer. Cultivars include 'Cerise Queen', cherry red with pale centres, and the pink 'Rosea'. This species may become invasive in some areas and needs controlling.

A. 'Moonshine'

This species bears pretty flattened heads of pale sulphur-yellow to bright yellow flowers throughout summer; it is a good species for cut flowers. It has delicate, feathery, silvery-grey leaves and an upright habit, reaching a height of 60 cm (about 24 in) with a spread of 50 cm (about 20 in). It should be divided regularly in spring to promote strong growth.

A. tomentosa

WOOLLY YARROW

A low, spreading plant with feathery grey-green leaves and flowerheads of bright yellow on 30 cm (about 12 in) stems. This species is excellent in the rock garden or as an edging plant.

ACONITUM
napellus

HELMET FLOWER, FRIAR'S-CAP

Native to Asia, Europe and America, this autumn/fall-flowering perennial is good for cooler climates. Plant in bold groups or allow to naturalize in woodland conditions. It has tall slender spires of helmet-shaped violet-blue flowers (some forms have pink or white flowers) and deeply divided mid-green leaves. It grows to 1.5 m (about 4½ ft) in height with a spread of 30 cm (about 12 in). It will do best in a moderately rich well-drained soil, in sun or partial shade, and must not be allowed to dry out during the growing season. Plants are easily increased by root division in winter, but once established they are best left undisturbed for several years. Transplant when dormant in winter. *A. napellus* is fully hardy. The poison aconite is extracted from the roots of this plant.

ACORUS
calamus

SWEET FLAG

This grass-like plant is a marginal water plant, needing a depth of up to 25 cm (about 10 in) of water. It is a semi-evergreen perennial with aromatic tangerine-scented leathery sword-like leaves. *Acorus* grows to 75 cm (about 30 in) high with a spread of 60 cm (about 24 in). It is fully hardy and grows best in full sun in an open position. Propagation is by division of the rhizomes in winter or early spring. Plants should be divided every three or four years. Cut away dead foliage in autumn/fall. The leaves of the cultivar *A. calamus* 'Variegatus' have cream variegation and take on a rosy tinge in spring.

ACTAEA
alba

WHITE BANEBERRY

From the eastern United States, this summer-flowering perennial is most notable for its handsome berries, though its flowers and foliage are attractive too. It forms a clump of fresh green, divided leaves with a spread of 45 cm (about 18 in), from which rise the fluffy white flowers on stems up to 1 m (about 3 ft) high. By late summer they have developed into spires of small, gleaming white berries on red stalks. The berries are poisonous, hence the name 'baneberry'. It prefers a site in partial shade, on a fertile, moisture-retentive soil. Propagate by division in spring or by seed in autumn.

ADONIS
aestivalis

This fully hardy herbaceous perennial has ranunculus-like red blooms in early spring, and feathery mid-green foliage. It grows in clumps with a height and spread of 25–30 cm (about 10–12 in). Best results are obtained when planted in a moist, fairly light soil that contains a considerable amount of composted material, peat or leafmould. It flowers in sun or light shade but wilts badly in extreme heat. Fertilize and water regularly, and propagate from seed in late summer or by division after flowering.

AETHIONEMA
armenum

syn. *A.* × *warleyense* 'Warley Rose'

A member of the Brassicaceae (which includes cress) family, and native to the Mediterranean area, this low evergreen short-lived sub-shrub is grown for its profusion of small bright rose-pink flowers in spring and summer. Foliage is handsome, with narrow, elongated bluish green leaves. It is a compact 15 cm (about 6 in) high and wide, making it an ideal plant to grow between paving stones or in a rock garden. It is fully hardy, and enjoys well-drained coarse-textured soil and full sun. Trim lightly after flow-

ering and propagate by softwood cuttings in spring or by seed in autumn/fall. This species will self-seed readily.

AGAPANTHUS

AFRICAN LILY, AGAPANTHUS

Native to southern Africa, these strong-growing perennials are popular for their fine foliage and showy flowers produced in abundance over summer. They have dark green, glossy, gracefully arching strap-shaped leaves. Flowers are blue or white, in many flowered umbels, borne on a long erect stem, often 1 m (about 3 ft) or more tall. Agapanthus are ideal for background plants or for edging along a wall, fence or driveway. Cut flowers are useful for bold arrangements in large containers and the plants also make excellent tub and container specimens. The genus is extremely tough, thriving in conditions of neglect, on hillsides and near the coast. The plants enjoy full sun but will tolerate some shade, and will grow in any soil as long as it is well watered. They naturalize readily, soon forming large clumps. Propagate by division in late winter, or from seed in spring or autumn/fall. Remove spent flower stems and dead leaves at the end of winter. Frost-hardy to half-hardy.

A. 'Blue Baby'

Growing 45–60 cm (about 18–24 in) high with a spread of 30 cm (about 12 in), this frost-hardy cultivar bears light blue flowers on rather open heads in summer.

A. campanulatus

Native to Natal in South Arica, this clump-forming perennial grows to a height of 1.2 m (about 4 ft) with a spread of 50 cm (about 20 in). In late summer, crowded umbels of pale blue flowers are borne on 1 m (about 3 ft) stems above narrow, deciduous, greyish green leaves. Frost-hardy. *A. c. patens* is a smaller, more slender variety, one of the daintiest of all the agapanthus.

A. praecox subsp. orientalis

A half-hardy species, this is probably the best known agapanthus. It has large dense umbels of rich blue flowers carried on strong stems over broad dark green leaves in late summer. It grows to 1 m (about 3 ft) high and 60 cm (about 24 in) wide, and is ideal for pot plants. Prefers full sun and moist soil.

Agapanthus campanulatus

Agapanthus 'Blue Baby'

Aethionema armenum

Acorus calamus

Adonis aestivalis

Agapanthus praecox subsp. *orientalis*

Achillea tomentosa

Alcea rosea

Agrostemma githago

Alchemilla mollis

Ajuga reptans 'Atropurpurea'

Alpinia purpurata

Ageratum houstonianum

AGERATUM
houstonianum
FLOSS FLOWER

Native to tropical Mexico, this
member of the Asteraceae family
(which also contains daisies) is a
popular and easily grown annual with
dull hairy heart-shaped leaves and
showy blue, lavender, mauve-pink or
white fluffy flowerheads. It should
flower throughout summer and into
autumn/fall if the ground is kept
moist and dead flowerheads are removed regularly. The tall cultivars
form clumps of 30 cm (about 12 in)
high and wide and are useful for
bedding and cut flowers. The dwarf
varieties form clumps of 15 cm
(about 6 in) high and wide and are
excellent for edging and containers.
Any well-drained soil is suitable,
preferably compost-enriched. They
are half-hardy and prefer a sunny
position with protection from cold
wind. Keep moist, especially during
spring and summer. Young plants
benefit from tip pruning and spent
flowers should be removed. Propagate from seed sown in spring.

AGROSTEMMA
githago
CORN COCKLE

This fast-growing showy annual
reaches a height of 1 m (about 3 ft),
with a spread of 30 cm (about 12
in), making it ideal for planting at
the back of an annual border. It has a
slender, many branched, willowy
habit with lance-shaped leaves.
Open, trumpet-shaped pink flowers, 8 cm (about 3 in) in diameter,
appear throughout summer. It is
fully hardy, growing best in full sun in
a well-drained soil. Propagate from
seed sown in early spring or autumn/
fall. Young plants should be thinned
to about 25 cm (10 in) spacing and
may need light staking if growing in
exposed areas. The tiny, round, dark
brown seeds are poisonous.

AJUGA
reptans
CARPET BUGLEWEED, BLUE BUGLE

This excellent perennial ground
cover forms a showy carpet in sun
or part shade. Bright blue flower

spikes appear in early spring above
the metallic green crinkled leaves.
There are various cultivars with
different coloured leaves: 'Burgundy Lace' has cream and maroon
variegated leaves; 'Atropurpurea',
dark purplish bronze; 'Multicolor',
white and pink and purple;
'Variegata', light green and creamy
white; and 'Jungle Beauty', dark
green with a tinge of purple. They
grow 10–30 cm high (about 4–12 in)
and spread rapidly from runners.
Fully hardy, they grow in most conditions but prefer shade and cool moist
soil. Those with variegated foliage do
better in sun. Propagate by division in
spring. Remove spent flowerheads
and watch for fungus disease. *Ajuga*
has been widely used as a healing
agent for wounds.

ALCEA
rosea
syn. *Althaea rosea*
HOLLYHOCK

A native of the eastern Mediterranean and central Asia, this stately
biennial was one of the first flowers to
be cultivated in the southern hemisphere. They are popular for their tall
spikes of flowers which can reach 2
m (about 6 ft). Flowers appear in
summer and early autumn/fall, and
come in a range of colours including
pink, cream and yellow. Foliage is
roundish and rough and the plant
spreads to about 60 cm (about 24
in). They are fully hardy but need
shelter from wind, benefiting from
staking in exposed positions. They
prefer sun, a rich, heavy well-drained
soil and frequent watering in dry
weather. Propagate from seed in late

summer or spring. Rust disease can
be a problem; spray with fungicide.

ALCHEMILLA
mollis
LADY'S MANTLE

This old-fashioned, low-growing
perennial is ideal for ground cover,
the front of borders or for rock
gardens. It is clump-forming, growing to a height and spread of 40 cm
(about 16 in). It has decorative,
wavy-edged leaves which hold dew or
raindrops to give a sparkling effect. In
summer, it bears masses of small
sprays of greenish yellow flowers,
similar to *Gypsophila*. They are fully
hardy, preferring partial shade, moist,
well-drained soil and a humid atmosphere. Propagate from seed or by
division in spring or autumn/fall, and
cut back to 3 cm (about 1½ in)
when they finish flowering.

ALPINIA
ORNAMENTAL GINGER

A genus named in honour of the
sixteenth-century Italian botanist
Prospero Alpino, it is grown for its
very showy flowers. Gingers are not
easy to grow successfully in pots
and will only flower in a warm,
moist position. They prefer a mild to
subtropical climate, although all but
A. purpurata will grow in a mild temperate climate. They need full sun to
part-shade. Frost-tender, they will
not survive below 16–18°C (about
61–64°F). Propagate by division of
rhizomes in spring or early summer.
Although edible, it is not the ginger
used commercially. The flowers are
used in the Pacific islands to make
garlands.

A. purpurata
RED GINGER

From Polynesia, the showy spikes
of fairly inconspicuous, small white
flowers in scarlet bracts, bloom
throughout the year and bring a vivid
splash of colour to the garden. The
glossy leaves are narrow and lance-
shaped. New plantlets sprout among
the flower bracts and take root when
the dying flower stems fall to the
ground under the weight of the growing plantlets.

A. zerumbet

syn. A. speciosa, A. nutens

SHELL GINGER, SHELL FLOWER

A tall plant, originally from China, in summer it bears racemes of waxy, ivory or white flowers with yellow lips and pink or red throats. It can grow to 3 m (about 9 ft) and needs partial shade, good soil and plenty of water to flower well.

ALSTROEMERIA

PERUVIAN LILY

Native to South America, these tuberous plants are among the finest of all perennials for cutting, but they do drop petals. Flowers are showy and multi-coloured, resembling miniature trumpet lilies held on thin wiry stems. They flower profusely from spring to summer. About 50 species exist, all growing well in sun or light shade in a well-enriched, well-drained acid soil. They soon form large clumps, bearing dozens of heads of flowers. Propagate from seed or by division in early spring. They are frost-hardy, but in cold winters protect the dormant tubers by covering with loose peat or dry bracken. Best left undisturbed when established, but one-year-old seedlings transplant well. Alstroemerias do well naturalized under trees or on sloping banks.

A. aurea

syn. A. aurantiaca

This is the most common and easily grown species, with heads of orange flowers, tipped with green and streaked with maroon. Leaves are twisted, narrow and lance-shaped. Several cultivars exist; 'Majestic' and 'Bronze Beauty' both have deep orange or bronzy orange flowers. They reach a height of 1 m (about 3 ft) with a spread of 60 cm–1 m (about 2–3 ft).

A., Ligtu hybrids

Leaves are narrow and twisted and flowers are widely flared in shades of pink, salmon, yellow or orange, sometimes streaked and spotted with other colours. They grow 60–80 cm tall (about 24–32 in) with a spread of 60 cm–1 m (about 2–3 ft).

AMARANTHUS

These bright showy annuals, native to the tropics, are grown for their brilliant foliage, curious flowers and adaptability to hot, dry conditions. They are popular bedding plants, with large and attractively coloured leaves and minute flowers borne in drooping tassel-like spikes. A sunny, dry position with protection from strong winds is essential, and they enjoy a fertile, well-drained soil, mulched during hot weather. Half-hardy. Prune when young to

Alpinia zerumbet

Alstroemeria, Ligtu hybrids

Alstroemeria aurea

Amaranthus tricolor 'Joseph's Coat'

thicken growth and propagate from seed sown in spring. Prepare soil for planting with plenty of manure, and water seedlings regularly. Protect from snails when young and watch for caterpillars and aphids.

A. caudatus

LOVE-LIES-BLEEDING, TASSEL FLOWER

This tall species, growing to 1.2 m (about 3½ ft) high and 50 cm (about 20 in) wide, has oval, pale green leaves and dark red flowers in long, drooping cords, their ends often touching the ground. Flowers appear in summer through to autumn/fall. In many old gardens this plant was used to give height in the centre of circular beds.

A. tricolor 'Joseph's Coat'

A bushy annual, growing to 1 m (about 3 ft) and 50 cm (about 20 in) wide. This plant is grown for its brilliant bronze, gold, orange and red variegated 20 cm (8 in) long leaves which retain their colouring into the late autumn/fall. Tiny red flowers appear in summer.

Amaranthus caudatus

ANAGALLIS

linifolia

PIMPERNEL

This charming little plant is grown for its brilliant blue or scarlet flowers of 1 cm (about ½ in) in diameter. They are good small rockery plants or can be used for edging large containers. They flower during summer and are low-growing, rarely exceeding 5 cm (about 2 in) in height, with a spread of 15 cm (about 6 in) or more. This species requires a sunny, well-drained spot in fertile, moist soil. They benefit from some shade in hot areas. Propagate from seed or by division in spring. Fully hardy.

ANAPHALIS

margaritacea

syn. A. yedoensis

PEARL EVERLASTING

Native to the northern hemisphere this perennial member of the Asteraceae family (which includes daisies) is valued for its papery, small white flowers which can be dried

Anagallis linifolia

Anaphalis margaritacea

for indoor decoration. It has lance-shaped, silvery grey leaves and the flowers are borne on erect stems in late summer. Bushy in habit, it grows to 60–75 cm (about 24–30 in) high and 60 cm (about 24 in) wide. Easily grown, it prefers a sunny situation (but will grow in semi-shade) and well-drained chalky soil. Do not allow to dry out. They are fully hardy. Propagate from seed in autumn/fall or by division in winter or spring. Prune back hard in winter.

Antirrhinum majus

Anchusa capensis 'Blue Angel'

Anchusa azurea

Anthemis tinctoria

Anemone × *hybrida* 'Honorine Jobert'

ANCHUSA

SUMMER FORGET-ME-NOT, ALKANET

Natives of Europe, north and south Africa and western Asia, this genus consists of about 50 species of annuals, biennials and perennials. They are larger than the forget-me-not (*Myosotis*) and have clearer, true blue flowers that do not fade easily. All species are suitable for herbaceous borders and are easily grown in beds and containers. Fully to frost-hardy, they grow best in a sunny position in deep, rich, well-

drained soil. In very hot areas planting in semi-shade helps maintain the flower colour. Feed sparingly and water generously. The taller species benefit from staking and the plants require plenty of room as they make large root systems. Cut flower stalks back after blooming to promote new growth. Propagate perennials by division in winter, annuals and biennials from seed in autumn/fall or spring. Transplant perennials when dormant in winter. These plants are popular with bees.

A. azurea
syn. *A. italica*

This fully hardy perennial grows to 1–1.2 m (about 3–3½ ft) high and 60 cm (about 24 in) wide. It has coarse, hairy leaves and an erect habit with tiers of brilliant blue flowers borne in spring to summer. Cultivars include the rich blue 'Morning Glory', light blue 'Opal' and deep blue 'Loddon Royalist'.

A. capensis 'Blue Angel'

A bushy biennial, grown as an annual, this *Anchusa* reaches a height

and spread of 20 cm (about 8 in). A native of southern Africa, it forms a compact pyramid of shallow, bowl-shaped sky-blue flowers in early summer. Frost-hardy. 'Blue Bird' is a taller—50 cm (about 20 in)—but equally striking cultivar.

ANEMONE
× hybrida
syn. *A. japonica, A. hupehensis*
JAPANESE WINDFLOWER

One of the most elegant plants for growing under trees or large shrubs, these vigorous branching perennials grow to a height of 60 cm to 1.3 m (about 2-4 ft) and a width of 60 cm (about 24 in). Leaves are deeply divided and dark green; tall, erect flower stems bear many large, saucer-shaped flowers in late summer and early autumn/fall. Flowers are white, pink or soft carmine red, single, semi-double or double; cut back stems as they fade. Plant in humus-rich, well-drained soil in full sun to half-shade. They adapt to almost any position. Propagate by division of an established clump in early spring before growth begins, or from seed sown in late summer. Fertilize in late winter or early spring. 'Honorine Jobert' has snow-white flowers with a yellow centre.

ANTHEMIS
tinctoria
GOLDEN MARGUERITE, YELLOW CHAMOMILE

A fully hardy easily grown perennial that is covered in late spring and summer with a dazzling display of daisy-like yellow flowers above fern-like, crinkled green leaves. The foliage of *Anthemis*, very aromatic when crushed, is used to make chamomile tea. They prefer sun and will thrive even in poor sandy or clay soils as long as they are well-drained. Strong growers, they form clumps 1 m (about 3 ft) high and wide and need cutting back and

breaking up into smaller clumps each season. Propagate by division in spring, or basal cuttings in spring or late summer. Prolong flowering by cutting back the spent stems.

ANTIRRHINUM
majus
SNAPDRAGON

Native to the Mediterranean region, this perennial is valued for its showy flowers that are borne over a long period from spring to autumn/fall. There are many cultivars (usually grown as annuals), ranging from tall—75 cm (about 30 in); to medium—50 cm (about 20 in); to dwarf—25 cm (about 10 in). They have a spread of 30–50 cm (about 12–20 in). Erect plants, they form dense bushes of many upright stems carrying spikes of frilly, two-lipped, sometimes double, flowers, in a range of colours including orange, yellow, red, purple, pink and white. They prefer a fertile, well-drained soil in full sun with some protection from wind. Plants should be dead-headed to prolong flowering and early buds can be pinched out to increase branching. Half-hardy. Propagate from seed in spring or early autumn/fall. Rust disease can be a problem.

AQUILEGIA
COLUMBINE

These graceful, clump-forming perennials, native to Europe, North America and much of Asia, are grown for their interesting form and varied colour range. They are also useful cut flowers, and the dwarf and alpine species make good rock garden plants. Foliage is fern-like and the flowers are mainly bell-shaped and spurred. Fully to frost-hardy, they flower during early summer and prefer a well-drained light soil, enriched with animal manure. Plant in an open, sunny site, protected from strong winds and with some shade in hot areas. They look

look their best in bold clumps with a foreground planting of other annuals. Keep moist and give plenty of liquid fertilizer during growth. In cold climates columbines are perennial and need to be cut to the ground in late winter, but growing them as annuals usually gives best results. Propagate from seed in autumn/fall and spring. The plants are short-lived, but self-seed readily. The common name, 'columbine', comes from the Latin for dove, as the flowers were thought to resemble a cluster of doves.

A. caerulea
BLUE COLUMBINE

This alpine species is a short-lived, upright perennial growing to 45 cm (about 18 in) in height with a spread of 15 cm (about 6 in). Big, powdery blue or white nodding flowers on branching stems appear in spring and early summer. It sometimes produces a few blooms in autumn/fall. It is fully hardy, and does best in rich soil. *A. alpina* is similar but has short spurs and usually all blue flowers.

A., McKana hybrids

A clump-forming, leafy perennial growing to 75 cm (about 30 in) tall with a spread of 30 cm (about 12 in). This strain includes an extensive range of pastel shades and bicolours. Flowers are large and noted for their delicate long spurs behind the petals. Fully hardy, they flower in spring or early summer.

A. vulgaris
GRANNY'S BONNETS

This is the true columbine, one of the parents of the modern hybrids. It is a variable species, growing to 1 m (about 3 ft) high with a spread of 50 cm (about 20 in). It bears funnel-shaped, short spurred flowers in colours of pink, crimson, white and purple, on long stems from the centre of a loose rosette of grey-green foliage that resembles maidenhair fern. Fully hardy, it flowers from spring to early summer.

ARABIS
caucasica 'Plena'
syn. A. albida

This fully hardy, evergreen perennial is suitable for ground cover in the rock garden, crevices in walls or bedding. It is sometimes used to overplant spring flowering bulbs. Easily grown, it forms dense clusters of thick foliage, up to 15 cm (about 6 in) high with a spread of 45 cm (about 18 in). It has loose, mid-green leaf rosettes and white, fragrant, double flowers appear in early to late spring. It requires a light, well-drained soil, rich in organic matter. Plant in full sun

(semi-shade in warmer climates) and cut back hard after flowering. Propagate from softwood cuttings in summer, or from seed or by division in autumn/fall.

ARCTOTIS
× hybrida
AFRICAN DAISY, AURORA DAISY

Native to southern Africa, these colourful, profusely blooming flowers are excellent for ground cover or mass planting on sloping sites. They are compact perennials, often grown as annuals, and reach a height of 50 cm (about 20 in) or more, and spread of 40 cm (about 16 in). Daisy-like 8 cm (about 3 in) flowers in shades of pink, white, yellow, red and orange, all with contrasting black and gold centres, are produced abundantly from winter until late summer. The blooms close in dull weather and in late afternoon. Leaves are chrysanthemum-like. These plants require full sun, regular watering, and a well-drained light soil with well-rotted compost and sharp sand added. Frost-tender. Propagate from seed in spring or autumn/fall, or from year-round stem cuttings.

ARGEMONE
mexicana
PRICKLY POPPY

This half-hardy perennial has prickly, white-marked greyish green leaves, and fragrant, yellow or white poppy-like flowers. The flowers are 8 cm (about 3 in) wide and appear in summer. It has a spreading habit, growing to 60 cm (about 24 in) high and 30 cm (about 12 in) wide. They grow best in full sun and very well-drained soil. Remove spent flowers to prolong flowering and propagate from seed in early summer. Transplant in autumn/fall. This species self-seeds readily and tends to become invasive. Native to North America, the genus is named from the Greek *argema*, a cataract, as the local Indians believed the plants had medicinal properties that would cure cataracts.

ARGYRANTHEMUM
frutescens
syn. Chrysanthemum frutescens
MARGUERITE, PARIS DAISY

Native to the Canary Islands, this bushy evergreen perennial is available in many colours. They bear many daisy-like flowerheads, both single and double, in spring and summer. Most grow to a height and spread of 1 m (about 3 ft). A. *frutescens* is half-hardy. Pinch out growing tips regularly to maintain shape, and cut back severely in summer.

Aquilegia, McKana hybrids

Aquilegia caerulea

Aquilegia vulgaris

Argemone mexicana (white form)

Arabis caucasica 'Plena'

Arctotis × *hybrida*

Argyranthemum frutescens

Armeria maritima

Artemisia stelleriana

Artemisia 'Powys Castle'

ARMERIA

maritima

SEA PINK, THRIFT

One of the best of the old cottage garden plants, thrift was in cultivation as early as 1578. It is a tufted evergreen perennial with a mound-like mass of narrow, dark green leaves, and dense flowerheads of small white to pink flowers. Flowers are produced in a flush in early spring and continue to bloom for most of the year. The plant grows to 10 cm (about 4 in) high and spreads to 20 cm (about 8 in), making it good for edging. Sandy soil and good drainage are essential and they thrive in hot, dry, sunny situations, particularly near the coast. The species is native to the mountains and rocky coasts of the Mediterranean and Asia Minor and resents wet conditions or heavy soils. Fully hardy. Propagate from seed in autumn/fall, or semi-ripe cuttings in summer.

ARTEMISIA

WORMWOOD

This is a large genus of plants and herbs, mostly native to arid regions in the northern hemisphere. Grown for their decorative silvery foliage that is often aromatic and sometimes repellent to insects. They have insignificant flowers but are an attractive addition to a flower border where their feathery foliage provides interest throughout the year. There are both shrubby and herbaceous, evergreen and deciduous species. Mostly fully to half-hardy, they prefer an open, sunny situation with light, well-drained

soil. Prune back lightly in spring to stimulate growth. Propagate from softwood or semi-ripe cuttings in summer or by division in spring. Transplant during winter.

A. arborescens

Evergreen perennial with silvery white foliage, reaching a height of 1.2 m (about 3½ ft) and spread of 75 cm (about 30 in). Small bright yellow flowers are borne in summer and early autumn/fall. Half-hardy. Trim well in spring. This is a good plant for the back of a border.

A. lactiflora

WHITE MUGWORT

A tall-growing, attractive Chinese species which grows like a Michaelmas daisy with many-branched heads of tiny milky white flowers blooming in summer. Foliage is fern-like and aromatic. This is a useful plant to contrast with stronger colours in a garden. Needs staking. It grows 1.2–1.5 m tall (about 3½ to 4½ ft) with a spread of 50 cm (about 20 in). Fully hardy.

A. 'Powys Castle'

This assumed hybrid between *A. absinthium* and *A. arborescens* is one of the most useful of the wormwoods, with its finely dissected silvery leaves and its gentle 60-90 cm (about 2-3 ft) mounding habit. Because it seldom flowers, it remains more compact and less leggy than other species; older plants, nevertheless, benefit from a hard cutting back in early spring as new shoots develop from the base. Use it to introduce a distinct foliage effect into a mixed border of perennials and shrubs; contrast it with

Aruncus dioicus

deep reds and purples. It prefers full sun but does well in light shade, provided the soil is well drained. Propagate from cuttings in summer.

A. stelleriana

Excellent planted in light sandy soils, this evergreen perennial has serrated, white-haired silver leaves, and slender sprays of small yellow flowers are borne in summer. It has a rounded habit and grows 30–60 cm (about 12–24 in) high and spreads up to 1 m (about 3 ft). Fully hardy.

ARUNCUS

dioicus

syn. *A. sylvester, Spiraea aruncus*

GOAT'S BEARD

A graceful woodland perennial useful for shady spots and moist situations. The clump-forming plants produce a mass of rich green, fern-like foliage and arching plumes of tiny silky white flowers in summer. Grows to a height of 2 m (about 6 ft) and spread of 1.2 m (about 3½ ft). It is a good specimen for planting beside a pool or creek. Fully hardy, the plant naturalizes readily and thrives in any well-drained moist soil, in full light or partial shade. Propagate from seed in spring or by division in spring or autumn/fall. Cut flowering stems back hard in autumn/fall.

ASTER

MICHAELMAS OR EASTER DAISY, ASTER

Native to the northern hemisphere, this large genus of perennials and deciduous or evergreen sub-shrubs

contains over 250 species. Easily grown, they vary in height from miniatures suitable for rock gardens to 2 m (about 6 ft) tall giants suitable for the back of a herbaceous border. Leaves are sometimes dark coloured, sometimes hairy. Showy, daisy-like flowerheads are usually produced in late summer or autumn/fall, in a wide range of colours, including blue, violet, purple, pink, red or white, all with a central disc of yellow or black. Grow in sun or partial shade in hot areas in a well-drained soil, preferably enriched with leafmould. Keep moist at all times and feed complete plant food in spring and summer. Shelter from strong winds and stake the taller species. Cut the long stems down to ground level and tidy the clumps when flowers have faded. Propagate by division in spring or late autumn/fall, or from softwood cuttings in spring. Replace plants about every three years; the most vigorous types are best lifted annually, and two or three strong side shoots planted again.

A. alpinus

A clump-forming plant, growing 15 cm (about 6 in) high and spreading to 45 cm (about 18 in). Large violet-blue daisies with yellow centres appear from late spring until early summer; the foliage is dark green. This species is from the higher mountains of Europe and is popular as a rock garden plant. Fully hardy, it prefers full sun and is easily grown in any but very light soil.

Artemisia lactiflora

Artemisia arborescens

Aster alpinus

A. frikartii 'Mönch'

A bushy free-branching plant, producing large, single soft lavender-blue daisy-like flowers with yellowish centres from mid-summer until late autumn/fall. Grows to a height of 75 cm (about 30 in) and spread of 45 cm (about 18 in). Fully hardy. One of the best asters for garden display and picking.

A. novae-angliae 'Barr's Pink'

An erect plant growing to 1 m (about 3 ft) tall, this cultivar produces bright rose pink flowers from late summer until autumn/fall. Fully hardy and mildew resistant.

A. novae-angliae 'Harrington's Pink'

The best-known of the *A. novae-angliae* cultivars, this cultivar produces lovely salmon-pink flowers with yellow centres in autumn/fall. Fully hardy, it grows to 1.2 m (about 3½ ft) tall, so it may need staking. It is well-branched and very showy when in bloom.

A. novi-belgii 'Mulberry'
NEW YORK ASTER

An upright plant bearing large, daisy-like semi-double, rich mulberry-red flowers with yellow centres in autumn/fall. Leaves are small, lance-shaped and dark green. Grows to 75 cm (about 30 in) tall with a spread of 45 cm (about 18 in). Fully hardy. Watch for mildew.

ASTILBE
GOAT'S BEARD

Native to the Orient, these easily grown fully hardy perennials are ideal used as a trouble-free ground cover in damp spots. They grow best on the edge of ponds and in damp hollows, but are also suitable for borders and rock gardens. Foliage is attractive and fern-like, and in young plants often a coppery red. Flowers appear in summer, in tall, fluffy plume-like panicles, in white, cream, many shades of pink, red and purple. Plant in rich, deep soil with plenty of water, in partial shade and do not allow to dry out. Propagate by division of established clumps from late winter to spring,

or from seed or division in autumn/fall. Astilbes make good cut flowers.

A. × arendsii

A leafy, clump-forming plant growing to 60–90 cm (about 2–3 ft) tall and as wide. These are hybrids produced from several different species, the height of which vary. They are available as named cultivars in a range of colours from red through pink to white. 'Fanal' is scarlet, 'Bridal Veil' is white and 'Rheinland' is deep rose, to name but a few. Flowers are produced in spikes in late spring to early summer. It has broad leaves with oval leaflets.

A. chinensis 'Pumila'

An attractive clump-forming plant with toothed, hairy, dark green leaves and dense, fluffy spikes of small, star-shaped mauve-red flowers. It grows to a height of 30 cm (about 12 in) and spreads quickly. Ideal for moist, shady borders or rock gardens. Benefits from extra fertilizer during the flowering period.

Astilbe × *arendsii*

Aster frikartii 'Mönch'

Aster novae-angliae 'Barr's Pink'

Astilbe chinensis 'Pumila'

Aster novi-belgii 'Mulberry'

Aster novae-angliae 'Harrington's Pink'

ASTRANTIA
major
MASTERWORT

Deeply lobed palmate leaves form a loose mound of foliage 45 cm (about 18 in) tall from which rise nearly bare stems to 60 cm (about 2 ft) or more, each topped by intricately formed soft pink or white daisy-like flowers. Each flower is actually many tiny flowers in a domed cluster, surrounded by petal-like bracts in the same col-

Aubrieta deltoidea

ours. Flowers are produced almost throughout summer. They prefer rich, moist soil in full sun or dappled shade and are good for cutting, which will prolong the flowering period. They have a tendency to seed themselves around.

AUBRIETA
deltoidea
ROCK CRESS

This miniature trailing perennial is an ideal plant for rock gardens,

Aurinia saxatilis

sunny dry banks, chinks in stone paving and walls or for border edges. It is a compact plant with greenish grey leaves and masses of starry flowers in mauve-pinks, mauve-blues and violets. It flowers for a long period in spring, often repeat flowering in autumn/fall. It forms a dense mat to 5 cm (about 2 in) high with a spread of 20 cm (about 8 in), and spills prettily over the edges of beds or containers. Fully hardy, it thrives in sun and any well-drained soil. Propagate from semi-ripe cuttings in late summer or autumn/fall or from seed sown in spring. Cut back hard after flowering. *Aubrieta* was named for an eighteenth-century French botanical artist.

AURINIA
saxatilis
syn. *Alyssum saxatile*
YELLOW ALYSSUM

Native to south-eastern Europe, this perennial blooms in early spring. It forms a neat mound of greyish green leaf rosettes and has showy flower sprays in shades of vivid yellow and gold that last for months. It is a woody rooted evergreen plant growing to 25 cm (about 10 in) high with a spread of 30 cm (about 12 in). Fully hardy, it needs sun and a moderately fertile, coarse, gritty, well-drained soil. It is highly regarded as a rock garden or wall plant and makes a good companion plant to tulips. Propagate from seed in autumn/fall or softwood or greenwood cuttings in early summer. Self-seeds readily. Cut back after flowering.

BAPTISIA
australis

Native to the eastern United States, this summer-flowering perennial is beautiful in both flower and foliage. The lobed leaves are blue-green and form a loose mound about 1.3 m (about 4 ft) high and 60 cm (about 24 in) across. The lupin-like flowers are borne on spikes from early to mid-summer; they are an unusual shade of deep blue. The seed pods can be dried for indoor decoration.

This plant does best in full sun and in a good, moisture-retentive soil. It has a deep root system, so propagation is best done by seed collected and sown as soon as it is ripe in autumn.

BEGONIA
BEGONIA

This large genus of perennial plants are grown for their colourful flowers and ornamental foliage. Most of the 1000-odd species can be grown outdoors only in areas with temperate to subtropical climates. Tuberous rooted or fibrous, they range in habit from dwarf to tall and scandent, some are hardy and others very sensitive to frost. All require a light, rich well-drained soil that is slightly acidic. They need shelter from wind and strong sunlight. There are various groups of begonias, each with different cultivation requirements.

Semperflorens group
BEDDING BEGONIA, WAX BEGONIA

Bushy, evergreen perennials, cultivars within this group are often grown as bedding annuals. They are also useful for bordering, especially in shaded gardens. Freely branching plants, with soft succulent stems, they have rounded glossy green, bronze or variegated 5 cm (about 2 in) long leaves. Flowers are showy, single or double in colours of bright rose-pink, light pink, white or red. They grow best in partial sun or shade and a well-drained soil. Propagate in spring from seed or stem cuttings and pinch out growing tips to encourage bushy growth. Frost-tender, these begonias can be dug up and potted for indoor winter use in frosty areas.

B. metallica
METAL-LEAF BEGONIA

A tall-growing, shrub-like begonia from Mexico with bronze-green leaves often splashed with white. The leaves are borne from white-haired stems and are covered with fine silver hairs, red beneath. In summer to autumn/fall pink flowers with red bristles appear. It goes well as an indoor plant.

B. 'Orange Rubra'

This cane-stemmed begonia can reach 60 cm (about 24 in). It has large, oval, light green leaves, sometimes with white spots that disappear with age. Clusters of orange flowers are produced throughout the year.

BELLIS
perennis
DOUBLE DAISY, ENGLISH DAISY

The common daisy of English lawns has given rise to a variety of garden

Astrantia major

Begonia metallica

Begonia 'Orange Rubra'

Baptisia australis

Bergenia cordifolia

Browallia americana

Bergenia stracheyi

strains with fully double flower-heads of red, crimson, pink or white, all with a gold centre. They grow to a height and spread of 15–20 cm (about 6–8 in) and make ideal front border, edging or rockery plants. They flower in spring and grow in sun or semi-shade and prefer well-drained, rich, moist soil. Keep an eye out for rust disease. They are usually grown as annuals or biennials from seed sown in summer. Remove spent flowerheads regularly to prolong flowering. The golden centre of the daisy gave the flower its name 'Deus eye', or the eye of god.

BERGENIA

A group of perennials with large, handsome, leathery leaves, the shape of which has earned them the name of elephant's ears. The species are native to Asia, and there are also many garden hybrids that have been developed over the last one hundred years or so. Clusters of flowers are borne on short, stout stems in spring. The evergreen foliage makes excellent ground cover, which is especially useful as bergenias thrive in sun or shade and are tolerant of exposed sites. The leaves often develop attractive red tints in winter; these colours develop best when the plants are grown in sun and on poor soil. Propagate by division in spring after flowering.

B. cordifolia
HEARTLEAF, SAXIFRAGA

Native to Siberia, this tough perennial has large, roundish, crinkle-edged, heart-shaped leaves and produces racemes of rosy red flowers on 30–40 cm (about 12–16 in) stems in spring. It is long-flowering and useful for cutting. Cultivars include 'Red' with deep carmine flowers and 'Purpurea', magenta pink. It grows to a height of 45 cm (about 18 in) and spread of 60 cm (about 24 in). Fully hardy, it makes an excellent border plant or trouble-free ground cover among deciduous trees and shrubs. Thrives in sun or shade and requires a fairly good soil with plenty of humus. Propagate by division from autumn/fall through to spring, after flowering. Water

well in hot weather and remove spent flowerheads to prolong flowering.

B. hybrids
ELEPHANT'S EARS

There are many handsome bergenia hybrids in a range of colours. They include 'Abendglut' (also known as 'Evening Glow') with deep magenta flowers and leaves that develop maroon tints in winter. 'Ballawley' bears bright crimson flowers, those of 'Silberlicht' (also known as 'Silver Light') are pure white, and 'Sunningdale' has carmine-pink flowers. They all flower in spring. Sizes range from 30–60 cm (about 12–24 in) in height and spread. Propagate by division in spring after flowering.

B. stracheyi

Native to the Himalayas, this ever-green perennial has relatively small, wedge-shaped, hairy-margined leaves that are carried more erectly than on most of the other bergenias. It produces sprays of cup-shaped, pale pink or white flowers in spring. Clump-forming, it reaches a height of 22 cm (about 9 in), with a spread of 30 cm (about 12 in). It is fully hardy.

BRACHYCOME

Native to Australia, these low-growing annuals and evergreen perennials are suitable for use as ground cover. They are mound-forming plants with finely divided, soft, fern-like foliage and bear hundreds of daisy-like flowers in many shades of blue, mauve, pink and white, centred in black and gold. They are showy border or bedding plants, the smaller species being excellent for rock gardens. Frost-hardy to half-hardy, they prefer a sunny situation, sandy loam or well-drained garden soil. A sheltered position is preferable, with plenty of root protection. Do not overwater as they prefer dry conditions. Pinch out early shoots to encourage branching and propagate from ripe seed or by divisions or stem cuttings in spring or autumn/fall. The Swan River daisy (*B. iberidifolia*) grows to a

Bergenia hybrids

height and spread of 50 cm (about 20 in). It is fairly fast growing with lacy green foliage. Small, fragrant daisy-like flowers of blue, pink, mauve, purple or white appear in summer and early autumn/fall.

BROWALLIA
americana
syn. *B. elata*

This moderately fast-growing perennial, related to the petunia, is usually grown as an annual. A bushy plant, it grows to a height of 60 cm (about 24 in) and spread of 15 cm (about 6 in). Makes a good pot or basket plant as well as growing well outdoors. In summer and early autumn/fall it bears clusters of showy semi-star shaped 4 cm (about 2 in) wide flowers in a rare shade of intense blue. It has oval, mid-green leaves. It can withstand temperatures down to 4°C (40°F), and grows best in partial shade in a rich soil with good drainage. Do not allow to completely dry out. Propagate from seed in spring, or in late summer for winter flowers. Pinch out young growing tips to encourage bushiness. The cultivar 'Vanja' has deep blue flowers with white eyes; 'White Bells' has ice white flowers.

BRUNNERA
macrophylla
SIBERIAN BUGLOSS

The small but intensely blue flowers show their relationship to the forget-me-not; they are held on slender stems 45-60 cm (about 18-24 in) tall above the bold mounds of heart-shaped basal leaves. Flowers appear

Bellis perennis

Brachycome iberidifolia

Brunnera macrophylla

in late spring to early summer, after which the new leaves grow to their full 15-20 cm (about 6-8 in) width. Clumps spread slowly underground but self-seed readily, becoming an excellent ground cover under trees and large shrubs. It prefers a rich, woodsy, moist soil, especially in sun; it is more tolerant of dry conditions only in shade. The cultivar 'Variegata' is one of the choicest of variegated foliage plants, with a thin white margin around each leaf. Alas, it is slow to propagate and difficult to find in nurseries.

Calceolaria integrifolia

Calocephalus brownii

Calceolaria × herbeohybrida

Callistephus chinensis

CALCEOLARIA

LADIES' PURSE, SLIPPER FLOWER

Mostly native to Central and South America, these charming annuals, biennials, evergreen perennials, sub-shrubs and scandent climbers make spectacular pot plants and garden plants, and are valued for their ability to flower profusely in partial shade. Flowers are pouch-like, usually yellow, sometimes red and heavily spotted on the lower lip. They are fully hardy to frost-tender. Most prefer sun, but several species will flower well in a shady cool site in moist, well-drained soil, with added compost and sharp sand. Propagate from seed in autumn/fall or softwood cuttings in summer or late spring. Provide shelter from heavy winds as the flowerheads are easily damaged. Needs to be pruned back to half height each winter.

C. × herbeohybrida

A compact bushy annual popular for spring display indoors. There are many named varieties, growing to a height of 20–40 cm (about 8–16 in) and spread of 15–25 cm (about 6–10 in). Flowers during spring and summer, bearing heads of red and yellow pouched flowers about 4 cm (2 in) wide. Leaves are oval and slightly hairy. Half-hardy.

C. integrifolia

An evergreen, sub-shrubby perennial, growing to 1.2 m (about 3½ ft) high with a spread of 60 cm (about 24 in). It has soft green, heavily wrinkled, clammy leaves, rust-coloured beneath, and in summer bears crowded clusters of wide, brilliant yellow to red-brown flow-

ers. Half-hardy. It is sometimes grown as an annual and during very cold winters may die down to near ground level. Prefers crowded conditions, an acid soil and only occasional watering.

CALENDULA
officinalis

POT MARIGOLD

This is a popular winter and spring flowering annual that remains in bloom for a long time. There are tall and dwarf forms, both bushy, the tall growing to a height and spread of 60 cm (about 24 in) and the dwarf to 30 cm (about 12 in). These fast-growing plants are among the easiest of all annuals to grow, and are useful for filling gaps in the winter and spring garden. They also provide good cut flowers for the cooler months. All forms have lance-shaped, strongly scented pale-green leaves and daisy-like single or double flowerheads. Tall cultivars include 'Geisha Girl' with double orange flowers; 'Pacific Beauty', pastel-shaded double flowers; 'Princess', crested orange, gold or yellow flowers; and the Touch of Red Series, double flowers in tones of deep orange-red. Dwarf cultivars include the Fiesta Series, double flowers in colours ranging from cream to orange; and 'Honey Babe', apricot, yellow and orange flowers. All cultivars are fully hardy and will thrive in almost any well-drained soil in a sunny situation. Propagate from seed sown in spring or autumn/fall. They also self-seed readily. Remove spent flowerheads to encourage prolonged flowering. Watch for mildew, snails and slugs.

Calendula officinalis

CALLISTEPHUS
chinensis

CHINA ASTER

An erect, bushy annual that is reputedly difficult to grow. This species needs sun, protection from wind and extremes of heat and a light sandy, fertile, well-drained soil with added lime. Water plants well and mulch in hot weather to keep the root system cool. It is a fairly fast-growing plant. There are various cultivars available, ranging from tall, up to 60 cm (about 24 in) with a spread of 45 cm (about 18 in) to very dwarf, up to 20 cm (about 8 in) with a spread of 30 cm (about 12 in). Leaves are oval, toothed and mid-green and the plants flower in summer and early autumn/fall in a wide range of colours including white, blue, pink and red. *C. chinensis* is half-hardy. Stake tall cultivars and remove spent flowers regularly. Propagate from seed in

mid-spring and watch for virus disease, aphids, foot rot and root rot.

CALOCEPHALUS
brownii

CUSHION BUSH

This dwarf, evergreen, spreading low shrub is native to Australia. It has a rounded habit, growing to 1 m (about 3 ft) high and wide, and makes a silvery mound with its intricate velvety grey branches and tiny scale-like leaves. It flowers in summer with pale cream rounded knobs that appear silver when in bud. Useful as an accent plant, a striking ground cover or a dwarf hedge. Frost-hardy, it prefers a sunny situation and well-drained soil. Propagate from semi-ripe cuttings or seed in late summer. Trim after flowering, pinch tips of young plants to promote bushy growth and watch for botrytis in damp conditions.

Caltha palustris

Campanula isophylla

Campanula carpatica

CALTHA
palustris
KINGCUP, MARSH MARIGOLD

Native to the temperate and cold regions of the northern hemisphere, this hardy marginal water plant is grown for its attractive flowers. It is a deciduous or semi-evergreen perennial, with glistening, buttercup-like golden yellow flowers borne in spring, and dark green, rounded leaves. Grows to a height and spread of 30 cm (about 12 in). Fully hardy, it is suitable for the margins of streams or ponds or in any damp spots. Prefers an open, sunny position and wet soil. Propagate by division in early spring, or from seed or by division in autumn/fall. Watch for rust which should be treated with a fungicide.

CAMPANULA
BELLFLOWER

Native to the temperate parts of the northern hemisphere, this large genus includes about 250 species of annuals, biennials and perennials. They are among the most showy of plants and are useful specimens for rockeries, borders, wild gardens and hanging baskets. Many of the species are classed as rock and alpine plants. Leaves vary in shape and size, sometimes appearing on upright stems and sometimes only as a cluster at the base. Flowers are mostly bell-shaped and blue, with some whites. All do best in a moderately enriched, moist, well-drained soil. They grow in sun or shade, but flower colour remains brightest in shady situations. Protect from drying winds and stake the taller varieties, which make good cut flowers. Remove spent flower stems. Feed regularly, particularly during the growing season. Propagate from seed or by division in spring or autumn/fall, or by softwood or basal cuttings in spring or summer. They are fully to half-hardy. Transplant during winter. Watch for slugs.

C. carpatica
CARPATHIAN BELLFLOWER

The slowly spreading clumps of basal leaves of this species make it good as an edging or rock garden

Campanula persicifolia 'Alba'

plant. From late spring through much of summer 30–38 cm (about 12–15 in) stems rise above the foliage, carrying up-facing, 2–5 cm (about 1–2 in) wide bowl-shaped flowers in blue, lavender or white. The most common cultivars available are the compact-growing 'Blue Chips' and 'White Clips', and the bright violet blue 'Wedgwood Blue'. They are always attractive plants, even when not in flower. Full sun to light shade is preferred, along with a well-drained soil. Divide established clumps to get more plants in early spring as growth begins, or sow from seed in autumn.

C. isophylla
ITALIAN BELLFLOWER

A dwarf, evergreen trailing perennial, growing to 10 cm (4 in) high with a spread of 30 cm (12 in). Native to the mountain slopes of northern Italy, it has star-shaped blue or white flowers in summer. Leaves are small and heart-shaped. 'Alba' has white flowers. Half-hardy. This is an ideal hanging basket specimen.

C. lactiflora

A strong growing perennial reaching a height of 1.2 m (about 3½ ft) and a spread of 60 cm (about 24 in). In summer, it produces immense pyramidal spikes containing large, nodding, bell-shaped lilac blue, occasionally pink or white, flowers. Leaves are narrowly oval. If cut back straight after flowering they may bloom again in late autumn/fall. Fully hardy, these plants can be naturalized among light grass and will thrive in either sun or semi-shade.

Campanula lactiflora

C. medium
CANTERBURY BELL

A biennial species, this is a slow-growing, erect clump-forming plant. It produces spires of bell-shaped single or double, white, pink or blue flowers, towering 1 m (3 ft) over a rosette of lance-shaped fresh green leaves that spreads to 30 cm (about 12 in). Flowers in spring and early summer. Grow as border plants in semi-shade. The common name is derived from the harness bells worn by medieval pilgrims' horses as they journeyed to Canterbury Cathedral in England.

C. persicifolia

Perhaps the best known *Campanula* with nodding, bell-shaped blue or white flowers borne above narrow, lance-shaped bright green leaves in summer. *C.p.* 'Alba' has white flowers. Pinch individual spent flowers off upright stems as soon as they fade. Fully hardy, it is a spreading, rosette forming perennial reaching a height of 1 m (about 3 ft) and spread of 30 cm (about 12 in).

Campanula medium

Catharanthus roseus

Campanula poscharskyana

Campanula portenschlagiana

Canna × generalis

Celosia cristata

Campanula takesimana

C. portenschlagiana

Native to the mountains of southern Europe, this is a low-growing evergreen plant, well suited to rock gardens. Grows to a height of 15 cm (about 6 in) with an indefinite spread. It has dense, small, ivy-shaped leaves, and a profusion of open, bell-shaped, violet flowers are borne in late spring and early summer. Plant in cool, part-shaded positions with good drainage. Fully hardy.

C. poscharskyana

A rampant, low-growing, spreading perennial with sprays of bell-shaped mauve-blue flowers from late spring onwards. It mounds up from 10 to 15 cm (about 4–6 in) with an indefinite spread and is fully hardy. Ideal for use as a ground cover, on walls, banks and in the front of mixed borders. Partial shade will prolong flowering.

C. takesimana

A native of Korea, this striking perennial has unusual large, bell-shaped flowers that are lilac-pink and spotted with a darker shade of the same colour on the inside. The large leaves form basal rosettes of foliage, and the roots tend to spread so the plant forms a large clump. Happy in sun or shade, this plant can be propagated by division in autumn or spring. The height and spread is 45 cm (about 18 in).

CANNA
× generalis

Native to tropical America, these robust, showy perennials grow from rhizomes and are valued for their striking flowers and foliage. Ideally suited to summer bedding displays and containers, they grow from 1.5–2 m (about 4½–6 ft) in height with a spread of 60 cm (about 24 in). The sturdy stems have bold, lance-shaped, green or bronze leaves and the summer flowers are red, pink, orange or yellow. Frost-tender, they require a sunny position and moist soil with plenty of well-decayed animal manure. Water well during the summer period to prolong flowering. Propagate in spring by division. In cold areas the roots need to be protected with mulch.

CATANANCHE
caerulea
CUPID'S DART

Native to the Mediterranean region, this fast-growing, herbaceous perennial reaches 60 cm (about 24 in) in height with a spread of 30 cm (about 12 in). Clump-forming, the slender leaves are grey-green and thin, leafless stems topped with daisy-like lavender-blue flowerheads are borne freely throughout summer. The flowers are suitable for drying. Requiring full sun, it is easily grown in most soil conditions, and is fairly drought tolerant. Relatively short-lived, it is best divided frequently; it will self-seed readily. It looks good among grasses in a meadow garden as well as in a sunny border. *Catananche caerulea* 'Major' is a somewhat untidy cultivar that will also look its best among long grasses in a meadow garden rather than a planting bed.

CATHARANTHUS
roseus
syn. **Vinca rosea**
MADAGASCAR PERIWINKLE

A native of Africa, this small relative of the frangipani is an evergreen spreading shrub, valued for its rose-pink to white, phlox-like flowers, which bloom from spring through to autumn/fall—and into winter as well in warmer areas. Grows to 60 cm (about 24 in) in height and spread. Frost-tender, it requires full light and a well-drained, compost-enriched soil. It will tolerate considerable heat. Older plants may become untidy and should be pruned to promote a bushy habit. A useful summer bedding plant in cool climates, this species is often grown annually from seed in spring, or greenwood or semi-ripe cuttings in summer.

CELOSIA
cristata
COCKSCOMB

Native to tropical Asia, this fairly fast-growing perennial is cultivated as an annual for summer bedding displays. Erect and bushy, it reaches 30–60 cm (about 12–24 in) high with a 30 cm (about 12 in) spread. Leaves are mid-green; rippled coral-shaped flowerheads appear in summer. Flowers are usually vivid red or yellow, though other colours are available. They are long lasting and make excellent cut flowers. Half-hardy, they require a rich, well-drained soil and constant moisture. Grows best in a sunny position and does well in hot summers. Propagate from seed in spring.

CENTAUREA
KNAPWEED

Mostly native to Europe, Asia and Africa, this large genus of annuals and perennials are grown for their graceful flowerheads which have thistle-like centres surrounded by finely rayed petals in shades of bright red, deep purple, blue and golden yellow. Some species are inclined to sprawl and need trimming back. All are suitable for cutting. Fully hardy, they need sun and well-drained soil. They are particularly useful in dryish conditions on chalky soil. Propagate by division or seed in autumn/fall, late winter or spring. Transplant during winter or spring. Centaureas have been grown since ancient times and were once used as a love divination.

C. cyanus
CORNFLOWER

One of the best known annuals, this fast-growing upright plant reaches a height of 1 m (about 3 ft) with a spread of 30 cm (12 in). It is a hardy species with lance-shaped grey-green leaves and a spring or early summer display of double daisy-like flowerheads in shades of pale and deep pink, cerise, crimson, white, purple and blue. Tall and dwarf cultivars are available. Best displayed in large clumps and will flower for months if deadheads are removed regularly. Once known as bluebottle, the wild form was used to make ink.

C. dealbata

A very leafy plant with light greyish green, deeply cut foliage. Lilac-purple to lilac-pink flowerheads appear in a mass from late spring onwards. An erect perennial, it grows to 1 m (about 3 ft) high with a spread of 60 cm (about 24 in). The cultivar 'Steenbergii' has larger, deep pink flowers.

C. hypoleuca 'John Coutts'

Deep rose-pink flowers are produced singly on stalks up to 60 cm (about 24 in) high in early summer, often with a second flush in autumn. This spreading perennial has long, lobed leaves, green on top and grey underneath, and forms a clump 45 cm (about 18 in) across.

C. moschata

SWEET SULTAN

A sweet-scented cottage garden plant introduced to cultivation over 350 years ago, this is a fast-growing, upright annual with lance-shaped, greyish green leaves. Large, delicate, fluffy flowers to 8 cm (about 3 in) across are produced in a wide range of colours in summer and early autumn/fall. Grows to 50 cm (about 20 in) high and spreads to 20 cm (about 8 in). An open position with protection from hot afternoon sun is best.

CENTRANTHUS
ruber

RED VALERIAN, KISS-ME-QUICK

Native to Europe, this perennial is often seen as a naturalized plant on dry banks and is ideal for dry rock gardens. It is grown for its dense clusters of small, star-shaped, deep reddish pink flowers that are borne

for a long period from late spring to autumn/fall. The cultivar 'Albus' has white flowers. Forms loose clumps of fleshy leaves and grows to a height of 60 cm to 1 m (about 2–3 ft) and spread of 50–60 cm (about 20–24 in). One of the easiest plants to grow, it requires sun and good drainage and will tolerate exposed positions and poor, alkaline soil. It is fully hardy. Propagate from seed in autumn/fall or spring; it self-seeds readily and may naturalize.

CEPHALARIA
gigantea

GIANT SCABIOUS

This handsome giant of a perennial is native to Siberia. It needs plenty of space to spread, as it grows to around 1.8 m (about 6 ft) high and 1.3 m (about 4 ft) across. It forms a huge clump of dark green, divided leaves from which rise many tough, thin stems around 1 m (about 3 ft) high, topped with primrose-yellow flowerheads that are rather like those of a scabious. Propagation can be done by division in spring or by seed in autumn. This plant is not particular as to soil, and does best in a site in full sun.

CERASTIUM
tomentosum

SNOW-IN-SUMMER

A vigorous, fast-growing ground cover, this perennial is ideal for a well-drained hot dry bank or rockery. It has tiny, silvery grey leaves, and masses of star-shaped white flowers are borne in late spring and

summer. It is particularly attractive when used as an underplanting against darker backgrounds. The foliage is dense and an effective weed-suppressant. It grows to 8 cm (about 3 in) high and spreads indefinitely, and is fully hardy. Water regularly but allow to dry out between soakings. Fertilize in early spring and propagate by division in spring. After flowering, remove spent flowers by clipping the top of the plant with shears.

CERATOSTIGMA
plumbaginoides

CHINESE PLUMBAGO, PERENNIAL LEADWORT

Native to western China, this bushy perennial grows to 45 cm (about 18 in) high with a spread of 20 cm (about 8 in). Valued for its tough constitution and attractive foliage and flowers, it has oval, mid-green leaves that turn a rich orange and red in autumn/fall. Flowers are plumbago-like, with small clusters of single cornflower blue blooms appearing on reddish, branched

stems in late summer and autumn/fall. Fully hardy, it requires an open sunny position, preferably sheltered from salty winds, and a well-drained light soil. Keep moist. Cut back severely in early winter to stimulate strong spring growth. Propagate by division in spring. It is useful to grow in front of a border or as a ground cover.

Centaurea cyanus

Centaurea moschata

Centaurea dealbata

Centaurea hypoleuca 'John Coutts'

Cerastium tomentosum

Ceratostigma plumbaginoides

Centranthus ruber

Cheiranthus cheiri

Clarkia amoena

Cleome hassleriana

Chrysanthemum carinatum

CHEIRANTHUS
cheiri

ENGLISH WALLFLOWER

These perennial flowering plants are well-known as winter and spring bedding subjects and have been part of the cottage garden for centuries. Some species are suitable for rock gardens. Short-lived species are best grown as biennials. The older types are sweetly scented while the newer cultivars have no fragrance but bloom well in the winter months. Fully to half-hardy, they do best in fertile soil in an open sunny position. Propagate from seed in spring or greenwood or softwood cuttings in summer. *C. cheiri* is a bushy perennial grown as an annual or biennial. Cultivars vary in height from tall, up to 60 cm (about 24 in) with a spread of 40 cm (about 16 in), to dwarf, with a height and spread of 20 cm (about 8 in). Fragrant 4-petalled flowers appear in spring in colours ranging from pastels to deep browns, bronze, orange, bright yellow, dark red and scarlet. All have lance-shaped leaves. It is fully hardy and self-seeding. They must not be allowed to dry out in summer and should be cut back after blooming and again in autumn/fall. They grow best in cooler areas.

CHELONE
obliqua

TURTLEHEAD

Of the several species of turtleheads native to eastern North America, this is the showiest and most garden worthy. Pairs of rich green leaves line 90 cm (about 36 in) tall vertical stems topped with short spikes of

curious rosy-purple tubular flowers in late summer and autumn. Best along streams or pond edges, they also adapt well to a moist border planting with rich soil in full sun or part-shade. Propagate by dividing clumps in early spring.

CHRYSANTHEMUM
CHRYSANTHEMUM

Native to temperate zones, this large genus is valued for its ease of culture, rapid growth and showy flowers. It includes annuals, perennials and sub-shrubs, most of which are evergreen. All have daisy-like flowers, each flowerhead in fact made up of a large number of individual florets. Colour range includes yellow, orange, brown, white, pink, red and purple. Leaves are usually deeply cut or divided, often feathery, and oval to lance-shaped. Stems are upright and often woody. Fully to half-hardy, chrysanthemums grow best in an open, sunny site in a rich, friable, well-drained soil. Feed and water regularly. Stake tall plants with canes and pinch out growing tips of young plants to encourage lateral branching. Suckers should not be allowed to develop until the plants have flowered. Propagate annuals by seed sown in spring; perennials by dividing basal growth or by striking cuttings taken from plant material that is in active growth in spring; and sub-shrubs by softwood cuttings in spring or hardwood cuttings in winter. The genus *Chrysanthemum* is currently undergoing revision. Some species have been reclassified and will be found in this chapter under their new names.

Diseases include chrysanthemum rust, white rust (difficult to control—the plant should be destroyed), powdery mildew, petal blight, and botrytis. Insect pests can also be a problem.

C. carinatum
syn. *C. tricolor*
PAINTED DAISY

This spectacular annual species is from Morocco and grows to 60 cm (about 24 in), spreading to 30 cm (about 12 in) with banded, multi-coloured flowers in spring and early summer. Hardy to half-hardy. 'Monarch Court Jesters' comes in red with yellow centres or white with red centres, and the Tricolor Series has many colour combinations. Excellent as bedding plants and cut flowers.

C. frutescens see
Argyranthemum frutescens

C. maximum see
Leucanthemum × *superbum*

C. morifolium see
Dendranthema grandiflora

CIMICIFUGA
racemosa

BUGBANE

These eastern American natives are bold additions to the summer garden, at the back of borders or in open woodland situations. Above large, divided, astilbe-like foliage rise 0.9-2.4 m (about 3-8 ft) tall racemes of tiny, fragrant, white flowers. They prefer partial shade and a deep, rich soil with regular watering but are generally carefree

perennials. Plant in spring or autumn, but do not disturb for years; they flower best when established, and seldom need staking.

CLARKIA
amoena
syn. *C. elegans*
FAREWELL-TO-SPRING

A free-flowering, hardy annual, this American native is fast-growing to a height of 60 cm (about 24 in) and spread of 30 cm (about 12 in). It has lance-shaped, mid-green leaves, thin upright stems, and in summer bears spikes of open, cup-like single or double flowers, in shades of pink. They make excellent cut flowers but remove leaves before putting them in water as they have an offensive smell. The plants require a sunny situation and a well-drained sandy soil that has low fertility; they do not flower well in rich soil. Allow to dry out between watering. Propagate by seed sown in autumn/fall or in spring in cool areas. Watch for botrytis, which can be a problem. The genus *Clarkia* is named after Captain William Clark, a Rocky Mountains explorer.

CLEOME
hassleriana
syn. *C. spinosa*
SPIDER FLOWER

Mainly native to tropical America, this fast-growing, bushy annual is valued for its unusual spidery flowers. An erect plant, it grows to 1.2 m (about 3½ ft) tall with a spread of 45 cm (about 18 in). It has hairy spiny stems and large, palmate leaves topped in summer with heads of airy, pink or white flowers with long protruding stamens. Flowers will last until winter. This species makes a good background bedding plant and is useful in new gardens for its rapid growth. Half-hardy, it requires sun and fertile, well-drained soil. Shelter from strong winds and water regularly. Taller growth can be encouraged by removing side branches and dead flowers should be removed. Propagate by seed in spring or early summer. Watch for aphids.

COBAEA
scandens
CUP-AND-SAUCER VINE

Native to Mexico and tropical Central America, this vigorous quick-growing perennial vine has dense foliage and abundant bell-shaped flowers that open yellow-green and turn from mauve to a translucent purple with age. There is an all-green version, usually sold as 'white'. Flowers throughout the year in mild climates and makes an attractive screen on a netting fence or trellis. It is a woody stemmed tendril climber growing to a height of 4–5 m (about 12–15 ft). Frost-tender, it is best grown as an annual in colder climates. It requires full sun, protection from cold winds and a rich, well-drained soil, kept moist. Propagate by seed in spring. Needs constant control in a confined space.

CODONOPSIS
clematidea

Native of Asia, this late-summer-flowering perennial thrives in cooler areas. The bell-shaped, pale blue blossoms are borne in late summer; they are prettily marked with orange and red on the inside. The greyish green foliage forms a rounded clump around 60 cm (about 24 in) high and wide, though the plant can reach double that height if it can twine up a support or through a shrub. For the best effect, plant it in a raised bed or on a bank where the inside of its nodding flowers can easily be seen. It does best in a light, well-drained soil in part or complete shade. Propagate by seed in autumn or spring.

COLEUS

Native to Indonesia and tropical North Africa, these annuals, perennials and evergreen sub-shrubs are grown for their brightly coloured and variegated foliage. In milder climates, they are popular pot plants and useful for bedding in sheltered places. *Coleus* grow best in bright, indirect light or partial shade and rich, well-drained or moist soil in a sheltered position. Feed and water liberally during the growing season to encourage strong leafy growth. In winter the soil should be kept almost dry. Potted plants develop brightest colours when pot bound. Pinch out young shoots to promote bushy growth. Frost-tender. Propagate from seed sown under glass in late winter or spring, or from softwood cuttings in spring or summer.

C. blumei

Native to Java, this bushy, fast-growing perennial is grown as an annual in more temperate climates.

Leaves are a bright mixture of pink, green, red or yellow and are a pointed oval shape with serrated edges. It grows to 50 cm (about 20 in) high with a spread of 30 cm (about 12 in), and prefers partial shade. Remove flower spikes.

C. thyrsoideus

Fast-growing, bushy perennial, also grown as an annual. This is a larger species, growing to 1 m (about 3 ft) high with a spread of 60 cm (about 24 in). Leaves are oval, mid-green with serrated edges and panicles of tubular bright blue flowers are borne in winter.

CONSOLIDA
ambigua
LARKSPUR, ANNUAL DELPHINIUM

A showy annual with upright, 0.6–1.5 m (about 2–5 ft) spikes of delphinium-like flowers in blue, violet, pink, carmine and white. Leaves are deeply lobed, like birds' feet. Plants bloom heavily in late spring and early summer, then gradually wither away. Sow seed in autumn for bloom the following year; once planted, they self-seed readily. Give them a sunny situation, and a well-drained soil. Water regularly for best growth. There are numerous seed strains, with variations in height and flower colour and with single or double flowers.

CONVOLVULUS

This is a large genus of dwarf, bushy and climbing perennials, annuals, evergreen shrubs and sub-shrubs from warm to temperate climates.

Coleus thyrsoideus

Convolvulus cneorum

Some species are now naturalized and strongly invasive; others, of only moderate vigour, are useful for spilling over walls, for rock gardens, hanging baskets and as a ground cover. They are fully hardy to frost-tender, flowering most prolifically in a sunny situation in poor to fertile well-drained soil. Little pruning is needed. Dead-head plants to prolong flowering. Propagate from seed sown in mid-spring, or from softwood cuttings in late spring and summer for perennials and sub-shrubs.

C. cneorum
SILVERBUSH

A dense, shrubby, evergreen, growing to 60 cm (about 24 in) or more, with narrow, silky, silvery green leaves and large white flowers, sometimes tinged with pink or cream, with yellow centres. Flowers from mid-spring to late summer. It is a useful plant for hot dry places and average soil, and is frost-hardy. It flowers best if lightly trimmed back every year.

C. sabatius
syn. *C. mauritanicus*
MOROCCAN GLORY VINE, BINDWEED

A trailing perennial with profuse, open, trumpet-shaped mauve-blue flowers from spring to autumn/fall. Slender stems and small, oval leaves. An excellent specimen for draping over walls and hanging baskets, it grows to a height of 15–20 cm (about 6–8 in) and spread of 30 cm (about 12 in). Half-hardy.

Convolvulus sabatius

Cobaea scandens 'White' form

Consolida ambigua

Coleus blumei

Coreopsis verticillata

Corydalis lutea

Convolvulus tricolor

C. tricolor
syn. C. minor

An interesting bedding annual with profuse trumpet-shaped blue or white flowers with banded yellow and white throats. Leaves are lance-shaped and mid-green. Grows to a height of 20–30 cm (about 8–12 in) and spread of 20 cm (about 8 in). Fully hardy, it blooms continuously through the warm weather.

COREOPSIS

This genus of easily grown annuals and perennials is valued for its daisy-like flowers in shades of gold or yellow, some bicolours. They are mainly summer-flowering and fully to frost-hardy. The perennials make excellent herbaceous border plants, looking striking with shasta daisies and blue delphiniums. They prefer full sun and a fertile well-drained soil but also grow well in coastal regions and on poor, stony soil. Propagate perennials by division of old clumps in winter or spring, or by spring cuttings. The annuals also prefer full sun and a fertile, well-

Coreopsis tinctoria

Cosmos atrosanguineus

Corydalis flexuosa

drained soil; they will not tolerate a heavy clay soil. Taller varieties may need staking. Propagate annuals from seed in spring or autumn/fall, and dead-head regularly.

C. tinctoria
TICKSEED

A fast-growing showy annual that produces clusters of bright yellow daisy-like flowerheads with red centres throughout summer and autumn/fall. Grows to a height of 60–90 cm (about 24–36 in) and spread of 20 cm (about 8 in). Fully hardy. Provide support with branched twigs or fine bamboo stakes. Makes good cut flowers.

C. verticillata

A strong, tall perennial, growing to 75 cm (about 30 in) with a spread of 60 cm (about 24 in). Produces abundant, large, daisy-like rich yellow flowers on elegant stems and is useful for cutting. Flowers from late spring until winter and does best in light, poorish soil. Leaves are bright green, divided and lance-shaped. It is fully hardy.

CORYDALIS

Native to Europe, Siberia and China, these dainty perennials have pretty, tubular flowers and ferny foliage. The flowering period is longest if the plants are grown in partial shade. Most species thrive in sun or part shade and in well-drained soil, though some species such as *C. cashmeriana* require a cool, shady spot and a retentive, lime-free soil that is rich in humus. Several species such as *C. lutea* self-seed freely, which makes these plants ideal for growing in cracks between paving or on walls. Propagate by seed in autumn.

C. flexuosa

A choice and charming perennial for the rock garden that forms a small clump of ferny, green foliage around 30 cm (about 12 in) wide and 15 cm (about 6 in) high. In spring masses of tubular, wedgwood-blue flowers are borne on short stems. It requires a cool spot in part shade and a moisture-retentive yet free-draining soil. Propagate by seed in autumn or spring.

C. lutea

Related to the bleeding hearts (*Dicentra* spp.), this long-blooming perennial covers itself with racemes of soft yellow flowers from spring to autumn, beautifully presented against the lush, fern-like foliage. The mounded plants are only 30 cm (about 12 in) tall and wide, but self-seed readily to form quite an acceptable ground cover. The best growth will be achieved in dappled shade, though more flowers are produced in full sun; they prefer a woodsy soil and steady moisture through the growing season. They are excellent for naturalising in stone walls, between paving stones or in a woodland garden.

COSMOS
MEXICAN ASTER

Native to Mexico and Central America, this small genus of annuals and perennials has been grown in gardens for over a century. Some annual species are particularly tall, ideal for the back of borders and excellent for late summer and autumn/fall cutting. They require a sunny situation with protection from strong winds and will grow in any well-drained soil as long as it is not over-rich. Mulch with compost or animal manure and water well in hot, dry weather. Fully to half-hardy. Propagate annuals by seed in spring and autumn/fall, half-hardy species by basal cuttings in spring. Remove dead-heads regularly, and in humid weather watch for insect pests and moulds.

C. atrosanguineus
BLACK COSMOS, CHOCOLATE COSMOS

A clump-forming perennial growing to 60 cm (about 24 in) in height and spread, black cosmos has very dark, blackish red flowers that have a chocolate scent, which is most noticeable on warm days. It flowers from late spring to autumn/fall. The pinnate foliage is broad compared to that of the annuals. Partially evergreen but it may die back completely in cold areas. Near hardy but demands excellent winter drainage or the rootstock may rot.

C. bipinnatus

An upright, bushy annual, growing to nearly 2 m (about 6 ft) in height with

with a spread of 50 cm (about 20 in). Though too tall for bedding, it is a fine border plant with large rose-pink, white or maroon flowerheads held against delicate feathery foliage. Half-hardy, it flowers in late summer and autumn/fall. In South Africa, it is often seen growing in grasslands along roads on the Transvaal Highveld in autumn/fall.

C. sulphureus

This annual has coarser foliage and blooms in many shades of yellow and orange in summer and early autumn/fall. Half-hardy, it is moderately fast-growing, reaching a height of 60 cm (about 24 in) and spread of 50 cm (about 20 in).

CRAMBE
maritima
SEA KALE

This robust, small perennial forms a mound of wide silvery green leaves and carries branching sprays of tiny white flowers in summer. Fully hardy, sea kale prefers an open sunny position, but will tolerate light shade, and a well-drained, neutral to alkaline soil. It grows to a height and spread of 60 cm (about 24 in). The leaf shoots are edible. Propagate from seed in spring or autumn/fall or by division in early spring. *C. cordifolia* is very similar.

CREPIS
incana
HAWKWEED

This dandelion-like, rosette-forming perennial is a good subject for a sunny rock garden or border and looks pretty in cracks and crevices. It grows to a height of 20 cm (about 8 in) and spread of 10 cm. Summer-flowering, with ragged, pink to orange flowerheads on stiff stems. Leaves are oblong, greyish green and hairy. Fully hardy, it is easily grown in either sun or shade and prefers a well-drained soil. Propagate by root cuttings in late winter. Self-seeds readily.

CYPERUS
papyrus
PAPER REED, PAPYRUS

This large perennial evergreen sedge has an indefinite spread and grows 1.5–2.5 m (about 4¹/₂–7¹/₂ ft) tall. Its sturdy leafless stems carry enormous umbels of spikelets in summer. Prefers a sunny situation in wet soil and can be grown in water. It is half-hardy.

DAHLIA
DAHLIA

This genus of bushy, tuberous perennials, native to Mexico, is named after the Swedish botanist, Andreas Dahl, a pupil of Linnaeus. Grown as bedding plants, they are valued for the wide range of colours, colour combinations, sizes and shapes of their flowers, which are excellent as cut flowers. Named varieties come and go with amazing speed, and every country has a different selection. So we have simply given representative examples of each type. Dwarf forms are also suitable for containers. Half-hardy and fast-growing, they have a

long flowering period from late spring to late autumn/fall. They grow best in a warm sunny position, preferably sheltered from strong winds, and in well-fertilized, well-drained soil. They must be fed monthly and watered well when in flower. Old and faded blooms should be removed to help prolong the flowering season. Flower size can be increased by disbudding—pinch out the two buds that grow with the centre bud on each stem and cut off the immediate laterals and all superfluous shoots. In very hot weather they benefit from a mulch of straw around the stems. All dahlias except for the dwarf forms will require staking. In areas prone to frost, the tubers should be lifted in late autumn/fall after foliage has died down, stored covered with

straw, and replanted when all frost danger has passed. In frost-free areas they can be treated as normal herbaceous perennials and left in the ground. Propagate dwarf forms from seed; others in spring from seed, basal shoot cuttings or by division of tubers. Watch for virus infection, thrips, earwigs, aphids and red spider mite.

Cactus dahlias

Derived from crosses between *D. variabilis* and *D. juarezii* from northern Mexico, this most popular type is distinguished by the long, recurved ray florets which give the flower a graceful outline. The varieties are classed as miniature, medium and giant, the size range being about the same as the decoratives. All are tall and need staking.

Cactus dahlia

Crambe maritima

Crepis incana

Cosmos bipinnatus

Cosmos sulphureus

Cyperus papyrus

A Field Trip to Lundy

Viewed from the mainland on a clear day, the windswept island of Lundy looms out of the sea haze, providing a tantalizing and imposing view of its fortress-like profile. A safe haven for pirates and marauders in centuries past, Lundy is now a sanctuary for wildlife, both land-based and marine. It has been owned by the National Trust for the past 25 years. As a measure of its importance, the surrounding waters were recently declared Britain's first Marine Nature Reserve.

Lundy lies 17 km (about 11 miles) off the coast of Devon in south-western England. Boat trips there operate regularly from the small, north Devon port of Bideford. After an invariably choppy sea-crossing lasting a couple of hours, the towering cliffs of Lundy are a welcome sight. After stepping ashore, regain your land legs and climb the steep slopes to admire stunning coastal scenery of granite headlands and cliffs stretching into the distance. The island comprises a flattish plateau, which in places rises almost 120 m (about 400 ft) from the sea, some cliffs being almost sheer. The eastern side is relatively sheltered from prevailing westerly winds while the western side is often battered by the full force of Atlantic gales. If your visit coincides with the peak flowering period, many of the views are framed by a foreground carpet of purple foxgloves (*Digitalis purpurea*).

Lundy's flowers are fascinating and varied. In May and June, thrift, or sea pink (*Armeria maritima*), and sea campion

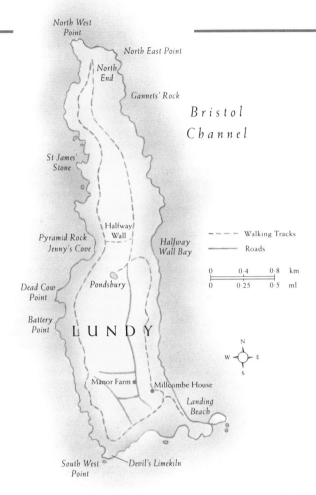

Foxgloves grow profusely on the islands off south-western England.

(*Silene vulgaris* subsp. *maritima*) provide a floral display on the western side, while short-cropped turf on the top of the island harbours Britain's best population of the intriguingly named dwarf adder's tongue-fern (*Ophioglossum azoricum*). There is even an endemic plant here—the Lundy cabbage (*Coincya wrightii*), which is found nowhere else in the world. The impact of these is diminished, however, by the abundant spikes of purple foxgloves that thrive in the eastern and southern parts of the island.

Although the foxglove is sometimes perennial, especially in ornamental settings, it is mostly considered a biennial in the wild. In the first year it produces rosettes of broad, oval to lanceolate leaves up to 30 cm (about 12 in) long with a distinctly hairy upper surface. In the second year a tall flowering spike is produced, which is usually branched and stands up to 2 m (about 6 ft) in height. Flowers appear on the spike over a period of a few weeks between May and August, opening from the bottom of the spike upwards as the spike itself lengthens. The individual flowers, lasting approximately one to two weeks, are tubular with an elongated, bell-shaped appearance. In the wild they are usually deep pink or purple, although white flower spikes are occasionally seen. In cultivation, the paler varieties tend to be more popular. The inner surface of the flower is usually spotted and hairy; this latter assists bees to pollinate the flowers.

Foxgloves are common along the north Devon coast and grow wild in a wide range of habitats. They do, however, prefer comparatively well-drained, neutral to acid soil. Typical sites would include sunny woodland glades, forest clearings, hillsides with broken or rocky soils and coastal cliffs; they will grow quite happily on recently disturbed ground. On Lundy they thrive on slopes which, although covered with bracken (*Pteridium aquilinum*), are almost completely lacking in tree cover. Growing in these conditions, the plant has to be tolerant of salt-spray and constant, sometimes violent, wind.

Rainfall in the west of Britain is comparatively high—1000–1200 mm (about 40–50 in) per year is not unusual—so the plant will need regular watering in a garden setting; however it will not tolerate becoming waterlogged. Foxgloves will also grow both in the open and in a sheltered position although they will not survive for long where the shade is too dense. Since it occurs from sea-level to moderate elevations inland, the foxglove is clearly tolerant of climatic variation.

If you want to see foxgloves at their best on Lundy, visit in mid-June. One of their most attractive settings is among the quarries and spoil workings halfway along the eastern side. Here you can see signs of where blocks of granite were hewn from the cliffs, although much of the evidence is now masked by plant growth, including introduced clumps of rhododendrons. For an alternative view, make your way to the top of the island where you may see small numbers of the rare Soay sheep and Lundy ponies (a breed exclusive to the island). A track runs north–south down the island's spine.

Whether you visit Lundy to see garden plants such as the foxglove growing in their native setting, or simply to experience the rugged splendour of the untamed coastal scenery, you will find it a captivating island, one which few visitors can bear to see only once.

Digitalis purpurea

Digitalis

Digitalis, the foxglove genus, consists of around 18 species of biennials and perennials and a few soft-wooded shrubs. Geographically they are centred on the Mediterranean (including North Africa), the majority growing wild in Britain and Europe. Apart from *D. purpurea*, several other *Digitalis* species are sometimes grown for ornament.

Despite being poisonous, the foxglove is one of Britain's most striking and distinctive plants, both in overall size and flower structure. The medicinal properties of *D. purpurea* are important—the leaves are a source of the drug digitalin, which is used to control and alleviate the symptoms of heart disease.

Foxgloves are represented in gardens chiefly by the ornamental strains of *D. purpurea,* for example, the well-known 'Excelsior' strain. The garden forms are more robust than the wild *D. purpurea* plants, and the flowers are packed more closely on the stem. Breeders have aimed for larger, more widely flared and richly spotted flowers displaying a more varied mix of colours. Garden foxgloves are also remarkably adaptable, thriving almost anywhere in temperate zones and in any normal, well-drained garden soil.

Digitalis is just one of almost 250 genera of the world-wide Scrophulariaceae family. Snapdragons (*Antirrhinum* spp.), a genus of annuals popular among gardeners, also belong to this family.

Digitalis purpurea

Collarette dahlias

These old-fashioned dahlias have single flowers which have a ruffle of short petals surrounding the disk like a lace collar. Usually they are in a contrasting colour from the main ray petals. Both tall, 2 m (about 6 ft), and dwarf, 35 cm (about 12 in), forms are available.

Decorative dahlias

Growing to about 2 m (about 6 ft), these have informal, fully double flowers with broad ray petals. They come in giant, medium and miniature varieties, the miniatures having flowers about 10 cm (about 4 in) across and the giants 35 cm (about 15 in) or more. All need staking.

Dwarf or bedding dahlias

Often grown as annuals, dwarf dahlias grow 35–40 cm (about 16 in) tall and do not need staking. The flowers are about 10 cm (about 4 in) across and either semi-double or fully double, like small editions of the tall decoratives. They are much

used for bedding and may be grown from seed sown in spring or by division of the tubers.

Pompon dahlias

These are tall growing—2 m (about 6 ft)—but bear small flowers, 4–5 cm (about 2 in) across. They are usually fully double, so much so that the flowers open into perfect spheres. They are very useful for cutting, to contrast with the larger types. Show dahlias, not often seen now, are similar in form but three times the size.

Waterlily or Nymphaea dahlias

These have fully double flowers with broad ray petals, smaller and more formal than the decoratives; most varieties are about 12–15 cm (about 5–6 in) wide. They grow 1.5–2 m (about 4½–6 ft) tall and need staking.

DELPHINIUM

This is a large genus of annuals and herbaceous perennials, most native to the northern hemisphere. The splendid mainly blue, pink, purple or

white spikes of cup-shaped, spurred flowers are useful for massed displays or for cutting. They range from tall spikes up to 2 m (about 6 ft) to dwarfs suitable for bedding. Best suited to cooler climate gardens, they can be grown as annuals in warmer climates. Grow in a sunny position, preferably sheltered from wind—the taller cultivars will need to be staked. A well-drained, moist, slightly alkaline, rich loam is ideal. Fully to half-hardy, they will not tolerate drought conditions. Feed with a complete fertilizer, water well, and provide a surface mulch of compost during the growing season. Remove flower spikes after they fade to encourage a second flush in late summer, and remove stems at the end of the flowering period. Spray with fungicide for mildew and black spot, and protect from slugs and snails. The name delphinium derives from the Greek *delphin*, for the dolphins the buds were thought to resemble.

D. belladonna

Fully hardy perennials with an upright branching form and 2 cm (about 1 in) wide, flowers in shades of blue or white. The single, sometimes semi-double, flowers which appear in summer on 30 cm (about 12 in) long spikes, are useful for cutting. It grows to a height of 1–1.5 m (about 3–4½ ft) and spread of 60 cm (about 24 in). Propagate by division or basal cuttings in spring.

D. elatum hybrids

These fully hardy, erect perennials flower in a range of colours from white to purple, usually with con-

trasting eyes. They grow to 1.5–2.2 m (about 4½–6½ ft) high with a spread of 75 cm–1 m (about 2½–3 ft). Tall, tapering spikes of evenly spaced semi-double flowers appear from summer through to autumn/fall. Cultivars include: 'Blue Bird', medium blue flowers with a white eye; 'Galahad', pure white; 'King Arthur', royal-purple with a white eye; 'Summer Skies', light blue with a white eye; 'Black Knight', violet-blue with a black eye; and 'Astolat', blush pink to rose. Propagate *D. elatum* hybrids by cuttings only; selections by seed in spring or autumn/fall.

D. grandiflorum
syn. D. chinense
BUTTERFLY DELPHINIUM

Perennial in its native Asian home, this plant is best treated as an annual in mild winter climates. It grows to a height of 45 cm (about 18 in) and spread of 30 cm (12 in). It has bright blue flowers and is useful as a bedding plant as it flowers over a long period during the summer months. Remove spent flowerheads regularly. 'Azure Fairy' is a pale blue form; 'Blue Butterfly', deep blue. Fully hardy.

DENDRANTHEMA
grandiflora
syn. Chrysanthemum morifolium
FLORIST'S CHRYSANTHEMUM

Hybrids of this perennial species make up the vast majority of cultivated chrysanthemums, and include a variety of flower forms, sizes and growth habits. Most

Waterlily or Nymphaea dahlia

Dwarf or bedding dahlias

Decorative dahlia

Pompon dahlia

Collarette dahlia

Delphinium belladonna

Delphinium elatum hybrids

flower in mid- or late autumn/fall, but flowering is often artificially delayed to fit in with exhibition seasons. The best cultivars for garden display and cut flowers are the intermediate decorative (e.g. 'Pink Poolys'), reflexed decorative (e.g. 'Amethyst'), anemone-centred (e.g. 'Powder Puff'), single (e.g. 'Kathleen Olsen'), pompon (e.g. 'Ping Pong'), spider (e.g. 'Nightingale') and charm (e.g. 'Ringdove'). Potted chrysanthemums can be planted out after the flowers have faded. *Dendranthema grandiflora* is the national flower of Japan.

DIANELLA
tasmanica
FLAX LILY

Native to south-east Australia, including Tasmania, this upright perennial is fibrous-rooted, spreading from underground rhizomes and sending up evergreen, strap-like leaves. Nodding, star-shaped, bright blue or purple-blue flowers are borne in branching sprays in spring and early summer, followed by shining deep blue berries. The plants grow from 50 cm to 1.2 m (about 20 in– 4 1/2 ft) in height with a spread of 50 cm (about 20 in), and are frost-hardy. They make interesting accent plants in sun or partial shade and require a well-drained, neutral to acid soil. Propagate by division, rooted offsets, or seed in spring and autumn/fall. It is invasive, but useful for naturalizing. Named after Diana, the ancient Roman goddess of hunting.

DIANTHUS
PINK

A very large genus including the carnation, maiden pink, cottage pink, sweet William, Chinese or Indian pink and many other cultivated annuals, biennials and evergreen perennials. Most species are popular as massed border plants and for cutting. Perennial species include some small-flowered plants, excellent for rock gardens and chinks in stone walls and between paving stones. The taller perpetual and spray carnations are generally grown in glasshouses. Fully to half-hardy, *Dianthus* likes a sunny position, preferably protected from strong wind, and well-drained, slightly alkaline, soil. Regular watering and twice-monthly feeding produces good flowers. The taller varieties will require staking. Prune stems back after flowering to encourage new growth. Propagate perennials by layering or cuttings in summer; annuals and biennials by seed in autumn/fall or early spring. Watch for aphids, thrips and caterpillars. Also susceptible to rust and virus infections.

Dianthus caryophyllus cultivars

D. × allwoodii
PERPETUAL FLOWERING PINK

Densely leafed, tuft-forming perennials of hybrid origin, with grey-green foliage and an abundance of erect flowering stems each carrying four to six fragrant, single to fully double flowers in shades of white, pink or crimson, often with dark centres and with plain or fringed petals. Flowers over a long season from late spring until early autumn/fall. Grows 30–50 cm (about 12–20 in) high with a spread of 20–25 cm (about 8–10 in). Frost-hardy.

D. barbatus
SWEET WILLIAM

A short-lived perennial, usually treated as a biennial, it self-sows readily and is useful for bedding and cut flowers. It is slow growing, to a height of 50 cm (about 20 in) and spread of 15 cm (about 6 in). In late spring and early summer, it bears many small, fragrant flowers, in bright reds, pinks and bicolors, on a flat-topped crown. It has bright green, grassy leaves. Frost-hardy. The dwarf cultivars, to about 10 cm (about 4 in), are usually treated as annuals.

D. caryophyllus cultivars
CARNATION

Fairly fast-growing evergreen perennials of short duration, carnations have a tufted erect habit with lance-shaped grey-green leaves and showy, perfumed, semi-double or double flowers. The range of colours includes pink, yellow, white and red. Striped flowers are called fancies; those edged in a contrasting colour,

Dendranthema grandiflora

Dianthus × allwoodii

Delphinium grandiflorum

Dianthus barbatus

Dianella tasmanica

picotees. The numerous cultivars are classified under 3 groups.

Annual or marguerite carnations

Evergreen perennials, usually grown as annuals. The 6 cm (about 2 1/2 in) wide flowers appear in sprays in spring to autumn/fall. They grow to 75 cm (about 30 in) high with a spread of 20 cm (about 8 in). Frost-hardy. 'Enfants de Nice' has fancy or picotee flowers; 'Chabaud', fringed, solid coloured flowers.

Border carnations

Bushy evergreen perennials, growing to a height of 80 cm (about 32 in) and spread of 30 cm (about 12 in). Frost-hardy, they are best suited to cooler climates. Flowers are smooth-edged or fringed, 8 cm (about 3 in) wide, and come in many colours. Spring or early summer flowering. Most varieties of border carnations carry a decided clove perfume.

Perpetual-flowering carnations

Evergreen perennials growing to 1 m (about 3 ft) high or more with a spread of 30 cm (about 12 in). They have a straggly habit and may need staking. Fully double flowers, usually fringed, are produced throughout the year. Half-hardy. Cultivars include: 'William Sim', bright red; Exquisite', deep pink; 'Arthur Sim', white with red markings; 'Harvest Moon', pale yellow; 'Calypso', pale pink; 'Mini Star', apricot. Disbud large-flowered varieties to give one flower per stem. Spray types produce about five flowers per stem and do not need disbudding.

D. chinensis
INDIAN PINK

This popular annual has a short, tufted growth habit, and grey-green lance-shaped leaves. In late spring and summer it bears masses of tubular, single or double, sweetly scented flowers in shades of pink, red, lavender and white. Slow growing to a height and spread of 15–30 cm (about 6–12 in), and fully hardy.

D. deltoides
MAIDEN PINK

Ideal for a rock garden or ground cover, this dwarf, mat-forming evergreen perennial is easily grown from seed or cuttings. It has tiny, lance-shaped leaves and bears small, single, fringed flowers in pink, cerise or white, mostly with a red eye, in spring and early summer. Grows to 15 cm (about 6 in) high with a spread of 30 cm (about 12 in), and is fully hardy. Cut back after flowering.

D. plumarius
GARDEN OR COTTAGE PINK

A loosely tufted, evergreen perennial growing 30–50 cm (about 12–20 in) in height with a spread of 25 cm (about 10 in). There are many named cultivars, bearing sprays of single or fully double sweetly scented flowers in red, pinks, purple-reds, mauves and whites. Many have fringed petals and a contrasting eye. Late spring flowering and frost-hardy. Useful at the front of the border or in rockeries.

DIASCIA
barberae

This low growing, rather fragile perennial, native to South Africa, is a useful addition to rock gardens and borders. It has small heart-shaped, pale green leaves, and bears clusters of twin-spurred, salmon pink flowers in spring through to early autumn/fall. Grows to a height of 15–20 cm (about 6–8 in) with a spread of 20 cm (about 8 in). They

Dichorisandra thyrsiflora

Dicentra formosa 'Alba'

Dianthus chinensis

Dicentra spectabilis

do best in rich, well-drained soil, in a sunny position in temperate climates and in partial shade in hotter areas. Fertilize lightly and water regularly when flowers are forming. Pinch out growing tips to increase bushiness and cut back old stems after flowering has finished. Propagate from seed in autumn/fall, softwood cuttings in late spring or from semi-ripe cuttings in summer.

DICENTRA

Herbaceous perennials native to the colder regions of northern Asia and North America, they are grown for their attractive sprays of pendent, heart-shaped pink, red or white flowers, which are carried on arching stems above lacy grey-green leaves. They flower from spring through summer. They grow to a height of from 8 cm (about 3 in) to 5 m (about 15 ft) and have a spread of up to 60 cm (about 24 in). Plant in a rich, well-drained soil of coarse texture with a liberal dressing of organic matter. Propagate by late winter

divisions, from spring basal cuttings or seed in autumn/fall.

D. formosa
WESTERN BLEEDING HEART

This spreading plant grows to 45 cm (about 18 in) high and has a spread of 30 cm (about 12 in). Dainty pink and red flowers appear throughout spring and summer. *D. f.* 'Alba' is a white-flowered form.

D. spectabilis
BLEEDING HEART

This species is a popular garden perennial. It grows to a height and spread of 60 cm (about 24 in). Pink and white flowers appear in late spring and summer.

DICHORISANDRA
thyrsiflora
BLUE GINGER, BRAZILIAN GINGER

An evergreen perennial with glossy, dark leaves which grow on their stems in spirals. Tall spikes of deep purple-blue flowers are produced

Dianthus plumarius

Diascia barberae

Dianthus deltoides

in summer and autumn/fall. Grows well in a tropical or subtropical area in the shade, such as beneath trees. Needs well-drained soil with acid peat and leaf mould. This plant will not survive the slightest frost and languishes in winter temperatures below 10°C (about 40°F). Requires adequate moisture at all times and high humidity in summer. Propagate by division in early spring or from stem cuttings taken during summer.

DICTAMNUS
albus
BURNING BUSH

Native to southern Europe and Asia, this long-lived, herbaceous perennial is grown for its early summer spikes of fragrant star-shaped white flowers with long stamens. Flowers are good for cutting. It has an upright habit, growing to 1 m (about 3 ft) tall with a spread of 60 cm (about 24 in) with lemon-scented, glossy, leathery, light green leaves. Fully hardy, it requires full sun, fertile well-drained soil and regular water. It is a slow-growing plant, taking 3 or 4 years to reach flowering size. Propagate from seed sown in late summer. Resents being disturbed once established. The whole plant gives off an inflammable oil which may ignite if a flame is held near it.

DIERAMA
pulcherrimum
LADY'S WAND, WANDFLOWER, ANGEL'S FISHING ROD

South African members of the same family (Iridaceae) as the Iris, these upright, summer-flowering corms have evergreen, strap-like foliage and arching stems which bear long, swinging tassels of tubular or bell-shaped deep pink flowers. The effect is particularly enchanting in a breeze or reflected in a pool. Grows to a height of 1.5 m (about 4½ ft) and spread of 30 cm (about 12 in). Requires sun and deep, rich, moist well-drained soil—water well in summer when in growth. Frost-hardy, it dies down partially in winter. Propagate by division of corms in spring or from seed in spring and autumn/fall. They resent disturbance and may be left in the ground for years.

DIETES

Native to southern Africa, these evergreen, rhizomatous perennials are grown for their attractive iris-shaped flowers. The flowers usually last only for a day but new buds open over a long period in spring and early summer. They have strong, sword-like leaves which form large and attractive clumps. All species will thrive in semi-shade or sun, and in humus-

rich, well-drained soil that does not dry out too quickly. Do not remove flower stems as they continue to flower for several years. Half-hardy, they are tough enough to use as low hedges and, once established, self-seed readily. Propagate from seed in spring or autumn/fall or by division in spring.

D. grandiflora
WILD IRIS

Wild Iris grows to a height and spread of 1 m (about 3 ft) and bears 10 cm (about 4 in) wide, white, iris-like flowers marked with mauve and orange-yellow. Its blooms last several days in summer.

D. iridioides
syn. D. vegeta

A smaller version of D. grandiflora, it has branching wiry stems carrying 6–8 cm (about 2½–3 in) wide, iris-like flowers, white with central yellow marks. Grows to a height of 60 cm (about 24 in) and spread of 30–60 cm (about 12–24 in), forming dense clumps. Its native habitat is in semi-shade under tall open trees.

DIGITALIS
FOXGLOVE

Natives of Europe, northern Africa and western Asia, these biennials and perennials, some of which are evergreen, are grown for the strong accent value of their tall flower spikes in the summer border. They are very effective planted in groups in a shrub border under taller trees to provide shade and wind protection. They come in many colours including magenta, purple, white, cream, yellow, pink and lavender. Fully to frost-hardy, they grow in most conditions, doing best in cool, humid climates in semi-shade and moist, well-drained soil. Cut flowering stems down to the ground after the spring flowering to encourage development of secondary spikes. Propagate from seed in autumn/fall; they self-seed readily. The medicinal properties of digitalis have been known since ancient times, and these plants are still used in the treatment of heart ailments today.

D. × mertonensis

Clump-forming, this perennial grows to 60 cm (about 24 in) in height with a spread of 30 cm (about 12 in). Summer-flowering, it bears spikes of tubular, cherry rose to salmon rose flowers over a rosette of soft, hairy, oval leaves. Divide after flowering. Fully hardy.

D. purpurea

The common foxglove, this short-lived perennial is grown as a bien-

Digitalis purpurea

Dietes iridioides

Dietes grandiflora

Digitalis × mertonensis

Dictamnus albus

Dierama pulcherrimum

nial. Ideal for providing a backdrop in a border or for naturalizing in open woodlands because of its upright habit, reaching a height of 1–1.5 m (about 3–4½ ft) and spread of 60 cm (about 24 in). Tall spikes of tubular flowers in shades of purple, white, pink, rosy magenta and pale yellow appear between late spring and early autumn/fall, above a rosette of rough, oval, deep green leaves. D. purpurea is fully hardy. All parts of the plant, especially the leaves, are poisonous.

Dorotheanthus bellidiformis

Dimorphotheca sinuata

DIMORPHOTHECA

AFRICAN DAISY, CAPE MARIGOLD

Indigenous to South Africa, these annuals, perennials and evergreen sub-shrubs are valued for their glossy daisy-like flowers which appear over a long season from early spring. They are useful for rock gardens, dry banks and the front row of borders—particularly as temporary fillers. They require an open sunny situation and a fertile, well-drained soil. Ideal for beach gardens. They are not good as cut flowers as they close on cloudy days and remain closed indoors. Light pruning after flowering helps extend the life of the plants. Dead-head to prolong flowering. Propagate annuals from seed sown in spring and perennials from semi-ripe cuttings in summer. Watch for botrytis.

D. pluvialis

RAIN DAISY

This annual is an excellent bedding plant producing small flowerheads, snowy white above, purple beneath, with brownish purple centres. It is low growing, reaching 20–30 cm

Dodecatheon meadia

(about 8–12 in) high with a spread of 15 cm (about 6 in) and half-hardy.

D. sinuata

syn. D. aurantiaca, D. calendulacea

This expansive annual species grows up to 30 cm (about 12 in). Its roughly serrated spoon-shaped leaves grow to 8 cm (about 3 in) long. Daisy-like flowers with yellow centres and orange outer petals which occasionally have yellow bases, appear from the beginning of spring until autumn/fall.

DIPLARRHENA
moraea

This iris-like perennial features elegant clusters of white flowers with yellow and purple centres, borne on wiry stems. Flowers are short-lived but appear in quick succession during spring and early summer. It has fans of strong, long, green strap-shaped leaves. Clump forming, it quickly grows to a height of 50 cm (about 20 in) and spread of 25 cm (about 10 in). Frost-hardy, it requires

Dimorphotheca pluvialis

a sunny position and well-drained, moist soil. Propagate by division in spring or autumn/fall, or by seed in spring.

DODECATHEON
meadia

SHOOTING STAR

This perennial, a member of the Primulaceae family (which includes the primrose) and native to North America, is good for hillside and mountain gardens, and is a beautiful poolside or bog plant. In spring it bears distinctive, nodding, cyclamen-pink flowers with reflexed petals and extended stamens. It has primula-like, clumped rosettes of pale green leaves, and ranges in height from 15 to 50 cm (about 6–20 in) with a spread of 50 cm (about 20 in). Best grown in semi-shade in a moist, well-drained acid soil. Fully hardy. Propagate from seed in autumn/fall or by division in winter. Dormant after flowering and difficult to transplant as it resents disturbance. The plant's common name derives from the fact that, once fertilized, the flowers turn skywards.

DOROTHEANTHUS
bellidiformis

ICE PLANT, LIVINGSTONE DAISY, BOKBAAI VYGIE

Native to South Africa, this small succulent annual is ideal for massed summer display in rockeries, banks, beds and planter boxes,

Diplarrhena moraea

Duchesnea indica

particularly if sown thickly so the plants can intermingle. It has daisy-like flowerheads in dazzling shades of yellow, white, red or pink. Grows to a height of 15 cm (about 6 in) and spread of 30 cm (about 12 in). Plant in an open sunny position—the flowers close in dull weather or if grown in shade. Grows well in poor but well-drained soil, and because of its salt-resistance is good for sea-side gardens. Do not overwater. Half-hardy. Propagate from seed in autumn/fall. Dead-head regularly and watch for slugs and snails.

DORYANTHES
excelsa

GYMEA LILY, SPEAR LILY, GIANT LILY

A bold plant from Queensland and New South Wales in Australia. It has stiff rosettes of 10–15 cm (about 4–6 in) wide, lance-shaped, light green leaves which at maturity can reach 1–2 m (about 3–6 ft) long. Globular heads of long-lasting, bright red flowers are borne on 5 m (about 15 ft) stems in summer. These eye-catching flowers drip with nectar. A half-hardy perennial preferring light, well-drained but moist soil in full sun or semi-shade. Propagate from seed in spring or suckers after flowering.

DUCHESNEA
indica

syn. Fragaria indica

A semi-evergreen trailing perennial that spreads rapidly by runners and is

Doryanthes excelsa

Epimedium grandiflorum

Echium wildpretti

Echinacea purpurea

Echinops ritro

Epimedium rubrum

Echium vulgare [dwarf]

useful for ground cover, bed edging, hanging baskets and pots. It has dark green leaves and bright, 2.5 cm (about 1 in) wide, yellow flowers from spring to early summer. Ornamental, strawberry-like small red fruits appear in late summer. Grows to a height of 10 cm (about 4 in) with an indefinite spread. Fully hardy, it is best grown in sun or semi-shade in well-drained, rich, cultivated soil. Propagate by division in spring, from seed in autumn/fall, or by rooting plantlets formed at the ends of runners in summer.

ECHINACEA
purpurea
syn. *Rudbeckia purpurea*
PURPLE CONEFLOWER

Native to North America, this showy summer-flowering perennial has large daisy-like, rosy purple flowers with high, orange-brown central cones. The 10 cm (about 4 in) wide flowers, borne singly on strong stems, are useful for cutting. Leaves are lance-shaped and dark green. Of upright habit, it grows to 1.2 m (about 4 ft) and spreads 50 cm (about 20 in). Fully hardy, it prefers a sunny situation and a rich, moist but well-drained soil. Regular deadheading prolongs flowering, and in cold climates the entire plant can be cut back in autumn/fall. Propagate by division or root cuttings from winter to early spring.

ECHINOPS
ritro
GLOBE THISTLE

This perennial of a genus native to northern Africa, Europe and western Asia, from Spain to India, is a useful plant for the herbaceous border, and its globe-like spiky flowers can be cut and dried for winter decoration. It has large, deeply cut, prickly leaves, downy beneath, with silvery white stems and round, thistle-like, purplish blue heads of flowers in summer. Of an upright habit, it grows to 1.2 m (about 4 ft) in height with a spread of 75 cm (about 30 in). Fully hardy, it requires full sun and a well-drained soil, and is generally

drought resistant. Propagate from seed in spring, by root cuttings or division in autumn/fall, or by division in late winter. Transplant during the winter or early spring months.

ECHIUM

Indigenous to the Mediterranean, Canary Islands and Madeira, this genus of annuals and evergreen shrubs, perennials and biennials is grown for their spectacular tall spires and bright blue or pink flowers in late spring and summer. Fully hardy to frost-tender, they require a dry climate, full sun or semi-shade, and a well-drained soil of light to medium quality. They grow unwieldly in soil that is too rich or damp. Coastal planting is ideal. Propagate from seed or cuttings in spring or summer. In mild climates they self-sow readily.

E. vulgare [dwarf]

This biennial has an erect, bushy habit. In its dwarf form it grows to a height of 30 cm (about 12 in) and a spread of 20 cm (about 8 in). It has lance-shaped, dark green leaves, and white, blue, pink or purple tubular flowers. Fully hardy, it is fast growing and may become invasive.

E. wildprettii
syn. *E. bourgaeanum*

A striking biennial from the Canary Islands, this evergreen plant makes a lovely rosette of narrow, silvery leaves and, in its second season, bears a single, bold spike of small, funnel-shaped, rich coral flowers. Frost-hardy, it needs perfect drainage and dies after fruiting. It has an erect habit, growing to a height of 2.5 m (about 7½ ft) or more with a spread of 60 cm (about 24 in).

EPILOBIUM
angustifolium
FIREWEED, GREAT WILLOW HERB

A tall, vigorous perennial native to northern and mountainous parts of North America, most widespread in areas that have been burned or logged recently. Drifts of rose-pink flowering spikes cover moist

mountainsides in late summer, creating a memorable sight. In the garden, fireweed is useful in a border or naturalized in a moist meadow. Growing 0.9–1.5 m (about 3–5 ft) tall, it will spread indefinitely unless confined by reducing watering or by pruning or containing the root system, so it should be planted with care. It is easily grown in moist soils in full sun or light shade. Propagate in spring by division of the roots; it also self-seeds readily.

EPIMEDIUM

This genus of spring-flowering perennials has flowers that are cup-shaped with long or short spurs. It is fully hardy and makes a good ground cover. It will do best in partial shade in a humus-rich, moisture-retentive but well-drained soil. Cut back just before new growth appears in spring; propagate by division in spring or autumn.

E. grandiflorum

This species is deciduous, except in mild climates, and has toothed leaflets often margined in red. Spidery, red-violet flowers with white spurs are held above the foliage on 30 cm (about 12 in) slender stems. It is best displayed as a specimen clump rather than as a ground cover. The cultivars 'Rose Queen' (pink) and 'White Queen' are the most readily available.

E. perralderanum

An ideal plant for ground cover in part- or full shade, this species forms a carpet of large, glossy, green leaves 30 cm (about 12 in) high. Small, bright yellow flowers are borne on thin, wiry stems in early spring. As with all epimediums, it is best to cut off the old foliage by late winter so the flowers can be seen at their best.

E. pinnatum subsp. colchicum
PERSIAN EPIMEDIUM

This subspecies is commonly grown for its larger yellow flowers in clusters at the top of 45 cm (about 18 in) stems. The leaves are bronzy and generally not toothed or spined, and are nearly evergreen. This makes an excellent ground cover, and is one of the best for dry shade.

E. rubrum

This hybrid can be variable, but generally has spiny leaves that are strikingly veined in red. Low mounds are topped by 30 cm (about 12 in) stems with crimson and white 2.5 cm (about 1 in) flowers in spring. It can be used as a ground cover.

E. × warleyense

Somewhat sparse as a ground cover, this species nevertheless works well in a woodland garden, producing beautiful flowers that combine coppery red with yellow centres. The leaves are spiny and semi-evergreen. It is one of the best hybrid epimediums.

EREMURUS,
Shelford hybrids

FOXTAIL LILY

This group of perennials is grown for its lofty spikes of close-packed flowers, magnificent for floral displays. They produce rosettes of strap-like leaves and in mid-summer each crown yields spikes of bloom with strong stems and hundreds of shallow cup-shaped flowers in a wide range of colours including white, pink, salmon, yellow, apricot and coppery tones. Grows to 1.5 m (about 4½ ft) in height with a spread of 60 cm (about 24 in). Frost-hardy, they prefer a sunny, warm position, protection from heavy winds, and well-drained soil. The Shelford hybrids may require staking. Protect the roots of this group with a layer of mulch in cold winters. Propagate from seed in autumn/fall or by division in late winter and early spring. Transplant when dormant.

Erigeron glaucus

Erinus alpinus

Erigeron karvinskianus

Eremurus, Shelford hybrids

Eryngium x oliverianum

Erodium pelargoniflorum

Eryngium variifolium

Eryngium tripartitum

ERIGERON

FLEABANE

This is a large genus of annuals, biennials and perennials, some evergreen, that are predominantly native to North America. They have mainly erect stems, capped by masses of pink, white or blue, daisy-like flowers that are striking in the front row of a mixed herbaceous border or rock garden. They flower between late spring and mid-summer. Fully to frost-hardy, they prefer a sunny position, sheltered from strong winds, and moderately fertile, well-drained soil. Do not allow to dry out during the growing season. Propagate by division of an established clump in spring or autumn/fall and remove spent stems after flowering. Can become invasive. Erigeron became popular garden plants for their supposed ability to repel fleas.

E. glaucus

SEASIDE DAISY

A perennial bearing lilac-pink flowers in summer. Clump-forming, it grows to 25 cm (about 10 in) in height with a spread of 20 cm (about 8 in). Leaves are long and hairy. Fully hardy.

E. karvinskianus
syn. E. mucronatus

This frost-hardy, spreading perennial is useful as an informal ground cover and in mild climates will bloom profusely throughout the year. The small 2 cm (about 1 in) wide, daisy-like flowers open white, fading to pink and wine-red. Grows 10–15 cm (about 4–6 in) in height with an indefinite spread. It has lax stems and narrow, lance-shaped, hairy leaves. Cut back hard from time to time. Native to Mexico. This plant is becoming a noxious weed in New Zealand.

ERINUS
alpinus

This small semi-evergreen perennial is native to the European alps and ideal for planting in wall crevices and rock gardens. It forms rosettes of soft, medium green leaves, and bears a profusion of starry, rosy purple or white flowers in late spring and summer. Grows 5–8 cm (about 2–3 in) in height and spread. It is short-lived but self-seeds freely. Fully hardy, E. alpinus grows well in either full sun or partial shade and requires a well-drained soil. Propagate from seed in autumn/fall.

ERODIUM
pelargoniflorum

Native to Turkey, this mound-forming, tufted perennial is related to the pelargonium and is ideal for rock gardens or alpine houses. It has prostrate woody stems and heart-shaped, lightly lobed green leaves. Umbels of white, purple-veined flowers are produced from late spring to autumn/fall. It has a shrubby habit, reaching a height of around 30 cm (about 12 in). It needs limy soil in a sunny situation and is prone to aphid infestation. Propagate by semi-ripe cuttings in summer. Half-hardy.

ERYNGIUM

SEA HOLLY

Mostly native to South America and Europe, these biennials and perennials are members of the same family as the carrot (Apiaceae), and are grown for their interesting foliage and spiny-collared blooms that usually have a bluish metallic sheen. They flower over a long period in summer and may be cut and dried for winter decoration. Fully to half-hardy, they require a sunny situation, good drainage and a sandy soil. Plants tend to collapse in wet, heavy ground during winter. Propagate species from fresh seed; selected forms by root cuttings in winter or by division in spring. Transplant when dormant in winter. The spiny appearance of the strongly coloured thistle-like bracts that surround the central flower give rise to the common name 'holly'.

E. x oliverianum

This fully hardy upright perennial grows to a height of 60 cm–1 m (about 2–3 ft) and spread of 45–60 cm (about 18–24 in). In late summer it bears large, rounded, lavender blue thistle heads. Leaves are jagged, mid-green and heart-shaped.

E. tripartitum

Native to the Mediterranean regions, this perennial is not as spiny as some of the other species. It has coarsely toothed, smooth dark green, wedge-shaped leaves and bears globular, grey-blue flowerheads on blue stems from summer through to autumn/fall. Fully hardy, it reaches a height of 1 m (about 3 ft) and a spread of 50 cm (about 20 in). It requires some support in exposed conditions. The flowers may be cut before they fade, and dried for winter decoration.

E. variifolium

Distinct for its variegated white and green foliage which forms an attractive evergreen mantle, this species has silvery-blue stems to 45 cm (about 12 in) which are topped by 2.5 cm (about 1 in) thistle-like flowers surrounded by similar silvery-blue bracts. Good for the front of the border, where the foliage will provide year-round interest.

ERYSIMUM
hieraciifolium
syn. *Cheiranthus | allionii*
SIBERIAN WALLFLOWER

Found in all parts of the northern hemisphere, this bushy evergreen perennial is suitable for rock gardens, banks and borders. It is short-lived and should be grown as a biennial. It has toothed, mid-green leaves and bears bright yellow or orange flowers in spring, putting on a dazzling display for a long period. Slow-growing, it reaches a height and spread of 30 cm (about 12 in). It is fully hardy, preferring light, well-drained fertile soil and a sunny position. Propagate in summer by cuttings, which root very easily, or from seed in spring—it self-seeds freely. Cultivars include 'Orange Bedder' which has scented, brilliant orange flowers.

ESCHSCHOLZIA
californica
CALIFORNIAN POPPY

This, the official floral emblem of California, is one of the brightest garden annuals, suitable for rock gardens, the front of borders, and gaps in paving. The cup-shaped flowers open out from grey-green feathery foliage into vivid shades of orange, bronze, yellow, cream, scarlet, mauve and rose. They flower from summer through to autumn/fall but close in dull weather so should be planted in a sunny situation. Of a slender, erect habit, they grow to 30 cm (about 12 in) high with a spread of 15 cm (about 6 in). Fully hardy, they grow well in poor, very well-drained soil and should be dead-headed regularly to prolong flowering. Propagate from seed sown in spring. They do not transplant easily so sow where the plants are to remain. Watch for snails.

EUPATORIUM
purpureum
JOE-PYE WEED

These are massive perennials, reaching 1.5–2.7 m (about 5–9 ft) in height with a spread of 1.2 m

(about 4 ft) or more. They provide a bold accent for the autumn garden, with their 30 cm (about 12 in) long leaves and large heads of tiny purplish flowers. Native to eastern and central North America, they are usually found where there is plenty of water. Useful in the large border, they perform best alongside water where they can get all the moisture they need for full growth. Give them full sun to part-shade and a rich, humusy soil. Cut to the ground each winter. Propagate in spring or autumn by division.

EUPHORBIA
MILKWEED, SPURGE

This large and varied genus of shrubs, succulents, perennials and annuals have in common a milky sap which may irritate the skin and can be poisonous. The spectacular flowerheads consist of a series of highly coloured cup-shaped bracts or modified leaves. There are many succulent species which are suitable for pot plants and for sandy or desert gardens. Fully hardy to frost-tender, they require either sun or partial shade and a moist but well-drained soil. Plants are increased from young basal cuttings in spring, division in early spring or early autumn/fall. They may also self-seed if conditions are suitable.

E. characias subsp. wulfenii

Beautiful blue-green leaves densely line the erect stems, which in spring are topped by broad flowerheads of intense chartreuse. Colour remains in the flowerheads until seeds ripen, when foliage yellows; cut to the ground to make room for new shoots. Plants are upright to 1.2–1.5 m (about 4–5 ft) with a spread of 1 m (about 3 ft). They are fairly drought tolerant.

E. marginata
SNOW-ON-THE-MOUNTAIN, GHOSTWEED

Native to central areas of North America, this bushy annual makes an excellent foil for brighter flowers. It has pointed oval, bright green leaves, sharply margined with white, and broad petal-like white

bracts surrounding small flowers in summer. Fairly fast-growing to 60 cm (about 24 in) tall with a 30 cm (about 12 in) spread. Half-hardy, it will endure colder conditions.

E. polychroma
syn. *E. epithymoides*

Native to central and southern Europe, this fully hardy, clump-forming herbaceous perennial is grown for its heads of bright chrome-yellow flowers produced from spring to summer. It has softly hairy, bright green leaves and a rounded, bushy habit, reaching a height and spread of 50 cm (about 20 in). *E. polychroma* 'Major' has yellowish green flowers in loose clusters.

EUSTOMA
grandiflorum
syn. *Lisianthus russellianus*
PRAIRIE GENTIAN

Native to America's mid-west, right down to Texas and New Mexico, this annual is grown for its flowers which are excellent for cutting, lasting up to 3 weeks in water. They are also useful as container plants. It has lance-shaped deep green leaves and 5 cm (about 2 in) wide, flared tulip-like flowers in colours of rich purple, pink, blue or white. Flowers appear in spring and again in autumn/fall. Of an upright habit, the plant is slow growing to a height of 60 cm (about 24 in) and spread of 30 cm (about 12 in). It is frost-tender, requiring a sunny situation and well-drained soil. In frost-free areas propagate from seed sown in early autumn/fall.

Erysimum hieraciifolium

Euphorbia polychroma 'Major'

Eustoma grandiflorum

Euphorbia marginata

Eschscholzia californica

Euphorbia characias subsp. *wulfenii*

EXACUM
affine
PERSIAN VIOLET

Native to the Yemeni island of Socotra, this showy miniature is useful both as an indoor pot plant and as a plant for outdoor sun or semi-shaded positions. It has shining, oval dark leaves and bears a profusion of tiny, fragrant, 5-petalled, saucer-shaped purple flowers with yellow stamens throughout summer. A biennial usually treated as an annual, it has a bushy habit and grows to a height and spread of 20–30 cm (about 8–12 in). It is frost-tender and enjoys rich, moist but well-drained soil. Indoors, they like diffused sun and a night temperature not below 15°C (60°F). Propagate from seed sown in early spring or late summer.

FELICIA

Native to South Africa, these annuals and evergreen sub-shrubs include some of the finest species of blue daisy flowers. They are particularly useful as container plants as they are seldom without blooms. They are fully hardy to frost-tender and require full sun and a dryish, well-drained gravelly soil enriched with organic matter; they will not tolerate wet conditions. Flowers are produced throughout spring and summer, and dead-heading can prolong the season. Prune straggly shoots regularly. Propagate by cuttings taken in autumn/fall and spring or from seed in spring.

F. amelloides
BLUE MARGUERITE

A bushy, evergreen shrub with roundish, bright green leaves and sky-blue flowerheads with bright yellow centres borne on long stalks. It has a spreading habit, growing to 60 cm (about 24 in) in height and width. Half-hardy, it is fast growing in temperate climates and useful for small formal hedges, rock gardens, path edgings, indoor pot plants or as a seaside plant. The flowers cut well for posies. Prune hard as soon as it becomes straggly to encourage new growth.

F. bergeriana
KINGFISHER DAISY

This mat-forming annual bears a mass of bright cobalt-blue daisy flowers with yellow centres, above hairy, lance-shaped grey-green leaves. The flowers only open in sunshine so plant in a sunny situation. It can be used for bedding or edging, window boxes or balcony containers. It is fast growing to a height and spread of 15 cm (about 6 in), and fully hardy.

FILIPENDULA
vulgaris
syn. *F. hexapetala*
DROPWORT

This fully hardy herbaceous perennial is grown for its attractive, deeply cut, fern-like foliage, and showy, crowded heads of tiny white flowers; some garden varieties are pink. Flowers are long-lasting and the foliage remains lovely long after flowering. These plants do well at the back of larger perennial borders, as long as the soil remains moist, and in waterside positions. Upright in habit, it grows to a height of 1 m (about 3 ft) and spread of 45 cm (about 18 in) and has fleshy, swollen roots. Fully hardy, this species will tolerate fairly dry conditions but prefers a moist soil in full sun or in semi-shade. Propagate by division in winter or from seed in spring and autumn/fall, and cut back when dormant in colder areas. Watch for powdery mildew.

GAILLARDIA
BLANKET FLOWER, INDIAN BLANKET

These annuals and perennials from the central and western United States have vividly coloured, daisy-like flowers. Some varieties make good cut flowers. The perennials are often short-lived and are better grown as biennials in cooler climates. They are easy to grow, requiring sun and any ordinary well-drained garden soil. Suits coastal areas. Fully to frost-hardy. Propagate from spring cuttings taken before the plants have bloomed or from seed in autumn/fall or spring.

G. aristata

A showy perennial with large, single, daisy-like cheerful orange flowers with red centres, and aromatic, divided leaves. Flowers are borne freely from early summer until early winter, and their bright colours enhance the shades of autumn/fall leaves. Grows to a height of 60 cm (about 24 in) with a spread of 50 cm (about 20 in) and may require staking. It is fully hardy but may be short-lived in damp conditions.

G. pulchella

An annual or short-lived perennial, this upright species has hairy, lance-shaped, grey-green leaves and ball-like flowers. Garden forms are usually double with many tubular flowers, creating a pompon effect. It is summer-flowering and comes in shades of crimson, red or pink, and yellow. Useful for creating bright patches in the border. Fast-growing to a height of 30–50 cm (about 12–20 in) and spread of 30 cm (about 12 in) and fully hardy.

Exacum affine

Felicia bergeriana

Gaillardia aristata

Gaillardia pulchella

Felicia amelloides

Filipendula vulgaris

GALEGA
officinalis
GOAT'S RUE

Indigenous to the goat country of
southern Europe and Asia Minor,
this fully hardy perennial has spikes
of small, pea-like mauve, pink or
white flowers over a long period in
summer. These are followed by
erect, long, narrow pods. It has an
upright habit with erect stems and
divided, lance-shaped, bright green
leaves. Grows to a height of 1.5 m
(about 4½ ft) and spread of 1 m
(about 3 ft) and requires staking.
Thrives in an open, sunny situation
in any deep, well-drained soil.
Propagate by division in winter or
from seed in autumn/fall and cut
faded flower stems to the ground.

Galega officinalis

GALEOBDOLON
argentatum
syn. *Lamiastrum galeobdolon*
'Variegatum', *Lamium galeobdolon*
'Variegatum'

This semi-evergreen carpeting perennial is much favoured as ground
cover in shaded places, particularly
under deciduous trees. It spreads fast
from runners, producing long trailing
stems of oval, coarsely-toothed, sil-
ver-marked mid-green leaves. It is
inclined to be rampant but can be
easily controlled. In summer it bears
racemes of tubular, two-lipped,
golden-yellow flowers. It grows to 30
cm (about 12 in) high with an indefinite spread. Fully hardy, it will grow
in sun or shade and any well-drained
soil. Propagate by division of rooted
runners in winter and cut back after
flowering.

Galeobdolon argentatum

GAURA
lindheimeri

Native to North America, this
bushy, long-flowering perennial is
useful for backgrounds and mixed
flower borders. It has loosely
branched stems covered with tiny
hairs, and from spring to autumn/
fall produces beautiful, pink-suf-
fused, small white flowers which
give a misty pink effect. Leaves are
lance-shaped and mid-green.
Grows to 1.2 m (nearly 4 ft) in height
with a spread of 1 m (about 3 ft), and
is fully hardy. It is easily grown, thriving in hot dry climates and preferring
full sun and a light sandy, well-
drained soil. Propagate from seed in
spring or autumn/fall or from cuttings
in summer.

GAZANIA

These low-growing perennials,
some grown as annuals, are valued
for their ease of culture and large,
brightly coloured flowers. Most modern variants are hybrids from a
number of South African species.

They are useful for bedding, rock
gardens, pots and tubs, and for binding soil on sloping land. Leaves are
either entire or deeply lobed, long
and narrow, and dark green on top,
silver-grey and woolly beneath. The
large daisy flowers are in a range of
colours from cream to yellow, gold,
pink, red, buff, brown and intermediate shades, usually marked with
bands or spots of contrasting colour
at the base of the petals. They open
in full sun and glow with a metallic
sheen. Flowering is over a long period
from early spring until summer. Grow
in full sun in sandy, fairly dry, soil.
Give an annual mulch of compost
and water during dry periods. They
are half-hardy and salt resistant so are
useful in coastal areas. Propagate by
division or from cuttings in autumn/
fall, or from seed in late winter to
early spring. Remove spent flowers
and dead leaves, and tidy up at the
end of the growing season.

G. 'Daybreak'

This carpeting perennial grows to a
height and spread of 20 cm (about 8
in). In cooler districts it is better
grown as an annual. Produces large,
orange, yellow, pink and bronze
daisy-like flowers. Unlike most
Gazania, flowers of this species remain open even in cloudy weather.

G. krebsiana

Originating in South Africa, this
stemless perennial has slender
lance-shaped leaves with a smooth
upper surface and a white downy
underside. Flowers are yellow to
orange-red with a contrasting darker
colour around their centres. Plant in
light, well-drained soil in full sun.

Gazania, Sunshine hybrids

G., Sunshine hybrids

Another carpeting perennial that is
better grown as an annual in cooler
climates. Grows to a height and
spread of 20 cm (about 8 in). There
is a large range of colours, many of
them with dark centres. The hybrids are often not quite as hardy as
the older species.

GENTIANA
GENTIAN

Natives of alpine meadows
throughout the world, these fully
hardy annuals, biennials and perennials, some of which are evergreen, are
valued for their brilliant blue flowers.
They are useful plants for rock gardens, peat beds and sloping hillside
gardens, doing best in cooler regions.
They prefer a well-drained, acid,
peaty-sandy soil with some humus.
Some species grow naturally on

Gaura lindheimeri

limestone soils. Plant in either sun
or semi-shade. Propagate by division in spring or from seed in au-
tumn/fall. Divide autumn/
fall-flowering species every 3 years
in early spring, planting out in fresh
soil. They are named after Gentius,
an Illyrian king who discovered the
medicinal value of their bitter roots.

Gazania 'Daybreak'

Gazania krebsiana

G. acaulis

syn. *G. excisa, G. kochiana*
STEMLESS GENTIAN

An evergreen, clump-forming perennial suitable for edgings or rockeries. In spring, and sometimes autumn/fall, it forms a striking carpet of trumpet-shaped, vivid blue flowers with green-spotted throats. Its foliage is compact, with tufted clumps of glossy green, narrow leaves. Grows to 2 cm (about 1 in) in height with a spread of 5–8 cm (about 2–3 in). *G. acaulis* needs a deep root run and will benefit greatly from a light application of lime.

G. asclepiadea

WILLOW GENTIAN

The arching stems of this species are clad with slender, willow-like leaves. In early autumn, many rich blue flowers are borne in the leaf axils on the upper part of the stems. This perennial forms a loose clump around 1 m (about 3 ft) high and 60 cm (about 2 ft) across. It does best in deep, moist, humus-rich soil in part of full shade. Propagate by division in early spring.

G. lutea

GREAT YELLOW GENTIAN

This perennial produces tubular yellow flowers in summer. Erect and unbranched, it grows to 1–2 m (about 3–6 ft) high and spreads to 60 cm (about 24 in). Its oval leaves grow to 30 cm (about 12 in) in length. This species is the main commercial source of gentian root which is used medicinally and as a flavouring in vermouth.

Geranium sanguineum

G. sino-ornata

An evergreen perennial, flowering in autumn/fall, bearing trumpet-shaped, deep blue flowers that are paler at the base and banded purplish blue. It is an easily grown species of prostrate, spreading habit, reaching a height of 5 cm (about 2 in) and spread of 30 cm (about 12 in). Prefers a moist, acid soil.

GERANIUM

CRANESBILL, GERANIUM

There are over 400 species of perennial geraniums, some of which are evergreen, found all over the world in cool, temperate and alpine regions. Grown for their attractive flowers, they are useful for rock gardens, informal ground covers and plants for the front of the border. They make small, showy clumps with pink to blue or purple flowers about 3 cm (1½ in) across. All flower in spring to summer. Fully to half-hardy, most species prefer a sunny situation and damp, well-drained soil. Propagate from semi-ripe cuttings in summer; seed in spring or by division in autumn/fall. Tidy up regularly to encourage bushy growth. Transplant during winter.

G. incanum

This half-hardy South African evergreen perennial grows up to 40 cm (about 16 in) in height and broadly spreads up to 1 m (about 3 ft). Its greyish green leaves are heavily lobed and have a spicy aroma. This frost-hardy plant produces cup-

Geranium 'Johnson's Blue'

shaped individual blooms, usually crimson in colour with deeper coloured veins.

G. 'Johnson's Blue'

Fully hardy, this rhizomatous perennial has cup-shaped lavender-blue flowers throughout summer. Leaves are deeply divided. It has a spreading habit, growing to a height of 30 cm (about 12 in) and spread of 60 cm (about 24 in). Propagate by division or cuttings only.

G. phaeum

MOURNING WIDOW

Native to Europe and western Russia, this clump-forming perennial has soft green, densely lobed leaves and 2 cm (about 1 in) wide lilac to brownish purple flowers that may or may not have a paler eye or basal zone. The flowers are borne on 60 cm (about 24 in) stems in late spring and early summer. This fully hardy geranium reaches a height of 75 cm (about 30 in) and a spread of 45 cm (about 18 in). The cultivar 'Lily Lovell' has white flowers.

G. sanguineum

BLOODY CRANESBILL

A fully hardy perennial useful as ground cover. It bears cup-shaped, bright purple-crimson, notched-petalled flowers throughout spring and summer. A much-branched species, it has deeply divided, dark green leaves. Grows to 25 cm (about 10 in) in height with a spread of 30 cm (about 12 in) or more and has a hummock-forming, spreading habit. There is a pretty pink version called 'Lancastriense'.

GERBERA

jamesonii

BARBERTON DAISY

Native to the Transvaal in South Africa, but much developed and improved in Holland, this is one of the most decorative of all daisies and is an excellent cut flower. It has orange-red or flame-scarlet flowerheads up to 10 cm (about 4 in) wide, borne singly on long stems in spring and summer from basal rosettes of large, jagged leaves. An evergreen perennial of upright habit, it grows to 60 cm (about 24 in) in height with a spread of 45 cm (about 18 in). Half-hardy, it requires an open, sunny position and a light, fibrous soil with free drainage. Keep somewhat dry during autumn/fall and winter. Fertilize monthly in spring and summer to produce large blooms. Propagate from cuttings of side shoots in summer, from seed in autumn/fall or early spring, or by division from late winter to early spring. Watch for white rust, root rot and wire worms.

Geranium phaeum 'Lily Lovell'

Gentiana sino-ornata

Gentiana asclepiadea

Gentiana acaulis

Gentiana lutea

Geranium incanum

Gerbera jamesonii

Geum × borisii

GEUM

These evergreen and herbaceous perennials are valued for their long flowering period from late spring until early autumn/fall. Flowering can be prolonged by regular dead-heading, and in frost-free areas they will flower almost continuously all year. They form basal rosettes of hairy, lobed leaves and bear masses of red, orange and yellow, single or double flowers with prominent yellow stamens. Good plants for mixed herbaceous borders and rock gardens, but require a lot of room to produce a good display. Fully hardy, they prefer a sunny, open position and moist, well-drained soil. Propagate by division or from seed in autumn/fall. Easily transplanted from divisions of older plants during winter or seedlings planted out in spring or autumn/fall.

G. × borisii

A clump-forming perennial with a constant succession of single, bright orange flowers borne on slender, branching stems above irregularly lobed leaves. Low-growing, it reaches a height and spread of 30 cm (about 12 in). A good rock garden plant.

G. 'Mrs Bradshaw'

A taller cultivar with rounded, double, orange-scarlet flowers borne in small sprays. Grows to a height of 60 cm (about 24 in) and spread of 45 cm (about 18 in) and is good for mixed herbaceous borders. Water well during hot weather.

GILIA
capitata
QUEEN ANNE'S THIMBLES

Native to the western mountains of the Americas, this erect, branching annual has mid-green, fern-like leaves and tiny, soft lavender-blue flowers that appear in a pincushion-like mass in summer and early autumn/fall. It is a good cut flower and useful border plant. It grows to a height of 50 cm (about 20 in) and spread of 20 cm (about 8 in). Fully hardy, it prefers a cool climate and requires full sun and a fertile, well-

Gomphrena globosa

Glechoma hederacea

drained soil. Water lightly and regularly. The intensity of flower colour can vary with soil type and situation. Propagate from seed sown outdoors in spring, or under glass in autumn/fall.

GLECHOMA
hederacea
GROUND IVY, RUNAWAY ROBIN

A European native, this evergreen perennial makes a good carpeting ground cover but is very invasive and should be kept away from heavily planted beds. Useful as a container and hanging basket plant. It has heart-shaped leaves and bears small clusters of insignificant mauve-blue trumpet flowers in summer. A pretty variegated cultivar has white marbling on the leaves. It grows to a height of 15 cm (about 6 in) and spreads rapidly. Fully hardy, it can be grown in either sun or shade in a moist, well-drained soil. Propagate by division in spring or autumn/fall, or by softwood cuttings in spring.

GLOBULARIA
cordifolia
GLOBE DAISY

An evergreen dwarf shrub found in Europe and the Mediterranean, this plant is ideal for sunny rockeries in cool temperate climates. It has creeping woody stems with unusual, tiny, spoon-shaped leaves, and produces solitary stemless round heads of fluffy mauve stamens from late spring until early summer. It forms a dome-shaped hummock, growing to a height of 2–5 cm (about 1–2 in) and gradually

Gilia capitata

Globularia cordifolia

spreading to 20 cm (about 8 in). Fully hardy, it requires full sun and well-drained neutral to alkaline soil. Water sparingly. Propagate by division or from seed in autumn/fall, or softwood cuttings in summer.

GOMPHRENA
globosa
GLOBE AMARANTH, BACHELOR'S BUTTONS

This bushy bedding annual from South-East Asia is valued for its papery, pompon-like flowers which are attractive dried for winter decoration. Cut flowering stems just before blooms are fully open and hang upside down in a cool, well-ventilated place until dry. The plant has oval hairy leaves and produces clover-like flowerheads in shades of pink, purple, yellow, orange or white in summer and early autumn/fall. Of an upright habit, it reaches a height of 30 cm (about 12 in) and spread of 20 cm (about 8 in) and is moderately fast growing. Half-hardy, it prefers a sunny situation and light, well-drained soil. Propagate from seed in spring when danger of frost is passed.

GUNNERA
manicata
GIANT ORNAMENTAL RHUBARB

Native of Brazil, this huge plant thrives in boggy soil and is usually grown on the margins of a pond. The massive leaves, borne on prickly stems, quickly unfurl in spring to form a clump around 2 m (about 6 ft) high and 2.4 m (about 8 ft) across. Long spikes of greenish flowers are borne in sum-

Geum 'Mrs Bradshaw'

Gunnera manicata

mer. Give the dormant crown a protective mulch of straw in winter. Propagate by seed in autumn or spring.

GYPSOPHILA
BABY'S BREATH

Native to Europe, Asia and North Africa, these annuals and perennials, some of which are semi-evergreen, are grown for their masses of small, dainty, white or pink flowers which make an excellent foil for bolder flowers. They are also a valuable cut flower for use with other flowers or foliage. Plant in full sun with shelter from strong winds. Fully hardy, they will tolerate most soils but do best in deep, well-drained soil that contains some organic matter in the form of compost or peat. They will grow well on limestone soils. Cut back after flowering to encourage a second flush of flowers. Propagate from cuttings of small lateral shoots in summer or from seed in spring or autumn/fall. Transplant when dormant during winter.

Helianthemum nummularium

Gypsophila elegans

G. elegans

Of dainty, erect habit, this bushy annual grows to a height of 60 cm (about 24 in) and spread of 30 cm (about 12 in). It makes delicate, pretty clumps in the garden and bears masses of tiny purplish white flowers in branching heads from summer to early autumn/fall. Leaves are lance-shaped and greyish green.

G. paniculata 'Bristol Fairy'

A short-lived perennial, mostly used as an annual. It has small, dark green leaves and bears sprays of tiny, white, double flowers in spring. An excellent garden plant, it should be resown every 3 weeks for continuous warm weather bloom. Grows 60–75 cm (about 24–30 in) in height with a spread of 1 m (about 3 ft).

HEDYCHIUM
GINGER LILY

Natives of South-East Asia, these semi-tropical perennials with fleshy rhizomes and sweetly scented flowers are ideal for sheltered borders. The large deep-green, paddle-shaped leaves are attractive in summer and die down in winter in cold areas. The showy flowers are short lived but borne profusely. In some species the flowers are followed by capsules with red or orange seeds. Grow in full sun or partial shade and rich, moist soil with a little sand for drainage. Water well in summer. Propagate by division of rhizomes from late winter to spring. Cut down to ground level as soon as flowers have finished and keep barely moist over winter. Ginger lilies are frost-hardy to frost-tender.

Hedychium gardnerianum

H. coronarium
WHITE GINGER LILY

A satiny white-flowered, sweet-scented species that in summer bears dense spikes of butterfly-like flowers with pastel yellow blotches. Leaves are lance-shaped with downy undersides. It has an upright habit and grows to 1.5 m (about 4½ ft) in height with a spread of up to 1 m (about 3 ft). Frost-tender.

H. gardnerianum
KAHILI GINGER

The best-known and easiest grown species, this plant produces spikes of short-lived, fragrant scarlet and yellow blossoms in late summer and early autumn/fall. Its leaves are greyish green and lance-shaped. It grows to 1.5 m (about 4½ ft) in height with a spread of 2 m (about 6 ft). Frost-tender. This plant is becoming a noxious weed in northern New Zealand.

HELENIUM
'Moerheim Beauty'
SNEEZEWEED

This upright perennial, native to North America, is grown for its sprays of daisy-like, rich orange-red flowers with prominent, chocolate-brown central discs. Flowers are borne in summer and early autumn/fall above dark green foliage. Easily grown, they give a vivid splash of colour to borders and are useful as cut flowers. They are slow growing to a height of 1 m (about 3 ft) and spread of 60 cm (about 24 in). Fully hardy, they enjoy hot summers and

Hedychium coronarium

Helenium 'Moerheim Beauty'

Gypsophila paniculata 'Bristol Fairy'

are best grown in full sun with shelter from strong wind, otherwise staking may be necessary. A rich, moist, well-drained soil is ideal. Dead-head regularly to prolong the flowering period, and propagate by division of old clumps in winter or from seed in spring or autumn/fall.

HELIANTHEMUM
nummularium

SUN ROSE, ROCK ROSE

Native mostly to the Mediterranean countries and North America, these evergreen, sun-loving sub-shrubby perennials are grown in rock gardens or as a ground cover for their brightly coloured flowers and neat, prostrate habit. The double cultivars retain their flowers until the evening, but the petals of the singles drop off in the afternoon. They have attractive foliage, varying from deep to greyish green and in spring are smothered with flowers in shades of red, pink, orange and yellow. They should be lightly cut back as soon as flowers fade to encourage a second flush of bloom in autumn/fall. Fully hardy,

they enjoy a warm sunny position in a freely drained, coarse soil; add a little peat or compost during dry periods. They do not do well in strongly acid soils. Good for cold winter areas and temperate climates. Propagate by semi-ripe cuttings in late summer and autumn/fall.

HELIANTHUS
SUNFLOWER

Native to the Americas, these tall, showy-flowered annuals and perennials are grown for their large daisy-like, golden-yellow blooms, which are on prolonged display from summer to autumn/fall. The plants have coarsely hairy, sticky-feeling leaves, and tall, rough stems which bear mostly yellow flowers with brown or yellow discs. They are effective planted against a dark green background. Fully hardy, they prefer full sun and protection from wind, otherwise staking will be necessary to support the tall stems. Soil should be well-drained. Fertilize in spring to promote large blooms and water deeply in dry conditions. They may become invasive and should be cut down to the base when they finish flowering. Propagate from seed or by division in autumn/fall or early spring. Watch for snails. These flowers were once worshipped by the Incas as living images of their Sun God.

H. annuus

An upright annual, fast growing to a height of 3 m (about 9 ft) or more. Large daisy-like, 30 cm (about 12 in) wide, yellow flowerheads with brown centres are borne in summer. They are coarse, leggy plants with heavily veined, mid-green leaves. The seeds produce a vegetable oil that has economic uses and are also used to feed parrots and poultry.

H. salicifolius

An upright perennial that is valuable for background planting. It grows to 2.2 m (about 6½ ft) in height and bears brilliant yellow, 7.5 cm (about 3 in) wide, single daisy-like flowers on branching stems in late summer or autumn/fall. The rich, dark green shining leaves are willow-like. They look good planted with late-flowering blue asters or salvias.

HELICHRYSUM

EVERLASTING, STRAWFLOWER, PAPER DAISY, IMMORTELLE

This large genus of mainly annuals and short-lived perennials are notable for their papery, daisy flowers, commonly called everlastings. The most spectacular species occur in Australia. They are fully hardy to frost-tender and require a warm, sunny situation and a moderately fertile sandy or gravelly soil with free

drainage. The plant adapts to most soils except heavy clay. Water regularly and shelter from strong winds. To use as dried decoration, cut flowers when just open, tie in bundles loosely wrapped in a paper sheath and hang upside-down in a well-ventilated place. Propagate perennials by division, seed or suckers in spring and annuals from seed in spring.

H. bracteatum

STRAWFLOWER, EVERLASTING DAISY

Native to Australia, this annual or short-lived perennial has an upright, branching habit and grows to a height and spread of 75 cm (about 30 in). It has tough, hollow stems, rough narrow leaves and from summer to early autumn/fall bears clusters of daisy-like blooms. Flowers are multi-coloured and have a crackly, papery finish. Half-hardy. 'Dargan Hill Monarch' is the name of the golden-flowered cultivar commonly grown which often lives for two or three years, while the many-coloured garden hybrids raised in Europe (red, pink, white, yellow) are definitely annuals.

H. hookeri

An evergreen shrub with a compact habit, growing to 1 m (about 3 ft) in height with a spread of 60 cm (about 24 in). Clusters of white flowers with greenish yellow bracts are borne in summer. Leaves are tiny and dark green. This species is frost-hardy.

HELICONIA

Beautiful, exotic plants from South America, they have large leaves and spikes of colourful bracts enclosing relatively insignificant flowers. Grow

Helianthus salicifolius

only in a warm, tropical garden with a winter minimum of 18°C (about 64°F). Plant in a humus-rich, well-drained soil in filtered sun and summer humidity. Water well during growing season. To encourage new growth remove all dead leaves and flowers. Propagate by division of rootstock in spring, ensuring there are two shoots on each division.

H. humilis

LOBSTER CLAW

The large, paddle-shaped, green leaves surround a flower stem of pointed, scarlet bracts tipped with green and inconspicuous white flowers. They are popular for flower arrangements.

H. psittacorum

PARROT'S FLOWER

A smaller species good for mass planting, H. psittacorum has long-stalked, lance-like, rich green

leaves. Narrow, glossy, orange-red bracts surrounding orange flowers with green tips, are produced in summer.

HELIOPSIS

'Light of Loddon'

Native to North America, this fully hardy, herbaceous perennial puts on a bright display in the summer border. It has rough, hairy leaves and strong stems which carry neatly shaped, bright yellow, double flowers in late summer. The flowers are dahlia-like and are good cut flowers, particularly in large arrangements. The plant grows to a height of 1.2 m (about 3½ ft) and spread of 60 cm (about 24 in). Fully hardy, it requires sun and a moist but well-drained soil. Dead-head regularly to prolong the flower display and cut back to ground level after flowering finishes. Propagate from seed or by division in spring or autumn/fall.

Heliconia humilis

Heliconia psittacorum

Helichrysum hookeri

Helichrysum bracteatum

Helianthus annuus

Heliopsis 'Light of Loddon'

Helipterum anthemoides

Helleborus niger

Helleborus lividus subsp. *corsicus*

Hemerocallis hybrid

Helleborus foetidus

Hemerocallis fulva

Hesperis matronalis

Helleborus orientalis

HELIPTERUM
anthemoides
PAPER DAISY

This perennial, particularly in its forms 'Paper Baby' and 'Paper Cascade', is very popular for rockeries, hanging baskets and dried arrangements. It has thin, wiry stems with small, greyish green leaves. The papery, daisy-like, 2.5 cm (about 1 in) wide flowers are carried throughout the year in most areas. It has a mounding habit and grows to 20 cm (about 8 in) in height with a spread of 30 cm (about 12 in). Near-hardy, it grows best in sun and poor, very well-drained soil. The species may be propagated from seed but the selected forms are propagated from cuttings taken in spring. Dead-head regularly to stimulate flower display and cut back occasionally to maintain dense growth.

HELLEBORUS
LENTEN ROSE

Native to southern Europe and western Asia, these perennials, some of which are evergreen, are useful winter and spring-flowering plants for cooler climates. They bear beautiful, open, cup-shaped flowers in shades of green and purple and are effective planted in drifts or massed in the shade of deciduous trees. Fully to half-hardy, they grow best in semi-shade and a moisture-retentive, well-drained soil that is heavily enriched with organic matter. Never let the plants dry out in summer. Cut off old leaves of deciduous species in early spring just as buds start to appear. A top-dressing of

compost or manure after flowering is beneficial. Propagate from seed or by division in autumn/fall or early spring, and watch for aphids. The plants have poisonous properties.

H. foetidus
STINKING HELLEBORE

A clump-forming, poisonous perennial with attractive, dark green, divided leaves that remain all year. In winter or early spring the clusters of pale green, bell-shaped flowers, delicately edged with red, are borne on short stems. It thrives in sun or shade in any reasonable soil. Propagation is best done by seed in spring, though established plants will often self-seed readily.

H. lividus subsp. corsicus
CORSICAN HELLEBORE

This is one of the earliest flowering *Helleborus*, with blooms appearing in late winter and early spring. It is a robust evergreen which produces large clusters of cup-shaped, nodding, 5 cm (about 2 in) wide, green flowers on an upright spike above divided, spiny, dark green foliage. It has a clump-forming habit, growing to a height of 60 cm (about 24 in) and spread of 45 cm (about 18 in). Frost-hardy, the flowers are long-lasting when cut.

H. niger
CHRISTMAS ROSE

Popular for its white, mid-winter flowers, often appearing in the snow, this is one of the more temperamental species. It is often worth covering the plant with a cloche before the flowers open, to protect them from the winter weather. Dark

green, deeply lobed leaves are evergreen; mounds are 30 cm (about 12 in) high with a spread of 30–45 cm (about 12–18 in). They prefer shade, a rich soil that is slightly alkaline, and need steady moisture.

H. orientalis

The most easily grown of the genus, this species is evergreen and clump-forming, growing to a height and spread of 45 cm (about 18 in). The large nodding flowers come in a great variety of colours from white, green, pink and rose to purple, sometimes with dark spots. Fully hardy, it flowers in winter or early spring. The dense foliage fades and can be trimmed back before flowering. Good cut flowers.

HEMEROCALLIS
DAYLILY

Native to Europe, eastern Asia and the Orient, these perennials, some of which are semi-evergreen or evergreen, are grown for their showy, often fragrant flowers, which come in a vibrant range of colours. Individual blooms last only for a day, but they are borne in great numbers on strong stems above tall, grassy foliage and continue flowering from early summer to autumn/fall. Grow in the herbaceous border, among shrubs, or naturalize in grassy woodland areas. Position carefully when planting as the flowers turn their heads towards the sun and the equator. Fully hardy, they prefer sun but will grow well and give brighter colours in part shade. Plant in a reasonably good soil that does not dry out. Propagate by division in autumn/fall or spring

and divide clumps every 3 or 4 years. Cultivars raised from seed do not come true to type. Watch for slugs and snails in early spring. Plants may also suffer from aphid or spider mite attack. The botanical name derives from the Greek and means beautiful for a day.

H. fulva

Clump-forming, growing to a height of 1 m (about 3 ft) and spread of 75 cm (about 30 in). It bears rich orange-red, trumpet-shaped, 7.5–12.5 cm (about 3–5 in) wide, flowers from mid to late summer. This plant has been in cultivation for centuries. 'Kwanso Flore Plena' is double-flowered.

H., hybrids

In the last 50 years, plant breeders in the USA, and lately Australia and the UK, have developed a huge range of daylilies. These bloom in late spring and intermittently until autumn/fall, and have flowers 8–15 cm (about 3–6 in) wide on plants ranging in height from 50 cm to 1 m (about 20–36 in) or more. Colours vary from cream to brilliant yellow, pale pink to red; many have contrasting shades in the throat. Evergreen types are best suited to mild climates; decidious to cool areas. Catalogues carry an ever-changing selection.

HESPERIS
matronalis
SWEET ROCKET

This perennial, found mainly in the northern hemisphere, is grown for its flowers which become very fragrant on humid evenings. It has smooth, narrowly oval leaves and branching flowerheads with white to lilac flowers borne in summer. Upright in habit, it grows to 75 cm (about 30 in) in height with a spread of 60 cm (about 24 in). Fully hardy, it prefers a sunny situation and will tolerate poor soil as long as it is well-drained and is not allowed to completely dry out. Plants have a tendency to become woody and are best renewed every few years. Propagate by division or from seed in spring or autumn/fall.

HEUCHERA
ALUM ROOT, CORAL BELLS

These evergreen perennials, indigenous to North America, are useful cultivated as ground cover or as rock garden or edging plants. They form neat clumps of scalloped leaves, often tinted bronze or purple, from which arise very slender stems bearing masses of dainty, nodding white, crimson or pink bell flowers over a long flowering season. Fully to frost-hardy, they grow well in either full sun or semi-shade, and like a well-drained, coarse, moisture-retentive soil. Propagate species from seed in autumn/fall or by division in spring or autumn/fall; cultivars by division in autumn/fall or early spring. Remove spent flower stems and divide established clumps every 3 or 4 years.

H. × brizoides
CORAL BELLS

This ever-enlarging group of hybrids represents the combined traits of several species. Most flower over a long period on stems reaching 60–76 cm (about 24–30 in) in height. 'Firebird' has large crimson flowers; 'Pearl Drops' is pure white. New cultivars are introduced each year, many now displaying variegated foliage.

H. 'Palace Purple'

This species is grown for its striking, purple, heart-shaped foliage and sprays of small white flowers in summer. It is clump forming, growing to a height and spread of 50 cm (about 20 in). The leaves last well for indoor decoration. Fully hardy.

H. sanguinea
CORAL BELLS

This is the most important species, with sprays of scarlet or coral-red flowers over round dark leaves. British and American gardeners have developed strains with a wider colour range—from pale pink to deep red—and slightly larger flowers. Bressingham hybrids are typical.

HIBISCUS
moscheutos
MALLOW ROSE

Native to North America, this herbaceous perennial grows to a height of 2 m (about 6 ft) and spread of 1–1.5 m (about 3–3½ ft). Single, hollyhock-like flowers, 10–20 cm (4–8 in) wide, are carried on robust, unbranched stems in late summer and autumn/fall. Colours vary from white to pink, some with deeper throat markings. Leaves are large, toothed, and softly hairy beneath. Suitable for the back of the herbaceous border and should be protected from strong winds. Frost-hardy, this hibiscus requires full sun and a well-drained, moderately rich soil. Remove spent canes in winter after the wood has died back to ground level. Transplant when dormant during winter. Fertilize in spring to encourage growth and water well during the flowering season. Prune to maintain shape. Propagate from seed or cuttings. Watch for root and collar rot, and for attacks by aphids, the hibiscus beetle, white fly and caterpillars.

HOSTA
PLANTAIN LILY

Natives of Japan and China, these easily grown, fully hardy perennials are valued for their decorative foliage. They all produce wide, handsome leaves, some being marbled or marked with white, others a bluish green. All-yellow foliage is also available. They do well in large pots or planters, are excellent for ground cover, and add an exotic touch planted on the margins of lily ponds or in bog gardens. Tall stems of nodding white, pink or mauve bell flowers appear in warmer weather. Both leaves and flowers are popular for floral arrangements. They prefer shade, and rich, moist, neutral, well-drained soil. Feed regularly during the growing season. Propagate by division in early spring.

H. lancifolia

A clump-forming plant growing to 50 cm (about 20 in) with a spread of 75 cm (about 30 in). It has narrow, lance-shaped, glossy, mid-green leaves. Racemes of trumpet-shaped pale lilac flowers are borne in late summer and early autumn/fall.

H. sieboldiana

A robust, clump-forming plant growing to a height of 1 m (about 3 ft) and spread of 1.5 m (about 4½ ft). It has large, puckered, heart-shaped bluish grey leaves and bears racemes of trumpet-shaped white flowers in early summer.

H. tokudama

This very slow-growing perennial, native to Japan, has racemes of trumpet-shaped pale mauve flowers that are borne above cup-shaped blue leaves in mid-summer. Clump-forming, it reaches a height of 45 cm (about 18 in) and a spread of 76 cm (about 30 in). There are several cultivars available: 'Aureo-nebulosa' has leaves with creamy yellow centres; 'Flavo-carcinalis' has heart-shaped leaves with creamy margins.

Hosta tokudama

Heuchera × brizoides

Hosta sieboldiana

Hibiscus moscheutos

Heuchera sanguinea

Heuchera 'Palace Purple'

Hosta lancifolia

Iberis sempervirens

Iberis umbellata

Hypericum cerastoides

Hunnemannia fumariifolia

Hypericum calycinum

HOUTTUYNIA

cordata 'Chamaeleon'

syn. *H.c.* 'Variegata', 'Court Jester', 'Harlequin'

A native of the Himalayas, Indonesia and Japan, this water-loving deciduous perennial makes a good ground cover but may become invasive. It is a vigorous plant, growing to 10 cm (about 4 in) in height with an indefinite spread. It grows from underground runners which send up bright red branched stems bearing aromatic leathery, heart-shaped leaves splashed with yellow and red. Small sprays of white flowers are borne in summer. Fully hardy, it prefers a damp, semi-shaded position and will grow in shallow water at the edge of streams and ponds. Propagate from runners in spring.

HUNNEMANNIA

fumariifolia

MEXICAN TULIP POPPY

One of the best yellow-flowered perennials, this relative of the Califor-

nian poppy is usually grown as an annual. It has an upright habit and is fast growing to a height of 60 cm (about 24 in) and spread of 20 cm (about 8 in). It has decorative, oblong, divided, bluish green leaves and bears rich, glowing yellow, single or semi-double, 8 cm (about 3 in) wide, tulip-shaped flowers in summer and early autumn/fall. Half-hardy, it prefers a warm, sunny position and slightly alkaline, well-drained soil. Dead-head plants regularly to prolong flowering and provide support in exposed areas. Water liberally during hot weather. Propagate from seed in spring—the plants do not transplant well so seed should be sown where the plants are to remain.

HYPERICUM

This large genus of perennials and deciduous, semi-evergreen or evergreen sub-shrubs and shrubs are grown for their bright yellow flowers with prominent showy stamens. In a mild temperate climate they provide year-round colour. There are prostrate species excellent for rock gardens and large flowered species striking in garden displays. Larger species need semi-shade and a fertile, not too dry, soil; the smaller types prefer full sun and well-drained soil. Most are frost resistant. Propagate perennials by seed or division in spring or autumn/fall, and sub-shrubs and shrubs by softwood cuttings in summer. Leaves are occasionally attacked by rust and should be sprayed with a fungicide if this occurs. Most species benefit from winter mulching.

H. calycinum

AARON'S BEARD, ROSE OF SHARON

An evergreen or semi-evergreen dwarf shrub with dark green foliage that grows to a height of about 30 cm (about 12 in) with an indefinite spread. It is a good ground cover and bears large yellow flowers, up to 10 cm (about 4 in) wide, from mid-summer to mid-autumn/fall. It is frost-hardy, grows in sun or shade, and is ideal for massed planting.

H. cerastoides

A deciduous sub-shrub with dense, oval, grey-green leaves, and terminal

Iberis amara

Houttuynia cordata 'Chamaeleon'

clusters of bright yellow, cup-shaped flowers in late spring and early summer. It has an upright, slightly spreading habit and grows to 30 cm (about 12 in) tall with a 50 cm (about 20 in) spread. Fully hardy, it is useful in rock gardens.

IBERIS

CANDYTUFT

These annuals and perennials are mainly from southern Europe, western Asia and the Mediterranean area. They are highly regarded as decorative plants and are excellent for rock gardens, bedding and bordering. Showy flowers are borne in either flattish heads in colours of white, red and purple, or in erect racemes of pure white flowers. They are widely used in floral arrangements. Fully to half-hardy, they require a warm, sunny position and a well-drained, light soil, preferably with added lime or dolomite. Water regularly. Propagate from seed in autumn/fall—they may self-sow but are unlikely to become invasive—or semi-ripe cuttings in summer.

I. amara

CANDYTUFT, HYACINTH-FLOWERED CANDYTUFT

Native to the United Kingdom and Europe, this fast-growing, fully hardy, annual has lance-shaped, mid-green leaves and produces showy, flattish heads of numerous, fragrant, small pure white flowers in early spring and summer. Of an erect, bushy habit, it reaches a height of 30 cm (about 12 in) and spread of 15 cm (about 6 in). Various strains are available. The Hyacinth-flowered Series has flowers in a variety of colours.

I. sempervirens

A low, spreading, evergreen perennial, this species is ideal for rock gardens. It has narrow, dark green leaves and dense, rounded heads of white flowers in spring. It is fully hardy, and grows to a height of 15–30 cm (about 6–12 in) and spread of 50–60 cm (about 20–24 in). The cultivar 'Snowflake' is most attractive. Lightly trim after flowering.

I. umbellata

GLOBE CANDYTUFT

Native to the Mediterranean region, this upright annual has lance-shaped, mid-green leaves and flattish heads of mauve, lilac, pink, purple, carmine or white flowers in late spring and summer. Of a bushy habit, it grows to a height of 15–30 cm (about 6–12 in) and spread of 20 cm (about 8 in). It is fully hardy. A useful cut flower.

IMPATIENS

This large genus of succulent annuals and mainly evergreen perennials are from the subtropics and tropics of Asia and Africa. They are useful for colourful summer bedding displays and for indoor and patio plants. Flowers come in an ever-increasing range of colours. Many hybrid strains are perennial in mild climates but in colder climates are usually grown as annuals. Frost-tender, they will grow in sun or semi-shade, many species doing well under over-hanging trees. They prefer a moist but freely drained soil, and need protection from strong winds. Tip prune the fast-growing shoots to encourage shrubby growth and more abundant flowers. Propagate from seed or stem cuttings in spring or summer. Their botanic name refers to the impatience with which they grow and multiply.

I. balsamina
GARDEN BALSAM

An erect, bushy annual with lance-shaped bright green leaves and small, camellia-like single or double spurred flowers produced in abundance throughout summer and early autumn/fall. Colour range includes blood-red, purple-red, pink, yellow and white, some spotted. It is fairly fast-growing to a height of 30–50 cm (about 12–20 in) and spread of 18–25 cm (about 7½–10 in). It is half-hardy and good for bedding displays in sunny situations.

I., New Guinea hybrids
BUSY LIZZIE

A group of fast-growing perennials that are also grown as annuals in cool climates. The result of extensive hybridizing from a New Guinean species, they are frost-tender and grow to a height and spread of 30–50 cm (about 12–20 in). Leaves are oval, pointed and bronze-green, or they may be variegated with cream, white or yellow. Flowers are flat, spurred, pink, orange, red or cerise, sometimes with white markings. 'Cheers' has coral flowers; 'New Guinea F1 Tango', deep orange; and 'Red Magic', scarlet. They do well in brightly lit positions indoors.

I. sodenii
syn. I. oliveri

This vigorous and profusely flowering, softwooded perennial has whorls of 4 to 10 waxy, oval, pale green leaves with toothed margins. Many white or pale lilac single flowers appear in autumn/fall to winter.

I. walleriana
syn. I. sultanii
BUSY LIZZIE

Native to tropical East Africa, this succulent, evergreen perennial is grown as an annual in cool climates. It has soft, fleshy stems with reddish stripes, oval, fresh green leaves and flattish spurred flowers ranging through crimson, ruby red, pink,

Impatiens balsamina

Incarvillea delavayi

Impatiens sodenii

Impatiens walleriana

Inula oculis-christi

orange, lavender and white, some variegated. There are many cultivars. Half-hardy, fast-growing and bushy to a height and spread of 30–35 cm (about 12–14 in). Flowers from late spring to late autumn/fall. A popular indoor plant and useful for bedding in partial shade. Water well.

INCARVILLEA
delavayi
PRIDE OF CHINA

This fleshy-rooted, clump-forming perennial is useful for rock gardens and borders. It has handsome, fern-like foliage and erect stems bearing 7.5 cm (about 3 in) long, trumpet-shaped, rosy purple flowers in summer. Best suited to cool, temperate climates, the plants grow to a height of 60 cm (about 24 in) and spread of 30 cm (about 12 in), but die down early in autumn/fall. Fully hardy, but should be protected with a compost mulch during cold winters. Grow in a sunny situation in rich, well-drained soil. Propagate from seed or by division of old clumps in spring or autumn/fall.

INULA
oculis-christi
EYE OF CHRIST

This showy, daisy-like perennial has lance-shaped, hairy, mid-green leaves, 8.5 cm (about 3 in) wide, yellow flowerheads, and blooms freely in summer. It is a spreading, fleshy-rooted plant growing to 45 cm (about 18 in) in height with a spread of a little more than that. Fully hardy, it requires a sunny position and fertile, moisture-retentive soil. Propagate from seed or by division of old plants in spring or autumn/fall. The genus is native to Asia, Africa and Europe and has been in cultivation since ancient times.

IRIS
IRIS

This genus of more than 200 species, almost all of which are worth cultivating, is native to the temperate regions of the northern hemisphere. The majority are clump-forming, rhizomatous perennials, although a significant number grow from bulbs (these can be found in

that chapter). The rhizomotous irises are divided into four groups: the bearded irises, sometimes called 'flag irises' and distinguished by the tuft of hairs (the 'beard') on the three lower petals; the beardless irises, which have none; the crested or Evansia irises, which have a raised crest in lieu of a beard and are mostly rather tender in cold climates; and the very rare and beautiful Oncocyclus irises, allied to the bearded types. These last are native to the eastern Mediterranean and need cold winters and hot, dry summers to flourish; the pale grey *I. susiana* is the most likely to be seen in specialist catalogues. All the rhizomatous irises have sword-shaped leaves, sometimes evergreen. As a rule they are cold hardy and prefer sun: some of the beardless types like very moist soil. All are easily grown and are propagated by division in late summer after flowering. There are many hybrids in all divisions, and the selection is constantly being updated. The varieties illustrated are simply indicative of the range available.

A Field Trip to the Guadalupe Mountains National Park

The prairie country of the USA is home to a host of wild-flowers, a number of which have found their way into gardens all over the world. Although the prairies are large, relatively flat expanses of many different grasses, extensive stands of one or a few wildflower species can sometimes occur, creating a wildflower lover's delight.

Driving along any of the major highways in Texas from March through to May, particularly following a season of good rainfall, you are likely to be greeted with a kaleidoscope of wildflowers.

Although the prairie country consists mainly of vast flat regions, you are always close to mountains, and the adventurous wildflower lover can move between different elevations to extend the viewing range, as the delayed spring of higher altitudes causes the lowland species to flower later.

One of the most distinctive of these prairie wildflowers is the daisy, Indian blanket (*Gaillardia pulchella*), with its bright, almost gaudy, colour scheme. Native to a wide area of the southern and central USA—from Arizona to Texas, north to Colorado and Nebraska and south into Mexico—it is found

A huge drift of Indian blanket creates a colourful expanse.

mainly on the sandy prairies and in the desert regions. Its scientific name, *Gaillardia pulchella*, which incorporates the name of Gailard de Charentoneau, a French patron of botany, and the Latin word for 'pretty', hardly conveys the vividness of its floral display. Its common name, Indian blanket, more appropriately describes its habit, after a good rainfall season, of spreading over wide areas of the prairie in a series of flamboyant patterns.

One of the best places to view *G. pulchella* is in the Guadalupe Mountains National Park, on the border between New Mexico and Texas. Travelling east from El Paso, take Route 62 for approximately 160 km (about 100 miles) until you reach the town of Pine Springs, just inside the park. From here, drive in a north-easterly direction, skirting the southern side of the park through the foothills of the Guadalupe Mountains and up to the border with New Mexico, which forms the park's northern boundary. Among these foothills, you will see that the Indian blanket is well-adapted to colonizing roadside verges, making it easy to find. At first you will see the odd flash of colour on a roadside bank and then, if you are lucky, a large expanse of pure Indian blanket will appear over a meadow or a disturbed area of soil. It is worth stopping at these spots to explore the subtle variations in size and colour of each population. These areas usually run into larger expanses of wildflowers further from the roadside—walking through these is a memorable experience.

The prairies often produce spectacular fields of wildflower mixtures and you may find the adaptable *G. pulchella* near other equally appealing flowers, such as the delicate white Queen Anne's lace (*Daucus carota*) and the strikingly blue Texas bluebonnet (*Lupinus texensis*).

The Indian blanket can grow on high plains to 1000 m (about 3300 ft) above sea level, where there are dramatic fluctuations between day and night temperatures, and is adaptable enough to grow in conditions ranging from desert to humid coastal areas. Being a prairie species, the Indian blanket needs full sun and room to spread. It is best suited to porous, well-drained soils which mimic those found in its natural habitat.

A fascinating aspect of the Indian blanket is the natural variation it shows when it is grown from seed. A wonderful range of colours is obtained with interesting zigzag patterns on the florets. It is frequently grown as an annual, and seed should be sown in autumn/fall. Alternatively, it can be easily propagated from soft-tip cuttings which, if renewed every six months or so, can produce flowers all year round. The Indian blanket itself can form a sprawling specimen up to 80 cm (about 32 in) if not kept in check by tip pruning. The flowers are, of course, its most outstanding feature, the individual heads being 4–6 cm (about 1.5–2.5 in) wide, with bristly scales found among the florets. The leaves are a pleasing greygreen, approximately 7 cm (about 3 in) in length, often with toothed margins.

The Indian blanket is a star attraction of the prairie wildflower country. Whether you wish to appreciate its ephemeral charm in the wild or cultivate it in your own garden, *G. pulchella* will always reward the you with both its adaptability and inspirational colouring.

Gaillardia pulchella

Gaillardia

Gaillardia is a genus of about 28 species of annuals and perennials in the daisy (Asteraceae) family, within which it falls into the sunflower tribe (Heliantheae). *Gaillardia* is centred in the USA and Mexico, with three of its species also being found in South America. Only two species are generally known in gardens, the yellow-flowered perennial *G. aristata* and the bicoloured annual Indian blanket, *G. pulchella*. Both have been selected over a hundred years for their size and for the colouring of the flowers. A range of hybrids has arisen between them, the earliest of which were believed to have appeared spontaneously. The results of deliberate breeding for new strains are known collectively as *G. × grandiflora*.

The most distinctive feature of *Gaillardia* is the circle of 'petals' (the ray-florets), which are wedge-shaped and toothed at the apex. These contrast in colour with the prominent dark centre of the flowerhead. Cultivated gaillardias are among the hardiest of garden flowers, tolerating extreme heat as well as cold and dryness, strong winds and poor soils.

Daisies form one of the largest flowering plant families with some 25 000 species in 1100 genera, including *Coreopsis*, *Cosmos*, *Rudbeckia* and *Echinacea*.

Gaillardia pulchella

Iris Pacific Coast hybrids

Iris Louisiana hybrid

Iris pallida 'Variegata'

Iris japonica

Iris ochroleuca

Iris ensata

Iris bearded hybrid

I. bearded hybrids

Often classed under *I. germanica,* which is only one of their ancestral species, the bearded irises are among the most beautiful and widely grown of late-spring flowers. Their sword-shaped, greyish foliage is handsome in its own right and the flower stems bear several flowers. They are available in an enormous range of colours—everything but true red—with many varieties featuring blended colours, contrasting 'standards' and falls, or a broad band of colour around basically white flowers (this pattern is called 'plicata'). They are divided into three groups: the dwarfs which grow to 15–20 cm (about (6–8 in) tall and flower earlier than the others; the intermediates which are usually about 1.5 m (about 4^1/$_2$ ft) tall and flower a fortnight or so later; and the tall bearded irises, last to bloom and growing 1 m (about 3 ft) tall or slightly higher. These are the most popular, and new introductions are available every year from breeders in the United States, the United Kingdom, and Australia and New Zealand. Some of the newer varieties, described as 'remontant', flower a second time in late summer or autumn, though rather erratically. All prefer a temperate climate, sun, and milky alkaline, well-drained soil, and flower most freely if not over-watered in summer.

I. ensata
syn. *I. kaempferi*
JAPANESE IRIS, HIGO IRIS

Native to Japan and cultivated there for centuries, the beardless *I. ensata* grows to a height of 1 m (about 3 ft) and bears purple flowers with yellow blotches in late spring. The many named garden varieties bear huge flowers, sometimes as much as 25 cm (about 10 in) wide, in shades of white, lavender, blue and purple, often blending two shades. The foliage dies down for the winter. The plants prefer rich, acid soil and plenty of moisture, even growing happily in shallow water, provided they are not submerged in winter. The similar but slightly smaller flowered *I. laevigata* can grow in water all year. Both feature in Japanese paintings.

I. japonica
syn. *I. fimbriata*
CRESTED IRIS

This 50 cm (about 20 in) tall species from Japan is the best known of the crested species. It forms large clumps of almost evergreen, mid-green leaves and bears sprays of many 7 cm (about 2^1/$_2$ in) wide, exquisitely ruffled, pale blue or white flowers in late winter and spring. It likes acid soil and a lightly shaded spot, and prefers a more or less frost-free climate. There is a variety with white-striped leaves, although this is rather shy flowering.

I. Louisiana hybrids

Mainly derived from *I. louisiana* and its allied species from the United States, these beardless irises are evergreen and bear flat, often ruffled flowers. In late spring several flowers appear together on stems which are usually a little over 1 m (about 3 ft). They come in a very wide range of colours—white, cream, yellow, blue, mauve, magenta and purple. They prefer sun and very moist soil and will grow permanently in shallow water at the edge of a pond. The flowers are excellent for cutting.

I. ochroleuca
SWAMP IRIS

This 1.2 m (about 3^1/$_2$ ft) tall, almost evergreen beardless iris from western Asia has mid-green leaves and produces white and yellow flowers in early summer. There is an all yellow variety called *monnieri*. Although they will grow in damp ground, they are perfectly happy in any rich, well-watered garden soil and sun.

I. Pacific Coast hybrids

These almost evergreen, beardless irises are mainly derived from *I. innominata, I. douglasiana* and other species native to the west coast of the United States. In late spring they bear 8 cm (about 3 in) wide flowers, usually beautifully marked and veined in a wide range of colours—cream, yellow, blue, mauve and bronze. They prefer acid soil and sun or light shade, and have the reputation of being difficult to transplant. Once a clump is established, leave it undisturbed. Water freely while the plants are growing, less generously in winter. Foliage is narrow and dark green.

I. pallida 'Variegata'

This splendid bearded iris from the Middle East features handsome leaves which are striped in grey-green and cream. Its pale blue, lightly scented flowers are borne on 1.2 m (about 3^1/$_2$ ft) high stems in late spring. Cultivation is the same as for the bearded irises.

I. pseudocorus
WATER FLAG

A beardless iris from Europe, the water flag has handsome, mid-green leaves and profuse bright yellow flowers in late spring. There is also a form with variegated leaves. Both prefer to grow in shallow water and rich soil, and are delightful, easily grown plants for a garden pond.

I. pseudocorus 'Variegata'

This cultivar has yellow-and-green-striped foliage during the spring months, which often turns green in summer. It is less vigorous than *I. pseudocorus.*

I. spuria hybrids

While *I. spuria, I. sibirica* and their allied species, mainly from eastern Europe and western Asia, are beautiful plants in their own right, they have been much hybridized. The more common hybrids bear many flowers on 1.2 m (about 3½ ft) high stems in early summer. The colours are mainly in the white to blue range. All prefer sun, rich soil, and lavish watering while they are growing and flowering.

I. unguicularis
syn. *I. stylosa*
WINTER IRIS, ALGERIAN IRIS

This evergreen, beardless species from north Africa is valued for its habit of bearing its scented flowers from autumn to spring. Whenever the weather is mild they are lovely for cutting and will last 3 or 4 days if cut in bud. The typical form is pale blue but there are also white and darker blue varieties available. Although frost-hardy, all flower best in a warm, sunny position where they don't get too much summer sun, and in slightly alkaline soil. The flowers on their 20 cm (about 8 in) stems will be more conspicuous if the luxuriant foliage is cut back in late autumn. They are loved by snails and precautions must be taken.

KIRENGESHOMA
palmata

From Japan comes this unusual perennial which thrives in cool,

moist conditions and needs a deep, lime-free soil in order to flourish. In late summer it bears pale yellow, shuttlecock-shaped flowers on arching stems 1 m (about 3 ft) high, forming a clump about the same distance across. It does best in part or complete shade. Propapage by division in autumn or spring.

KNIPHOFIA
RED-HOT POKER, TORCH LILY, TRITOMA

Native to southern Africa, these stately perennials, some of which are evergreen, can be relied upon to make a brilliant display in the garden for a long time. They are upright, tufted plants with long, grass-like foliage and tall bare stems carrying showy, brightly coloured, tubular flowers in dense racemes. Fully to half-hardy, they require an open position in full sun and a well-drained soil with plenty of water in summer. They tolerate wind well and are often seen growing close to the coast. They are excellent cut flowers, looking very good when combined with agapanthus. Propagate species from seed or by division in spring; cultivars by division in spring.

K. hybrids

A great many hybrids have been developed over the years, using *K. uvaria* and other species. Nurseries tend to stock these named selections more than any of the other species. Heights range from 30 cm (about 12 in) to 1.3 m (about 4 ft). Flower colour varies from creamy whites, through yellows and oranges to hot corals and scarlet; many have two or three colours per flower. The flowering season also varies from spring through late summer. 'Atlanta' has soft red flowers.

K. uvaria

A tall perennial with large, strap-shaped, strongly channelled leaves and dense racemes of tubular scarlet flowers that become orange-yellow with age. Flowers in late summer and autumn/fall and grows to a height of 1.2 m (about 3½ ft) with a spread of 50 cm (about 20 in). It is fully hardy.

Kniphofia 'Atlanta'

Iris pseudacorus 'Variegata'

Iris spuria hybrid

Iris pseudacorus

Kniphofia uvaria

Iris unguicularis

Kirengeshoma palmata

Lavatera trimestris

Lamium maculatum

Lathyrus odoratus

Leucanthemum × superbum

Leonotis leonurus

Kochia scoparia f. trichophylla

KOCHIA
scoparia f. trichophylla
SUMMER CYPRESS, BURNING BUSH

This very bushy annual, native to southern Europe, is grown for its narrow, lance-shaped, 5–8 cm (about 2–3 in) long, soft, light green leaves that turn a brilliant reddish brown in autumn/fall. The flowers are dull and inconspicuous. It is useful for bedding and for pot plants. Moderately fast-growing, it reaches a height of 90 cm (about 36 in) and spread of 60 cm (about 24 in). It is half-hardy and prefers an open, sun-exposed position, warm and sheltered from harsh winds—provide support in very windy areas. Soil should be moderately fertile and well-drained. Tip-prune young plants to encourage denser growth. Propagate from seed in spring.

LAMIUM
maculatum
DEAD NETTLE

A semi-evergreen perennial, native to Europe and the Middle East, where they are often treated as weeds, this plant is a popular flowering ground cover. It has mauve-tinged, deeply toothed leaves with central silvery stripes and carries clusters of pinkish flowers in spring and summer. Mat-forming, it grows to a height of 25 cm (about 10 in) with a spread of 1 m (about 3 ft). It can be invasive. Fully hardy, the plants prefer full or partial shade and a moist, well-drained soil. Propagate by division of the root mass in autumn/fall or early spring. There are several cultivars.

LATHYRUS
odoratus
SWEET PEA

Native to Italy but much 'improved' by gardeners, this vigorous, climbing annual is grown for its abundant and sweetly scented flowers. Flowers 5 cm (about 2 in) wide and in colours of white, cream, pink, blue, mauve, lavender, maroon and scarlet bloom, several to the stem, from late winter to early summer. It is an excellent cut flower. The plant has oval, mid-green leaves with compound tendrils and grows to 2 m (about 6 ft) in height. There are dwarf non-climbing cultivars available, suitable for bedding. Fully hardy, the climbers will need a good support such as wire netting or lattice, and are ideal for covering sunny walls or fences. They should be grown in full sun and a deep, well-fertilized soil with plenty of lime. Water regularly. Propagate in autumn/fall from seed, which should be soaked for an hour or two before planting.

LAVATERA
trimestris
ANNUAL MALLOW

This shrubby annual, native to the Mediterranean, is grown mainly for its silken, trumpet-shaped, brilliant white or pink flowers that closely resemble a hibiscus. Flowers are 8 cm (about 3 in) wide and appear from summer to early autumn/fall. They are short-lived but are borne in profusion, benefiting from regular dead-heading. Leaves are oval, lobed and mid-green. It has an erect, branching habit and is moderately fast-growing to a height of 60 cm (about 24 in) and spread of 50 cm (about 20 in). Fully hardy, mallows are best in temperate climates and require a sunny position and well-drained soil. Propagate from seed in spring or early autumn/fall. L. trimestris 'Silver Cup' has lovely dark pink flowers.

LEONOTIS
leonurus
LION'S EAR, WILD DAGGA

Native to Africa, this semi-evergreen shrubby perennial is popular in all temperate climates. A striking plant, growing to 2 m (about 6 ft), it bears tall stems with whorls of tawny orange, furry, tubular flowers in late summer and autumn/fall. Leaves are lance-shaped and aromatic. It requires a sunny position and rich well-drained soil. Do not over water. These plants are fairly drought resistant and do well in coastal situations. They are half-hardy, and if damaged by frost will usually come into new growth in spring. Propagate from seed in spring or greenwood cuttings in early summer, and cut back to 15 cm (about 6 in) above ground level in early spring. There is a white variety.

LEUCANTHEMUM
× superbum
syn. *Chrysanthemum maximum*
SHASTA DAISY

This robust perennial grows to a height and spread of 1 m (about 3 ft). It has large, daisy-like white flowerheads with golden centres. The flowers are carried high over the dark, shiny, toothed leaves in summer. Cultivars are always white but there are many single and double flowers, some with fringed petals. Divide and replant every 2 years.

LIATRIS
spicata
syn. *L. callilepis*
GAY FEATHER, BLAZING STAR

This low-growing perennial from the USA is a desirable cut flower and a good butterfly and bee-attracting plant. The flowers are lilac-purple and are produced in crowded, fluffy spikes—like a feather duster—in late summer. They open from the top downwards, the opposite of most flowering spikes. The species has thickened, corm-like rootstocks and basal tufts of grassy, mid-green foliage. Clump-forming, it grows to a height of 60 cm (about 24 in) with a spread of 30 cm (about 12 in). The plants require a sunny situation and well-drained light soil of reasonable quality. They are fully hardy but do not like high humidity. Propagate by division in early spring or from seed in spring or autumn/fall. Transplant when dormant during winter.

LIBERTIA
grandiflora
NEW ZEALAND IRIS

An easily grown, rhizomatous perennial, native to New Zealand and valued for its foliage, decorative seed pods and flowers. It has grass-like, brown-tipped, dark green leaves. In early summer it produces tall, wiry, lightly branched flower stems with dainty white flowers, followed in autumn/fall by golden brown seed capsules. Loosely clump-forming, it grows to a height of 75 cm (about 30 in) and spread of 60 cm (about 24 in). Frost-hardy, it requires a sheltered, sunny or partially shaded position and well-drained, peaty soil with plenty of moisture in spring and summer. Propagate by division in spring or from seed in spring or autumn/fall. They naturalize freely.

LIGULARIA

Originally from the temperate regions of Europe and Asia, these perennials produce large, daisy-like flowers in summer. Some species grow up to 2.5 m (about 7½ ft) and 1 m (about 3 ft) wide. Fully hardy to half-hardy, they prefer a moist, well-drained soil and will grow in either sun or semi-shade. Propagate by division in spring or from seed in spring or autumn/fall. Prone to attack by slugs and snails.

L. dentata 'Desdemona'
syn. *Senecio clivorum* 'Desdemona'

A compact perennial, grown for its striking foliage and showy heads of daisy flowers. It has kidney-shaped, long-stalked, leathery, brownish green leaves and bears clusters of large, 7.5 cm (about 3 in) wide, orange-yellow flowerheads on long branching stems in summer. Clump-forming, it grows to a height of 1.2 m (about 4 ft) and spread of 60 cm (about 24 in). Fully hardy, this species will grow happily at the edge of ponds.

L. tussilaginea 'Aureomaculata'
LEOPARD PLANT

This herbaceous perennial is grown for its foliage and flowers. It has variegated gold and white leaves with clusters of daisy-like flowers arising from branched stems in late summer. This species grows to a height and spread of 60 cm (about 24 in). A frost-tolerant plant ideal for a damp, shady area although it will also grow in the sun. Plant in damp fertile soil. Cut stems down to the base in autumn/fall.

LIMONIUM
STATICE, SEA LAVENDER

These sub-shrubs and perennials, sometimes grown as annuals, are popular for their papery, many coloured flowers, which can be cut and dried for decoration. Flowers should be cut just as they open and hung upside down to dry in a cool, airy place. They are good mixed border plants and are easily grown in full sun and well-drained, sandy soil. Their tolerance to seaspray and low rainfall make them a good choice for seaside and low maintenance holiday house gardens. Plants will benefit from light fertilizing in spring while flowerheads are developing. Propagate by division in spring, from seed in early spring or autumn/fall, or from root cuttings in late winter. Transplant during winter or early spring.

Liatris spicata

L. latifolium

A fully hardy, tall-stemmed perennial bearing clusters of lavender-blue or bluish white flowers for a long period over summer. Clump-forming, it grows to a height of 30 cm (about 12 in) and spread of 45 cm (about 18 in), with large leaves. The dried flower stems have a delicate, misty appearance.

L. sinuatum

This statice is a bushy, upright perennial, almost always grown as an annual. It produces dense rosettes of oblong, deeply-waved, dark green leaves and bears masses of tiny blue, pink or white papery flowers on winged stems. Flowers in summer and early autumn/fall. It is fairly slow-growing to a height of 50 cm (about 20 in) and spread of 30 cm (about 12 in).

Libertia grandiflora

Limonium latifolium

Limonium sinuatum

Ligularia dentata 'Desdemona'

Ligularia tussilaginea 'Aureomaculata'

LINARIA
maroccana 'Fairy Bouquet'
TOADFLAX

Native to Morocco, this fast-grow-ing, bushy annual is a useful bed-ding plant, giving a long and colourful display of flowers in spring. It bears sprays of small, snapdragon-like flowers in colours of gold, pink, mauve, apricot, cream, purple and yellow. It has lance-shaped, pale green leaves, and grows to a height of 10–15 cm (about 4–6 in) and spread of 10 cm (about 4 in). Fully hardy, it prefers sun or light shade and a well-drained, neutral soil. Water well in early stages of growth. Propagate from seed in spring or autumn/fall. It self-seeds freely. Cut back hard after the first flush to encourage plants to flower again.

LINUM
FLAX

These annuals, biennials, perenni-als, sub-shrubs and shrubs, some of which are evergreen, are distributed widely in temperate regions. They are grown for their profusely blooming flowers. The plants are useful in a rock garden or border. They are fully to half-hardy; some species need shelter in cool cli-mates. Grow in a sunny spot in humus-rich, well-drained, peaty soil. Prune the perennial species back hard after flowering. Propagate the annuals, biennials and perenni-als from seed in autumn/fall and perennials by division in spring or autumn/fall. Transplant from late autumn/fall until early spring.

L. grandiflorum 'Rubrum'
SCARLET FLAX

Native to Algeria, this annual has small, rounded, flattish, deep red flowers and lance-shaped, grey-green leaves. Flowers best in cool summers. The flowering period is short but can be extended by sow-ing seed at monthly intervals. It has a slim, erect habit and is fairly fast-growing to a height of 50 cm (about 20 in) and spread of 15 cm (about 6 in). It is fully hardy.

L. narbonense
FLAX

A perennial native of the Mediter-ranean region, this most handsome of all the blue flaxes has deep, sky-blue, funnel-shaped flowers that last for many weeks in summer borne on slender stems. It has soft, green leaves and forms a clump 45 cm (about 18 in) high and wide. It needs a well-drained soil and a sheltered site in full sun in order to flourish and is both drought and frost resistant. Propagation is by seed.

L. perenne
syn. L. sibiricum

A vigorous, upright perennial native to Europe, forming a shapely bushy plant 30 cm (about 12 in) high with a spread of 15 cm (about 6 in). It has slender stems with grass-like leaves and clusters of open, funnel-shaped light blue flowers are borne throughout summer. A pure white cultivar, 'Alba', is also available. It is fully hardy. Propagate by seed or by cuttings.

LIRIOPE
muscari
LILYTURF

This clumping evergreen peren-nial—one of 5 species of a genus native to Vietnam, Japan and China—is a useful casual ground cover or path edging. It has grass-like, shining, dark green leaves and bears erect spikes of rounded, bell-shaped, violet flowers in late sum-mer. It grows to a height of 30–60 cm (about 12–24 in) with a spread of 30 cm (about 12 in), with flower spikes held just above the foliage. It prefers shade and well-drained, moderately fertile soil. The foliage should be cut back hard in late winter when it becomes ragged. Propagate by division in early spring or from seed in autumn.

LOBELIA

This large genus of annuals and perennials is widely distributed in temperate regions, particularly America and Africa. Growth habits vary from low bedding plants to tall herbaceous perennials. They are all grown for their ornamental flowers and neat foliage and make excellent edging, flower box, hanging basket and rock garden specimens. Some are suitable in wild gardens or by the waterside. They are best grown in a well-drained, moist, light loam enriched with animal manure or compost. Most grow in sun or semi-shade but resent wet conditions in winter. Prune after the first flush of flowers to encourage repeat flower-ing, and fertilize weekly with a liquid manure during the season. Fully hardy to frost-tender. Propa-gate annuals from seed in spring, perennial species from seed or by division in spring or autumn/fall and perennial cultivars by division only. Transplant from late autumn/fall until early spring.

L. cardinalis
CARDINAL FLOWER

A clump-forming perennial, useful for growing in wet places and be-side streams and ponds. From late summer to mid-autumn/fall it pro-duces spikes of brilliant scarlet-red

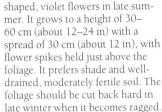

Linum perenne

Linaria maroccana 'Fairy Bouquet'

Linum narbonense

Lobelia cardinalis

Liriope muscari

Linum grandiflorum 'Rubrum'

Lobelia erinus 'Cambridge Blue'

flowers on branching stems above green or deep bronzy purple foliage. Grows to a height of 1 m (about 3 ft) and spread of 30 cm (about 12 in). It requires moist soil and semi-shade and is half-hardy. 'Queen Victoria' is a well-known cultivar.

L. erinus 'Cambridge Blue'
EDGING LOBELIA

This slow-growing compact annual is native to South Africa. It has a tufted, sometimes semi-trailing, habit with dense oval to lance-shaped leaves. It bears small, 2-lipped blue flowers continuously through spring, summer and early autumn/fall. Grows to a height of 10–20 cm (about 4–8 in) and spread of 10–15 cm (about 4–6 in), and is half-hardy. Water sparingly and feed regularly. Excellent for edging, rockeries, pots and hanging baskets.

L. 'Vedrariensis'

A clump-forming perennial that is an excellent border plant, growing to a height of 1 m (about 3 ft) and spread of 30 cm (about 12 in). It produces racemes of 2-lipped violet-blue flowers in late summer. Leaves are dark green and lance-shaped. Frost-hardy, it prefers full sun, but should not be allowed to get too dry.

LOBULARIA
maritima
syn. *Alyssum maritimum*
SWEET ALYSSUM, SWEET ALICE

Native to southern Europe and western Asia, this fast-growing, spreading annual is a widely popular edging, rock garden or window box plant. It produces masses of tiny, honey-scented, 4-petalled white flowers over a long season from spring to early autumn/fall. Lilac, pink and violet shades are also available. It has a low, rounded compact habit with lance-shaped greyish green leaves and grows to a height of 8–15 cm (about 3–6 in), and a spread of 20–30 cm (about 8–12 in). Fully hardy, it grows best in a dryish position in full sun and likes a fertile, well-drained soil. Good for coastal and beach situations. Shear back after flowering to encourage continuous flowering. Propagate from seed in spring.

Lobularia maritima

LOTUS
berthelotii
CORAL GEM

Native to the Cape Verde and Canary Islands, this semi-evergreen, trailing perennial is suitable for hanging baskets, ground cover or spilling over rockeries, banks or the tops of walls. It has hairy, silvery branches of fine needle leaves and clusters of pea-like scarlet flowers cover the plant in spring and early summer. Grows to 30 cm (about 12 in) tall with an indefinite spread. It requires a fairly sunny situation and well-drained coarse soil, preferably with a little added peat or other organic matter. Frost-tender, it suits warm coastal gardens. Tip-prune young shoots to encourage dense foliage. Propagate from cuttings taken in summer or from seed in spring or autumn/fall.

LUNARIA
annua
syn. *L. biennis*
HONESTY

A fast-growing biennial, native to southern Europe and the Mediterranean coast, this plant is grown for its attractive flowers and curious fruits. It has pointed oval, serrated, bright green leaves, and bears heads of scented, four-petalled rosy magenta, white or violet-purple flowers in spring and early summer. These are followed by circular seed pods with a silvery, translucent membrane, which are used in dried floral arrangements. Erect in habit, it grows to a height of 75 cm (about 30 in) and spread of 30 cm (about 12 in). Fully hardy, it will grow in either

Lobelia 'Vedrariensis'

sun or shade, but prefers partial shade and a moderately fertile, well-drained soil. Propagate from seed in spring or autumn/fall. This plant self-sows readily in most climates.

LUPINUS
LUPIN

A large genus of annuals and perennials mainly native to North America and southern Europe, grown for their ease of culture, rapid growth and large spikes of showy pea flowers in a range of colours including blue, purple, pink, white, yellow, orange and red. They are useful grouped with bearded irises in bedding schemes and are good naturalized. Grow in cool climates in an open, sunny position and a well-drained alkaline soil. They enjoy high humidity and should be mulched in dry areas. Spent flowers should be cut away to prolong plant life and to prevent self-seeding. Fully to frost-hardy. Propagate species from seed in autumn/fall and selected forms from cuttings in early spring. Watch for

Lotus berthelotii

Lupinus hartwegii

Lunaria annua

slugs and snails. The foliage adds nitrogen to the soil when dug in.

L. hartwegii
HAIRY-FOLIAGED LUPIN

Native to Mexico, this annual has compact, erect growth to 70 cm (about 28 in) high with a spread of 40 cm (about 16 in). It has hairy, palmate, dark green leaves, and slender spikes of pea flowers in shades of blue, white or pink are borne abundantly in late winter, spring and early summer. Fast-growing.

L., Russell hybrids

This fine strain of strong-growing perennial lupines bear long spikes of large brilliant, strongly coloured flowers (in shades of cream, pink, orange, blue or violet), some of which are bicoloured, in late spring and summer. They produce a magnificent clump of handsome, deeply divided, mid-green leaves, growing to a height of 90 cm (about 3 ft) with a spread of half that. There are also dwarf strains, such as the 60 cm (24 in) high 'Lulu'. Cut back flowering stems to ground level in late autumn/fall and divide and replant clumps between autumn/fall and early spring every two or three years.

L. texensis

TEXAS BLUE BONNET

A fast-growing, bushy annual reaching a height of 30 cm (about 12 in) and spread of 20 cm (about 8 in), this species has bright green palmate leaves and bears dark blue and white flowers in late spring. Easily grown, it thrives in poor soils, and is quick to flower from seed. This is the state flower of Texas.

LYCHNIS

Native to the temperate regions of the northern hemisphere, these annuals, biennials and perennials are grown for their attractive summer flowers, borne in cymes in white through to reds and magenta. They are fully hardy, and easily grown in cool, elevated places, preferably on sunny sites with an easterly or southerly slope to minimize soil temperatures. They grow in any well-drained soil and an annual feeding in late winter to early spring is beneficial. Remove spent stems after flowering and dead-head frequently to prolong the flowering period. Propagate by division or from seed in autumn/fall or early spring. They self-seed readily. These plants have been cultivated for many centuries.

L. coronaria

ROSE CAMPION

A clump-forming perennial, sometimes grown as a biennial, this plant grows to a height of 60 cm (about 24 in) and a spread of 45 cm (about 18 in). It forms a dense clump of silvery white, woolly leaves, and branched grey stems carry bright scarlet flowers throughout summer. Fully hardy, it thrives in most areas and self-sows readily. 'Alba' is a white-flowered cultivar. In ancient times the flowers were used for garlands and crowns.

L. × haagena

MALTESE CROSS

A short-lived, clump-forming perennial, growing to a height of 45 cm (about 18 in) with a spread of 30 cm (about 12 in). In summer it bears clusters of large, 5-petalled white, salmon, flame and scarlet flowers. Foliage is mid-green. It is weak-growing and should be regularly propagated from seed.

LYSICHITON
camtschatcensis

SKUNK CABBAGE

Native to Siberia and northern Japan, this deciduous perennial is a marsh plant, useful for planting in damp, boggy soils and on pond edges. It has handsome, arum-like, pure white spathes surrounding spikes of small insignificant flowers. These are borne in spring and are followed by tufts of bold, bright green foliage, arising from a creeping rhizome. Grows to a height of 75 cm (about 30 in) and spread of 60 cm (about 24 in). Fully hardy, it prefers full sun but will tolerate semi-shade. They require a cold and frosty winter climate and are happy growing in both running and still water. Propagate from seed in late summer.

LYSIMACHIA
punctata

GARDEN LOOSESTRIFE, GOLDEN LOOSESTRIFE

A clump-forming perennial seen at its best planted in bold drifts or groups. It has mid-green leaves and lightly branched stems that in summer carry a great massed display of brilliant yellow, starry flowers, produced in whorls near the top of the stem. They are suitable for bedding, rock gardens or beside pools and streams. It grows erect to a height and spread of around 70 cm (around 28 in). Fully hardy, it prefers a sunny situation and moist but well-drained soil. Propagate by division in autumn/fall, winter or early spring, or from seed in autumn/fall. Its common name is derived from 'louse-strife', as the plant was grown to repel lice.

MACLEAYA
cordata

syn. Bocconia cordata

PLUME POPPY

Native to China and Japan, this tall perennial grows to 1.5 m (nearly 5 ft) or more. It belongs to the Papaveraceae family, which includes poppies. It has large, rounded, deeply veined, heart-shaped grey-green leaves, and bears large, feathery, terminal flower spikes of cream tinted with pink in summer. An evergreen, it is one of the most attractive foliage plants available for the herbaceous border. Fully hardy, it requires

Lysichiton camtschatcensis

Lychnis coronaria

Lychnis × haagena

Lupinus, Russell hybrids

Lupinus texensis

Macleaya cordata

Matthiola incana

a sunny, sheltered situation and well-drained soil, and prefers a cool climate. Water well during the growing season and mulch during winter. It exudes a yellow sap when cut. Propagate by division in early spring or from root cuttings in winter. It spreads from underground stems and may become invasive.

MALCOLMIA
maritima
VIRGINIA STOCK, VIRGINIAN STOCK

An attractive little annual from the Mediterranean, this plant is valued for its ability to flower quickly from seed as soon as 4 to 6 weeks after seed is sown. It is very useful for edging, for paths, crevices and window boxes, and for growing over spring-flowering bulbs. It has oval, grey-green leaves, and bears 2 cm (1 in) wide, fragrant flowers in shades of pink, red, mauve and white from spring to autumn/fall. It has an erect habit and is fast-growing to a height of 20 cm (about 8 in) and spread of 5–8 cm (about 2–3 in). Fully hardy, it requires sun and fertile, well-drained soil. Propagate from seed sown at frequent intervals from spring to early autumn/fall for a long flowering season. Self-seeds readily.

MALVA
moschata
MUSK MALLOW

Useful for naturalizing in a wild garden or odd corner, this fully hardy perennial has narrow, lobed, divided

leaves with a sticky, hairy texture, which emit a musky, cheesy odour when crushed. A native of Europe, it bears profuse spikes of saucer-shaped pink flowers in summer. 'Alba', the white cultivar, is also very popular. It has a bushy, branching habit and can grow to a height of 1 m (about 3 ft). It requires a sunny situation and will thrive in a wide range of soil and climatic conditions. Propagate from seed in autumn/fall and cut plants back after first flowers have faded. Watch for rust disease.

MATTHIOLA
STOCK

This genus of annuals, biennials and perennials is native to the Mediterranean region. They are grown for their soft grey-green foliage and densely clustered, highly scented flowers in shades of white, lilac and purple, deep reds and pinks, and yellow. They are fragrant

Malva moschata

and long-lasting as cut flowers. Grow in a sheltered position in sun or semi-shade, and in a fertile, well-drained new soil that has been freshly turned with manure and lime. Tall and dwarf, single and double varieties have been developed. Tall cultivars may need support. Over fertilizing will encourage leaf growth at the expense of the flowers. Fully hardy to frost-tender. Sow seed of annuals in late summer to early autumn/fall; perennials under glass in spring. Watch for botrytis, downy mildew, club root, aphids and flea beetle.

M. incana
STOCK

This upright biennial or short-lived perennial from southern Europe is best grown as an annual. It has a bushy habit and grows up to 60 cm (about 24 in) in height with a spread of 30 cm (about 12 in). These stocks are fully hardy with lance-shaped, grey-green leaves, and fragrant, 7–15 cm (about 3–6 in) long spikes of mauve flowers borne in spring. There are many varieties and strains available, the best selected for a high percentage of double flowers.

M. 'Mammoth Column'
syn. *M.* 'Giant Column'

This is a cultivar from *M. incana* which grows taller, reaching 75 cm (about 30 in) in height. Each plant produces a single, 30–40 cm (about 12–16 in) tall spike of scented flowers in spring, in mixed or separate colours. When the main spike is finished, cutting the plant back will promote more flowers.

MAZUS
radicans

This prostrate carpet-forming New Zealand perennial has a strong stem and stout upright branches. The limbs are covered with egg-shaped to linear foliage which often has a downy reverse. In summer, bluish purple to pink or white 5-lobed cylindrical flowers with a yellow centre appear. These are followed by egg-shaped seed pods containing many seeds. Plant in medium soil allowing full sun. Propagate from seed or by division at the beginning of spring.

Malcolmia maritima

Mazus radicans

Matthiola 'Mammoth Column'

MECONOPSIS

A genus of short-lived perennials that are mostly native to the Himalayas. They bear large, exotic flowers with papery petals and a bold, central boss of stamens on tall stems in early summer. They need a moist but not over-wet, lime-free soil with plenty of humus and a cool site in part- or full shade which is sheltered from strong winds. Propagate from seed in late summer.

M. betonicifolia
BLUE POPPY, TIBETAN POPPY

This clump-forming perennial bears pure, sky-blue, saucer-shaped, 5–8 cm (about 2–3 in) wide, satiny flowers with yellow stamens in late spring and early summer. Oblong, hairy, mid-green leaves are produced in basal rosettes. Grows to a height of 1 m (about 3 ft) and spread of 45 cm (about 18 in). A fully hardy woodland species, it prefers a cool climate. Plants do not bloom in the first season, die down completely over winter, and produce fine flowerheads the next spring.

M. cambrica
WELSH POPPY

Native to western Europe and including Great Britain, these perennial poppies are more easily grown than the blue poppy and make a welcome addition to the garden when allowed to naturalize with shrubs and bulbs or when added to flower borders. The slightly hairy, mid-green leaves are deeply divided and form basal tufts. Lemon-yellow or rich orange blooms are freely borne in late spring. It has a spread-

Meconopsis betonicifolia

ing habit, reaching 30 cm (about 12 in), with a height of 30–45 cm (about 12–18 in). Fully hardy, it is a short-lived species that nevertheless self-seeds readily.

MERTENSIA
virginica
VIRGINIA BLUEBELL

Native to the cooler parts of North America, this perennial is one of the loveliest of all blue spring flowers. It has smooth, oblong, soft blue-green foliage, and bears clusters of rich blue, tubular 2.5 cm (about 1 in) long flowers, 20 or more on each stem. It is effective planted with daffodils and polyanthus and is seen at its best naturalized in woodlands or alongside streams. Fully hardy, it grows to a height and spread of around 45 cm (about 18 in). Plant in shade and a deep, well-drained soil. Propagate by division in spring or from seed or by division in autumn/fall.

MIMULUS

These annuals and perennials are characterized by tubular flowers with flared mouths, often curiously spotted and mottled, which have been likened to grinning monkey faces. The flowers come in a large range of colours including brown, orange, yellow, red and crimson. Mainly native to the cool Pacific coastal areas of Chile and the USA, most species are suited to bog gardens or other moist situations, although some are excellent rock garden plants. Grow in full sun or partial shade in a wet or moist soil.

Propagate perennials by division in spring and annuals from seed in autumn/fall or early spring.

M. cardinalis

Native to the south-western USA and Mexico, this herbaceous perennial grows to 90 cm (about 36 in) or more in height, with a spread of around 30 cm (about 12 in). It has sharply toothed, hairy, mid-green leaves and produces racemes of yellow-throated scarlet flowers from summer through to autumn/fall. This species needs a sheltered position as it has a tendency to sprawl if battered by rain and wind. It will tolerate fairly dry soil.

M. moschatus
MONKEY MUSK

A small, creeping, water-loving perennial growing to a height and spread of 15–30 cm (about 6–12 in). It bears snapdragon-like, pale yellow flowers, lightly dotted with brown, in summer to autumn/fall. It is fully hardy. This plant was once grown for its musk scent but, mysteriously, it has been odourless for many years.

MINA
lobata
syn. *Ipomoea versicolor, Quamoclit lobata*

Native to Mexico and Central America, this vigorous, short-lived twining climber is a perennial usually grown as an annual. It is deciduous or semi-evergreen with three-lobed bright green leaves, and bears racemes of small, tubular, dark red flowers fading to orange

then creamy yellow. Flowers appear from late summer until late autumn/fall. The plant climbs to a height of 5 m (about 15 ft) and quickly provides a dense leafy cover over a suitable supporting structure. Half-hardy, it requires a warm position and a rich well-drained soil.

MIRABILIS
jalapa
MARVEL OF PERU, FOUR-O'CLOCK-FLOWER

This bushy tuberous perennial is grown for its fragrant, trumpet-shaped, crimson, pink, white or yellow flowers that open in late afternoon and remain open all night, closing again at dawn. Good as pot plants, bedding plants or as a dwarf hedge. They are native to tropical America, summer-flowering, and grow to around 1 m (about 3 ft) high with a spread of 60–75 cm (about 24–30 in). They require a sheltered position in full sun with a fertile well-drained soil. In frosty areas tubers are best lifted and stored like dahlias over winter; in mild climates

Meconopsis cambrica

Mimulus cardinalis

Mertensia virginica

Mina lobata

Mimulus moschatus

they can be left undisturbed and gradually make large clumps. Propagate from seed or by division of tubers in early spring.

MOLUCCELLA
laevis
BELLS OF IRELAND, SHELL FLOWER

This summer-flowering annual, native to Syria, is grown for its spikes, surrounded by shell-like, apple green calyces which are very popular for fresh or dried floral work; the tiny white flowers are insignificant. Rounded leaves are pale green and nettle-like. The plant is fairly fast growing to a height of 60 cm (about 24 in) and spread of 30 cm (about 12 in), and has an erect, branching habit. Half-hardy, it grows best in a sunny, open position and a rich very well-drained soil. Propagate by sowing seed directly into its flowering position in early spring. Water moderately and feed monthly with a balanced fertilizer.

MYOSOTIDIUM
hortensia
CHATHAM ISLAND FORGET-ME-NOT

Native to the Chatham Islands off the coast of New Zealand, this evergreen, clump-forming perennial is the giant of the forget-me-not family, growing to a height and spread of around 60 cm (about 24 in). It has a basal mound of large, glossy, rich-green, pleated leaves, and in spring and summer bears large clusters of bright blue flowers, slightly paler on the edges, on tall flower stems. Half-hardy, it requires semi-shade and a humus-rich moist soil. It can withstand salt winds and benefits from a mulch. Propagate by division in spring or from seed in summer or autumn/fall. Once growing well, they should not be disturbed and will naturalize freely.

MYOSOTIS
FORGET-ME-NOT

This genus of annuals and perennials includes 34 New Zealand natives among its 50 or so species, but those most commonly cultivated come from the temperate regions of Europe, Asia and the Americas. They are grown for their dainty blue (sometimes pink or white) flowers that complement plants of stronger colour in the spring garden. Most species are useful in rock gardens, border displays or as ground cover under trees and shrubs.Fully hardy, they prefer either a semi-shaded woodland setting or a sunny spot with the protection of other larger plants. Soil should be fertile and well-drained. They are rarely affected by pests or diseases and respond well to feeding in the pre-flowering period. Discard plants

after flowering. Propagate from seed in autumn/fall. Once established they self-seed freely. Myosotis is derived from the Greek for 'mouse ear', referring to the pointed leaves. The flowers have long been associated with love and remembrance.

M. alpestris
ALPINE FORGET-ME-NOT

This fully hardy, short-lived perennial (usually grown as an annual or biennial) forms clumps to a height and spread of 10–15 cm (about 4–6 in). In late spring and early summer, it bears clusters of dainty, bright blue, pink or white flowers with creamy yellow eyes. Plant in gritty soil in semi-shade.

M. 'Blue Ball'

This fully hardy, slow-growing perennial is usually grown as an annual. It has a bushy, compact habit, growing to a height of 20 cm (about 8 in) with a spread of 15 cm (about 6 in), and bears tiny, deep blue flowers in spring and early summer. It is good for edging.

M. colensoi
NZ FORGET-ME-NOT

The best known New Zealand forget-me-not, it adapts well to garden conditions, unlike most of the other species. It has rounded, slightly hairy, greyish green to silver leaves and small white flowers in late spring and summer. It forms a dense clump 5 cm (about 2 in) tall with a 30 cm (about 12 in) spread. Grow in sun or partial shade and moist well-drained soil. Suits rockeries or alpine pans. Propagate from seed in autumn/fall, by division in early spring or from rooted offsets.

M. scorpioides
syn. M. palustris
WATER FORGET-ME-NOT

A deciduous to semi-evergreen perennial, ideally grown as a marginal water plant for muddy situations or in very shallow water. It grows to a height and spread of 30 cm (about 12 in). It bears small blue flowers, with a yellow, pink or white eye, throughout summer. It is fully hardy.

Myosotis alpestris

Myosotis scorpioides

Mirabilis jalapa

Moluccella laevis

Myosotis colensoi

Myosotidium hortensia

Myosotis 'Blue Ball'

Nemophila insignis

Nertera granadensis

Neomarica caerulea

NELUMBO
nucifera
SACRED LOTUS

A deciduous, perennial, marginal
water plant, this is the giant of the
Nymphaeaceae (water lily) family,
growing 1–1.4 m (about 3–4½ ft)
above the water surface and spreading to 1.2 m (about 3½ ft). Large
fragrant, pink or white 25 cm
(about 10 in) wide flowers are
borne above large, shield-shaped,
pale green leaves. It is a subtropical
species and requires an open, sunny
position and 60 cm (about 24 in)
depth of water. Flowers develop
into unusual seed pods, resembling
salt-shakers. Remove faded foliage
and divide overgrown plants in
spring. Propagate from seed in
spring. This vigorous plant grows
well in large ponds. Buddha is often
depicted in the centre of a lotus.

NEMESIA
strumosa

Indigenous to southern Africa, this
colourful, fast-growing annual is a
popular bedding plant. They are
also useful for planting between
summer-flowering bulbs, in rock
gardens and window boxes. They
are bushy plants with lance-shaped,
pale green and prominently toothed
leaves, growing to a height of 20–
30 cm (about 8–12 in) and spread
of 25 cm (about 10 in). Large, trumpet-shaped flowers in colours of
yellow, white, red or orange are
borne in spring on short terminal
racemes. The plants prefer a well-
dug, moderately fertile, mildly acid
or neutral, well-drained soil, and a
wind-sheltered, sunny position.

Nemesia strumosa

They cannot tolerate very hot, humid climates. Prune spent flowers to
prolong flowering and pinch out
growing shoots of young plants to
encourage a bushy habit. Propagate
from seed in early autumn/fall. The
most cultivated of its genus, N.
strumosa has spawned a range of
hybrids and cultivars of varying
heights and colours. 'Blue Gem' is a
compact annual, fast-growing up to
20 cm (about 8 in). It bears trumpet-shaped, small, clear blue flowers that are a good foil for stronger
coloured spring plants.

NEMOPHILA
insignis
syn. N. menziesii
BABY BLUE-EYES

A charming little Californian
wildflower, this fast-growing, spreading annual is a useful ground cover
under shrubs such as roses, in rock
gardens and edges, and is particularly effective overplanted in a bed
with spring bulbs. It bears small,
bowl-shaped, sapphire-blue flowers
with a well-defined concentric ring

of white in the centre. It has dainty,
serrated mid-green foliage, and
grows to a height of 20 cm (about 8
in) and spread of 15 cm (about 6
in). It is best planted in a cool,
partly shaded site in fertile, well-
drained soil that does not dry out in
summer. These plants dislike heat
and transplanting. Propagate from
seed sown outdoors in early au-
tumn/fall. Watch for aphids.

NEOMARICA
caerulea
WALKING IRIS

Native to Brazil, this iris-like,
rhizomatous, evergreen perennial
yields an amazing number of flowers,
but is essentially a garden plant as
they are not suitable for cutting. It
has tall, straight, sword-like leaves in
basal fans, and produces a succession
of triangular sky-blue flowers with
white, yellow and brown central
marks. Flowers are short-lived but
are borne over a long period in
summer. The plant grows to a
height of 1 m (about 3 ft) and
spread of 1–1.5 m (about 3–4½ ft),

Nelumbo nucifera

and is frost-tender. Plant in a fertile,
moist, humus-rich soil in a partially
shaded position. Water well in summer and ensure the soil does not
dry out in winter. Propagate from
seed in spring or by division in
spring or summer. Transplant from
late autumn/fall until early spring.

NEPETA
× faassenii
CATMINT

A bushy, clump-forming perennial,
useful for separating strong colours in
the shrub or flower border, and very
effective when used with stone, either
in walls, paving or rock gardens, or as
an edging plant. It forms spreading
mounds of greyish green leaves that
are aromatic when crushed, and the
numerous flower stems carry hundreds of small, pale violet-blue flowers throughout summer. Grows to a
height and spread of 45 cm (about 18
in). Fully hardy, it prefers cool conditions and a sunny situation but will
grow in semi-shade. Any moderately
fertile, well-drained soil will suit. Cut
back old growth to within 15 cm
(about 6 in) of soil level in winter
when the plants become untidy.
Propagate by division in early spring
or from softwood cuttings in spring
and summer.

NERTERA
granadensis
syn. N. depressa
BEAD PLANT

A carpeting perennial, grown
for the mass of spherical, orange or
red, bead-like berries it bears in
autumn/fall. It has a prostrate
habit, growing to 1 cm (about ½ in)

in height with a spread of 10 cm (about 4 in) and forming compact cushions of tiny bright green leaves with extremely small, greenish white flowers in early summer. Half-hardy, it thrives in a cool, sheltered, semi-shaded site in gritty, moist but well-drained sandy soil. Water well in summer but keep dryish in winter. It is an excellent alpine house plant. Propagate by division or from seed or tip cuttings in spring. There is a variety with purple-tinged foliage.

NICOTIANA
FLOWERING TOBACCO

These annuals and perennials, some of which are grown as annuals, are mainly of South American origin and are an ornamental species of tobacco. The older species are grown for the fragrance of their warm-weather flowers which usually open at night; the newer strains have flowers that remain open all day but have limited perfume. They are half-hardy to frost-tender, requiring full sun or light shade and a fertile, moist, but well-drained soil. Propagate from seed in early spring. The flowers are good for cutting, although the plants are sticky to handle. Watch for snails and caterpillars.

N. alata
syn. N. affinis

A short-lived perennial, often grown as an annual, this half-hardy plant bears clusters of attractive, tubular flowers in white, red or various shades of pink. The flowers open towards evening and fill the garden with scent on warm, still nights. Rosette-forming, it has oval, mid-green leaves and grows to a height of 1 m (about 3 ft) with a spread of 30 cm (about 12 in). It flowers through summer and early autumn/fall.

N. × sanderae

A half-hardy, slow-growing bushy annual, reaching to a height of 40 cm (about 16 in) and spread of half that. In summer and early autumn/fall it bears long, trumpet-shaped flowers in shades of white, pink, red, cerise, bright crimson and purple. Flowers stay open during the day and are fragrant in the evening.

NIEREMBERGIA
hippomanica var. violacea 'Purple Robe'
syn. N. caerulea

Native to Argentina, this small, bushy perennial, best grown as an annual, is ideal for edgings and massed beddings, rock gardens and window boxes. In summer and early autumn/fall it bears a profusion of cup-shaped, open, dark bluish purple flowers with yellow throats. It has much-branched, thin, stiffly erect stems and narrow, lance-shaped, deep-green, slightly hairy leaves. Moderately fast-growing to a height and spread of 15–20 cm (about 6–8 in). Half-hardy, it prefers a moist but well-drained soil and a sunny situation. Cut well back after flowering. It increases readily by underground runners and may become invasive. Propagate by division in spring, from semi-ripe cuttings in summer or seed in autumn/fall. Fresh stock should be raised every two or three years.

NIGELLA
damascena
LOVE-IN-A-MIST, DEVIL-IN-A-BUSH

A fully hardy annual, grown for its attractive flowers, native to the Mediterranean and western Asia. It has spurred, many-petalled blue or white flowers in spring and early summer, almost hidden in the bright green, feathery foliage followed by rounded green seed pods that mature to brown. Both flowers and seed pods are good for floral decoration. Upright and fast-growing, it reaches 60 cm (about 24 in) high with a spread of 20 cm (about 8 in). Plant in a sunny situation in a fertile, well-drained soil; fertilize monthly and water regularly. The plants have a short blooming season and can be dead-headed to prolong flowering; successive sowings can also be made. Propagate from seed in autumn/fall. It self-sows readily.

NYMPHAEA
WATER LILY

This genus of deciduous and evergreen, perennial aquatic plants with fleshy roots is named for the Greek goddess Nymphe. They are grown for their floating leaves and attractive brigh flowers that come in shades of white and cream, brilliant yellows and oranges, pinks and deep reds, blues and purple. There are hardy and tropical varieties. Hardy water lilies grow in all climates and flower freely throughout summer, both flowers and foliage floating on the water surface. Faded foliage should be removed. Divide the tuber-like rhizomes and replant in spring or summer every three or four years. Tropical water lilies are all frost-tender, requiring a very warm, sunny situation. They flower from mid-summer into autumn/fall, and have large, scented flowers held above the water surface. In cooler areas, the tubers should be lifted and stored in moist sand over the winter. All species need still water and annual fertilizing as they are gross feeders. Propagate from seed or by separating plantlets in spring or early autumn/fall. Watch for insects, particularly aphids; goldfish in the pool will eat most pests.

N. alba

A deciduous, hardy species with floating dark green leaves and cup-shaped, semi-double, fragrant 10 cm (about 4 in) wide, white flowers with golden centres. Spreads to 3 m (about 9 ft).

N. 'Aurora'

A smaller hardy cultivar, also deciduous, with floating olive green leaves blotched with purple. Semi-double flowers are star-shaped, 5 cm (about 2 in) wide and turn from cream to yellow, to orange, to blood-red. Spreads to 75 cm (about 30 in).

N. candida

This dainty, dwarf species is ideal for a miniature pond. It bears small, pure white cup-shaped flowers.

Plant with around 15–23 cm (about 6–9 in) of water over the crown of the plant.

N. × helvola

A true miniature water lily which bears soft yellow, star-shaped, semi-double flowers. The leaves are handsome too, being dark olive green splashed with maroon. Plant with around 23 cm (about 9 in) of water over the crown of the plant. It is the smallest of the miniature water lilies.

N. Laydeckeri hybrids

These compact hybrids are excellent for small ponds, as they are very free flowering yet produce comparatively little foliage. Colours range from soft rose-pink to deep pink and rosy-crimson. Plant with 23–30 cm (about 9–12 in) of water over the crown of the plant. They have a spread of around 60 cm (about 24 in). N. × laydeckeri 'Fulgens' is a hardy perennial with star-shaped, semi-double crimson to magenta flowers.

Nicotiana alata

Nicotiana × sanderae

Nierembergia hippomanica var. *violacea* 'Purple Robe'

Nigella damascena

Nymphaea alba

Nymphaea 'Aurora'

N. nouchali var. caerulea
syn. *Nymphaea caerulea*
BLUE LOTUS

Native to tropical Africa, this species has long, rounded complete leaves over 30 cm (12 in) wide. The leaves have a green surface with purple edges and markings beneath. After the first year, lightly fragrant, pale blue, lilac or pink flowers bloom in spring. This species is easily grown in a tub and is suitable for the greenhouse.

N. marliacea 'Carnea'

This elegant water lily has dark green leaves and star-shaped semi-double, soft pink flowers with golden centres 15–25 cm (about 6–10 in) across. Plant with 50 cm (about 20 in) of water over the crown of the plant. It flowers in summer.

N. odorata
WHITE POND LILY

This perennial, native to America, has large, white, fragrant and many-petalled flowers appearing in summer. It prefers the still waters of ponds and marshes in an open, sunny position and is frost-resistant. Propagate by division.

OENOTHERA
EVENING PRIMROSE

Native to North America but widespread elsewhere, this genus of annuals, biennials and perennials is grown for the masses of short-lived flowers borne during summer. Most species are pollinated by night-flying insects and only release their lovely fragrance at night. Some members of the genus do not even open their petals during the day. They are fully to frost-hardy and grow best in a well-drained sandy soil in an open sunny situation. They will tolerate dry conditions. Propagate from seed or by division in spring or autumn/fall, or from softwood cuttings in late spring. Evening primrose oil has a great variety of health benefits. The oil is extracted from the plant's tiny seeds which contain essential fatty acids.

O. biennis

A showy plant, this upright biennial has large, scented, yellow flowers that grow in long sprays and open in the evening. Foliage is light green. It is frost-hardy and fast-growing to a height of 1.5 m (nearly 5 ft) and spread of 60 cm (about 24 in).

O. missouriensis

A spreading perennial that forms mats of dark green leaves and has short-stemmed, bell-shaped, 10 cm (about 4 in) wide, canary yellow flowers, sometimes spotted red. Flowers open at sundown and are borne over a long period throughout spring and summer. It is fully hardy and grows to a height of 10 cm (about 4 in) and spread of 40 cm (about 16 in) or more.

O. speciosa
WHITE EVENING PRIMROSE

A short-lived rhizomatous perennial bearing spikes of fragrant, saucer-shaped, pink-tinted white flowers in profusion. Fresh flowerheads open daily throughout the summer. The small leaves often turn red in hot or cold weather. Clump-forming, it grows to 45 cm (about 18 in) in height with a spread of 30 cm (about 12 in) or more, and is frost-hardy.

Oenothera speciosa

OSTEOSPERMUM

This genus of annuals and ever-green, semi-woody perennials is mostly indigenous to South Africa. The tough plants are useful for rock gardens, dry embankments, or the front rows of shrub borders, particularly as temporary filler plants. They produce large daisy-like flowers in the white and violet, purple, blue range, and flower for many weeks in winter and spring. They prefer a warm, temperate climate and require moderately fertile, well-drained soil. An open, sun-exposed position is essential. Light pruning after flowering helps maintain shape. Propagate from cuttings of non-flowering shoots or from seed in summer.

O. ecklonis
SAILOR BOY DAISY, FREEWAY DAISY

An evergreen with either upright or straggling habit, this half-hardy perennial grows to a height and spread of

Nymphaea marliacea 'Carnea'

Nymphaea nouchali var. *caerula*

Oenothera biennis

Osteospermum ecklonis

Nymphaea hybrid

Oenothera missouriensis

45 cm (about 18 in). It has lance-shaped, mid-green leaves and bears 7.5 cm (about 3 in) wide daisies, glistening white with deep reddish violet centres, and streaked with bluish mauve underneath the petals. Flowers from early summer to autumn/fall.

O. jucundum

syn. *O. barberae, Dimorphotheca barberae*

TRAILING MAUVE DAISY, PINK VELD DAISY, FREEWAY DAISY

This frost-hardy, evergreen perennial grows to a height and spread of 45 cm (about 18 in). It is clump-forming with mid- to dark green, lance-shaped to rectangular leaves, and produces abundant purplish pink daisies with darker central discs throughout autumn/fall and early summer. The flowers close on cloudy days. 'Whirligig' has pink or white flowers and curled petals.

OURISIA
macrophylla

Native to New Zealand, this perennial has a carpet-forming habit. It reaches up to 10 cm (about 4 in) high and 15 cm (about 6 in) wide. The light green, downy foliage is egg-shaped to elliptical and develops on long, purple-tinted stalks. In late spring to early summer an abundance of small white blossoms appear. It requires total shade and fertile, damp soil. It is reluctant to grow in dry climates, preferring moist peat beds or shady walls. Propagate from seed or by division in spring.

OXYPETALUM
caeruleum
syn. *Tweedia caerulea*

Pale blue starry flowers, ageing to purple, are borne in summer and early autumn/fall on this herbaceous twining climber. They are followed by 15 cm (about 6 in) long, boat-shaped, green seed pods. The flowers are suitable for picking but the cut stems must be burnt to seal the sticky white sap. The plant has heart-shaped grey-green leaves covered with a hairy down, and grows to a height of 1 m (about

3 ft). Frost-tender, it requires a sunny situation and rich, well-drained soil. It should be grown as an annual in cooler climates. Propagate from seed in spring and pinch out tips of buds to encourage a branching habit. This species, from Uruguay and Brazil, is the only member of its genus to be cultivated widely. It belongs to the Asclepiadaceae family, which is the favoured source of food for the monarch caterpillar.

PACHYSANDRA
terminalis

This creeping perennial, a native of Japan, has leathery, ovate leaves with saw-tooth tips, clustered at the ends of short stems. Tiny white flowers, sometimes pink or purple-tinted, appear in terminal clusters in early summer. This frost-resistant evergreen makes good ground cover and likes moist, well-drained soil in a shady site. It grows to a height of 10 cm (about 4 in) with a spread of 20 cm (about 8 in). Propagate by division in early spring.

PAEONIA
PEONY

Some species of these deciduous shrubs and perennials display showy seed pods in addition to the lobed foliage and full round flowerheads for which this genus is renowned. Many species are from western China and the Himalayas; some from Siberia and Mongolia. Others are of European origin, including *P. officinalis* which, although poisonous, has been used as a remedy for everything from gout, cramps and asthma to bladder and kidney problems, as well as serving as a diuretic, sedative and antispasmodic. Sow seed in autumn/fall or propagate by division in autumn/fall or early spring. Germination from seed can take as long as three years. Use root cuttings from tuberous species in winter. To start the deciduous tree peonies, use grafts in winter or semi-ripe cuttings late in summer. Soil should be moist and fertilized, although too much animal manure or

poorly drained soil may bring on botrytis.

P. 'Bowl of Beauty'

Big flowers appear on this perennial between late spring and mid-summer. A dense cluster of slender, creamy-white petaloids nest in the centre of broad, pink outer petals. The plant grows to a height and spread of 1 m (about 3 ft). This frost resistant perennial enjoys semi-shade. The variety is typical of the Chinese peonies, derived mainly from *P. lactiflora* which comes in a huge range of colours and forms.

Osteospermum jucundum

Oxypetalum caeruleum

Paeonia 'Bowl of Beauty'

Pachysandra terminalis

Ourisia macrophylla

A Field Trip to Grindelwald

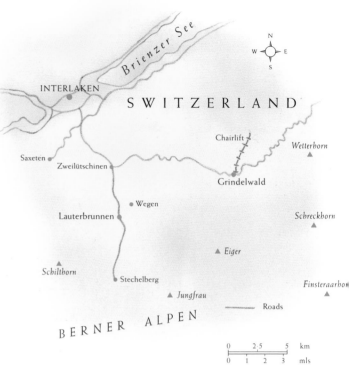

Visit the picture-postcard town of Grindelwald between December and March and you will find thousands of brightly clad skiers trudging through the slush and ice. Return again in July and Grindelwald will have undergone a transformation, with colourful windowboxes full of geraniums adorning attractive alpine houses.

The town nestles in the mountains of the Bernese Oberland, sitting against the backdrop of the Swiss Alps, These mountains, with their wooded lower slopes, alpine meadows and snow-capped peaks, include among their number the towering Eiger.

Although Grindelwald at times suffers from an inundation of visitors, it does have two important advantages for the plant enthusiasts who visit. Firstly, it is surrounded by some superb alpine meadows and pastures which are incredibly rich in colourful species; secondly, the same chairlifts that

The great yellow gentian, with a spectacular mountain backdrop.

transport hopeful skiers to the *piste* during the winter months operate throughout the year and can save hours of foot-slogging toil. Within a few short minutes, you can be free of the hustle and bustle of urban Grindelwald below and admire the clear views and brilliant flowers which in summer include one of the Alps' most spectacular species, the great yellow gentian (*Gentiana lutea*).

The Grindelwald chairlift has intermediate stations before you reach the highest point. One of the best ways to explore the region, assuming you are sufficiently fit and energetic, is to walk down the slopes from one of these stop-off points. The network of paths and tracks are signposted and route maps are available.

The highest ski-station is well above the tree-line and in the highest zone of vegetation before areas of permanent snow are reached. A succession of flowers appears from May onwards, as the snows retreat, and these include the spring gentian (*G. verna*) and the trumpet gentian (*G. acaulis*). One of the region's most enchanting plants also occurs here, the aptly named alpine snowbell (*Soldanella alpina*), and it is one which usually cannot wait for the snow to melt. Nodding flower-spikes of these fringed flowers often force their way through the snow itself.

After you descend a hundred metres or so (a few hundred feet) you come to some truly vivid alpine meadows. Throughout the summer months these flower-rich pastures are home to small herds of cattle, noisily identified by their jangling cow-bells. Everywhere you look there are such plants as alpine pasque-flower (*Pulsatilla alpina*), alpine bartsia (*Bartsia alpina*) and alpine butterwort (*Pinguicula alpina*), as well as numerous cranesbills, bedstraws, cinquefoils and orchids. It is in this region, on slopes and banks, that you are most likely to come across some brightly coloured stands of great yellow gentian.

Further down the mountainside, towards Grindelwald, the meadows become increasingly lush and full of grasses and rich flowers such as red campion (*Silene dioica*) and dandelion (*Taraxacum officinale*).

Here and there, as you are descending the slopes above Grindelwald, you walk through stands of native conifer forest. These are mainly comprised of white fir (*Abies alba*)—in winter their sagging, snow-laden branches make a delightful spectacle. On the forest floor colourful plants such as the yellow wood violet (*Viola lutea*) and the twinflower (*Linnaea borealis*) are there to be seen. If you look carefully you may find the diminutive and easily overlooked lesser twayblade orchid (*Listera cordata*).

Gentiana lutea is among the most striking and distinctive of all these plants, and its appearance is enhanced by the invariably stunning settings in which it grows.

The species produces a robust basal rosette, each leaf of which is broadly lanceolate or ovate in outline and pointed at the tip. The leaves are bluish green in colour with strongly marked veins, and can be up to 30 cm (about 12 in) long. From June until August, stout and upright flower-bearing spikes appear, rising from the basal rosette. These reach a height of up to 2 m (about 6 ft) or more and are hollow and unbranched. Whorls of large, bright yellow flowers are arranged up the stem with pairs of clasping leaves below. These are similar in appearance to the basal leaves but smaller in size. The individual flower corollas are coloured deep yellow, or occasionally reddish, and are about 2 cm (about 1 in) long; they have five to nine lobes which spread out in star-shaped fashion.

Great yellow gentian is a hardy, long-lasting perennial, like all the species that grow in the Alps and central European mountains, Here the combination of a short growing season and a prolonged winter has favoured the adaptation of very hardy plants indeed. The first heavy snows in the Alps can come as early as October, although the lower slopes are not usually covered until Christmas. Sub-zero temperatures and a blanket of snow are then the norm until April, when the thaw begins.

Great yellow gentian can be found in many of the mountainous areas of Europe, but while some of these may rival the Bernese Oberland for scenic splendour, few can match it for the ease with which you can reach the plant's natural habitat. Whether you visit Grindelwald or one of the many other alpine resorts, you will surely have a botanical field trip to remember and cherish.

Gentiana lutea

Gentiana

Gentians are members of the genus *Gentiana* and its more recent sister-genera *Gentianella* and *Gentianopsis*. The group consists of around 400 species of mostly perennial herbs found in most parts of the world, although in the tropics only in higher mountain regions. The areas richest in gentian species are the mountains of western China and the neighbouring Himalayas. The Alps of Europe boast equally attractive species, including *G. lutea* which is widespread throughout the upland and mountain regions of central Europe. The roots of *G. lutea* are important in herbal medicine and its infusions and brews serve as useful tonics; a potent liqueur is also distilled from the fermented root.

Intense deep blues and sky blues are the flower colours most commonly associated with gentians, but whites and creams are also frequent, and *G. lutea* has a brilliant yellow flower.

The family Gentianaceae contains about 80 genera, including woody shrubs, annuals and perennials. Others that may be familiar to gardeners include the prairie gentian (*Eustoma*), popular as a cut flower, and the Persian violet (*Exacum*), which is grown as an indoor plant.

Gentiana lutea

P. mlokosewitschii

From late spring to mid-summer, this European perennial bears big, open, pale to bright yellow flowers atop soft green leaves with hairy undersides that are sometimes tinged purple at the edges. Grows to a height and spread of 75 cm (about 30 in). The species enjoys semi-shade and is resistant to frosts.

P. officinalis

A tuberous species, this perennial reaches 60 cm (about 24 in) in height and spread, bearing single, purple or red, rose-like flowers in spring through mid-summer. Frost-hardy, it is a native of Europe and likes good soil and ample water. Of similar size, the hybrid 'Rubra Plena' bears flowers that are fulsome clusters of many small, mid-magenta petals. A more compact hybrid, 'China Rose', bears darker green foliage and flowers with yellow-orange anthers.

PAPAVER

POPPY

With their characteristic cupped petals, and nodding buds turning skywards upon opening, poppies are popular bedding flowers. They are fully hardy and prefer little or no shade and moist, well-drained soil. Sow seed in spring or autumn/fall; many species self-seed readily.

P. alpinum

This alpine poppy is a miniature Iceland poppy. A short-living perennial, this tuft-forming semi-evergreen grows 20 cm (about 8 in) high with a spread of half that, and has fine, greyish leaves. It bears white or yellow flowers through summer. Use on banks or in rock gardens.

P. nudicaule

ICELAND POPPY

This tuft-forming perennial is in fact almost always grown as an an-nual. It bears large scented flowers, coloured white, yellow, orange and pink and with a crinkled texture, in winter and spring. The plant has pale green leaves, long hairy stems, and grows to a height of 30–60 cm (about 12–24 in) with a 10 cm (about 4 in) spread. Give this native of North America and Asia Minor full sun. Sow in late summer to early autumn. The species is good for rock gardens and cutting.

P. orientale

ORIENTAL POPPY

This frost-hardy perennial bears spectacular single or double flowers in early summer. Originally from Asia, varieties offering different colours abound, but a common feature is the dark basal blotch on each petal. Foliage of hairy, lance-like, bluish green leaves can become straggly. The plant will grow to a height and spread of 45 cm (about 18 in) and may need support.

P. rhoeas

CORN POPPY, FIELD POPPY

The cupped flowers on this fast-growing annual from Asia Minor are small, delicate, scarlet and single, although cultivated varieties (Shirley poppies) offer hues including reds, pinks, whites and bicolours. Double-flowered strains are also available. It will grow 60 cm (about 24 in) high with a 30 cm (about 12 in) spread. Flowering time is early summer, and the leaves are light green and lobed. Give them all full sun.

P. somniferum

OPIUM POPPY

The green leaves on this fast-growing annual have a greyish cast, are lobed and elliptical with serrated edges. It blooms in summer, displaying big flowers in white, pink, red or purple, usually as doubles. The fully hardy species from the Middle East likes sun. Opium poppies are cultivated for the milky sap extracted from their seed capsules, source of the narcotic drug opium and its derivatives. Garden varieties are not very potent, but homemade opium is still illegal, and nervous nursery owners can be reluctant to stock the opium poppy.

PARADISEA

liliastrum

ST BRUNO'S LILY, ST BERNARD'S LILY

Racemes of scented, white, funnel-shaped flowers bloom on long, thin stems in early summer on this perennial from Italy. The leaves have a greyish cast and are strap-like, ar-

Paeonia mlokosewitschii

Papaver somniferum

Paeonia officinalis

Papaver orientale

Papaver nudicaule

Papaver alpinum

Papaver rhoeas

Paradisea liliastrum

Parochetus communis

Pelargonium cucullatum

Pelargonium crispum

ranged in a basal rosette. The roots are fleshy clusters. Fully hardy, plant where it is sunny but cool, or in semi-shade. Its soil must drain well but retain moisture. Propagate by division or from seed in spring or autumn/fall, although with division you might miss one season of flowering.

PAROCHETUS
communis

SHAMROCK PEA

It is the flowers that are pea-like on this evergreen, ground-hugging, wide-spreading perennial. The flowers are bright blue and bloom for most of the year. The leaves resemble clover. An alpine house environment best suits this half-hardy species, although in moderate climates it is a successful ground cover. Plant it in partial shade in moist, coarse soil. Use rooted runners to propagate by division at any time of year. Don't be alarmed if it vanishes without apparent cause; marginal bits will live from which you can make divisions to re-establish it.

PATERSONIA
glabrata

AUSTRALIAN IRIS, SNAKE FLOWER

Violet 3-lobed flowers appear on this upright perennial in spring and summer. Its leaves are strap-like and clump-forming. Plant this frost-hardy species in well-drained soil in full sun. Sow seed in autumn/fall, and once planted, don't disturb it. It will grow to 30 cm (about 12 in) or more with a similar spread. This is a native of the eastern states of Australia.

Patersonia glabrata

PELARGONIUM

GERANIUM

These frost-tender perennials are often grown as annuals for summer bedding in colder climates. In warmer climates with long hours of daylight, they flower almost all the time, although they do not do well in extreme heat and humidity. Plant in pots or beds. The site should be sunny with light, well-drained, neutral soil. If in pots, fertilize regularly and cull dead-heads. Avoid over watering. Use softwood cuttings for propagation in spring through autumn/fall. The species in this genus are mainly from South Africa. Including hybrids and cultivated varieties, the genus is divided into three large groups: zonal, ivy-leaved and regal or show geraniums.

P. crispum

LEMON GERANIUM, FINGER-BOWL GERANIUM

The lemon-scented leaves on this upright plant are small and lobed with crinkled margins. Pink flowers up to 25 mm (about 1 in) across often have darker markings. Grows to 1 m (about 3 ft) with a 30–50 cm (about 12–20 in) spread. *P. c.* 'Variegatum' has variegated leaves.

P. cucullatum

This South African upright perennial grows to 2 m (about 6 ft) high. It has readily branching downy stems covered with broad, light green foliage. The erect leaves are funnel-shaped and have wavy edges. In spring to summer, lustrous reddish purple flowers with deeper coloured veins appear. The flowers are up to 5 cm (about 2 in) in diameter.

Pelargonium × domesticum

P. × domesticum

REGAL GERANIUM, REGAL PELARGONIUM, MARTHA WASHINGTON GERANIUM

Often just called 'pelargonium', the regal types are shrubby perennials with stiff, pleated leaves and clusters of large flowers, wide open and often blotched or parti-coloured. They flower in late spring and come in shades from white through pink to red and purple. They are much grown as pot plants, and are tender—in cool areas a greenhouse is needed. Cut back hard after blooming to keep the bushes compact.

Pelargonium peltatum

Pelargonium × zonale

Peltiphyllum peltatum

Penstemon barbatus

Pelargonium 'Orange Ricard'

P. 'Orange Ricard'

Masses of large, semi-double coral flowers bloom on this variegated-leaved zonal geranium. It grows vigorously to 60 cm (about 24 in), spreading over half that.

P. peltatum
IVY-LEAVED GERANIUM, HANGING GERANIUM

Originating in South Africa, this species has narrow trailing or climbing stems up to 1 m (about 3 ft) long. Its bright green leaves have five sharp lobes and are up to 7 cm (about 3 in) across. The foliage is similar in appearance to ivy. Flowers can range from purplish red-pink to white and appear in spring and summer.

P. tomentosum
PEPPERMINT GERANIUM

A strong refreshing smell of peppermint comes from the large-lobed, heart-shaped, greyish green velvety leaves on this sprawling geranium. It produces insignificant, purple-

Penstemon × gloxinoides

veined white flowers in clusters. Give it at least partial shade. The species climbs to 60 cm (about 24 in), spreads widely or hangs. Limit its spread by pinching out the growing tips. Older plants present poorly and are better replaced.

P. × zonale
ZONAL GERANIUM

This South African species is rarely seen in gardens, however its hybrids, the zonal geraniums, are among the most popular of all the summer flowers. Bushy aromatic perennials, they can be grown either from seed or cuttings. Zonal geraniums are frost tender and can be grown as annuals in cold climate areas.

PELTIPHYLLUM
peltatum
UMBRELLA PLANT

A good plant for around ponds, this perennial, indigenous to North America, has lobed, peltate leaves

Pelargonium tomentosum

(hence the species name, meaning shield-shaped) that grow up to 60 cm (about 24 in) across. In spring it bears pale pink flowers, some forming into panicles, on hairy stems. Foliage growth follows flowering. It grows 1.2 m (about 4 ft) in height and half that in spread. Plant this fully hardy species in moist soil in a sunny or shaded location. Propagate by division in spring. In full growth the umbrella plant is not easily contained.

PENSTEMON

This large genus includes shrubs, sub-shrubs, annuals and perennials, all of which do best in fertile, well-drained soil and full sun. Most of the species are native to North America, but hybrids are grown worldwide for their showy flower spikes in blues, reds, white and bicolours. Tall varieties suit sheltered borders; dwarf strains are bright in bedding schemes. Cut plants back hard after flowering.

Propagate from seed in spring or autumn/fall, by division in spring, or from cuttings of non-flowering shoots in late summer (the only method for cultivars). The genus comprises mainly evergreens and semi-evergreens.

P. barbatus
syn. Chelone barbata
CORAL PENSTEMON, BEARD-LIP PENSTEMON

The scarlet flowers on this frost-hardy perennial are tubular with 2 lips. They bloom on racemes from the middle of summer to early in autumn/fall above narrow, lance-shaped, green leaves. The plant grows to 1 m (about 3 ft) high, with a spread of 30 cm (about 12 in). Plant this semi-evergreen in well-drained soil in a sunny location.

P. × gloxinioides
BEARD TONGUE

These hybrids between P. hartwegii and P. cobaea are the most widely grown penstemons in gardens. They include the two-toned, strong-growing 'Huntington Pink'; the tall, dark 'Midnight' and not-so-tall but also dark 'Prairie Dusk'; and one that flowers profusely called 'Apple Blossom'. All grow about 80 cm (about 32 in) tall and are fine plants for the middle of a border.

P. heterophyllus 'True Blue'
VIOLET PENSTEMON

A good addition to rock gardens, this frost-hardy semi-evergreen shrub reaches 25 cm (about 10 in) in height and somewhat more in spread. In late spring through early summer, blue tube-shaped flowers bloom from short side shoots. Its lanceolate leaves are pale green. Used for ground cover, this North American native has been dubbed 'Blue Bedder' in some regions.

P. pinifolius

This is a sprightly perennial best suited to a well-drained rock garden. A native of the south-west United States, it loves heat and needs little in supplemental water beyond the normal rainfall. Flowers are typically two-lipped and bright orange-red, and are produced for much of the summer. The leaves are needle-like.

PEROVSKIA
atriplicifolia
RUSSIAN SAGE

This tall, tough sub-shrub produces soft, grey-green foliage, beautifully complementing the haze of pale, lavender-blue flowers which appear on panicles in late summer and autumn. Plants are upright to 4.5 m (about 5 ft), with a spread of 1 m (about 3 ft) or more. Given full sun, a well-drained, not too rich soil and only moderate water, these plants will live for a long time. Cut to the ground in late autumn. Divide in autumn or early spring.

PETUNIA
PETUNIA

'Petun' means 'tobacco' in a South American Indian dialect; and petunias are indeed relatives of the tobaccos (Nicotiana), their leaves having a similar narcotic effect on humans, and both genuses belonging to the same family as potatoes (Solanaceae). Always grown as annuals, these perennials like well-drained, fertile soil and a sunny location. They thrive where summers are hot, but need shelter from the wind. Available are hues of white, purple, red, blue, pink and a mix. Fairly fast-growing, the branching plant has dark green elliptical leaves. Flowers of some of the larger grandiflora hybrids are damaged by rain but others, mainly the multiflora hybrids, are more resistant. Sow seed early in spring. Pinching back hard encourages

branching. Give fertilizer every month only until the onset of hot weather. Cucumber mosaic and tomato spotted wilt can attack these species, which need regular deadheading. Petunias are some of the most popular flowers in the world, finding widespread use as bedding plants and in window boxes, hanging baskets and planters.

P. 'Bonanza'

A multiflora type, this has frilly double flowers in trumpet shapes which display in a multitude of colours.

P. 'Cascade'

A wide range of colours is available from this grandiflora series. The plants bear their flowers singly and have trailing stems, most suitable for hanging baskets.

PHACELIA
campanularia
CALIFORNIA BLUEBELL

True to its common name, the flowers on this fast-growing annual are blue and shaped like bells. Appearing in spring and early summer, the flowers are small, only 2.5 cm (about 1 in) across. The bushy, branching plant is delightful in a rock garden or border; it grows about 20 cm (about 8 in) high, with a 15 cm (about 6 in) spread. Its leaves are dark green and serrated. Plant in well-drained, fertile soil and full sun, to approximate the conditions of its native home, California's Mojave Desert. Propagate from seed in spring or early autumn/fall.

Petunia 'Bonanza'

Penstemon heterophyllus 'True Blue'

Petunia 'Cascade'

Perovskia atriplicifolia

Phacelia campanularia

Penstemon pinifolius

PHLOMIS
russeliana

A native of Syria, this easily grown plant thrives in any ordinary soil given a reasonable amount of sun. The large, heart-shaped, fresh green leaves make excellent ground cover, forming clumps around 30 cm (about 12 in) high and up to 60 cm (about 24 in) across. In summer it bears stout stems around 1 m (about 3 ft) high topped with several whorls of hooded, butter-yellow flowers. Propagate by division in spring or by seed in autumn.

PHLOX

These evergreen and semi-evergreen annuals and perennials, mostly native to North America, are grown for their profuse, fragrant flowers. The name phlox means 'flame', an appropriate epithet for these brightly coloured, showy flowers, popular in bedding and border displays. Grow in fertile soil that drains well but remains moist in a sunny or partially shaded location.

P. drummondii
ANNUAL PHLOX

This annual grows fairly rapidly to a bushy 40 cm (about 16 in) height, half that in spread. The species has a number of cultivars, including some dwarf strains which grow to 10 cm (about 4 in). *P. drummondii* bears closely clustered, small flattish flowers with 5 petals in summer and autumn/fall, in reds, pinks, purples and creams, and has lanceolate light green leaves. It is resistant to frosts but not to droughts. Sow seed in spring.

P. paniculata
SUMMER PHLOX, PERENNIAL

This tall perennial can grow to more than 1 m (about 3 ft), although height varies a little among the many named varieties. In summer it bears long-lasting, terminal flowerheads comprising many small, 5-lobed flowers. Colours range through violet, red, salmon and white according to variety. Eelworm is this species' enemy.

Watch out also for spider-mites and mildew. Propagate from root cuttings in winter or by division early in spring. Give it mulch in winter. It is fully hardy.

P. stolonifera
CREEPING PHLOX

A native of the woodlands of southeastern North America, this delightful creeper makes an excellent ground cover in shaded situations. Low mats of deep green evergreen foliage increase by rhizomes. Spring flowers in pink, blue or white are held above the foliage on 30 cm (about 12 in) stems. It will tolerate sun in cool areas; otherwise it needs shade and a woodsy soil.

P. subulata
MOSS PHLOX, CREEPING PHLOX

The flowers that bloom through spring in terminal masses on this prostrate alpine perennial are mauve, pink, white and shaped like stars, the petals being notched and open. The fully hardy, evergreen species is suited to growing in rock gardens where it will get sun. Its fine-leaved foliage will grow carpet-like to 10 cm (about 4 in) high with a spread twice that. Start in spring or summer using cuttings from non-flowering shoots. Trim back after flowering.

PHORMIUM
NEW ZEALAND FLAX

Grown for the dramatic effect of their stiff, vertical leaves, these large, clumping plants are extremely hardy in most conditions. In summer they produce panicles of flowers which are attractive to nectar-feeding birds. *P. tenax* grows to 2 m (about 6 ft) tall, while *P. colensoi* about half that height. They make splendid container plants as well as useful garden plants in almost any climate as they are fairly frost-hardy. They respond well to generous watering and permanently moist conditions. Propagate from seed or by division in spring. The plants produce a fibre which has been used commercially but which is now largely confined to traditional Maori crafts.

P. cookianum 'Tricolor'
NEW ZEALAND FLAX

This handsome, evergreen upright perennial plant with bold spiky leaves is ideal for adding some foliage interest to the garden. It prefers full sun and a reasonably retentive yet well-drained soil. The erect, sword-like leaves, reaching around 1.2 m (about 4 ft) high in a clump 45 cm (about 18 in) across, are prettily striped with red, yellow and green, which sounds garish but is in fact extremely effective. It also bears panicles of tubular, pale yellowish green flowers. Propagate by division in spring. Frost damage can be a problem in colder parts of the country, in which case the plant can be grown in a large container and overwintered in an unheated greenhouse or conservatory.

P. hybrids

These hybrids of *P. tenax* and *P. colensoi* are the most varied in foliage colour, and are often of more compact growth habit than their parents. Foliage colour varies from bronze or purplish chartreuse to pink and salmon; the leaves may be variegated with vertical stripes of two or more colours. New cultivars are introduced from New Zealand each year. Some have the unfortunate habit of reverting to a plain green foliage with age. Among the best are 'Bronze Baby' (reddish-brown, to 1 m/3ft), 'Maori Chief' (green and rose-red stripes, to 1.5 m/5 ft) and 'Tom Thumb' (green with bronze margins, to 60 cm/2 ft).

Phlox subulata

Phlox paniculata

Phlomis russeliana

Phlox drummondii

Phlox stolonifera

Phormium tenax

Polemonium caeruleum

Polygonatum | hybridum

Polygonum affine

Physostegia virginiana

P. tenax 'Purpureum'

The stiff, pointed, strap-like leaves of this cultivar are plum-purple to dark copper, and grow to 2.5 m (about 7½ ft) long. Panicles of reddish flowers on purplish blue stems appear in summer.

PHYSOSTEGIA
virginiana
OBEDIENT PLANT, GALLIPOLI HEATH

If you move a flower on this herbaceous perennial, it will not spring back into position but will obediently stay put, thanks to a stalk with a hinge-like structure. The showy flowers, which bloom in erect terminal spikes late in summer, are tubular, have 2 lips and are available in pale pink, magenta ('Vivid') or white. The leaves are lance-shaped and serrated. Plant this fully hardy species in sun in fertile soil that drains well but remains moist. Propagate by division in spring. This native of North America will grow to 1 m (about 3 ft) and make a striking display planted in clumps in a mixed border.

PLATYCODON
grandiflorus
BALLOON FLOWER, CHINESE BELL FLOWER

This perennial originates from Japan and China. In summer, balloon-like buds open out into 5-petalled flowers like bells, coloured blue, purple, pink or white. The serrated elliptical leaves with a silvery blue cast form in a neat clump up to 60 cm (about 24 in) high and half that in spread. Plant the fully hardy species in full sun in well-drained sandy soil. Use rooted basal cuttings of non-flowering shoots to propagate in summer, sow seed in spring or autumn/fall, or divide clumps in spring.

PLECTOSTACHYS
serphyllifolia
syn. *Helichrysum petiolare* 'Microphyllum'

Formerly classified as a member of the *Helichrysum* genus, this sprawling, frost-tender sub-shrub has felt-like stems and tiny leaves of silvery grey. Though the flowers are insignificant, the foliage and form pro-

vide an excellent addition to container and windowbox gardens in cold regions, or a year-round low mound of silver for mild gardens. They adapt to either full sun or part shade, but need a well-drained soil and only moderate amounts of water. Pinch growing tips to encourage branching. Propagate by cuttings in summer.

PODOPHYLLUM
peltatum
MAY APPLE

A vigorous, spreading perennial for the woodland garden, appearing before the leaves on deciduous forest trees. Deeply lobed peltate leaves around 30 cm (about 12 in) tall practically hide creamy white spring blossoms resembling single roses; edible yellow or rose-pink fruit follow. Deep, woodsy soil is preferred, with ample water in a lightly shaded position. It spreads rampantly to form a bold ground cover, so it is not for the small garden. Propagate by dividing the rhizomes in early spring.

POLEMONIUM
caeruleum
JACOB'S LADDER

Yellowy orange stamens provide a colourful contrast against the blue of this perennial's bell-shaped flowers when they open in summer. The flowers cluster among lance-shaped leaves arranged in many pairs like the rungs of a ladder, hence its common name. The plant grows in a clump to a height and spread of

up to 60 cm (about 24 in) or more. The stem is hollow and upstanding. Grow this species in well-drained soil in sun or semi-shade. Propagate by division in early spring, from seed or by division in autumn/fall. A native of temperate Europe, it suits cooler climates.

POLYGONATUM
| hybridum
syn. *P. multiflorum*
SOLOMON'S SEAL

The elegant Solomon's seal is native to temperate areas of the northern hemisphere. A hardy plant, it does best in cool to cold areas where it will produce tubular, bell-shaped flowers in spring. A drooping stem grows to about 90 cm (about 36 in). White, green-tipped flowers hang down from the stem at the leaf axils. The broadly oval leaves rise off the stem like sets of wings. Rhizomes should be planted in autumn/fall to

winter in a moist, shady spot in well-drained soil. The rhizomes can be divided in winter. It is difficult to grow from seed.

POLYGONUM
affine
KNOTWEED

The green of this evergreen perennial's small, shiny, lance-like leaves becomes bronze in winter. It spreads 30 cm (about 12 in) or more, forming a mat to about the same height. The flowers it bears in dense spikes in late summer and autumn/fall are small, red and funnel-shaped. Sunny or shady locations are fine for this fully hardy plant in soil that drains well or a dry position in a bank or rock garden. Sow seed or propagate by division in spring or autumn/fall. The genus name means 'many knees', referring to the plant's swollen nodes.

Plectostachys serphyllifolia

Platycodon grandiflorus

Podophyllum peltatum

Phormium tenax 'Purpureum'

Pontederia cordata

PONTEDERIA
cordata
PICKEREL RUSH, PICKEREL WEED

This fully hardy marginal water plant from North America grows to 75 cm (about 30 in) with a 45 cm (about 18 in) spread. Its tapered, heart-shaped leaves are dark green and shiny. Blooming in summer, the deciduous perennial produces intense blue flowers in dense, terminal spikes. Plant it in full sun in up to 25 cm (about 10 in) of water. Cull flowers as they fade. Sow seed or propagate by division in spring.

PORTULACA
grandiflora
MOSS ROSE, SUN PLANT

This annual, native to South America, grows slowly, attaining a height of up to 20 cm (about 8 in) and a spread of 15 cm (about 6 in). Its small, lance-shaped, fleshy leaves are bright green and its branching stems are prostrate. Its large open flowers, which may be single or double, bloom in red, pink, yellow or white, in summer through early autumn/fall. Plant this half-hardy plant as ground cover or in a rockery or border, in well-drained soil in a sunny location. The flowers close in dull conditions and overnight. Sow seed in spring. Watch out for aphids.

POTENTILLA
CINQUEFOIL

The flowers of this large genus of deciduous shrubs and perennials are small and rounded, growing in clusters. Although the species all thrive in full sun in temperate climates, cultivars producing pink, red and orange blooms will be better coloured if protected from very strong sun. Plant all in well-drained, enriched soil. The species are indigenous to the northern hemisphere, from temperate to arctic regions. Perennials are generally frost-hardy and propagated by division in spring or from seed or by division in autumn/fall. Some species are used medicinally for such ailments as diarrhoea, cramps, mouth sores, enteritis, fever and jaundice. The root bark of one species is said to stop nose-bleeds, and even internal bleeding.

P. 'Monsieur Rouillard'

The flowers borne on this cultivar through summer are saucer-shaped and double, in deep red hues. Its dark green leaves resemble those of a strawberry plant. This perennial matures into a clump 45 cm (about 18 in) wide and high.

P. nepalensis

A profusion of flowers in shades of pink or apricot with cherry-red centres appears on the slim branching stems of this Himalayan peren-

nial throughout summer. With bright green, strawberry-like leaves, this frost-hardy species reaches a height of 30 cm (about 12 in) or more and twice that in breadth. Plant it in well-drained soil.

PRATIA

This genus includes 20 species of predominantly carpet-forming perennials native to New Zealand, Australia, Africa and South America. The species have multiple branching stems and little lobed leaves. A profusion of starry flowers is followed by globular berries. These plants range from frost- to semi-hardy and generally enjoy damp but porous soil, total sun or partial shade and protection from the elements. Water liberally during the growth period and sparingly in winter. Some species are susceptible to slugs if over moist. They make excellent rockery specimens, but they have a tendency to overrun the garden. Propagate by division or from seed in autumn/fall.

P. angulata

This frost-hardy New Zealand creeper has wide, rounded, deep green leaves with roughly serrated edges. In spring white starry flowers with purple veins appear in the leaf axils, followed in autumn/fall by globular, reddish purple fruits. This species will tolerate full sun and enjoys damp soil.

P. pedunculata

A creeping perennial with small leaves, this species is good for ground cover as it is low-growing and spreads widely into a carpet, taking root at its nodes. A native of the coast and tablelands of eastern Australia, it blooms profusely in spring and early summer. Its 5-petalled flowers are star-shaped and usually mid-blue or paler to the point of white, although sometimes of a more purple hue. It also bears small berries. The species prefers moist soil in a sunny position, with partial shade from hot noonday sun. It is frost-resistant. Propagate from seed or by division in autumn/fall.

PRIMULA
PRIMULA, PRIMROSE

Fragrant, colourful flowers on stems above a rosette of basal leaves is characteristic of this genus, mostly from the temperate regions of the northern hemisphere. The flowers can be flat, trumpet-shaped or bell-shaped. Primulas like fertile, well-drained soil, partial shade and ample water. Propagate from seed in spring, early summer or autumn/fall, or by division or from root cuttings. Remove dead-heads and old foliage after blooming. There is a primula for virtually every posi-

Portulaca grandiflora

Potentilla nepalensis

Pratia pedunculata

Pratia angulata

Potentilla 'Monsieur Rouillard'

tion and purpose. Primula groups include: Candelabra, Polyanthus and Auricula. A floury substance called 'farina'—the term for the flour ground from cereal grains—covers the leaves, stems and sepals of some primulas.

P. denticulata
DRUMSTICK PRIMULA, DRUMSTICK PRIMROSE

The name of this frost-hardy Himalayan perennial refers to the toothed profile of the leaves, which are mid-green and broadly lanceolate. A neat and vigorous grower, it reaches a height and spread of 30 cm (about 12 in). It blooms in early to mid-spring, when open flowers of pink, purple or lilac, with yellow centres, crowd in rounded terminal clusters atop thick hairy stems.

P. florindae
HIMALAYAN PRIMROSE

Growing 60 cm–1 m (about 2–3 ft) high, this fully hardy perennial blooms in spring. The flowers—up to 60 of them to an umbel—are bright yellow and hang like little bells against a backdrop of broad, mid-green leaves with serrated edges.

P. japonica
JAPANESE PRIMROSE

Forming a clump up to 60 cm (about 24 in) high and 50 cm (about 20 in) across, this fully hardy native of Japan blooms from thick stems in spring to early summer. Its shiny flowers are pink or deep red, although the cultivar 'Postford White' offers a white, flattish round flower. This perennial has elliptical, serrated, pale green leaves.

P. malacoides
FAIRY PRIMROSE

Small, open flowers bloom in spiral masses on this frost-tender perennial, sometimes grown as an annual. It is a native of China. The single or double flowers range in colour from white to pink to magenta. Its oval-shaped, light green leaves have a hairy texture, as does its erect stem. The species reaches a height and spread of 30 cm (about 12 in) or more.

Primula vulgaris

Primula florindae

P. obconica
POISON PRIMROSE

Dense flower clusters grow in an umbellate arrangement on hairy, erect stems on this perennial. A native of China, it grows to 30 cm (about 12 in) high and as much or more in spread. Flowering time is winter through spring. The yellow-eyed, flattish flowers, 2.5 cm (about 1 in) across, range in colour from white through pink to purple. The light green leaves are elliptical, serrated and form a basal rosette. This is popular as a container plant.

P. × polyantha
POLYANTHUS

This fully hardy perennial, sometimes grown as an annual, reaches 30 cm (about 12 in) in spread and height. Large, flat, scented flowers in every colour but green bloom on dense umbels in winter through spring. Polyanthus are cultivars derived from *P. vulgaris* crossed with the cowslip (*P. veris*) and have been grown since the seventeenth century.

Primula malacoides

P. viallii

This 60 cm (about 24 in) tall perennial species from Yunnan Province in China is remarkable for carrying its purple flowers in short spikes, quite unlike any other primula. The buds are paler than the open flowers, giving the inflorescence a two-tone effect. Foliage is lush and bright green. A cool, moist climate is needed.

P. vulgaris
ENGLISH PRIMROSE, COMMON PRIMROSE

This is one of the most familiar wildflowers in Europe and it likes its cultivated conditions to mirror its cool woodland native environment. It is low-growing to around 30 cm (about 6 in), usually frost-resistant, and produces a carpet of bright flowers in spring. The flattish flowers are pale yellow with dark eyes (but the garden forms come in every colour), and bloom singly on hairy stems above rosettes of crinkled, lance-shaped, serrated leaves. Both leaves and flowers are edible.

Primula obconica

Primula denticulata

Primula viallii

Primula japonica

Primula x polyantha

PRUNELLA
grandiflora
LARGE SELF-HEAL

Purple, 2-lipped flowers grow in erect spikes above leafy stubs in spring and summer on this hardy, semi-evergreen perennial. A native of Europe, it is good for ground cover or rock gardens, having a spread and height of 50 cm (about 20 in). Plant in moist, well-drained soil in a sunny location. Propagate by division in spring. Trim out old flower stems before they seed. The species is a member of the Lamiaceae family (as is mint), of a genus that includes woundwort, and is said to be beneficial for wounds, throat irritations, thrush, diarrhoea, fits, convulsions, worms and stomatitis.

PULMONARIA
angustifolia
BLUE COWSLIP

Dark blue flowers, sometimes tinged pink, bloom through spring

Pulsatilla vulgaris

Raoulia australis

Reseda odorata

on this frost-resistant European perennial. The flowerheads have a 5-lobed tubular shape and are held above basal rosettes of mid-green foliage. The plant grows to a height and spread of 25–30 cm (about 10–12 in). Plant in moist, well-drained soil in shade. Propagate by division in spring or autumn/fall. It is a relative of lungwort, used by ancient herbalists to treat wounds, diarrhoea, haemorrhoids and respiratory ailments; its effectiveness for the last condition having been inferred from its lung-shaped leaves.

PULSATILLA
vulgaris
syn. *Anemone pulmonaria*
PASQUE FLOWER

Nodding, six-petalled flowers bloom in spring on this fully hardy perennial from Europe. The yellow centres of the flowers are a stark colour contrast to the petals, which can range through white, pink and red to purple. The finely divided leaves are pale green. Reaching 25

cm (about 10 in) in height and spread, the species is good in a sunny rock garden, in well-drained soil rich in humus. Avoid disturbing the roots. Sow seed when fresh or propagate using root cuttings in winter.

RAMONDA
myconi
syn. *R. pyrenaica*
BALKAN PRIMROSE, PYRENEAN PRIMROSE, ROSETTE MULLEIN

From branched, reddish brown stems this perennial produces flattish flowers—5-petalled and resembling African violets—in hues of white, pink, blue, lavender or purple, with yellow, pointed anthers. The flowers bloom late in spring and early in summer. Reaching a height and spread of 8–10 cm (about 3–4 in), this fully hardy evergreen, from the mountains of southern Europe, bears rosettes of rounded leaves that are wrinkled and hairy (more so on the undersides), with wavy and toothed edges. Grow in a rock garden or shallow pot. Add fragments of limestone to a potting mix of sand, loam and leafmould. Keep moist and shade from full sun. Propagate by rooting offsets in early summer or by leaf cuttings or seed in early autumn/fall.

RANUNCULUS
aconitifolius
FAIR MAIDS OF FRANCE

Cultivated to produce pure white, single or double flowers, this perennial native of central and southern

Ramonda myconi

Prunella grandiflora

Pulmonaria angustifolia

Europe flowers in terminal clusters on robust branched stems from spring to summer. Its dark green leaves have 3 or 5 lobes with saw-edges. The plant grows to 60 cm (about 24 in) high over a slightly lesser spread; it is fully to half-hardy. The species is native to southern and central Europe. The genus name derives from the Latin for 'frog' as some are aquatic plants, although these are not widely cultivated. The genus includes two species of buttercups that are popular folk cures for arthritis, sciatica, rheumatism and skin conditions including the removal of warts. Sow seed when fresh or propagate by division in spring or autumn/fall.

RAOULIA
australis
GOLDEN SCABWEED

Suitable for rock gardens, this native of New Zealand lays down a solid carpet of silvery leaves 1 cm (about $\frac{1}{2}$ in) deep over a spread of 25 cm (about 10 in). In summer it produces miniscule flowerheads of fluffy yellow blooms. The stems are prostrate, spreading and mat forming. Plant this perennial in moist, well-drained, acidic soil that has been well composted. Give it an open, sunny location. It is frost-resistant but drought-tender. Sow seed when fresh in late summer or propagate by division in spring.

RESEDA
odorata
MIGNONETTE, LITTLE DARLING

A moderately fast-growing annual, renowned for the strong fragrance of its flowers. The conical heads of small greenish flowers with dark orange stamens are otherwise unspectacular, although they do attract bees and are suitable for cutting. Flowering is in summer through early autumn/fall. Remove dead-heads to prolong flowering. Plant it in well-drained, fertile soil in sun or partial shade. Sow seed in spring or autumn/fall. It will grow to 60 cm (about 24 in) high and about half that in spread.

Ranunculus aconitifolius

Rheum palmatum 'Atrosanguineum'

Rodgersia aesculifolia

RHEUM
palmatum 'Atrosanguineum'

A cousin of the rhubarb we eat, this fully hardy perennial bears panicles of small, bright red flowers that open early in summer. It has deep green leaves with decoratively cut edges, and reaches up to 1 m (about 3 ft) in height and 60 cm (about 24 in) in spread. Grow in deep, rich soil that drains well but retains moisture. Give it a sunny or partially shaded location. Propagate from seed or by division in spring or autumn/fall. *R. palmatum* itself has white flowers.

RHODOCHITON
atrosanguineum
syn. *R. volubile*
PURPLE BELLS

A native of Mexico, this evergreen leaf-stalk climber is mostly grown as an annual. The flowers it bears in late spring through late autumn/fall comprise a long, finger-like, dark purple corolla protruding from a bell-shaped calyx in a redder hue of purple. Its leaves are ovate to heart-shaped with sparsely spiky edges. The plant is good for ground cover or for planting on trellises or fences, where it will grow to 3 m (about 9 ft). It thrives in sun and well-drained soil. Propagate from seed early in spring.

RICINUS
communis
CASTOR OIL PLANT

The purgative of universal renown comes from the seeds of this species, native to Asia. The evergreen

Ricinus communis

shrub, which is alone in its genus, is mostly grown as an annual. Rounded, prickly seed pods appear following the summer display of woolly clusters of red and greenish flowers. The plant's leaves are large, glossy and divided deeply into elliptical lobes. It grows rapidly, reaching 2 m (about 6 ft) in height and spread. This drought- and frost-resistant species takes to most soils and likes a sunny, open location. They may require support in exposed areas. Propagate by sowing seed. Some warn that the whole plant (but especially the seeds) contains an irritant that can poison the blood.

RODGERSIA

Native to China and Japan, these handsome, moisture-loving perennials are attractive both in foliage and flowers. However, they tend to be grown more for their bold, architectural leaves than for their plumes of fluffy flowers which are borne in mid- to late summer. The stems unfurl in mid-spring and spread out to form a fan of leaves on top of

stout stems. Their liking for moist soil makes them excellent plants for marshy ground at the edge of a pond or in a bog garden in sun or part shade. They are best grown in a site sheltered from strong winds, which can damage the foliage, and preferably in semi-shade although they will tolerate full shade. Propagate by division in spring or by seed in autumn.

R. aesculifolia

Large, lobed, bronze-tinted leaves are borne on hairy stalks, forming a clump around 60 cm (about 24 in) high and wide. The large, cone-shaped clusters of small, starry flowers are cream or pale pink, and are borne in mid- to late summer on stout stalks up to 1.2 m (about 4 ft) high.

R. pinnata

The bold, dark green leaves are arranged in pairs, above which are borne clusters of creamy pink flowers. It grows to a height of 1 m (about 3 ft) with a spread of 75 cm (about 30 in).

Rodgersia pinnata

Rhodochiton atrosanguineum

Roscoea cauteloides

Rudbeckia fulgida 'Goldsturm'

Rudbeckia hirta

Salpiglossis sinuata

Rodgersia podophylla

Romneya coulteri

R. podophylla

Suited to pond surrounds, this rhizomatous perennial has unusual leaves comprising 5 to 9 large leaflets, with a touch of copper to their green colour. Multi-branched panicles of star-shaped flowers bloom in mid-summer in a froth of cream. Plant in moist soil and protect from strong wind. Tolerates full shade, but is better in partial shade. Propagate by division in early spring or from seed in autumn/fall. This frost-hardy species grows to a height of

1–1.2 m (3–4 ft) and a spread of 75 cm (about 30 in).

ROMNEYA
coulteri
CALIFORNIA TREE POPPY, MATILIJA POPPY

This summer-flowering, shrubby Californian perennial produces large sweetly scented, poppy-like flowers with white colour highlighted by the gold of fluffy stamens. The silvery green leaves are deeply divided, their edges sparsely fringed with hairs. Sensitive to disturbance but a vigorous grower once established, this fully hardy species forms a bush up to 2.4 m (about 8 ft) high, with a spread of 1 m (about 3 ft). Grow it in well-drained soil in full sun. In colder climates, protect the roots. Sow seed in early spring.

ROSCOEA
cauteloides

Bearing a yellow flower similar to an orchid in summer, this frost-hardy tuberous perennial grows to 25 cm

(about 10 in) with a 15 cm (about 6 in) spread. Glossy leaves are lance-shaped, erect and wrap into a hollow stem-like structure at their base. Grow this species in cool soil that is rich in humus. Keep the soil moist in summer. Choose a sunny or semi-shaded location. When it dies back, top-dress with mature compost or leafmould. Propagate by division in spring or from seed in winter or autumn/fall.

RUDBECKIA
CONEFLOWER

These North American annuals, biennials and perennials are popular for their bright, daisy-like flowers with a prominent dark-coloured central cone (hence their common name). Plants range from 60 cm–2 m (about 2–6 ft) tall, depending on species, and spread up to 1 m (about 3 ft) wide. The summer and autumn/fall blooms provide good cut flowers. Grow in moist soil in a sunny position. Start from cuttings in spring. Propagate from seed or by division in spring or autumn/fall.

R. fulgida 'Goldsturm'

This upstanding perennial bears flowerheads like daisies, yellow with central black cones. Growing 60 cm (about 24 in) high with a spread of 30 cm (about 12 in) or more, the plant has narrow lanceolate green leaves. Both sunny and shaded locations are suitable. It is very fashionable for massed plantings in meadow-style gardens.

R. hirta

The flowerheads on this branching annual are big, daisy-like and bright yellow, with central cones of green or purple. Its leaves are mid-green and lance shaped. It reaches 30 cm–1 m (about 1–3 ft) tall, with a spread of 30 cm (about 12 in). Grow in a sunny position in well-drained soil.

SALPIGLOSSIS
sinuata
PAINTED TONGUE

Offering a variety of flower colours including red, orange, yellow, blue and purple, this species from Chile blooms in summer and early autumn/fall. The 5 cm (about 2 in) wide, heavily veined flowers are like small flaring trumpets. The lanceolate leaves are light green. A fast grower, this branching annual reaches a height of 40–50 cm (about 16–20 in) and a spread of at least 40 cm (about 16 in). It is both frost- and drought-tender. Grow it in well-drained, rich soil in a sunny location, supporting its stems. Watch out for aphids. Propagate from seed early in either spring or autumn/fall.

Salvia elegans

Salvia azurea

SALVIA

SAGE

This large and widely distributed genus of annual and perennial herbs and shrubs includes species whose leaves are used as edible herbs as well as for a host of folk remedies. The genus is named from the Latin *salveo*, to save or heal. The leaves of most species are aromatic, and many produce decorative garden displays with spikes of small thimble-shaped flowers with two lips. Establish these species in fertile well-drained soil in a sunny location. Propagate annuals from seed and perennials by division in spring or from softwood cuttings in spring and summer.

S. azurea

BLUE SAGE

Dense spikes of white or deep blue flowers bloom in terminal spikes in summer and autumn/fall on this perennial. The narrow green leaves have a grey cast. This native of North America grows to 2 m (about 6 ft). It is drought-tender but resistant to frost.

S. elegans

syn. *S. rutilans*

PINEAPPLE-SCENTED SAGE

A smell of pineapples comes from this perennial's oval leaves, which are toothed and hairy. Growing to a height and spread of 1 m (about 3 ft), the half-hardy species blooms in summer and autumn/fall, producing scarlet flowers in spiral clusters.

S. farinacea 'Blue Bedder'

MEALY-CUP SAGE

This species is grown as an annual in regions that have cold winters and sometimes also in warmer climates. Growing to 45 cm (about 18 in), the perennial bears its violet-blue flowers in slender racemes on whitish stems. This cultivar was developed in North America.

S. nemorosa

syn. *S. virgata* var. *nemorosa*

Many slender, erect spikes of pinkish purple flowers bloom in summer on branching racemes on this perennial. Growing 1 m (about 3 ft)

high, with a 45 cm (about 18 in) spread, this fully hardy species has rough leaves of narrow elliptical shape.

S. splendens

SCARLET SAGE

This native of Brazil, which is grown as an annual, produces dense terminal spikes of scarlet flowers in summer through early autumn/fall. The leaves are toothed ellipses. It grows to 30 cm (about 12 in) with a similar spread. In hotter climates, give it a little shade. This species is half-hardy.

S. uliginosa

Long racemes of blue flowers appear on this branching species in summer and autumn/fall, amid serrated, elliptical to lance-shaped leaves. Growing to 2 m (about 6 ft) with a spread of 45 cm (about 18 in), it has slender, curving stems. Its soil should be moist. This species originates in South America.

SANGUISORBA
canadensis

CANADIAN BURNET

A native of eastern North America, this vigorous perennial loves full sun and a moist soil. The handsome, pinnate leaves are fresh green and form a clump around 60 cm (about 24 in) wide, above which are borne masses of white, bottlebrush flowers in late summer. The tall flowers stems, up to 2 m (about 6 ft) high, sometimes benefit from staking. Propagate by division in spring or by seed in autumn.

Salvia splendens

Salvia farinacea 'Blue Bedder'

Salvia nemorosa

Salvia uliginosa

Sanguisorba canadensis

SANVITALIA
procumbens
CREEPING ZINNIA

A native of Central America, this summer-flowering, fully hardy annual produces masses of bright yellow flowerheads like 2.5 cm (about 1 in) daisies with black centres. It is a prostrate species with mid-green, ovate leaves, growing to 15 cm (about 6 in) high and spreading easily twice that. Grow it as ground cover or in a hanging basket, in fertile well-drained soil in a sunny position. Sow seed in situ in spring or early autumn/fall.

SAPONARIA
ocymoides
SOAPWORT

Ideal for banks, rock gardens or trailing over walls, this tough alpine perennial, a native of Europe, forms a thick carpet from which profuse terminal clusters of small, flattish flowers, coloured pink to deep red, bloom in late spring and early summer. Grow this fully hardy species in sun in sandy, well-drained soil. Propagate from softwood cuttings in early summer or seed in spring or autumn/fall. The common and generic names refer to the juice of the plant's crushed leaves which, lathered in water, can be used as a soap substitute.

SARRACENIA
flava
YELLOW PITCHER PLANT

This insectivorous plant, native to North America, has cylindrical, yellowish green pitchers (modified leaves) marked in red and with a hooded top. The pitchers secrete nectar which, together with the bright colours of the plant, attract insects which become trapped and are absorbed into the plant. Strongly scented, yellow or greenish yellow flowers are borne on long stems in late spring to summer. During the growth period it requires wet conditions, and in winter, when dormant, cool moist conditions are preferred. Grow in full sun or part-shade. Frost-tender, it requires a minimum temperature of 5°C (about 40°F).

SAXIFRAGA

Both the foliage and blooms on these perennials are equally appealing. The genus comprises some 370 species of evergreens and semi-evergreens. Their natural territory includes temperate, alpine and subarctic regions but many garden hybrids have been cultivated, and they serve well in rock gardens, in edges and as ground cover. The flowers are mostly white, sometimes spotted with pink, but other colours are also available. Use rooted offsets for propagation in winter or seed in autumn/fall. The genus name combines two Latin terms, 'rock' or 'stone' and 'to break', suggestive of either the hardiness of their rooting system or their reputed medicinal effect on bladder stones.

S. caespitosa
MOSSY SAXIFRAGE

This frost-hardy perennial grows low over a spread of 15 cm (about 6 in). White flecks adorn its small leaves, which cluster into leafy masses. Flowers with open, flared back petals, in white or, more commonly, a shade of pink, bloom in early spring. Grow it in moist soil in a sunny, open position.

S. paniculata
syn. *S. aizoon*
LIVELONG SAXIFRAGE

This summer-flowering evergreen perennial from central Europe bears terminal clusters of 5-petalled white flowers, often with spots of reddish purple on erect stalks. Other colours include pale pinks and yellows. The bluish green leaves, which are stiff and strap-like with saw edges, form a rosette below the flower stems. The species grows to a height and spread of 20–25 cm (about 8–10 in).

S. stolonifera
syn. *S. sarmentosa*
MOTHER OF THOUSANDS

Geranium-like leaves are a feature of this perennial, which is a native of eastern Asia. The rounded glossy leaves are olive green with silver veins, purplish pink on the under-

Sanvitalia procumbens

Saxifraga paniculata

Saponaria ocymoides

Sarracenia flava

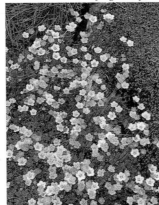

Saxifraga caespitosa

Scaevola aemula

Scabiosa atropurpurea

Scaevola 'Mauve Clusters'

Saxifraga stolonifera

Schizanthus pinnatus

Scabiosa caucasica

sides. In spring through early summer, oddly petalled white flowers are borne in delicate panicles on thin, erect stalks. One petal on the tiny flowers seems to outgrow its 4 companion petals. This frost-tender species makes a good ground cover or container plant. It grows to a height of 15–20 cm (about 6–8 in) and spreads 30 cm (about 12 in) by runners.

SCABIOSA
SCABIOUS

This genus of annuals and perennials, found widely in temperate climates, produces tall-stemmed, honey-scented flowers ideal for cutting. Blooms of multiple flowerets with protruding filaments, giving a pincushion-like effect, are a feature. Flower colours range from pinkish white to deep purple. Most species will thrive in full sun in well-drained, alkaline soil. Propagate annuals from seed in spring; perennials from cuttings in summer, seed in autumn/fall, or by division in early spring.

S. atropurpurea

This bushy annual produces flowers from summer through to early autumn/fall, provided blooms are cut or dead-headed. The dome-shaped flowerheads are some 5 cm (about 2 in) wide and fragrant, mainly crimson but also in white,

pink, purple and blue. Sizes vary from 50 cm (about 20 in) for dwarf forms, up to 1 m (about 3 ft) high for taller plants. This fully hardy species has lobed, lance-like foliage.

S. caucasica
PINCUSHION FLOWER

Flat, many petalled flowerheads in pink, red, purple or blue hues, with pincushion-like centres, often in a contrasting colour, make these summer-flowering annuals popular for borders and cut flowers. A busy plant with lobed mid-green leaves, it reaches a height and spread of 50–60 cm (about 20–24 in). The native species is from the Caucasus, and there are many fully hardy cultivars.

SCAEVOLA
FAN FLOWER

The distinctive flowers of this genus of about a hundred evergreen perennials and small shrubs found in tropical and subtropical regions, particularly of Australia and the islands of the Pacific, all have 5 petals shaped like fans. They come in many colours, from white to mauves and blue. The plants are excellent as ground cover or in rockeries or hanging baskets. They like sun or partial shade and well-drained soil. Propagate from cuttings in spring and summer.

S. aemula
FAIRY FAN FLOWER

The thick, coarsely toothed, dark green leaves on this perennial herb grow along spreading stems to form ground-hugging cover not more than 50 cm (about 20 in) high. Its spread is typically 1 m (about 3 ft). Spikes of large mauve-blue flowers with yellow throats bloom in spring and summer. This species, native to the sandy coastal regions of Australia, resists drought, frost and salt spray.

S. 'Mauve Clusters'

This spreading perennial flowers profusely in spring and summer. The small flowers present as mauve masses against a backdrop of bright green leaves. Growing very close to the ground, the frost-hardy cultivar spreads as much as 2 m (about 6 ft).

SCHIZANTHUS
pinnatus
syn. S. wisetonensis
BUTTERFLY FLOWER, POOR MAN'S ORCHID

These attractive plants, native to Chile, are grown for their exotic blooms and pale green, fern-like foliage. The orchid-like flowers come in a range of colours from white, pinks and mauves to scarlet and purple, all with speckled yellow throats. They need fertile well-drained soil, partial shade, and protection against both frost and heat. They

grow into a bush up to 1 m (about 3 ft) high, with a 30 cm (about 12 in) spread, although there are more compact cultivars. They are usually grown in containers or greenhouses for winter and spring flowers, but make fine spring- and summer-flowering bedding plants in mild climates. Propagate from seed in late summer and autumn/fall. Encourage young plants into bushy growth by nipping off growing tips. A light feeding of bone meal encourages flowering. Watch for aphids.

A Field Trip to Dochu La

The flight to Bhutan from the cities of Calcutta and Delhi passes over a region of stark contrast. As your light aircraft crosses the flat expanse of the Bangladesh plains, which can be either dry and dusty or completely flooded, you will see far to the north the snow-covered peaks of the world's tallest mountains, hanging suspended above an ever-present haze. As your descent begins, you pass closely over a myriad of ridges and slopes still completely clothed in pristine forest. Soon you slip into the Paro valley and land at the airstrip which services Bhutan's capital, Thimphu, which has a population of 20 000. Walk down the steps and treat yourself to the rarified Himalayan air, with spectacular scenery whichever way you look.

This was certainly not the way that plant collectors in the nineteenth and early twentieth century arrived in the kingdom, but Bhutan's diversity of plant species was a big enough incentive for them to endure the hardship of a long overland journey through India to reach these botanical crown jewels. Many of our most attractive garden plants originated in the

forests of Bhutan, ranging from large-flowering *Magnolia* and *Rhododendron* species, shrubby *Pieris* and *Daphne* species, to *Impatiens* and *Primula*. Nowhere else in the world can you see as many species from the *Primula* genus. The best time to see *Primula denticulata* in Bhutan is April. Spring weather is often clear and cold at night but pleasantly warm during the day.

Bhutan is a small Bhuddist country to the east of the famous Indian districts of Darjeeling and Sikkim, with Tibet to the north. The interior is protected physically by ranges of forested hills and a scarcity of roads, while its culture is maintained intact by a monarchist government committed to conservation of the environment. Fortunately for both the visitor and the Bhutanese, its policy of sustainable tourism, designed to protect the country's fragile natural and cultural riches, allows only limited access.

Thimphu, the base for your field trip, lies 30 km (about 19 miles) to the east of the airstrip. The road from here climbs east out of the Thimphu valley and, after about 20–25 km (about 12–15 miles), reaches a pass called the Dochu La. Most visitors travel to the pass by taxi, coach or jeep, the hardy returning part of the way on foot. A trekking path winds downhill for about 15 km (about 9 miles), passing through open forest with clearings. The walk back to the road junction at Simtokha takes about four hours.

The view from Dochu La at 2800 m (about 9100 ft) allows a glimpse of distant snowy peaks, but the forests in the foreground are even more spectacular. The birches, oaks and firs always make an impressive combination, but in spring the gaze is really drawn to the multiple splashes of bright colour. These include the intense red of the tree rhododendron (*Rhododendron arboreum*), the stark and beautiful candles of the

A carpet of drumstick primulas at Dochu La.

Campbell magnolia (*Magnolia campbellii*) on branches otherwise bare of leaves; and the bright pink *Rhododendron kisangi*, this last species only recognized as a separate species in the 1980s and named after the queen of Bhutan.

In clearings on the ground and along the sides of the path, the round pink heads of the drumstick primula or primrose (*Primula denticulata*) can be seen. Common throughout the mid-altitudinal range and the most easily seen member of its genus in the Himalayas, *P. denticulata* is particularly impressive, with tall, flowering stalks and large, round umbels of flowers—a growth form which gives the plant its colloquial name. The leaves form a compact rosette. At flowering time they are a fresh, pale green, often closely packed in the rosette and tending to curl downwards along the edges. After flowering the leaves become much larger, up to 30 cm (about 12 in) long. The flowers are usually pink or purple, the intensity of colour varying considerably, although occasionally they can be white. Around Dochu La, drumstick primulas are mainly tall with purplish pink flowers. In other areas, where Bhutan's wild deer and yak or domestic flocks of sheep have been grazing, the stem may be very short and the flowers appear to sit down on the leaves.

In this area the drumstick primula can be found in shrubberies and on open slopes, but not in the shade of the forest interior. Like other primulas it grows close to water, often along the damp edges of paths. In the 1930s, the plant collector, Frank Kingdon Ward, said during one of his Himalayan expeditions: 'Primulas have a strong social sense. They hate to be alone. On the other hand they loathe all but their own kind. Each primula species stands up for its own rights, but once security is attained, then it is primulas against the world; at least the alpine world.'

The drumstick primula's natural range covers a wide diversity of habitat and climate. The species can withstand heavy frosts and in its highest Himalayan locations, up to 4500 m (about 14 750 ft), it will often spend some months under snow. In summer, its presence in open, rather than shaded, situations shows its ability to withstand long days of intense sunshine and heat.

In the Dochu La pass groups of tall pink drumstick primulas compete for your attention with the wildlife. Parties of small, brightly coloured birds move through the trees and understorey of bamboo and daphne—warbler-sized babblers and flycatchers, and the iridescent red and green sunbirds which perch among the rhododendrons to sip nectar. Overhead the occasional mountain hawk-eagle soars, and yellow-billed magpies flap across to their fir tree perches. It may be possible to glimpse muntjac deer or yellow-throated marten; these forests also hold small numbers of the elusive lesser, or red, panda.

Yet despite these distractions, a swathe of *P. denticulata* is spectacular enough to halt your progress. In this area particularly, the species grow in large concentrations, making the area flush with pink, with the whole scene framed by tall Himalayan firs and a glorious blue sky. It is a scene not easily forgotten, a reminder of the magnetic attraction which originally drew explorers to these mountains—and to their botanical treasures—a hundred years ago.

Primula denticulata

Primula

Primulas, or primroses, are botanically members of the genus *Primula* , which consists of as many as 500 species. They are concentrated in temperate Asia, more particularly in China and the Himalayas; smaller numbers of species occur in other areas of the world. *Primula denticulata* occurs right throughout the Himalayas, from Afghanistan to south-eastern Tibet and to Burma in the east. Its seed only reached England in the mid-nineteenth century. Some of the most popular English wildflowers are *Primula* species, namely the primrose, cowslip and oxlip (*P. vulgaris*, *P. veris* and *P. elatior* respectively).

Hardly any other genus offers such a treasury of perennials to the cool-climate gardener. With spikes of flowers in almost every colour known in nature and often with two or more colour zones in a flower, they attract the attention of enthusiasts and collectors. Their scale is generally small though there are a few that send up spikes 1 m (about 3 ft) in height. In warmer temperate climates a few species succeed, for instance fairy primula (*P. malacoides*), which is usually treated as an annual, poison primula (*P. obconica*) and the more brilliantly coloured polyanthuses, (*P.* × *polyantha*), which are treated as spring annuals in warmer areas.

The Primulaceae family contains 20 or so genera, most of them confined to the northern hemisphere. Another well-known genus (*Cyclamen*) contains the tuberous cyclamens.

Primula denticulata

Sempervivum arachnoideum

Sedum spurium

Sempervivum tectorum

Schizostylis coccinea 'Grandiflora'

Sedum rosea

Sedum spectabile

SCHIZOSTYLIS
coccinea 'Grandiflora'
KAFFIR LILY, RIVER LILY

Spikes of cupped, gladiolus-like flowers provide bright splashes of crimson against long grassy foliage on this rhizomatous perennial, which blooms in autumn/fall. A South African native, it grows to a height of 40 cm (about 16 in) or more and a spread of about half that. Like most of its genus, it is a good source of cut flowers. Grow this frost-hardy species in moist, fertile soil. Give it some shade only where exposed to hot weather. Water amply during summer. Propagate by division every three years in spring. There are white and pink cultivars, the best known being the pale pink 'Mrs Hegarty'.

SEDUM
STONECROP

There are about 600 species and eight groups in this genus, comprising annuals, biennials, perennials, shrubs and sub-shrubs, mostly succulents. They serve well along borders and in rock gardens. Common features are the small overlapping leaf and cyme-type flowering. Their natural territory is wide: from the Far East and Europe to tropical mountain regions. Any soil is suitable, but they need sun. Propagate perennials from seed in spring or autumn/fall, or by division or from softwood cuttings in spring through mid-summer. Propagate annuals and biennials from seed sown under glass in early spring or outdoors in mid-spring.

S. rosea
syn. *Rhodiola rosea*
ROSEROOT

The tightly massed heads of pink buds produced by this perennial in late spring or early summer open to small star-shaped flowers, in pale purple, green or yellow. The saw-edged, elliptical leaves are fleshy. This fully hardy species grows into a clump 30 cm (about 12 in) in height and spread. The name comes from the scent of the fleshy roots, used in making perfume.

S. spectabile
SHOWY SEDUM

Spoon-shaped, fleshy, grey-green leaves grow in clusters on the branching erect stems of this perennial. Butterflies flock to the flattish heads of little pink star-like flowers which bloom late in summer. This Asian native grows to a height and spread of 45 cm (about 18 in). It is drought- and frost-resistant.

S. spurium

This summer-flowering, semi-evergreen perennial bears small blooms in big, rounded flower-heads; colours range from white to purple. Hairy stems carrying saw-edged elliptical leaves spread widely into a carpet 10 cm (about 4 in) deep, suitable for covering banks and slopes. It is frost-hardy.

SEMPERVIVUM
HOUSELEEK

These fully hardy, evergreen perennials with distinctive small rosettes of fleshy, elliptical or strap-shaped leaves spread into a dense carpet, making good cover for walls, banks and rock gardens. Found in Europe, northern Africa and western Asia, their star-shaped flowers comprise 8 to 16 petals. Gravelly soil and sun are preferred. Flowering does not begin for several years. Propagate in summer from offsets left after the rosettes die following flowering.

S. arachnoideum
COBWEB HOUSELEEK

The web of white hairs covering the green, triangular-leaved rosettes of this species undoubtedly inspired its name. This evergreen produces pink to crimson flowers in loose terminal clusters through summer. A native of the European Alps, it grows to a height of 30 cm (about 12 in) and about half that in spread.

S. tectorum
COMMON HOUSELEEK, ROOF HOUSELEEK, HENS AND CHICKENS

The rosettes of this species are reddish tipped, sometimes red throughout. The flowers are a purple to rosy red and appear in one-sided terminal clusters on 30 cm (about 12 in) high stems in summer. The plant has a spread of about 20 cm (about 8 in) and a height of 10–15 cm (about 4–6 in). Applying bruised leaves to the skin has a cooling effect and is said to relieve burns, insect bites, skin problems and fever. The juice is used by some on warts and freckles. Shingles, haemorrhoids, and worms are also said to benefit from houseleek. In the Middle Ages, the plant was grown on house roofs to ward off evil spirits and lightning.

SENECIO

This genus of annuals, perennials, shrubs, sub-shrubs and climbers are grown for their foliage and daisy-like flowerheads. The shrubby species do very well in coastal gardens. Grow them in full sun and well-drained soil.

S. cruentus
CINERARIA

This plant is native to the Canary Islands; it grows 30–60 cm (about 12–24 in) tall and as wide, with deeply cut leaves; its lower stems often become woody with age. The terminal clusters of daisy-like flowers can be white, pink, red, blue or violet. They can be pruned off to encourage branching and a good dense form. They are very tolerant of heat and drought, salt air and poor soil.

S. elegans
WILD CINERARIA

This semi-hardy, moderately fast-growing hairy annual has an erect habit growing to 60 cm (about 24 in) tall. Its branching stems are covered with variable dark green leaves that range from entire to pinnate, up to 8 cm (about 3 in) long. In spring to summer, daisy-like purplish pink flowers appear in dome-shaped terminal clusters.

SIDALCEA
'Rose Queen'

The flower spikes borne in summer by this fully hardy perennial resemble hollyhocks. The large, cupped flowers are dark pink. The divided leaves form a basal clump with a spread of 60 cm (about 24 in). Overall height of this species is 1.2 m (about 4 ft) and tall plants may need staking. Establish in well-drained soil in sun. Propagate from seed or by division in spring or by division in autumn/fall.

SILENE
CAMPION, CATCHFLY

These annuals and perennials feature 5-petalled summer flowers, baggy calyces and a multitude of small, elliptical, often-silky leaves. Some of the species do well potted; others make good ground cover, with numerous stems forming a mound. Widely distributed throughout temperate and cold climates of the northern hemisphere, these fully to half-hardy evergreens like fertile, well-drained soil and full or partial sun. To propagate, use seed in spring or early autumn/fall or softwood cuttings in spring.

S. coeli-rosa
syn. *Agrostemma coeli-rosa, Lychnis coeli-rosa, Viscaria elegans*

This upstanding annual bears pinkish purple flowers with white centres in summer. Its green leaves have a greyish cast. It grows rapidly to 50 cm (about 20 in), with a spread of 15 cm (about 6 in).

S. vulgaris subsp. *maritima*
SEA CAMPION

This deep-rooted perennial bears a multitude of white flowers like pompons on branched stems in spring or summer. Its calyces are greenish and balloon-like; its lanceolate leaves have a greyish cast. Reaching about 20 cm (about 8 in) in height and spread, it can be grown on top of walls, in beds or containers. Cut the stems occasionally to bring on new growth. The species grows wild on cliffs along the European seaboard. It is adaptable to most soils and positions and is frost-resistant but drought-tender.

SISYRINCHIUM

These natives of South and North America can self-destruct in seasons of prolific blooming. This is because the flower stem kills off the leaf stem from which it sprouted. The genus includes fully to half-hardy species of annuals and perennials. Establish them in moist soil that drains well. Although tolerant of semi-shade, they prefer sun. They readily self-seed, or can be propagated by division in late summer to autumn/fall or by seed in spring or autumn/fall. It is easy to mistake the narrow leaves of the seedlings for grass.

S. graminoides
syn. *S. angustifolium, S. bermudiana*
BLUE-EYED GRASS

This semi-evergreen perennial blooms in spring, producing terminal clusters of small pale to dark purple flowers like irises, with yellow throats; some yellow with darker veins. The stalks are flattened and winged. The plant grows to 60 cm (about 24 in).

Sisyrinchium graminoides

Silene coeli-rosa

Silene vulgaris subsp. *maritima*

Senecio elegans

Sidalcea 'Rose Queen'

Senecio cruentus

Sisyrinchium striatum

Soleirolia soleirolii

Solanum pseudocapsicum

S. *striatum*

SATIN FLOWER

Long, narrow and sword-shaped, the leaves on this frost-resistant, semi-evergreen perennial are grey-green. In summer it bears slender spikes of little cream flowers, striped purple. The species, which originates in Chile, grows 45–60 cm (about 18–24 in) high, with a 30 cm (about 12 in) spread. There is also an attractive variegated form.

SMILACINA

racemosa

FALSE SPIKENARD, FALSE SOLOMON'S SEAL

Red fleshy fruits appear on this perennial after it blooms in spring through mid-summer, producing lemon-scented white flowers in feathery sprays above fresh green, elliptical leaves. Growing to 90 cm (about 36 in) high and a spread of about half that, this fully hardy plant likes semi-shade and moist soil of acidic pH. It is a native of North America.

SOLANUM

pseudocapsicum

JERUSALEM CHERRY, WINTER CHERRY, CHRIST-MAS CHERRY

The small scarlet berries that appear on this species after flowering are poisonous to eat but in some northern hemisphere countries are used as Christmas decorations. The starry white flowers, precursors to the berries, bloom in summer. A native of the Mediterranean, this frost-tender evergreen grows sedately into a bushy, velvety leaved shrub

about 1.2 m (about 4 ft) high and wide. It is perhaps best grown as an annual, even in wild areas, in which case it should grow to 65 cm (about 26 in) tall. Several varieties with differently coloured fruit are available. The species is related to the potato, eggplant and tomato, as well as some less edible plants.

SOLEIROLIA

soleirolii

syn. *Helxine soleirolii*

BABY'S TEARS, MIND-YOUR-OWN-BUSINESS, PEACE-IN-THE-HOME

Indigenous to the Mediterranean, this creeping herbaceous perennial has small, round, bright green leaves and tiny white flowers, which occur singly in the leaf axils. Grow in moist soil and semi-shade. It will survive frost even if its leaves are killed. It spreads widely and can be invasive unless contained; hanging baskets are ideal.

SOLIDAGO

GOLDENROD

Hay fever sufferers have had cause to dread the plants in this genus, although breeders have tried to reduce their pollen output. If left unchecked, these rhizomatous perennials become invasive and weedy. The more compact garden cultivars have good foliage.

S. 'Golden Wings'

This perennial grows to 1.5 m (about 5 ft) high with a spread of 1 m (about 3 ft). It has downy, lance-shaped leaves with serrated margins, and produces small bright

Smilacina racemosa

Solidago 'Golden Wings'

yellow flowers in feathery panicles early in autumn/fall.

S. species and hybrids

Growth of these perennials is generally upright, with heights varying from 30 cm (about 12 in) to 1.2 m (about 4 ft) or more. Flowering occurs in late summer and autumn, the tiny flowers clustered in large masses in racemes or panicles. They are easily grown in full sun, average soil and with moderate water. Divide in autumn or spring. 'Golden Mosa' is a good, light yellow.

X *SOLIDASTER*
luteus
syn. × *S. hybridus, Aster luteus*
YELLOW ASTER

When this perennial's daisy-like flowers first open at their mid-summer blooming, both their disk and rays are gold, although the rays quickly fade to creamy yellow. The flowers cluster in flattish heads, 10 cm (about 4 in) across, on downy stems branched near the top. The leaves are narrow and mid-green. Grows to 60 cm (about 24 in) high and spreads somewhat more than that. This fully hardy species likes well-drained soil and full sun.

STACHYS
byzantina
syn. *S. lanata, S. olympica*
LAMB'S EARS, LAMB'S TONGUE

This genus of late spring- or summer-flowering perennials, shrubs and sub-shrubs is fully hardy to frost tender to a minimum of 5°C (41°F). They grow in any well-drained soil and are particularly tolerant of poor soil. Propagate by division in spring. The leaves of *S. byzantina* give this perennial its common name: tongue-shaped, they are thick and whitish. Unfortunately their woolly surface turns mushy if rained on heavily. Frost also does damage. Nonetheless it makes a good ground cover or border plant, growing 30–50 cm (about 12–20 in) high, with a 60 cm (about 24 in) spread. Mauve-pink flowers appear in summer; nip the buds at the onset of blooming to make the

foliage lusher. Establish in well-drained soil in full sun.

STOKESIA
laevis
STOKES' ASTER

This fully hardy perennial from the south-east of North America has evergreen rosettes, its narrow leaves green, basal and divided. The summer-flowering, blue-mauve or white blooms have a shaggy appearance, reminiscent of cornflowers. They last well as cut flowers. The plants grow to a height and spread of about 40 cm (about 16 in). Establish in well-drained soil in full sun. Water regularly in summer. Propagate from seed or root cuttings.

TAGETES
MARIGOLD

These annuals are used in beds or for edges. Plant seed in spring. To prolong flowering, cull the dead-heads. Watch out for attack by botrytis and slugs.

T. erecta
AFRICAN MARIGOLD, AZTEC MARIGOLD

A strong aroma comes from the glossy dark green leaves of this bushy annual from Mexico. The leaves' margins are deeply incised. The stems are upstanding and branching. It grows to about 50 cm (about 20 in) in height and spread. Orange or yellow daisy-like flowers bloom in summer and autumn/fall. The flowers can be as large as 10 cm (about 4 in) across. The species resists frost and drought. It suits most soils and likes a sunny, open location. Propagate from seed.

Tagetes erecta *Stokesia laevis*

Stachys byzantina

X *Solidaster luteus*

Solidago 'Golden Mosa'

T. patula
FRENCH MARIGOLD

The double flowerheads produced in summer and early autumn/fall by this bushy annual resemble carnations. They bloom in reds, yellows and oranges. The leaves are deep green and aromatic. This fast-grower reaches 30 cm (about 12 in) in height and spread. Like *T. erecta*, it is a native of Mexico. This marigold was introduced to European gardens via the south of France—hence its common name.

TANACETUM
coccineum 'Brenda'
syn. *Pyrethrum* 'Brenda', *C. coccineum*
PYRETHRUM

Immortality came to Ganymede as a result of drinking tansy, a species of this genus that even in recent times has been used (despite being potentially quite poisonous even when applied externally) for promoting menstruation and treating hysteria, skin conditions, sprains, bruises and rheumatism. Confined mainly to the northern hemisphere, the species of this genus are today appreciated more for their daisy-like flowers. They are relatives of the chrysanthemum. The foliage of many of the perennials carries a strong fragrance. The leaves are feathery and scented on *T. coccineum* 'Brenda'. Its single flowerheads are magenta, appearing from late spring to early summer. The species grows 60 cm (about 24 in) high with a spread of 45 cm (about 18 in) or more.

TELEKIA
speciosa
syn. *Buphthalmum spesiosum*

Not highly recommended for the garden, this coarse, invasive perennial might nonetheless find a place around pools. The shape of the leaves varies from the base, where they are shaped like hearts, to the stems, where they are elliptical. Its scented flowers, which bloom in summer, are like gold daisies. It grows 1.2–1.5 m (about 3½–4½ ft) tall with a spread of up to 1.2 m (about 3½ ft). Propagate by division in spring or by seed in autumn/fall.

TELLIMA
grandiflora

A native of North America, this late-spring-flowering perennial makes excellent ground cover for a cool, part-shaded site so it is ideal for planting under shrubs or in a woodland garden. It does best in a reasonably well-drained soil. The heart-shaped, purple-tinted green leaves are semi-evergreen and form a neat clump around 60 cm (about 24 in) high. Racemes of small, bell-shaped, creamy flowers are borne on 60 cm (about 24 in) stems, well above the foliage. Propagate by division in spring or by seed in autumn.

THALIA
dealbata
WATER CANNA

This aquatic perennial from the south-east of North America tolerates cool water, although it is frost-tender. Growing to 2 m (about 6 ft) in height and 60 cm (about 24 in) or more in spread, it carries blue-green leaves that are broadly elliptical to lanceolate with long stalks and a mealy whitish coating. Its stems are erect and unbranching. Its summer blooms are followed by decorative seed heads. The flowers, which occur in tall spikes, are violet and waxy, their six petals forming a tube. Establish the species in loamy soil in sun.

THALICTRUM
MEADOW RUE

A genus known for its fluffy, showy flowers, these perennials overall have a delicate presentation. The branches of their slender upstanding stems often intertwine. The leaves are finely divided and columbine-like. Blooming in summer and spring, the flowers, which lack petals, have four or five sepals and conspicuous stamen tufts. They serve well in borders, particularly as contrast to perennials with bolder blooms and foliage, and in the margins of bush gardens. Grow in any well-drained soil in a position with sun or light shade. Propagate from seed when fresh in autumn/fall or by division in spring. The genus has its roots in Europe, northern Africa, northern Asia, the Himalayas and Tibet.

T. aquilegiifolium
GREATER MEADOW RUE

This spring-flowering perennial, which is a native of Europe, bears lilac or greenish white flowers in fluffy clusters on strong stems. Each grey-green leaf comprises three or seven small, elliptical, saw-edged leaflets composed into a feather-like arrangement, something like maidenhair fern. Growing 1 m (about 3 ft) high, the species has a spread of 45 cm (about 18 in). It is resistant to frost but is drought-tender. Establish it in rich, damp soil in a protected location with partial shade. Propagate by seed sown in spring.

T. delavayi
syn. *T. dipterocarpum* of gardens
LAVENDER SHOWER

Rather than fluffy heads, this species bears a multitude of nodding, lilac flowers in loose panicles, their yellow stamens prominent. Flowering time is from the middle to the end of summer. The finely divided leaves give the mid-green foliage a dainty appearance. Reaching 1.2 m (about 3½ ft) high, this species has a spread of 60 cm (about 24 in).

Thalictrum aquilegiifolium

Thalia dealbata

Tagetes patula

Tanacetum coccineum 'Brenda'

Telekia speciosa

Thalictrum delavayi

THUNBERGIA
alata
BLACK-EYED SUSAN

A black 'pupil' at the centre of each flat, golden-orange flower gives this plant from southern and eastern Africa its common name. Flowering occurs from early summer to early autumn/fall. A twisting climber, the plant grows fairly rapidly up to 3 m (about 9 ft). Its leaves are heart- or pear-shaped, with sparsely toothed edges. It prefers well-drained soil and a sunny, protected location. It is both frost and drought tender. Use cuttings or seed for propagation.

TIARELLA
cordifolia
FOAMFLOWER, COOLWORT

This vigorous spreading evergreen, a North American native, blooms profusely in early to late spring, producing terminal spikes of tiny, pink-tinged, white flowers with 5 petals. Its leaves are mostly pale green, lobed and toothed, with dark red marbling and spots, although the basal leaves take on an orange-red hue. Its height and spread when in flower are 30 cm (about 12 in) or more. Establish in moist well-composted soil in semi-shade. Propagate from seed or by division.

TITHONIA
rotundifolia 'Torch'
MEXICAN SUNFLOWER

Flowerheads resembling bright orange or red daisies up to 8 cm (about 3 in) across appear on this slow-growing annual in summer and early autumn/fall. Growing to 90 cm (about 36 in) high with a spread of 30 cm (about 12 in), this half-hardy species carries rounded lobate leaves. Establish it in well-drained soil in full sun. Propagate by seed sown under glass in late winter or early spring.

TORENIA
fournieri
WISHBONE FLOWER

This branching annual from tropical Asia has light to dark green, ovate or elliptical leaves with toothed edges. Its flowers, borne in summer and early autumn/fall, are pansy-like and deep purplish-blue, turning abruptly paler nearer the centre, and with a touch of yellow. Frost-tender, it grows fairly rapidly to a height of 30 cm (about 12 in) and a spread of 20 cm (about 8 in). Establish in rich, moist soil that drains well, in partial shade. Propagate from seed. Red, pink and white varieties are available.

TRADESCANTIA
virginiana
COMMON SPIDERWORT

A native of eastern North America, this perennial has dull green, strap-like leaves that grow up to 40 cm (about 18 in) long. It has an erect stem with spreading branches, and reaches a height of 45–60 cm (about 18–24 in) with a spread of 60 cm (about 24 in) or more. It bears small, 5 cm (about 2 in) wide, deep blue flowers with three petals in late spring to autumn/fall. This frost-resistant species is the foundation of many cultivars. Give it a protected location, in moist to dry soil, and fertilize. Propagate by division.

TRILLIUM
grandiflorum
WAKE ROBIN

The wild wake robin, a native of North America, has 3-petalled white flowers which fade to pale pink in spring, above deep green leaves. It is a perennial for a shaded spot in a cool climate where it will be long lived and easy to grow. The double-flowered form is beautiful but very rare and expensive. There are several other species, all with 3-petalled red or pink flowers.

TROLLIUS
europaeus
GLOBE FLOWER

The stem on this perennial from northern and central Europe is smooth, hollow and upstanding, branching at the apex. Its spring flowers are yellow and terminal, its 5 to 15 petal-like sepals forming a rounded shape 5 cm (about 2 in) across. Forming each mid-green leaf are 3 to 5 lobes arranged palmately, each lobe incised deeply. This frost-resistant species grows to a height of 60 cm (about 24 in) with a 45 cm (about 18 in) spread. Establish it in moist rich soil, in a protected location with some shade. Propagate from seed in spring or autumn/fall, by division in spring or autumn/fall.

Thunbergia alata

Tradescantia virginiana

Torenia fournieri

Tithonia rotundifolia

Tiarella cordifolia

Trollius europaeus

Trillium grandiflorum

Tropaeolum majus 'Alaska'

Veratrum nigrum

Tropaeolum peregrinum

x *Venidio-arctotis* cultivars

Verbascum nigrum

TROPAEOLUM

NASTURTIUM

Bright flowers are the attraction of this genus of annuals, perennials and twining climbers, whose natural territory extends from Chile to Mexico. Frost-hardy to frost-tender, most species prefer moist, well-drained soil and a sunny or semi-shaded location. Propagate from seed, basal stem cuttings or tubers in spring. Watch out for aphids and the caterpillars of the cabbage moth.

T. majus

GARDEN NASTURTIUM, INDIAN CRESS

The stem is trailing and climbing on this fast-growing, bushy annual. Its leaves are rounded and variegated with radial veins. It blooms in summer and autumn/fall, its 5-petalled flowers spurred, open and trumpet-shaped, in many shades of red or yellow. It grows to a spread of 30 cm (about 12 in) and a height up to

Verbascum olympican

twice that. Avoid fertilizing this plant, which is resistant to frost but not to drought, and let it have sun. The spicy-flavoured leaves and flowers of this species are used to add taste to salads. There are several varieties with single or double flowers and compact or trailing habit. 'Alaska' has single flowers and prettily variegated leaves.

T. peregrinum
syn. *T. canariense*

CANARY CREEPER

This frost-tender South American annual vine climbs to over 2 m (about 6 ft). Its grey-green leaves have 5 broad lobes and radial veins. In summer to early winter, it bears small, trumpet-shaped yellow flowers; the upper pair of its 5 petals are bigger and fringed. The stems are slender and trailing or climbing. It is adaptable to most acid soils in a protected, partially shaded position and is drought-tender.

X VENIDIO-ARCTOTIS CULTIVARS

MONARCH OF THE VELD

In summer, these branching perennials bear large flowers like daisies in numerous hues. Most commonly grown as annuals, the plants carry lobate green leaves that have a greyish cast on the upper side and are almost white beneath. They grow sedately to a height and spread of 50 cm (about 20 in). Only half-hardy, they are from a hybrid genus that enjoys well-drained, fertile soil and sun. The plants are best propagated in late summer using semi-ripe cuttings. In frosty climates they are grown as annuals. Old plants should be replaced annually.

VERATRUM
nigrum

BLACK FALSE HELLEBORE

This species is a rare perennial from southern Europe and Asia. It carries long, narrow, terminal spikes of small, purplish brown flowers with six petals that bloom from late summer. The big, pleated, elliptical leaves are arranged spirally into a sheath around the stout, erect stems. This fully hardy species grows to a height of 2 m (about 6 ft) and a spread of about half that. Establish it in moist rich soil, in a protected location in sun or semishade. Propagate *V. nigrum* in early spring from seed or by division. *V. album,* with cream, 6-petalled star-shaped flowers, and *V. viride,* with pale green 6-petalled flowers on terminal spikes, are very similar to this species. Protect from snails. All species are poisonous.

VERBASCUM

MULLEIN

Large, often complex, basal rosettes develop on these evergreens from Europe and the more temperate zones of Asia. Including both very large and some very coarse species, the genus offers much variety in the foliage, with leaves ranging from glossy to velvety. Summer flowering is mainly in the form of tall narrow spikes. There are frost-resistant through to fully hardy species. Establish all species in well-drained soil, and an open, sunny location though they do tolerate shade. Propagate from seed in spring or late summer or root cuttings in winter. Some species self-seed readily.

V. nigrum

BLACK MULLEIN, HAG TAPER

Long spikes of yellow flowers with almost black centres appear on this native of Morocco in summer through autumn/fall. The species' mid-green leaves taper to a point and carry a dense layer of hairs. This semi-evergreen, which is fully hardy, grows to a height and spread of around 1 m (about 3 ft). Most well-drained soils are suitable. Give it an open sunny location. Black mullein is used as a herbal remedy for colic, coughs and spitting blood. Applied externally, it is said to relieve haemorrhoids. Witches of the Middle Ages were thought to use the plant in their love potions and brews, hence the name 'hag taper'.

V. olympican

Not a long-lasting species, this semi-evergreen perennial grows sedately up to 1.5 m (about 4¹/2 ft) with a spread of 60 cm (about 24 in). Its stems and leaves are hairy. The rosette-forming leaves are large, elliptical and silver-grey and spikes of 5-lobed yellow flowers appear in summer.

VERBENA

VERBENA

Because of a susceptibility to mildew, these biennials and perennials are considered best grown as annuals. Originating in Europe, they are characterized by small, dark, irregularly shaped and toothed leaves. They bloom in summer and autumn/fall. Half-hardy, they do best where winters are not severe. Establish in medium, well-drained soil, in sun or at most semi-shade. To propagate, use seed in autumn/fall or spring, stem cuttings in summer or autumn/fall, or division in late winter. You can also propagate in spring by division of young shoots. An agreeably spicy aroma is associated with most verbenas.

V. × hybrida

This trailing perennial bears slightly hairy leaves. It blooms in summer to autumn/fall, its fragrant flowers appearing in dense clusters 2 cm (about 1 in) across, many showing off white centres among the hues of red, mauve, violet, white and pink. Use this species in summer beds and containers. Avoid being heavy handed with fertilizers or the plants will yield more leaves than they will flowers.

V. venosa
syn. V. rigida

A South American native, this tuberous-rooted perennial is an excellent species for seaside cultivation as it is nearly fully hardy in mild areas. It reaches a height of 45–60 cm (about 18–24 in) and a spread of 30 cm (about 12 in). Dense spikes of pale violet to magenta flowers are borne from mid-summer.

VERONICA
SPEEDWELL

These perennials are widespread through temperate regions. Although their flowers are usually blue, they encompass a wide variety of foliage and of size, with a height range from 30 cm (about 12 in) to over 1.2 m (about 4 ft). Hardiness ranges from frost-resistant to fully hardy. Establish them in well-drained, fertilized soil in sun. To propagate, use seed in autumn/fall or spring, division in early spring or autumn/fall, or either softwood or semi-ripe cuttings in summer.

V. austriaca subsp. teucrium

A spreading perennial forming a low mound of foliage around 45 cm (about 18 in) across, from which rise the flower stems 30 cm (about 12 in) high, which comprise many tiny blooms in deep true blue. The flowers are borne in late summer. Hybrids include 'Crater Lake Blue', 'Royal Blue' and 'Blue Fountain'. This plant prefers full sun and a well-drained soil.

V. gentianoides

This mat-forming plant has wide, dark green leaves from which rise stems of the palest blue, almost white flowers in late spring. They reach 45 cm (about 18 in) in height and spread.

V. prostrata

This perennial from Europe and parts of Asia has woody, branching stems and variable foliage, although all tooth-edged. The flowers are small and blue, with widely flared petals, occurring in upright spikes in spring and early summer. This species spreads widely into a mat of indefinite coverage, however it only reaches 30 cm (about 12 in) in height.

Veronica prostrata

Verbena × hybrida

Veronica gentianoides

Veronica austriaca subsp. teucrium

Verbena venosa

Viola reichenbachiana

Veronica spicata

Vinca minor

Viola cornuta

V. spicata

DIGGER'S SPEEDWELL

A European species, this fully hardy perennial reaches a height of 60 cm (about 24 in) and a spread of up to 1 m (about 3 ft). Its stems are erect, hairy and branching. Spikes of small star-shaped blue flowers bloom in summer. The leaves of this species are mid-green, linear to lanceolate in shape.

VINCA

PERIWINKLE

Shiny green leaves are common on these vining perennials and sub-shrubs from Russia and Europe. The flowers are widely flared with five lobes. Hardiness ranges from frost- and drought-resistant to fully hardy. Any soil is good provided it is not too dry. If you want ground cover, provide these evergreens with shade to semi-shade. If you want flowers, let them have more sun. Propagate by division in autumn/fall through spring, or from semi-ripe cuttings in summer.

V. major

GREATER PERIWINKLE

The leaves have a dark green gloss and are heart-shaped to pointed ovate on this tenacious evergreen vine from the Mediterranean. Widely spreading, with an erect woody stem, the species climbs as high as 3 m (about 9 ft). Brilliant blue flowers, 5 cm (about 2 in) across, are borne in late spring through early autumn/fall. It is drought-resistant and frost-resistant, and can also be aggressive and invasive.

V. minor

LESSER PERIWINKLE

The slender woody stems on this European evergreen creeper will cover ground over a distance of 3 m (about 9 ft) to lay down a mat of glossy, dark green leaves of pointed elliptical shape. The small flowers it produces in mid-spring through early summer are bluish lilac, purple or white. This species, like *V. major,* is often aggressive and invasive.

VIOLA

PANSY, VIOLET

Although the sweet violet (*V. odorata*) gives one of the best loved of flower perfumes, many of the other species are less fragrant. Their leaves can be solitary or in clumps, lightly to heavily textured, kidney to heart-shaped. Their hardiness ranges from half- to fully hardy. The annuals are suited to summer bedding, although big beds of them are needed if you want sufficient yield to pick. The perennials and sub-shrubs are good in beds and rock gardens. Some species have runners and are invasive. Most species do best in lean or fertile soil that drains well and retains moisture, with some preferring an acidic pH. Grow them in sun or shade. All bloom in spring.

V. cornuta

HORNED VIOLET

V. cornuta was originally a broad-faced violet with a short spur in the back. The plant is rhizomatous and has oval toothed leaves. The

Vinca major

flowers are flat faced and usually range in colour from pale blue to deep purplish blue. A short-lived perennial, it is often grown as an annual for winter bedding in mild regions, or spring-summer bedding in areas of cool summers. Plants grow 15–30 cm (about 6–12 in) tall and wide. The flowers are 2.5 cm (about 1 in) across. A native of Europe, it prefers well-composted, moist soils in a protected shady position. It is frost-resistant but drought-tender. Propagate by seed or by division.

Viola hederacea

Viola × wittrockiana

V. hederacea

syn. *V. reniformis, Erpetion reniforme*
AUSTRALIAN NATIVE VIOLET

The tiny 5-petalled, scentless flowers that bloom on short stems on this creeping perennial from the south-east of Australia are lilac or white and solitary. They appear in spring, summer and autumn/fall. The plant's stems are prostrate, suckering and mat forming, spreading widely but reaching only 5 cm (about 2 in) in height. Its leaves are rounded and kidney-shaped, deep green and with irregular edges. Partially shade this frost-resistant but drought-tender species. Propagate *V. hederacea* by division in spring or autumn/fall.

V. odorata

VIOLET, SWEET VIOLET

A sweet perfume wafts from the flowers on this spreading, rhizomatous perennial from Europe, which grows 7 cm (3 in) high over 15 cm (about 6 in) or more in spread. Its dark green leaves are a pointy kidney shape with shallow toothed edges. Spurred, flat-faced flowers in violet, white or rose, bloom from late winter through early spring. Boasting many cultivars, this fully hardy species readily self-seeds and can be propagated by division in autumn/fall. The plants like well-composted, moist soil and a protected location in semi-shade.

V. reichenbachiana

WOOD VIOLET

This perennial bears small, flattish, pink, mauve or pale blue flowers in spring and summer. Its kidney-shaped leaves are green. Although an invasive species—spreading widely, growing to only 5 cm (about 2 in)—it can serve over a bank or in natural settings. Propagate from rooted runners in autumn/fall.

V. riviniana Purpurea group

A neat, clump-forming perennial with rounded, purple-green leaves and purple flowers borne on short stems in spring and early summer. The leaves are usually retained through the winter. This plant thrives in part or full shade, so it is good under larger plants or for a woodland garden. They reach 5–10 cm (about 2–4 in) in height, with a spread of 22 cm (about 9 in).

V. sororia 'Freckles'

A new introduction with attractive flowers that are white and heavily speckled with blue. The flowers are borne in late winter and spring; they are shown off well by the fresh green leaves. Height and spread reach 10–15 cm (about 4–6 in).

V. tricolor

HEARTSEASE, WILD PANSY, JOHNNY JUMP UP, LOVE-IN-IDLENESS, PINK OF MY JOHN

Originating in the United Kingdom, this short-lived perennial or annual produces neat flowers with appealing faces from spring to autumn/fall, displaying shades of yellow, blue, violet and white. It has soft, angular, branching stems, and lobed ovate to lanceolate leaves, and grows to a height and spread of 5–15 cm (about 2–6 in). Frost-resistant, it prefers a sunny, open location and is adaptable to most soils. Propagation is by seed; it also readily self-seeds.

V. × wittrockiana

PANSY, VIOLA

This group of predominantly bushy perennials are almost always grown as biennials or annuals. Offering flowers of a great many hues, the species bloom in late winter through spring and possibly into summer in cooler climates. The flowers grow up to 10 cm (about 4 in) across and have 5 petals in a somewhat flat-faced array. Its mid-green leaves are elliptical, sometimes with toothed margins. Slow- to moderately fast-growing, these plants reach about 15–20 cm (about 6–8 in) in height with a spread of 20 cm (about 8 in). Propagate from softwood cuttings in spring. The usual distinction is that pansies have black blotches, violas none, but there are now intermediate types with pale-coloured markings.

Viola odorata

Viola tricolor

XERANTHEMUM

annum
IMMORTELLE

A good source of dried flowers, this annual blooms in summer, producing heads of purple daisy-like flowers; whites, pinks and mauves and doubles are also available. The leaves are silvery and lanceolate on this fully hardy species, which grows 60 cm (about 24 in) high with a 50 cm (about 20 in) spread. Grow in any well-drained soil and full sun.

YUCCA
YUCCA

Huge clumps—in some species reaching to 13 m (about 40 ft)—are formed by the spear-like leaves of these evergreen plants from North and Central America. Yuccas carry showy clusters of flowers, mostly white, at the end of stalks which can measure 3 m (about 9 ft) or more. They need well-drained soil and full sun. If you grow them in containers, do not over water and ease off even more outside the growth season. Propagate from seed, root cuttings or by division in spring. Although not all are desert species, the yuccas are drought- and frost-resistant.

Y. filamentosa
ADAM'S NEEDLE

Like 1 m (about 3 ft) long green spears, the leaves on this evergreen plant form a basal rosette. The leaves are edged with white threads. The flowers that bloom in terminal spikes from the middle to the end of summer are white and bell-shaped. This species is native to south-eastern North America and grows to 2 m (about 6 ft) high with a 1.5 m (about 5 ft) spread. It is fully hardy.

Y. gloriosa
SPANISH DAGGER, MOUND LILY

The stout erect stem on this evergreen plant has a tufted crown of stiff, spear-like leaves, which start out with a greyish cast but, as they mature, turn a deeper green. The white bell-shaped flowers appear in very long terminal spikes in summer right through to autumn/fall. This native of eastern North America reaches a height and spread of 1 m (about 3 ft).

Y. whipplei
OUR LORD'S CANDLE

Distinct from the other species of yucca by its very narrow, grey-green leaves that form a nearly perfect sphere, this Californian native is only hardy in the warmest parts of the country near the sea. Occasionally it produces a tall flowering spike several feet tall and covered densely with creamy white flowers, sometimes tinged with purple. It is extremely drought-tolerant and needs a hot, sunny position. An evergreen, it grows to a height of 2 m (about 6 ft) with a spread of 1.5 m (about 4½ ft). Propagate by seed.

ZANTEDESCHIA
ARUM LILY, CALLA LILY, PIG LILY

These tuberous perennials, indigenous to South Africa, are characterized by the classic lily shape comprising an enfolding spathe like a funnel with a central finger-like spadix. The leaves are glossy green and arrow shaped. Mostly evergreens in warm climates, this genus includes frost-tender to frost-resistant species, most being drought-tender. Establish in well-drained soil. Some prefer full sun, others partial shade. Propagate using offsets in winter.

Z. aethiopica
WHITE ARUM LILY, LILY OF THE NILE

The large flowers that appear on this species in spring are white, the spadix yellow. Although normally deciduous, the perennial can stay evergreen if given enough moisture. You can grow it around pools in water 15–30 cm (about 6–12 in) deep. Growing 60 cm–1 m (about 2–3 ft) high with a 30–50 cm (about 12–20 in) spread, the plant produces many large broad leaves.

Z. rehmannii
PINK ARUM LILY, PINK CALLA

The spathe on this summer-flowering species is rosy purple with paler

Zantedeschia aethiopica

Yucca gloriosa

Xeranthemum annum

Yucca whipplei

Yucca filamentosa

Zinnia angustifolia

margins, enclosing a yellow spadix. Its arrow-shaped leaves are glossy green, basal, semi-erect and about a handspan long. It grows 40 cm (about 16 in) high with a spread of 30 cm (about 12 in). The species is half-hardy, and likes well-composted soil, a protected location and partial shade.

ZAUSCHNERIA
californica
CALIFORNIAN FUCHSIA

The common name refers both to the species' Californian origin and to its flowers that are indeed like fuchsias. These are bright red, appearing in terminal spikes on erect slender stems in late summer and early autumn/fall. The evergreen shrub has lance-like, 2 cm (about 1 in) long leaves, and grows to a height and spread of 50 cm (about 20 in). Give it light, well-drained soil and a sunny, open location. This species is not resistant to frost or drought.

ZINGIBER
zerumbet
WILD GINGER

A clump-forming ginger plant from India and Malaysia with very narrow, 30 cm (about 12 in) long leaves. On separate, tall stems, are overlapping cones of green bracts that age to red, surrounding white and gold flowers. Used to hot equatorial areas, it is frost-tender to a minimum 18°C (about 64°F) and needs a humid atmosphere in part-shade with plenty of water during growth period. Plant in moist, hu-

mus-rich soil. Propagate by division of rhizomes in spring. The rhizomes, unlike the edible ginger of *Zingiber officinale*, are bitter to eat, but can be used in potpourri.

ZINNIA
ZINNIA

The flowerheads on these half-hardy annuals are like dahlias. Establish them in fertile soil that drains well in a sunny position. They need frequent dead-heading. Sow seed under glass early in spring. Found through Mexico, Central and South America, this genus is an excellent source of cut flowers. Propagate by seed under glass in early spring.

Z. angustifolia
syn. *Z. linearis*
LITTLE STAR

This native of Central America grows hairy green leaves of elliptical shape. Its abundant flowers are orange-yellow. The plant is trailing in habit, with matt green leaves. A fast-growing annual, it reaches a height of 40 cm (about 16 in) and a spread of 30 cm (about 12 in). There is a very pretty white form.

Z. elegans
YOUTH-AND-OLD-AGE

This sturdy annual from Mexico is the best known of the zinnias. The flowerheads are purple, and bloom in summer to autumn/fall. It grows fairly rapidly to 60–75 cm (about 24–30 in), with a smaller spread. Its deep green leaves are linear to lanceolate. Hybrids offer hues of white,

Zinnia elegans

red, pink, yellow, violet, orange or crimson in flowers up to 12 cm (about 5 in) across. Grow in rich, loamy soil in an open, sunny location.

Z. haageana 'Old Mexico'
syn. *Z. mexicana*

The 6–8 cm (about 2½–3 in) wide single or double flowers on this annual are yellow and bronze. It flowers in summer and early autumn/fall. A fast-grower, this Mexican species reaches 60 cm (about 24 in) high, with a 20 cm (about 8 in) spread, its stem erect and branching. It is drought-resistant and frost-tender. 'Persian Carpet' is another well-known strain, with a few more petals.

Zauschneria californica

Zinnia haageana 'Old Mexico'

Zingiber zerumbet

Zantedeschia rehmannii

CHAPTER 3

Shrubs

*N*o garden is complete without the cohesive atmosphere that shrubs supply. With their multi-stemmed growth they fill in the garden picture between the lower growing annuals and perennials and the taller growing background trees. They unite the house and garden, make wonderful barriers for both sight and sound and can be grouped with one another to form eye-catching displays of colour almost all year round.

Shrubs are generally classified as decidu-ous or evergreen, although in more temperate areas some fall between these two groups and are termed partly or semi-deciduous.

Evergreen shrubs provide the perma-nent structure of a garden so necessary in the overall landscape design, espe-cially in winter when the deciduous types are dormant. In this regard they make excellent backgrounds for decidu-ous plants. Also, consider the advantage of permanent plant foliage against a plain house or fence wall or where a division of garden space is needed.

Deciduous shrubs can provide the contrast elements of garden design. Their ever-changing attributes give continued interest. In winter their bare branches can look magnificent against green backgrounds or a winter skyline, then plants such as the bright yellow forsythias and the flowering quinces in the pink shades tell us the cold is almost over. We can look forward to an unsur-passed parade of colour through spring provided by a myriad of well-loved and proven shrubs. As summer progresses the shrub garden can form a dense, cool background highlighted by spectacular show stoppers like the tibouchinas, crepe myrtles and oleanders.

Keep this continuous colour show in mind when designing and choosing the plants for the shrub garden as it is possible to have a plant in bloom almost year-round.

Colour through Foliage

Colour is not the sole domain of flowers in the shrub garden. There are many plants clothed with a fantastic display of coloured leaves. Many of these make striking accents in an otherwise green shrubbery, indeed in tropical and humid subtropical areas plants such as acalyphas and crotons take the place of flowering plants and replace those that are traditionally used to provide autumn colour in colder areas.

Shrubs with silver or grey foliage can be used to create wonderful landscapes and are often combined with white flowering plants to great effect. Also there are the variegated forms, some of which need to be planted where they are sheltered from drying winds and hot afternoon sun otherwise they tend to burn. On the other hand, gold-leafed plants and those with gold markings need to be planted in full sun to retain their colour. The shade loving vari-egated forms of *Aucuba japonica* are the exceptions to this rule.

Roses are perhaps the best loved of all flowers.

Remember also to include in your list of essential shrubs those plants with berries which highlight the foliage and make marvellous displays indoors. Holly is one cold country favourite. Then, in warmer climates, the pigeon berry (*Durante repens*) with its display of bright yellow berries can be a real eye-catcher as can the showy ardisias with their long-lasting red or white berries providing added interest to a deeply shaded area.

Scented Shrubs

Plants not only give visual pleasure; a fragrant shrub can provide a subtle sense of joy as its scented foliage, if brushed against, or its flowers release their distinctive perfume. Daphne, boronias, lavenders, rosemary, gardenias and the lilacs are all beautifully scented and well worth including on your shopping list. They are examples of the many plants which can be placed near an outdoor living area where their perfume can be appreciated as you sit at leisure. Others, such as the night scented *Cestrum nocturnum*, some may find overpowering on a summer's evening and are best positioned where you pass by, such as beside a front gate or entrance path.

Accent Points

The dramatic statements that an accent plant can provide are sometimes overlooked. These shrubs, used sparingly, act as a focal point, drawing the eye through the landscape to another section of the garden.

They are choice plants, chosen for a particular growth pattern such as a weeping standard or for their arresting shapes like those of the *Acer palmatum* cultivars. Though usually more expensive, if well positioned they give a garden that individual look.

Soil

Most shrubs will tolerate a wide range of soil types, as long as it is well drained and reasonably fertile, however there are a number of garden favourites which need to have an acidic soil. Soil is measured on a pH scale ranging from very acid (1) to very alkaline (14) and although soil solutions don't reach these extremes a plant is considered to be acid loving if it enjoys a pH level in the low 6 range. Three that immediately

Most of the over 30 000 varieties of camellias are decended from Camellia japonica.

come to mind are camellias, azaleas and rhododendrons but there are other shrubs which will thrive in similar conditions and help to give variety to a shrub border. Other shrubs to interplant with them include the heaths and ericas, magnolias, the American laurel (*Kalmia*) and the various species of *Pieris*. These plants thrive in soils that have had loads of compost, peat moss and organic mulches added to them.

Planting

A shrub border is best planned wide enough to accommodate at least two shrubs in depth, with the taller, easy care evergreens at the back and the plants which require more attention, in the form of pruning, or which are to be grown for cutting, planted towards the front. Often there is room to interplant these with ground-hugging shrubs to act as a mulch keeping both weeding and watering requirements to a minimum. And it makes sound gardening sense to plant out a complete bed at the one time—not only do some plants resent being disturbed, but the ability for shrubs to establish a good root system within a well-established border is very limited.

Prepare a garden bed a few weeks prior to planting, digging it over well and adding well-rotted compost or other decayed organic matter. This humus helps to break up heavy soils making it more porous and so more

easily drained and provides light, sandy type soils with moisture-retentive materials.

Pruning

Pruning is often unnecessary for shrubs, but some do require annual attention to ensure continued high quality blooms. These shrubs can be divided into two categories—those that produce flowers on new or the current season's wood and those that form the flower buds in the previous season. Flowers that appear on last season's canes include forsythia, weigela and kerria. These and similar shrubs do best if the flowering canes are cut well back once the flowers are finished to enable the developing new shoots ample room to develop.

When shrubs produce flowers on the current season's growth, the flowers usually appear towards the end of summer on spring growth. These are best pruned in late winter, or in colder areas once all possibility of frost is over. Shaping is the main requirement here, taking thin or dead wood back to the main trunk and shortening vigorous shoots. Plants in this category include the late summer flowering shrubs such as tibouchina, fuchsias and abutilon as well as hibiscus and luculia. Bearing this in mind, it is possible to choose plants for a garden shrubbery that require very little attention and still be assured of a colourful display that is as easy care as a garden can possibly be.

Abelia × grandiflora

Abelia schumannii

Abutilon × hybridum

Abuliton megapotamicum 'Variegatum'

Acacia acinacea

ABELIA

Native to Japan, the Himalayas and India, these dense, low-branching evergreens are widely grown in temperate climates the world over. They flower in summer, bearing fragrant, pink or white flowers and a sprinkling of deep red bracts. They prefer sun or part-shade and do best when well watered. They flourish in all but the coldest regions, where they may survive in deciduous form. If conditions are very cold, abelias prefer the shelter of a wall or bushes. Plant out in early spring or autumn/fall. Deadwood should be removed in late spring and older branches pruned after flowering. Trim lightly all over during winter. The fine growth that follows trimming makes it an excellent choice for a pleasantly decorative hedge. Propagate from cuttings in summer.

A. × grandiflora

This, the best known of the group, is a hybrid of a number of Chinese species. It has oval, glossy, bronze-green foliage, and fragrant, pink-tinged, white flowers which appear from mid-summer to mid-autumn/fall. When there is new foliage, or when the flowers have fallen, leaving behind red bracts, the entire bush takes on a reddish tone. It grows to a height and spread of 2–3 m (about 6–9 ft).

A. schumannii
SCHUMANN'S ABELIA

Also from China, Schumann's abelia has larger flowers which are a deeper mauve-pink than *A. grandiflora*. Its yellow-blotched, pink-

and-white, bell-shaped flowers appear from mid-summer and last until mid-autumn/fall. Its dense habit makes it a suitable choice for a hedge. It grows to a height and spread of 1.5 m (about 4½ ft).

ABUTILON
CHINESE LANTERN, FLOWERING MAPLE

Grown for the beauty of their variegated, maple-like leaves as much as for their delightful, colourful, lantern-shaped flowers, these leggy evergreen or semi-evergreen shrubs are grown in glasshouses in cold conditions or in the open when warmer. They prefer full sun or part-shade and a rich, moist, fertile and well-drained soil. Improve the flower yield by regular pinching back to ensure branching and hence budding. If necessary, tie to a support if lax. Raised from seed sown at any time, *Abutilon* will germinate within 3 weeks or less and should flower within 12 months. The varieties named here however will come true only from cuttings (take these from firm, new tips later in the season and struck with heat in a sand/peat mixture). Often raised as indoor plants, they bloom best when rootbound. Popular with flea beetles and aphids.

A. × hybridum
FLOWERING MAPLE

These open, soft-wooded shrubs have green, heart-shaped leaves with a furry texture. They bear bell-shaped flowers, in shades of white, cream, pink, yellow, orange and red (often veined in contrasting tone), from spring to autumn/fall. In the

growing season, young plants may need tip pruning to promote bushy growth. Mature specimens should have the previous season's stems cut back hard annually in early spring. It grows to a height and spread of 2 m (about 6 ft). Propagate from softwood or semi-ripe cuttings from summer to winter. Slightly tender, they are best grown as conservatory plants in cold climates.

A. megapotamicum 'Variegatum'
BIG RIVER ABUTILON, TRAILING ABUTILON

One of the hardiest of the genus, this sprawling evergreen is a native of Brazil. It has long, slender branches and pendant, bell-shaped, yellow and red flowers appearing in spring to autumn/fall. They appear among oval, lightly serrated leaves variegated with yellow blotches. Normally it is trained against a wall, but it may be used as a dense ground cover. Prefers sun, well-drained soil and is half-hardy. It grows to a height and spread of 3 m (about 9 ft).

ACACIA
MIMOSA, WATTLE, MYALL, ACACIA

One thousand species of evergreen, semi-evergreen and deciduous trees and shrubs, found in Africa, North America and most predominantly Australia. They grow fast and are usually short-lived. The flowering season is variable and brief, with a spectacular explosion of fragrant yellow that blows away to leave dry pea pods. The flowers are actually a mass of stamens and produce pollen in abundance—birds and bees

love them. Instead of leaves, many species have phyllodes—flattened leaf-like stalks—that serve the same function. The fruits are round or extended pods containing seeds that are exceptionally resilient—they may survive for up to 30 years. Light watering in dry seasons and light pruning after flowering will prolong life. They require well-drained soil and full sun to thrive. Propagate from seed or cuttings. Borer, leaf miner, acacia scale and galls can be a problem.

A. acinacea
GOLD DUST WATTLE

This is an evergreen, many branched shrub with slender leaves, 1.3 cm (about ½ in) long. It flowers in late winter to late spring, either singly or in clusters. It grows to a height and spread of 2 m (about 6 ft). *A. acinacea* likes an open, sunny, well-drained position. It is half-hardy, tolerates periods of dryness well and prefers a light to medium soil. The obliquely oblong, bright green phyllodes grow to about 1.5 cm (about ½ in) long.

A. boormannii
syn. *A. hunteriana*
SNOWY RIVER WATTLE

This small, rounded, evergreen tree or shrub grows to a height and spread of 3–4 m (about 9–12 ft), producing bright yellow balls of flowers in spring. *A. boormannii* tolerates the cold well. It produces narrow, dark green phyllodes and is best propagated from the suckers that appear around the main trunk.

A. pravissima
OVENS WATTLE, ALPINE WATTLE

This arching evergreen shrub is half-hardy and grows to a height and spread of 6 m (about 18 ft). Its phyllodes are triangular, spine-tipped and dull green. Small heads of bright yellow flowers appear in late winter or early spring.

ACER
MAPLE

Maples have been grown in cool climates all over the world for centuries, but when we think of *Acer*, we think of Japan, where its cultivation reached the level of an art form. Maples are grown for the delicate beauty of their foliage, although they do have small red flowers on drooping stems, which are followed by two-winged fruits and seeds which can glide for miles. They prefer cool, moist conditions and fertile, well-drained soil. They do best when protected from full sun, otherwise the leaves will burn. They colour beautifully in the autumn—particularly if the soil is neutral or slightly acid. Mainly deciduous, they are propagated by seed as soon as ripe, or in autumn/fall (cultivars by grafting). Avoid pruning where possible, apart from removing dead branches.

A. palmatum 'Dissectum Atropurpureum'
JAPANESE MAPLE, CUT LEAF MAPLE

This cultivar of the deciduous Japanese mountain maple has normally reddish purple leaves, which turn brilliant red in autumn/fall. The flowers are small, also reddish to purple, and appear in spring. The plant grows sideways rather than vertical, to a maximum spread of about 6 m (about 18 ft). It can only be propagated by grafting and is a slow grower—hence it is often expensive to buy. It prefers sunlight, moist soil, and is fully hardy. Protect from the sun to prevent leaf burn.

A. palmatum 'Dissectum Viridis'

The green cut-leaf maple resembles the purple, but it is slightly more able to stand the sun.

AESCULUS
BUCK-EYE, HORSE CHESTNUT

Native to various parts of Europe, North America and Asia, these deciduous shrubs are grown for their handsome leaves, flower clusters and shining brown fruits (known as chestnuts or 'conkers'). They require fertile, deep, well-drained soil and will grow in either a sunny or semi-shaded situation, favouring cooler climates. Grow species from seed in autumn, and cultivars by grafted cuttings in late winter or by budding in late summer. Prune only to remove dead branches. Young leaves may be prone to leaf spot.

A. parviflora
BOTTLEBRUSH BUCKEYE

Suitable for small gardens, this wide-spreading, suckering species reaches 3–4 m (about 9–12 ft) in height and has huge conical panicles of red-centred white flowers that are freely produced in late summer. It has the advantage of flowering later in the season and offers good autumn colour. It spreads by means of rooted suckers, which may be detached and planted in spring. Fully hardy.

A. pavia
RED BUCKEYE

This species, which has a shrubby habit with a rounded head, grows to a height of 4 m (about 12 ft) and a spread of 3 m (about 9 ft). The leaves are a glossy dark green, comprising 5 narrow oval leaflets. Beautiful large heads of 4-petalled bright red flowers are produced in early to mid-summer. It is fully hardy.

AGAPETES
serpens
syn. *Pentapterygium serpens*
FLAME HEATH

This squat, semi-epiphytic shrub sends out slender, arching branches from a tuberous rootstock. The evergreen leaves are red-tinted on the upper side only. Bright red tubular flowers, hanging in loose pairs, appear in spring and summer. It grows to a height and spread of just under 2 m (about 6 ft). *A. serpens* prefers a well-drained, humus-rich soil (neutral to acid), and full light or part-shade. Propagate in spring from seed, or in late summer from semi-ripe cuttings.

Acacia boormannii

Acacia pravissima

Aesculus parviflora

Acer p. 'Dissectum Atropurpureum'

Acer p. 'Dissectum Viridis'

Aesculus pavia

Agapetes serpens

ALYOGYNE
huegelii
syn. Hibiscus huegelii

LILAC HIBISCUS

A native of Western Australia, this dense, semi-deciduous desert shrub blooms in late spring and summer, bearing lilac, hibiscus-like flowers. Formerly a member of the hibiscus genus, it has now been reclassified. The leaves are lobed and slightly hairy with irregularly serrated margins. It prefers full sun, and well-drained soil. Avoid watering—seasonal rainfall is adequate. It grows to a height and spread of 1.5 m (about 4½ ft). Prune often for compact growth. Propagate from semi-hardwood cuttings in summer.

AMELANCHIER
alnifolia

Native to North America, this deciduous, upright shrub is grown for its profuse flowers, autumn colouring and edible fruit. The creamy white, star-shaped flowers, which are not all that long-lasting, are borne in erect spikes during spring; they are followed by edible, purple-black, round berries in summer. Slow growing, A. alnifolia can reach up to 4 m (about 12 ft) in height and 3 m (about 9 ft) in spread on maturity. They are fully hardy, preferring sun, well-drained, moisture-retentive soil and cool climates. Autumn colouring is best in acid or neutral soils. Propagate by seed sown when ripe or by layering in spring; pruning is generally not required. Fireblight can often be a problem.

ANDROMEDA
polifolia

BOG ROSEMARY

A native of sub-arctic areas, this dainty, spreading evergreen will only grow in cool climates or mountain conditions. It has glossy, mid-green leaves and produces pitcher-shaped clusters of pink flowers in spring and early summer. It prefers full sun or partial shade and a moist, humus-rich, acid soil—it thrives naturally in peat bogs. Fully hardy, it grows to a height and spread of 60 cm (about 24 in). Propagate from seed or by division of root runners. Andromeda are named after the Greek mythological figure who survived an attack by a sea monster—an apt choice given that all the other former members of the genus have been reclassified—only A. polifolia survives.

ANISODONTEA
hypomandarum
syn. A. capensis, Malvastrum capensis

Grown for their attractive flowers, these evergreen bushy shrubs have an erect habit, and can reach a height of 1 m (about 3 ft) with a spread of 60 cm (about 24 in). Bowl-shaped, deep pink flowers highlighted by darker veins are borne from spring to autumn. They prefer a sunny position and well-drained soil. Useful container plants, they require heavy watering when in full growth but prefer dryish soil at other times. Tip prune to maintain shape in the growing

season. Propagate by semi-ripe cuttings in late summer or by seed in spring. Frost-tender to a minimum 3–5°C (37–40°F).

ARBUTUS
unedo 'Compacta'

STRAWBERRY TREE

Native to Ireland and southern Europe, this slow-growing, evergreen shrub has a compact habit, growing to a height of 4 m (about 12 ft) and a spread of 2 m (about 6 ft). It has rough, shreddy brown bark and oblong, shiny-toothed, dark green leaves; in autumn the branches are covered with panicles of urn-shaped white flowers that resemble lily-of-the-valley. Last seaon's strawberry-like, orange-red fruit ripen amongst the flowers and, while the fruit is edible, they are flavourless. Arbutus are frost-hardy but need a spot sheltered from strong coastal winds. They prefer full sun and a well-drained, fertile, acid soil. Propagate by seed in autumn or by semi-ripe cuttings in late summer. They do not transplant readily. Prune only to remove dead wood.

ARCTOSTAPHYLOS

BEARBERRY, MANZANITA

These evergreen shrubs are grown for their foliage, flowers and fruit. Some species make excellent ground covers, suitable for interplanting between larger shrubs. They have leathery leaves and pendent, urn-shaped flowers followed by red or black berries. Fully hardy to frost-tender to a minimum 7°C (44°F), they require an acid, lime-free, well-drained soil and full sun. Salt tolerant, Arctostaphylos are suitable for seaside gardens although they need shelter from strong winds. Propagate by semi-ripe cuttings in summer or by seed in autumn. Pruning is generally not necessary.

A. manzanita

Native to California, this erect shrub grows to 2 m (about 6 ft) or more in height and spread. It has long, crooked branches, peeling, reddish

brown bark and oval, greyish green leaves. Small, urn-shaped white to pink flowers are produced in spring, followed by deep red fruit. Frost-hardy.

A. uva-ursi

A useful ground cover, this vigorous, low-growing, mat-forming plant reaches a height of 10 cm (about 4 in) and a spread of 50 cm (about 20 in). It is native to most of the cooler temperate areas of the northern hemisphere. Arching stems are covered in somewhat glossy bright green leaves, while small, pendent, pink-flushed white flowers are produced in spring. These are followed by red, globular fruit. Fully hardy. A. uva-ursi 'Nana' is a more compact version that is useful for rockeries as it does not run.

ARDISIA

CORALBERRY

This genus of evergreen shrubs and trees, native to the area stretching from the East Indies to Japan and Korea, are grown for their flowers, fruits and foliage. They are half-hardy to frost-tender, to a minimum 10°C (50°F), and need humus-rich, well-drained soil that is not too dry. Propagate by seed in spring or by semi-ripe cuttings in summer.

A. crispa
syn. A. crenata, A. crenulata

CORALBERRY, SPICEBERRY

This evergreen upright shrub with its slender trunk may be found in subtropical climates worldwide. It

Arctostaphylos uva-ursi

Amelanchier alnifolia

Alyogyne huegelii

Andromeda polifolia

Anisodontea hypomandarum

Arbutus unedo 'Compacta'

Arctostaphylos manzanita

grows to a height and spread of 1 m (about 3 ft) and is a frequent feature of Japanese gardens, where its whirled arrangement of berries are used to delightful effect. Fragrant, star-shaped, white or pink flowers appear in early summer, followed by berries, which may survive a year or more. Frost-tender, it does best in partial shade and a humus-rich, well-drained soil. Sow seed in spring or plant cuttings in summer.

A. japonica

Native to Japan and China, this small, broad-leaved evergreen shrub grows to 45 cm (about 18 in) in height. It has elliptic, leathery, glossy dark green leaves that are sharp toothed and crowded at the ends of the branches. Clusters of small white flowers appear from late spring to summer; these are followed by red berries. Frost-tender, it requires a partly shaded, wind-sheltered position in a mild climate. Seeds germinate readily when cleaned of their fleshy covering and sown in spring. *A. j.* 'Variegata' has variegated leaves.

ARONIA
arbutifolia 'Brilliant'
RED CHOKEBERRY

Native to North America, this deciduous shrub is grown for its flowers, fruit and vivid autumn foliage. Growing to around 2 m (about 6 ft) in height, it spreads slowly by suckering to at least 2 m (about 6 ft) in width. It has an upright habit when young, arching as it matures. Small white flowers (often stained or tinged pink or light red outside) with red anthers appear in spring, followed by bright crimson berries. Dark green foliage changes to a brilliant red in autumn, lasting to early winter. Fully hardy, it is best grown in light, fertile, well-drained soil in full sun or semi-shade, preferably in a cool, moist climate. Propagate from softwood or semi-ripe cuttings in summer, by division from early autumn to spring or from seed in autumn.

ARTEMISIA
ludoviciana
syn. A. purshiana
WESTERN MUGWORT, WHITE SAGE

Native to central North America and Mexico, this herbaceous species is grown for its aromatic, sometimes coarsely toothed lance-shaped leaves, which are densely white-felted beneath and grey/white-haired above. Bell-shaped greyish white flowerheads are produced in summer. A bushy, invasive species, it reaches a height of 1.2 m (about 4 ft) with a spread of 60 cm (about 24 in). Fully hardy, it prefers a light, well-drained soil and a sunny situ-

ation. Cut back to almost ground level in autumn/fall, and watch for the appearance of cream-coloured root aphids on the leaves. Propagate by division any time from autumn to spring.

AUCUBA
japonica
JAPANESE LAUREL, GOLD-DUST TREE, SPOTTED LAUREL

Thriving in shade, while producing colourful fruits under a dense cover, this cool-climate mountain native of Japan grows in all but the most barren of soils. A bushy evergreen, it has stout, green shoots and glossy, dark green, oval leaves, heavily splashed with gold. Small, purple, star-shaped flowers appear in mid-spring. Red, egg-shaped berries follow, but only if at least one male plant is grown to every two females (the females are the ones that bear fruit). Cut old shoots back in spring to restrict growth. Hardy to frost-hardy, it grows to just under 3 m (about 9 ft) in height and spread. Propagate from semi-hardwood autumn/fall cuttings.

AZARA
microphylla

This elegant, evergreen native of Chile has deep green, oval leaves and in spring bears vanilla-scented, yellow flowers with masses of stamens. It grows to a height and spread of 5 m (about 15 ft), thriving in sun or shade. It requires fertile, well-drained soil. Frost- to half-hardy, it suits a mild, temperate garden. Propagate from semi-ripe cuttings in summer.

BACCHARIS
pilularis 'Twin Peaks'

A native of California, this evergreen shrub grows to a height of 30 cm (about 12 in) with a spread of 1 m (about 3 ft). It has small, oval, bright green leaves on spreading branches and tiny white flowers. It is adaptable to most soils in any sunny position and is drought and frost resistant. Propagate from seed or by cuttings.

BAECKEA
virgata

This dainty, woody, evergreen, native to the east coast of Australia, is prized for its elegant profusion of white, tea-tree-like flowers, which appear in summer. It bears thin leaves up to 1.5 cm (about ½ in) long and prefers well-drained, moist soil and full sun or semi-shade conditions. It grows to a height of 4 m (about 12 ft) with a spread to 3 m (about 9 ft). Propagate either from young cuttings or ripe seeds, if they can be caught before dispersal.

Baeckea virgata

Aronia arbutifolia 'Brilliant'

Aucuba japonica

Ardisia japonica

Baccharis pilularis 'Twin Peaks'

Ardisia crispa

BANKSIA
BANKSIA, BUSH HONEYSUCKLE

Named after the botanist, Sir Joseph Banks, who discovered this evergreen in 1770, banksias are found in every state of Australia, particularly in the south-western regions. Foliage and habit vary, but all species are characterized by colourful flowerheads, odd, woody follicle fruits, and adaptation to harsh conditions. The slender, tubular flowers arranged in neat, parallel rows along a spike usually appear in spring. All species prefer well-drained and sandy soil. They do best in full sun or part-shade conditions. Frost-hardy to frost-tender. Containerized plants need moderate watering during growth periods. Propagate from seed in early spring or autumn/fall. Do not allow pot seedlings to become pot-bound prior to planting. Banksias are closely related to the Protea genus, found around the Cape of Good Hope, and scientists cite this as evidence that the continents were once joined as part of the supercontinent 'Gondwanaland'.

Artemisia ludoviciana

Azara microphylla

Berberis thunbergii

Banksia ericifolia

Begonia fuchsioides

Boronia heterophylla

Berberis ottawensis 'Superba'

Banksia integrifolia

Berberis darwinii

Bauhinia galpinii

B. ericifolia
HEATH BANKSIA

This wiry, freely branching shrub has fine, glossy foliage and an upright, copper to orange, bottlebrush spike about 10–25 cm (about 4–10 in) long. It flowers in autumn/fall to winter. It is found freely in coastal, sandstone ridges, but adapts to inland conditions. It grows to about 4 m (about 12 ft) in height and spread.

B. integrifolia
COAST BANKSIA

This gnarled, evergreen has a lime-yellow flower spike up to 15 cm (about 6 in) long. The leaves are grey-green above; white below. It grows 15 m (about 50 ft) tall with a 7 m (about 21 ft) spread.

BAUHINIA
galpinii
NASTURTIUM BAUHINIA, PRIDE OF DE KAAP, PRIDE OF THE CAPE

The most spectacular shrub in the genus *Bauhinia*, this low-spreading bush (occasionally a climber) is

native to Africa. It has 2-lobed leaves and sweet smelling, bright red flowers—borne in small racemes—which appear in late summer and autumn/fall. It prefers light, fertile, well-drained soil and full sun and dislikes cold or salty wind. It grows to a height of 3 m (about 9 ft) with a spread of around 2 m (about 6 ft). Prune after flowering and propagate from seed in spring.

BEGONIA
fuchsioides

This evergreen, multi-stemmed begonia has dark green, oval, serrated leaves. Small, single, white flowers are borne in spring and autumn/fall. It grows to 1 m (about 3 ft) tall with a 30 cm (about 12 in) spread. It prefers good light and moist but well-drained soil. Best propagated from soft tip cuttings or seed if available.

BERBERIS
BARBERRY

Species from this genus of evergreen, semi-evergreen and deciduous shrubs from Europe, Asia and the Americas are among the most popular for cool climate gardens. The leaves are shiny and saw-toothed, and the flowers, which resemble very small daffodils, are a delight, especially when offset against the red or purple foliage, which may change colour in late summer or autumn/fall. They prefer sun or part-shade, any but water-logged soil, and are fully to frost-hardy. Smaller species are excellent in rockeries, while taller species

make good, dense hedges. Propagate from seed in autumn/fall.

B. darwinii
DARWIN BARBERRY

This is a native of Chile and Argentina. It grows to a height and spread of 3 m (about 9 ft), producing an abundance of orange to yellow flowers among dark green leaves from mid- to late spring. Then blue-coloured berries appear in turn. It is fully hardy. Water heavily only in dry seasons. Prune lightly to shape after flowering if desired, but be prepared to lose some berries. Propagate from semi-ripe cuttings in summer.

B. ottawensis 'Superba'
syn. B. o. 'Purpurea'

Developed at the Ottawa Experimental Station in Canada, this deciduous shrub is grown for its attractive arching habit and dark maroon/purple leaves that turn to orange-scarlet and purple in autumn/fall. Small umbels of cup-shaped, red-tinged yellow flowers appear in late spring, and are followed by glossy, bright scarlet berries. Fully hardy, it reaches a height and spread of 2.5 m (about 7½ ft).

B. thunbergii

This is a deciduous species from Japan. Its pale to mid-green, oval leaves turn brilliant, orange-red in autumn/fall. Small, red-tinged, pale yellow flowers erupt in mid-spring. Bright red, egg-shaped fruits follow. It is fully hardy and grows to 1.5 m (about 4½ ft) and 3 m (about 9 ft) wide. The dwarf cultivar 'Red Pygmy', with purple tinted leaves, is very popular. It grows to about 80 cm (about 32 in) tall and wide.

BORONIA
heterophylla
KALGAN BORONIA

Native to Australia, boronias are found in lightly covered, sandy bushland, and are admired for their sweet smelling flowers. These evergreens do best in very well-drained soil with an acid pH balance (moistened peatmoss may be added to retain moisture). They prefer shady conditions and are half-hardy to frost-hardy. The genus is related to two other fragrants—*Citrus* and *Murraya*. Light pruning after flowering improves the look, and can prolong the life of short-lived species. Water potted plants lightly, less when not in full growth. *B. heterophylla* is a frost-hardy species with finely divided, bright green leaves. In spring it bears fragrant, bell-shaped flowers in bright magenta-pink. It grows to a height of 1.5 m (about 4½ ft) and spread of 1 m (about 3 ft). Seed germination is unpredictable, so propagate from small, firm-tipped cuttings struck in coarse sand.

BOUGAINVILLEA
species

These extremely useful climbers are popular for their brilliant papery bracts, borne for a very long period and often overpowering the foliage. Half-hardy to frost-tender, they grow rapidly in fairly frost-free gardens, or they can be grown indoors in cooler climates. They are semi-evergreen or evergreen in warmer climates, but can be deciduous in cooler climates. They are good grown in containers and tubs, trained into arches and standards or even as hedges and ground covers. Root restriction encourages flowering; the plants need to be cut back after blooming. They require fertile, well-drained soil, full sun and plenty of water during summer. Propagate from semi-ripe cuttings in summer or from hardwood cuttings when dormant. Some cultivars, such as B. 'Pink Champagne' (with coral-pink bracts) and B. 'Limberlost Beauty' (with double white flowers), can be kept shrubby.

BOUVARDIA

These evergreens come from Mexico and Central America and are grown for the spectacular beauty of their flowers, though they also have a reputation for fragrance (largely undeserved). Bouvardias are untidy and require pruning after flowering to maintain shape—cut back stems half- to three-quarters. Frost-tender,

Bouvardia hybrids

they prefer full light and fertile, well-drained soil. Water heavily in summer and add diluted liquid fertilizer when the shrub is flowering. Propagate in spring from softwood cuttings or root cuttings. Whitefly and mealy bug may present problems.

B. hybrids

There are a number of hybrid bouvardias available, mainly derived from *B. longiflora*. They are spreading shrubs to about 1 m (about 3 ft) tall, with clusters of flowers in shades from white to bright red; some, such as the pink 'President Garfield', have double flowers. They make excellent, long blooming pot plants, and used to be very popular conservatory plants. Scent is apt to be lacking.

B. longiflora
syn. B. 'Humboldtii'

This thin-stemmed, spreading evergreen is the only *Bouvardia* that is truly fragrant. It bears exquisite, white flowers, each with four tubular-shaped petals, in terminal clusters during autumn/fall and winter. It has small lance-shaped leaves and grows to a height and spread of 1 m (about 3 ft) or more. Cold resistant only to 13–15°C (55–59°F) when flowering—7°C (44°F) at other times.

BRACHYGLOTTIS
RANGIORA

These evergreen shrubs and trees, native to the North Island of New Zealand, are grown for their hand-

some foliage and attractive appearance. The terminal panicles of tiny, greenish flowers borne in spring are insignificant. Hardiness varies considerably among the species. They do best in a damp, compost-rich soil, in full light or partial shade. Potted specimens should be watered freely in summer. Prune regularly and pinch back occasionally to maintain habit. Propagate from semi-ripe cuttings in summer.

B. greyi
syn. Senecio greyi

This many-branched evergreen belongs to the same family (Asteraceae) as daisies—though its petite, bright yellow, daisy-like flowers that appear in summer and autumn/fall are less interesting than its hair-covered, leathery, green-grey leaves. Half- to fully hardy, it prefers full sun or part-shade and well-drained soil. Plants in a pot should be watered freely in summer. It grows to a height and spread of 1 m (about 3 ft). Propagate from cuttings in late summer.

B. monroi
syn. Senecio monroi

A neat, compact shrub, *B. monroi* bears terminal racemes of bright yellow flowers in summer. Half-hardy, it grows to a height and spread of 60–90 cm (about 24–36 in). The leaves are olive-green to brownish green above and hairy underneath and have crinkled margins.

Bouvardia longiflora

Brachyglottis greyi

Bougainvillea sp.

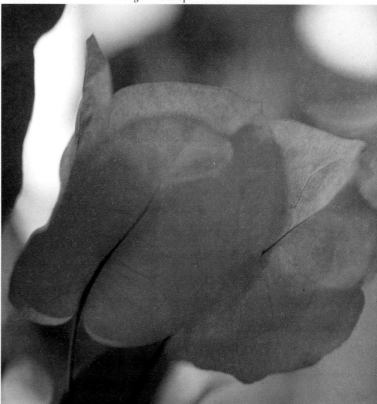

Brachyglottis monroi

BRUGMANSIA

ANGEL'S TRUMPET

These exotic-looking but robust, evergreen or semi-evergreen shrubs are native to the Andes mountains. Hardiness varies considerably among the species. They prefer full sun or half-shade and fertile, well-drained soil. Propagate from seed in spring, or greenwood or semi-ripe cuttings in summer. Keep moist during the growing season. Prune in early spring to maintain shape. Specimens in containers should be watered freely. Be prepared for disoriented snails—the sap contains a narcotic. *B. stramonium* (Jimson weed) is an annual and a fairly common weed, with white flowers and prickly seed capsules. It is dangerously hallucinogenic and poisonous.

B. × candida
syn. *Datura candida*

This semi-evergreen shrub has a rounded habit, growing to 4 m (about 12 ft) in height with a spread of 3 m (about 9 ft). It is grown for its elegant, pendulous, greenish-tinted white flowers which are extremely fragrant, especially at night. Flowers are borne from summer to autumn/fall. It can withstand temperatures down to minus 10°C (50°F) and prefers full sun and a well-drained soil.

B. sanguinea
syn. *Datura sanguinea*

This species grows cream and scarlet, trumpet-shaped flowers up to 20 cm (about 8 in) long, each with a spathe-like calyx, in summer to autumn/fall. *B. sanguinea* has oval leaves and is frost-tender. It grows to a height and spread of 4 m (about 12 ft).

B. suaveolens
syn. *Datura suaveolens*

This round-headed tree or shrub produces thin, oval leaves to 30 cm (about 12 ft) long, and funnel-shaped, double, white flowers which appear in autumn/fall and winter. Green, egg-shaped berries follow. Half-hardy, it grows to a height and spread of 2–4 m (about 6–12 ft).

BRUNFELSIA

pauciflora

BRAZIL RAINTREE, YESTERDAY-TODAY-AND-TOMORROW

This stunning, rounded, evergreen shrub from South America is widely enjoyed for the varying displays of fragrant blue flowers on the one plant. In spring, this tropical beauty produces rich, purple flowers, which gradually fade to pale blue and then to white. The shrub has lance-shaped, glossy, leathery leaves, and prefers full sun to part-shade and fertile, humus-rich, well-drained soil. It is frost-tender. Water plants in containers only moderately. It grows to 2 m (about 6 ft) in height and spread. Propagate from summer cuttings. Mealy bug and whitefly may present problems.

BUDDLEJA

BUTTERFLY BUSH

The spicy, fragrant blooms of *Buddleja* attract butterflies from far and wide—hence the common name. Found in Asia, Africa and the Americas, there is little variation in the foliage between species—all have pointed, crepe-textured, large leaves, but the bloom varies—the tubular florets may be arranged in whorls, globes, single spikes or branched racemes. Most do best in fertile, well-drained soil, and are fully hardy to frost-tender. Propagate these arching deciduous shrubs and trees from semi-ripe cuttings in summer.

B. alternifolia

WEEPING BUTTERFLY BUSH

Native to north-west China, this large, deciduous or semi-evergreen species grows 3–5 m (about 9–15 ft) tall. It is best grown as a single-stemmed standard to display its elegant form and flowers. It has slender, arching shoots and narrow leaves, dark green above and greyish white below. Many clusters of sweetly perfumed lilac-mauve flowers with deep violet throats appear in early summer. Prune in late winter by removing half the number of older shoots to make way for new material from the lower branches. Fully hardy.

B. davidii
syn. *B. variabilis*
BUTTERFLY BUSH, SUMMER LILAC

This deciduous or semi-evergreen, arching shrub is the most widely known. It has dark-green, long, lance-shaped leaves with white-felted undersides. Small, honey-scented, purple, lilac or white flowers appear in long panicles in summer to autumn/fall. A fully hardy species from China, it grows to a height of 5 m (about 15 ft) and spread of 3 m (about 9 ft).

Brugmansia suaveolens

Brunfelsia pauciflora

Brugmansia × candida

Buddleja davidii

Brugmansia sanguinea

Buddleja alternifolia

B. globosa

This deciduous or semi-evergreen species from South America grows to a height and spread of 4 m (about 12 ft) and is valued for its fragrant, bright orange flowers in ball-like heads which appear in spring and summer. Its leaves are long, dark green and wrinkled. It likes full sun, good drainage and is frost-hardy.

B. salviifolia

This dense, vigorous, semi-evergreen native of southern Africa bears terminal clusters of delightful, sweet-smelling, lilac flowers. It has finely serrated 12 cm (about 5 in) long grey-green leaves. Propagate from hardwood cuttings in autumn/fall. Susceptible to frosts, it grows to a height and spread of about 2 m (about 6 ft).

BURCHELLIA
bubalina
SOUTH AFRICAN POMEGRANATE

The only species in its genus, this small shrub originates in South Africa and is valued for its leaves and summer flowers. It grows 2–3 m (about 6–9 ft) high and has shiny, rounded, deep green leaves. In late spring to summer, dark orange-red, cylindrical flowers appear at the branch tips in dense terminal clusters containing up to 10 blooms. This frost-tender shrub enjoys full shade in extremely hot areas, but generally needs good light with partial shade. Prune as soon as flowering finishes. Propagate from semi-ripe cuttings in summer.

Buxus sempervirens

Buddleja salviifolia

BURSARIA
spinosa
PRICKLY BOX

Australian sheep farmers hate this spiny, evergreen bush—they claim it is forever snagging the wool of passing sheep. However, the fragrance and charm of the tiny white flowers make it popular in Australian gardens and also in the USA, particularly California. In summer the flowers are massed in panicles towards the ends of the branches, after which attractive, brown fruits appear. These contrast nicely with the small, shiny leaves, making the plant an attractive choice for flower arrangements. It is also excellent for hedging, though it is of course thorny. It prefers full sun and well-drained soil. Resistant to frost, it grows to a height of 10 m (about 30 ft) and a spread of 6 m (about 18 ft). Propagate from seed or semi-ripe cuttings.

BUXUS
BOX

These densely foliaged evergreen shrubs are native to Mediterranean Europe, Japan and Central America. The flowers are insignificant but the foliage is ideal for hedging, edging and topiary; the plants have been used in this way for centuries. They thrive in sun or semi-shade and any soil that is not waterlogged. They are best set out (use semi-ripe cuttings) in early spring or late summer, watered regularly and, as they grow (which is very slowly), pinched to shape. Trim and shear regularly as separate plants grow

Bursaria spinosa

Buddleja globosa

together. Promote new growth by cutting back stems to 30 cm (about 12 in) or less in late spring.

B. microphylla var. *japonica*
syn. *B. japonica*

This evergreen, bushy variety bears a rounded mass of small, oblong, glossy, dark green leaves. It is resistant to frost, requires full sun and will tolerate moist soil. It grows to a height and spread of 2.5 m (about 7 ft). Perfect for hedging and screening.

B. sempervirens

This is almost identical to *B. microphylla* but grows to twice the height. However, the form most often seen, 'Suffruticosa', grows to only about 80 cm (about 32 in) and is the type used to make clipped edgings in formal Italian or French style gardens.

CAESALPINIA

These deciduous shrubs, trees and climbers are valued in warm cli-

Buxus microphylla var. *japonica*

Caesalpinia gilliesii

mates worldwide for their brilliant flowers. Found in tropical and subtropical areas, they do best in soil that retains moisture, and prefer full sun and plenty of water. Named after a sixteenth-century Italian botanist, *Caesalpinia* are half-hardy to frost-tender. Propagate from seed in autumn/fall or spring, or from softwood cuttings in summer.

C. gilliesii
DWARF POINCIANA

C. gilliesii is sometimes incorrectly called 'Bird of paradise'—this name really belongs to *Strelizia reginae*. This rather prickly deciduous shrub or small tree is grown for the short racemes of bird-like, yellow flowers with long, red stamens that appear in summer. It has finely-divided, dark green leaves. In cooler areas it may be seen as a wall shrub. It prefers full sun, a well-drained soil and is half-hardy. It grows to a height of 4 m (about 12 ft) and a spread of 6 m (about 18 ft). Propagate from seed in autumn/fall.

Burchellia bubalina

C. pulcherrima
syn. *Poinciana pulcherrima*
BARBADOS PRIDE

This is the most common species of *Caesalpinia*. An erect or spreading, prickly, evergreen shrub, it has fern-like leaves and in summer bears racemes of orange-red to yellow, cup-shaped flowers for most of the year. It prefers full sun and well-drained soil. It grows to a height and spread of 3 m (about 9 ft) and tolerates the cold poorly—minimum 5°C (about 40°F). Propagate from seed in autumn/fall.

CALLIANDRA
tweedii
RED POWDER PUFF

Native to Central and South America and related to the *Acacia*, this evergreen shrub grows to a height and spread of 3 m (about 9 ft). In late autumn/fall to spring it bears striking flower heads made up of many red-stamened florets—like all species in the genus, *Calliandra*, it has no petals. The bipinnate leaves each have more than 100

leaflets. This picturesque plant prefers full sun and well-drained soil, and tolerates the cold poorly—it will not survive in temperatures below 7°C (about 44°F). The Greek genus name reflects its characteristics (*kallos*: beauty and *andros*: stamens). Propagate from seed in spring or by semi-ripe cuttings in autumn/fall.

CALLICARPA
BEAUTY BERRY

The attraction of these upright, deciduous shrubs lies in the luxurious bunches of glossy, purplish, lilac berries they bear in summer. The pale green, crepe-textured leaves (often bronze-tipped when young) and tiny, lilac flowers in spring are of little interest. Ungainly plants, they should be pruned in winter. Use the fruiting stems for indoor decoration. They grow best in fertile, well-drained soil and prefer full sun or semi-shade conditions. They grow to a height and spread of 2 m (about 6 ft) and are fully frost-hardy. Propagate from softwood cuttings in summer. There

are several species, all very much alike: *C. bodinieri* is usually thought to be the best; *C. dichotoma* has pale purple flowers in late spring and summer followed by small, clustered, lilac-violet fruits in autumn and early winter.

CALLISTEMON
BOTTLEBRUSH

Native to Australia, these woody and sometimes papery-trunked evergreen shrubs are popular in Ireland, the USA, Mediterranean countries, Hong Kong and South Africa and wherever frost is not severe. Often weeping in habit, they are grown for their magnificent flowers, which closely resemble a bottle brush. From the tips of the flower spikes, new leaves grow, leaving long-lasting, woody, seed capsules behind. A favourite with birds, *Callistemon* prefer full sun and a moist soil—many species will tolerate soggy, almost boggy, conditions. Propagate from semi-ripe cuttings in summer. Tent caterpillar may present a problem about this time.

C. citrinus
LEMON BOTTLEBRUSH

The forms of this species all thrive and flower profusely in dry or damp conditions. Many cultivars exist, including 'Anzac', which bears white bottlebrush-like flowers with yellow tips, and grows to 1 m (about 3 ft); 'Burgundy', with masses of burgundy bottlebrush flowers in summer, growing to 2.5 m (about 7½ ft); 'Mauve Mist', with

delightful, mauve-pink flowers in spring and growing to 2 m (about 6 ft); and 'Splendens' with spikes of bright red flowers.

C. viminalis
WEEPING BOTTLEBRUSH

This graceful weeping evergreen shrub or small tree flowers mostly in spring, producing clusters of bright red flowers. It grows to 7 m (about 21 ft) in height and spread, producing long, narrow, oblong leaves. Half-hardy, it tolerates most soil conditions.

CALLUNA
vulgaris
SCOTTISH HEATHER, LING

A familiar sight as natural cover on moors and heaths in northern Europe, this bushy evergreen is a native of Europe and Asia Minor. A densely spreading bush, its small leaves are arranged in pairs. It has spikes of bell- to urn-shaped, single or double flowers, usually pink, mauve or white, which appear from mid-summer to late autumn/fall. The shrub does well in rockeries and where mulched with pebbles. Salt, wind and drought resistant, it makes good ground cover, preferring a gritty, well-drained, acid soil with regular water. Grows to a height of 60 cm (about 2 ft) and a width of 50 cm (about 20 in). Propagate from autumn/fall cuttings. Several cultivars with coloured leaves, e.g. 'Multicolor', are available.

CALYCANTHUS
ALLSPICE, WINTERSWEET

Native to North America, these hardy, deciduous shrubs are grown for their pleasant fragrance and attractive flowers. The whole plant, including the mature wood, is aromatic. They prefer fertile, deep, moist, well-drained soil in sun or partial shade and require little attention apart from light cutting back after flowering. Propagate from seed in autumn/fall or from softwood cuttings in summer. Plant in autumn/fall to spring.

Callicarpa bodinieri

Callistemon citrinus   *Callistemon viminalis*

Calliandra tweedii

Caesalpinia pulcherrima

Calluna vulgaris 'Multicolor'

Camellia granthamiana

Calycanthus floridus

Camellia j. 'Aldolphe Audusson'

C. floridus

CAROLINA ALLSPICE

This species occurs naturally from Virginia to Florida in North America. It has a bushy, well-shaped habit, growing to a height and spread of 2 m (about 6 ft). The fragrant flowers have masses of petals and are an unusual reddish brown colour; they are borne in late spring or early summer. Foliage is dark green, and fragrant, pear-shaped fruit are also produced.

C. occidentalis

CALIFORNIAN ALLSPICE, SPICE BUSH

A bushy shrub with a height and spread of 3 m (about 9 ft), this species has large, bright green leaves and fragrant, brownish purple-red, many-petalled flowers that are borne in summer. It prefers an open, sunny aspect and moist soil.

CAMELLIA

CAMELLIA

Though associated with Japanese culture, the majority of this genus of evergreen, woody shrubs and trees are actually from mainland China and the Indo-Chinese peninsula. They are found in mountainous, subtropical areas, growing in partial shade. In Japan these lush plants are grown in part for the oil content of their seed capsules, but elsewhere most camellias are cultivated for their luxurious flowers and shiny foliage. Over 30 000 varieties now exist, most of which are descendants from *C. japonica*. They prefer semi-shade in the open and a well-drained, neutral to acid soil. During frost or snow periods, move in containers to the shelter of evergreen trees. White or pink varieties need to be screened from direct sun or their flowers will discolour. Propagate from cuttings in late summer or mid-winter, or graft in spring or winter. To trim the shape,

Camellia japonica

prune camellias during or immediately after flowering. *C. sinensis* is not grown for flowers but for its leaves, which are used to make tea. Legend has it that enterprising British East India agents attempted to export some specimens out of China, after tea had become fashionable in Europe in the mid-seventeenth century. However, Chinese officials substituted *C. japonica* instead—a beautiful plant, but quite useless for tea making. The popularity of *C. japonica* as a flowering plant took off soon after. *C. j.* 'Elegans' is a prized cultivar with large, rose-pink flowers.

C. granthamiana

This half-hardy, evergreen shrub from Hong Kong flowers in late autumn/fall. The flowers are single, up to 15 cm (about 6 in), white, and saucer-shaped, with a row of a maximum 8 petals surrounding a central boss of yellow stamens.

C. japonica

Native to Japan, Korea and eastern China, this evergreen shrub contains much variation in habit, foliage, floral form and colour. The flowers may be single to very double, in shades from white to red. It flowers in winter in temperate conditions and in spring in very cold areas. It grows to 7 m (about 21 ft),

Calycanthus occidentalis

Camellia japonica 'Desire'

Camellia japonica 'Elegans'

with a similar spread. Prefers a cool soil, adequate moisture and a protected environment. Shade from the burning afternoon sun. Watering is essential in dry areas, or the buds will fail to open.

C. japonica 'Adolphe Audusson'

This well-established cultivar has better resistance to cold than other varieties. It grows large, saucer-shaped, dark red flowers and prominent yellow stamens. They are semi-double with 2 or more rows of 9–21 petals. The leaves are dark green and broadly lance-shaped.

C. japonica 'Desire'

This fairly new camellia is greatly admired for its perfect formal double shape and delicate pink and white colouring. It blooms early.

Camellia sasanqua

Camellia sasanqua 'Yuletide'

Camellia japonica 'Lady Vansittart'

Camellia reticulata 'Captain Rawes'

Camellia japonica 'Kingyo-Tsubaki'

Camellia sasanqua 'Hiryu'

Camellia japonica 'Yamato Nishiki'

Camellia lutchuensis

C. japonica 'Kingyo-Tsubaki'

Sometimes called the 'Fishtail' or 'Mermaid' camellia, because of its distinctive lobed leaves, this ancient Japanese cultivar bears abundant single flowers in an attractive shade of bright pink from early in the season. It has a rather weeping habit.

C. japonica 'Lady Vansittart'

Medium-sized, saucer-shaped, 'semi-double', white flowers, flushed rose-pink, appear in winter to early spring. This upright shrub has unusual, holly-like, twisted, mid-green foliage.

C. japonica 'Yamato Nishiki'
syn. *C. japonica* 'Brocade of Old Japan'

The large, single flowers of this spreading shrub are streaked in pink and red. The centre features a flare of gold-tipped stamens. The plant's leaves are small and lance-shaped.

C. lutchuensis

This recently introduced species from China is a little tender but well worth growing for the long display of dainty, white flowers with only 3 petals but the strongest, sweetest perfume of any camellia. The plant is fairly fast growing, upright when young and spreading at maturity.

C. reticulata

A favourite among enthusiasts, with its upright habit and handsome, serrated foliage. Found naturally in the forests of southern China, it grows slowly, up to a height of 10 m (about 30 ft). The species bears large, saucer-shaped, single, rose-pink and red flowers in spring; the cultivars have large (20 cm—about 8 in—or more) double flowers in shades of pink or red. 'Captain Rawes', the oldest, has been joined by many in recent years. The leaves are large, oval and leathery. Less cold-hardy than *C. japonica,* it is a taller, more open grower.

C. sasanqua

This upright native of southern Japan is another lovely evergreen and it is the most sun-tolerant of all camellias. It is a fast-growing, slender and dense species, which produces an explosion of fragrant, single, white (occasionally red or pink) flowers in autumn/fall. These flowers usually shatter within a day or so of opening. The leaves are lance-shaped, glossy and bright green. *C. sasanqua* will thrive in a sunny spot.

C. sasanqua 'Hiryu'

Suitable for hedges, this popular cultivar bears double, pink flowers.

C. sasanqua 'Yuletide'

Suitable for formal or container planting, it bears a profusion of deep red flowers throughout the winter months.

C. sinensis

TEA

A variable shrub/tree, cultivated in warm, temperate parts of eastern and southern Asia, its processed young leaves are used to make tea. Some varieties are also used as ornamental hedge plants. The flowers are small, scented and white.

C. × williamsii

This is a hybrid group between *C. japonica* and *C. saluensis,* including numerous popular and attractive cultivars. Most popular of these are 'Donation', 'E. G. Waterhouse', 'Elsie Jury' and 'J. C. Williams', but there are many others, almost all in shades of pink.

C. × williamsii 'Donation'

This spectacular cultivar makes both an excellent tub specimen and garden plant. It is quite prolific; a compact upright shrub, it bears large, semi-double, orchid-pink flowers in the winter months.

CANTUA
buxifolia

MAGIC FLOWER, FLOWER-OF-THE-INCAS

This beautiful native of the Andes mountains develops a leggy habit with slender, weeping branches. It grows to a height and spread of 4 m (about 9 ft). An evergreen, soft-stemmed, bushy shrub, it becomes bowed down by the sheer weight of its bright red or purplish, trumpet flowers in mid- to late spring. Preferring full sun and well-drained soil, it is drought resistant and half-hardy, showing a considerable resistance to cold, especially in a sheltered position. The shrub requires support for best display. Light-tipped pruning after flowering helps keep its shape. Propagate from semi-ripe cuttings in summer.

CARISSA
macrocarpa

NATAL PLUM, AMATUNGULU

Native to South Africa, this fast-growing, dense, thorny hedge plant grows to a height of 3 m (about 9 ft) and a spread of 2 m (about 6 ft). The leaves are leathery and glossy and in spring large, white, frangi-pani-like flowers appear followed by fruit, which is rich in vitamin C. Half-hardy, it needs a well-composted soil, partial shade and regular watering. Propagate from seed.

CARMICHAELIA
odorata

SCENTED BROOM

Native to New Zealand, this leafless, broom-like, many-branched shrub bears clusters of fragrant, pea-like, purple-veined flowers from spring to summer, followed by small, ovoid pods. Instead of leaves, it bears flattened, green shoots. This shrub does best in a well-drained humus-rich soil in semi-shade. Deadwood should be cut out in spring. Frost-hardy, it grows to a height and spread of just under 2 m (about 6 ft). Propagate from seed in spring or cuttings in summer. The genus, *Carmichaelia* is named after Captain Dugan Carmichael, a Scottish army officer who collected botanical specimens in the early nineteenth century in India, South Africa and Mauritius—but curiously never in New Zealand.

Carissa macrocarpa

Cantua buxifolia

Camellia × williamsii 'Donation'

Camellia × williamsii

Camellia sinensis

Carmichaelia odorata

CARPENTARIA
californica

Like many other Californian natives, this sturdy, evergreen shrub is drought resistant, but dislikes the air pollution in city gardens. Half-hardy, it thrives in full sun and likes a rich, damp, well-drained soil. It has glossy, long, narrow, dark green leaves and fragrant, yellow-centred, white flowers which appear in summer. Withhold water in winter to prolong life, and prune regularly after flowering to prevent scragginess. Grows to a height of 3 m (about 9 ft). Propagate from seed in autumn/fall or from cuttings in summer.

CARYOPTERIS
× *clandonensis*

This deciduous, bushy, sub-shrub is prized for its masses of delicate, purple-blue flowers from late summer to autumn/fall. The leaves are irregularly serrated, oval, and grey-green. Frost-hardy, preferring full sun and light, well-drained soil, it grows to a height and spread of 1 m (about 3 ft). Propagate by greenwood or semi-ripe cuttings in summer or by seed in autumn/fall.

CASSIA
artemisioides

SILVER CASSIA, FEATHERY CASSIA, DESERT CASSIA

Native to Australia, this wiry, upright to spreading evergreen is a dry climate, frost-tender shrub. It is a member of the same family (Leguminosae) as peas and beans, it bears spikes of delightful, buttercup-like, yellow flowers from winter to early summer. Each leaf has 6 to 14 silver-grey leaflets covered in a fine down. It prefers an open, sunny position, and fertile, well-drained soil, although it will tolerate wetter conditions if the water is allowed to drain freely. It grows to a height and spread of 1–2 m (about 3–6 ft). Cut back hard in spring and propagate from semi-hardwood cuttings, or from seed in spring.

CEANOTHUS

CALIFORNIA LILAC

Originating in Mexico and the western states of the USA, this genus of over 50 species of evergreen or deciduous shrubs prefers cooler areas. *Ceanothus* species thrive in many parts of England, Europe and the cooler southern states of Australia. Despite the name, members of this genus are not lilacs. They bloom in much greater varieties of shades of blue, violet, mauve, pink and purple than true lilacs. They are grown for their small but densely-clustered flowers, which develop in showy terminals or panicles. The evergreen species are the more popular. Half-hardy, all species do best in a sheltered spot in an open sunny position, preferring a light, gravelly, well-drained soil. To prune, cut deadwood from evergreens in spring, and trim side shoots after flowering. Propagate from seed in spring or from leafy, semi-hardwood cuttings taken in summer.

C. 'Gloire de Versailles'

This sturdy, vigourous, deciduous shrub has mid-green leaves that are broad and oval. It does best in full sun and well-drained soil. It is fully hardy and, in mid-summer to early autumn/fall, bears racemes of pale blue flowers. Grows to a height and spread of 1.5 m (about 4½ ft).

C. impressus

This evergreen, bushy shrub does best in full sun and well-drained soil. Frost-hardy, it bears deep blue flowers which appear in clusters from mid-spring to early summer. The leaves are small, dark green, and crinkled. It grows to 1.5 m (about 4½ ft) with a spread of 3 m (9 ft).

C. thyrsiflorus

CALIFORNIAN LILAC

This evergreen, many-branched, bushy species, growing to a height and spread of 6 m (about 18 ft), has rounded clusters of pale blue flowers that are borne abundantly in late spring and early summer. The

Cassia artemisioides

Ceanothus 'Gloire de Versailles'

Ceanothus impressus

Carpentaria californica

Caryopteris × clandonensis

Ceanothus thyrsiflorus

leaves are a glossy rich green. It produces black fruits that dry when ripe. It is particularly useful for seaside gardens and prefers a sunny, sheltered site. Frost-hardy. A popular prostrate form, *C. t.* var. *repens*, which grows to 1 m (about 3 ft) high, is very useful in a mixed border.

CESTRUM
BASTARD JESSAMINE

While some enjoy the scent from some species of this genus of deciduous/evergreen shrubs and semi-scrambling climbers, others find it overpowering and unpleasant. All agree that the showy flowers are a delight. These shrubs like a sunny position and fertile, well-drained soil. Generally not frost-hardy, they like plenty of water and regular fertilizer during the warmer months. Plants in containers should be freely watered during active growth, less at other times. Cut out the older canes every year. Propagate from soft-tip cuttings in the summer.

C. aurantiacum

Mostly evergreen, this semi-scrambling shrub is deciduous in colder climates. Frost-tender, it grows to a height and spread of 2 m (about 6 ft), though it stays a rounded shrub if cut back. In summer, tubular, bright orange flowers appear in large trusses, followed by white berries. The leaves are oval and bright green. Prune annually—and remove dead stems by cutting to the base after flowering.

C. elegans
syn. C. purpureum
PURPLE CESTRUM

Native to Mexico, this vigorous evergreen grows to a height of 3 m (about 9 ft) and has many long, flexible stems arching gracefully outwards to form a vase-shaped bush to 3 m (about 9 ft) wide. The leaves are dark green, soft and velvety, but have an unpleasant odour when crushed. Dense racemes of faintly perfumed, nodding, purplish red flowers are borne from late summer to winter, followed by drooping clusters of deep red fruits. Frost-hardy.

Cestrum nocturnum

C. 'Newellii'

This arching, evergreen cultivar grows to a height and spread of 3 m (about 9 ft). It has large, green, broadly lance-shaped leaves and bears clusters of crimson flowers in late spring and summer; followed by berries in a matching shade of crimson.

C. nocturnum
NIGHT-SCENTED JESSAMINE

This spreading, evergreen tropical and subtropical shrub with dark green leaves comes originally from the West Indies. In summer, it bears clusters of greenish white to cream flowers, which give off intense fragrance, especially after dark. It prefers full sun and a well-drained soil. It grows to a height of 3 m (about 9 ft) and a spread of 2 m (about 6 ft).

CHAENOMELES
speciosa
FLOWERING QUINCE, JAPONICA

This dense, thorny, many-branched shrub from China is grown not so much for its fruit as for its flowers. The spherical, greenish fruits make excellent jelly. They follow the winter–spring bloom of attractive, clustered, red, white, pink or orange flowers. In colder climates *C. speciosa* is popular with flower arrangers because, when indoors, its bare but budded stems will open when placed in water. The plant prefers sun and well-drained soil and is fully hardy. After flowering, cut back side shoots on wall-trained shrubs to two or three buds and shorten shoots growing away from the wall during the growing season.

Chaenomeles speciosa

Cestrum 'Newellii'

Cestrum aurantiacum

Take leafy, semi-hardwood cuttings in summer or autumn/fall, the latter also being the best time to plant seed. Fireblight and chlorosis may present problems. The shrub grows to 3 m (about 9 ft) with a spread of 5 m (about 15 ft).

CHAMAECYPARIS
obtusa

HINOKI CYPRESS

Native to China and Japan, this fully hardy conifer can grow to a height of 30 m (about 95 ft) and a spread

Chamaecyparis obtusa

of 5 m (about 15 ft). There are, however, many dwarf cultivars, such as 'Duncanni', 'Minima' and 'Gnome'. This species has aromatic, blunt-tipped, bright green glossy leaves and very small orange-brown cones which ripen to brown. The crown is broadly conical and the foliage very dense. Stringy red-brown bark, which is used for roof shingles in Japan, shreds into coarse, parallel strips. This tree is dedicated as 'the Tree of the Sun' in Japan. It does well on slightly acid, moist soils.

Clerodendrum thomsoniae

Chorizema cordatum

Cistus ladanifer

Cistus salviifolius

Choisya ternata

Cistus 'Brilliancy'

Chimonanthus praecox

CHIMONANTHUS

praecox

WINTERSWEET

This twiggy, deciduous shrub, native to China and Japan, is grown for the rich, fragrant scent of its dainty, brown and pale yellow flowers with purple centres. It has rough, glossy, oval, dark green leaves. It needs constant moisture to thrive, preferring full sun and a fertile, well-drained soil. Propagate from seed in late spring and early summer, and by layering in autumn/fall. It grows to 3 m (about 9 ft) in height and spread.

CHOISYA

ternata

MEXICAN ORANGE BLOSSOM

Originally from Mexico, this drought-resistant, moderately frost-hardy plant prefers a sunny but sheltered position and a fertile, well-drained soil. It grows to a height and spread of 2 m (about 6 ft). Fragrant, white flowers, similar to orange blossom, appear in spring. The bright green, glossy leaves are also scented. Propagate from semi-ripe cuttings in summer.

CHORIZEMA

cordatum

HEART-LEAFED FLAME PEA

This gaudy, popular native of Western Australia bears sprays of yellow or orange-red pea-like flowers in spring. A thin-branched, scrambling shrub, it has heart-shaped, light green leaves. It does best in a sandy loam and likes to be watered regularly. Without pruning, it turns into a climbing plant, so prune annually to keep it a tidy shape. It prefers shady conditions and grows to a height of 1 m (about 3 ft), with a spread of 1.5 m (about 4½ ft). Propagate from seed in spring or semi-ripe cuttings in summer. Frost-free climates are preferred.

CISTUS

ROCK ROSE

This genus of spreading evergreens is famous for its drought resistance and ability to thrive in poor or sandy conditions, such as exposed banks or seaside cliffs. Native to the shores of the Mediterranean, *Cistus* species produce delightful, freely borne but short-lived flowers; these only last a day, but are quickly replaced. However in cold areas they need shelter and are frost hardy. Regular pinching back will maintain shape. Propagate by seed in autumn/fall or by softwood or greenwood cuttings in summer (cultivars and hybrids by cuttings in summer only), and grow the young plants on in pots. Of the many *Cistus* spe-

cies, *C. x purpureus* is a very popluar and much grown variety that produces rose-crimson flowers with deep maroon blotches and golden yellow stamens.

C. 'Brilliancy'

This straggling cultivar grows to 1.5 m (about 4½ ft) tall with a 1 m (about 3 ft) spread. In summer it bears pretty, little, rose-pink flowers with crimson blotches near the central stamens, set off by elliptic, grey-green leaves with downy undersides. Fully-hardy, it likes full sun and well-drained sandy soil.

C. ladanifer

LADANUM BUSH

This open, upright evergreen bears striking, large, white flowers in summer, bearing triangular, red markings at the base of each petal. The narrow leaves are dark green and sticky. Frost-hardy, it likes full sun and well-drained soil. It grows to a height and spread of 1 m (about 3 ft). The leaves are the source of the fragrant, medicinal resin ladanum; not to be confused with laudanum, a form of opium.

C. salviifolius

This is a bushy, dense, evergreen bearing white flowers in late spring and early summer. Slightly smaller than *C. ladanifer*, its flowers have yellow blotches at the centre. It also prefers the same conditions.

CLERODENDRUM

These picturesque flowering evergreen or deciduous shrubs are found mostly in Africa, South-East Asia and Australia. They vary tremendously in habit, from upright tree to climbing varieties. *C. bungei*, for instance, is grown for its large, heart-shaped, coarsely serrated leaves and its rounded clusters of small, fragrant, rose-red flowers. Thriving in humus-rich, well-drained soil, they all do best in full sun, with partial shade in summer. Water all year round, especially in summer. Stems will require support. Crowded growth should be thinned out in spring. Propagate from semi-hardwood cuttings in autumn/fall. Whitefly, mealy bug and red spider mite may present problems.

C. thomsoniae

BLEEDING HEART

This woody-stemmed, climbing shrub from western tropical Africa bears clusters of crimson flowers with white, bell-shaped calyces in summer. Leaves are a deep green oval shape. It reaches 3 m (about 9 ft) tall and prefers partial shade and well-drained soil. It requires temperatures above 16°C (about 61°F).

C. trichotomum

This deciduous, upright, tree-like shrub grows to a height and spread of 3 m (about 9 ft). From late summer to mid-autumn/fall it bears clusters of fragrant, tubular white flowers with red calyces. These are followed by blue berries.

C. ugandense

BLUE BUTTERFLY BUSH

This is an open, evergreen shrub, grown for its delicate flowers in two shades of blue with long, arching stamens. It grows to a height of 3 m (about 9 ft) and spread of 2 m (about 6 ft). It has serrated, oval leaves and does best in partial shade and well-drained soil. Does badly below 5°C (about 40°F). Prune after flowering to keep it compact.

CLETHRA
alnifolia

SWEET PEPPER-BUSH

This bushy, deciduous, rounded shrub, native to eastern North America, has oval, serrated leaves and bears a profusion of dainty, spicily fragrant, bell-shaped flowers in summer to autumn/fall. It prefers a well-drained, moist, peaty, acid soil in semi-shade conditions and year-round watering. Prune back after bloom by removing the oldest canes. Grows to a height and spread of 3 m (about 9 ft). Propagate from spring seed, soft-tip cuttings, or best of all, from the suckers it produces.

CLIANTHUS
puniceus

KAKA BEAK, PARROT'S BILL

Known to have been cultivated by the Maori before European settlement, this weeping evergreen is a native of New Zealand. *C. puniceus* is grown for the drooping clusters of red, claw-like flowers it bears in spring and early summer, and for its green, fern-like foliage. It is best grown outdoors in a sunny area, with well-drained, sandy, alkaline soil. It is half-hardy to hardy. In cooler areas it should be under glass. Feed with animal manure and water regularly. It has a rambling, spreading habit, so prune after flowering to maintain shape. Snails can be a problem. It grows to a height and spread of 4 m (about 12 ft). Propagate from summer cuttings or from scarified seed. In Europe it is sometimes grafted onto *Colutea arborescens*.

COLEONEMA
pulchrum

DIOSMA, BREATH OF HEAVEN

This spreading shrub is a native of South Africa. While not a member of the same family as heath, they do have heath-like foliage and are com-monly planted along banks or alongside lawns. They can also be trained as a low hedge. The soft, bright green leaves give off a sweet-scented fragrance when crushed. Terminal clusters of pink flowers appear from late winter to spring. The shrub does best in a well-drained, neutral to acid soil and needs a sunny to half-shaded spot. Water potted specimens moderately during the growing season, less so at other times. Winter moisture stimulates flowering. Clip after blooming to maintain shape. Grows to a little over 1 m (about 3 ft) in height and spread. Propagate from soft tip cuttings in summer.

COPROSMA

MIRROR PLANT, TAUPATA, LOOKING-GLASS PLANT

These lush, spreading, evergreen shrubs are native to New Zealand. Some species produce decorative red or orange berries, but they are mostly grown for their glossy foliage. All species grow well in warm, humid conditions, in a well-drained soil that is not over-rich. They are salt resistant and do well in a seaside environment. Hardiness varies considerably, some species requiring a minimum temperature of 5°C (about 40°F). Water all plants heavily in summer and moderately at other times. A regular, light pruning helps maintain shape. Propagate from seed in spring or from semi-ripe cuttings in late summer.

C. × kirkii

The foliage of this smaller-leafed hybrid varies; most frequently narrow, oblong, glossy, bright green leaves are set opposite or in clusters. A variety with leaves variegated in grey-green is also available. Squat and densely branched, the half-hardy shrub is useful as a dense ground cover, and for erosion control, especially on coastal sites. Grows to 40 cm (about 16 in) high with a 1–2 m (about 3–6 ft) spread.

C. repens
syn. *C. baueri*
TAUPATA

This evergreen shrub, which at first has a spreading habit and then later becomes erect, grows to a height and spread of 2 m (about 6 ft). It has bright, shiny, oval leaves, often with variegations. The insignificant flowers that appear in late spring are followed (on female plants only) by orange-red, egg-shaped berries from late summer to autumn/fall. It is tolerant to all kinds of soil conditions, including sandy soil. Withstanding salt winds as well as it does, it is no surprise that it flourishes in coastal areas. Prune back to prevent dense growth.

Clianthus puniceus

Clerodendrum ugandense

Coleonema pulchrum

Clethra alnifolia

Coprosma × kirkii

Clerodendrum trichotomum

Coprosma repens

A Field Trip to the Magallanes Region

The story is told that, in the closing years of the eighteenth century, James Lee, a famous English nurseryman, was showing a client around his establishment in Hammersmith. The visitor remarked that he had seen a plant, far more beautiful than anything in Mr Lee's collection, growing in a humble house in Wapping. Lee found the house and a magnificent species of *Fuchsia*. After much negotiation he obtained the plant for the princely sum of six guineas.

The plant was *Fuchsia magellanica* and it has been one of the most important parents of our modern *Fuchsia* hybrids, thanks to its early introduction, its reputation for hardiness, the range of its different forms and colour variants and, of course, its own delicate beauty.

About 95 per cent of the naturally occurring fuchsia species are native to Central and South America, mainly in the moist, cool forests of the Andes. Two of these, including *F. magellanica*, are native to Chile and that country's most southern city, Punta Arenas, is the base for our field trip.

As you move south of the capital, Santiago, the climate changes progressively from dry, almost Mediterranean, to a zone of heavy rainfall around Los Lagos (the Lake Region). The rainfall becomes even heavier, the further south you go, to the point where some of the western Patagonian islands receive an astonishing 4000 mm (about 158 in) annually. *F. magellanica* occurs throughout this region and down to the southern part of the continent.

Punta Arenas, with a population of 90 000, is the capital of the Magallanes region of Chile, and the most southern city of this size in the world. It is a cold and windy place even in the warmer months from October through to March. Despite the cold, it is a good idea to time your visit for early autumn/fall, when the southern, or Antarctic, beech trees (*Nothofagus* species) are turning to red and gold. This also coincides with the later part of the flowering period for *F. magellanica*. As you travel toward the south of the Brunswick Peninsula, you will see many southern beeches covering the hillsides, some of them growing sideways due to the prevailing winds. The area around the Strait of Magellan has not changed greatly since its discovery by Ferdinand Magellan in 1520. Tierra del Fuego (Land of Fire) is but a line on the eastern horizon and looking south, you will see masses of snow-capped mountains above a green plain.

At various spots along the road south you are likely to find a delightful yellow violet (*Viola magellanica*), the occasional Chilean fire tree (*Embothrium coccineum*), which is a relative of grevillea and waratah and has similar red spider flowers, and a primitive flowering, glossy-leaved shrub or small tree, *Drimys winteri*.

Approximately 100 km (about 62 miles) south of Punta Arenas, in the area around Fuerte Bulnes, you will find mixed beech forests of evergreen *Nothofagus betuloides* and some

Torres del Paine National Park, in the Magallanes region.

The flowers of Fuchsia magellanica *contrast well with its foliage.*

Fuchsia magellanica

deciduous *Nothofagus antarctica* and *N. pumilio*. As you glance around, you are likely to see numerous *Fuchsia magellanica* plants covered in edible black berries about 1.5 cm (about ½ in) wide. They are quite common in this open woodland, enjoying the dappled light under the beech trees, where they grow into flaky-barked shrubs 2 m (about 6 ft) high and wide. The leaves are 3–4 cm (about 1½–2 in) long, sitting in an unusual pattern on their stems—mostly in opposite pairs, but also in threes and sometimes fours. The sepals are a striking crimson and the petals themselves are a pinkish purple and form a long tube. Flowers of many unrelated plants in this part of the world are reddish and tube-like, to attract the various species of tiny hummingbird.

Other plants to be seen in this woodland include various *Acaena* species which you are likely to collect in your socks, for this ground cover member of the rose family has burrs for fruit. Some barberry shrubs (*Berberis ilicifolius*) with spiny stems and prickly leaves, are found here, as are more Chilean fire trees. Many flowering stalks of the orchid genus *Chloraea* emerge from the grazing grass that covers most of the areas between the trees.

There are patches of boggy ground where you can find a yellow-flowered *Ranunculus* (buttercup) species, and a little herb with red spikes of fruit, *Gunnera magellanica*. The tree-tops are home to an interesting group of shrubby parasites (*Missodendron* species) that only occur on the southern beech trees of Chile. Some look like old man's beard lichen; others resemble button mushrooms; and others are reminiscent of the unrelated European mistletoe. *F. magellanica* grows in parts of the forests that are well drained, though fairly moist. The soil here is a loamy type with a rich, organic top layer.

Although *F. magellanica* is fairly common throughout the southern region of Chile, nothing can compare with seeing it in the wild and majestic area of the Strait of Magellan—an area steeped in history, extreme in location, and the place where the plant was first recorded and collected over 200 years ago. Not a field trip for the faint-hearted, but one that will impress you with the splendour of the setting.

Fuchsia

The genus *Fuchsia* comprises around 100 species, from the north to the southern tip of South America centred on the Andean mountain chain. Some species are found in eastern South America and there are five species in the Pacific, one in Tahiti and four in New Zealand. *F. excorticata*, from New Zealand, forms a tree to 12 m (about 40 ft) tall with a trunk to 60 cm (about 2 ft) in diameter! Variable in flower shape and colour, *F. magellanica* is possibly the most cold-hardy species and was introduced to the British Isles as early as 1788, and has since become naturalized in some milder, wetter areas.

Fuchsias are known to most gardeners through numerous named hybrids, grown as indoor plants in cold climates or as outdoor shrubs in milder climates, where they are also popular in tubs and hanging baskets. These hybrids derive from South American species such as *Fuchsia magellanica* and *F. coccinea*, with some genes from *F. fulgens* and *F. arborescens*, both from Mexico.

Fuchsia belongs to Onagraceae, the evening primrose family, which has 21 genera worldwide, with about 640 species.

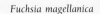

Fuchsia magellanica

Cornus nuttallii

Coronilla glauca

Corokia cotoneaster

Corokia × virgata

Cornus alba

Cordyline banksii

CORDYLINE
banksii

Native to New Zealand, this evergreen reaches a height and spread of 1.5–3 m (about 4–9 ft). In late spring and summer it bears panicles of delightfully fragrant, white flowers, set among long, drooping, dark green leaves. It does best in medium, well-drained soil in a protected, shaded position. Water potted plants moderately during active growth, less at other times. Propagate from stem cuttings in summer, or from seed in spring.

CORNUS

DOGWOOD, REDTWIG, BUNCHBERRY, CORNEL, CLUSTERBERRY

Attractive winter bark followed by a beautiful spring bloom, and then by autumn/fall foliage and fruit bloom make this genus of twiggy, deciduous shrubs a gardener's delight. Native to the cooler regions of the USA and Asia, they are popular in cold to cool-temperate climates. The main attraction is the

bracts which surround the clusters of small flowers. These later turn into fruit, giving rise to the names 'clusterberry' and 'bunchberry'. The various species all do best in sun or semi-shade and need a fertile, well-drained soil. They are fully to half-hardy. Cut back stems to almost ground level annually. Propagate from seed or rooted layers struck in a humid, sand-peat mixture.

C. alba
RED-BARKED DOGWOOD

This deciduous, upright then spreading shrub from northern Europe and Asia has shoots that turn an attractive, deep red in winter before the appearance of the foliage. The normally dark green, oval leaves turn red-orange in autumn/fall. Star-shaped, creamy white flowers appear in late spring and early summer and are followed by round white berries, which are often blue-tinted. Propagate from softwood cuttings in summer or hardwood cuttings in autumn/fall and winter. Grows to a height and spread of 3 m (about 9 ft) and is

fully hardy. Varieties with variegated leaves or yellow stems are available.

C. nuttallii
MOUNTAIN DOGWOOD, PACIFIC DOGWOOD

This spectacular, conical deciduous tree grows to a maximum height and spread of 5 m (about 12 ft). Its tiny, white flowers, surrounded by bracts, appear in spring followed by red to orange berries. The oval, green leaves turn red and gold in autumn/fall. *C. nuttallii* is fully hardy.

COROKIA

These evergreen shrubs are suitable for mild coastal areas where they have a good tolerance to wind and salt. They require full sun and a fertile, well-drained soil. Propagate from softwood cuttings in summer.

C. cotoneaster
WIRE NETTING BUSH

This sparse and hardy, evergreen bush is a native of New Zealand. Difficult to control, it grows zigzag

fashion in all directions. It has small, round, dark green leaves and fragrant, yellow flowers that appear in spring and summer. *C. cotoneaster* is frost- to half-hardy, but in very cold areas it will need some protection from the wind. It grows to a height and spread of 3 m (about 9 ft). Shear regularly after flowering to promote dense growth.

C. × virgata

This evergreen shrub, native to New Zealand, bears pretty yellow, star-shaped flowers in spring followed by bright orange, egg-shaped berries. The glossy green leaves have a downy undersurface. Frost-hardy, it adapts to most soils and conditions, but does best in full sun and a fertile, well-drained soil. It grows to a height and spread of 3 m (about 9 ft). Cultivars include: 'Red Wonder', with bright red berries, 'Yellow Wonder', with golden fruits, and 'Bronze Lady', so-called for its leaf colour in maturity.

CORONILLA
glauca

CROWN VETCH

This dense shrub is a native of the Mediterranean region. If grown in a sunny spot in a well-drained soil, it will thrive and bear yellow, fragrant, pea-like flowers from mid-spring to early summer. The leaves are a pleasant, blue-grey colour, each with 5 or 7 leaflets. Frost-hardy, it grows to a height and spread a little over 1.5 m (about 4½ ft). Use seed, summer cuttings, layers or divisions to propagate this delightful and rewarding, evergreen shrub.

CORREA

AUSTRALIAN FUCHSIA

The dense, evergreen Australian natives in this genus range from ground covers to 1.5 m (about 4½ ft) tall shrubs. They bloom in late winter if conditions are right. Their long, bell-shaped flowers are rich in honey. They prefer a semi-shaded spot, and a fertile, moist but well-drained soil. More mature plants will tolerate a drier soil. When planting out, a slightly alkaline soil is recommended. Water potted specimens moderately when in flower, less at other times. Prune to keep them well-shaped and compact. Although tender to frost, they are easy to grow. Propagate from seed in spring or semi-ripe cuttings in summer. *Correa* is named for the eighteenth-century Portuguese botanist, Jose Correa de Serra.

C. alba

WHITE CORREA

This is a low, compact, rounded shrub with rounded, downy leaves 4 cm (about 1½ in) long. White (sometimes pink), bell-shaped flowers, opening to star-shaped blooms, appear in winter. It grows to a height of 1.5 m (about 4½ ft) and a spread of 1 m (about 3 ft). As it tolerates salt spray, it does well in coastal gardens, and makes an excellent sand binder.

C. 'Dusky Bells'

This spreading, dense, evergreen shrub takes its name from the delightful dusky pink, bell-shaped flowers that appear from autumn/fall to spring. It grows to 60 cm high (about 2 ft) with a spread of 1 m (about 3 ft) and does best in shady conditions. It has bright green, oval leaves.

C. pulchella

Ideal for foreground planting, this evergreen species forms an attractive leafy bush up to 1 m (about 3 ft) in height with a spread of 1.5 m (about 4½ ft). It has slender stems and dark green oval leaves that are slightly aromatic when bruised. Small, pendent, bell-shaped, salmon-scarlet, orange-vermilion or coral-red flowers are borne from autumn to early spring. It prefers higher-grade, well-drained acid soils and full sun or partial shade. Frost-hardy.

CORYLOPSIS

WINTER HAZEL

Native to China and Japan, these hardy deciduous shrubs are grown for their fragrant catkins of yellow flowers, which are produced before the hazel-like leaves. The leaves often colour well in autumn/fall. They require a loamy acid soil containing organic matter and semi-

shady, sheltered conditions. Propagate from seed in autumn/fall or from softwood cuttings in summer; layer low branches if necessary. The flowers may be damaged by frost even though the species is fully hardy. Prune only to remove dead wood.

C. pauciflora

Fragrant, bell-shaped flowers, smelling of cowslips, are borne on this dense shrub from early to mid-spring. It has a bushy habit, reaching a height and spread of 2 m (about 6 ft). Densely branched, it has slender, twiggy growths and bright green leaves that are bronze when young. Fully hardy, but it requires shelter from cold winds.

C. spicata

WINTER HAZEL

Native to Japan, this deciduous, many-stemmed shrub is popular in Britain, Australia and New Zealand. It grows slowly to a height of 2 m (about 6 ft) and a spread of 3 m (about 9 ft). The leaves of this spreading shrub are dull, bristle-toothed and pale green. In late winter, small, fragrant, lemon-green, bell-shaped flowers appear in drooping racemes. It prefers a neutral to mildly acid soil rich in leafmould, and semi-shady conditions. Propagate from softwood cuttings in summer or from seed in autumn/fall. Purple-leaved clones are available.

CORYNABUTILON

vitifolium

syn. *Abutilon vitifolium*

BLUE ABUTILON

This tall, open, evergreen shrub, native to Chile, is prized for the masses of delicate, purplish blue flowers that bloom in spring. The oval, serrated leaves resemble maple foliage. One of only three species in the genus, the shrub is closely related to *Abutilon* and some botanists prefer to include it in that genus. *C. vitifolium* does best in full sun or partial shade with fertile, well-drained soil. Tip prune new growth to encourage bushiness. Water well during growth, less at other times. Tie wayward-growing species to a support if necessary. The shrub grows to a height of 4 m (about 12 ft) with a spread of 3 m (about 9 ft). Propagate from semi-hardwood cuttings in summer.

COTINUS

coggygria

syn. *Rhus cotinus*

VENETIAN SUMACH, SMOKE TREE, WIG TREE

This tall-growing, deciduous shrub, found in southern Europe and in Asia, is grown chiefly for its splendid autumn/fall colour and unusual flowers. Its rounded leaves, nor-

mally oval and light green, turn a glorious yellow-red in autumn/fall, more so in colder areas. Its fruits are unimpressive, as are its flowers—masses of tiny flower stalks forming pale grey clusters from late summer. The tiny stems left after the flowers fall give the appearance of puffs of smoke—hence the name. Smoke tree does best in fertile soil that is

not too rich. It needs full sun or semi-shade and is fully hardy. It grows to a height and spread of 5 m (about 15 ft). Prune back to growth buds by two thirds in winter. Propagate from greenwood or softwood cuttings in summer, or from seed in autumn/fall. There are purple-leaved forms available, however they aren't so bright in full colour.

Correa pulchella

Correa alba

Cotinus coggygria

Corylopsis spicata

Correa 'Dusky Bells'

Corynabutilon vitifolium

Cotoneaster lacteus

Cotoneaster microphyllus

Crinodendron hookerianum

Cotoneaster multiflorus

Cotoneaster apiculatus

Cotoneaster horizontalis

COTONEASTER

COTONEASTER, ROCKSPRAY

This genus of mostly evergreen bushes comes from Europe, North Africa and northern Asia. They are from the same family (Rosaceae) as the quince; the Greek *kotoneon* and *aster* together mean 'like a quince', and the genus name is pronounced 'kotonee-aster', not 'cotton-easter'. Cotoneasters are perhaps the most popular of berry-bearing shrubs anywhere—having the added attraction of tolerating almost any kind of soil condition (except waterlogged soil). They do thrive a little better, however, when the soil is dry and alkaline. They are also very drought resistant, and are fully frost-hardy. They are eminently suitable for use as an arching, specimen shrub, but may be used for hedging, or for ground cover. Evergreen species do well in either sun or semi-shade, but deciduous varieties and cultivars prefer full sun. Propagate from cuttings in summer or seed in autumn/fall.

C. apiculatus

CRANBERRY COTONEASTER

Native to the foothills of the western Himalayas, this low shrub has a trailing habit when young but on maturity reaches a height of 1 m (about 3 ft) with a slightly broader spread. The leaves are tiny, roundish and a glossy dark green in colour. Pink flowers are borne in spring, followed by glossy scarlet fruit in autumn/fall that lasts well into winter. Mostly evergreen in warm climates, this species can be deciduous in cooler conditions.

C. dammeri

This trailing, evergreen shrub grows to a height of 30 cm (12 in) with a spread of 1 m (about 3 ft). In summer it bears striking, white flowers with purple anthers, followed in autumn/fall by red fruits. Frost-hardy, it is vulnerable at times to fireblight. The leaves are glossy, dark green and oval.

C. horizontalis

WALL SPRAY

This low-growing, deciduous bush from China has horizontal, herringbone branches which spread along the ground—hence the name. As the plant matures, these branches grow in height. From late spring to early summer, it bears attractive pinkish white flowers, which are followed by bright red berries. The glossy, green leaves tend to redden in late autumn/fall. *C. horizontalis* is sturdy and makes an excellent addition to a rock garden. Fully hardy, it grows to a height of 50 cm (about 20 in) and a spread of 1.5 m (about 4^1/$_2$ ft).

C. lacteus

This large evergreen shrub is native to western China. It has an arching habit and can be trained by pruning to tree-like form or it can be used successfully for hedging. Cup-shaped white flowers with purple anthers are borne in spring, followed by abundant, long-lasting, bright red fruit. When fruiting, the branches of the tree are pendulous with the weight of the berries. It reaches a height of 3–4 m (about 9–12 ft), with a spread of around 4 m (about 12 ft). Fully hardy.

Cotoneaster dammeri

C. microphyllus

A small evergreen native to the Himalayas and south-western China with an open, irregular, spiky habit, this shrub grows to 1 m (about 3 ft) in height with a spread of 2 m (about 6 ft). Pruning will give it a more compact growth habit. It has small, oval, dark green leaves and white flowers with purplish anthers that appear in late spring, followed by spherical, bright red fruit which often crowd the branches. Fully hardy, it prefers light to medium, well-drained soils in an open, sunny position and is useful for covering bare banks and walls.

C. multiflorus

syn. *C. reflexus*

Native from Caucasus to China, this deciduous shrub reaches a height of 4 m (about 12 ft). It has arching, pendulous branches and oval to rounded leaves. White flowers, in clusters of 3 to 12, are freely borne from late spring to early summer; these are followed by red, berry-like fruit. This species prefers a position in full sun.

Cotoneaster salicifolius

C. salicifolius

WILLOW-LEAVED COTONEASTER

The long, slender, arching branches of this vigorous evergreen make it a graceful addition to any garden. Small, white flowers are borne in winter and the clusters of bright red berries appearing in autumn/fall are a delight. The leaves are narrow, lance-shaped and dark green. Fully hardy, it grows to a height and spread of 5 m (about 15 ft).

CRINODENDRON

hookerianum

syn. *Tricuspidaria lanceolata*
LANTERN TREE

This stiff-branched, evergreen native of Chile generally grows as a bush with a rounded top. In spring, red, lantern-like flowers appear, hanging from the leaf axils. Its leaves are coarse-toothed and leathery. It prefers moist, well-drained, slightly acid soil and partial shade. Frost-hardy, it grows to a height and spread of 3 m (about 9 ft). Propagate from softwood cuttings in summer or seed in autumn/fall.

CUPHEA
ignea
syn. *C. platycentra*
CIGAR FLOWER, PUA KIKA

The most common of the cupheas, this native of Central America is popular in temperate to subtropical areas. A petite sub-shrub with bright green leaves, it can grow untidily however, so remove flowered shoots after bloom to maintain a compact habit. Tubular orange-red flowers appear in autumn/fall, each with a white ring at the mouth. *C. ignea* prefers fertile, well-drained soil and full sun conditions. Water freely in full growth, not too much at other times. Half-hardy to frost-tender, it does poorly in cold conditions—it will die back to the ground in frost—but when conditions are suitable, it will grow to a height and spread of 75 cm (about 30 in).

CYTISUS
BROOM, ATLAS BROOM

Among the brightest and gaudiest of the Fabaceae family, this genus of flowering, arching deciduous or evergreen shrubs is native to the Mediterranean area and the islands of the Atlantic. The abundant, pea-like flowers range in colour from shades of pink, red, cream and pure yellow to tan. They prefer full sun and well-drained soil that is not too rich. They do not transplant well, so set in the final position early on. Brooms are ideal at the back of mixed borders or as rock plants. The species are best propagated from semi-ripe cuttings in summer or from seed in autumn/fall.

C. × praecox
WARMINSTER BROOM

This semi-weeping, deciduous shrub bears pale yellow, pea-like flowers in spring. These have a characteristically acrid smell. The tiny, silky leaves are grey-green. Fully hardy, *C. × praecox* prefers sunny conditions and a well-drained soil. It grows to a height and spread of 1.5 m (about 4½ ft).

C. scoparius
SCOTCH BROOM

This deciduous, arching shrub is a native of Europe. Valued for its profusion of bright yellow flowers that appear in spring and early summer, it is fully frost-hardy. It prefers a well-drained soil and full sun. *C. scoparius* grows to a height and spread of 1.5 m (about 4½ ft). In some countries, such as New Zealand, it has become a weed.

DABOECIA
cantabrica
IRISH HEATH

This straggling, evergreen shrub, a native of Ireland, grows to a height and spread of 50 cm (about 20 in). It prefers a peaty, well-drained but moist, slightly acid soil. A slow-growing bush, it flowers throughout the year except in winter, bearing pinkish purple, urn-shaped flowers. The leaves are oval to lance-shaped, dark green above, silver-grey below. It prefers full sun in cooler areas and semi-shade elsewhere. Named after Ireland's St Dabeoc, *D. cantabrica* is frost-hardy—though the top may be damaged by cold winds and frost. Prune to produce fresh growth from the base. It makes a perfect choice for lining sandstone paths or in rockeries. Propagate from semi-hardwood cuttings kept under glass.

DAHLIA
excelsa
TREE DAHLIA

This woody, tuberous, bushy perennial is grown for its magnificent, autumn/fall bloom of single, large, pink, slender flowers with yellow centres, that grow to 10 cm (about 4 in) across. They are eminently suitable for cutting. *D. excelsa* has thick, bamboo-like stems and grows to a height of 4–5 m (about 12–15 ft). Half-hardy, it needs well-drained soil and a sunny position. Propagate in spring from seeds, basal shoot cuttings or by division of tubers. Cut the plants back hard in autumn/fall. *D. imperialis* is very similar but has white flowers.

Daboecia cantabrica

Cytisus scoparius 'Burkwoodii'

Cytisus × *praecox*

Dahlia excelsa

Cuphea ignea

DAPHNE

Found everywhere except the tropics, these evergreen, semi-evergreen or deciduous shrubs are grown for their delightfully fragrant, tubular flowers that appear in winter and spring. They thrive in semi-shady conditions and prefer a slightly acid, fertile, peaty soil that is well-drained but not too dry. Water lightly and use a small amount of complete fertilizer after flowering. Excessive watering will cause collar rot. Transplanting is not recommended, so choose the site carefully. It is best to grow daphnes in a raised spot, with the root junction above soil level. Between summer waterings allow the soil to dry out. The genus is named after the nymph in Greek mythology, who, rather than face the unwanted affections of the pursuing sun god Apollo, turned into a flowering shrub.

Daphne odora

Desfontainea spinosa

Deutzia 'Rosalin'

Daphne tangutica

Daphne × burkwoodii

Daphne cneorum

D. × burkwoodii

The dense clusters of fragrant, white and pink flowers of this upright, semi-evergreen shrub appear in late spring, and sometimes for a second time in autumn/fall. Its leaves are pale to mid-green and lance-shaped. Fully hardy, it prefers a sunny spot with well-drained soil. It grows to a height and spread of 1.5m (about 4½ ft).

D. cneorum

Native to the sub-alpine areas of central Europe, this pretty species is one of the best rock garden varieties. An evergreen with a bun-shaped habit, it grows to 22 cm (about 9 in) in height with a spread of 2 m (about 6 ft). Trailing branches are clothed with deep green, narrowly oblong leaves, while sweetly perfumed, deep rose-pink flowers are borne in dense clusters in late spring. The plant often has a repeat flowering in autumn. Fully hardy, it does best in humus-rich soil.

D. genkwa

A beautiful plant for inclusion in a flower or shrub border or among daffodils this deciduous species, native to western China, has an upright, open habit and slender branches. It reaches a height and spread of 1.5 m (about 4 ½ ft). The oval leaves are reddish green when young, turning to dark green. Faintly perfumed lavender-blue flowers appear in clusters along the naked branches in mid- to late spring. It prefers soils of limestone origin and ranges from fully hardy to frost-hardy, depending on the summer heat.

D. odora

The most popular of the genus, this moderately frost-hardy, evergreen, bushy shrub from China grows to a height and spread of 1.5 m (about 4½ ft). It bears fragrant, white to purplish pink flowers from mid-winter to early spring and has glossy, dark green, oval leaves. As a cut flower, it lasts well indoors. The form with yellow-margined leaves is said to be more tolerant of cold.

D. tangutica

Native to western China, this evergreen bears clusters of perfumed, white-stained, rosy-purple flowers in mid- to late spring. It has dark leathery leaves and stout shoots. Fully hardy, it has a bushy habit, growing to a height and spread of around 1 m (about 3 ft).

DESFONTAINEA

spinosa

This compact, evergreen native of the Andes Mountains superficially resembles a holly with its spiny, glossy, dark green leaves—hence the name. But the delightful, showy, orange-scarlet tubular flowers appearing in mid-summer put paid to the illusion. Frost- to half-hardy, *D. spinosa* prefers moist, peaty, preferably acid soil. In dry conditions it needs some shade and in cold areas does better in shelter. Even in these optimal conditions it grows slowly, to a height and spread of 1.5 m (about 4½ ft). Propagate from semi-ripe cuttings in summer.

DEUTZIA

These deciduous, arching bushes appear fairly nondescript until late spring or early summer, when a profusion of flowers appears— white, pink or bicoloured depending on the species. Related to *Philadelphus*, which it resembles, the genus *Deutzia* is a native of China, Japan and the Himalayas. The shrubs prefer fertile, moist but well-drained soil and do best in full sun, although they require semi-shade in warmer areas. Give fertilizer in early spring to encourage a full flower yield. Prune heavily to encourage bloom—remove about half the old wood. Propagate from softwood cuttings in summer.

D. 'Rosalin'

This deciduous hybrid shrub of uncertain parentage produces clus-

Daphne genkwa

Deutzia × rosea

ters of pink flowers from late spring through to summer. It has a rounded, bushy habit, reaching a height of 2 m (about 6 ft) with a spread of around 1.5 m (about 4½ ft). It does particularly well in pots and will flower early if brought into a greenhouse in mid-winter.

D. × rosea

This compact, bushy, arching shrub produces massed clusters of beautiful, bell-shaped, pale pink flowers in spring and early summer. Its leaves are dark green, oval and deciduous and it grows to a height and spread of 75 cm (about 2½ ft). *D. x rosea* is fully hardy, and prefers a moist soil and partial shade.

D. scabra

This upright, deciduous shrub bears dense clusters of pink-tinged white blooms in spring. Its leaves are dark green and oval and it grows to a height of 3 m (about 9 ft) with a spread of 1.5 m (about 4½ ft). Fully hardy, it prefers a moist soil and partial shade. Propagate from cuttings struck under glass.

DIPELTA
floribunda

This tall, stiff, open shrub is grown for its spring appearance of fragrant, pale pink flowers, with throats flushed in yellow, and for its pale brown, peeling bark. The green, pointed leaves are deciduous. A native of China, it is not often found in Western gardens. Fully hardy, it thrives in sun or semi-shade and requires fertile, well-drained soil to do really well. A member of the same family (Caprifoliaceae) as honeysuckle, it grows to a height and spread of 4 m (about 12 ft). Prune old shoots after flowering and propagate from softwood cuttings in summer.

DODONAEA
viscosa

STICKY HOP-BUSH

This dense, fast-growing, short-lived bush is grown for the showy clusters of green fruits in summer, that follow its insignificant bloom. The sticky, glossy, pale green leaves are deciduous. Native to Australia and New Zealand, it does well in any warm climate. *D. viscosa* grows to a height of 3 m (about 9 ft) or more and a spread of 1.5 m (about 4½ ft), with reddish brown, peeling bark and thick branches. It prefers a well-drained soil, and sun or partial shade. To keep its shape, cut back in summer after flowering. Water specimens in containers frequently when in full growth, less at other times. Propagate from seed in spring or semi-ripe cuttings in summer; it will strike in any location.

DREJERELLA
guttata

syn. *Beloperone guttata, Justicia brandegeana*
SHRIMP PLANT

The salmon to rose-pink, or pale yellow bracts surrounding the white flowers of this attractive, evergreen shrub, resemble a shrimp—hence its name. Native to tropical Mexico, it grows best in fertile, well-drained soil, and colours best under partial shade. It flowers mainly in summer. It can survive temperatures as low as minus 4°C (about 25°F) by behaving like a perennial when the tops are frozen back. A weak, sprawling plant, it needs regular pruning to maintain its shape and encourage new, flowering wood. Water potted plants freely when in full growth, less at other times. It grows to a height of 1 m (about 3 ft) and a spread of 60 cm (about 2 ft). Propagate from tip or semi-hardwood cuttings.

DRYANDRA

Native to Western Australia, these bushy shrubs are grown for the small, yellow or orange flowers in rounded domes, that grow in late winter to spring. Their elongated, saw-toothed leaves are evergreen. They prefer full light or partial shade, and do best in a well-drained, light, sandy soil without a large amount of nitrates or phosphates. They can withstand about minus 3°C (about 27°F). They grow to a height and spread of 2 m (about 6 ft). Water moderately. Propagate from seed in spring, and remember that these shrubs are susceptible to root rot and can be difficult to establish in some areas. There are several species.

DURANTA
repens

syn. *D. plumieri*

GOLDEN DEWDROP, PIGEONBERRY, BRAZILIAN SKYFLOWER

Found naturally in the area stretching from Florida, USA, to Brazil, this handsome, weeping shrub makes an ideal windbreak or hedge in warmer climates. It bears delightful but tiny, violet-blue flowers in summer, which are followed by a shower of yellow berries. (These are poisonous, so keep children away.) The dark green, oval leaves are deciduous. Frost-tender, *D. repens* grows quickly to a height of 3 m (about 9 ft) with a spread of 2 m (about 6 ft). It does best in a well-drained soil and in full light or partial shade. Prune for shape (the plants can be clipped as a hedge) and water potted plants when growing. Propagate from seed in spring or from semi-ripe cuttings in summer. Whitefly can cause problems.

Drejerella guttata

Dryandra nobilis

Dipelta floribunda

Duranta repens

Deutzia scabra

Dodonaea viscosa

Elaeagnus pungens

Enkianthus campanulatus

Edgeworthia papyrifera

Elaeagnus pungens 'Maculata'

Epacris impressa

Eremophila glabra

EDGEWORTHIA

papyrifera
syn. *E. chrysantha*
PAPERBUSH, YELLOW DAPHNE

This open, rounded shrub is native to eastern Asia. Once used in Japan for paper-making, it has tough, fibrous branches, so flexible they can be knotted without breaking. In late winter and early spring, it bears sweet-smelling heads of rounded, tubular, yellow flowers. The oval, dark green leaves are deciduous. It is frost-hardy, except for the flowerheads. It likes moist, well-drained, leafy soil and full sun or partial shade. The position should be chosen carefully as it does not transplant well. It grows to a height and spread of 1.5 m (about 4¹/₂ ft). Propagate from semi-ripe cuttings in summer or seed in autumn/fall.

ELAEAGNUS

WILD OLIVE, OLEASTER, SILVERBERRY

These dense, spreading, mainly evergreen shrubs are favourites for hedging and as a backdrop. Found all over the northern hemisphere, they grow well in poor soil and are frost-hardy. Deciduous species prefer full sun; evergreens thrive in sun or partial shade. Hedges are best trimmed in late summer. Propagate from seed in autumn/fall or semi-ripe cuttings in summer.

E. pungens
syn. *E. japonica*

This is the most common of the genus. A frost-hardy, evergreen bush with long, prickly, horizontal branches, it is excellent for hedges, growing to a height of 3 m (about 9 ft) and a spread of 5 m (about 15 ft). In autumn/fall it bears fragrant, tiny, bell-shaped, cream flowers. The glossy, oval leaves—dark green above, silvery with brown spots beneath—are deciduous.

E. pungens 'Maculata'

This bushy, slightly thorny shrub grows to a height and spread of 4 m (about 12 ft). Its glossy, dark green leaves, which feature a large, central, yellow patch, are evergreen. Mid- to late autumn/fall sees the appearance of sweet-smelling, bowl-shaped, creamy white flowers. Half-hardy, it likes a well-drained soil and full sun.

ENKIANTHUS

campanulatus
CHINESE BELLFLOWER

Related to azaleas and heaths, these cool-climate, tree-like shrubs are originally from China and Japan where the flowers are gathered in large numbers to celebrate New Year. In spring the open, spreading habit is gaily adorned with small, bell-shaped, red-veined, creamy flowers. The shrub is deciduous; tufts of dull green leaves turn bright red in autumn/fall. Fully to frost-hardy, *E. campanulatus* does well in sun or partial shade in a moist, acid, peaty soil. Like all the species of *Enkianthus*, it does not tolerate air pollution well and does best in a country garden. Propagate from semi-ripe cuttings in summer or seeds in autumn/fall.

EPACRIS

impressa
VICTORIAN HEATH

This erect, leafless, evergreen, heath-like shrub is perfect for rock gardens as it likes fast drainage, preferring a sandy soil with full sun or partial shade. Native to south-eastern Australia and Tasmania, *E. impressa* bears pendent, tubular, white, pink or red flowers in late autumn/fall to spring. Evergreen, with short, red-tipped leaves, it grows to a height and spread of 1 m (about 3 ft). It does well in pots, provided it is pruned back in spring after flowering, and the soil is sandy. Use liquid manure rather than chemical fertilizer. Propagate from young cuttings dipped in rooting hormone, keeping them constantly moist. It is also easily grown from seed (when this is commercially available).

EREMOPHILA

EMU-BUSH, POVERTY BUSH

Native to the outback areas of Australia, this genus is appropriately named 'lovers of lonely places'. Evergreen, bun-shaped shrubs, they do best in a sunny, open position and require well-drained, slightly alkaline soil. Frost-hardy, they dislike moist conditions and will thrive when conditions are very dry—they can go for years without water. Throughout most of the year they bear tubular flowers of varying colour. Propagate from semi-ripe tip cuttings in autumn/fall. Grow on for at least a year before planting out.

E. glabra
EMU-BUSH

This tenacious shrub bears red, yellow or green flowers mostly during spring. Frost-hardy, it grows to a height of 1.5 m (about 4¹/₂ ft) and a spread of 1–3 m (about 3–9 ft). Its lance-shaped, silvery grey leaves are evergreen. It thrives in arid conditions.

E. maculata
SPOTTED EMU-BUSH

From winter to spring, this rounded shrub produces tubular, yellow, pink, white or red flowers.

Eremophila maculata

Erica × darleyensis

Erica carnea

Erica cinerea

Erica erigena 'W.T. Racklift'

Evergreen, with oval or linear, grey-green leaves with spotted throats, it grows to a height and spread of 2 m (about 6 ft). Half-hardy, it prefers dry, sunny conditions.

ERICA

HEATH, HEATHER

This genus of evergreen shrubs is native to southern Africa, parts of northern Africa and much of western Europe. Related to azaleas and rhododendrons, it boasts some of the most popular flowering plants, partly because of the long flowering season. They are very particular, however, requiring an acid soil that is porous and left constantly moist with unpolluted rainwater—any hint of lime in the soil and they will do badly. Avoid animal manure. They bear tubular, waxy flowers of varying lengths, and small linear leaves grouped around a stem. Propagate from seed—kept moist and sheltered—or from tip cuttings taken in autumn/fall or early winter. *E. arborea* from eastern Europe,

rarely grown in gardens, supplies the 'briar' (bruyère) from which tobacco pipes are made.

E. carnea
syn. *E. herbacea*

This evergreen, spreading shrub makes good ground cover. From early winter to late spring, it bears bell-shaped to tubular flowers in shades of red and pink (sometimes white). Its mid- to dark green leaves are arranged in whorls. It will withstand some lime in the soil and shady conditions. Grows to a height of 30 cm (about 12 in) and spread of 50 cm (about 20 in) or more.

E. cinerea
BELL HEATHER

From early summer through to early autumn/fall, this compact native of Europe bears bell-shaped flowers in shades of pink, white and dark red. It has mid- to deep green, needle-like, evergreen leaves. It does best in a dry, warm position with an acid soil. Numerous attractive cultivars bear blooms of varying hue.

E. × darleyensis
DARLEY HEATH

Named after Darley Dale, the location of a large English nursery, this low-growing evergreen hybrid reaches a height of 45 cm (about 18 in) and a spread of 1 m (about 3 ft) or more. It has a loose, open habit that is improved by regular pruning. The needle-like leaves are pink, cream or red in new spring growth and are dark glossy green in maturity. Pale rose pink, white or purple flowers with deep crimson anthers

are borne from early winter to late spring. It grows well in limy soils and is one of the hardiest and most adaptable of the heaths.

E. erigena 'W.T. Racklift'
IRISH OR MEDITERRANEAN HEATHER

An evergreen, upright shrub reaching a height of 60 cm (about 24 in), this cultivar has dense, dark green foliage and bears clusters of urn-shaped creamy white flowers from late winter to late spring. It is lime-tolerant and frost-hardy.

Eriogonum umbellatum

Erica vagans

E. mammosa
RED SIGNAL HEATH

A loose open shrub growing to 1 m (about 3 ft) or more, this evergreen native to the Cape of Good Hope, South Africa, needs regular pruning to maintain a dense shape and encourage flowering. Long, dark green foliage contrasts with pale green twigs, while dense clusters of tubular reddish purple flowers are borne in summer and autumn. The cultivar 'Coccinea' is a bright scarlet. Half-hardy.

E. mediterranea

As the name suggests, this attractive species is native to Mediterranean countries. An upright evergreen, it grows to 2.5 m (about 7 ft) high with a spread up to 2 m (about 6 ft). In winter and early spring it bears pinkish mauve, bell-shaped flowers. The mid-green leaves are shaped like a needle. Frost may damage the top of the plant, but it will recover from the base; generally it is frost-hardy. Many attractive, fragrant cultivars exist; most not more than 80 cm (about 32 in) in height or width.

E. tetralix
CROSS-LEAVED HEATH, BOG HEATHER

Native to the British Isles and western Europe, this evergreen has an erect habit that spreads on maturity. Low growing, it reaches a height of 30 cm (about 12 in) and a spread of 1 m (about 3 ft) in old age. Bell-shaped, pale pink flowers are borne from summer to early autumn. Its small, needle-like, grey-green leaves

are arranged in fours, in the shape of a cross, up the stem. Fully hardy, it prefers moist, non-limy soil.

E. vagans
CORNISH HEATH

This fully hardy species is the most vigorous of the native heaths and will tolerate limy soils. A dense twiggy evergreen with a broad, flat-topped crown, it reaches a height and spread of 75 cm (about 30 in). The leaves are mid-green and needle-like, while bell-shaped, pale purple, white or pink flowers are borne in spike-like racemes from mid-summer to late autumn. Prune to maintain shape and increase flowering.

ERIOGONUM
umbellatum

This evergreen is grown for its attractive heads of tiny bright yellow flowers, borne in summer and turning copper with time. It is a useful rock plant, growing to a height of 8–30 cm (about 3–12 in) and a spread of 15–30 cm (about 6–12 in). It has a prostrate to upright form and the dense green leaves have white, downy undersides. In cooler, wetter areas some shelter is required. Propagate from semi-ripe cuttings in summer or from seed in spring or autumn. Perennial root clumps can be divided in spring. Remove spent flowerheads to prolong flowering.

ESCALLONIA

This genus of ornamental, mostly evergreen shrubs are native to the temperate parts of South America, mainly the Andes region; they are grown for their showy bell-shaped flowers and glossy green foliage. Fast growing, they are suitable for smaller gardens as specimen plants at the back of an herbaceous border; they are also good for making dense, informal hedges. Being wind resistant, they are used widely as windbreaks in mild coastal areas. Frost-hardy, but in cooler areas the more tender species should be sheltered by growing against a south- or west-facing wall. Propagate from cuttings taken in late summer. They

Erica mediterranea

Erica tetralix

Erica mammosa

flourish in moderately fertile, well-drained soil and a sunny situation. Regular, light pruning will improve the flowers and foliage.

E. 'Apple Blossom'

Wind-resistant and ideal for hedging in coastal gardens, this attractive, bushy, dense evergreen bears apple-blossom pink flowers in early to mid-summer. It has dark green, glossy leaves. Half-hardy, and preferring well-drained soil and full sun, it grows to a height and spread of 2 m (about 6 ft). After flowering, trim the hedges and wall-trained plants. Propagate from softwood cuttings in summer.

E. × exoniensis

A large, vigorous hybrid reaching a height of 4–5 m (about 12–15 ft), this plant has highly lustrous deep green leaves with paler undersides, and produces 10 cm (about 4 in) tall panicles of blush-pink or white flowers in mid-spring to late autumn/fall.

E. rubra

A Chilean native, this large evergreen reaches a height and spread of 3 m (about 9 ft) and sometimes more in sheltered situations. It is best kept pruned to encourage dense foliage. The glossy leaves are slightly aromatic, while tubular pink to crimson flowers are borne from summer to early autumn.

EUONYMUS

SPINDLE BUSH

These evergreen or deciduous shrubs, with the occasional tree and climber, are prized for their foliage, their odd, spindle-shaped seed pods, and the breathtaking autumn/fall colour of deciduous species. Found world-wide, the deciduous shrubs are grown in cool, temperate climates, while the evergreens are more suited to warmer conditions. Fully to frost-hardy, all need sun or semi-shade and well-drained soil. Propagate from semi-ripe cuttings in summer or seed in autumn/fall.

E. alatus

JAPANESE SPINDLE TREE

This slow-growing deciduous shrub from China and Japan is grown mainly for its splendid autumn/fall colour and display of purple fruits with scarlet seeds. It is of stiff and open habit to about 2.5 m (about 7½ ft) high and 2 m (about 6 ft) wide, with pointed, oval leaves which turn brilliant crimson in autumn/fall. The tiny greenish spring flowers are insignificant. It is fully hardy.

E. europaeus

SPINDLE TREE

A 2–3 m (about 6–9 ft) tall deciduous shrub from Europe, the spindle tree takes its name from the use of its hard, perfectly straight branches in weaving in the days before the mechanical loom. Fully hardy, it is grown in gardens for its lavish display of fruits, whose carmine red calyces split to reveal orange seeds. The tiny greenish spring flowers are insignificant and although the slender pointed leaves colour in autumn/fall, they are of less account than the fruit.

Euonymus alatus

Escallonia rubra

Escallonia 'Apple Blossom'

Euonymus europaeus

Escallonia × exoniensis

Euphorbia pulcherrima

Eupatorium megalophyllum

Euonymus j. 'Aureomarginatus'

Euonymus fortunei

Euphorbia milii

Euphorbia fulgens

E. fortunei
EMERALD AND GOLD

This open shrub is grown as a ground cover or shrub to about 1 m (about 3 ft) tall. As a ground cover it has an indefinite spread. From early to mid-summer it bears greenish white flowers. An evergreen, it has dark green and gold leaves.

E. japonicus 'Aureomarginatus'

This dense, upright evergreen grows to a height of 1–2 m (about 3–6 ft). It has oval, yellow-margined leaves and small, star-shaped, green flowers in summer. Frost-hardy, it makes a suitable choice for a hedge. The plain green variety is freer (on female plants) with its pretty coral pink berries.

EUPATORIUM
megalophyllum
MIST FLOWER

This erect shrub is a native of southern Mexico. In spring, it bears striking clusters of lilac flowers. The large, dark green leaves of this

evergreen shrub are veined and have pale undersides. It will not survive even the mildest of frosts. It requires full sun or partial shade and does best in a moist but well-drained soil. It seeds profusely—to prevent it taking over, prune lightly after flowering or in spring. Tip back new shoots in summer to maintain shape. Potted plants should be watered freely in full growth, less so at other times. It grows to a height of 1.5 m (about 4½ ft) and a spread of 2 m (about 6 ft). Propagate from slim, semi-hardened cuttings with short internodes. Two-spotted mite and whitefly may cause problems.

EUPHORBIA
MILKWEED, SPURGE

This genus contains over 1000 widely varying species of shrubs, perennials and succulents. Each species bears a spectacular show of coloured bracts rather than true flowers, and the milk sap is always poisonous. The shrubs do well in sun or partial shade and in moist but well-

drained soil. Propagate from seed in autumn/fall or spring, from basal cuttings in spring or summer, or by division in early spring or early autumn/fall.

E. fulgens
SCARLET PLUME

This evergreen, arching shrub grows to a height of 1.5 m (about 4½ ft) and a spread of 60 cm (about 24 in). In winter to spring, its long branches bear sprays of flowers, each cluster surrounded by red bracts. It has mid- to deep green, oval to lance-shaped leaves. It tolerates frost poorly and is suited to warmer areas only. Propagate from hardwood cuttings in summer.

E. milii
syn. E. splendens
CROWN OF THORNS

This slow-growing, ferociously thorny, semi-succulent shrub is a native of Madagascar. Deciduous in cooler areas, it is drought resistant and grows to a height of 1 m (about 3 ft) and a spread of 75 cm (about 2½ ft). It is excellent in rock gar-

dens or in cavities and is often used as a low hedge in coastal areas. Throughout the year and especially in spring, it bears tiny, yellowish flowers, enveloped by bright red bracts, whether there are pale green leaves on the branches or not. It does not tolerate frost well—hardy only down to 5–7°C (about 40–44°F). It prefers a sunny spot and well-drained soil.

E. pulcherrima
POINSETTIA, CHRISTMAS PLANT

The hollow-stemmed poinsettia is the showiest and most popular of the genus. A native of Mexico, it does best in well-drained soil, and plenty of water. From late autumn/fall to spring, small, greenish-red flowers appear, surrounded by bright-red, pink or white bracts. The oval, green leaves may be evergreen or deciduous. It is not at all frost-hardy—even a light frost will kill it. Prune poinsettias back hard to encourage shoot growth. Grow them in pots for pleasant, indoor, winter decoration, although the colour will not be as good as when grown out-

Fatsia japonica

doors in subtropical or tropical climates where it will grow 4 m (about 12 ft) tall and wide.

EURYOPS
pectinatus
BRIGHTEYES, RESIN BUSH

A native of South Africa, this shrubby evergreen grows well in most temperate conditions. Excellent for rock gardens and borders, it likes sun, partial shade in hot conditions, and a moist, well-drained, gravelly soil. From winter to spring it bears delightful, bright yellow, daisy-like flowers. It has a spreading habit, with grey-green leaves. Water in the hot months and prune after blooming to maintain the shape. Half-hardy, it grows to a height of 1 m (about 3 ft) with a spread of 75 cm (about 2½ ft). Propagate from softwood cuttings in summer.

EXOCHORDA
racemosa
PEARL BUSH

This deciduous, arching shrub, native to China, is grown for the delightful, upright clusters of white flowers it bears in late spring. These appear from bare wood and the buds resemble a string of pearls—hence the name. Another species, *E. x macrantha* 'The Bride', also produces prolific large white flowers. *E. racemosa* has oblong, deep blue-green leaves and grows to a height and spread of 4 m (about 12 ft). Plant the shrub in loamy but well-drained, acid soil in a sunny position. Thin out old shoots after flowering—this will improve the bloom. Fully hardy, it needs regular watering. Propagate from softwood cuttings in summer or seed in autumn/fall.

X FATSHEDERA
lizei
TREE IVY

This bi-generic hybrid (a botanical rarity) is the offspring of *Fatsia japonica* 'Moseri' and *Hedera helix* 'Hibernica' (Irish ivy). Popular as a house plant, it is also used extensively as ground cover; otherwise it may be trained against a wall. It prefers partial shade, and does best

in moist but well-drained, fertile soil. Frost-hardy, it reaches 2 m (about 6 ft) tall with a spread of 3 m (about 9 ft). Small, white flowers appear in autumn/fall. It bears glossy, deep green leaves; on x *F. lizei* 'Variegata' the leaves have a narrow creamy white edge. Pinch back to keep from falling over. Propagate in summer from semi-ripe cuttings.

FATSIA
japonica
syn. *Aralia japonica, A. sieboldii*
JAPANESE ARALIA

Japanese aralia is one of the world's most loved house plants. It may also be cultivated as a spreading bush, or trained into a single-stemmed tree. It bears splendid, large, rounded, deeply lobed, glossy, dark green leaves under almost any conditions. There is also a variegated form. Dense clusters of tiny, white flowers appear in autumn/fall, followed by small, black berries. It does best in sunny or shaded areas and prefers a well-drained, fertile soil. Frost-hardy, it prefers shelter from cold winds. Propagate from semi-ripe cuttings in summer or from seed in autumn/fall or spring.

FORSYTHIA
GOLDEN BELLS

Profuse blooms of yellow flowers are the principal attraction of this genus of deciduous shrubs. Vase-shaped and deciduous, they are easy to grow in rich, well-drained soil. They are frost-hardy to minus 25°C (about minus 13°F). Propagate by division or from semi-hardwood cuttings taken in summer. The genus was named in the eighteenth century in honour of William Forsyth, gardener to King George III of England. *F. suspensa* has bright golden yellow pendulous flowers and is fully hardy.

F. x intermedia

This compact, deciduous, arching or spreading shrub bears yellow flowers in spring. Its leaves are dark green and lance-shaped. It grows to a height of 3 m (about 9 ft) with a spread of 2 m (about 6 ft).

Exochorda racemosa

Euryops pectinatus

Forsythia x intermedia

x Fatshedera lizei

F. × *intermedia* 'Beatrix Farrand'

This bushy, arching, deciduous shrub bears masses of yellow flowers about 6 cm (about 2½ in) across in spring. Mid-green, oval, serrated leaves soon follow. Fully hardy, it does best in full light and in a well-drained soil. It grows to a height and spread of 2 m (about 6 ft). The flower clusters are most dense on the previous year's growth, which is encouraged by pruning after flowering.

Fremontodendron californicum

FOTHERGILLA
major

MOUNTAIN WITCHHAZEL

This spreading, cool-climate shrub is native to the USA, where it thrives in remote, mountain areas. This, the best known of only 4 species in the genus, grows to a height of 2 m (about 6 ft) and a spread of 1.5 m (about 4½ ft). Fragrant, snowy white, puffball flowers appear in spring, and again in autumn/fall. The dark-green leaves, slightly blue beneath, turn yellow in autumn/fall. Fully frost-hardy, this species does best in a moist, peaty, acid soil and prefers partial shade. Propagate from softwood cuttings in summer.

FRANCOA
appendiculata

BRIDAL WREATH

From summer to early autumn/fall, this evergreen perennial bears racemes of delightful pale pink flowers on graceful erect stems. It bears

Forsythia × i. 'Beatrix Farrand'

crinkled, hairy, oval, dark green leaves. Frost-hardy, *F. appendiculata* will thrive best in full sun or partial shade. Plant in fertile, well-drained soil. It grows to a height of 60 cm (about 2 ft) with a spread of 45 cm (about 1½ ft). Propagate from seed or by division in spring .

FREMONTODENDRON
californicum

FLANNEL BUSH

This sun-loving, evergreen or semi-evergreen shrub is prized for its bright yellow flowers that bloom from spring to mid-autumn/fall. Its lobed, dark green leaves are white-felted underneath. A native of California, it thrives in arid, even desert conditions, with full sun, and a well-drained, sandy soil. Frost-hardy, it grows to a height of 6 m (about 18 ft) with a spread of 4 m (about 12 ft). It is advisable to wear gloves when handling the plant as it is covered in hairs which can cause allergic reactions. It does not transplant very well, so choose the final location carefully. Propagate from seed or softwood cuttings in summer or from seed in autumn/fall or spring.

FUCHSIA

FUCHSIA, LADIES' EARDROPS

Native to the rainforests of South America, these exotic evergreen and semi-evergreen shrubs and trees are grown for the splendid, pendulous, tubular flowers born from early summer to late autumn/fall. These hang from axils, most heavily at the

ends of arching branches. Each flower consists of four reflexed sepals and four or more petals, often in a contrasting colour. Fuchsias prefer a partially shaded, sheltered position and will thrive in almost any soil, as long as it contains plenty of organic matter. They require plenty of water (sometimes twice a day in summer)—but avoid watering in full sun. Prune back drastically to prevent the plant from becoming too woody, and to maintain shape. They are frost-hardy to frost-tender. Propagate from softwood cuttings in any season. Red spider mite may cause problems, also guard against leaf-eating caterpillars or looper.

F. 'Gartenmeister Bonstedt'

This lax shrub produces large, tubular, orange to brick-red flowers—abundantly, if conditions are mild with plenty of sun. It is quite useful as a garden hedge. Plant at intervals of 75 cm (about 2½ ft), or as a pot or garden shrub. The leaves of this cultivar are a dark, bronzed red.

F. *magellanica* var. *gracilis*

This upright, frost-hardy evergreen bears small, red, tubular flowers, with purple petals and red sepals. Black fruits follow.

F. *magellanica* var. *gracilis* 'Alba'

If growth continues unchecked, this cultivar can grow to a considerable size. Prune it back to maintain its shape. This shrub bears attractive, pale pink flowers.

Fuchsia 'Gartenmeister Bonstedt'

Fothergilla major

Francoa appendiculata

Fuchsia magellanica var. *gracilis* 'Alba'

Gamolepis chrysanthemoides

Fuchsia magellanica unnamed cultivar

Fuchsia procumbens

Fuchsia magellanica var. *gracilis*

F. magellanica cultivars

F. magellanica has given rise to a large number of cultivars, very popular as pot plants and (in mild winter areas) as garden shrubs for a shaded spot. They can have single or double flowers, in shades of white, pink, red, mauve or purple, often with the petals and sepals in contrasting colours. They range in height from less than 1 m (about 3 ft) to almost 1.5 m (about 4½ ft). They are evergreen and will thrive best in fertile, well-drained soil. Prune in late winter for bushiness and propagate from softwood cuttings.

F. procumbens

TRAILING FUCHSIA

Native to New Zealand, this prostrate, evergreen shrub grows to a height of 10 cm (about 4 in) with an indefinite spread. It bears erect,

orange-tipped, purple and green flowers among small, heart-shaped leaves, followed by large, red berries. Half-hardy, it is excellent as a ground cover, or in rock gardens and hanging baskets.

GAMOLEPIS
chrysanthemoides
PARIS DAISY

Admired for its ability to flower continuously throughout the year, this rounded shrub bears delightful yellow, daisy-like flowers, carried on single stems. Its glossy, green, irregularly serrated leaves are evergreen. Half-hardy, it prefers full sun and does best in moist but well-drained, loamy soil. Prune regularly to maintain shape and water all year round. Remove wilted flowers to promote continuous blooming. It self-seeds profusely; otherwise propagate from cuttings. It grows to

a height of 1.5 m (about 4½ ft) and a spread of 1 m (about 3 ft).

GARDENIA
GARDENIA, CAPE JASMINE

Gardenias provide some of the most attractive, fragrant blooms to be found in warm climate gardens world-wide. Unfortunately they are mostly frost-tender, and will not do well at temperatures below 5°C (about 40°F): in Europe and most of the USA they need greenhouse culture. They do best in full sun to partial shade, and like a rich, peaty, well-drained, neutral to acid soil. Shorten strong shoots after blooming to maintain a good shape. Water potted plants generously in full growth, less so at other times. Some pests can pose problems—notably mealybug and whitefly. Propagate from semi-ripe cuttings in summer, or greenwood cuttings in spring.

Garrya elliptica

Gardenia thunbergia

Gaultheria shallon

G. augusta 'Florida'

This cultivar grows slowly up to a height and spread of 1.5 m (about 4½ ft). From summer to winter it bears fragrant, double, white flowers. It is an evergreen, with glossy, oval, dark green leaves.

G. thunbergia
TREE GARDENIA

An exceptionally beautiful and desirable shrub, this tree gardenia grows to a height and spread of 3 m (about 9 ft) or more. It does best in temperate to warm conditions. In autumn/fall, it bears fragrant, large, white, terminal flowers, set among glossy, deep green leaves.

GARRYA
elliptica
SILK TASSEL BUSH

This extraordinary, bushy, dense shrub is cultivated almost exclusively for its curtain of grey-green catkins, which grow up to 20 cm (about 8 in) in length—shorter on female plants which, however, bear decorative bluish berries. These appear from mid-winter to early spring, and may be damaged by frosts. Native to the west coast of the USA, G. elliptica may grow to a height of 5 m (about 15 ft) with a spread of 3 m (about 9 ft). Frost-hardy, it prefers full sun or part-shade and well-drained soil to thrive, doing particularly well on the coast or inland. It has leaves that are dark green and leathery. Propagate from semi-hardwood cuttings taken in summer.

Gaultheria procumbens

Gardenia augusta 'Florida'

GAULTHERIA

This large genus contains over 200 small evergreen flowering shubs; they are natives of countries around the Pacific, as well as the Himalayas, eastern North America and eastern Brazil. They are grown for their shining green foliage, bell-like flowers and attractive berries. Fully to half-hardy, although young growth can be affected by spring frost. They require a moist, acid soil with added peat and shade to semi-shade, growing well in association with rhododendrons and camellias. Propagate from seed in autumn or from semi-ripe cuttings in summer.

G. procumbens
PARTRIDGE-BERRY, WINTER-GREEN, CHECKERBERRY

Native to north-east America, this creeping evergreen species is a useful ground cover, reaching a height of 5–15 cm (about 2–6 in) and a spread of around 1 m (about 3 ft) or more. The shiny, dark green, leathery leaves take on a reddish tinge in winter, while in summer bell-shaped white or pink flowers appear. These are followed by bright red berries. It prefers a moist, mildly acid soil and partial shade. A useful rockery plant, it is fully hardy.

G. shallon
SHALLON

Native to western North America, this bushy evergreen species rapidly spreads by suckers to form wild thickets, making it useful where bold ground cover is required, especially under trees. Mid- to dark green leaves are carried on red shoots, and racemes of urn-shaped, pink-tinged white flowers are borne in late spring and early summer. These are followed by purple-black berries. Fully hardy. It reaches a height and spread of around 1.3 m (about 4 ft), and may be cut back after flowering to control growth. Propagate by division in autumn/fall and spring.

GENISTA
DYER'S GREENWEED, BROOM

In ancient times, members of this genus of deciduous shrubs and trees were grown to make dyes. Nowadays, they are grown solely for the fragrance and beauty of their blooms. Native to the Mediterranean areas of North Africa, southern Europe and Asia Minor, they make good seaside shrubs. They do well in hot, sunny conditions but are quite hardy nonetheless, and will survive a prolonged freeze. Grow in a not-too-rich, well-drained soil. They will not do well if transplanted. Prune tips to encourage a bushy look. Propagate in spring from sown seed or from semi-hardwood cuttings in summer.

Genista monosperma

Genista aetnensis

Genista pilosa 'Vancouver Gold'

Grevillea 'Boongala Spinebill'

Gordonia axillaris

Genista lydia

Genista tinctoria

G. aetnensis

MOUNT ETNA BROOM, SICILIAN BROOM

This rounded, somewhat weeping shrub/tree is native to Sicily and North Africa. Frost-hardy, it prefers full sun and a moist soil. Growing to 10 m (about 30 ft) in height and spread, it is almost leafless, but in summer bears an explosion of small, golden yellow flowers.

G. lydia

This deciduous dwarf species native to Europe with its prostrate habit and long, arching branches is ideal for growing in a large rock garden, training over walls or covering banks. It has blue-green leaves and masses of golden yellow, pea-like flowers, freely borne in terminal clusters in late spring or early summer. It has a domed habit and reaches a height of 45–60 cm (about 18–24 in) and spread of 60 cm (about 24 in) or more. Fully hardy, it is adaptable to most soils and positions.

G. monosperma

This deciduous, broadly bushy shrub is native to Spain and North Africa. Spectacular in spring when in full bloom, it bears fragrant, white, pea-shaped flowers on long, arching branches. It grows to a height and spread of 3 m (about 9 ft). The fruit are laterally compressed smooth pods containing 5 to 10 seeds. Propagate from semi-hardwood cuttings in autumn/fall.

G. pilosa 'Vancouver Gold'

Useful on a bank or as a ground cover, this deciduous species grows to a height and spread of 30 cm (about 12 in) and has a domed habit. It is variable, either growing as a prostrate form with a tangled mass of shoots or as a bush with erect shoots. It has narrow, mid-green leaves and small yellow flowers borne in profusion in early summer. Propagate from semi-ripe cuttings in summer. It is fully hardy.

G. tinctoria

DYER'S GREENWEED

Fully hardy, this squat, deciduous, spreading shrub grows to a height of 75 cm (about 2½ ft) and a spread of 1 m (about 3 ft). In summer, golden-yellow, pea-like flowers appear, set among thin, dark green leaves. It does best in full sun with a well-drained soil.

GORDONIA
axillaris

CRÊPE CAMELLIA

This handsome, glossy-leaved plant may reach tree-size after many years—up to 9 m (about 30 ft)—in mild climates. Normally, however, it is seen as a shrub, growing to 2–3 m (about 6–9 ft). A native of China, Taiwan and Vietnam, it bears cream-white, saucer-shaped flowers with a mass of yellow stamens in autumn/fall to spring. Although evergreen, sometimes a few of its leathery, lance-shaped leaves turn rich scarlet or gold at the same time. Half-hardy, it prefers a sunny spot, with a well-drained, acid soil. Potted plants should be watered moderately, less so in winter. Propagate from late summer cuttings.

GREVILLEA

GREVILLEA, SPIDER FLOWER

The most popular and decorative of native Australian shrubs and trees, this genus numbers some 250 species, and again as many cultivars. Extremely variable in habit, foliage and flowers, most grevilleas are found in the south-western part of Western Australia. There are also a few species native to Malaysia. Well sought after as garden plants, many are adaptable and easy to grow with a long flowering period. Popular with honey-seeking birds, they will grow in most soils, but do best in one that is well-drained, slightly dry, gravelly and neutral to acid. Most are only moderately frost-hardy to minus 5°C (about 23°F). They appreciate the occasional addition of a light fertilizer, but avoid using phosphorus. Flowers are borne on heads, sometimes globular, sometimes elongated and one-sided, like a toothbrush. The fruits that follow are leathery capsules that split to release one or, more commonly, two seeds. Propagate from seed in spring or from firm tip cuttings taken in late summer. They can also be grafted. Strong roots develop early and it is important not to disturb these when potting on. Grevilleas are generally pest free.

G. 'Boongala Spinebill'

This attractive cultivar bears long, dense heads of deep red flowers for most of the year. A spreading, frost-hardy, evergreen shrub, it has serrated, green leaves and grows to a height of 2 m (about 6 ft) and spread of 4 m (about 12 ft).

A Field Trip to the Cape Floral Kingdom

The southern tip of the African continent encompasses the 'Cape Floral Kingdom', the name botanists have given to the southern Cape Province and its extraordinarily rich flora. This is a diverse region—the coastal plains are largely sand and limestone and further inland, the undulating landscape is formed from shales and clays. The Cape Fold Mountains dominate the skyline to the north-east of Cape Town and Table Mountain. They are composed of steeply tilted acid sandstones, which yield a shallow soil that is deficient in the nutrients required for plant growth and hence of no value for agriculture or even the grazing of livestock. On their slopes though, and in many areas of similar soil in the southern Cape, there has developed the famous 'Fynbos' vegetation—a low scrub of extraordinary botanical diversity.

Of the world's great floral kingdoms, the Cape Floral Kingdom occupies the smallest area, but for its size it has a higher concentration of plant species (about 8500) than anywhere else on earth.

A feature of the Fynbos vegetation is the concentration of genera and species of the Proteaceae family. Richest in species are the *Protea*, *Leucadendron* and *Leucospermum* genera. In spring you can travel to any one of the mountainous areas within 250 km (about 160 miles) of Cape Town and find yourself in a world of flowers.

Low-growing vegetation on the South West Cape Mountains slopes.

Of the many species of *Protea*, one of the best known and most widely distributed in Cape Province is the wagon tree (*Protea nitida*), a shrub or smallish tree of varying size and shape. It is typically small and bushy, appearing a distinct greyish white from a distance, usually 5 m (about 15 ft) high with a trunk up to 50 cm (about 18 in) in diameter. The crown of foliage is rounded and irregular. The flowerheads (inflorescences), normally creamy white, may be present all year round but their bloom peaks between May and August. They are typical protea blooms, with globes up to 16 cm (about 6½ in) wide when open.

In early colonial days in South Africa, the attractive, reddish coloured wood of the wagon tree was used for furniture, wagon building and wagon brake blocks, hence the common name. The bark was also used for tanning, while the mature leaves produced a tolerably good black writing ink extracted with a solution of iron salt.

A field trip to view the wagon tree can be made at any time, as the species flowers all year round. However the best time to visit the Cape Floral Kingdom is in spring to early summer (September to December), because there is a great profusion of other flowers to be seen at this time. Head out from Cape Town along the N1 national road towards the Transvaal. Approximately 30 km (about 18 miles) north-east of Cape Town is the town of Paarl, in the heart of one of the richest and longest-settled agricultural areas in South Africa. You will pass orchards and vineyards, for this is also the centre of the country's wine production.

From here there are two possible routes. If you proceed on the old N1 over the Du Toitskloof Pass, within 5 or 10 minutes you will be in the typically rugged sandstone mountains of the Cape. As you go up the pass you will have your first glimpse of the Fynbos flora and see *Protea nitida* almost on the shoulders of the road. There are many places to stop and stroll around, but the best is yet to come.

The wagon tree, with other Fynbos plants.

Protea nitida

As you continue over the pass and go slowly down the other side, you will find the sunny eastern slopes on your right are covered in groups and single specimens of both the wagon tree and another *Protea* species, the sugarbush (*P. repens*). The early Dutch settlers extracted a syrup from the nectar-rich flowers of this plant, and at times it was their only source of sugar.

The alternative route is via the R303 district road after Paarl, crossing the Berg River. This will take you to the historic town of Franschhoek (where French Huguenots settled at the end of the seventeenth century). From here continue on up the Franschhoek Pass where you will find a floral profusion equal to that of the Du Toitskloof Pass. Apart from proteas and other Proteaceae, the Fynbos on these mountain slopes contains many species of *Erica* (the heath genus), most of which have colourful flowers. This is an amazingly diverse genus with almost 600 species in the southern Cape Province alone. Although *Erica* is also well known in Europe and the Mediterranean, that far larger region has fewer than one-twentieth the number of species. Other colourful wildflowers in the Fynbos include some lovely members of the daisy family, and spring-flowering bulbs such as watsonias, to name but a few.

From Franschhoek it is some 50 km (about 30 miles) back to Cape Town. After your field trip, it is worthwhile visiting Kirstenbosch National Botanic Garden, famous as much for its magnificent setting on the slope of Table Mountain as for its collections of South African native plants. Stroll to the magnificent Castle Rock and then walk through the Protea Garden. Here you will again find yourself in native Fynbos vegetation, rich in a number of beautiful species, including *Protea nitida* of course. Another attraction of this wonderful garden is the view, with the Cape Peninsula laid out below and, more distantly, the mountains behind Paarl and Stellenbosch where you have already been.

Protea

When the eminent Swedish botanist Linnaeus was systematically renaming all known plant and animal species in the mid-eighteenth century, he was so impressed by the range of form in one genus of African shrubs that he named it *Protea* after the Greek god Proteus, who had the ability to change at will into any of a myriad of forms.

Protea later lent its name to a major plant family, the Proteaceae, which includes many genera and species in Australia as well as in Africa, with smaller numbers in South America, New Caledonia, New Guinea and Indonesia. It is one of the most clear-cut examples of a plant group that originated in the super-continent Gondwana, predating its break-up into the present southern hemisphere land masses.

The astoundingly beautiful, symmetrical and long-lasting flowerheads of many Proteaceae have contributed to their popularity as cut flowers, to the extent that they are now a major item of international trade. Foremost are species of *Protea* itself, grown in Australia, New Zealand, California and Israel as well as in their native South Africa. The more striking species of Proteaceae are all adapted to highly nutrient-deficient soils and their cultivation requirements are frequently specialized. Most are only suited to milder temperate areas.

Protea cynaroides

Grevillea 'Robyn Gordon'

Grevillea rosmarinifolia

Grevillea lavandulacea

Grewia occidentalis

G. 'Robyn Gordon'

A popular and attractive hybrid (from *G. banksii* and *G. bipinnatifida*), this sprawling, evergreen shrub bears large, rich red, drooping flowerheads all year round. It has dark green, fern-like leaves with silky undersides. Moderately frost-hardy, it is vulnerable to leaf spot in damp conditions. Prune to encourage dense growth. It grows to a height of 1 m (about 3 ft) and a spread of up to 2 m (about 6 ft).

G. rosmarinifolia
ROSEMARY SPIDER-FLOWER

Native to New South Wales, Australia, this dense shrub is grown for its needle-shaped, rosemary-like leaves, which are mid- to deep green above and pale green below, and its rose red to pink or white summer flowers. An evergreen with a rounded habit, it reaches a height and spread of 2 m (about 6 ft). Half-hardy, it will survive some light frost.

GREWIA
occidentalis

LAVENDER STAR, CROSSBERRY

Native to Africa, this fast-growing evergreen, the most popular of the genus, is widely grown in the southern USA, especially California. In summer it bears pink and mauve, star-shaped flowers. Shiny, oval, light green leaves complete the picture. It is frost- to half-hardy and likes moist but well-mulched, well-drained soil. Grows to a height and spread of 3 m (about 9 ft). Pruning will maintain a compact habit. Propagate from seed or cuttings.

GRISELINIA
littoralis

Native to New Zealand, this fast-growing tree or shrub is a popular seaside plant in Ireland and in New England and California in the USA. It is grown for its shining, oval, apple-green leathery leaves. It bears insignificant tiny, yellow-green flowers in spring. Small, black berries follow the bloom. *G. littoralis* is resistant to wind and salt, making it

G. lavandulacea

One of the most variable of the genus, this bushy, compact shrub bears small, crowded, abundant clusters of crimson to pink (sometimes white) flowers over the entire bush for most of the year. The leaves are short and broad, silvery grey, usually covered in hairs but sometimes smooth. Hardy, frost and drought resistant, it grows to a height of 1 m (about 3 ft) or less with a spread of 2 m (about 6 ft). It is suitable for hedges in parks and gardens.

a perfect choice for a hedge or windbreak in coastal areas. Drought resistant, it likes fertile, well-drained soil in full sun or partial shade. It is frost- to half-hardy and grows to a height and spread of 6–12 m (about 16–36 ft). Propagate from semi-ripe cuttings in summer or seed in spring and autumn/fall.

HAKEA

PINCUSHION TREE, NEEDLE BUSH

Members of this variable genus of shrubs and small trees are native to Australia but are now popular in Mediterranean areas, southern California and New Zealand. Strongly fragrant, they do best in dry, gravelly, well-drained soil that is slightly acid. The leaves vary; they are mostly hard and needle like. The flowers resemble those of grevilleas—instead of petals they have stamens sitting in cups of joined sepals. These are usually small and grow in pairs, often clustered into a long head. Frost-hardy to frost-tender, these plants like plenty of sun. Potted specimens should be watered moderately in full growth, less so at other times. Propagate from seed (pre-treated by nicking or immersion in near-boiling water) in autumn/fall or semi-ripe cuttings in summer. Collar rot is occasionally a problem.

H. laurina

PINCUSHION PLANT

A loose, gangly plant with weeping branches, this tall, smooth-barked

Griselinia littoralis

shrub is extremely popular. In winter to spring it bears delightfully fragrant, crimson or cherry flowers, with protruding, white styles, that resemble pins in a pincushion. The leaves are broad, stalked, and grey-green, with prominent veins. Half-hardy, it grows to a height of 3–6 m (about 9–18 ft) with a spread of 3 m (about 9 ft). Propagate from seed in autumn/fall or from semi-ripe cuttings in summer.

H. sericea

This evergreen, rounded shrub grows to a height of 3–5 m (about 9–15 ft) and a spread of 2–3 m (about 6–12 ft). It bears clusters of small, fragrant, tubular white or pale pink flowers. Its needle-like leaflets are very sharply pointed. Half-hardy.

HALIMIUM

lasianthum

syn. H. formosum

SUNROSE

This stunning, low-spreading evergreen is a native of Spain and Portugal. It has grey-green foliage and in spring and summer bears open, golden flowers, each petal marked with a central, red blotch. Although frost-hardy, it needs shelter in colder areas. Water sparingly, except in drought conditions, ensuring it has a well-drained soil and full sun. Related to *Cistus*, it is admirably suited for coastal gardens. It grows to a height of 75 cm (about 30 in) and a spread of 1.5 m (about 4½ ft). Propagate from semi-ripe cuttings in summer.

HAMAMELIS

WITCH HAZEL

These fine winter-flowering deciduous shrubs from east Asia and eastern North America are grown for their curious fragrant or yellow flowers and their autumn colour. The flowers are good for cutting, while the plants are suitable for use as specimen trees, in borders and for woodland planting. They require a cool, moist climate, a well-drained, peaty acid soil and a sunny or semi-shaded site protected from

cold winds. Propagate species from seed in autumn/fall and selected forms from softwood cuttings any time in summer. Cut back straggly branches after flowering. Fully hardy.

H. × intermedia

A vigorous, free-flowering hybrid, this plant has broadly oval, mid-green leaves that turn yellow in autumn and large, fragrant, spidery flowers with yellow or copper-tinted crimped petals that appear from mid- to late winter. It has an open spreading habit, reaching a height and spread of around 3 m (about 9 ft). Several forms are available. Propagate from seed in autumn/fall.

H. mollis

CHINESE WITCH HAZEL

Native to central and western China, this is probably the best known species with sweetly fragrant, rich, golden-yellow flowers flushed red at the base. The flowers appear in massed clusters along the twigs in mid- to late winter. The mid-green, softly hairy leaves turn a deep golden-yellow in autumn/fall. It has an upright, open habit, reaching a height and spread of 4 m (about 12 ft).

H. vernalis

OZARK WITCH HAZEL

Native to the central United States, this erect, suckering shrub has a

Hamamelis vernalis

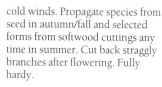

Halimium lasianthum

Hakea laurina

Hebe × andersonii

denser habit than the other species. Mid-green leaves turn yellow in autumn/fall, while the pungently scented clusters of small, spidery, pale to tawny yellow flowers appear in mid- to late winter. It grows to a height and spread of 1–2 m (about 3–6 ft). This species is good for growing beside lakes and streams as it tolerates fairly moist soils. The best known form is 'Sandra', which has vivid autumn colouring.

H. virginiana
VIRGINIAN WITCH HAZEL

Native to eastern North America and Canada, this is the species that produces the preparation known as witch hazel. Small, fragrant, curled and twisted yellow flowers unfurl in autumn/fall, before the leaves fall. Broadly oval, dark green leaves turn buttercup yellow in autumn. It has an open, upright habit, growing to a height of 3–4 m (about 9–12 ft) with a slightly smaller spread. It withstands cold better that the other species.

HEBE
VERONICA, SHRUB SPEEDWELL

Most of these evergreen shrubs are native to New Zealand but some

Hebe × franciscana 'Blue Gem'

species are to be found naturally in Chile and New Guinea. They are all grown for the luxurious, dense spikes of tiny, 4-petalled, purple, white or cerise flowers. Resistance to salt and sea winds make them eminently suited to coastal areas. They are good as dense hedges or thick ground covers. Half-hardy to about minus 5°C (about 23°F), they require well-drained soil and full sun or semi-shade. Propagate from semi-ripe cuttings in summer. There

are a great many cultivated species and hybrids.

H. × andersonii

This is a bushy, half-hardy, evergreen shrub that grows to a height and spread of 2 m (about 6 ft). It bears dense spikes of small, lilac flowers in summer. The leaves are dark green. A form with cream-variegated leaves is available.

H. × franciscana 'Blue Gem'

From summer to early winter, this spreading evergreen bears dense spikes of small, violet-blue flowers and has oblong, densely arranged, mid-green leaves. It grows to a height of 60 cm (about 24 in) with a spread of 1 m (about 3 ft).

H. hulkeana

This upright, open, evergreen shrub bears masses of small, pale lilac flowers in spring and early summer. Its attractive, oval, serrated, glossy, dark green leaves have red margins. It grows to a height and spread of 1 m (about 3 ft).

Hamamelis virginiana

Hebe hulkeana

H. speciosa

This desirable species boasts deep green foliage and purple brushes of flowers that appear in terminal clusters in summer and winter to spring. Half-hardy, it grows to a height of 1.5 m (about 4½ ft) with a spread of 1 m (about 3 ft). Numerous, brightly coloured cultivars exist, with flowers ranging from purple and deep red to pale lilac, pink and white.

HELICHRYSUM
selago

Native to the mountain regions of New Zealand, this erect evergreen shrub grows up to 45 cm (about 18 in). It has a conifer-like appearance; its rigid stems are covered with dense, triangular scale-like foliage. Terminal clusters of downy cream flowers sporadically appear at the tips of the branchlets.

HELIOTROPIUM
arborescens
syn. H. peruvianum
CHERRY PIE, HELIOTROPE

This attractive shrub is much-prized for the clusters of fragrant, purple to lavender flowers it bears from late spring to autumn/fall. A native of South America, it grows fast 75 cm (about 30 in) tall and 1 m (about 3 ft) wide. It is a branching, evergreen species with dark green, wrinkled leaves. Tender to frost, it needs rich, fertile,.well-drained soil and full sun. In very dry areas, it is best raised in a semi-shady position and the soil kept moist. Potted specimens should be regularly watered in full growth, but moderately at other times. Cut back to half in early spring to promote a bushy look. Propagate from seed in spring or semi-ripe cuttings in early autumn/fall. The name comes from the unusual way the flowerheads turn towards the sun.

HIBISCUS
ROSE OF CHINA, ROSE MALLOW, ROSE OF SHARON, SHRUB ALTHEA

These beautifully exotic, flowering, evergreen or deciduous shrubs, perennials and annuals hail from all continents, but particularly the countries around the Indian ocean—eastern Africa, Madagascar and Malaysia—as well as the Pacific Islands, Australia and China. Popular in warm to tropical gardens, they bear large, showy flowers, many of which last as little as one day—longer in colder conditions. The flowering season is long, however, lasting from late spring into autumn/fall, and the range of colours is impressive. They thrive in full sun, in a well-drained, rich, slightly acid, sandy soil. Water regularly and fertilize during flower-

ing. Trim after flowering to maintain shape. Propagate from cuttings taken in spring and summer. Potential pests include aphids, caterpillars, whitefly, tip borer and the hibiscus beetle. The genus is the floral emblem of Hawaii, where some of the most stunning hybrids are grown, and several beautiful species grow wild.

H. mutabilis
CONFEDERATE ROSE, COTTON ROSE

This delightful native of China grows to a height and spread of 6 m (about 24 ft). Frost-hardy, it bears large, hairy, heart-shaped leaves, with single, white flowers that fade to deep rose-pink. These appear in autumn/fall. Prune regularly in winter to maintain shape.

H. rosa-sinensis
ROSE OF CHINA, SHOEFLOWER

Native to China, this tall shrub bears coral-red flowers virtually all year in a frost-free climate. The wild form is less often seen in gardens than the numerous dazzling cultivars, many bred in Hawaii, which come in single or double and every colour but blue. Plants range in height and spread from 1–3 m (about 3–9 ft) and have evergreen, glossy leaves. They prefer full sun in tropical or subtropical climates where they are as important in gardens as roses are in temperate climates. In cold climates they can be grown in tubs in a greenhouse or as indoor plants. Water freely in summer, prune in spring after cold weather is over, and propagate from cuttings in summer. The name 'shoeflower' comes from the West Indian custom of polishing shoes with a hibiscus flower.

H. rosa-sinensis 'Apple Blossom'

This cultivar bears large, single, pale pink flowers. It grows vigorously to 4 m (about 12 ft) or more.

H. rosa-sinensis 'Cooperi'

Ideal for potting and excellent as an indoor decoration, this shrub bears small, light, open, scarlet flowers. It grows to a height of 1.5–3 m (about 4½–12 ft) and has variegated white, cream and pink foliage.

Hebe speciosa

Hibiscus rosa-sinensis

Hibiscus rosa-sinensis 'Cooperi'

Helichrysum selago

Hibiscus r.-s. 'Apple Blossom'

Heliotropium arborescens

Hibiscus mutabilis

Hydrangea macrophylla

Hydrangea aspera var. *aspera*

Hovea lanceolata

H. rosa-sinensis 'Madonna'

A Hawaiian cultivar, growing to about 2 m (about 6 ft) with large single flowers, cream with cerise-red throats.

H. rosa-sinensis 'Sabrina'

This cultivar bears fully double, bright cerise-red flowers and grows about 2 m (about 6 ft) tall.

H. syriacus

ALTHEA, ROSE OF SHARON

This colourful, upright, deciduous shrub is the hardiest of the genus. It flowers freely in summer in varying shades of white, pink, soft red, mauve and violet-blue. The single, semi-double and double flowers are bell-shaped. It has small, glabrous leaves and grows to 4 m (about 12 ft) tall with a spread of 1–2 m (about 3–6 ft). Prune hard in winter to keep it healthy.

H. syriacus 'Ardens'

This popular hibiscus bears large, mauve flowers with crimson centres. An upright shrub, it grows to a height of 3 m (about 9 ft).

H. syriacus 'Blue Bird'

This shrub bears single, violet-blue flowers with red centres. It grows to a height of 2 m (about 6 ft).

HOVEA
lanceolata

PURPLE PEA-BUSH

This lovely bush, covered in purple, pea-like flowers in spring, prefers full or semi-shade—the cover of taller shrubs and trees is ideal. It does best in a fertile, well-mulched

H. rosa-sinensis 'Madonna'

soil with good drainage. After flowering, prune lightly. Half-hardy, it grows to 2 m (about 6 ft) tall and 1 m (about 3 ft) wide. Propagate from scarified seed.

HYDRANGEA

HYDRANGEA

These lush, popular, deciduous and evergreen shrubs are native to China, Japan and North America and they grow profusely in the summer months. They need constant watering, as they transpire heavily from the stems and large, saw-toothed leaves. The sun damages their foliage, so always position them in the shade, or in full sun only in areas that are frequently cloudy. They are fully to frost-hardy. Hydrangeas are grown for the striking and attractive, domed fertile flowers which appear mid-summer. Each head consists of small flowers surrounded by larger petal-like sepals. Prune immediately after flowering—this encourages strong, vigorous growth for the following season. Propagate from softwood cuttings in summer.

Hibiscus syriacus 'Blue Bird'

H. aspera var. aspera
syn. *H. villosa*
STAR HYDRANGEA

This delicate beauty, native to eastern Asia, bears broad heads of blue or purple flowers in the centre of the shrub, and larger, white flowers towards the periphery. A deciduous upright shrub, it grows to a height and spread of 3 m (about 9 ft) and is fully hardy.

H. macrophylla

HORTENSIA

This deciduous, bushy shrub from Japan flowers in mid- to late summer, the colour depending on the pH of the soil. In soils with a pH of up to about 5.5, blue or purple flowers bloom; above this level they are pink. White flowers are unaffected by soil pH. There are two types—hortensias, with dense, domed heads; and lacecaps, with flat, open heads. Trim winter-damaged growth back to new growth and in summer, remove spent flowers. It is frost-hardy, has oval, serrated, green leaves and grows to a height and spread of 2 m (about 6 ft).

Hibiscus syriacus 'Ardens'

Hibiscus syriacus

Hibiscus rosa-sinensis 'Sabrina'

Hydrangea macrophylla 'Blue Wave'

Hypericum patulum

Hydrangea paniculata 'Grandiflora'

Hydrangea quercifolia

Hypoestes aristata

Hypericum 'Rowallane'

Hymenolepis parviflora

H. macrophylla 'Blue Wave'

This deciduous, bushy shrub with flat heads of blue to pink flowers appearing in summer, has oval, green, serrated leaves and grows to a height and spread of 1.5 m (about 4½ ft). It is the best known Lacecap type.

H. paniculata 'Grandiflora'

PEEGEE HYDRANGEA

This deciduous, open, upright shrub bears large, conical, terminal panicles of white bloom. Greenish to begin with, they gradually turn to pink as summer progresses. To obtain larger panicles, prune back hard in spring. Fully hardy, it grows to a height and spread of 3 m (about 9 ft).

H. quercifolia

OAK-LEAFED HYDRANGEA

The dark green foliage of this deciduous, bushy shrub turns a brilliant red and purple in autumn/fall. It bears white flowerheads from mid-summer to mid-autumn/fall. Frost-hardy, it grows to a height and spread of 2 m (about 6 ft).

HYMENOLEPIS

parviflora

syn. *Athanasia parviflora*
COULTER BUSH

This spreading, slightly woody shrub comes from the south-western Cape of South Africa. It grows to 1.5 m (about 4½ ft) high and bears small, golden-yellow flowers on large, flattened heads in early summer. The leaves are needle-like and 'branched'. Plant in rich, well-drained soil in full sun. Prune regu-

larly to remove old stems and maintain shape.

HYPERICUM

ST JOHN'S WORT, GOLDFLOWER, AARON'S BEARD, ROSE OF SHARON

These showy perennials, annuals and shrubs are easy to grow in mild, temperate climates worldwide. Larger species require sun or semi-shade, and fertile soil that is slightly moist. Smaller species do better in full sun and well-drained soil and make excellent rock plants. They are fully to half-hardy. Prune annually to prevent legginess and to maintain shape. Prune seed-pods to maintain vigour. Propagate small species from 5 cm (about 2 in) cuttings taken in late spring; for larger shrubs, from 12 cm (about 5 in) cuttings of non-flowering shoots in summer.

H. patulum

This evergreen, upright shrub bears large, golden yellow, erect flowers from mid-summer to mid-autumn/fall. It has dark green, oval leaves

and grows to a height and spread of 1 m (about 3 ft). *H. patulum* is frost-hardy. 'Hidcote', raised in the famous English garden of that name, is the best known cultivar.

H. 'Rowallane'

In mid-summer to mid- or late autumn/fall, this attractive, arching shrub bears delightful, bowl-shaped, yellow flowers, set among green, oval leaves. Frost-hardy, it grows to a height and spread of 1.5 m (about 4½ ft).

HYPOESTES

aristata

This bushy shrub is native to South Africa, and grows to a height of 1 m (about 3 ft) with a spread of 60 cm (about 24 in). In late winter, it bears terminal spikes of attractive, small, tubular, pink to purple flowers, set among mid-green, oval leaves. It prefers full sun and a moist, well-drained soil. Prune as required, and water frequently in the summer months. Propagate from stem cuttings in spring or summer.

ILEX

HOLLY

These popular and well-known, slow-growing, evergreen shrubs and trees are grown for their green, spiny leaves and the red, yellow or black berries borne in summer, autumn/fall or winter by female plants. Male and female plants must be grown together to obtain the berries. The shrubs bear clusters of small, white or greenish blossoms, but these are not significant. They need a moist, well-drained soil with plenty of leaf mulch and prefer sun or partial shade. Half-hardy, they do best when pruned hard in late spring. Propagate from semi-hardwood cuttings in early autumn/fall. Watch for holly leaf miner and holly aphid. Holly was invested with mystical properties by Europeans during the Middle Ages as it defied the winter, retaining both leaves and berries.

I. × altaclarensis 'Wilsonii'

This female evergreen grows vigorously to a height of 6 m (about 18 ft) and a spread of 4 m (about 12 ft). It has broad, spiny, dark green leaves and produces masses of large scarlet fruits. Good for hedging or as a specimen plant, these are also useful plants for industrial or maritime areas as they can resist pollution and harsh coastal conditions. Frost-hardy.

I. aquifolium cultivars

ENGLISH HOLLY, COMMON HOLLY

The bright red, winter berries and glossy, spiny, dark green leaves of these plants make popular traditional Christmas ornaments. Growing to about 5 m (about 15 ft) or more according to cultivar, this hardy evergreen is available in a number of garden varieties, some without spines on the leaves.

I. cornuta

CHINESE HOLLY

This dense, rounded species from China is self-fertile and frost-hardy. Better suited than other species to mild-winter areas, it grows to a height of 4 m (about 12 ft) with a spread of 5 m (about 15 ft). The leaves are rectangular with a spine at each corner, and bright red berries appear in summer. This too is excellent as a Christmas holly.

I. crenata

BOX LEAVED HOLLY, JAPANESE HOLLY

A Japanese native, this spreading evergreen has very small, smooth, dark green, oval, sharply pointed leaves. Small, glossy black berries are borne by the female plant in autumn/fall and winter. It is a densely branched shrub, completely different to the prickly leaved native species. It grows to a height of 5 m (about 15 ft) with a spread of 3 m (about 9 ft). It is useful as a hedge plant and is fully hardy.

I. glabra

INKBERRY

This dense evergreen has an upright habit, reaching a height of 2.5 m (about 7½ ft) and a spread of 2 m (about 6 ft). It has small, smooth-edged, dark green leaves and bears black berries. Fully hardy.

I. 'Golden King'

This magnificent female shrub or small tree is excellent, both as a specimen plant or as a hedge. Its principal attraction is the deep green, shiny leaves, with yellow borders that turn white as they get older. Frost-hardy, it grows to about 5 m (about 15 ft) with a spread of 3 m (about 9 ft). To bear its red berries, pollinate with a male cultivar such as 'Silver Queen'.

INDIGOFERA

decora

syn. *I. incarnata*

FALSE INDIGO, SUMMER WISTERIA

This delightful shrub, a native of China and Japan, bears racemes of pink and white pea-shaped flowers in summer. It has glossy, dark green leaves with oval leaflets. Frost-hardy, it grows to a height of 60 cm (about 24 in) and a spread of 1 m (about 3 ft). It needs full sun and fertile, well-drained soil. Drought resistant, it is a handy plant for dry gardens where the soil is poor. Prune to shape from an early age and propagate from softwood cuttings in summer, or from seed in autumn/fall.

ITEA

These evergreen and deciduous shrubs, mainly from tropical and temperate Asia, are grown for their showy, fragrant autumn flowers and prickly, holly-like leaves. They are frost-hardy, although in cooler areas they need the protection of a wall. They will thrive in anything but very dry soil and prefer a semi-shaded position but will tolerate full sun. Propagate from softwood cuttings in summer and plant in autumn/fall or spring. This is a useful plant for a specimen or for growing in a shrubbery.

I. ilicifolia

SWEETSPIRE

This handsome, bushy, evergreen shrub, native to western China, has leaves resembling those of holly, only narrower. It bears long racemes of small, greenish or cream flowers

Ilex × altaclarensis 'Wilsonii'

Ilex glabra

Ilex cornuta

Ilex aquifolium cultivar

Ilex 'Golden King'

Ilex crenata

Indigofera decora

Juniperus sabina

Jasminum nudiflorum

Juniperus chinensis

Juniperus conferta

Itea ilicifolia

Juniperus horizontalis

Itea virginica

Jasminum mesnyi

in late summer to early autumn/fall. It does best in moist, deep, rich soil, preferring partial shade. Hardy to minus 15°C (about 5°F), it grows to a height and spread of 3 m (about 6 ft). Propagate from softwood cuttings in summer.

I. virginica
VIRGINIA WILLOW, VIRGINIA SWEETSPIRE

This is the only species native to eastern North America. Its finely toothed, deciduous, bright green leaves have no prickles and do not fall until early winter, when they sometimes turn red. It bears fragrant, creamy white flowers in semi-erect panicles during summer. This species is hardier and smaller than *I. ilicifolia*, reaching only 1–1.3 m (about 3–4 ft) in height.

JASMINUM
JASMINE, JESSAMINE, PIKAKE

These deciduous, semi-evergreen or evergreen shrubs, and woody-stemmed, twining or scrambling climbers, are native to Asia, Europe and Africa. Grown for their yellow, white or pink, star-shaped flowers, they are fully hardy to frost-tender. Water regularly and prune occasionally to maintain their habit. The shrubs can easily be trained as climbers if their heads are not cut back. Propagate from ripe wood cuttings in summer, by layers, or from seed.

J. mesnyi
syn. *J. primulinum*
PRIMROSE JASMINE, YELLOW JASMINE

Native to China, this evergreen, rambling shrub bears large, semi-

double, golden blooms on arching canes, in late winter and spring. Its dark green leaves are made up of 3 leaflets. Half-hardy, it does well in all but the hottest climates, and prefers full sun and a well-drained soil. *J. mesnyi* grows to a height and spread of 3 m (about 9 ft).

J. nudiflorum
WINTER JASMINE

This is a rambling, deciduous, arching shrub from China. It is best suited to a cool or cold climate, where it will happily bear masses of bright yellow flowers on slender, leafless, green shoots in winter and early spring. Fully hardy, it prefers a well-drained soil and full sun. It grows to about 1.5–2 m (about 4½–6 ft) tall. Propagate from semi-hardwood cuttings in spring.

JUNIPERUS
JUNIPER

These evergreen conifers make excellent garden plants. They provide year round interest and need little attention. Plant in rock gardens to provide scale, or to act as a foil for other plants. They do well in all but the coldest conditions, requiring full sun and a dry, sandy soil. All species and cultivars are best propagated from tip cuttings, as they root easily. Some cultivars can be propagated by grafting. Aphids are sometimes a problem.

J. chinensis
CHINESE JUNIPER

Native to China, Mongolia and Japan, this is one of the most popu-

lar and frequently grown junipers. It grows as a conical tree to 18 m (about 60 ft) or as a spreading shrub reaching a height of 1–5 m (about 3–15 ft), with a spread of 3–5 m (about 9–15 ft). Both the spiny-pointed juvenile and the scale-like adult leaves are found together on the tree. The leaves are dark green and aromatic, while round, fleshy, glaucous white, berry-like fruits are produced. The plant has stringy brown bark. Fully hardy. There are several cultivars in a variety of forms.

J. conferta
SHORE JUNIPER

This shrubby, prostrate, dwarf conifer does quite well in a salty, coastal environment. It has dense, glossy, aromatic, needle-like, soft green leaves on spreading branches. Fully hardy, it grows to a height of up to 15 cm (about 6 in) and a spread of

up to 2 m (about 6 ft), and makes an excellent ground cover.

J. horizontalis
CREEPING JUNIPER

A native of north-east America, this prostrate, mat-forming species is a useful ground cover, eventually spreading to 2 m (about 6 ft) or more, with a height of up to 30 cm (about 12 in). It has aromatic, awl-shaped, blue-green or grey leaves and pale blue berries. Fully hardy.

J. sabina
SAVIN JUNIPER

The dark green leaves of this vigorously spreading, shrubby bush, a native to Europe and the Caucasus, give off an unpleasant odour when bruised or crushed. It has flaking, red-brown bark. Fully hardy, it can grow to 4 m (about 12 ft) but dwarf forms, about 1 m (about 3 ft) tall, are more often seen in gardens.

Justicia carnea

Kolkwitzia amabilis

Juniperus sabina 'Tamariscifolia'

Kerria japonica

Kunzea baxteri

J. sabina 'Tamariscifolia'

This bushy conifer grows to a height of 1 m (about 3 ft) with a spread of 2 m (about 6 ft). Its bright green or blue-green, needle-like leaves are arranged in tiers.

JUSTICIA
carnea
syn. *Jacobinia carnea, J. pohliana*
BRAZILIAN PLUME FLOWER

This strikingly handsome, evergreen shrub bears spikes of white, pink or rose-purple flowers in summer to autumn/fall. It has pointed, veined, deep green leaves. In colder climates, it needs to be grown under glass, as it is a frost-tender, tropical or subtropical plant. It does best in fertile, well-drained soil, and requires full light and partial shade. Water potted specimens freely in full growth, less so at other times. Prune back hard in early spring—this will encourage branching and prevent growth from becoming too tall and straggly. *J. carnea* grows to a height of 1.5 m (about 4½ ft) with a spread of 75 cm (about 30 in).

Kalmia latifolia

Propagate in spring or early summer by softwood or greenwood cuttings. Caterpillars and snails can be a problem.

KALMIA
latifolia
MOUNTAIN LAUREL

The charm and fragrance of this American native make it a favourite among shrub enthusiasts. It has dark, glossy, laurel-like leaves and bears small, purple-rose to rose-red flowers in late spring and early summer. *K. latifolia* grows to a height of 3 m (about 9 ft) and a spread of 3.5 m (about 10½ ft). Fully hardy, it thrives in a moist, peaty, acid soil and prefers sun or

semi-shade. Propagate by layering in summer, otherwise (with more difficulty) from softwood cuttings in summer, or seed in autumn/fall.

KERRIA
japonica
JAPANESE ROSE, GLOBE FLOWER, BACHELOR'S BUTTONS

The golden blossom of this species, the only one in its genus, will light up a garden corner in spring. The flowers, which appear at the end of lateral shoots on arching branches, also make delightful cut flowers. The leaves are double-toothed and bright green. Fully hardy, it likes partial shade and a well-drained soil. Prune back heavily to promote full

growth and, every now and then, give it a heavy watering. It grows to a height of 2 m (about 6 ft) and a spread of 3 m (about 9 ft). Grow from cutting layers in summer, or by division in autumn/fall.

KOLKWITZIA
amabilis
BEAUTY BUSH

The only species in its genus, this attractive plant is native to China. Its deciduous, arching branches bear delightful, bell-shaped, pink flowers with yellow throats, from late winter to early spring. It has peeling bark and dark green, oval leaves. *K. amabilis* likes a well-drained soil, rich in leafmould, and prefers full sun. Fully hardy, it grows to a height and spread of 3 m (about 9 ft). After flowering, prune old, weak or damaged shoots. Propagate from softwood cuttings in summer.

KUNZEA
baxteri
TICK BUSH

This rounded, wiry-stemmed evergreen from Australia is popular for the fluffy, bottlebrush-like, long-stamened, red flowers it bears in spring. The leaves are tiny and heath-like. Frost-tender, *K. baxteri* prefers well-drained, sandy, neutral to acid soil and does best in full light. Potted specimens should be watered moderately when in full growth, less at other times. It grows to a height and spread of 3 m (about 9 ft). Propagate from tip cuttings in summer.

Lantana camara

LAGERSTROEMIA

Native to tropical Asia, north Australia and the Pacific islands, these deciduous or evergreen shrubs do best in warm climates in hot, dry situations. They are grown for their profuse creped, crinkly flowers that appear in colours from soft pink to crimson and purple according to the variety. They prefer fertile, well-drained soil, preferably light to sandy, and full sun. Prune after flowering to retain a shrubby shape, or leave to grow to a small tree. They may be grown as tub plants on patios, where they should be watered well during the full growth period but less at other times. Frost-hardy to frost-tender, to a minimum 3–5°C (37–40°F). Propagate from seed in spring, from hardwood cuttings in winter or from semi-ripe cuttings in summer.

L. indica
CRÊPE MYRTLE, PRIDE OF INDIA

This deciduous, vase-shaped bush bursts into bloom in spring, bearing luxuriant trusses of pink, white or purple petals. Its small, oval, short-stalked leaves are deciduous and colour prettily in autumn/fall. Half-hardy, it prefers a fertile, well-drained soil and full light. Cut back the previous season's stems to maintain a bushy habit or allow the plant to grow unpruned into a small tree. Water potted plants freely in full growth, less at other times. It grows to 6 m (about 18 ft) tall with a 5 m (about 15 ft) spread. Propagate from hardwood cuttings in winter, semi-ripe cuttings in summer, or seed in spring.

L. indica hybrids

Several cultivars of *L. indica* are usually available in nurseries in colours of pink, white and purple. 'Petite Snow' has large, snowball clusters of glistening white flowers. 'Seminole' has colourful clusters of long-lasting rich pink flowers produced in a succession of blooms lasting several months.

LANTANA

Native to tropical America, the West Indies and tropical and western

Lavandula angustifolia

Africa, these evergreen shrubs are mostly classed as weeds in tropical and subtropical regions. However, two species and their cultivars are useful garden or greenhouse shrubs and are grown for their flowers in mild climate gardens, where they should be treated as tender bedding plants. They prefer a fertile, well-drained soil and full light. Containerised plants should be top-dressed anually in spring and watered well when in full growth, less at other times. Tip prune young growth to promote a bushy habit and propagate from semi-ripe cuttings in summer or from seed in spring. They are generally not affected by pests, but watch out for whitefly and red spider mite.

L. camara

Useful for covering banks and as small hedges, wall or container plants, this species has flowers that open yellow or yellow-red and age to red and white. The tiny flowers appear amongst the deep green foliage in dense, domed heads from spring to autumn. It is a rounded, spreading shrub with a height and spread of 1–2 m (about 3–6 ft). Frost-tender, to a minimum 10–13°C (50–55°F). There are various forms and cultivars ranging in colour from yellow to red, pink and white, changing colour as they age.

L. montevidensis
syn. L. sellowiana

The dainty, arched stems of this trailing or mat-forming, evergreen shrub make a wonderful ground cover or small hedge. Throughout the year, but particularly in summer, it bears heads of magenta or

Lantana montevidensis

Lagerstroemia indica

Lagerstroemia indica hybrid

white posy-like flowers, each with a yellow eye. It grows to a height of 30 cm (about 12 in) and a spread of 1.5 m (about 4½ ft). Native to the Americas, it does best in fertile, well-drained soil and a sunny position. When in full growth, potted specimens should be well watered, but this is not important at other times. To keep the habit bushy, tip prune occasionally. Propagate from semi-ripe cuttings in summer, or seed in spring. Whitefly and red spider mite may present problems. *L. camara* 'Chelsea Gem' and a few other species are considered noxious weeds in some countries.

LAVANDULA

LAVENDER

These fragrant, flower-bearing plants come from southern Europe. Cultivated commercially for the perfume industry, they are also grown for their evergreen foliage and attractive bloom. They prefer full sun and fertile, well-drained soil, that is not too rich in nitrates

and phosphates. Fully to half-hardy, lavender tend not to bloom profusely in warm conditions. Excellent as hedges, they need a light trimming in spring to keep the habit neat. Propagate in summer from semi-ripe cuttings.

L. angustifolia
syn. L. officinalis, L. spica
ENGLISH LAVENDER

This dense, bushy, evergreen shrub is native to the Mediterranean countries of southern Europe. It is grown mainly for the long-stemmed heads of mauve, scented flowers that appear from spring to autumn/fall— these are easily dried for lavender sachets, pot pourri and the like. It bears small, furry, grey leaves that turn green as the plant ages. Fully hardy and makes an excellent hedge; trim it in spring to maintain the shape. It grows to a height of 1 m (about 3 ft) and a spread of 1 m (about 3 ft). The flowers of *L. angustifolia* and *L. stoechas* are used in the distillation of oil of lavender.

Leptospermum laevigatum

Leucadendron salignum

Leptospermum petersonii

Lavandula stoechas

Leptospermum s. 'Red Damask'

L. dentata
FRENCH LAVENDER

A native of the Mediterranean region, the dense spikes of tubular, mauve-blue flowers of this bushy, evergreen shrub appear in autumn/ fall to late spring. Its aromatic leaves are serrated, fern-like and grey-green. Frost-hardy, it grows to a height and spread of 1 m (about 3 ft). *L. dentata* is drought and frost resistant and is adaptable to most soils.

L. stoechas
SPANISH LAVENDER, BUSH LAVENDER

This evergreen, dense, bushy shrub is frost-hardy and grows to a height and spread of 60 cm (about 24 in). In late spring and summer, it bears terminal spikes of fragrant, deep purple flowers. The leaves are aromatic and silver-grey. Propagate from cuttings in summer.

LEPTOSPERMUM
TEA-TREE, MOONAH

Ideal for the informal landscape garden, this genus of evergreen trees and shrubs is native to Tasmania and south-eastern Australia, as well as New Zealand. Well suited to cooler conditions, they have found their way into the gardens and parks of Europe and America, where many hybrids and cultivars have been developed. Profuse, small flowers—white, pink or red—appear in spring. Drought, wind and even salt resistant, they do well in coastal areas if not too exposed, and prefer a fertile, well-drained soil and full sun. Propagate from semi-ripe cuttings in summer. History has it that Captain James Cook prepared a brew from a New Zealand species for his crew as a remedy for scurvy—hence the common name, 'tea-tree'.

L. laevigatum
COASTAL TEA-TREE

Native to the eastern states of Australia, this tall, bushy shrub or tree bears attractive, small, white flowers in spring and early summer. The evergreen leaves are small, oval and leathery. Frost-hardy and preferring a moist soil, it grows to a height of 5 m (about 15 ft) and a spread of just under 3 m (about 9 ft). It is an excellent plant for the seaside, but not in South Africa where it has become a much-hated weed.

L. petersonii
syn. *L. citratum*
LEMON-SCENTED TEA-TREE

This evergreen shrub or small tree, a native of the eastern states of Australia, bears delightful, white flowers in spring and early summer. The narrow, lance-shaped leaves turn from red to green as the plant matures, giving off a characteristic lemon scent when bruised or crushed. The stem is graceful with slender branches and a lightly textured crown. It prefers light to me-dium, well-drained soil and does best in an open, sunny position. Drought resistant but frost-tender, *L. petersonii* grows to a height of 4 m (about 12 ft) and a spread of 2 m (6 ft).

L. scoparium 'Red Damask'
MANUKA

This upright, evergreen shrub grows to a height and spread of just under 3 m (about 9 ft). Frost-hardy, it has purple-tinged, dark green leaves and in spring and summer, bears sprays of double, dark red flowers. It prefers light, moist, well-drained soils in an open, sunny position, and is drought- and frost-hardy. There are many other cultivars of this native of Australia and New Zealand, many bred in the USA. They have white, red or pink flowers.

LEUCADENDRON
salignum
SILVER TREE

This genus, native to South Africa, is grown principally for its foliage, as the bloom is insignificant. The stiff, upward-pointing leaves may be silky or smooth and, as well as green, may be coloured gold, pink or silver. The male and female flowers are borne on separate plants— the female flowers are woody cones, the male flowers a mass of stamens. Colourful bracts (modified leaves) surround both male and female plants for several months of the year. *L. salignum,* an evergreen shrub with branching stems, bears small, yellow to red flowers, surrounded by colourful bracts, in autumn/fall and winter. It has silvery, lance-shaped leaves (the outer foliage may turn yellow in spring). Frost-hardy, it may grow to a height of 1.5 m (about 4½ ft) with a spread of 1 m (about 3 ft). Species do best in full light and well-drained, sandy, peaty soil—preferably without too much phosphate or nitrogen. Potted specimens should be well watered during periods of growth, less at other

Lavandula dentata

times. Propagate from seed or from cuttings in spring.

LEUCOSPERMUM
cordifolium
syn. *L. nutans*
SPELDEKUSSING, PINCUSHION BUSH

Native to South Africa, these spreading evergreen bushes have been raised successfully in warm, open temperate areas worldwide, including western USA and Australia. Grown for both flowers and foliage, they prefer a Mediterranean-type climate and a sandy, well-drained soil with few nitrates or phosphates. A sunny, protected position suits them best. *L. cordifolium,* a well-branched evergreen shrub, is grown for the delightful profuse bloom of pinkish orange, pincushion-like flowers it bears. These are long lasting when cut and much sought after by florists; they are cultivated extensively in Hawaii as well as in South Africa and Australia. Its leaves are green and lanceolate while the stem is short and has spreading branches. It grows to a height of 1–2 m (about 3–6 ft) with a spread of a little over 1 m (about 3 ft). Potted plants should be watered moderately during growth, less at other times. Propagate any time in spring from seed.

LEUCOTHOE
fontanesiana
syn. *Andromeda fontanesiana*
DOG HOBBLE, FETTERBUSH

Belonging to the Erica family, this evergreen species native to the mountains of the south-eastern United States is grown for its showy foliage and flowers. It has an arching habit, growing to a height of 1–2 m (about 3–6 ft) with a spread of 3 m (about 9 ft). The leaves are dark glossy green, lance-shaped and sharply toothed. Branches are gracefully arched and are laden with long panicles of waxen, white, lily-of-the-valley-type flowers that open below shoots from mid- to late spring. It prefers a moist, peaty, acid soil and shade or semi-shade. Propagate from semi-ripe cuttings in summer, and tip prune young plants during their first years. Fully hardy.

LIGUSTRUM
PRIVET

These deciduous, semi-evergreen and evergreen shrubs enjoy a mixed popularity. They can be difficult to remove once established, and they spread rapidly and can easily become weeds. Some species, however, are popular as hedge shrubs. Leaf size varies among the species, but they all have small, creamy white flowers in dense clusters with a strong odour. Fully to frost-hardy, they do best in sun or semi-shade—variegated forms require a fully sunny position. Cut back in mid-spring to restrict growth. Propagate from semi-ripe cuttings in summer.

L. japonicum
JAPANESE PRIVET

Native to Japan and Korea, this evergreen with its dense, compact habit grows to a height of 3 m (about 9 ft) and spread of 2.5 m (about 7½ ft). It has very deep green, oval, lustrous leaves crowded on the stem, resembling box leaves on a larger scale. Heavy conical panicles of tubular white flowers with four lobes appear from mid-summer to early autumn/fall. Frost-hardy. Propagate from semi-ripe cuttings in summer.

L. lucidum
CHINESE OR WAX-LEAF PRIVET

Native to China, Korea and Japan, this evergreen shrub with its upright habit reaches a height of 10 m (about 30 ft) and a spread of 8 m (about 24 ft). It has large, oval, glossy, dark green leaves and bears panicles of creamy white tubular flowers with four lobes in late summer and early autumn/fall. Frost-hardy, it needs protection from cold north and east winds. It has been declared a weed in some areas.

Leucospermum cordifolium

L. ovalifolium 'Aureum'
GOLDEN PRIVET

This upright, dense shrub, native to Japan, grows to a height of 4 m (about 12 ft) with a spread of 3 m (about 9 ft). In mid-summer it bears dense panicles of small, tubular, white flowers which give off a sickly odour. These are followed in turn by spherical, black fruits. The glossy, oval, green leaves have yellow borders. L. ovalifolium 'Aureum' is fully hardy. Prune out

Ligustrum quihoui

Ligustrum lucidum

any green shoots as soon as they appear or they will take over the shrub.

L. quihoui

A native of China, this elegant, evergreen shrub is one of the best species of the genus, producing panicles of white flowers up to 50 cm (about 20 in) long in autumn/fall. It has dark green oval leaves and grows to a height of 3 m (about 9 ft) with a spread of 2 m (about 6 ft).

Leucothoe fontanesiana

Ligustrum japonicum

Ligustrum ovalifolium 'Aureum'

Lonicera tatarica

Lonicera × purpusii

Lonicera nitida

Lonicera fragrantissima

Ligustrum sinense

L. sinense
CHINESE PRIVET

This semi-evergreen or deciduous, bushy shrub bears fragrant, tubular, white flowers in mid-summer, set among pale green, oval leaves. Small, black-purple berries follow. Fully hardy, *L. sinense* grows to a height of 4 m (about 12 ft) with a spread of 3 m (about 9 ft).

LONICERA
HONEYSUCKLE, WOODBINE

These deciduous, semi-evergreen shrubs and woody-stemmed, twin-

Loropetalum chinense

ing climbers are grown for the delightful, scented flowers and the foliage that suit them admirably as a cover for sheds and pergolas. Found worldwide in warm and temperate climates, they do best in a fertile, well-drained or moist soil in sun or semi-shade. They are fully hardy to frost-tender, to a minimum 5°C (40° F). Prune to remove dead growth or to restrict their often rampant spread—position the shrub where there is plenty of room. Mostly deciduous, the shrubby species of *Lonicera* should be propagated from cuttings taken in late summer. Aphids may pose a problem.

L. fragrantissima
WINTERSWEET

This deciduous or semi-evergreen bushy, spreading shrub, the most fragrant of the species, is native to China. It grows to a height of 2 m (about 6 ft) and a spread of 4 m (about 12 ft). Fully hardy, it bears paired, creamy, tubular, sweetly fragrant flowers in winter and early spring. Its leaves are oval, heart-shaped and green, and appear shortly after the flowers. Prune after flowering to control size and the plant's tendency to straggle.

L. nitida

This bushy, dense, evergreen shrub makes an excellent hedging specimen; it is adaptable to most soils in an open, sunny position and is drought tender. Growing to a height of 2 m (about 6 ft) and a spread of 3 m (about 9 ft), it bears insignificant, cream flowers, in pairs, in late spring. These are followed in turn by small, rounded purple berries.

Moderately frost-hardy, it has glossy, green, small, oval leaves. It can be clipped as a formal hedge.

L. × purpusii

This deciduous or semi-evergreen hybrid bears small clusters of fragrant, creamy white, short-tubed flowers with yellow anthers in winter and early spring. It is a dense, bushy shrub with a height and spread of up to 2 m (about 6 ft). The oval leaves are dark to mid-green. Fully hardy.

L. tatarica

Native to southern Russia, this deciduous shrub has an erect habit, growing to a height and spread of 3 m (about 9 ft). It has dark green oval leaves with blue-green undersides and tubular to trumpet-shaped white, pink or red flowers, borne in late spring and early summer. These are followed by red, globular berries. Fully hardy.

LOROPETALUM
chinense

FRINGE FLOWER

Native to China, this well-branched, rounded, evergreen shrub is prized for the attractive, creamy white flowers it bears in clusters all along the branches during winter and spring. The 5 cm (about 2 in) oval leaves are light green. Half-hardy, it needs full light or semi-shade, and does best in a well-drained soil that is neutral to acid. Potted specimens should be watered freely in full growth, but only moderately at other times. Little pruning is required, except to remove twiggy

Mahonia lomariifolia

Mahonia aquifolium

growth. The shrub grows to a height and spread of 1.5 m (about 4½ ft), although it can grow larger if very happy. Propagate from semi-ripe cuttings in late summer or by layering in spring.

MAGNOLIA

These evergreen, semi-evergreen and deciduous shrubs and trees hail from China. Grown for the pleasing, often sweet-scented, waxy, tulip-shaped flowers, they thrive in a fertile, well-drained soil. If the soil is sandy, add manure and leafmould before planting. Magnolias need shelter from strong winds, and prefer full-light to shady conditions. Little pruning is required, as they continue to flower on the same wood for several years. The very old branches with woody spurs may be removed to encourage new growth. Propagate from semi-ripe cuttings in summer or from seed in autumn/fall. Alternatively, graft in winter.

M. quinquepeta
syn. M. liliiflora

This deciduous, bushy species is native to China. From mid-spring to mid-summer, it bears handsome, purple, tulip-like flowers set among dark green, oval leaves. Fully hardy, it grows to a height of 4 m (about 12 ft) and a spread of 5 m (about 15 ft).

M. stellata
STAR MAGNOLIA

This dense, slow-growing, deciduous shrub is a native of Japan. Prized for the delightful, white, star-like flowers it bears in late winter and early spring, it is fully hardy and grows to a height and spread of 3 m (about 9 ft). It has narrow, pale green, elongated, oval leaves.

MAHONIA
OREGON GRAPE, HOLLY GRAPE, MOUNTAIN GRAPE

Useful as hedges or windbreaks, these evergreen shrubs are also grown for their dense panicles of open, yellow flowers. These are followed by blue-black fruits that make excellent jam. Low-growing species are also useful for ground

cover. Plant in fertile soil that is well-drained but not too dry. In cold conditions, they require full sun; in warmer climates, partial shade will see them thrive. Propagate from seed in autumn/fall or from semi-ripe cuttings in summer.

M. aquifolium
OREGON GRAPE

This evergreen, open shrub, native to North America grows to 1 m (about 3 ft) tall with a 1.5 m (about 4½ ft) spread. In early spring, it bears attractive, yellow flowers, followed by blue-black, globular berries. Its leaves are divided into bright green leaflets and turn bronze in winter. It prefers light to medium, well-drained soils in an open, sunny position and is fully hardy. Propagate from seed sown in spring.

M. lomariifolia
MOUNTAIN GRAPE

This evergreen, moderately frost-hardy, very upright shrub, is native to Yunnan Province, China. It grows to a height of 3 m (about 9 ft) with a spread of 2 m (about 6 ft), bearing bright yellow spikes in terminal clusters in late autumn/fall to winter. These are arranged like the spokes of an inverted umbrella and are set among narrow, holly-like, spiny leaflets. Black berries appear after the bloom. It prefers well-composted, well-drained soils in an open, sunny position.

M. repens
CALIFORNIAN HOLLY GRAPE

A dwarf species spreading by underground stems, this evergreen shrub is native to the western United States, between the Rocky Mountains and the coast. It is useful as a ground cover, especially for uneven, rocky ground where mowing is difficult. Reaching a height of 30 cm (about 12 in) and a spread 2 m (about 6 ft), it has an upright habit and is fully hardy. The blue-green leaves have bristle-like teeth and often turn reddish in autumn/fall in cooler climates. Fragrant, deep yellow flowers are borne in dense clusters from mid- to late spring, followed by showy, dark blue berries.

Magnolia stellata

Magnolia quinquepeta

Mahonia repens

Melaleuca incana

Malvaviscus arboreus

MALUS
sargentii

A Japanese native, this small, bushy, deciduous crab apple has pink-tinted buds which open to a profusion of white blossom in late spring. This display is followed by long-lasting, deep red fruits. The stems are erect, slender and branching, while the 3-lobed leaves are glossy, oval and dark green and have serrate margins. It has a spreading habit, growing to a height of around 2.5 m (about 7½ ft) with a spread of 3 m (about 9 ft). Fully hardy, it prefers a well-drained soil and a sunny situation. Prune to retain shape in winter, cutting out any dead or damaged wood. Propagate by grafting in mid-winter or by budding in late summer. Watch out for caterpillars, aphids and red spider mite. Fireblight, apple scab and honey fungus may also be a problem.

MALVAVISCUS
arboreus
TURK'S CAP, SLEEPY MALLOW

This evergreen, rounded shrub, a native of Mexico, is grown for the rich, red, hibiscus-like flowers it bears in summer, and for its bright green, soft-haired leaves. It prefers a well-drained but moist soil, and thrives in full sun or partial shade. Cut flower stems back hard in winter to maintain the shape. Potted specimens should be well watered in the growing season, but only moderately at other times. Frost-tender, *M. arboreus* grows to a height and spread of 3 m (about 9 ft).

MELALEUCA
HONEYMYRTLE, PAPERBARK

As well as being grown for their showy blossom and their general appearance overall, the magnificent shrubs of this genus (which also includes trees) are also useful for hedging and screening. They do best in a light, well-drained soil that is relatively free of nitrogen, but they will tolerate a wide range of soil conditions, even waterlogged soil. They do well in coastal areas and will assume interesting shapes. Many species have a fragrant, honey scent that will attract birds. Potted specimens should be watered moderately, less so in colder temperatures. Pruning into a hedge shape will encourage growth. Propagate from seed sown in spring, or from semi-hardwood cuttings from summer to mid-winter.

Melaleuca nesophylla

M. hypericifolia

This evergreen, rounded shrub, native to New South Wales and Queensland, Australia, grows to a height and spread of 3 m (about 9 ft). In summer it bears large, orange-red flowers in dense, bottlebrush spikes. These appear among lanceolate, mid- to pale green leaves that turn bronze-tipped in winter. The fruits are small, woody capsules. *M. hypericifolia* is half-hardy. If the shrub is pruned back hard in spring, it will produce long stems of foliage for flower arrangements.

M. incana

This pendulous, evergreen shrub is grown for its narrow, grey-green leaves and spring appearance of dainty, creamy-yellow, bottlebrush flowers. Half-hardy, it grows to a height of 3 m (about 9 ft) with a spread of 2 m (about 6 ft). *M. incana* is native to New South Wales, Australia.

M. nesophylla
WESTERN TEA MYRTLE

This evergreen, bushy shrub is native to Western Australia and in summer, bears flowers that are brushes of mauve, gold-tipped stamens, fading to white to give the plant a multi-coloured effect. Its leaves are oval, broad, smooth and grey-green. Frost-hardy, it grows to a height of 3 m (about 9 ft) with a spread of 2 m (about 6 ft).

MELASTOMA
affine
syn. *M. denticulatum*, *M. polyanthum*
NATIVE LASIANDRA, PINK LASIANDRA

This tropical, bushy shrub from India and Australia grows to 2–3 m (about 6–9 ft) tall. The ovate leaves are bright green with 3–5 prominent veins. Large pinkish purple, mauve or, more rarely, white flowers up to 7 cm (about 3 in) wide, are borne on terminal clusters. The flowers are short lived but bloom most of the year, peaking in summer, followed by purple berries which can be eaten. This plant will grow in a wide range of soils but

Malus sargentii

Melaleuca hypericifolia

likes well-drained soil in full light or part-shade. Can be kept in a pot and needs abundant water during growth and moderate amounts at other times. Propagate from fresh seed or cuttings which strike readily in spring or summer. It may be attacked by red spider mite or whitefly. In some countries it has run wild and in Hawaii is considered a pest.

MELIANTHUS
major
HONEY FLOWER, TOUCH-ME-NOT

This sprawling, evergreen bush is a native of South Africa. Growing to a height and spread of 2–3 m (about 6–9 ft), it is prized for the luxuriant foliage and brownish-red, tubular flowers on terminal spikes that appear in spring and summer. The leaves have oval, blue-grey, serrated leaflets. Half-hardy, it does best in fertile, well-drained soil and will thrive in a sunny position. It can be pruned hard in early spring to keep it compact, although it will then flower less freely. Propagate from seed in spring or from greenwood cuttings in summer. The leaves have a strong, unpleasant smell when bruised, hence the common name 'touch-me-not'.

MICHELIA
figo
PORT WINE MAGNOLIA, BANANA SHRUB

Native to western China, this evergreen shrub bears small, strongly scented, wine-coloured flowers, set among glossy, oval leaves. The flowers smell strongly of bananas. It does best in a well-drained, humus rich, neutral to acid soil. Half-hardy but drought-tender, *M. figo* does best in a protected spot in full light or partial shade. Pruning is not really necessary. Keep potted specimens well watered when in growth. The shrub grows to a height and spread of 3 m (about 9 ft). Propagate from semi-hardwood cuttings taken in summer or autumn/fall.

MIMULUS
aurantiacus
syn. *M. glutinosus, Diplacus glutinosus*
MONKEY MUSK

This evergreen shrub, native to North America, is grown for the beautiful crimson or yellow-orange, tubular flowers that appear in spring and summer, offset by narrow, glossy, lance-shaped leaves with margins that roll slightly inwards. Half-hardy, it prefers full sun to partial shade and a moist, even wet, soil (though it will adapt to most soil conditions). It grows to a height and spread of 1 m (about 3 ft). Propagate from seed in autumn/fall.

Melianthus major

MYOPORUM
parvifolium
CREEPING BOOBIALLA

This evergreen, spreading to prostrate shrub is native to southern and western Australia. Half-hardy, it grows to a height of 15 cm (about 6 in) and spread of 80 cm (about 32 in). Grow in an open, sunny position in a light to heavy, well-drained soil. Clusters of white, tubular flowers appear in summer, followed by purple, globular berries. The semi-succulent leaves are narrow, blunt and thick. Propagate from seed in spring, or semi-ripe cuttings in late summer.

MYRICA

Grown for their foliage and fruits, these evergreen or deciduous shrubs are of almost cosmopolitan distribution. They need plentiful water in summer, and so are ideal for waterside gardens in a sunny situation. Plants are aromatic and most varieties have insignificant small, petal-less flowers on short catkins in spring. Propagate from seed when ripe, from suckers removed at planting time or by layering in spring. Frost-hardy to frost-tender, to a minimum 5°C (40°F).

M. californica
CALIFORNIAN BAYBERRY

This handsome evergreen has been valued for many years for the wax coating on its dark purple fruit, which is still used for candle-making by craftspeople. It has a varying growth habit, reaching 3–18 m (about 9–60 ft) in height with a spread of 2–6 m (about 6–18 ft). The leaves are oval, serrated and apple-green and clusters of berries appear in autumn/fall, lasting until mid-winter. Frost-hardy.

M. pensylvanica
BAYBERRY, CANDLEBERRY, WAX MYRTLE

Native to eastern North America, this handsome deciduous shrub reaches a height of 2–3 m (about 6–9 ft). It has an erect habit with

Melastoma affine

Myrtus communis

Michelia figo

Myoporum parvifolium

Mimulus aurantiacus

aromatic, dark green leaves and waxy, greyish white fruits from winter through to spring.

MYRTUS
MYRTLE

Popular for hedges and screens, most species of the evergreen genus, *Myrtus*, also make elegantly handsome, potted plants. All bear long-stamened flowers with a pleasant fragrance, followed by handsome, edible berries. The leaves give off a strong scent when crushed. Myrtles

do best in full sun and fertile, well-drained soil. Drought resistant and half-hardy, they will survive down to minus 8°C (about 18°F).

M. communis
COMMON MYRTLE, GREEK MYRTLE

From early summer, this bushy, evergreen shrub bears dainty, fragrant, white flowers, set among glossy, dark green leaves. The flowers are followed by purple-black berries. Frost-hardy, *M. communis* grows to a height and spread of 3 m (about 9 ft). Propagate from seed.

A Field Trip to Mount Kinabalu

Mount Kinabalu in Sabah, on the island of Borneo, is a plant hunter's paradise. It is a bridge for the flora and fauna of both northern and southern hemispheres, and thousands of plant enthusiasts have made the pilgrimage to climb Mount Kinabalu, 'the botanist's Mecca'. It is also one of the places where the vireya rhododendrons can be seen. Many of these are epiphytic, and have unusual sunset colouring.

The journey from the closest town, Kota Kinabalu, takes about a day and you will then need to allow two days on the mountain, staying overnight in accommodation near the summit. You need to book an authorized guide at Kinabalu National Park Headquarters. Take warm clothing because, although this is the tropics, the upper parts of the mountain can be cold.

The journey to park headquarters will take you through typical lowland rainforest. The trees here are enormous, creating a heavy canopy that allows little or no sunlight through to the forest floor.

Park headquarters, where you start your climb, is at an altitude of 1500 m (about 5000 ft). Here in the lower montane zone, the trees, mainly oaks, are smaller than in the lowland rainforest. Lush ferns grow everywhere. The common tree fern (*Cyathea contaminans*) thrives, its graceful fronds reaching up to 4 m (about 12 ft) in length. Look up into the trees and you will see bird's nest ferns perched on forks in the branches, from which tangles of vines hang. Orchids also abound in this rich environment. The crimson and white nun's orchid (*Phaius tankervillae*) and the delicate white and gold angel orchid (*Coelogyne venusta*) are common.

After about two hours you will reach the Kamborangoh Shelter, situated at an altitude of 2286 m (about 7500 ft); then take the by-pass trail from here to Carsons Camp. The trees in this upper montane zone are smaller, up to 6 m

(about 18 ft). There are more orchids here, but it is the rhododendrons which will take your breath away. The magnificent *Rhododendron lowii* is everywhere, the shrubs almost obscured by masses of bright yellow flowers. The leaves are thick and long and the waxy, funnel-shaped flowers are 8 cm (about 3 in) wide. The flowers are usually yellow but sometimes pinkish yellow in colour. Along the track are located other *Rhododendron* species. *R. brookeanum* has smaller leaves and flowers, which are yellowish pink to red with white centres and often lemon-scented. You may see it growing as an epiphyte. *R. rugosum* and *R. fallacinum* have pink to apricot flowers. *R. stenophyllum* has orange to red, bell-shaped flowers and needle-like foliage. The carnivorous pitcher plant (*Nepenthes tentaculata*) also grows here.

Lows Peak
(4100 m, 13455 ft)

▲ Ugly Sisters
▲ Donkey's Ears

South Peak
(Puncak Tun Mustapha)
Sayat Sayat Hut
Panar Laban
Rock Face

Panar Laban
(H) ■ Burlington House
New Hut
Gua Pakka ▲ ■ Shelter
(Paka Cave)
(H)

S A B A H

Layang Layang   Old Carsons Camp
(2600 m, 8500 ft) (H) (Tapak Perkhemahan lama)
Shelter ■   Radio Sabah Transmitter
Kamborangoh ■   TV Complex

Power Station ▲

- - - - Treking Path
——— Roads
(H) Helipad

Park HQ to
Sayat Sayat Hut
is 9 hours

(H)
■ Park HQ
← Kota Kinabalu   Ranau →

Rhododendron ericoides

Rhododendron crassifolium

Rhododendron lowii

The summit of Mount Kinabalu, seen from park headquarters.

Mount Kinabalu is home to many rhododendrons, some of which are only found here. They are amazingly vigorous and luxuriant; if you take a moment to really study your surroundings you will see why. The soil is light but rich and covered in leaves. The rainfall and humidity are high and the rhododendrons are lightly shaded from the strong sun.

Mount Kinabalu is also rich in animal and birdlife, including the leopard, mongoose and Malay bear, but unfortunately these are unlikely to be seen as most keep well away from the tracks. Orang-utans are occasionally spotted near the trails and you may see small monkeys swinging in the trees.

Continuing on past Carsons Camp, at an altitude of 2713 m (about 8900 ft), the vegetation on either side of the track is thick with bamboo and more rhododendrons. At times the whole path will be clouded with mist and you will notice the temperature getting cooler.

After about two hours you reach Paka Cave, at an altitude of 3200 m (about 10 500 ft). This 'cave', not much more than the underside of a rock, is where Sir Hugh Low and Spencer St John, two of the region's earliest explorers, sheltered for several icy nights. The trees here include twisted, gnarled forms of the manuka or tea tree (*Leptospermum*). You may see green mountain blackeyes and the brown mountain bush warbler. You will also see the endemic *Rhododendron ericoides*, an unusual species with needle-like leaves and scarlet, 1 cm (about ½ in) long flowers.

As you climb higher the soil virtually disappears and the vegetation becomes sparse against the granite background. Very few plants can survive the fierce winds, strong sun and abundant rain. Some that do survive have adapted to the extreme conditions by assuming a bonsai-like form. Another unusual rhododendron grows at this altitude—*R. buxifolium*, which has leathery leaves and scarlet flowers.

Soon you reach the huts where you will spend the night. The best time to climb the rest of the way to the summit is at dawn; by late morning Lows Peak will be enveloped in mist. The last short leg of your climb is devoid of any vegetation but the stark granite landscape has a beauty all its own.

Rhododendron

In 1848 the renowned botanist Professor Lindley wrote: 'When Mr Hugh Low returned from his visit to Borneo, he was so obliging as to place in my hands some drawings and dried specimens of certain species of Rhododendron which occur in that island *growing upon trees*. They are found to be distinct from all previously known … '

Low's collections from Sarawak contained some of the first botanical specimens of what we now call the vireya, or Malesian, rhododendrons, technically members of *Rhododendron* sect. *Vireya*. This group has around 280 recognized species (out of a total of around 800 for the genus *Rhododendron* as a whole), mostly confined to the region between mainland Asia and Australia. By far the largest number, over 150, occur on the island of New Guinea; Borneo has 34, Sumatra has 26, the Philippines has 24, and there are 15 on the Malay Peninsula. Australia has a single native species, *R. lochiae*.

Many vireyas grow as epiphytes on trees, while others grow on cliffs or rocky mountain summits, on raw clay landslips, or in high mountain bogs at altitudes of up to about 4500 m (about 14 760 ft). Both leaves and flowers range in size from tiny to very large, while flower colours tend towards yellows, oranges and scarlets, although whites and pinks are also frequent.

In the last 30 to 40 years many of the New Guinea species have been brought into cultivation and hybridized, and are popular in mild humid areas.

Rhododendron brookeanum

Nerium oleander 'Album'

Nerium o. 'Splendens Variegatum'

Nandina domestica 'Nana'

Nerium oleander

Myrtus ugni

Nerium oleander 'Punctatum'

Nandina domestica

M. ugni
CHILEANGUAVA

This handsome, upright, densely branched, shrub is native to Chile. In spring, it bears cup-shaped, pink flowers, set among glossy deep, green, thick, small, round leaves. Edible dark red fruits follow the bloom. Half-hardy, it grows to a height of 1.5 m (about 4½ ft) with a spread of 1 m (about 3 ft).

NANDINA
SACRED BAMBOO, HEAVENLY BAMBOO

Not a true bamboo, the stems of these evergreen and semi-evergreen shrubs from China and Japan will grow to a height of nearly 3 m (about 9 ft) but with a spread of only about 1 m (about 3 ft). This makes the genus popular with landscape gardeners, who also grow the species for the handsome, reddish foliage which appears in autumn/fall and winter. Small, yellow-centred, white flowers appear in summer and autumn/fall, followed by glossy, red fruits. Frost-hardy,

they prefer a sheltered, sunny position, and fertile, well-drained, but not too dry soil. In spring, prune untidy, aging stems to the base. Propagate from semi-ripe cuttings or seed in summer.

N. domestica
SACRED BAMBOO, HEAVENLY BAMBOO

This upright evergreen shrub is a native of Japan and China. In summer, it bears small, white, upright, star-shaped flowers in sprays; these are followed (on female plants) by red berries. It has narrow, lance-shaped, sheathing leaves that turn purplish-red in winter. Frost-hardy, it prefers a moist soil and sunny position, although it will grow in light shade. Thin out the older branches every few years.

N. domestica 'Nana'

This dwarf shrub is particularly popular, probably because it colours so strongly in winter. An evergreen or semi-evergreen, it grows to a height of 30–60 cm (about 12–24 in) with a spread of 4 m (about

12 ft). Frost-hardy, it rarely flowers. Given sufficient direct sun, its bright green leaves will turn scarlet in autumn/fall to winter. *N. domestica* 'Nana' is eminently suitable for a mixed border or rockery.

NERIUM
OLEANDER, ROSE-BAY, ROSE LAUREL

These evergreen shrubs are grown for their delightful flowers, which bloom in a variety of colours—pink, white, red and cream. They have dark, glossy spear-shaped leaves. Although they do best in full sun and a well-drained soil, they do extremely well in a variety of conditions—dry, semi-arid; salty coastal areas; and in soil with poor drainage—and flourish from tropical to warm-temperate climates. Ideally the shrub should be pruned to promote branching, and when potted, should be watered regularly when in full growth. Propagate from semi-ripe cuttings in summer, or from seed in spring. The plant is poisonous, but so bitter even goats will not eat it.

N. oleander

This evergreen, upright, bushy shrub grows rapidly to a height of 2–4 m (about 6–12 ft) with a spread of 3 m (about 9 ft). Native to the Mediterranean, it bears open, white or pink flowers from spring to autumn/fall in terminal sprays set among narrow, long, dark green leaves. *N. oleander* is half-hardy.

N. oleander 'Album'

This cultivar bears single, white flowers with a cream centre.

N. oleander 'Punctatum'
syn. N.o. 'Monsieur Belaguier'

This upright, evergreen shrub bears clusters of delightful, pale pink, single flowers from spring through to autumn/fall. It has deep-green, leathery leaves. Frost-tender, it grows to a height and spread of 3 m (about 9 ft).

N. oleander 'Splendens Variegatum'

This evergreen cultivar bears deep pink, double flowers from spring to autumn/fall. It has leathery, dark green leaves with yellow margins. The plain-leaved version is splendid, also bearing flowers in great profusion.

OCHNA
serrulata
BIRD'S EYE BUSH, MICKEY MOUSE PLANT

This evergreen shrub is native to southern Africa. It is grown for the terminal clusters of attractive, yellow flowers set among oval, glossy, serrated leaves, and for the black, glossy berries set in red calyces that follow the bloom. It prefers full light in an open, sunny position, and a light, sandy, well-drained soil. Water potted plants moderately in full growth. If necessary, prune shrubs in spring. Frost-tender, it grows to a height and spread of just under 2 m (about 6 ft). Propagate from semi-ripe cuttings in summer, and from seed in spring. *O. serrulata* self-sows readily and therefore can become a pest.

OLEARIA
DAISY BUSH

These dense, evergreen shrubs are native to Australia and New Zealand, and are grown for their foliage and delicate, pale, daisy flowers. They do well in seaside gardens, providing good, wind-resistant shelter. They do best in full sun and moist, well-drained soil. Prune annually and dead-head regularly to prevent them becoming woody and straggly. Propagate from semi-ripe cuttings in summer.

Olearia arborescens

Ochna serrulata

O. arborescens

In summer, this many-branched, spreading tree-like shrub bears oval, daisy-like flowers in panicles at the ends of the branches. It has oval, serrated leaves. Half-hardy, it likes a moist soil and full sun. It grows to 5 m (about 15 ft) tall and 3 m (about 9 ft) wide.

O. macrodonta
LARGE-TOOTHED TREE ASTER

Native to New Zealand, this shrub is popular in the USA and UK. It grows 3–6 m (about 9–18 ft) tall and in summer bears many small, white, daisy-like flowers in terminal clusters. The ovate to oblong leaves, white felted below, have coarse toothed margins.

O. phlogopappa
DUSKY DAISYBUSH

This erect, evergreen shrub, native to New South Wales, Tasmania and Victoria, Australia, is grown for the white, pink or mauve, daisy-like flowers it bears from mid-spring to early summer. The grey-green leaves are oblong and serrated. Frost-hardy, it grows to a height and spread of 2 m (about 6 ft).

OSMANTHUS
FRAGRANT OLIVE, KWAI FA

The slow-growing, evergreen shrubs or small trees in this genus are grown for their fragrance produced from small, almost invisible, flowers. The scent resembles that of jasmine and gardenias and lasts from autumn/fall through to spring.

Olearia macrodonta

Olearia phlogopappa

Frost-hardy to half-hardy, they prefer fertile, well-drained soil and tolerate either sun or shade. Cut back after flowering to restrict growth, and propagate from semi-ripe cuttings in summer. The flowers of *Osmanthus* species are traditionally used by the Chinese to scent and sweeten their tea. Hybrids between *Osmanthus* and the closely related *Phillyrea* are called *Osmarea*: they look just like *Osmanthus* and are grown in the same way.

O. delavayi
syn. *Siphonosmanthus delavayi*

One of the most popular species, this evergreen, rounded, bushy shrub is a Chinese native. It has arching branches, small, glossy, dark, serrated leaves and clusters of highly scented white tubular flowers freely produced from mid- to late summer. Frost-hardy, it reaches a height and spread of around 2–3 m (about 6–9 ft). It is a good hedging plant.

Osmanthus delavayi

Osmanthus h. 'Variegatus'

O. fragrans
SWEET OSMANTHUS

This erect, branching, evergreen shrub is native to the Himalayas, India and Japan. It grows to a height of 5 m (about 15 ft) with a spread of 3 m (about 9 ft). Sprays of small, white, very fragrant flowers appear in spring and again in autumn/fall. *O. fragrans* has glossy, broad, green leaves and is half-hardy.

O. heterophyllus 'Variegatus'
syn. *O. illicifolius variegatus*

Native to China, this erect, branching, evergreen shrub or tree bears small, white, delightfully fragrant flowers in the leaf axils, in autumn/fall. It has holly-like leaves; there is a form with yellow-bordered foliage. Frost-hardy, it grows to a height of 6 m (about 18 ft) with a spread of 3 m (about 9 ft).

PACHYSTEGIA
insignis

This low-growing, spreading, evergreen shrub, native to New Zealand, is grown for its white, daisy-like flowers with yellow centres borne in winter. It has leathery, dark green, shiny leaves and likes a well-drained soil in a protected, sunny position; it will tolerate partial shade. Frost-hardy, it grows to 1 m (about 3 ft) tall with a 2 m (about 6 ft) spread. Propagate from seed or cuttings.

PAEONIA
PEONY

Native to Tibet, western China and Bhutan, peonies do best in colder temperatures. The shrubs of the genus (which also includes perennials) are called 'tree peonies'. These are woody and deciduous, bearing brightly coloured flowers that range from white to darkest red, to purple, orange and yellow. They do best in a cool, lightly shaded spot, especially in mild-winter climates—it is best to plant them in the shade of other shrubs, otherwise the sun will damage the blooms. However, where they are able to become properly dormant in winter, they are better with half-day sun. Peonies

like a moist, well-drained soil, rich with humus and preferably with some lime. Propagate from hardwood cuttings in autumn/fall or by grafting in winter. Protect young plants from frost and watch out for botrytis, especially in soggy soil. Difficult to propagate, plants are expensive and grafting is the usual method.

P. lutea

A deciduous, upright shrub, native to China, *P. lutea* bears single, yellow flowers in late spring to early summer. Its dark green leaves have sawtoothed edges. Frost-hardy, it grows to a height and spread of 2 m (about 6 ft).

P. suffruticosa
MOUTAN, TREE PEONY

This deciduous, upright shrub, a native of China, grows to a height and spread of 1–2 m (about 3–6 ft). In spring it bears single or double, cup-shaped, huge, red, pink, white or yellow flowers (depending on variety: there are many) set among large, compound, mid-green leaves. It is frost-hardy.

PARAHEBE
VERONICA

Found mainly in New Zealand, these dense, shrubby evergreens have a prostrate, decumbent habit, making them excellent for border edgings or for rock gardens. Frost-hardy, they prefer full sun, and a well-drained, peaty, sandy soil. Propagate from semi-ripe cuttings in early summer.

P. catarractae

Perhaps the most decorative of the genus, this species has at first a rapid spreading habit and then grows upwards. In spring, it bears racemes of small, white, funnel-shaped flowers tinged with purple, among oval, serrated leaves. Frost-hardy, it grows to a height and spread of 30 cm (about 12 in).

P. lyallii

This semi-evergreen, frost-hardy, prostrate shrub, a native of New Zealand, grows to a height of 15 cm (about 6 in) with a spread of up to 25 cm (about 10 in). In early summer, it bears terminal spikes of small, white or pink flowers, set among oval, serrated, leathery green leaves.

P. perfoliata
syn. *Derwentia perfoliata*
DIGGER'S SPEEDWELL

A native of New South Wales and Victoria, Australia, this evergreen shrub is grown for the beautiful, deep blue flowers it bears in spring, set among broad, sessile, leathery, silver-grey leaves. Frost-hardy, it does best in a well-drained, peaty,

Paeonia suffruticosa

Osmanthus fragrans

Parahebe lyallii

Paeonia lutea

Parahebe catarractae   Pachystegia insignis

sandy soil, in a sunny or partially shaded position. Well suited as a rockery plant or for border edging, *P. perfolia* grows to a height and spread of 60 cm (about 2 ft). Propagate from semi-ripe cuttings in early summer.

PAXISTIMA
canbyi
syn. *Pachistima canbyi*

Grown for its foliage, this evergreen shrub with its spreading habit reaches a height of 15–30 cm (about 6–12 in) and a spread of 20 cm (about 8 in). It is a useful ground cover, preferring a shady position with moist soil rich in organic matter. The leaves are linear or oblong, and short, drooping spikes of tiny greenish white flowers are borne in summer. Propagate from semi-ripe cuttings in summer or by division in spring. This species is fully hardy.

PENTAS
lanceolata
syn. *P. carnea*
EGYPTIAN STAR, STAR CLUSTER

Native to the tropics of Africa and the Arabian peninsula, this erect, straggling shrub grows to a height of 60 cm (about 24 in) and a spread of 1 m (about 3 ft). It is grown for the spring/summer appearance of clusters of tubular, red, pink, lilac or white flowers, set among bright green, hairy leaves. Frost-tender, it does best in fertile, well-drained, sandy soil and an open, sunny position. Pinch back regularly to maintain a compact habit and to encourage bloom. Water generously when in full growth. Propagate from seed in spring or from softwood cuttings in summer.

PERNETTYA
mucronata
PRICKLY HEATH

Native to the southern tip of South America, this evergreen shrub bears white, urn-shaped, heath-like flowers in late spring and early summer, set among small, pointed, heath-like leaves. Small, bright berries of variable colour appear in autumn/fall and winter. It does best in a well-drained acid soil and prefers sun or semi-shade. Densely branched when young, it gets leggy when more mature and will require cutting back hard. It grows to a height and spread of 1 m (about 3 ft). Propagate by division or from seed in summer or spring, or from softwood cuttings in summer to be sure of the berry colour.

PHILADELPHUS
MOCK ORANGE, SYRINGA

These suckering, deciduous shrubs come from Europe, Asia and the Americas and are among the most popular of flower-bearing shrubs because of their delightful orange-blossom fragrance. Very versatile plants, they are ideal for pathways, in open borders or as wall shrubs. Hardiness varies considerably among the species. They need sun and a fertile, well-drained soil. Thin out after bloom, and propagate from softwood cuttings in summer. Keep warm and moist until the roots establish themselves. Syringa is the old Roman name, now used by botanists as the genus name for the lilac.

P. coronarius
MOCK ORANGE

This species is a native of Europe and South-East Asia. Fully hardy, it grows to a height and spread of 3 m (about 9 ft). It bears terminal clusters of fragrant, creamy white flowers in spring, and oval leaves that have hairy veins underneath.

P. 'Lemoinei'

From early mid-summer, this slightly arching, upright, deciduous shrub bears small, very fragrant, white flowers, set among oval to lance-shaped leaves. Fully hardy, it grows to a height and spread of 1.5 m (about 4½ ft).

P. lewisii
MOCK ORANGE

A native of North America, this deciduous shrub grows to a height of 3 m (about 9 ft) with a spread of 2 m (about 6 ft). It has oval green leaves and white, fragrant, 4-petalled, solitary flowers. Frost resistant but drought tender.

Pentas lanceolata

Pernettya mucronata

Philadelphus coronarius

Philadelphus 'Lemoinei'

Parahebe perfoliata

Philadelphus lewisii

P. mexicanus
MEXICAN MOCK ORANGE, EVERGREEN MOCK ORANGE

Native to Mexico, this evergreen shrub bears single, cream, very fragrant flowers, set among oval green leaves. Moderately frost-tender, it grows to a height of 3 m (about 9 ft) and a spread of 2 m (about 6 ft). It prefers a partially shaded, protected position.

P. 'Virginal'

Fully hardy, this vigorous, upright shrub grows to a height and spread of a little under 3 m (about 9 ft). From late spring to early summer, it bears large, fragrant, semi-double flowers set among dark green, oval leaves.

PHLOMIS
fruticosa
JERUSALEM SAGE

This evergreen shrub, a native of southern Europe, is grown for the strikingly beautiful, yellow flowers it bears in whorls, from early to mid-summer, among oval, wrinkled, woolly green leaves. Frost-hardy, it does best in full sun. Drought, frost and salt resistant, it tolerates coastal areas quite well and grows to a height and spread of about 75 cm (about 30 in). Prune back to about half in autumn/fall to keep its habit neat. Propagate from seed in spring or from cuttings in summer.

PHOTINIA
CHINESE OR JAPANESE HAWTHORN

Grown mostly for their shiny foliage, species of this genus of semi-deciduous shrubs and trees make excellent hedges. They bear insignificant, white, acrid-smelling flowers in spring followed by blue-black berries The young foliage is brilliantly coloured, maturing to rich green. Fully hardy, photinias do best in a fertile, well-drained soil and require sun or semi-shade. Prune regularly to keep their habit dense and to promote new growth. Propagate by layering, or by grafting on to hawthorn stock.

P. × fraseri

This group of evergreen hybrids has leathery, dark green, glossy leaves that are crimson to coppery red in their new spring growth. Small white flowers are borne in spring. They grow well in neutral and chalky soils and are frost-hardy. 'Robusta' bears large, laurel-like leaves and has coppery red new growth, reaching a height of 4–5 m (about 12–15 ft). 'Red Robin' reaches up to 3 m (about 9 ft) in height and has bright ruby-red young leaves, while 'Birmingham' reaches 5 m (about 15 ft) in height and spread and has purple-red new growth.

P. glabra
PHOTINIA HEDGE

A native of eastern Asia, this species grows to a height of 3 m (about 9 ft) and a spread of 2 m (about 6 ft). As its name suggests, it makes an excellent hedging shrub. The tiny white flowers appear in flat terminal clusters in late spring, followed by blue-black berries. The leaves are elliptical to oblong and glossy green. *P. glabra* is frost-hardy. Selected cultivars are grown for their brilliant red young leaves and make excellent hedges; clipping usually brings on several flushes of young growth.

P. serrulata

This species, native to China, has glossy, oval, serrated, dark green leaves. In spring, it bears small, white flowers and these are followed in turn by red berries. Fully hardy, it grows to a height of up to 6 m (about 18 ft) with a spread of 4 m (about 12 ft).

PHYGELIUS
CAPE FUCHSIA

Related to *Penstemon* and *Antirrhinum* (snapdragon) rather than *Fuchsia*, these erect, evergreen undershrubs—perennials in some winter conditions—are native to the Cape of Good Hope, South Africa. They are grown for the handsome, red flowers they bear in summer, set among dark green, oval leaves. They do best in sun or semi-shade and like a fertile, well-drained soil that is not too dry. Excellent in a rock garden, they grow to a height of 1 m (about 3 ft) and a spread of 50 cm (about 20 in). Propagate from softwood cuttings in summer. *P. capensis* and *P. aequalis*, both red, are the best known species; there are several hybrids available with flowers in red, yellow or orange.

PHYSOCARPUS
opulifolius
COMMON NINEBARK

Native to eastern North America, this deciduous shrub is grown for its showy leaves and spring flowers. They are good plants for the front row of a shrub border, where their attractive pendulous form can be seen to best advantage. Broadly oval, lobed, mid-green leaves change to dull yellow in autumn/fall, and clusters of tiny white, sometimes pink-flushed flowers are borne in early summer. The pale to dark brown bark peels when mature. It requires a fertile, moist, well-drained, preferably acid soil and an open, sunny position. Fully hardy, they grow to a height of 3 m (about 9 ft) and a spread of 5 m (about 15 ft). Propagate from softwood cuttings in summer and thin established plants occasionally.

PIERIS
ANDROMEDA, PEARL FLOWER, LILY-OF-THE-VALLEY BUSH

These fairly dense, bushy, evergreen shrubs, native to the colder regions

Physocarpus opulifolius

Photinia × fraseri

Philadelphus mexicanus

Phlomis fruticosa
Photinia glabra

Philadelphus 'Virginal'

Photinia serrulata

Phygelius aequalis

of North America and Asia, are related to the *Azalea* and are grown for their small, urn-shaped flowers. Slow growing, they do best in a mildly acid soil that is well-drained and rich with leafmould. They prefer a sheltered spot in shade or semi-shade and are fully to frost-hardy, although young plants may be killed by frost in spring. They also like a humid atmosphere—this maintains the colour and freshness of the foliage. Dead-head after flowering as this improves the growth. Propagate from semi-ripe or soft tip cuttings in early summer.

P. formosa

This tall, bushy evergreen is native to China and the eastern Himalayas. It grows to a height and spread of 4 m (about 12 ft) and is frost-hardy. The large leaves are a glossy deep green, reddish when young, and it produces large panicles of white, sometimes pinkish-tinged flowers from mid- to late spring. *P. formosa* var. *forrestii* 'Wakehurst' has pure white flowers and brilliant red young foliage, while 'Henry Price' is bronze-red.

P. forrestii

RED LEAF PEARL FLOWER

This bushy, dense, evergreen species is a native of China. In spring it bears terminal sprays of white flowers, set among small oval leaves that are bronze when young and turn dark green when older. Frost-hardy, it grows to a height and spread of 2 m (about 6 ft).

P. japonica

JAPANESE PEARL FLOWER

This rounded, bushy, dense, evergreen shrub is a native of Japan. In spring it bears dense sprays of pendent, white flowers that resemble lily-of-the-valley. Though flower buds develop in autumn/fall, they do not open until spring. When young, the small, glossy leaves are oval, turning bronze as the plant matures. Fully hardy, *P. japonica* grows to a height and spread of 2 m (about 6 ft). There are selected cultivars with even more brilliant young foliage.

PIMELEA
prostrata

This low-spreading shrub, native to New Zealand, has small, leathery leaves and profuse white to pink, fragrant flowers appearing in terminal clusters. Frost-hardy, it prefers a light, porous soil with plenty of leafmould, and dappled sunlight. Propagate from semi-hardwood cuttings in late summer.

PINUS
mugo

DWARF PINE, MOUNTAIN PINE, SWISS MOUNTAIN PINE

This shrubby, spreading conifer is native to the Pyrenees in Europe. It bears purple, scaly, 5 cm (about 2 in) long cones that ripen over two years. Its leaves are long, dark green needles, arranged in clusters of two or three. It prefers a well-drained,

light to medium, acid soil and an open, sunny position. Evergreen and frost-hardy, it grows to a height of 5 m (about 15 ft) with a spread of 3 m (about 9 ft).

PITTOSPORUM

MOCKORANGE, PITTOSPORUM

These handsome, evergreen, fragrant shrubs and trees are found in China, Japan, Africa, New Zealand, Australia and the Pacific. Grown for their fragrance and ornamental foliage, they like a leaf-rich, well-drained soil and regular moisture. They are frost-hardy to frost-tender and generally do best in mild climates. Some species prefer sun, others sun or partial shade. Propagate from seed in autumn/fall or spring, or from semi-ripe cuttings in summer. There are a great many cultivated species and hybrids.

P. crassifolium

KARO

A New Zealand native, this erect shrub is ideal for planting as a

windbreak by the sea; it is also useful for underplanting among taller trees to stop ground drought. Evergreen, with a dense, bushy habit, it reaches a height of 4 m (about 12 ft) and a spread of 3 m (about 9 ft). The leaves are oblong and dark green with woolly white undersides. Clusters of small, fragrant, reddish purple flowers are borne in spring. Frost-hardy, and in fact one of the hardiest of the pittosporums. It prefers sun.

Pimelea prostrata

Pieris japonica

Pinus mugo

Pittosporum crassifolium

Pieris forrestii

Plumbago auriculata

P. tenuifolium
KOHUHU

This evergreen tree grows to a
height of 10 m (about 30 ft) with a
spread of 6 m (about 18 ft). A native
of New Zealand, it bears glossy,
oval, mid-green leaves with undulating margins, and bears dark purple, honey-scented flowers in
spring. It is half-hardy. There are
several cultivars, with variegated or
purple-toned leaves, much sought
after by flower arrangers.

P. tobira
JAPANESE PITTOSPORUM, MOCK ORANGE

Grown for its highly polished dark
green leaves and its very fragrant,
orange-scented, creamy, star-
shaped flowers, this evergreen is
native to China and Japan. The
flowers open white in late spring,
becoming creamy yellow with age.
Pods open to show bright orange
seeds. Frost-hardy, it does well
grown against a warm wall. Bushy-
headed and dense, it is slow growing to a height of 6 m (about 18 ft)
and spread of 4 m (about 12 ft).
This is one of the best flowering
pittosporums. *P. t.* 'Variegatum' has
greyish green leaves blotched and
edged with white. It prefers a sunny
situation.

PLATYCLADUS
orientalis
syn. *Thuja orientalis, Biota orientalis*
BIOTA, CHINESE THUJA, CHINESE ARBORVITAE

Native to northern and western
China, this large shrubby conifer
has a dense habit, growing to a
height of 5–12 m (about 15–37 ft)
or more with a spread of around 5

Pittosporum tenuifolium

m (about 15 ft). It has an irregularly
rounded crown with erect, flattened
foliage sprays. The leaves are dark
green, the bark fibrous and the egg-
shaped cones are glaucous until
mature, when they turn brown.
There are several popular cultivars
of this species, including the dwarf
'Aurea Nana', which grows to a
height and spread of 60 cm (about
24 in) and has golden-green foliage.
Grow in humus-rich soil in sun or
shade, although plants are more
shapely in full sun. Propagate from
seed in spring or from cuttings with
a heel in late summer. Plant in au-
tumn/fall or spring.

PLUMBAGO
auriculata
syn. *P. capensis*
CAPE LEADWORT

This evergreen, lax-growing shrub,
originally from South Africa, bears
pale blue or white flowers in terminal clusters from spring to autumn/
fall. Half-hardy, it has oblong, pale
green leaves. Fast growing, it likes a
fertile, well-drained soil and full

Pittosporum tobira 'Variegatum'

light or semi-shade. It is quite suitable as an informal hedge or to
disguise fences and walls, as it
climbs to a height of 5 m (about 15
ft). Water regularly in full growth,
less so at other times. Whitefly may
pose problems. Propagate from
semi-ripe cuttings in summer. *P.
auriculata* 'Alba' is a white cultivar.
P. capensis is said to have been used
by the ancient Romans as a cure for
lead poisoning.

POLYGALA
MILKWORT, LANGELIER, BLUECAPS,
SEPTEMBERBOSSIE

These evergreen shrubs are native to
South Africa. Well branched above,
somewhat leggy below, they are
ideal as temporary filler behind
slow-growing plants or as a background. They are grown mainly for
their pea-like flowers. Fully hardy
to frost-tender, plant in full light or
partial shade, in moist, well-drained
soil. Water potted plants well during full growth, less at other times.
Cut lanky stems back hard in late
winter. Propagate from semi-ripe

Polygala x *dalmaisiana*

cuttings in late summer, or seed in
spring.

P. chamaebuxus
BASTARD BOX

This evergreen shrub, a native of
alpine Europe, grows to a height of
20 cm (about 8 in) with a spread of
40 cm (about 16 in). Racemes of
small, pea-like, yellow and white
flowers appear in spring and early
summer. It has tiny, oval, dark
green leaves and is fully hardy.

P. × dalmaisiana

This showy, long-flowering hybrid shrub has narrow oval leaves and pea-like, rosy purple flowers that have a curious tuft of hairs at the tip of the flower keel. The flowers appear in spring. It grows to a height and spread of 1.5 m (about 4 ft). Propagate from seed in spring or from semi-ripe cuttings in late summer.

POTENTILLA
fruticosa 'Tangerine'

The yellow flowers of this dense, deciduous shrub carry a hint of reddish orange. The flowers appear from early summer to autumn/fall amid flat, mid-green leaves comprising 5 or 7 narrow elliptical leaflets arranged palmately. Sow seed in autumn/fall or propagate using greenwood or softwood cuttings in

summer. The arching shrub reaches 60 cm (about 24 in) in height with a spread of 1.5 m (about 4½ ft). A native of Europe, Asia and North America, it is adaptable to most soils and positions and is frost-hardy but drought tender.

PROSTANTHERA
rotundifola
MINT-BUSH

This 3 m (about 9 ft) tall, evergreen shrub is grown for the delightful clusters of mauve or violet flowers it bears in spring. It has small, fragrant, deep green leaves. Native to the southern and south-eastern states of Australia, it needs a fertile, well-drained soil and full light or partial shade to thrive. Potted plants should be watered well, less so when not in full growth. Prune after flowering. Propagate from semi-ripe

cuttings in late summer, or from seed in spring.

PROTEA
PROTEA, SUGAR BUSH, HONEY FLOWER

The beauty of the gigantic blooms of these evergreen shrubs make them a popular choice for a sunny spot in a garden with the right soil conditions—sandy, well-drained, low on phosphates and nitrates, and preferably acid (though some species tolerate an alkaline soil). Native to South Africa, the genus has relatives in South America, New Zealand and Australia. Often difficult to grow, all species need protection in the winter for a year or two after planting. Potted specimens in full growth should be watered now and then. Keep well ventilated if under glass. They last well after fading and after cutting—hence their popularity in

arrangements. Proteas are half-hardy. Propagate from cuttings taken in summer (seed germination is erratic). The genus is named after the mythical Greek god, Proteus, who could change into any shape he desired. The flowers are widely grown in Hawaii for the flower shops of the USA.

P. cynaroides
KING PROTEA

This species bears large, open flowerheads with pink, petal-like bracts, in winter, spring or summer. The leathery leaves are round and dark green. A lovely shrub, it is half-hardy and grows to a height and spread of 1.5 m (about 4½ ft). Like all proteas, the size of the shrub bears little relationship to that of the flowers—the flowerheads grow to 30 cm (about 12 in) wide. It is the floral emblem of South Africa.

Potentilla fruticosa 'Tangerine'

Prostanthera rotundifolia

Protea cynaroides

Platycladus orientalis

Prunus 'Shimidsu Sakura'

Protea neriifolia

Prunus glandulosa 'Rosea Plena'

P. neriifolia
OLEANDER-LEAVED PROTEA, BLACK PROTEA

The flowerheads of this species are fragrant, silvery pink, black-tipped and grow to 10 cm (about 4 in). These appear from autumn/fall to early spring. *P. neriifolia* has narrow, oblong, oleander-like leaves. It grows to a height and spread of 3 m (about 9 ft).

PRUNUS
BUSH CHERRY, CHOKEBERRY

Best known as a genus of popular, fruiting trees, *Prunus* also contains some delightful ornamental plants, mostly from North America. Grown for the autumn/fall colour of their foliage, as well as their fruits and flowers, they seem to tolerate any soil that is not excessively wet. Superficially they resemble the rose,

but as would be expected in a genus with over a hundred species and cultivars, there is widespread variation. All their leaves are oval to oblong. Deciduous species prefer full sun, while the evergreens do best in sun or shade. The evergreens should be propagated from semi-ripe cuttings in summer or autumn/fall, the deciduous species from seed in autumn/fall or hardwood cuttings in winter.

P. glandulosa 'Rosea Plena'
BUSH CHERRY

In late spring, this dainty, suckering, deciduous shrub bears handsome, rose-pink flowers, set among green, oval leaves. It grows to a height and spread of 1–1.5 m (about 3–4¹/₂ ft). After flowering, prune young shoots close to the old wood.

Pyracantha angustifolia

Pseudowintera colorata

Prunus laurocerasus

P. laurocerasus
CHERRY LAUREL

A dense, bushy shrub that eventually becomes spreading and open, this species bears racemes of small, white flowers in mid- to late spring. These are set among glossy, dark green, oblong to oval leaves. After the bloom, grape-like clusters of glossy, black, cherry-like fruits make their appearance. Frost-hardy, *P. laurocerasus* grows to a height of 6 m (about 18 ft) with a spread of 10 m (about 30 ft). Both the cherry laurel and the Portugal laurel respond very well to clipping and make splendid hedges.

P. 'Shimidsu Sakura'
JAPANESE CHERRY

This cultivar has a broad, flattened crown with wide, spreading branches. In late spring it produces pink-tinted buds that open to fringed, large, double white flowers hanging along the branches in long-stalked clusters. The leaves turn orange and red in autumn/fall. Fully hardy, it reaches a height of 5 m (about 15 ft), with a spread of 10 m (about 30 ft).

PSEUDOWINTERA
colorata
syn. *Drimys colorata*
ALPINE PEPPER TREE, HOROPITO

A spreading, bushy, evergreen shrub, native to New Zealand, this

shrub grows to a height of 1–2 m (about 3–6 ft) with a spread of 1.5 m (about 4½ ft). The aromatic green leaves, with scarlet markings and a silvery underside, are its main attraction—these turn purple in the winter months. The greenish, spring and summer bloom is insignificant. It prefers a light to medium, moist, humus-rich, well-drained soil in full light or partial shade. Potted plants should be watered frequently in summer. Prune to maintain the shape. Propagate from seed in spring or autumn/fall, or from semi-ripe cuttings in summer.

PUNICA
granatum var. *nana*
DWARF POMEGRANATE

This deciduous, rounded shrub grows slowly to a height and spread of 30–90 cm (about 12–36 in). Native to Asia, it bears red, funnel-shaped flowers in summer, set among light green, oblong leaves. Small, orange-red fruit follow the bloom—these fruits are edible only in warm climates. Frost- to half-hardy, it does best in a sunny, sheltered position and likes a coarse, gravelly, well-drained soil. Water well in dry conditions. Prune lightly at the end of each winter to maintain its compact habit. Propagate from semi-ripe cuttings in summer, or from seed in spring.

PYRACANTHA
FIRETHORN

Though these arching, evergreen shrubs bear delightful profusions of tiny, white flowers in spring, they are mostly grown for the impressive display of berries that follows in autumn/fall. These tend to colour better in cooler conditions. Dense and spiny, they do well as hedges, espaliers and ground covers. If grown against a wall, cut back long shoots after flowering. Grow in fertile soil in a sheltered, sunny position. Propagate from semi-ripe cuttings in summer. Scab and fireblight may cause problems.

Punica granatum var. *nana*

P. angustifolia
FIRETHORN

This dense shrub, native to western China, grows to a height and spread of 3 m (about 9 ft). In early summer, it bears small, white, open flowers set among dark green, oblong leaves followed by orange berries. It is frost-hardy.

P. cocchinea

Grown for its flowers and fruits, this dense, bushy shrub is native to southern Europe and western Asia. The spiny, toothed leaves are a glossy, rich green, and dense clusters of small white flowers are borne in early summer. These are followed by spherical coral-red fruits. Fully hardy, it reaches a height and spread of around 4 m (about 12 ft). It is one of the best known of all the firethorns. 'Lalandei' is a vigorous cultivar with broader leaves and larger, bright orange berries.

P. crenulata
syn. *Crataegus crenulata*
NEPAL FIRETHORN

This sturdy, erect, half-hardy shrub grows rapidly to a height and spread of 3–4 m (about 9–12 ft). Native to Nepal and China, *P. crenulata* bears numerous white, open flowers in early summer which are followed in turn by a profusion of small, dark red berries. The glossy leaves are narrow and blunt.

P. hybrids

There are a number of attractive hybrids in this genus, most of them cultivated with the objective of developing disease resistance. *P.* × 'Orange Glow' and *P.* × 'Orange Charmer' have orange-red fruit and are scab resistant; *P.* × 'Buttercup' has a spreading habit and rich yellow fruit; *P.* × 'Golden Charmer' is scab resistant and has orange-yellow fruit; *P.* × 'Shawnee' has a vigorous, wide-spreading habit with abundant light orange fruit; and *P.* × *waterei* has a vigorous, dense habit and a profusion of bright red fruit. Propagate from semi-ripe cuttings in summer; the hybrids can be susceptible to fireblight.

RAPHIOLEPIS
INDIAN HAWTHORN, YEDDO HAWTHORN

These dense, evergreen shrubs, grown for their fragrant bloom and foliage, are native to subtropical South-East Asia. Frost- to half-hardy, they like plenty of sun but, in hot climates, prefer semi-shade. They do best in a light to medium, well-composted, well-drained, sandy soil and in a sheltered position, ideally against a wall. They bear panicles of five petalled flowers, followed by berries, among alternate, leathery, dark green, oblong leaves. Coastal areas suit them best but, in colder areas, they need to be grown under glass. Propagate from seed or cuttings in summer.

Rhamnus californicus

Rhamnus alaternus

Raphiolepis × delacourii

Raphiolepis indica

R. × delacourii

A rounded, evergreen shrub that grows to a height and spread of 2 m (about 6 ft), R. × delacourii is grown for the rose-pink flowers it bears in early summer, and the blue-black berries that follow in winter. Its oval, leathery leaves are toothed at the ends. R. × delacourii is a hybrid between R. indica and R. umbellata.

R. indica
INDIAN HAWTHORN

This bushy, evergreen shrub is native to southern China. In spring or early summer it bears clusters of fragrant, star-shaped, white flowers, set among serrated, oblong leaves. Fully hardy, it grows to a height of just under 1 m (about 3 ft) and a spread of 2 m (about 6 ft). It prefers well-composted, moist, well-drained soils in an open, sunny position.

RHAMNUS
BUCKTHORN

This genus of deciduous or evergreen shrubs with its inconspicuous flowers are grown for their fruits and foliage. They will grow in either sun or semi-shade and prefer a fertile soil. Deciduous species should be propagated from seed in autumn/fall, and evergreen species from semi-ripe cuttings in summer. They are frost-hardy.

R. alaternus
BUCKTHORN

This erect, branching, evergreen shrub, native to southern Europe, grows to a height of 6 m (about 18 ft) with a spread of 3 m (about 9 ft). It bears tiny, greenish flowers in axillary racemes, which are followed by black, rounded, pea-sized fruits. The leaves are dark green and oval with saw-toothed margins. R. alarternus likes a protected, shady position and a light to medium, well-drained soil. Drought, frost and salt resistant, it is popular as a screening plant and makes an excellent clipped hedge in European coastal gardens. A variety with variegated leaves is popular. Propagate from semi-ripe cuttings in summer. This shrub is becoming a noxious weed in some countries.

R. californicus
COFFEEBERRY

This evergreen shrub is a native of western North America. It has oblong or oval leaves and grows to a height of 3 m (about 9 ft) with a spread of 1.5 m (about 4½ ft). It produces red fruit which become purple-black as they mature.

RHODODENDRON
RHODODENDRON, AZALEA

The rhododendrons are an enormous genus of some 600 species (almost all garden-worthy) and countless cultivars, native mainly to the temperate regions of Europe, North America and Asia, although with important representatives in the highlands of tropical South-East Asia and one species (R. lochae) in Australia. They are admired for their handsome leaves and showy, bell or funnel-shaped flowers. The flowers are borne at the ends of the previous year's shoots, often in clusters, mainly in spring although both winter and summer flowers are fairly common. Just about all of them share an intense dislike of lime, but where soils suit they are among the most desirable of all flowering shrubs. As a general rule, they like a shaded to semi-shaded position with a cool root run and acid, perfectly drained soil with abundant humus. No regular pruning is required, although they can be cut back quite severely in early spring if needed. Propagation is by layering, from cuttings, or by grafting, most species being fairly slow to strike. Their usually shapely habit and compact root systems make them first rate subjects for container growing, and they are among the easiest of all shrubs to transplant, even when mature. Red spider, lace bug, thrips, caterpillars and leaf miners can be troublesome.

The genus is divided into some forty 'series', but horticulturally there are three most important divisions. First, there are the azaleas, formerly given a genus of their own (the distinguishing mark being that azaleas usually have 5 stamens, the rest of the genus 10 or more); then the subtropical species and their

Rhododendron × gandavense

Rhododendron 'White Gumpo'

Rhododendron luteum hybrid

hybrids, mostly of the series Vireya and usually called vireya rhododendrons or simply vireyas; and the rhododendrons proper, which are very variable in habit, from dwarfs growing 25 cm (about 10 in) high or less to small trees, and, generally, preferring a cooler climate than the other two groups do. We shall deal with each in turn, illustrating merely a representative or two of each of the main types.

AZALEAS

These divide naturally into two groups, the deciduous azaleas and the evergreen kinds. The deciduous azaleas bear their flowers either on bare branches before their leaves or with the young foliage; they are available in just about every colour but blue, the yellow-to-flame range being the most distinctive and popular. The flowers are usually followed by brilliant autumn/fall foliage. Fully hardy, they are happiest in cool to cold climates. The evergreen azaleas are on the whole less cold hardy, and several of them are distinctly tender. They are of great importance in warm-temperate climates and as flowering pot plants.

R. × gandavense
GHENT AZALEAS

The Latin title is traditional, but effectively these are simply mollis-type azaleas with double flowers.

R. Gumpo azaleas

These are a small group of cultivars from Japan, a trifle more hardy than the Indicas. They are prostrate shrubs about 50 cm (about 20 in)

Rhododendron simsii 'Eureka'

tall (less with pruning) but spreading about 1.5 m (about 4½ ft) wide. They are suitable for ground cover in mild-winter climates, and have 8 cm (about 3 in) flowers in shades from white to red. They are late bloomers and their flowers may be damaged by the sun.

R. indica azaleas

Derived mainly from the southern Chinese *R. simsii,* and half-hardy at best, these are the most important rhododendrons in warm-temperate climates. They make rounded shrubs from 1–3 m (about 3–9 ft) tall, according to variety, with slightly hairy, dull green leaves. There are very many named varieties. Some flower throughout winter, but most are spring blooming. Bloom is most profuse in the white to red and purple range, the flowers usually being about 8 cm (about 3 in) wide. Single-flowered cultivars tend to be bigger growers than the doubles which are, under the name 'Belgian indicas', much cultivated under glass in Europe as Christmas-flowering pot plants.

Rhododendron Kurume azalea

R. Kurume azaleas

Mainly derived from the Japanese *R. obtusum,* these are the most frost-hardy of the evergreen azaleas. They grow to about 2 m (about 6 ft) high and wide, but are very slow and usually seen smaller than that. Foliage is dark green and oval, and the densely bushy plants are so smothered in bloom in their spring season that the leaves are quite obscured. The individual flowers are small, about 3 cm (about 1½ in) across, single or double, and come in every shade from white through pink to red and purple. They take their name from the province of

Japan where the leading varieties originated. In Japan, they are often sheared into formal shapes, although at the cost of some bloom.

R. luteum hybrids
MOLLIS AZALEAS

These are the best known of the deciduous azaleas, bearing wide open flowers in shades from white, cream, yellow, pale to deep pink and orange to red in early spring. They grow mostly 2–3 m (about 6–9 ft) high and wide, with mid-green leaves that turn brilliant shades in autumn/fall. There are many named varieties; some are sweetly scented.

VIREYAS (Malesian rhododendrons)

Native as they mostly are to such inaccessible places as the highlands of Indonesia, Borneo and New Guinea, the vireyas are still fairly new in cultivation, and there is still much work to be done in sorting out which of the species are going to prove easy to cultivate and popular. They are, however, among the most exciting new developments in gardening, at least in warm-temperate and subtropical climates—in areas with more than the mildest of frosts they need greenhouse cultivation—and hybrids are already being raised. Evergreen, they are mostly shrubs about 1–1.5 m (about 3–4½ ft) tall, with dark green, leathery, often glossy leaves, which are apt to be tinted russet when young. They flower in spring, although many continue intermittently throughout the summer into the autumn/fall. Flower size and shape varies, from 2–8 cm (about 1–3 in), from funnels to wide open bells, and some are sweetly scented. Colours range from white to orange, taking in sunset shades of gold coral and salmon pink on the way. The usual conditions of cultivation suit them.

R. jasminiflorum
VIREYA RHODODENDRON

This small, evergreen rhododendron bears fragrant, white flowers any time of the year among midgreen, oval leaves. It grows to a height and spread of 50 cm (about 20 in).

R. javanicum
VIREYA RHODODENDRON

Growing to a height and spread of 1 m (about 3 ft), this rhododendron bears red to orange flowers with purple stamens in autumn/fall. It has oval, lightly-veined green leaves.

R. lochae
AUSTRALIAN RHODODENDRON

Notable as the only species from Australia, this is a fairly typical vireya, growing about 1.5 m (about 4½ ft) tall in gardens, although capable of much more. It has glossy dark leaves and bears 3 cm (about 1½ in) wide, bell-shaped red flowers in late spring. It is rather tender.

RHODODENDRONS

Apart from the deciduous azaleas, all the rhododendrons are evergreen and, typically, bear their flowers in large domed clusters. They are a very varied lot, and we give simply a few typical species to illustrate the range.

R. arboreum

Native to the Himalayas, this species grows to a 10 m (about 30 ft) tall tree in the wild, although in cultivation it is usually only about half that. It has long, dull green leaves, often with silvery tinted undersides, and bears big clusters of red to pink flowers in spring. It is frost-hardy and one of the chief parents of the popular Hardy hybrids.

R. augustinii

Native to central China, this fully hardy, bushy species can grow to about 3 m (about 9 ft) high and wide, although it is usually rather less in gardens. It has small leaves, giving the bush an appearance like an evergreen azalea. The wide open flowers, borne in small clusters, vary in colour from blue to violet; in the best forms they are the purest blue seen in the genus. *R. augustinii* has been the parent of several very choice blue-flowered hybrids.

R. auriculatum

Another native of western China, this bushy, wide-branching shrub bears fragrant, white or pink, funnel-shaped flowers in summer. Its leaves are large, oblong and hairy. Fully hardy, it grows to a height of 6 m (about 18 ft) with a spread of 4 m (about 12 ft). It is notable for its very late season of flowering.

R. 'Chrysomanicum'

This shrubby, bud-tender specimen bears delightful, primrose-yellow flowers in spring and has hairy, green leaves. Unlike most species of

Rhododendron jasminiflorum

Rhododendron lochae

Rhododendron auriculatum

Rhododendron arboreum

Rhododendron javanicum

Rhododendron augustinii

Rhododendron 'Chrysomanicum'

Rhododendron, it does well in full sun and in warmer areas. Frost-hardy, it grows to a height and spread of just over 1 m (about 3 ft).

R. ciliicalyx

This spreading shrub grows to a height and spread of 2 m (about 6 ft). It has shiny, dark green leaves. Its fragrant white or white-tinged rose flowers bloom in spring. *R. ciliicalyx* tolerates minus 8°C (about 18°F) or lower and grows at altitudes of up to 3000 m (about 9600 ft) in the southern China–Burma–Himalaya region.

R. 'Fragrantissimum'

In the summer months this rhododendron bears trusses of fragrant, white flowers, tinted with pink. It makes an excellent plant for house decoration in a large tub, trained around a framework of bamboo. It can be susceptible to frosts; however, in a greenhouse it will give very little trouble and flower freely.

R. Hardy hybrids

The most widely grown of the rhododendrons, the Hardy hybrids are mostly large, domed shrubs 3 m (about 9 ft) or more tall, with large, dull green leaves. They flower spectacularly in spring, bearing many almost spherical clusters of wide open flowers in shades of white, pink, red or purple; very rarely cream or yellow. There are very many named cultivars, varying a little in hardiness, from frost-hardy to fully hardy. The usual conditions of cultivation apply.

R. maccabeanum

This magnificent species is typical of a group from the Himalayas which are noted for their extremely large and handsome leaves. It is an evergreen shrub or tall tree to about 10 m (about 30 ft) tall, with large leathery leaves, deeply corrugated above, woolly white beneath, and clusters of yellow flowers in spring. It is frost-hardy, but appreciates a sheltered position.

R. ponticum

Native to Spain, this is an evergreen shrub that grows to a height of 4 m (about 12 ft) and spread of 2 m (about 6 ft). It bears delightful, loose clusters of expanding, tubular, rose-pink flowers among green, oblong to lanceolate leaves. This species is one of the best rhododendrons for mild-winter climates, and it is much used as an understock on which to graft choicer species and hybrids.

R. trichostomum
syn. *R. sphacranthum*

One of the most desirable of dwarf rhododendrons, of which there are many, this evergreen species from western China makes a compact shrub, growing sometimes to 1.2 m (about 3½ ft) in height, but usually a bit less, spreading about 80 cm (about 32 in) wide. This species bears small leaves and white or rose pink flowers in clusters in late spring. Several varieties of wild origin are grown; they vary from half-hardy to frost-hardy. Give it sunshine in cool areas, shade elsewhere.

R. yakushimanum

This upright, dense, native of Japan bears rounded, terminal clusters of expanding, tubular flowers in late spring. It has deep green, wrinkled leaves. *R. yakushimanum* grows to a height of 1 m (about 3 ft) with a spread of 2 m (about 6 ft). It has been the parent of many hybrids, which retain its shapely, compact growth, as well as its beautiful flowers. It is perhaps the most desirable of the rhododendrons for small gardens in temperate to cool climates.

Rhododendron Hardy hybrid

Rhododendron 'Fragrantissimum'

Rhododendron ciliicalyx

Rhododendron trichostomum

Rhododendron maccabeanum

Rhododendron yakushimanum

Rhododendron ponticum

A Field Trip to the Blue Mountains

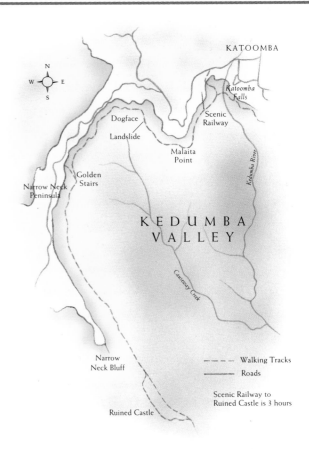

About a two-hour drive west of Sydney, Australia, takes you to the Blue Mountains, an area encompassing one of the country's most important national parks, and a haven for a variety of native plants, birds and animals. The Blue Mountains is also home to one of the largest populations of the waratah *(Telopea speciosissima)*, a strikingly distinctive native shrub and the floral emblem of the state of New South Wales.

The waratah blooms from October to December (spring to early summer in Australia). This is a good time to explore the Blue Mountains as it can be quite cold in winter, sometimes down to –4°C (about 24°F), and the whole area is often covered in an eerie, dense mist. In summer the average maximum temperature is a mild 23°C (about 73°F). Even when travelling in the middle of summer you should be prepared for a sudden change in the weather—a glorious warm day can suddenly turn quite cold.

A dry winter and spring can turn the whole of the Blue Mountains into a giant tinderbox and bushfires have ravaged the area many times. The waratah is a highly fire-adapted species, sprouting rapidly from a large woody underground stem (lignotuber) which withstands the fiercest bushfires and produces new growths within a month or two. Due to the fires, most wild plants are multi-stemmed with about 1–5 flowerheads per stem.

The best way to see the waratah is to start by taking the Scenic Railway at Katoomba. The railway runs the length of

The Three Sisters —a famous landmark of the Blue Mountains.

an almost sheer cliff face to the valley below and is so steep it is more like an amusement park ride than a train trip. It once served a coal mine and you will pass by openings to old mines and the remains of a horse-drawn tramway. A walking track at the bottom of the railway leads to a rock formation known as the Ruined Castle. The round trip on this walk will take you about 6 hours.

The first part of the walk is through tall open forest which contains the white-trunked Blue Mountains ash *(Eucalyptus oreades)* and the smooth-barked apple gum *(Angophora costata)*, easily recognized by its twisted, bumpy trunk. The Australian bush is quite different from the forests and woodlands of Europe and America. The abundant eucalyptus trees give an overall impression of grey rather than the green of a European forest. The trees of the open forest are taller and the soil there is deeper than on the exposed ridgetops and the extra moisture due to runoff causes many of the trees to be covered in moss.

Soon you will find yourself in a rich, cool rainforest. The lush green vegetation includes the lilly pilly *(Acmena smithii)*, which bears pinkish berries in winter. These berries were once part of the local Aborigines' diet. Other plants you will see include the strap water fern *(Blechnum patersonii)* and rough tree fern *(Cyathea australis)* and rainforest trees such as the yellow sassafrass *(Doryphora sassafras)*, which has fragrantly scented leaves, and the magnificent coachwood *(Ceratopetalum apetalum)*. In this area and also in the open forest you may also be lucky enough to see a lyrebird preening its magnificent plumage. The lyrebird has a fanned tail of feathers which opens in similar fashion to that of a peacock. It is also a wonderful mimic.

The New South Wales waratah—a colourful note in bushland.

Telopea speciosissima

After the rainforest you climb a steep track leading to a ridge and the Ruined Castle. The trees here are smaller than those of the open forest and the vegetation more sparse. Walk a little further on and you will come upon the singularly striking red flowers of the waratah, which grows in profusion on the ridgetops and hillsides beneath the shelter of eucalypts such as red bloodwood (*Eucalyptus gummifera*). The soil is very sandy and covered in leaves and twigs. The understorey here contains a number of attractive shrubs including the old man banksia (*Banksia serrata*), which has leathery leaves and creamy yellow bottlebrush-like flowers. Like the waratah, it also blooms in spring and summer.

Undoubtedly, the most distinctive plant in the area is the waratah. Both its common and botanical names mean 'to be seen from afar'. In 1793, Sir James Smith, President of the Royal Society, wrote in his book *A Specimen of the Botany of New Holland* (Australia): 'The most magnificent plant which the prolific soil of New Holland affords is, by common consent both of Europeans and Natives, the Waratah'. It grows to about 3 m (about 9½ ft) with foliage of leathery, coarsely serrated leaves. The large heads of closely packed flowers, encircled by bright red bracts and carried on strong stems, are an adaptation to bird pollination. Large nectar-feeding birds such as the wattle-bird and noisy miner are frequent visitors, their colour vision enabling them to spot the flowerheads from a long way off.

Other birds commonly seen here are grey currawongs, striking crimson rosellas and white-eared honeyeaters. Bold currawongs come quite close, particularly if you have some food to share. The area is also home to the ring-tailed possum and another 'bat-like' possum, the sugar glider. You may also glimpse shy wallabies.

Before you start your return journey, take time to climb to the top of the Ruined Castle and enjoy the panoramic views. The plants and wildlife alone would make this walk worthwhile but the magnificent scenery makes it unforgettable.

Telopea

The waratahs belong to a remarkable group of trees and shrubs found on both sides of the South Pacific Ocean—the Proteaceae (see A Field Trip to the Cape Floral Kingdom, page 193), a family significant for its strong evolutionary association with Gondwana.

The true waratah genus (*Telopea*) consists of four or five species (an isolated population in north-eastern New South Wales may be a distinct species). *T. speciosissima* is confined to a small area on the central coast of New South Wales and inland for less than 100 km (about 62 miles). The Braidwood waratah (*T. mongaensis*) is also found in New South Wales. It has bright red, loosely packed flower-heads. The Gippsland waratah (*T. oreades*) can be found in the damp ranges of south-eastern New South Wales and eastern Victoria. It has small heads of crimson flowers. The Tasmanian waratah (*T. truncata*) is similar to the Gippsland waratah but has more conspicuous flowers. The latter has proved hardy under sheltered conditions in the British Isles.

Waratahs are grown for cut flowers in South Africa, Israel and California as well as in their native south-eastern Australia.

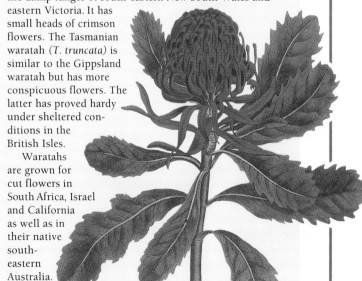

Telopea speciosissima

RHUS
aromatica

Grown for its brilliant autumn/fall hues, this deciduous, bushy shrub has deep green, divided, ash-like foliage which turns reddish purple or orange. Insignificant, small, yellow flowers are borne in mid-spring before the foliage appears; they are followed by small, hard, spherical red fruit. It reaches a height of 1 m (about 3 ft) and a spread of 1.5 m (about 4½ ft). Grow in any moderately fertile soil in a sunny position. Plant in autumn/fall to spring and propagate from root cuttings in winter, from seed in autumn/fall or from semi-ripe cuttings in summer. Prune regularly to maintain bushiness. Fully hardy. Many *Rhus* species are poisonous to a lesser or greater extent and can cause extremely painful rashes.

RIBES
sanguineum
FLOWERING CURRANT

This deciduous shrub is native to the west coast of the USA. Growing to a height and spread of about 2 m (about 6 ft), it bears handsome sprays of spicily fragrant, dainty, rose-pink flowers in spring, followed in turn by blue-black berries. The dark green, toothed leaves are also aromatic. Fully to frost-hardy, *R. sanguineum* needs full sun and fertile, well-drained soil to thrive. Propagate from hardwood cuttings taken in autumn/fall. There are several cultivars, differing in their precise shade of pink. Of the other *Ribes* species, *R. alpinum* is a shade-tolerant plant that makes a good low hedge and produces insipid-tasting scarlet fruit, while *R. odoratum* has clusters of rich yellow flowers and edible purple berries.

RONDELETIA
amoena
RONDELETIA, YELLOW-THROATED RONDELETIA

This erect, branching, evergreen shrub is native to Central America. Growing to a height of 3 m (about 9 ft) and spread of 2 m (about 6 ft), it is grown for the dense, rounded

Rosa foetida bicolor

Ribes odoratum   *Ribes sanguineum*

Rondeletia amoena

clusters of pink, tubular, scented flowers it bears in spring. It has dark green, oval leaves. Half-hardy, it does best in a fertile, well-drained soil in full light or partial shade. Keep potted specimens well watered in full growth. Prune back annually in early spring, taking flowered shoots back to within a few nodes of the previous year's growth. Propagate from seed in spring or semi-ripe cuttings in summer.

ROSA
ROSA

The rose is perhaps the best loved of all flowers, and it is prosaic to describe the genus as one of late spring or summer flowering deciduous shrubs, with prickly branches, pinnate leaves and terminal inflorescences; the flowers being (in wild roses) almost always 5 petalled, usually pale pink or white, sometimes red, purple or yellow; often, although by no means always, fragrant; and followed by red or orange fruits called 'hips'. Such a description does not account for the charm of the flowers, which has led gardeners to develop many thousands of hybrids and garden cultivars, often flowering intermittently from late spring or early summer until the autumn/fall. Most have many more petals than 5, which are arranged in a variety of flower forms, and in a much wider variety of colours: every shade of red and pink, white, yellow, orange, mauve, purple, coral; everything that is but true blue; many cultivars feature blends and variegations of two or more colours. Scent is variable, some cultivars offering intense fragrance, others virtually none. The plants range from only a few centimetres (about an inch) tall to giant, long limbed plants which are always treated in gardens as climbing plants and so are included in this book in the chapter on climbers. Names come and go from the catalogues with alarming speed: and we shall here simply list the most important classes accepted by the World Federation of Rose Societies, illustrating a typical variety or two of each, and departing from strict

Rosa glauca

alphabetical order to place them roughly in their historical sequence. Some of the Chinese species and their hybrids are half-hardy, but most roses are fully hardy. They all prefer sun and rich, well-drained soil. Pruning consists of removing weak or elderly branches and shortening the rest, and is carried out either immediately after bloom (for spring-only types) or in winter (for 'repeat-flowering' types). Aphids, caterpillars, scale insects, mildew, black spot, rust, and various virus diseases may prove bothersome; seek guidance as to which varieties are most resistant in one's local conditions. Roses are normally propagated by budding in summer, although many of the strongest varieties grow readily from cuttings taken in late summer or autumn/fall.

WILD ROSES

There are between one and two hundred species of *Rosa*, distributed very widely throughout the northern hemisphere. All tend to be variable and to interbreed freely, hence the uncertainty in the number. They are mostly arching shrubs, some climbers, and probably about half are garden-worthy. We describe only a few, to give an idea of the range.

R. foetida
AUSTRIAN OR PERSIAN BRIAR

This deciduous, rather rangy 1.5 m (about 4½ ft) tall shrub from Iran is of great historical importance as the chief ancestor of the modern yellow garden roses. It comes in two forms: *R. f. lutea*, the Austrian Yellow, with brilliant deep yellow flowers about 8 cm (about 3 in) across; and *R. f. bicolor*, the Austrian Copper, identical except for its brilliant orange-red petals with yellow reverses. Both flower in late spring and have a strong, sharp scent which many dislike—hence the name *foetida* meaning 'smelly'. The name Austrian briar comes from the rose having been introduced in northern Europe from Austria in the sixteenth century. There is a double yellow version known as 'Persian Yellow', introduced from Iran in 1837. All forms are frost-hardy but rather susceptible to black spot.

R. glauca
syn. R. rubrifolia

This 2–3 m (about 6–9 ft) tall, arching shrub from central Europe is grown mainly for its decorative grey foliage. It is plum-tinted when young and when the plant is grown in full sun; it is much sought after by flower arrangers. The small pink, late spring flowers are rather fleeting and of less account, but the red-brown hips are generously borne and decorative. Fully hardy, most forms are thornless or mostly so.

Rhus aromatica

Rosa moyesii

Rosa pimpinellifolia

Rosa rugosa

Rosa gallica 'Cardinal Richelieu'

Rosa virginiana

R. moyesii

This tall, deciduous shrub from China is grown both for the deep red colour of its spring flowers and the spectacular display of large, bottle-shaped scarlet hips in autumn/fall. It is a gawky grower to about 3 m (about 9 ft), and several more compact selected forms have been introduced, the best known of which is the 2 m (about 6 ft) tall and wide 'Geranium'. All are fully hardy.

R. pimpinellifolia

syn. *R. spinossissima*

BURNET ROSE

Native to northern Europe, including the British Isles, this densely thicketing, fully hardy shrub grows to about 1 m (about 3 ft) high. It has many straight prickles and fern-like leaves (their resemblance to salad burnet gives rise to both its common and scientific names). The fragrant, 5 cm (about 2 in) wide flowers are borne in spring and are very variable in colour, from white through pale yellow, and pale pink to purple. Black hips follow in autumn/fall, when the leaves assume muted tints. Double-flowered varieties have been cultivated since the eighteenth century, and in recent years the species has been used in the breeding of extremely frost-resistant garden roses.

R. rugosa

JAPANESE ROSE, RAMANAS ROSE

This 1.5–2 m (about 4½–6 ft) tall, densely thicketing (and very thorny) rose from Japan, Korea and northern China is one of the very best of all flowering shrubs. It is fully hardy, densely furnished with bright green, quilted (rugose) leaves and bearing flowers from spring to autumn/fall. These are about 10 cm (about 4 in) across in the best forms, and may be white, pink or violet. They are scented of cloves, and followed by 2 cm (about 1 in) globular hips. The foliage colours clear yellow in autumn/fall. In the wild it grows within sight of the sea, and is invaluable for seaside gardens and sandy soil. It is perhaps the best of all roses for hedging. There are a number of garden varieties with single and double flowers. The species has entered into the breeding lines of modern shrub roses and climbers, giving them great resistance to disease and cold.

R. virginiana

This 1.5 m (about 4½ ft) tall, clump-forming, late spring blooming shrub from eastern North America is one of the most desirable of Wild roses. The leaves are glossy and dark green. The bright pink or white flowers, 8 cm (about 3 in) across, are borne in small clusters. The leaves colour brilliantly in autumn/fall, and there is usually a lavish display of orange-red hips. It is fully hardy.

OLD GARDEN ROSES

These are the groups which were developed before the rather arbitrary date 1867, when 'La France', first of the hybrid Teas (large-flowered bush roses) was introduced. They fall into two main groups: the old European roses, mainly derived from the Mediterranean species *R. gallica* and spring or early summer flowering only, and including the Gallicas, Albas, Damasks, Centifolias and Moss roses; and those which were bred from crosses of these with repeat-flowering roses from China, bred there from *R. chinensis*. These include the China roses, the Teas, Bourbons, Portlands, and Hybrid Perpetuals as well as the Noisettes, most of which are climbers.

R. gallica and varieties

GALLICA ROSES

Derived directly from *R. gallica,* these varieties are mainly upright bushes, growing to about 1.2 m (about 3½ ft) high and a bit less wide, with small prickled, rough-textured leaves and flowers in shades of pink, crimson and purple, often striped or blended. The flowers are usually about 8 cm (about 3 in) wide, carried erect, and mainly very fragrant. The double varieties open flat and often 'quartered', a style of flower common in all the European old roses. Fully hardy, they are early summer flowering only. Mildew may be a problem.

Damask roses
syn. *R. damascena*

These are thought to have originated as hybrids between *R. gallica* and the otherwise insignificant *R. phoenecia*. They are rather lax growing shrubs from 1.2–2 m (about 3½–6 ft) in height, with matt-textured light green leaves and flowers in shades of pink or white. Most are very fragrant. The majority flower in summer only, although there is a small group called Autumn Damasks which repeat sparingly in autumn/fall. All are fully hardy.

Alba roses

These derive from *R. alba,* not a true species but thought to be of hybrid origin. They are strong, prickly bushes, usually about 2 m (about 6 ft) tall and wide, with grey-green leaves and flowers in refined shades of white or pink, almost always very fragrant. Fully hardy, they need only very light pruning.

Centifolia or Provence roses
syn. *R. centifolia, R. provincialis,* cabbage roses

These are of garden origin, and make floppy bushes, usually from 1.5–2 m (about 4½–6 ft) tall, with coarsely toothed leaves, many sharp prickles, and nodding, very double flowers in white or pink; a few show deeper tones. The term cabbage roses comes from the globular flower shape. Fully hardy, they are intensely fragrant. They benefit from discreet staking to control their lax habit.

Moss roses
syn. *R. centifolia muscosa*

These arose mainly as sports of Centifolia varieties, although some are forms of the Damask roses. They resemble their parents except for the strongly developed, resinous glands on the sepals, which resemble fragrant moss. They are available in shades of white through crimson, and a few are sparingly repeat flowering.

They were great favourites in Victorian times. Most are fully hardy.

R. chinensis and varieties
CHINA ROSES

Introduced from China at the end of the eighteenth century, the Chinas are mainly compact shrubs, from 50 cm–1.2 m (about 20 in–3½ ft) tall, with distinctively pointed leaves. They flower very continuously from spring to autumn/fall; many will flower all year in frost-free climates. The flowers are usually about 5 cm (about 2 in) wide and carried in clusters. They come in shades of true red or pink, and the flowers become deeper in colour as they age; most are only mildly fragrant. Half to frost hardy, they are pruned in winter.

Tea roses
syn. *R. odorata*

The Teas, so called because of a fancied resemblance between their

scent and that of freshly prepared tea leaves, are thought to have been derived in China from crosses between *R. chinensis* and the climbing rose *R. gigantea.* They are mainly bushes growing to about 1.5 m (about 4½ ft) high and wide (taller in mild climates) although some are climbers. Leaves are smooth and often glossy. Flowers are large, to 12 cm (about 5 in), usually carried singly on rather weak flower stalks, and borne almost all year in mild climates; from late spring to autumn/fall elsewhere. They are of elegant form, and mainly in delicate shades of pink, white, apricot or yellow. Few are more than half-hardy. Prized by Victorian gardeners, they are outstanding in subtropical climates.

Bourbon roses

Derived originally from crosses between China roses and Damasks, these are mainly fully hardy, arch-

Rosa 'Crested Moss' (Moss)

Rosa 'Celeste' (Alba)

Rosa damascena 'Kazanlik'

Rosa 'Coupe d'Hébé' (Bourbon)

Rosa 'Monsieur Tillier' (Tea)

Rosa chinensis

Rosa centifolia 'Bullata'

ing shrubs about 1.5 m (about 4½ ft) tall; a few are best treated as climbers. Flowers are mainly double, opening cupped or flat, and very fragrant. They are available in shades from white to red and purple. Most varieties are repeat flowering, although some are not very generous about it. Foliage is smooth, and the stems only lightly armed with prickles.

Portland roses

Derived from crosses between the gallica types and China roses, the portlands are mostly erect shrubs about 1.2 m (about 3½ ft) tall, with luxuriant, smooth leaves and 10–12 cm (about 4–5 in) wide flowers, usually fully double and quartered, in shades of white, pink, red or purple. Fully hardy, they are repeat blooming, although the amount of autumn/fall bloom depends on how generously the bushes are fertilized and watered.

Hybrid Perpetual roses

These are derived from crosses of all the old types, and were the leading garden roses from about 1840 until World War I; few of the many thousands of varieties then raised are available now. They are mostly tall shrubs, to 2 m (about 6 ft), with long lax branches which may be bent over horizontally and tied down to short stakes to create a great mass of summer flowers. Whether there will be a comparable autumn/fall show depends on the variety; many are distinctly stingy unless very generously manured, and the term 'perpetual' is nurseryman's salesmanship. The flowers range from white through pink to crimson and purple, and most varieties are very large in flower—to 15 cm (about 6 in) or slightly more—and fragrant.

MODERN GARDEN ROSES

These include the types developed since the 1870s, and represent the bulk of roses grown today. They are classed as Bush roses (either large or cluster flowered) which make compact, upright bushes about 1 m (about 3 ft) tall (although often rather more in mild climates) and flower from late spring to autumn/fall; Shrub roses, which are taller, less upright growers, mostly repeat-flowering; Miniatures, which are repeat-flowering bushes growing only about 30 cm (about 12 in) tall or less, with leaves and flowers reduced in proportion; and Climbers, which may or may not be repeat flowering.

Large-flowered bush roses
syn. Hybrid Tea roses

Derived originally from crosses between Hybrid Perpetuals and Tea roses, but also incorporating the blood of R. foetida and one or two other species, these are perhaps the most important of all classes of roses. They are mainly upright bushes, displaying large, 12–18 cm (about 5–7½ in), flowers singly on strong stems from late spring or early summer to autumn/fall, and are pre-eminent for cutting. Growth varies from 1 m (about 3 ft) to twice that, depending on climate and conditions. Most are fully hardy, although some winter protection will still be needed in extreme winter climates such as those of the mid-western USA. The range of colours is enormous; just about everything but blue and bright green is available. Fragrance is variable, some varieties being very richly scented, others almost scentless. So is vigour and resistance to disease, and local knowledge should be sought in selecting varieties.

Polyantha roses

Mainly of historical importance now, these dwarf bushes grow to about 35 cm (about 14 in) tall. They bear small, scentless flowers in large clusters from late spring to autumn/fall. They are available in shades from white through pink and salmon to red. Mildew may be a problem. The only variety to have retained general favour is the lovely pale pink 'Cécile Brünner'.

Cluster-flowered bush roses
syn. Floribunda roses, Hybrid Polyantha roses

Originated in the 1920s from crosses between large-flowered bush roses and polyanthas, the cluster roses rival the large-flowered roses in popularity, and interbreeding between the two has led to the division becoming rather indistinct; they can be mingled freely in beds if one so chooses. The cluster types are generally a little shorter in growth, and bear smaller blooms in clusters of 5 to 20 or so from early summer to autumn/fall. The individual flowers range from 6–10 cm (about 2½– 4 in), and can be single to fully double, informally shaped or in the high-centred form traditional for the large-flowered roses. Most are excellent for cutting. They are available in the full range of colours, but strong fragrance is exceptional. The best varieties are strongly disease resistant and fully hardy.

Patio roses
syn. Dwarf Floribunda roses

These are not a recognised class, but are becoming very popular. They are short-growing, cluster-flowered bush roses, usually about 50 cm (about 20 in) tall, but otherwise resemble the taller-flowered varieties. They are useful for the front of a mixed rose bed, for small spaces, or for growing in pots, but their stems are rarely long enough for cutting.

Rosa 'Peace' (Large-flowered)

Rosa 'Iceberg' (Cluster-flowered)

Rosa 'Jaques Cartier' (Portland)

Rosa 'Général Jacqueminot' (Hybrid Perpetual)

Rosa 'Cécile Brünner' (Polyantha)

Rosa 'Marlena' (Patio)

Rosa 'Flower Carpet' (Ground cover)

Russelia juncea

Ruscus aculeatus

Miniature roses
syn. Fairy roses, *R. chinensis minima*

Derived originally from exceptionally dwarf China roses crossed with bush roses, the Miniatures are scaled down bush roses, usually growing to about 35 cm (about 14 in) with flowers about 3 cm (about 1½ in) wide. The bushes are smaller if propagated from cuttings, although budded plants, which tend to grow larger, to about 50 cm (about 20 in). Bushes grown from cuttings are excellent for growing in containers and rockeries; the larger, budded plants are useful for giving touches of low, bright colour in the garden. All the usual bush rose colours are available, but few varieties have much in the way of scent. They are usually very free and continuous in bloom, and delightful for small flower arrangements. Most are fully hardy.

Modern shrub roses

These are something of a mixed bag, with several sub-groups, but most are too tall and robust for growing in beds in the usual way;

they are placed in the garden as other deciduous flowering shrubs are, and can be used to great effect in mixed borders. Among the recognised groups are the Hybrid Musks, large, arching bushes with sprays of very fragrant flowers resembling cluster-flowered roses; 'landscape roses', a fairly new group, mostly resembling the cluster roses in habit but claimed by their originators to be exceptionally easy to grow and needing no pruning; 'English roses', raised by the English grower David Austin who has sought to unite the grace and full petalled, scented flowers of the old European roses with the repeat flowering habit and brighter colours of the bush roses.

Ground cover roses

These are a very recent development, and are best thought of as prostrate or trailing shrub roses, which can be used as ground cover, although very few (as yet) are really sufficiently dense or evergreen enough to smother weeds. They have flowers resembling the smaller and more informal cluster roses.

Salix purpurea

They are fully hardy, and most varieties are repeat flowering. Few have much fragrance.

RUSCUS
aculeatus
BUTCHER'S BROOM, BOX HOLLY

A rough, erect, branching, evergreen shrub, *R. aculeatus* is native to northern Africa. In spring it bears tiny, star-shaped, green flowers, followed by bright red berries. The 'leaves' are actually extensions of the stem, ending in spines and the flowers and fruit are borne in the centre, apparently on the leaves. Useful for dry, shady sites, it does well in sun or shade, and prefers a heavy, moist, alkaline soil. Fully hardy, it grows to a height of 75 cm (about 2½ ft) and a spread of 1 m (about 3 ft). Propagate by division in spring but remember that male plants will not bear fruit. Butcher's broom is so called because in days gone by, butchers used the brush of the spiky stems to brush down their chopping blocks.

RUSSELIA
juncea
syn. *R. equisetiformis*
CORAL PLANT

This erect, slender shrub is a native of Mexico. It is grown for the clusters of handsome, red, tubular flowers it bears all year round, set among tiny, green leaves. *R. juncea*

Rosa 'Rise 'n Shine' (Miniature)

does best in a light, humus-rich, well-drained soil and prefers a sunny spot. Fast-growing, it is well suited to spilling over a wall, or as a seaside specimen. It is frost-tender, and grows to a height and spread of just under 1 m (about 3 ft). Propagate from stem cuttings or by division in spring.

SALIX
purpurea
PURPLE OSIER OR WILLOW

Native to Europe, to Siberia and Japan, south to North Africa and Turkey, this deciduous, bushy species has a spreading habit and grows to 5 m (about 15 ft) in height and spread. It bears catkins of both sexes: the male ones have yellow anthers, while the female ones are insignificant; both are borne on slender purplish shoots in spring prior to the leaves. The narrow, oblong, deep green leaves are often borne in opposite pairs, making the species distinctive. Fully hardy. *S. p. gracilis* is a dwarf form with a compact habit.

SALVIA
africana-lutea

This bushy, evergreen shrub bears bi-labiate brown flowers, fading to red then brown. The foliage is soft, light-grey and aromatic. It does best in a sunny position with a well-drained, fertile soil. Propagate from

Rosa 'Buff Beauty' (Modern shrub)

softwood cuttings in spring and summer. Of the other *Salvia* species, *S. greggii* bears spikes of bright carmine or reddish purple flowers, while *S. guaranitica* has spikes of long, dark blue flowers with a white base.

SAMBUCUS
canadensis
AMERICAN ELDER

Native to south-eastern Canada and the United States, this strong-growing deciduous shrub has an irregular broad outline with many stout branches arching outwards from the base. It reaches a height and spread of 4 m (about 12 ft). The leaves are mid-green, changing to yellow in autumn/fall and colouring best in cool, moist climates. Small, star-shaped white flowers are borne in summer, followed by round, purple-black fruits. The variety 'Aurea' has butter-yellow foliage and cherry-red fruits. Plant in autumn/fall to spring and propagate species from seed in autumn/fall, softwood cuttings in summer or from hardwood cuttings in winter. Fully hardy.

SANTOLINA

Small, aromatic evergreens from the Mediterranean regions, these shrubs are grown for their scented, usually silvery-grey foliage and dainty, button-like yellow flowerheads. They are useful for covering banks, as a shrubby ground cover, in the front of shrub borders and rock gardens or as a low hedge. They require a well-drained soil and a sunny situation. Cut back old wood to encourage new growths from the base immediately after flowering and remove dead flowerheads and stems in autumn/fall. Propagate from semi-ripe cuttings in summer. Frost-hardy.

S. chamaecyparissus
COTTON LAVENDER, LAVENDER COTTON

This low-spreading, aromatic shrub, native to mild, coastal areas of the Mediterranean, grows to a height and spread of 1 m (about 3 ft). It bears bright yellow, rounded flowerheads on long stalks in summer, set among oblong, greyish green leaves. Cotton lavender does best in a sunny spot in soil that is well drained but not too rich. Water from time to time and dead-head continually. Straggly old plants should be pruned to a neat rounded habit in early spring. Hardy, it grows to a height of 75 cm (about 30 in) with a spread of 1 m (about 3 ft). Propagate from semi-ripe cuttings in summer.

S. virens
syn. *S. rosmarinifolia*
HOLY FLAX

Native to Spain, Portugal and southern France, this evergreen species

has green, thread-like 2–5 cm (about 1–2 in) long leaves and produces heads of bright yellow flowers in mid-summer. It has a dense, bushy habit, reaching a height of 60 cm (about 24 in) with a spread of 1 m (about 3 ft). Frost-hardy. The cultivar 'Primrose Gem' has paler yellow flowers.

SARCOCOCCA
CHRISTMAS BOX, SWEET BOX

Evergreen, low-growing, hardy shrubs, these plants are native to the Himalayas, western China and south-east Asia. They are grown for their fragrant winter flowers and ornamental berries and are ideal for planting in shady areas under trees. Preferably grow in any well-drained, moisture-retentive soil on a sheltered, shady site; they will, however, tolerate sun. Propagate from seed in autumn/fall or from semi-ripe cuttings in summer, and plant in autumn/fall or spring. They are useful for winter cutting for indoor decoration and are fully to frost hardy.

S. hookeriana

Native to western China, this suckering species has an erect, dense habit, reaching a height of 1.5 m (about 4½ ft) with a spread of 2 m (about 6 ft). The leaves are dark green and lance shaped with slender points. Tiny white or pink-tinted flowers are produced in the leaf axils in winter, followed by purple-black fruits. Fully hardy.

S. ruscifolia
SWEET BOX

The most commonly grown, this species is native to central China. It has an upright, arching habit, reaching a height and spread of 1 m (about 3 ft). Small, fragrant, milky-white flowers appear in winter, followed by brilliant, scarlet-red berries. The leaves are oval, deep lustrous green above and paler beneath. Frost-hardy.

Sarcococca ruscifolia

SENECIO
petasitis
VELVET GROUNDSEL

This erect, branching, evergreen shrub bears large, terminal panicles of sparsely petalled small, yellow flowers in mid-winter. The foliage is handsome and lobed. It prefers full sun in a protected position and a rich, moist, well-drained soil. It makes an excellent coastal garden shrub. Frost-tender, it grows to a height and spread of 1.5 m (about 4½ ft). Propagate from semi-ripe cuttings in summer.

SENNA
corymbosa
syn. *Cassia corymbosa*
AUTUMN CASSIA

This fast-growing shrub has light green foliage and large, dense clusters of bright yellow flowers that cover the shrub in autumn/fall. It grows to a height of 2.5 m (about 7½ ft) with a spread of 2 m (about 6 ft). Propagate from cuttings.

Senna corymbosa

Salvia africana-lutea

Sarcococca hookeriana

Santolina chamaecyparissus

Salvia guaranitica

Sambucus canadensis

Senecio petasitis

Santolina virens

SKIMMIA
japonica

This dense, round, evergreen shrub, native to the cooler parts of Asia, is resistant to air pollution, and so is a good choice for town gardens and parks. In early spring it bears clusters of tiny, white flowers. If male and female plants have been grown together, bright red berries will follow in summer and last well into autumn/fall. The leaves are aromatic, mid- to dark green and glossy. *S. japonica* prefers a well-drained, acid soil and shade or semi-shade—poor soil or too much sun will cause chlorosis. Fully hardy, it grows to a height and spread of 1.5 m (about 4½ ft). Propagate from cuttings in summer.

SOPHORA
prostrata

This native of New Zealand is much prized for the clusters of pea-shaped, pale yellow flowers that appear in summer amid small, oval leaflets. Frost-hardy, it prefers a rich, moist, well-drained soil, in a sunny position, and grows to a maximum height and spread of 2 m (about 6 ft). Propagate by scarified seed under glass in autumn/fall.

SPARMANNIA
africana
AFRICAN HEMP

This erect, spreading, evergreen shrub or small tree, native to southern Africa, bears clusters of delightful, white flowers all year round, amid large, heart-shaped, light green leaves. It is available in both single- and double-flowered types. It does best in fertile, well-drained soil. Water freely when in full growth, less so at other times. Prune hard every few years to control size. *S. africana* is frost-tender and it grows to a height and spread of just over 3 m (about 9 ft). Propagate from cuttings in spring. The genus is named after Dr Andes Sparmann, a Swedish naturalist aboard Captain Cook's historic second voyage.

SPARTIUM
junceum
SPANISH BROOM

This sparse, twiggy, almost leafless, deciduous shrub is native to southern Europe. In spring it bears long, showy spikes of bright yellow, pea-shaped flowers. The leaves are very small and sparse. *S. junceum* does best in a sunny spot in soil that is well-drained but not too rich. It is very suitable for a ground cover or as a hedge, especially in seaside areas. Prune in early spring to maintain a compact habit. Frost-hardy, it grows to a height and spread of 3 m (about 9 ft). Propagate from seed in autumn/fall. Plants are not very long lived, but are a good choice where a fast-growing plant is needed to fill in while slower growers are maturing.

SPIRAEA
SPIREA, MAYBUSH, GARLAND FLOWER, BRIDAL WREATH

Native to the northern hemisphere, these thick, often arching, deciduous or semi-evergreen shrubs are grown for their beautiful springtime bloom of pink, white or crimson flowers. Fully hardy, they do best in a fertile, moist, well-drained soil in full sun. A layering of manure in autumn/fall and early spring will help bring out the best quality bloom. Cut back spent heads to the old wood. Propagate from softwood cuttings in summer.

S. 'Anthony Waterer'

This fully hardy, upright, deciduous shrub bears crimson-pink flowers from late spring to early summer. It grows to a height and spread of 1 m (about 3 ft). The red foliage turns green as the shrub ages.

S. cantoniensis

This deciduous shrub, with arching, slender stems, is native to China and Japan. It grows to a height and spread of 2 m (about 6 ft) and is prized for its showy clusters of white flowers that appear in spring. These are set among narrow, diamond-shaped leaves with saw-toothed margins.

Spiraea cantoniensis

Sophora prostrata

Sparmannia africana (double)

Spiraea 'Anthony Waterer'

Spartium junceum

Skimmia japonica

Staphylea colchica

Sutherlandia frutescens

Streptosolen jamesonii

Spiraea vanhouttei

Spiraea thunbergii

S. thunbergii

Another native of Japan and China, *S. thunbergii* is a dense, deciduous shrub that bears clusters of single, white flowers in early spring. The leaves are narrow and long and turn orange in autumn/fall. It grows to a height and spread of 1 m (about 3 ft).

S. vanhouttei

BRIDAL WREATH

This compact, deciduous shrub bears dense clusters of white flowers amid dark green, diamond-shaped leaves in spring. It grows to a height of 3 m (about 9 ft) with a spread of 2 m (about 6 ft).

STAPHYLEA
colchica

BLADDER NUT

This deciduous, upright shrub is native to the Caucasus in Europe. From spring to early summer it bears delicate, erect, daffodil-like, trumpet-shaped flowers, set among serrated, trifoliate leaves. Pale green

inflated pods follow the bloom. *S. colchica* does best in a moist, leaf-rich soil, and in a shaded spot in hotter areas. Fully hardy, it grows to a height and spread of 3 m (about 9 ft). Propagate from cuttings in summer or seed in autumn/fall.

STREPTOSOLEN
jamesonii

FIREBUSH, ORANGE BROWALLIA, MARMALADE BUSH

This rather lax, branching ever-green, a native of Colombia, bears terminal clusters of orange, phlox-like flowers in spring; a yellow variety is also available. It has narrow, oval leaves. Full sun suits it best and it will thrive in a well-drained, humus-rich soil. Water well in full growth, less at other times. Tip prune regularly when young to help develop its shape. *S. jamesonii* is ideal as a shrub border plant. Cut back flowered shoots after the bloom. Frost-tender, it grows to a height and spread of 2 m (about 6 ft). Propagate from softwood or semi-ripe cuttings in summer.

SUTHERLANDIA
frutescens

DUCK PLANT, CANCER BUSH

Originating in South Africa, this erect semi-evergreen shrub is ex-tremely attractive but short lived. With an expansive habit and reach-ing up to 1.5 m (about 4½ ft) when potted, it is valued for its foliage, flowers and fruit. The vivid green, pinnate leaves are composed of up to 21 lance-shaped downy leaflets. In late spring, pendent deep red-orange flowers appear along slender stems, followed by inflated seed pods. Locate in full sun in fertile, well-drained soil. Propagate from seed or root cuttings in spring.

SYMPHORICARPOS

SNOWBERRY, WAXBERRY

These showy, cold-climate shrubs are grown for the clusters of long-lasting, pink-tinted or puffy white berries that follow their spring bloom of small, bell-shaped flowers. Native to the colder areas of China and North America, their arching habit

bends almost double under the weight of flowers and fruit. They are fully hardy and prefer filtered sun and a rich, acid soil. Propagate from softwood cuttings in summer or by division in autumn/fall. *S. x chenaultii* is a dense shrub that pro-duces spikes of pinkish flowers, followed by pinkish white berries.

S. orbiculatus

CORAL BERRY, INDIAN CURRANT

Native to North America, this erect, slender, deciduous shrub bears white or pink flowers in late summer, set among dark green, oval leaves that turn bronze in autumn/fall. Round, purple-red berries follow the bloom. It grows to a height and spread of 1–1.5 m (about 3–4½ ft).

Syringa 'Maréchal Foch'

Syringa × *persica*

Syringa 'Souvenir de Louis Spaëth'

Syringa vulgaris

Symphoricarpos rivularis

S. rivularis

syn. *S. albus* var. *rivularis*

This deciduous, thicketing shrub bears pink or white flowers in summer, appearing among dark green, rounded leaves. Large, white fruits follow. It grows to a height and spread of 1.5 m (about 4½ ft). There is a form with variegated leaves.

SYRINGA

LILAC

These vigorous, open, deciduous bushes, native to Europe and north-eastern Asia, are much loved. They are grown for the delightful fragrance of their flowers, which form in dense panicles in any shade of red, pink, white, mauve, purple, or even yellow, most being cultivars of the Turkish *S. vulgaris*. The leaves are oval and medium sized. Lilacs are fully hardy, and require cold, dormant winter conditions to bloom the following spring. They do best in a deep, fertile, well-drained, preferably alkaline soil, in full sun. Prune after flowering to maintain the shape. Dead-head for the first few years. Propagate by grafting or from softwood cuttings in summer. Grafted plants should be set with the graft union well below the soil surface.

S. laciniata

This species is a graceful form with prettily dissected 3- to 9-lobed leaves that produces small panicles of lilac flowers in mid-spring.

Syringa laciniata

Syringa meyeri 'Palibin'

S. 'Maréchal Foch'

This deciduous, bushy, upright shrub grows to a height and spread of 3 m (about 9 ft) and bears large panicles of fragrant, crimson-pink flowers in spring, among heart-shaped, mid-green leaves.

S. meyeri

This deciduous shrub, native to China, has small, dark lilac flowers that occur in small sprays in spring and narrowly oval leaves. It grows to a height and spread of 1 m (about 3 ft). *S. meyeri* 'Palibin' has pale pink flowers.

S. × persica

PERSIAN LILAC

Native to Afghanistan, *S.* × *persica* is a deciduous, bushy, compact shrub. In spring it bears profuse sprays of small, delightfully fragrant flowers set amid narrow, pointed, dark green leaves. It grows to a height and spread of just under 2 m (about 6 ft). It will grow in warmer winter climates than most lilacs.

S. 'Souvenir de Louis Spaëth'

In late spring, this lilac shrub bears long, thin panicles of sweet-smelling, deep purple-red flowers set among dark green, heart-shaped leaves. It grows to a height and spread of 5 m (about 15 ft).

S. vulgaris

COMMON LILAC

Native to south-eastern Europe and naturalized elsewhere, this large, upright, deciduous shrub grows to a height of 3–4 m (about 9–12 ft) with a spread of 2–3 m (about 6–9 ft). It has strong, upright growth, and on maturity develops a broadly rounded crown. Dark green, heart-shaped to ovate leaves turn dull yellow in autumn/fall. Sweetly perfumed lilac-coloured flowers are borne in erect panicles in spring. There are single, double and semi-double varieties, in colours ranging from white, through pale mauve, violet, purple and pink to carmine red.

TAMARIX

TAMARISK

The deciduous shrubs and small trees of this genus, native to the deserts and salty areas of Europe, Africa and Asia, are grown for their impressive foliage and the panicles of small flowers they bear. Being wind and salt resistant, these shrubs do particularly well in exposed, coastal positions, and make excellent hedges. They do best in a fertile, well-drained soil in a sunny position. All are frost-hardy. Early spring-flowering species should be pruned back to about half, once the flowerheads are spent, while late spring- and summer-flowering species are best pruned in winter. Propagate from semi-hardwood cuttings in late summer or from hardwood cuttings in late autumn/fall.

T. gallica
FRENCH TAMARISK

Native to the Canary Islands and Sicily, this deciduous, irregularly branched, upright shrub grows to a height of 4 m (about 12 ft) with a spread of 6 m (about 18 ft). In spring and summer, it bears terminal racemes of pink, star-shaped flowers set amid tiny, blue-grey leaves. *T. gallica* is frost-hardy.

T. parviflora

This graceful, arching, deciduous shrub grows to a height and spread of 4 m (about 12 ft). Native to Mediterranean Europe, it bears terminal racemes of inconspicuous, pink flowers, set amid tiny, blue-green, sessile leaves. *T. parviflora* is frost-hardy.

TAXUS
cuspidata
JAPANESE YEW

An evergreen, spreading conifer reaching a height and spread of 5 m (about 15 ft), although it can grow up to 15 m (about 50 ft) in the wild. It has long, dark, matt-green leaves, yellowish green beneath and sometimes colouring red-brown in cold weather. The fruit is glossy scarlet. This fully hardy conifer will tolerate very dry and shady conditions; seed-raised plants will grow taller more quickly. Another species, *T. x media*, grows to 3–6 m (about 9–18 ft) and bears cup-shaped, bright red fruits.

TECOMA
stans
syn. Bignonia stans, Stenolobium stans
YELLOW ELDER, YELLOW BELLS

Native to Central America, this erect, branching, evergreen shrub grows to a height of 5 m (about 15 ft) with a spread of 3 m (about 9 ft). It bears gorgeous, golden yellow, tubular flowers right through the warmer months, set among fern-like leaves with narrow leaflets. Half-hardy, it thrives in a rich, moist, well-drained soil and does best in a protected, sunny position.

Potted plants require an occasional watering when in full growth. Prune *T. stans* annually after blooming to maintain its habit. Propagate from soft-tip or semi-hardwood cuttings in summer.

TECOMARIA
capensis
syn. Tecoma capensis
FIRE FLOWER, CAPE HONEYSUCKLE

This evergreen, shrubby climber can be grown either as a shrub or climber. It bears tubular, fiery orange-red flowers in spring to summer, set among saw-toothed, dark green leaflets. Resistant to drought and salt, it does well in coastal areas, growing to a height and spread of 2–3 m (about 6–9 ft). *T. capensis* is half-hardy. It does best in fertile, well-drained soil and likes an open, sunny position. It will climb if not pruned hard annually. Crowded stems should be thinned out in spring. Propagate from semi-ripe cuttings in summer or from seed in spring. Yellow, dark red and pink forms are available.

TELOPEA
speciosissima
NEW SOUTH WALES WARATAH

This is a genus of bushy, tree-like shrubs, grown for their striking flowerheads. These consist of multiple, curved florets, surrounded by common bracts. Waratahs can be difficult to grow, and only really do well in a damp, sandy, neutral to acid loam, covered in leafy mulch. Half-hardy, they do best in dappled shade, though they will tolerate full sun. Potted specimens should be watered well in full growth, not so much at other times. Prune regularly to keep them compact. Propagate by layering in winter or from seed in spring. In its natural state in the Australian bush, its bright spring flowers can be easily spotted from a distance, hence the Aboriginal name of 'Waratah', meaning 'seen from afar'; the botanical name has the same significance. *T. speciosissima* is an upright, bushy, evergreen shrub that bears red, globular heads 15 cm (about 6 in) across, surrounded by bright red bracts in spring and early summer. It has leathery, wedge- to oblong-shaped leaves with saw-toothed margins. It grows to a height and spread of just under 3 m (about 9 ft). It is native to and the floral emblem of the state of New South Wales, Australia.

TERNSTROEMIA
gymnanthera

An attractive evergreen with glossy, oval, mid- to deep green leaves, this dense shrub which is a native of south-east Asia bears hanging, 5-petalled white flowers in summer that are followed by berry-like, bright red fruits in autumn/fall. It has a rounded appearance and reaches a height and spread of 2 m (about 6 ft). They will grow in either full sun or semi-shade, and require a well-drained, neutral to acid soil that is rich in organic matter. Straggly growth can be pruned in spring if required. Propagate from semi-ripe cuttings in late summer or from seed when ripe. Half-hardy.

Tamarix gallica

Taxus cuspidata

Tecomaria capensis

Ternstroemia gymnanthera

Tamarix parviflora

Telopea speciosissima

Tecoma stans

Teucrium chamaedrys

Tibouchina urvilleana

Thevetia peruviana

Teucrium fruticans

Tetrapanax papyriferus

Thuja occidentalis 'Rheingold'

TETRAPANAX

papyriferus

syn. *Fatsia papyrifera*

RICE PAPER PLANT

This upright, evergreen, branching shrub native to southern China is grown mainly for its large, felted, deeply lobed leaves, but the creamy white flowers it bears in late summer and autumn/fall, and the small black berries that follow, are added attractions. *T. papyriferus* is the only species in the genus. It prefers a humus-rich, moist but well-drained soil and does well in either full sun or partial shade. It tolerates salt-laden winds and so is excellent for coastal gardens. Too large for pots, it is suitable for courtyards. Half-hardy, it grows to a height of 4 m (about 12 ft) with a spread of 5 m (about 15 ft). Propagate from suckers or seed in early spring, and prune as and when needed to control the plant's size.

TEUCRIUM

GERMANDER

Mainly native to the Mediterranean, this genus was named for King Teucer of Troy, who reputedly used the plants medicinally. Evergreen or deciduous, they are useful shrubs for dry areas because of their ability to withstand hot, dry conditions and poor soils. They are grown for their flowers and foliage and prefer light, well-drained soil and sunny conditions. Low-growing species do best in poor soils. Propagate from softwood or semi-ripe cuttings in summer, and plant in autumn/fall to spring. Fully to half-hardy.

T. chamaedrys

GERMANDER

This hardy, sub-shrubby alpine species is native to Europe and south-western Asia. It bears spikes of pale to deep rosy-purple flowers in summer and has toothed ovate leaves, glossy deep green above and grey beneath. It grows to a height and spread of around 30 cm (about 12 in).

T. fruticans

BUSH GERMANDER

Native to southern Europe, this upright evergreen grows to a height and spread of around 1.5 m (about 4½ ft). It is mostly enjoyed for the attractive, blue, tubular, double-lipped flowers it bears in spring, set among aromatic, oval, slivery grey leaves. Half- to frost-hardy, it needs a well-drained soil and full sun. Trim old flowerheads to promote new growth. *T. fruticans* makes a good, low, neat hedge, and does well in seaside gardens. Propagate from softwood or semi-ripe cuttings in summer.

THEVETIA

peruviana

syn. *T. neriifolia*

YELLOW OLEANDER

Native to tropical America, this upright, spreading evergreen bears fragrant, yellow, petunia-like flowers from winter to summer, set among spidery, short-stemmed, lance-shaped leaves. Frost-tender, it does best in well-watered, well-drained, sandy soil, in full sun. Potted plants should be watered moderately in full growth, less at other times. Tip young stems in winter to promote branching. Propagate from semi-ripe cuttings in summer, or from seed in spring. *T. peruviana* is sometimes called the 'be-still bush' because of the distinctive movement of its leaves in a breeze. The plant is intensely poisonous and should not be planted where it might pose a danger to children.

THUJA

occidentalis 'Rheingold'

AMERICAN ARBOR-VITAE, NORTHERN WHITE CEDAR

This attractive little conifer grows slowly to a height of 1–2 m (about 3–6 ft) and a spread of 1.5–3 m (about 4½–9 ft). It is grown for its rounded habit and its yellow, summer foliage that turns bronze in winter. Fully hardy, it tolerates most types of soil but prefers a shady position. Prune to shape or to restrict size. Propagate from hardwood cuttings taken from a young plant and strike in humid conditions, between late autumn/fall and late winter.

TIBOUCHINA

urvilleana

syn. *T. semidecandra*

GLORY BUSH, LASIANDRA

This upright, branching native of South America is grown for the delightful clusters of purple flowers it bears from summer to early winter, set among prominently veined, hairy, oval leaves. It needs a rich, well-drained, acid soil and full sun. In very hot areas it will do reasonably well in dappled shade. To promote bushiness, pinch out growing tips regularly. Keep the soil moist during spring and summer. Frost-tender, *T. urvilleana* grows to a height of 3 m (about 9 ft) with a spread of 2 m (about 6 ft). Propagate from greenwood or semi-ripe cuttings in late spring or summer. There are several cultivars available, with flowers in varying shades of purple or strong pink.

VACCINIUM

macrocarpon

syn. *Oxycoccus macrocarpon*

AMERICAN CRANBERRRY

Native to eastern North America, this evergreen is commercially grown in that country and several cultivars are known. It bears pink nodding flowers in summer, followed by relatively large red fruit.

Prostrate in habit, it forms mats of interlacing wiry stems with alternate leaves, spreading to around 90 cm (about 36 in) when fully mature. Grow in acid, peaty, permanently moist soil in full sun, and propagate by layers in spring or from seed when ripe. Plant in autumn/fall to spring. Fully hardy.

VIBURNUM

SNOWBALL TREE, CRANBERRY BUSH, GUELDER ROSE, LAURUSTINUS

These deciduous or evergreen shrubs and trees are grown for their fragrant flowers, fruits and beautiful autumn/fall foliage. Fully to frost-hardy, the hundres-odd species and many more varieties grow best in sun or semi-shade in a rich, moist, well-drained soil. Remove spent flowerheads regularly and prune annually to maintain shape. Propagate from cuttings in summer or from seed in autumn/fall. Mildew and spider mite may cause problems.

V. × bodnantense

A deciduous hybrid, this viburnum is one of the best frost-resistant, winter-flowering shrubs. It bears clusters of fragrant, white-flushed rose-pink flowers from late autumn/fall right through to winter. It has an upright, rather stiff habit and reaches a height and spread of 3–4 m (about 9–12 ft). The leaves, which are toothed and dull green, are bronze-tinged when young. There are several forms grown, 'Dawn' being the most commonly cultivated.

V. × burkwoodii

BURKWOOD VIBURNUM

This bushy, open, semi-evergreen shrub bears wide, globular clusters of scented flowers that open pink, but fade to white. Its oval, dark green leaves turn red in autumn/fall. Fully hardy, it grows to a height and spread of 2.5 m (about 7 ft).

V. × carlecephalum

A deciduous, spring-flowering hybrid with large, rounded heads of fragrant, creamy white flowers that are pink when in bud. The dark green foliage often turns red in autumn/fall. It has a rounded, bushy habit and grows to a height and spread of around 3 m (about 9 ft). Fully hardy.

V. carlesii

KOREAN VIBURNUM

This upright, deciduous shrub grows to a height and spread of just over 2 m (about 6 ft). In spring it bears fragrant, snow-white and pink flowers, followed by round, black berries. Its dull green, woolly, oval leaves turn red in autumn/fall.

V. davidii

Native to China, this compact, wide-spreading evergreen species is one of the few viburnums grown for its leaves rather than its flowers. Its leathery, deeply veined leaves form a dome, over which dense clusters of small white flowers appear in late spring. If male and female plants are grown together, the flowers are followed by decorative turquoise-blue berries. Suitable as a ground cover, it reaches a height of 80 cm (about 32 in) with a spread of 1.5 m (about 4½ ft). Fully hardy.

V. dentatum

Native to the eastern United States, this erect deciduous shrub reaches a height of 3 m (about 9 ft) or more, with a spread of 2–3 m (about 6–9 ft). It has coarsely toothed, heavily veined mid-green leaves that take on attractive autumn/fall colours. Clusters of white flowers are borne in spring, followed by blue-black fruits in autumn/fall.

V. farreri

syn. V. fragrans

A deciduous shrub from western China, bearing the name of the great plant explorer who discovered it. It is a 3 m (about 9 ft) tall deciduous, frost-hardy shrub whose leaves turn red in the autumn/fall. Its main feature is the fragrance of its clustered pale pink flowers which are reliably borne all through the winter. It is adaptable to most soils but prefers an open, sunny position.

Viburnum × burkwoodii

Viburnum × bodnantense

Vaccinium macrocarpon

Viburnum farreri

Viburnum carlesii

Viburnum davidii

Viburnum dentatum

Viburnum × carlecephalum

Viburnum tinus

Viburnum plicatum 'Mariesii'

Viburnum lantana

Viburnum opulus 'Nanum'

V. lantana
WAYFARING TREE

A deciduous shrub with an upright habit, this plant grows vigorously to a height of 5 m (about 15 ft) and a spread of 4 m (about 12 ft). The oval, grey-green leaves are densely downy underneath and turn red in autumn/fall. Flattened clusters of small white flowers are borne in late spring and early summer, followed by red berries that ripen to black.

V. opulus 'Nanum'
GUELDER ROSE

Native to Europe and North Africa, this deciduous, bushy shrub bears heavily scented, delicate, white lacecap flowers in late spring and early summer. They are followed by large clusters of transluscent berries in autumn/fall. The leaves are dark green, lobed and maple-like, reddening in autumn. It is a vigorous species, growing to a height and spread of 4 m (about 12 ft). 'Nanum' has a dense dwarf habit but flowers very sparsely. Fully hardy.

V. opulus 'Sterile'
syn. *V. o.* 'Roseum'
GUELDER ROSE

This vigorous, bushy, deciduous shrub, native to Europe, Asia and northern Africa, grows to a height and spread of 4 m (about 12 ft). In spring and early summer, it bears flattened heads of flowers that are green at first and later turn white. The oval, green leaves turn red in autumn/fall.

V. plicatum 'Mariesii'

In late spring and early summer, this bushy, deciduous shrub bears large, rounded heads of flowers with white bracts. The dark green leaves turn red in autumn/fall. Fully hardy, it grows to a height of 3 m (about 9 ft) and a spread of 4 m (about 12 ft).

V. prunifolium
BLACK-HAW VIBURNUM

Native to the eastern United States, this shrubby, deciduous species grows to a height of 5 m (about 15 ft) and has a short main trunk and conical head when mature. The dark green, *Prunus*-like leaves change to orange and scarlet in autumn/fall, and clusters of white flowers are borne in spring. These are followed by blue-black fruit with a whitish bloom; the fruit is very attractive to birds. Young shoots are a reddish green, while the trunk becomes grey with age.

V. tinus
LAURUSTINUS

This bushy, evergreen shrub bears clusters of honeysuckle-fragrant, pinkish white flowers in winter, set amid oval, dark green, glossy leaves. Frost-hardy, it grows to a height and spread of 3 m (about 9 ft). Recommended as a hedge plant, although not for enclosed court-yards where the smell of the fallen leaves can be offensive.

V. trilobum
syn. *V. americanum*
CRANBERRY BUSH, HIGHBUSH CRANBERRY, SQUAWBUSH

Native to northern North America, this species is almost identical to *V.*

Viburnum trilobum

Viburnum prunifolium

Viburnum opulus 'Sterile'

opulus but has leaf stalks with small glands.

VITEX
agnus-castus

CHASTE TREE

Native to Europe and Asia, *V. agnus-castus* grows to a height and spread of 2–3 m (about 6–9 ft). This open, deciduous, spreading shrub bears dense, upright clusters of small, dark blue or white flowers in late summer. The grey-green, compound leaves are aromatic. It is frost- to half-hardy and prefers full sun and well-drained soil. It is best propagated from semi-ripe cuttings in summer or from seed in spring.

WEIGELA

FAIRY TRUMPETS, WEIGELA

These decidious, fountain-shaped shrubs bear brilliant, though short-lived, masses of pink, white or red trumpet flowers in the warmer months. However, their leaves fall early in autumn/fall without colouring, leaving the branches bare for most of the winter. They do best in a sunny position in a rich, well-drained soil. Water them well during the growing season and prune out older branches after flowering. Propagate from softwood cuttings in summer.

W. florida

A native of China and Korea, this deciduous, arching shrub bears delightful, deep rose-pink, trumpet-shaped flowers in late spring and early summer. The leaves are serrated, mid-green, small and oval. Fully hardy, it grows to a height and spread of 2.5 m (about 7 ft). It prefers rich, well-drained soils in an open, sunny position and is frost resistant.

W. florida 'Eva Ratke'

This cultivar bears crimson flowers from purplish red buds from late spring to early summer. Fully hardy, it grows 1.5 m (about 4½ ft) tall and wide with a dense, erect habit.

W. florida 'Variegata'

In late spring and early summer, this cultivar bears an abundance of funnel-shaped, pink flowers, set among green leaves with creamy white margins.

WESTRINGIA
fruticosa
syn. *W. rosmariniformis*

MORNING LIGHT, COAST ROSEMARY

This rounded, compact, evergreen shrub grows to a height and spread of 1.5 m (about 4½ ft). Native to New South Wales and Queensland, Australia, it is grown for the delicate, white to pale mauve flowers it bears in spring, set among light, greyish green, broad leaves arranged in whorls of four. It is a fast grower but is short lived. Moderately frost-hardy, it does best in a sunny position in a fertile, well-drained soil. Water potted plants regularly during full growth. Propagate from seed in spring or from semi-ripe cuttings in late summer.

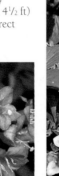
Wiegela florida 'Eva Ratke'

Wiegela florida

Vitex agnus-castus

Westringia fruticosa

Weigela florida 'Variegata'

CHAPTER 4

Trees

*T*he backbone of a garden, trees are fundamental to the landscape. Whatever their size, these plants form the basis of the type of garden being aimed for, be it a lush rainforest atmosphere, a cold country woodland or a single specimen highlight for a small courtyard.

A tree is a plant, either broad leafed or coniferous, with a single, woody stem reaching to a height of at least 4 m (about 12 ft) when mature. Palms and tree ferns, although they do not have the same type of woody stem, are generally included for horticultural purposes because their growth habit and landscape uses are similar to that of trees.

Trees can form windbreaks in larger gardens, are invaluable as noise inhibitors, provide privacy from overlooking houses or unit buildings and soften the skyline in the urban environment.

They are growing structures in gardens, chosen for a particular purpose, though many will provide bonus points to add to their initial attractiveness as they mature. Trees planted to provide shade may well provide a horizontal branch to support a swing, or branches to form a climbing frame for adventurous children. Birds will soon inhabit suitable trees for nesting or food gathering among blossom and fruits while keeping a sharp eye on the insect population in the garden below.

Choosing the Right Tree

Never buy a tree on impulse. It is a permanent part of the garden structure, after all trees can take around 20 years to arrive at any semblance of maturity, so it is necessary to get the selection right first time. Take time before you go to the nursery, read as much as you can about a tree's growing habits such as its estimated mature height and spread, as well as its seasonal displays. What at first appears to be a bewildering choice will soon be whittled down to a couple of possible contenders for a particular spot in the garden.

Climate and soil requirements also need to be considered. It is preferable to grow a tree climatically suited to your area. If you're new to a neighbourhood, walk through the parks and look over garden fences to see which trees are growing well.

Evergreen or Deciduous?

Trees are most often sought after for their shade value. Consider then the choice of evergreen or deciduous. Perhaps an evergreen is what's needed in a screening situation or in the tropics where year-round sun protection over a patio is needed. A deciduous tree will provide summer shade and winter sun. There is an ever changing display each season, ranging from the fine tracery of bare branches in winter to soft green new spring growth, a welcoming dense cover in summer then a wonderful autumn/fall display, often with flowers and colourful fruit as well.

The colourful contribution trees make to the landscape often comes because of their foliage colour. Consider the soft blue-grey foliage of some of the conifers and eucalypt species or *Pyrus salicifolia* which meld so well with the

Shape and height are two important considerations when selecting trees.

white and pastel blues and pinks favoured by cottage gardeners. Then there's the variegated foliaged trees which provide a welcome accent in an otherwise green landscape, but it's the intensity of yellow/orange/red tones that really capture a gardener's heart.

Cold country gardeners have any number of trees in all sizes and shapes from which to make a rich display of colour before winter sets in. Temperate gardeners are not so fortunate. However, beautiful displays can be assured with *Nyssa sylvatica*, *Ginkgo biloba* or in larger gardens the majestic *Liquidambar styraciflua*.

Getting the Proportions Right

For the home gardener, perhaps the most important consideration in choosing a particular tree is its mature height and spread. Proportion is the catchword here for both aesthetic and practical reasons. A large, dense tree planted too close to a house may shade it too well, making rooms very dark and cutting off any perspective view through the windows. It may also rob the surrounding garden of light and root room. In such a situation it may be better to choose a smaller, more openly branched tree which both frames the view and allows ample light into a room, for example *Cassia fistula*, *Betula pendula*, *Pistacia chinensis* or *Zelkova serrata*.

Planting

It takes a few years for a tree to become self-sufficient even though it may be quite large when planted out. New roots need time to establish to forage for nutrients and to anchor the plant. Consequently, all trees, but in particular those planted as specimen trees, need to be given great care in their early years. Before planting, check the tree will not be hindered above by overhead wires or that underground pipes will not be invaded by vigorous root systems.

Good drainage is essential as few plants will thrive with wet feet. Wide planting holes, ample surrounding soil cultivation and even raising the bed are some ways of overcoming a drainage problem, but if the soil is very heavy, the addition of gypsum or coarse sand may be required as well. As soil in the container and the surrounding garden soil are often quite different in texture, it's important to combine these two to allow new roots to venture easily into

Deciduous trees provide a delightful display of autumn/fall colour.

their new surrounding. Do this by digging a shallow (just a little deeper than the container) yet wide hole, at least twice the diameter of the root ball, and fill the base with a friable mixture composed of about half the existing soil and a rich humus mix. Carefully remove the plant from the container, taking special care not to damage the main trunk, and place the root ball in position, together with up to three stakes. At this point check that the roots are not tangled or wound round in circles. If they are they need to be gently teased out and straightened, otherwise they will continue in this circular fashion eventually causing the plant to wither. Continue to fill the hole with the soil mix firming it in and around the trunk by hand, but ensuring that the tree is planted only as deep as it was in the container. Once it is firmly in position water well to get rid of any remaining air pockets. The remaining soil mix can be used to form a raised circle around the plant. Then, to conserve moisture, a layer of organic mulch can be added. This mulch, weeds and low-growing ground covers should be kept well away from the trunk to discourage collar or other root rot fungus.

If planting in a lawn, cut away a circle of turf at least 1 m (about 3 ft) in diameter to ensure the tender roots of the newly planted tree will not have to compete with those of voracious lawn

grasses. Keep the surface of this area well mulched to retain as much moisture as possible and to deter weeds competing for the available nutrients.

Trees need to be staked to ensure the leader, main trunk, is not damaged while still young and tender. Place the stakes in position at the time of planting, then attach the plant to these with tree ties or a length of old rag tied in a figure of eight to ensure the trunk remains steady when buffeted by strong winds. Don't use wire as it can cut into the trunk.

Deciduous trees are usually planted in the dormant state; evergreens, in temperate areas, are best planted out in autumn/fall while the soil is still warm. In colder areas, evergreens with new, tender growth will avoid frost damage if planted out in late spring.

Pruning

Trees rarely need pruning in maturity except after storm damage or for the removal of diseased branches, however young trees often benefit from being given a helping hand to balance their shape or to develop a higher branching system where they overhang a path. If noticed early enough unwanted new shoots can be rubbed off very easily by hand, a technique which doesn't leave unsightly scars on the often beautiful trunks of these majestic garden plants.

Abies concolor

Abies procera 'Glauca'

Acacia dealbata

Abies cephalonica

Acacia baileyana

Acer buergerianum

Acer ginnala

ABIES

SILVER FIR, BALSAM

These 40 diverse species of conical conifers are cold-climate evergreens. Prized for their aromatic wood and sap, their usefulness to the timber and pharmaceutical industries has threatened many species with extinction. Their name comes from the Latin *abeo*: 'I rise': some attain majestic heights of 100 m (about 320 ft) growing 1 m (about 3 ft) a year. In autumn/fall the spiral branches show seed-bearing cones, not pendent but growing upright, which distinguishes *Abies* from similar conifers like the spruces. The soft, spindle-shaped leaves are flat and round-edged, often bearing two parallel silver lines on the underside. Most species are too large for the average garden, being better suited to a country property. Fully hardy, they prefer moist soil, partial shade and a cool climate. Prune in late winter to encourage shape and limit size; propagate from seeds from ripened cones. The classic European Christmas tree belongs to this genus.

A. cephalonica

GRECIAN FIR

This upright conifer grows to 30 m (about 95 ft) high, and has a conical crown. Its cylindrical cones are 10–15 cm (about 4–6 in) long and brown when mature. The glossy, dark green leaves have white-green undersides.

A. concolor

WHITE FIR

Originally from California and Mexico, this conifer can grow to 30

m (about 95 ft). It has grey-green leaves and an open crown. Its green cylindrical cones ripen to brown.

A. procera 'Glauca'

The attractive blue foliage and smooth, silvery bark identify this upright conifer. It grows to 30 m (about 95 ft) high. Its cylindrical cones are 15–20 cm (about 6–8 in) long and purplish brown. The leaves are glaucous. If the tree dries out cracks will appear in the wood and bark.

ACACIA

WATTLE, ACACIA

This extremely diverse genus contains over 1000 short-lived evergreen, semi-evergreen and deciduous species, mostly native to Australia and Africa. Growing 5–20 m (about 15–65 ft) high, they are valued for their beautiful dense golden blossoms and rapid growth. Most species have flat, spindle-shaped stalks (phyllodes) instead of conventional leaves. A few develop pinnate, fern-like fronds or compound leaves. The fruit is a long, legume-like pod. Heat-treated seeds may be used for propagation, mimicking the way seeds are released in bushfires. Untreated seeds have been known to last 50 years. Renowned for their ability to survive drought, acacias grow best in warm climates with well-drained soil and full sun; few can be described as more than half-hardy. To extend their life, completely top dead branches and prune soon after flowering ends. Watch for borers, leaf miner and acacia scale. White Australian settlers used acacias to build

wattle-and-daub huts; hence the common name.

A. baileyana

COOTAMUNDRA WATTLE

Native to Australia, this elegant, half-hardy evergreen grows to 6 m (about 18 ft). In late winter to early spring, soft golden blossoms appear on drooping branches. The foliage is silver-blue pinnate leaves, rather than phyllodes, 5 cm (about 2 in) long. Ugly circular swellings may appear on the limbs as a result of gall wasp; remove and burn affected limbs.

A. dealbata

SILVER WATTLE, MIMOSA

This frost-hardy evergreen produces beautiful lemon-coloured flower clusters. It is popular in Europe and the USA, where it is known as mimosa. While it may grow to 30 m (about 95 ft), the average height is 12 m (about 37 ft). Silver-blue compound leaves, 13 cm (about 5 in) long, contrast with the soft pink seed pods, which are 5–10 cm (about 2–4 in) long.

ACER

MAPLE

Originating in the cool-temperate zones of the northern hemisphere, these deciduous trees and shrubs are prized for their decorative bark and magnificent foliage. Species vary considerably in shape and size: some grow to 40 m (about 130 ft) in cool mountain regions; others in coastal zones reach 3–5 m (about 9–15 ft). Hand-shaped leaves with sharply pointed fingers colour dramatically in autumn fall. Some spe-

cies produce little flowers followed by 2-winged fruit, or keys, that 'fly' long distances on the wind. Maples prefer cool or temperate climates with rich, well-drained soil and will not flourish in dry heat or tropical conditions. Provide full sun or partial shade; shelter from the wind to avoid leaf burn. A neutral to acid soil encourages optimum leaf colours. Propagate from seed in autumn/fall; budding in summer. *Acer*, meaning 'sharp', has been used since the days of the Romans; the name is thought to derive from the use of the wood for spears.

A. buergerianum

TRIDENT MAPLE

This species attains a spread of 8 m (about 24 ft) while growing to a height of 10 m (about 30 ft). Its shiny, dark green leaves turn orange-purple in autumn/fall, giving a brilliant and lasting show of colour.

A. ginnala

AMUR MAPLE

Growing up to 10 m (about 30 ft) high and wide, this maple originated in China and Japan. It has clusters of fragrant white flowers in summer, and 3-lobed, cordate, mid-green leaves which turn a vibrant red, making the tree a visual delight in autumn/fall.

A. griseum

PAPER-BARK MAPLE

Native to China, this slow-growing species can reach 10 m (about 30 ft) high and wide, and will suit a small garden. Its common name is derived from the way the pale brown dead bark peels off in strips to expose new coppery orange bark. Its leaves consist of 3-lobed leaflets that open a pink-brown, then turn dark green and finally red and orange in autumn/fall.

A. japonicum

DOWNY JAPANESE MAPLE, FULL-MOON MAPLE

This bushy tree can reach 14 m (about 45 ft) in height with a similar spread. Originally from Japan, its mid-green leaves have 7–11 lobes, which turn red at the tips in autumn/fall. It bears bright red flower clusters along with its spring leaves. This species needs to be protected from strong winds. *A. j.* 'Vitifolium' attains much the same proportions but has broader, more rounded leaves that turn brilliant crimson and orange in autumn/fall.

A. macrophyllum

OREGON MAPLE, BIG LEAF MAPLE

This rounded species, growing to 30 m (about 95 ft) with a spread of 22 m (about 70 ft), bears pendent yellow flowers followed by light green fruit. The large, sharply lobed leaves turn yellowish orange in autumn/fall.

A. negundo 'Aureo-variegatum'

BOX ELDER, GHOST TREE

This attractive, fast-growing cultivar reaches 5–6 m (about 15–18 ft). Small yellow-green flowers appear in bunches on slender stalks in early spring. Distinctive compound leaves, 3 to 5 oval-shaped leaflets edged with yellowish gold, give the tree a remarkable appearance; it does not change colour in autumn/fall. The species itself has plain green leaves and is fast growing to 15 m (about 50 ft). It comes from North America.

A. palmatum

JAPANESE MAPLE

There are many cultivars of this popular species, both trees and shrubs, and all have striking foliage. A deciduous, shapely tree with a bushy head, it grows 3–5 m (about 9–15 ft) in mild-winter areas and can reach 15 m (about 50 ft) in cool-temperate zones. The 5-pointed leaves are deeply recessed. They turn from mid-green to bronze in spring and reddish orange in autumn/fall. Avoid pruning and provide protection from the wind.

A. platanoides

NORWAY MAPLE

This very hardy maple, reaching 25 m (about 80 ft) high and 15 m (about 40 ft) wide, is a favourite for city streets as it is tolerant of pollution. Its clusters of bright yellow flowers appear in spring before the broad, lobed, light green leaves. In autumn/fall the leaves turn yellow and reddish brown. The Norway maple has many distinct forms.

A. platanoides 'Crimson King'

NORWAY MAPLE

Native to Europe, this grand tree grows to 15–18 m (about 50–60 ft). Immature leaves turn blood red in autumn/fall, while the mature leaf changes from bright green to yellow or orange. Deeply recessed, with few lobes, the leaves are 15 cm (about 6 in) long and 20 cm (about 8 in) wide. Small yellow flowers with red edges appear in clusters in mid-spring.

A. pseudoplatanus

SYCAMORE

This fast and easily grown shade tree from Europe and west Asia will reach its greatest height of 18 m (about 60 ft) in cool, hilly country. Long clusters of attractive flowers are conspicuous in spring, while its leaves are divided into 5 lobes with blunt teeth and are broader than they are long. In Scotland, a wine is made from the sap of this species.

A. rubrum

RED MAPLE

A native of North America, this round-headed tree provides much colour throughout the season. Growing to 30 m (about 95 ft), it bears clusters of small red flowers on reddish branches in spring before the 3- to 5-lobed leaves appear. Yellowish green at first, they turn a lustrous deep green above and blue-white underneath; in autumn/fall they change again, to a brilliant red. Plant in deep, fertile soil in a protected, semi-shaded position.

A. saccharinum

syn. ***A. dasycarpum***

SILVER MAPLE, WHITE MAPLE, RIVER MAPLE

The main source of sugar and syrup for the first settlers of North America, this fast-growing tree—to 30 m (about 95 ft)—carries its small red flowers in spring before the 5-lobed, mid-green leaves with silvery white undersides appear. The leaves then turn yellow, and occasionally red, in autumn/fall. Often planted in parks and along roadsides in Britain, this tree has an open appearance.

Acer japonicum

Acer palmatum

Acer griseum

Acer negundo 'Aureo-variegatum'

Acer macrophyllum

Acer platanoides

Acer platanoides 'Crimson King'

Acer saccharinum

Acer rubrum

Acer pseudoplatanus

Albitzia lophantha

Aesculus × carnea

Aesculus californica

Ailanthus glandulosa

Albitzia julibrissin

Alberta magna

Agathis robusta

Agathis australis

AESCULUS

HORSE CHESTNUT, BUCKEYE

This genus of hardy, deciduous flowering trees and shrubs is grown for its ease of cultivation and for its erect panicles of showy flowers, followed by seed cases which can be prickly. Growing to 30 m (about 95 ft), they are a favourite for parks and roadsides. They require a fertile, well-drained soil and do best in sun or partial shade. Pruning is not generally necessary. The new palmate leaves can be subject to leaf spot in spring, which may eventually cause the whole leaf to wither. Propagate the species from seed in autumn/fall, cultivars by grafting in late winter. The famous schoolyard conker is the seed case of *A. hippocastanum.*

A. californica
CALIFORNIAN BUCKEYE

This shrubby tree can reach a height and spread of 10 m (about 30 ft). The small leaves are made up of 5–7 dark green leaflets, and fragrant white, occasionally pink, flowers appear in spring and early summer.

A. × carnea
syn. *A. rubicunda*
RED HORSE-CHESTNUT, BUCKEYE

This deciduous hybrid between the Indian and European horse-chestnuts is valued for its beautiful foliage and well-rounded shape. It grows slowly to 10–20 m (about 30–65 ft) and is fully hardy. The dark green, divided leaves are prone to leaf spot when immature. Large, upright clusters of rich pink blossoms appear in late spring to early summer, followed by the fruit. This species prefers a cold winter to cool-temperate climate. Suitable for parks or large gardens, it needs a rich, moist, well-drained soil and full sun or partial shade. Leaves burn easily. Propagate from seed in autumn/fall; by grafting in late winter. Pruning is generally unnecessary but the tree may be lopped in winter. The white species *A. hippocastanum* is a splendid tree, larger than the red.

AGATHIS

KAURI, TENNIS BALL TREE

These tall, erect, evergreen conifers, native to the South Pacific, are slow growing and average between 40 and 60 m (about 130–190 ft) in height. Unlike most conifers, the waxy, simple leaves are deep green and slightly curved. The large cones are also unusual, resembling small pineapples or tennis balls and developing at the union of the branch and branchlet. The trees prefer warm temperatures and full sun, and will grow in most soils. Prune to encourage shape or limit size and propagate from seed. Highly valued for their timber, which is relatively straight and free of knots, the trees are a copious source of copal resin which is used in varnish.

A. australis
KAURI PINE, KAURI

Reaching heights up to 35 m (about 110 ft), this grand, long-living New Zealand evergreen has a slender, conical shape, developing a spreading level crown in maturity. Its narrow elliptical foliage is mid-green turning to coppery brown in colder weather. Inconspicuous male and female flowers develop separately on the same tree, and are followed in autumn/fall by globular, egg-shaped cones. This half-hardy species prefers moderate temperatures, damp soil and full sun. Prune regularly and propagate from cold-treated seed. This tree is highly valued worldwide as a source of Kauri gum, copal lacquer and timber.

A. robusta
QUEENSLAND KAURI, TENNIS BALL TREE

This tall tree is a native of the Pacific region and highly valued for its knot-free timber. A frost-hardy evergreen, the species slowly reaches a lofty height of 18–30 m (about 60–95 ft). Its deep green, waxy leaves are 5–10 cm (about 2–4 in) long and ovular. Globe-shaped cones, 7–12 cm (about 3–5 in) long, grow at the union of the branches and resemble tennis balls—hence the nickname. The species also yields a gummy resin, copal, which is used to manufacture varnish. The tree prefers warm-temperate to tropical regions. Propagate from seed.

AILANTHUS
glandulosa
syn. *A. altissima*
TREE OF HEAVEN

Native to China, this broad, deciduous shade tree reaches 6–18 m (about 18–60 ft). It is valued for its attractive, unusual foliage: deep green, fern-like leaves, 60 cm (about 24 in) long, with 15–30 oval leaflets. Inconspicuous groups of tiny green flowers, with an unfortunate odour, bloom in mid-summer, followed by reddish orange, winged seed pods. Able to withstand the worst city smog, this fully hardy tree graces many world capitals. It does best in subtropical areas but will survive in most climates, preferring full sun or partial shade and deep, rich soil. Prune severely in spring to create a shrub. Propagate from seed in autumn/fall, and suckers or root cuttings from the female tree in winter. Because of its tendency to sucker, it is classified as a noxious weed in Victoria, Australia.

ALBERTA
magna

This small, slow-growing, evergreen tree from South Africa reaches a height of 4 m (about 12 ft). It is grown for its shiny, oval-oblong, dark green leaves that look like laurel leaves, and the erect clusters of tubular, orange-red flowers from late autumn/fall to spring, followed by scarlet calyces in summer. It prefers a moist, well-drained soil in a warm, temperate coastal climate in full sun or semi-shade. Protect against cold and salty winds and give plenty of water in summer. Frost-tender, it does best above 10°C (about 50°F). Propagate from seed in autumn/fall or separate root cuttings or suckers for true-to-type plants.

ALBITZIA
SILK TREE

This genus comprises over 100 species of deciduous trees and shrubs native to the tropical and subtropical areas of Asia, Africa and Australia, with one species in Mexico. They are distinguished from their close relatives in the *Acacia* genus by their stamens, which are knitted together. Trees vary in height, 6–25 m (18–75 ft), and are noted for their very unusual foliage: opposing pairs of bipinnate leaves form along a central stalk and fold up at night. Clusters of small flowers, spiky or downy, form large, globular crowns similar to bottlebrushes. Plants refuse to bloom in pots but are still worthwhile for their foliage. They prefer full sun with protection from the wind. Plant in a light, compost-enriched soil and propagate from seed in late autumn/ fall to early spring. The genus was named after an Italian naturalist, F. degli Albizi, who first cultivated *A. julibrissin* in 1759.

A. julibrissin
PINK SILK TREE

Found in the area between Iran and Japan, this is a squat tree with a broad crown. Reaching a height of 10 m (about 30 ft), it has large, pale to mid-green pinnates. An abundance of translucent pink, downy blossom appears in late spring to early summer. The species is hardy to minus 12°C (about 10°F), and is valuable as the only fern-leaved tree for cool-temperate climates.

A. lophantha
CAPE LEEUWIN WATTLE, TREE-IN-A-HURRY

This 6 m (about 18 ft) evergreen tree from Western Australia is valued for its rapid growth—it can grow 3 m (about 9 ft) in its first year. The leaves are doubly pinnate, the summer flowers greenish. Frost-tender, it is rather short lived and best used for immediate effect.

ALECTRYON
excelsa
syn. *A. excelsus*
TITOKI

Native to New Zealand, this thickly foliaged, spreading evergreen grows 6–10 m (about 18–30 ft) tall. Its squat trunk is covered with distinctive, dark brown-black bark and the branches are reddish brown and downy. The foliage is asymmetrically bipinnate and grows up to 40 cm (about 16 in) long. Tiny red or cream-coloured blossoms develop in multi-branched clusters, followed by brown seed pods. The fruit splits open to reveal a deep red interior and glossy black seed. Plant in light, sandy soil with full sun or partial shade and water regularly. Propagate from seed in autumn fall. The hardwood timber is used to make carpentry tools and furniture.

ALNUS
ALDER

These birch relatives are slender upright trees, deciduous and fully

Alnus glutinosa

hardy. Reaching heights of 25–30 m (about 80–95 ft) they have attractive, slightly arching branches. Highly valued for their ability to survive in extremely wet locations due to their strong root system, they are often found by rivers, in moist gullies or swamps. Small, conical male flowers and pendulous, spiky female flowers appear in spring. The leaves are long stemmed and shiny. The genus will survive in a range of climates, from cool to warm-temperate to subtropical. Propagate from seed in autumn/fall, bud cultivars in late spring and hardwood cuttings in early winter. The timber is extremely water-resistant; once prized by shipbuilders, it was also used for the wooden piles that have supported the city of Venice for hundreds of years.

A. cordata
syn. *A. cordifolia*
ITALIAN ALDER

A fast-growing, attractive, pyramidal tree which can attain 30 m (about 95 ft), the Italian alder is native to Corsica and Italy. Purple and yellow male catkins appear in late winter/ early spring before the tree is densely covered with oval, pointed, deep green leaves 4–10 cm (about 2–4 in) long. The cone-shaped fruits are produced in groups of 3 and persist on the tree. It grows well in any soil. As it will tolerate dusty conditions, it is often used to line motorways.

A. glutinosa
COMMON ALDER

This conical deciduous tree grows rapidly to 10–18 m (about 30–60

Alectryon excelsa

Amelanchier lamarckii

ft). Hanging yellow catkins (male) and tiny upright ones (female) are borne in early spring, followed in mid-spring by shiny, heart-shaped leaves with slim stalks. The species bears round, fruit-like tiny pine cones in autumn/fall. It grows best by the water.

A. jorullensis
MEXICAN ALDER, EVERGREEN ALDER, TOORAK GUM

Native to Mexico and Central America this fast-growing erect evergreen reaches 12–15 m (about 37–50 ft). Its drooping branches are light grey and papery. The deep green, lanceolate leaves are heavily veined and saw-toothed. Small, stretched seed pods appear in late spring and mature in summer. Conical fruit ripens in autumn/fall. It is half-hardy.

AMELANCHIER
lamarckii

Belonging to a genus of deciduous trees which are native to the temperate regions of the northern hemisphere, this tree grows to 6 m

Alnus jorullensis

(about 18 ft) high and 4 m (about 12 ft) wide. The immature leaves are bronze, turning green in summer before colouring beautifully to yellow and red in autumn/fall. Star-shaped white flowers open in early spring. A hardy species, it should be planted in sun or partial shade in a light, neutral to acid soil. Propagate from seed in autumn/fall or by layering in late autumn to early spring. Pruning is generally not necessary. The species can be susceptible to fireblight, which blackens and shrivels the flowers.

Araucaria bidwillii

Arbutus menziesii

Arbutus unedo

Araucaria araucana

Aralia elata

Angophora costata

ANGOPHORA
costata

SMOOTH-BARKED APPLE, RUSTY GUM, SYDNEY RED GUM

This tall, elegant tree originates in the sandstone areas of Australia's east coast. It grows up to 20 m (about 65 ft), has a sturdy, trunk and an irregular open crown of many twisting branches. Uneven annual peeling reveals fresh pink bark, often stained red from the tree's sap; it then turns grey. The 7–16 cm (about 3–6½ in) red and green leaves are lance shaped and pendulous. Immature foliage is bright pink or red turning to green, with a prominent yellow central rib. In spring and summer the tree produces tiny cream flowers with multiple stamens and five lobes. The woody, seed-bearing fruit is greyish brown and flat-topped, like a gumnut. A warm-temperate climate with full sun or partial shade is ideal for this half-hardy tree. Propagate from seed in winter.

ARALIA
elata

ANGELICA TREE

This deciduous South-East Asian native is valued for its abundant foliage and flowers. A small tree or tall shrub, it varies in height from 3 to 10 m (about 9–30 ft). Its enormous, shiny, deep green leaves, 1 m (about 3 ft) long and 60 cm (about 25 in) wide, divide twice into serrated leaflets. The spiny leaf stalks, covered in fine hair, turn red in autumn/fall. Small white or pink flowers cluster together forming large globe-shaped heads in late summer to early autumn/fall. The species has a tendency to sucker, sending out stocky, sharp, thorny shoots, and in smaller gardens is best grown in pots. Frost-hardy, it requires full sun or partial shade and protection from the wind. Plant in a rich, well-drained soil. Propagate from seed in autumn/fall; sucker and root cutting in winter.

ARAUCARIA

The 18 conifers in this genus are native to the South Pacific region, where coniferous species rarely originate. These upright, slender trees grow 30–50 m (about 95–160 ft) tall and make popular indoor plants when immature. Stiff outstretched branches which are shed periodically, radiate out from the trunk.Adaptable to all but cold climates, Araucarias will grow in poor soil and like full sun. Water only when the root surface appears dry. Propagate from seed in spring.

A. araucana
syn. A. imbricata

MONKEY PUZZLE, CHILE PINE

Brought to Europe from South America by the Spanish in the seventeenth century and popular in Victorian England, this slow-growing conifer has a very distinctive habit and can eventually reach a height of 30 m (about 95 ft). The lower branches often fall, exposing the thick grey bark. Its branchlets are covered with overlapping, dark green, flat, 1–3 cm (about ½–1 in) needles tipped with spines. The male and female flowers do not grow on the same tree, and cones can take up to 3 years to mature. This is a good tree for a windy, coastal position.

A. bidwillii

BUNYA BUNYA PINE

Native to the south-eastern rainforests of Queensland, Australia, this slow-growing species is valued for its shapely appearance and timber. Its upright scaly trunk supports drooping branches which umbrella out at the apex. The stiff, shiny green leaves that whorl around the ends of the radial branches are lance-shaped and stalkless. Scaly cylinders of yellowish green male flowers appear in spring; followed on the same tree in summer by oval, scaly green female flowers. Heavy upright cones, 30 cm (about 12 in) long and 20 cm (about 8 in) wide, appear at the top of the tree every two years. These scaly, pineapple-like fruit ripen from green to brown. Each scale contains an edible red seed, a traditional Aboriginal delicacy. The tree flourishes in coastal districts and reasonably moist inland areas, growing best in fertile volcanic soil.

ARBUTUS

This genus contains some 20 species of frost-hardy, evergreen trees and shrubs. Valued for their attractive, egg-shaped leaves and decorative bark, they are native to an area reaching from California to the Mediterranean. Bell-shaped flower clusters bloom in spring, followed in summer by orange-red spherical fruit, 1 cm (about ½ in) in diameter, which may take up to a year to mature. Arbutus do well in both cool and warm-temperate climates. They are attractive planted in tubs, where root constriction causes earlier blooming and fruiting. Plant in a well-drained, slightly acid soil; protect from sea breezes and full sun. Propagate from seed in spring, cuttings in summer and layering in autumn/fall or spring. *Arbutus* is Latin for 'strawberry', but the raw fruit is tasteless. It is used to make wine and jam in Italy and Spain.

A. menziesii

MADRONE

This native of North America, Canada and Mexico is valued for its timber. Moderately fast growing, it reaches 10–15 m (about 30–50 ft) on average but may grow to 30 m (about 95 ft), making it the tallest of its genus. The knotted branches are reddish, the smooth bark a lighter red that peels away in large sheets. Smooth-edged leaves are deep-green on top and blue-grey underneath. White flowers form in triangular clusters, followed by orange or red fruit.

A. unedo

IRISH STRAWBERRY TREE, CANE APPLE

A native of Ireland and southern Europe, this small tree grows up to 8 m (about 24 ft). It is valued for its attractive foliage and its bark, used for tanning. Pink or white flowers form in clusters of 30 to 50 in autumn/fall and early winter. A species with a shrubby habit, it is suitable for hedges and backdrops.

ATHROTAXIS
selaginoides

KING WILLIAM PINE, KING BILLY PINE

Originating in the mountains of Tasmania, Australia, this evergreen conifer is frost-hardy. It grows exceedingly slowly to 30 m (about 95 ft) and has tiny dark green leaves, narrow and sharply pointed. This tree only starts producing an abundance of branches and branchlets halfway up its straight trunk, which made it attractive to early boatbuilders. The reddish brown bark matures to grey and is scored with long vertical grooves. Unimpressive globe-shaped cones, containing 6 rectangular winged seeds, appear in spring and take up to a year to ripen. The tree prefers a moist, cool-temperate climate and rich, well-drained soil. Plant in full sun or partial shade.

BANKSIA
serrata
SAW BANKSIA, RED HONEYSUCKLE, OLD MAN

An evergreen Australian native, this tall shrub or medium tree grows to 3–10 m (about 9–30 ft). Its sturdy, twisted trunk is often grooved, the bark a dark grey. The gnarled branches are thinly covered with dark green, rectangular or lanceolate serrated leaves. The silvery grey flowers produce prominent whorled stigma stems, similar to bottlebrushes, and are 7–10 cm (about 3–4 in) long. Seed-bearing grey tubular cones, 13–15 cm (about 5–6 in) long, appear in summer. These contain black winged seeds, which are released during bushfires. This salt-resistant coastal species will grow in temperate or warmer climates and prefers light sandy soil with full or partial shade. It is half-hardy. Banksias are named after renowned English botanist Sir Joseph Banks.

BAUHINIA
variegata 'Candida'
syn. *B. variegata* 'Alba'
WHITE MOUNTAIN EBONY

Native to the warm-temperate and tropical zones of Asia, Africa, America and Australia, this predominantly deciduous genus contains over 300 species. The rotund trees produce much-valued flowers that are large and scented, often resembling orchids, while the leaves are two-lobed. *B. variegata* 'Candida' has large white or lemon-green flowers up to 10 cm (about 4 in) in diameter. They bloom in early spring and are most impressive after a cool winter, when leaves are prematurely shed. Water trees well during spring, when the flowers are in bloom. Frost-tender, they should be grown in full sun, protected from cold winds and sea breezes. Propagate from seed or cuttings in spring. Bauhinias are named after the brothers Jean and Gaspard Bauhin, sixteenth-century Swiss botanists.

BEAUCARNEA
recurvata
syn. *Nolina recurvata, N. tuberculata*
PONY-TAIL PALM, ELEPHANT'S FOOT

A slow-growing tree from southern USA and Mexico, it is not in fact a palm but is related to yuccas, adapting to the arid tropics in a similar manner. The swollen base stores water in times of drought, and tapers to a smooth, palm-like trunk with 2 m (about 6 ft) long thin recurving leaves sprouting from the top. It is sparsely branched and makes an attractive plant for a dry spot. It will only grow outdoors in mild to warm climates and in well-drained, fertile soil, preferring full sun and a minimum temperature of 7°C (about 44°F). Water well when growing, but sparingly at other times. Potted specimens need full light and moderate water, allow to dry out between waterings. Propagate from seed or suckers in spring, or stem-tip cuttings in summer.

BETULA
BIRCH

This genus contains over 35 species, native to the northern hemisphere. Tall and elegant, these fully hardy deciduous trees are valued for their slender, weeping branches and shimmering foliage. Growing to 18–30 m (about 60–95 ft), they have broad serrated leaves that turn gold in autumn/fall. Pendent fruit contains winged seeds. Brightly coloured grey, red-brown, white or yellowish black bark is shed in long strips. Birches will grow in any well-drained soil, provided they receive plentiful water and full sun. Pruning is unnecessary. Propagate from seed, by grafting in late winter or from softwood cuttings in early summer. Once used to make school canes and domestic brooms, birch timber is highly prized by Scandinavia's furniture industry. North American Indians traditionally used the leathery, waterproof bark to make canoes.

B. nigra
BLACK BIRCH, RIVER BIRCH

This tree of pyramidal habit can reach a height of 15 m (about 50 ft) and forms an irregular crown. Its often drooping branches enhance the delicate, diamond-shaped, ragged-edged leaves, which are a shiny green. The bark, reddish brown when young, turns black as it ages. As with all birches, the root system is shallow and the tree will need watering during a drought.

B. papyrifera
PAPER BIRCH, CANOE BIRCH, WHITE BIRCH

This is a round-headed, vigorous species with an open habit that can reach a height of 30 m (about 95 ft), although it is often shorter. Its 3–10 cm (about 1½–4 in) long serrated, dull green leaves turn yellow in autumn/fall. It bears yellow catkins in spring. The bark of young trees is reddish brown, but as they mature it turns white and peels off in long, horizontal strips.

B. pendula
SILVER BIRCH, EUROPEAN BIRCH, WHITE BIRCH

This popular ornamental garden tree is native to Europe and Asia. It

Banksia serrata

Betula papyrifera

Betula nigra

Athrotaxis selaginoides

Bauhinia variegata 'Candida'

Betula pendula

Beaucarnea recurvata

is widely conical and rapidly grows up to 20 m (about 65 ft). The species has silvery white bark turning to black, and thinly stalked, diamond-shaped leaves 2–7 cm (about 1–3 in) long. Seed-bearing cones, lemon-green and 2 cm (about 1 in) long, appear in spring. If kept moist, the tree will survive in most climates other than the tropics and subtropics. It is, however, happiest in cold climates.

B. pendula 'Dalecarlica'
syn. *B. pendula* 'Laciniata'
CUT-LEAF BIRCH, SWEDISH BIRCH

A slim and attractive tree, this cultivar reaches a height of some 10 m (about 30 ft). It has distinctive white bark and its branches are gently arching. The leaves are deeply cut with saw-toothed margins.

BOLUSANTHUS
speciosus
SOUTH AFRICAN WISTERIA WILD WISTERIA, TREE WISTERIA, RHODESIAN WISTERIA

This deciduous South African native is the only species in its genus. It is valued for its slender appearance and wisteria-like blooms. Averaging 6 m (about 18 ft) tall, this tree has slightly arching branches covered with uneven fernlike foliage. The immature frosted green leaflets become lustrous in maturity. In spring, beautiful bluish purple, pea-type flowers appear, followed by legume-type seed pods. This frost-tender species will thrive best in full sun and rich porous soil. Give it plenty of water. But once it is established it will survive long dry spells. Propagate from heat-treated seed in summer.

BUTEA
monosperma
syn. *B. frondosa*
FLAME OF THE FOREST, PALAS

This magnificent deciduous tree is valued for its flowers, foliage and sap, which is used to make astringents. A native of Bangladesh, Burma and East India, it slowly grows up to 10 m (about 30 ft). The leaves, 20 cm (about 8 in) long, are composed of three leaflets, greyish blue on the surface and silvery underneath. Big clusters of orange-red flowers, similar to the pea's, precede the foliage in spring. The grey seed pods are legume-shaped and covered in down. This species prefers a damp, warm location but also tolerates saline conditions. Frost-tender, it does best in tropical climates. Pruning is not required. This species is named after the eighteenth-century Earl of Bute. There is a yellow-flowered variety.

CALLICOMA
serratifolia
BLACK WATTLE, BUTTERWOOD

This frost-hardy Australian native evergreen is the only species in its genus. It grows up to 10 m (about 30 ft) with slim, arching branches and a dense crown. Branchlets, flower stems and leaf undersides are downy. Shiny green, serrated foliage is either wide and lanceolate or oval and narrow, with a prominent midrib. Creamy yellow blossoms cluster in thick puffballs, similar to the wattle's, in spring and early summer. This tree prefers damp, rich soils and requires plentiful water in summer. Shelter from cold winds and sea breezes. Prune when immature to encourage shape; propagate from seed in autumn/fall. Like the acacia, this tree was used by early white Australians for their wattle-and-daub constructions.

CALOCEDRUS
decurrens
syn. *Libocedrus decurrens*
INCENSE CEDAR

Valued for its shapely, conical habit and attractive foliage, this species is frost-hardy and grows slowly to 12–22 m (about 38–70 ft). Shiny, dark bluish green leaves adhere to the branches in flat clusters. The tubular cones grow in three splayed segments. This tree likes partial shade and well-drained soil of indifferent quality. It does well in the heat of summer and makes an ideal windbreak. If immature plants are liberally watered they will become drought-resistant in maturity. Propagate from seed.

CALODENDRUM
capense
CAPE CHESTNUT

This warm climate evergreen is native to South Africa. Decorative and dome-shaped, it grows to 8–15 m (about 24–50 ft). Its shiny oval leaves 10–15 cm (about 4–6 in) long, are similar to those of the lemon tree. They are marked with dots, only discernible when held to the light. Clusters of light pink to pale lavender flowers appear in spring and early summer. Half-hardy, this tree prefers warm climates but not dry exposed areas and requires regular watering. Plant in rich, well-drained soil and full sun. This species will stand pruning if necessary to keep its shape. Propagate from seed in spring or, more effectively, from semi-ripe cuttings in summer.

CARPINUS
HORNBEAM

This genus of deciduous trees comes from the northern hemisphere, where they can grow to 25 m (about 80 ft). They are often planted as specimen trees. The long, male, yellow-green catkins are most attractive. Hardy, the trees like a sunny or partially shaded position in well-drained soil. Propagate in autumn/fall from seed, which forms clusters of winged nuts. In Britain hornbeams are clipped for hedges, and often pollarded or coppiced. The wood is extremely hard and is used in the making of butcher's blocks and mallets.

C. betulus
COMMON HORNBEAM, EUROPEAN HORNBEAM

This species forms a magnificent round-headed tree when allowed to grow to its full height of 25 m (about 80 ft) and spread of 20 m (about 65 ft). However, it is equally suitable for hedging. It pointed, double-toothed, deep green leaves turn yellow-orange in winter. The yellow-green catkins flower from late spring into atumn/fall, when the clusters of 8-paired nutlets appear. Its fluted bark is a silver-grey colour. A smaller-growing cultivar, 'Fastigiata', is more suited to a garden.

C. caroliniana
AMERICAN HORNBEAM, BLUE BEECH, WATER BEECH

A native of North America, this species grows to 10 m (about 30 ft) high and wide. Its oval, pointed,

Carpinus betulus 'Fastigiata'

Callicoma serratifolia

Bolusanthus speciosus

Betula pendula 'Dalecarlica'

Butea monosperma

Calocedrus decurrens

Calodendrum capense

sharply toothed, mid-green leaves turn delicate shades of red and orange in autumn/fall. The green catkins, which flower in spring, are followed by clusters of winged nuts. This is a graceful tree with grey, fluted bark.

CASSIA
CASSIA

This genus contains over 500 diverse species of evergreen, deciduous and perennial plants, ranging from fully hardy to frost-tender. Varying from 9 to 15 m (about 27–50 ft) tall, they are among the most popular and beautiful of flowering trees and shrubs. Their fern-like foliage has a variable number of alternating leaflets. Their predominantly yellowy, dish-shaped flowers, some scented, bloom at different times of the year, appearing in some species in long, drooping sprigs; in others, at the end of stiff stems. All produce long, legume-like seed pods, up to 60 cm (about 24 in) long. Cassias readily cross-fertilize, producing a vast array of hybrids. They require sunny, spacious locations and like fertile, well-drained soil. Water these plants liberally when in flower. While all species tolerate radical pruning, they are best left to grow freely. Propagate from seed in spring, and from cuttings in late summer. Cassias are used for tanning as well as in the pharmaceutical industry.

C. fistula
INDIAN LABURNUM, GOLDEN SHOWER

This attractive, tropical native of India and Sri Lanka grows rapidly up to 10 m (about 30 ft). It has pinnate leaves, 20 cm (about 8 in) long, which are composed of 4 to 18 oval leaflets. Light to vivid yellow flower clusters form in thick, drooping racemes. The seed pods are dark brown and 60 cm (about 24 in) long and give cassia pulp which is used for medicinal purposes. Plant in full sun.

C. javanica
JAVA SHOWER, APPLE BLOSSOM CASSIA, APPLE BLOSSOM SENNA

Native to Java and Malaysia, this evergreen has either a spreading or columnar shape, depending on the climate, and grows up to 10 m (about 30 ft). Feathery, greenish grey foliage is made up of 12–24 oval-shaped leaflets, 5 cm (about 2 in) long. Pale pink flowers, becoming more vivid with age, appear in large thick sprigs during spring and summer. Black seed pods, 30–60 cm (about 12–24 in) long, form on the long arching branches. This frost-tender species will not survive in temperatures under 10°C (about 50°F).

C. multijuga
GOLDEN SHOWER

This half-hardy evergreen originates in Brazil and Guyana and grows rapidly to 7 m (about 21 ft). It is either round-crowned or tall and narrow, with pendent branches. Its fern-like leaves are made up of 36–80 rectangular leaflets, 2 cm (about 1 in) long. Attractive orange yellow blooms form in dense clusters during spring and summer. The flat seed pods are 15 cm (about 6 in) long.

CASTANEA
sativa
SWEET CHESTNUT, SPANISH CHESTNUT, EUROPEAN CHESTNUT

Growing to 30 m (about 95 ft), this statuesque, deciduous tree was probably introduced to Britain by the Romans from its native southern Europe. It has long, lanceolate, mid-green, toothed leaves with prominent veining. The long yellow catkins appear in summer and are followed by green, spiny husks which enclose the edible nuts, which are traditionally used for roasting and stuffings. Hardy, it should be grown in any sunny position in well-drained, fertile soil. Propagate from seed in autumn/fall and grow on for up to 5 years before planting in its final site. Chestnut wood is often used for fence palings as it can withstand most weather conditions.

CASTANOSPERMUM
australe
BLACK BEAN, MORETON BAY CHESTNUT

This Australian species, the only one in its genus, is valued for its timber and shade. A slow grower, it reaches 9–18 m (about 27–60 ft) and develops a broad, open crown. Shiny, dark green compound leaves of 5 to 7 leaflets are 30–45 cm (about 12–18 in) long. Orange-red or occasionally yellow, the pea-type flowers bloom in spring and summer, at which time the tree should be liberally watered. Long, tubular seed pods containing big poisonous 'chestnuts', 5 cm (about 2 in) across, appear in autumn/fall. This frost-tender tree prefers warm locations. Plant in an open sunny location in well-drained soil. Propagate from seed or ripe cuttings. The attractive timber is used to make furniture.

CASUARINA
glauca
SWAMP SHE-OAK

This handsome, fast-growing Australian native, one of 30 species of the genus of evergreen trees and shrubs valued for their shade and extremely tough timber, grows 15–20 m (about 50–65 ft) tall. It has greenish blue branches and

tough, deep grey bark with long vertical grooves. The small, greyish brown cones are 1 cm (about ½ in) long and tubular. Small red flowers grow among the twigs, appearing in late spring. These trees adapt to a wide range of conditions, from poor arid soil to swampy saltwater marshes. They are excellent sand-binders but are prone to suckering. Propagate from seed in spring. The timber has been used for traditional Aboriginal hunting weapons as well as tool handles.

Castanea sativa

Carpinus caroliniana

Cassia fistula

Castanospermum australe

Cassia multijuga

Casuarina glauca

Cassia javanica

Catalpa bignonioides

Celtis occidentalis

Cedrus deodara

Cephalotaxus harringtonia

Cedrela sinensis

Cedrus atlantica

CATALPA
bignonioides
INDIAN BEAN TREE, CIGAR TREE

Native to North America, this deciduous tree is valued for its large foliage and flowers. It grows up to 15 m (about 50 ft), spreading broadly in later life. Pale green or yellow, heart-shaped leaves are 18–25 cm (about 7½–10 in) long, grouped in threes. Bell-shaped and perfumed, the flowers are white, pink or lemon, variegated with purple and yellow. They appear in summer in thick upright clusters, 18–30 cm (about 7½–12 in) tall, later replaced by drooping tubular seed pods. This tree likes full sun, shelter from the wind and rich, well-drained soil. Propagate from seed in autumn/fall, cultivars by budding and cuttings in summer.

CEDRELA
sinensis
syn. *Toona sinensis*
CHINESE CEDAR, CHINESE TOON

This deciduous native of China is not a cedar, although in the timber trade its red timber is called cedar. Reaching heights of up to 12 m (about 38 ft), it is valued for its large foliage: beautiful pink, fernlike leaves, later changing to green, appear in early spring and grow 30–60 cm (about 12–24 in) long. Perfumed white flowers appear in drooping clusters in spring. This species likes full sun and rich, well-drained soil. Prune in winter to encourage shape. Propagate from seed in autumn/fall, cuttings in winter. In some areas locals eat the onion-scented young leaves.

CEDRUS
CEDAR

This genus of conifers contains four species of tall, conical trees greatly valued for their timber. Native from Africa to India, some species grow up to 45 m (about 145 ft) tall. The spiraled foliage is grey-green and needle-shaped. They have woody, egg-shaped cones which bear seed scales. These fully hardy trees prefer cool temperatures, full sun and rich, well-drained soil. Too large for the average garden, they are better suited to country properties. Propagate from seed; some cultivars by grafting. Cedars have an ancient lineage; their timber was greatly valued by the Greeks and Romans.

C. atlantica
MT ATLAS CEDAR, ATLANTIC CEDAR

Originating in North Africa, this fast-growing species reaches heights of up to 15 m (about 50 ft). The pale green or blue-grey, spindly foliage is distinctively short at 2 cm (about 1 in). Erect, light green to purple flowers bloom in summer. The brown male and pale green female cones take 2 years to mature. While young, this tree may be grown in a tub.

C. deodara
DEODAR, INDIAN CEDAR

The largest of its genus, this magnificent Himalayan native reaches a towering 30 m (about 95 ft). Tiered branches droop slightly at the extremities where the silvery grey leaves develop. Male and female cones grow on separate branches and the 5–10 cm (about 2–4 in) cones have flat tops. This species will grow in various climates, from arid inland to cooler mountain areas. Height is determined by soil quality and the amount of water the tree receives. Suitable for pots, it may be replanted when up to 2 m (about 6 ft) tall. In Britain, this species is slightly tender.

CELTIS
occidentalis
COMMON HACKBERRY

Belonging to a genus of deciduous trees, this species can reach a height and spread of 20 m (about 65 ft). It is grown for its striking, oval, sharply toothed green leaves, which become yellow in autumn/fall. It bears tiny, nondescript, spring flowers and produces round, yellow-red fruits in autumn which turn a deep purple. It prefers an open, sunny position in well-drained soil and should be propagated from seed in autumn/fall. Fully hardy.

CEPHALOTAXUS
harringtonia
JAPANESE PLUM YEW

Originating in China, this bushy, decorative conifer grows to 5 m (about 15 ft). Its slightly flattened needles are deep green on top, grey below. This upright foliage grows in whorls around the branch shoots. Male and female flowers bloom on separate trees in spring. These are followed in summer and autumn/fall by plum-sized, edible green fruit. Though the species is quite hardy, it cannot survive in climates too cold or hot. Plant in good, slightly acid, well-drained soil with protection from the midday sun. Propagate from seed.

CERCIDIPHYLLUM
japonicum
KATSURA TREE, KATSARU TREE

In Britain this species rarely reaches the height of 30 m (about 95 ft) attained in its native China and Japan. This member of a genus of deciduous trees is grown for the spectacular changing colour of its ovate foliage: pinkish in spring, turning a deep green in summer, and finally a variety of yellows and

Cercis siliquastrum

Chorisia speciosa

Chamaecyparis lawsoniana

reds in autumn/fall, especially striking on acid soils. The male and female spring flowers are carried on separate trees. Protect from late frosts and winds, which could kill the young shoots, and plant in moist, well-drained, preferably acid soil in a sunny or partially shaded position. Propagate from seed in autumn/fall. Because of its light weight and fine grain, the wood is prized in its native country by furniture makers.

CERCIS

REDBUD, JUDAS TREE

This genus consists of 7 small, ornamental trees and shrubs, native to North America, southern Europe and Asia. They are grown for their beautiful, pea-like flowers. Deciduous species reach 12 m (about 37 ft) with fine multiple branches. It is straight out of these limbs that the pink, white or purple, stalkless flowers appear at the end of winter. Numerous flat seed pods, 10 cm (about 4 in) long, follow the blooms and endure until the following winter. These trees prefer rich porous soils and full sun. They do not like being moved, so transplant when young. Propagate from seed in autumn/fall and bud cultivars in summer. According to legend, Judas Iscariot hanged himself from the bough of one of these trees after betraying Christ.

C. canadensis

RED BUD

Native to the USA, this erect tree or shrub grows up to 13 m (about 40

Cercidiphyllum japonicum

Chionanthus virginicus

ft) tall and has heart shaped leaves. The young, reddish purple flower buds turn light pink when open. They are 1 cm (about ½ in) in diameter. Seed pods are brown and approximately 9 cm (about 3½ in) long.

C. siliquastrum

JUDAS TREE, LOVE TREE

This small, bushy tree develops a rounded crown and is fully hardy. It originates in southern Europe and Asia Minor and grows up to 13 m (about 40 ft). An abundance of bright pinkish purple or white flowers, 2 cm (about 1 in) across, blossom in spring before the leaves appear. These are heart shaped and 7–10 cm (about 3–4 in) long. Propagate from seed.

CHAMAECYPARIS

FALSE CYPRESS

Native to the USA and eastern Asia, the 8 conifers comprising this genus are extremely variable in colour and habit. They may be shrubby and

Cercis canadensis

Chamaecyparis pisifera

small, or erect and tall, up to 30 m (about 95 ft). Their small leaves vary considerably in colour, from green to greyish blue. Branches may be stiff or arching, tiered or constant. All species are easily propagated, withstand transplanting and do not require pruning—hence their popularity as possibly the most commonly cultivated genus of evergreens. They prefer cool-temperate conditions and full sun. Propagate from seed; cultivars by cuttings. Once classified as true cypresses, they were placed in their own genus early this century.

C. lawsoniana

LAWSON CYPRESS, PORT ORFORD CEDAR

This native of the USA is prized for its quality timber and impressive appearance. It has a triangular shape, later becoming open-crowned and columnar, and is variable in height up to 30 m (about 95 ft). Tiny, deep green scales cover the slender, slightly arching branches, giving the tree a felty appearance. Narrow rectangular cones of both genders appear on the same tree. The species thrives best in cool conditions and rich, damp soil. There are many garden varieties with narrower habit.

C. pisifera

SAWARA CYPRESS

This fully hardy species is shaped like a pyramid. It grows to a height of 30 m (about 95 ft) and has stiff branches and reddish brown bark with raised vertical lines. The deep green leaf scales have white margins. This species bears rectangular, yellowy brown cones.

CHIONANTHUS

virginicus

FRINGE TREE, OLD MAN'S BEARD

Native to North America, this fully hardy deciduous species slowly grows to 3–10 m (about 9–30 ft) tall, as a slender small tree or large shrub. It has an open crown and is valued for its attractive flowers. The flowers are dainty and white, and appear in late spring in drooping terminal clusters, 20 cm (about 8 in) long— hence the name 'old man's beard'. The large, shiny, dark green leaves are rectangular and turn gold in autumn/fall. This species prefers cool temperatures and the rich, moist soils of riverbanks. Plant in a position with full sun.

CHORISIA

speciosa

FLOSS SILK TREE, BRAZILIAN KAPOK TREE

This tree is native to the subtropical zones of Brazil and Argentina. An erect species with a lofty crown, it grows to 15 m (about 50 ft). Its tapering trunk is covered with vicious spikes and its branches are long and uplifted. Compound leaves are shaped like hands, made up of saw-toothed leaflets 12 cm (about 5 in) long. Resembling the hibiscus, the variegated flowers have 5 petals and range in colour from light pink to purple with white or yellow throats, marked with red or brown. The species needs full sun, a warm climate and prefers rich, well-drained, loamy soil. Water liberally when in flower, in autumn/fall. Propagate in spring from seed sown in sand and treated with bottom heat.

Cladrastis lutea

Cornus capitata

Clusia rosea

CITHAREXYLUM

FIDDLEWOOD

Native to South America and the Caribbean, this genus of evergreen and half-evergreen decorative timber trees grow up to 15 m (about 50 ft). They have an attractive compact appearance and a dense crown. Plant in fertile crumbly soil with good drainage. In summer, water plentifully and prune tips to encourage good shape. Propagate from ripe seed or half-ripe cuttings in spring. The timber is used in cabinet-making. The genus name was derived from the Greek *kithara*, a lyre, and *xylon* wood, as the timber was used to make lyres in ancient times.

C. quadrangulare

JAMAICAN FIDDLEWOOD

Valued for its impressive autumn/fall foliage, this Jamaican native evergreen grows to 6–12 m (about 18–37 ft) tall. Its rectangular to elliptical leaves have distinctive elongated tips and are neither serrated nor veined. They turn a golden, reddish brown in autumn/fall and endure through winter. When young, this tree requires shelter from frost. Propagate from hardwood cuttings at the end of winter.

C. spinosum

syn. c. subserratum

Valued for its foliage, this semi-evergreen is native to the West Indies. Growing quickly to 10–15 m (about 30–50 ft), it is conical or shrubby with a broad, open crown. The vivid green, oval leaves are heavily serrated and turn a beautiful rusty bronze in winter. Tiny white flowers grow in slender erect sprays from mid-summer to winter, followed by small pendent seed pods. The species is only just frost-hardy and requires liberal water when in flower. Plant in fertile, crumbly soil with full sun. Prune tips in early summer to encourage shape. Propagate from seed or cuttings in spring.

CLADRASTIS

lutea

YELLOW WOOD

Native to east Asia and the USA, this fully hardy deciduous species has very fragrant flowers and thick foliage. It grows to 11 m (about 34 ft) or more, with a broad, dome-shaped crown. The attractive compound leaves have 7 to 9 deep-green, ovate leaflets and are 10 cm (about 4 in) long. Foliage turns from deep green to vivid yellow in autumn/fall. Magnificent white flower clusters follow, although not every year. This species takes 10 years to flower. It likes cool weather and will grow in adequate soil provided there is good drainage. Propagate from seed in autumn/fall. The common name

comes from the bright yellow colour of its freshly cut timber. which is used to make dye.

CLUSIA

rosea

COPEY, AUTOGRAPH TREE

This shrubby tree is slow-growing to 16 m (about 50 ft). The lustrous, deep green leaves are oval, and in summer it bears 5 cm (about 2 in) cup-shaped, pink flowers, followed by globe-shaped, greenish fruit with a sticky resin. Grow in well-drained soil in semi-shade with a minimum temperature of 2–5°C (about 35–40°F). If in a pot, water moderately, less during colder weather. Propagate by layering in spring or from semi-ripe cuttings in summer.

CORDYLINE

australis

NEW ZEALAND CABBAGE TREE, GIANT DRACENA, GRASS PALM, SAGO PALM, PALM LILY

A palm-like tree from New Zealand, it is extremely hardy, although slow-growing. The tall central stem has a rosette of slender, strap-like leaves growing to 1 m (about 3 ft) in length. From late spring to summer, large sprays of tiny, scented, white flowers appear. This tree grows well in almost all conditions but prefers fertile, well-drained but moist soil and full sun to part-shade. It makes an excellent potted plant that needs moderate watering with less in winter. Propagate from seed or suckers in spring or stem cuttings in summer. Among its many common names, it was called 'cabbage tree' because early settlers used the young, tender leaves instead of cabbage.

CORNUS

DOGWOOD

This is a large genus from the temperate northern hemisphere, with over 100 species varying from small shrubs to forest rees. They can be either evergreen or deciduous, and their attraction can be coloured bark, autumn/fall foliage or showy flowers, though the actual flowers are insignificant and the display comes from the 4 bracts which surround the flower cluster. In many species the flowers are followed by long-lasting berries. Fertile soil and drought-free, cool but not frosty climates are preferred.

C. capitata

syn. Dendrobenthamia fragifera

HIMALAYAN STRAWBERRY, BENTHAM'SCORNEL

This Himalayan evergreen or semi-evergreen has wide, spreading branches and grows up to 13 m (about 40 ft) high and wide. Pendent, greenish grey leaves are 7–10

Citharexylum spinosum

Cordyline australis

Citharexylum quadrangulare

(about 40 ft) high and wide. Pendent, greenish grey leaves are 7–10 cm (about 3–4 in) long. The bracts are creamy yellow, 6–8 cm (about 2½–3 in) wide. The plump, dark pink fruit resembles strawberries. This tree does best in cool coastal climates and acid soil.

C. controversa

Originally from China and Japan, this deciduous species with layered branches can grow to 15 m (about 50 ft). Its ovate, alternate, bright green leaves turn purple in autumn/fall, and the 4–9 cm (about 2–3 in) clusters of white flowers are borne in summer. It is fully hardy. There is a variegated form, 'Variegata', which is propagated by grafting in winter.

C. florida

DOGWOOD

Originating in the USA, this slim or shrubby deciduous species slowly reaches 6–18 m (about 18–60 ft). It is valued for its abundant pink or white spring flowers and deep green, egg-shaped, large veined leaves, 7–10 cm (about 3–4 in) long, that turn vivid, reddish purple in autumn/fall. It requires deep, rich, acid soil.

C. kousa

Originating in Japan and Korea, *C. kousa* grows to a height of 7 m (about 21 ft) and has a spreading habit. It has oval, pointed, mid-green leaves which turn deep red in autumn/fall. In early summer white flower bracts, around 3 cm (about 1½ in) wide, surround the tiny, purple-green flowers and are followed by strawberry-like fruits in late summer. The variety 'Chinensis' has larger bracts and flowerheads.

C. mas

CORNELIAN CHERRY

Native to south-east Europe, this deciduous species with an open, shrub-like habit grows as wide as it does high, up to 5 m (about 15 ft). Its small yellow flowers are carried in late winter/early spring on the bare thick stems of the previous season's growth. The dark green

leaves that follow are opposite and pointed and turn bronze-purple in autumn/fall. The edible, oval, bright red berries, which can be made into preserves and jellies, ripen towards the end of summer. It prefers chalk soil though it will grow in any except acid soils.

CORYLUS
avellana 'Contorta'
CURLY HAZEL, CRAZY HAZEL

Corylus avellana is the hazel nut, a native of Europe and western Asia. This cultivar is grown more for its strange appearance than for its nuts. It grows to 6 m (about 18 ft), a dense mass of contorted stalks and shoots with wide serrated leaves. Sleek, greenish yellow catkins, 5 cm (about 2 in) long, appear on its bare limbs in winter. The tree also produces edible brown nuts. Fully hardy, it requires full sun or partial shade and deep, rich, well-drained soil. Propagate from cuttings in autumn/fall or by grafting in summer. The foliage is prone to mildew and the nuts susceptible to insects.

CORYNOCARPUS
laevigata
syn. *C. laevigatus*
KARAKA

This New Zealand evergreen has a dense, rounded crown and grows 6–12 m (about 18–37 ft) in height. The complete rectangular leaves are lustrous, deep green or streaky and up to 20 cm (about 8 in) long. Clusters of small, creamy green flowers are followed in autumn/fall or winter by yellowy orange, egg-shaped fruit which contain an extremely poisonous seed. This semi-hardy species prefers damp, moderate climates and full sun or partial shade with well-drained soil. Water regularly while in flower and propagate in summer from seed or half-ripe cuttings.

CRATAEGUS
HAWTHORN, THORN

This large, diverse genus of ornamental deciduous trees and shrubs originates in Europe, Asia Minor

and Africa. Members of the Roseaceae family, they have beautiful rose flowers and cruel thorns. Height varies between 5 and 14 m (about 15–45 ft). The spiky branches, usually spreading, develop finely serrated rose-type leaves, divided into lobes. Fragrant double or single flowers bloom in spring, often white but also in shades of pink, followed by long-lasting ornamental fruit, white, pink, orange, yellow or bright red and of varying size. Species enjoy a cool climate, though some are frost-tender. They will survive in most

soils provided they are not too damp. Propagate from seed in autumn/fall; cultivars by budding in late summer. The genus name from the Greek *kratos*, 'strength', refers to their durable wood.

C. coccinea 'Plena'
SCARLET HAWTHORN

This species, from North America, grows to 4–7 (about 12–21 ft) in height. It has roundish, fine-toothed leaves that turn a rich red in autumn/fall and bright pink flowers. These are followed by long-lasting red berries.

Cornus florida

Cornus mas

Cornus kousa

Corylus avellana 'Contorta'

Corynocarpus laevigata

Crataegus coccinea 'Plena'

Cornus controversa

C. laevigata 'Paul's Scarlet'
syn. *C. oxyacantha*
DOUBLE-RED HAWTHORN

This decorative, deciduous tree reaches 8 m (about 24 ft). It is much admired for its flowers, ornamental fruit and dense foliage. Egg-shaped leaves with deeply cut lobes are 5 cm (about 2 in) long on spiky, broadly spreading branches. Strongly scented, double red or deep pink flowers bloom in late spring to early summer. Red fruit endures through autumn/fall. This frost-hardy tree prefers a cool climate, full sun and well-drained soil. Propagate by budding in late summer. Susceptible to fireblight.

C. × lavallei
syn. *C. × carrierei*

This deciduous garden hybrid is a vigorous grower—to 7 m (about 21 ft) high, with a greater spread, up to 10 m (about 30 ft). It has glossy, oval, dark green leaves which in late autumn turn red and often endure on the almost thornless branches

Crataegus × lavallei

Crataegus laevigata 'Paul's Scarlet'

Crataegus phaenopyrum

until well into winter. The white flowers appear in erect clusters in late spring, while the orange-red fruit ripen in late summer or early autumn/fall.

C. phaenopyrum
syn. *C. cordata*
WASHINGTON THORN

This small, attractive species has a round shape and grows up to 10 m (about 30 ft). Its shiny deep green foliage is heart-shaped and deeply lobed. Clusters of white flowers appear in summer, followed by shiny orange-red spherical fruit. This species is fully hardy and suitable for most gardens in cool climates.

C. pubescens
syn. *C. mexicana, C. stipulacea*
MEXICAN HAWTHORN

This frost-hardy semi-evergreen quickly reaches 6–10 m (about 18–30 ft) and has a dense crown with serrated foliage, 8 cm (about 3 in) long. The tree bears clusters of single flowers 2 cm (about 1 in) across. The leaves turn orange-red in autumn/fall; edible, golden yellow or red fruit follow.

CRYPTOMERIA

A member of the Taxodiacaea family, this genus has only the one species of evergreen conifer. Originating in China and Japan, it plays an important part in the Japanese timber industry as the wood is strong. To flourish it needs moist, fertile soils in a sheltered, sunny or partially shaded site, preferably with good rainfall. Propagation is from

Crataegus pubescens

Cryptomeria japonica 'Elegans'

heel cuttings in late summer or early autumn/fall, or from seed in spring. There are a number of cultivars available, many of which keep their juvenile foliage. These should be propagated from cuttings rather than seed. In Japan the tree is often found near temples.

C. japonica
JAPANESE CEDAR

This is a hardy, fast-growing tree with a narrow conical crown and a spreading base; it can reach 35 m (about 110 ft) in height. It has long, awl-like dark green leaves which are arranged in a spiral fashion. It bears round, dark brown cones, and its soft, fibrous, orange-brown bark sheds in long strips. A native of South America, it prefers light, moist, humus-rich soil in a protected, partially shaded position. Unusually in a conifer, if cut down to the ground or coppiced it will grow new shoots.

C. japonica 'Elegans'
BRONZE JAPANESE CEDAR

This erect triangular Asian conifer up to 5–12 m (about 15–37 ft) is highly valued for its fascinating needle-like foliage that develops in soft feathery whorls and drapes to the ground. Leaves turn from deep green in summer to rich golden rust in autumn/fall. It prefers cool conditions but will survive in the heat with regular watering. Plant in cool, damp soil and shelter from cold winds; it will withstand transplanting up to a reasonable size. Propagate from cuttings. The wood is rather weak and it is rare for a mature tree not to lean.

Cryptomeria japonica

× Cupressocyparis leylandii

× CUPRESSOCYPARIS
leylandii
LEYLAND CYPRESS

When cones of *Cupressus macrocarpa* were fertilized naturally by pollen from *Chamaecyparis nootkatensis*, the result was one of the fastest-growing of all conifers— up to 1 m (about 3 ft) a year. Its pyramidal shape can attain a height of 30 m (about 95 ft), but it is more often grown as a hedge or wind-break and pruned in late summer to the desired height. It has small, grey-green triangular needles borne in flat, slightly drooping sprays, and numerous, globular, brown cones. Fully hardy, it will grow in any deep, well-drained soil, preferably in full sun. Propagate from cuttings taken from the current season's growth. For hedges or a row of featured specimens, plant 60 cm (about 24 in) apart. There are several good forms available.

CUPRESSUS
CYPRESS

Native to Europe, Asia, the USA and Central America, this diverse genus of evergreen coniferous trees and shrubs may be tall and slender or open and squat, ranging from 1 to 45 m (about 3–145 ft) high. They make symmetrical shade trees or hedges. Golden green or bluish grey needle-like foliage changes to tiny leaf scales in maturity. Their globose, scale-covered cones may hang on the branches for years. They prefer cool to warm-temperate regions, can survive in arid, sandy soil and are ideal for coastal locations

Cupressus s. 'Swane's Golden'

where they can enjoy full sun. Prune frequently to promote fresh growth. Mature plants will not survive transplanting. Propagate from cuttings in winter or cold-treated seed from the end of autumn/fall to late winter. The trees are susceptible to leafroller caterpillars, beetles, weevils and canker. Cypresses are traditionally associated with death and mourning.

C. arizonica

ARIZONA CYPRESS, ROUGH-BARKED ARIZONA CYPRESS

Originating in Arizona and sometimes confused with *C. glabra*, this pyramidal species will grow to 15 m (about 50 ft). Its mature foliage is grey-green and does not display the white spots of the smooth cypress. It has short-stalked, large, round cones, up to 2.5 cm (about 1 in) across, and a brown stringy and furrowed bark. It is grown both as a specimen tree and as a hedge.

C. macrocarpa

MONTEREY CYPRESS

This stately tree from California is noted for its handsome habit, conical when young and developing picturesque, spreading branches with maturity. The wild form has dark green needles, but several 'golden' leaved cultivars are popular. It is not a tree for bitterly cold climates, although it is frost-hardy. It is very resistant to salt winds and much used as a shelter tree; and, as it takes clipping very well, for tall hedges. Propagate from cuttings or seed. It is prone to cypress canker.

C. sempervirens 'Swane's Golden'

SWANE'S GOLDEN PENCIL PINE

C. sempervirens itself is a familiar sight in Italian gardens, where its green, pencil-slim spires can be as high as 30 m (about 45 ft). It is notable for having the largest cones of the genus. 'Swane's Golden', which originated in Australia, is not nearly so tall growing. It is admired for its yellow leaves but has proved a little more frost-tender than the green cyprus. Its spreading root system makes it unsuitable for smaller gardens. Take cuttings from good stock; avoid overfertilizing.

C. torulosa

HIMALAYAN CYPRESS, BHUTAN CYPRESS

This Himalayan native has an erect triangular shape, broadening in maturity, and grows 10–20 m (about 30–65 ft) tall. Thick, bluish green foliage gives it a soft appearance. Its globose cones ripen from purple to reddish brown. This conifer prefers warm conditions and does not need pruning. It will survive for many years in a tub and makes an excellent hedge tree.

CUSSONIA
spicata

SPIKED CABBAGE TREE, LITTLE CABBAGE TREE

This fascinating South African evergreen has a thick rounded crown and an upright smooth trunk. It grows to 6 m (about 18 ft) and produces extremely large, serrated compound leaves to 25 cm (about 10 in) long on dense stalks. Inconspicuous yellow flowers appear above the canopy in spring to summer. Grow in well-drained soil in full sun. It is frost-tender.

DAIS
cotinifolia

SOUTH AFRICAN DAPHNE, POMPON BUSH

This small deciduous tree originates in South Africa Growing to 4–5 m (about 12–15 ft) tall, it has a rounded dome and multiple branches. Its greenish blue leaves grow to 8 cm (about 3 in) long and are egg-shaped. At the end of spring, convex terminal clusters of fragrant, pinkish purple, starry flowers bloom and endure after withering. This half-hardy species enjoys full sun or partial shade and porous soil. Propagate from seed in spring and half-ripe cuttings in summer. The stringy bark is used to make twine.

DAVIDIA
involucrata

DOVE TREE, HANDKERCHIEF TREE

This native to China, the only species of its genus, is valued for its unusual white bracts. Growing to 6–12 m (about 18–37 ft), this deciduous ornamental develops a rounded appearance. Its broad, egg-shaped leaves up to 15 cm (about 6 in) long, are succeeded in late spring by small, deep-set, brownish red flowers. Two white bracts (commonly mistaken for petals) of unequal lengths surround the flower. The longer leaf resembles a birch or handkerchief; hence the common names. Purplish green, pear-shaped seed pods follow, each encasing a single nut. Plant in full sun or partial shade in rich, porous soil. It is frost-hardy. Propagate (with some difficulty) from cuttings or seed in spring. The genus is named after Pére David, the French missionary who discovered it.

DIOSPYROS
kaki

KAKI, CHINESE PERSIMMON, DATE PLUM, KEY FIG

Valued for its fruit, timber and stunning autumn/fall foliage, this graceful, slow-growing deciduous tree is native to China and Japan. It may reach 13 m (about 40 ft) but is more usually 6 m (about 18 ft) tall. In autumn/fall the egg-shaped leaves

turn the most striking colours: scarlet, yellow, orange and purple. Insignificant, yellowish white female flowers develop into delicious, golden red fruit, or persimmons. Up to 7 cm (about 3 in) in diameter, these are the size and shape of a tomato. This tree enjoys warm summers, rich, fertile soil and frequent watering. It is best propagated by grafting, though seed may be used. A relaltive of the ebony, its precious timber is used to make oriental cabinets and golf 'woods'.

Diospyros kaki

Cupressus torulosa

Cupressus macrocarpa

Cupressus arizonica

Davidia involucrata

Cussonia spicata

Dais cotinifolia

A Field Trip to Norfolk Island

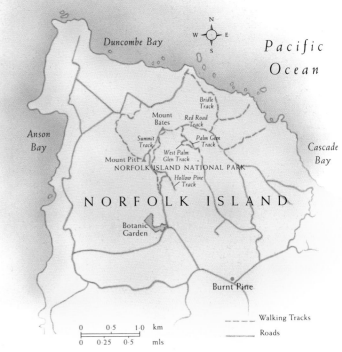

The stately splendour of Norfolk Island pines (*Araucaria heterophylla*) can't be fully appreciated until you see them growing in their own home—Norfolk Island.

Norfolk Island is a tiny island in the Pacific Ocean, about 1700 km (about 1050 miles) north-east of Sydney, Australia. You can fly to Norfolk Island from Sydney or from Auckland, New Zealand. As your aircraft approaches the island, you can see the steep basalt cliffs and gently rolling hills, and catch your first glimpse of its most dominant feature—great stands of Norfolk Island pines They can be seen both in the open and in the densely wooded areas where they can be seen towering over the canopy.

Norfolk Island has a pleasant, mild, subtropical climate with an average yearly rainfall of 1326 mm (about 52 in). The best time to visit is in summer, when the mean temperature is 25°C (about 77°F); in winter it is about 18°C (about 65°F).

The best place to see the island's most interesting and beautiful flora is Norfolk Island National Park. There are up to 170 native plant species, about 40 of which are found only on Norfolk Island. It is a good idea to visit the Botanic Garden on Mission Road before you explore the National Park. Here you can familiarize yourself with some of the flora so you can more easily identify it when you are in the park. The National Park contains some 8 km (about 5 miles) of walking tracks. A good place to start exploring these is from the summit of Mount Pitt, the highest point of the island. You can walk or drive to this area from Burnt Pine.

As you wind your way up the mountain the towering pines and palms create a canopy that, in places, obscures the sky. The rich soil here is home to many fern species, including the smooth tree fern (*Cyathea brownii*), which is considered to be the world's tallest. The view from the summit is magnificent; you can see the whole of Norfolk Island and neighbouring Nepean and Phillip Islands, and all around an endless expanse of sea.

From Mount Pitt take the Summit Track to Mount Bates, winding your way through some thick forest. The trees here include the Norfolk Island hibiscus, also known as the white oak (*Lagunaria patersonii*), which produces splendid pink flowers in spring (September to November). The pepper tree (*Macropiper excelsum*), too, is fairly abundant. This shrub grows up to 3 m (about 9 ft), producing yellow flower spikes followed by spikes of yellow to orange fruit which was used in preserves by the early settlers.

Follow the Red Road Track from Mount Bates through more hardwood forest and large stands of Norfolk Island pines and you may see the epiphytic orchid *Taeniophyllum muellerii*, commonly known as the minute orchid, growing on the trunks and branches. On the forest floor is *Oplismenus*, a creeping native grass which has tiny reddish flowers.

Looking south from Anson Bay, Norfolk Island.

Lichen covers the limbs of some pines in the island's north-east.

Araucaria heterophylla

The Palm Glen Track leads you through one of the island's most attractive areas where you will see great stands of the Norfolk Island palm (*Rhopalostylis baueri*), a magnificent tree reaching heights of 10 m (about 30 ft). The West Palm Glen Track leads through more stands of palms and a lush tree fern forest. Here you will see the smooth tree fern again, also the smaller rough tree fern (*Cyathea australis*) and the rare king fern (*Marattia salicina*).

Wildlife in the area includes the scarlet robin, a delightful but endangered endemic bird which is black with a bright red breast. The Norfolk Island morepork (a small owl) makes its nest in a hollow of the Norfolk Island pine, as do many of the island's native birds. Another threatened species, the Norfolk Island green parrot, an attractive bird with jewel green plumage, makes its home among the branches. The white tern, a sea bird and the island's emblem, also nests here.

After you have walked back to Mount Pitt—the round trip is 4 km (about 2½ miles)—take the track to Hollow Pine. Here stands a magnificent Norfolk Island pine which is hollow at the base. An escaped convict is said to have lived for seven years in a similar pine before he was finally captured.

The area surrounding Hollow Pine is rich in native flora. Many parts of the island have been affected by the encroachment of weeds but here volunteers have assisted in the battle against unwanted introduced species.

Before European settlement, the island was almost covered in rainforest. When Captain Cook first landed, the Norfolk Island pines came right down to the water's edge. Clearing of the land started within days of settlement in 1788, and now less than 1 per cent remains as it was when Cook saw it. Planting of the pines is now being done on a large scale. These may take up to 80 years or more to reach their full height of up to 70 m (about 220 ft), but eventually the island may once again be almost covered by these magnificent trees.

As the Pitcairners of Norfolk Island say: 'If we do not live to see them grow, our children will.'

Araucaria

The unique conifer genus *Araucaria* consists of 19 species, distributed in a remarkable geographical pattern. On one side of the Pacific Ocean there are two species in eastern Australia, one of which occurs in New Guinea which also has an endemic species; Norfolk Island has just one species but nearby New Caledonia has 13 species. Across the Pacific in South America there are just two species, the spectacular 'monkey puzzle' in Chile and southern Argentina, and the Parana pine in south-central Brazil. This sort of distribution suggests the genus originated and diversified before Gondwana, the southern supercontinent, began splitting apart over 100 million years ago.

The araucarias make beautiful ornamental trees where space is sufficient and the climate is suitable. The most cold-hardy is the Chilean monkey puzzle (*Araucaria araucana*), which actually requires cool climates such as that of southern England. The next most hardy is the Australian bunya pine (*A. bidwillii*). Some of the species, such as the Norfolk Island pine and the New Caledonian pine (*A. columnaris*), are noted for their tolerance of salt-laden winds.

Araucaria heterophylla

Embothrium coccineum

Erythrina crista-galli

Elaeocarpus reticulatus

DOMBEYA

tiliacea

syn. *D. natalensis*

NATAL CHERRY, WILD PEAR, CAPE WEDDING FLOWER

This evergreen is native to Africa and certain islands in the Indian ocean. It has slim multiple trunks and branches and grows quickly to 8 m (about 24 ft) with a spread of 4 m (about 12 ft). Its bark is brownish black and the heart-shaped leaves erratically serrated. In late autumn/fall to early winter, white, fragrant flowers tinged with pink appear in clusters of 2 or 4 at the end of long stalks. This species prefers warm, sunny or partially shaded locations and will not survive below 5°C (about 40°F). It also needs light to medium, well-drained soil. It is susceptible to white fly and red spider mite. Water generously while flowering, less when temperatures are low, and prune afterwards. Propagate from seed and cuttings. The genus was named after Jacob Dombey, an eighteenth-century botanist.

ELAEOCARPUS

reticulatus

syn. *E. cyaneus*

BLUEBERRY ASH, BLUE OLIVEBERRY

This Australian evergreen is valued for its foliage, flowers and fruit. A tall shrub or small tree, it reaches 10 m (about 30 ft) with an erect trunk and spreading crown. The shiny, lanceolate foliage is sharply lobed and finely veined. In spring and summer, clusters of pink or white frilly-edged flowers appear on fine stalks. Bright blue berries follow, globe-shaped and 1 cm (about ¹/₂ in) in diameter. This frost-tender tree tolerates a minimum temperature of 5°C (about 40°F). The species requires a damp, shady location and plentiful water while in flower. Prune back summer growth at the start of winter to control its size. Propagate from seed in spring, or from cuttings in summer.

EMBOTHRIUM

coccineum

CHILEAN FIREBUSH

Native to Chile and Argentina, this evergreen or semi-evergreen small tree or spreading bush varies in height between 3 and 10 m (about 9–30 ft) and has shiny dark green, lance-shaped leaves. These are woody and narrow, growing up to 10 cm (about 4 in) long. Terminal clusters of scarlet, tubular flowers bloom in an impressive display from late spring to early summer. The plant will produce flowers from an early age, provided it is well watered. A cool-temperate species, it enjoys a damp, cool location with acid soil and good drainage. Propagate from suckers in spring or seed in autumn/fall.

ERYTHRINA

crista-galli

COCKSCOMB CORAL TREE, CRYBABY TREE

These deciduous and semi-evergreen trees and shrubs originate in the tropical and warm-temperate areas of Africa, Asia, central America, the Caribbean and Hawaii. They are usually grown in these areas as ornamentals. *E. crista-galli* is a deciduous species that rapidly reaches 4–10 m (about 12–30 ft) and spreads broadly. Its prickly, 3-leafed foliage develops at the end of thorny stems. Rich crimson flowers bloom in loose terminal clusters from summer to autumn/fall. The woody seed pods are 38 cm (about 15 in) long. This species requires full sun and moist soil; it can survive the occasional frost. Prune in winter; an attractive gnarled trunk will develop without pruning but then the crown will be full of dead branches. Propagate from seed in spring or from cuttings in summer. Prone to attack by two-spotted mite.

EUCALYPTUS

GUM TREE, EUCALYPT

This diverse genus of mainly Australian natives contains over 600 species of evergreen trees and shrubs, prized for their beauty, shade, oils, hardwood and honey. Foliage varies from linear to heart-shaped; young and adult leaves differ markedly, making identification difficult. All species have distinctively lidded flower buds with densely packed stamens, blooming in spring or summer in shades of white, red or yellow. Trees vary from frost-hardy to frost-tender and differ greatly in size, shape and habitat: some low, multi-trunked species are excellent sand-binders, able to survive for a year without rain in the arid inland; other gnarled, salt-resistant species thrive in swamps; others still, straight and tall, prefer cool mountain areas. Plant eucalypts in isolation with full sun in rich, well-drained soil; trees do not transplant well. Prune in spring and early winter. Propagate from seed in autumn/fall and late winter. Eucalypts were first brought to Europe by Captain Cook's Australian expedition.

E globulus

syn. *E. globulus* subsp. *globulus*

TASMANIAN BLUE GUM, BLUE GUM, SOUTHERN BLUE GUM

Perhaps the most beautiful of all eucalypts, this column-shaped species is the floral emblem of its native Tasmania in Australia. A fast grower, it may exceed 70 m (about 220 ft). The thick trunk sheds its smooth grey bark. The juvenile leaf is silvery blue and circular, the mature leaf a deep green, sickle shape, up to 45 cm (about 18 in) long and fragrant. Single cream blossoms develop along slender stalks in spring and summer. This drought-resistant species occurs naturally in coastal areas. It prefers a mostly frost-free climate. Probably the most frequently planted gum outside Australia, this species is used for paper pulp, building timber and eucalyptus oil.

E. gunnii

syn. *E. divaricata*

CIDER GUM

This fast-growing gum is one of the few hardy enough to grow well in Britain (even though its leaves are frost-tender), where it can attain a height of 25 m (about 80 ft). Native to Tasmania, its juvenile foliage—which can last up to 4 years—is round, silver-grey, and a favourite with flower arrangers. The mature foliage is lanceolate and blue-green, and yellow-white flowers appear in clusters in mid-summer. The smooth bark is pale pink-grey, ageing to a dark brownish grey. To

Dombeya tiliacea

Eucalyptus globulus

retain the juvenile foliage, cut back hard in early summer and the resulting suckers will produce new, young growth.

E. pauciflora
syn. *E. coriacea*
CABBAGE GUM, WHITE SALLY

Originating in south-eastern Australia, this hardy, spreading tree can grow to 15 m (about 50 ft) high. It has smooth, white, peeling bark and glossy red to orange shoots. The grey-green adult foliage is broadly lanceolate, and clusters of white flowers appear in summer.

EUCRYPHIA

This genus consists of deciduous and evergreen trees and shrubs native to Australia and America. They grow to 10–15 m (about 30–50 ft) high and are planted for their foliage and striking, often scented flowers. While hardy, they require a sheltered, sunny or partly shaded position with a cool, moist root run in well-drained, non-limed soil. In winter the young shoots should be protected from frost. Propagate from a semi-ripe heel cutting, and tip prune the leading shoots to encourage bushiness.

E. cordifolia

A native of Chile, this semi-ever-green tree grows to a height of 12 m (about 37 ft) with a spread of 3 m (about 9 ft). It has oval leaves with undulating margins and large, open, solitary, white flowers that are 6 cm (about 2½ in) across. It prefers rich, acid soils in a protected, partially shaded position and is frost resistant.

E. × nymansensis

A natural hybrid, this slender ever-green is vigorous, growing to 15 m (about 50 ft). Its shiny dark green leaves can be either simple or pinnate (with 3 to 5 leaflets), and cover the erect branches. Creamy white flowers are borne in late summer in profuse clusters, providing the tree is sheltered from wind. This species will tolerate limed soils.

FAGUS

BEECH

Native to Europe and North America this small cool-climate genus includes some of the world's most popular deciduous trees. They are valued for their autumn/fall foliage and their timber, used to make furniture. Reaching up to 30 m (about 95 ft) they are well rounded with dense crowns. Foliage varies in shape, size and colour, ranging from yellow to purple. Inconspicuous flowers bloom in late spring, followed in late autumn/fall by the pyramid-shaped nuts in their

Eucaplyptus pauciflora

Eucryphia cordifolia

Eucryphia × nymansensis

Fagus grandifolia

prickly oval seed pods. Although edible, beechnuts are not particularly tasty and are usually used as stock fodder. The purple-leaved trees like full sun; the yellow-leaved prefer partial shade. All species enjoy well-drained, limed soil.

F. grandifolia
syn. *F. americana*
AMERICAN BEECH

This broad-spreading deciduous tree will grow as wide as it does high—to 10 m (about 30 ft). The ovate leaves are light green when immature, darkening to a deep green in summer and ultimately a yellow-brown before they drop in autumn/fall.

Fagus sylvatica f. *purpurea*

Fagus sylvatica

Fraxinus americana

F. sylvatica
EUROPEAN BEECH

Triangular in shape with a broad spreading crown and drooping branches, this fast grower reaches up to 40 m (about 130 ft). Young foliage is oval, downy and light green, maturing to deep glossy green. Leaves turn a vivid golden orange in autumn/fall. It prefers cold climates and partial shade and will do best in well-drained alkaline soils. Prune in summer and propagate from seed in autumn/fall, budding in late summer.

F. sylvatica 'Pendula'

This cultivar is a weeping variety with pendulous branches, and is a slow grower to 3 m (about 9 ft).

F. sylvatica f. purpurea
COPPER BEECH, PURPLE BEECH

This form has purple-green leaves that turn copper in autumn/fall. It requires full sun. True colour can be achieved from seed. In Germany it is considered unlucky to plant a proper beech near the house—the tree is thought to attract lightning. It stands clipping and can be used for tall hedges.

FRANKLINIA
alatamaha

The *Franklinia* genus belongs to the Theaceae family and consists of one species, a deciduous tree that will grow to 5 m (about 15 ft). It is cultivated for its large, cup-like, white flowers, which appear in late summer, and for the long, lustrous, green leaves which turn a rich red colour in autumn/fall. While hardy, it needs a hot summer to flourish. It enjoys well-drained but moist, non-limed soil. To propagate, softwood cuttings may be taken in summer or hardwood cuttings early in winter. It can also be grown from seed in autumn/fall.

FRAXINUS
ASH

Native to the northern hemisphere, this well-known genus contains about 60 deciduous timber trees and shrubs. They are extremely variable in size, ranging from 15 to 50 m (about 50 to 160 ft). Dense flower clusters which are insignificant in most species appear in early spring, followed by distinctive feathery foliage up to 30 cm (about 12 in) long, divided into 3 to 13 leaflets. Decorative drooping clusters of small, winged seeds develop from the flowers. These fully hardy trees will endure a broad range of temperatures provided that they are planted in deep, fertile soil with sufficient moisture and full sun. Propagate from heat-treated seed in autumn/fall, or by budding in summer.

F. americana
WHITE ASH

Originating in North America, this deciduous tree is fast growing and can reach 26 m (about 85 ft); it has a domed crown. It bears large, dark green, opposite leaves consisting of 5–9 lanceolate leaflets. Silver coloured underneath, the leaves occasionally become purple or yellow during autumn/fall.

Fagus sylvatica 'Pendula'

Franklinia alatamaha

Fraxinus oxycarpa 'Raywood'

F. ornus

MANNA ASH, FLOWERING ASH

Originating in southern Europe and Asia Minor, this spreading tree can grow up to 20 m (about 65 ft) with a rounded crown. The compound foliage comprises 5 to 9 leaflets, which turn from deep green to reddish purple in autumn/fall. Fragrant white flowers appear in abundance in early spring, during which time a sweet substance called manna is exuded from fissures in the bark.

F. oxycarpa 'Raywood'

CLARET ASH

This robust and fast-growing tree, a cultivar of Australian origin, is valued for its autumn/fall leaves and attractive shape. The tree grows to 10–15 m (about 30–50 ft), developing a stocky trunk and rounded crown. The deeply lobed foliage is made up of 7 to 9 narrow leaflets which turn from shiny deep green to a claret red in autumn/fall. This frost-hardy tree will withstand hot conditions if regularly watered.

F. pennsylvanica

syn. **F. pennsylvanica** var. **subintegerrima**

RED ASH, GREEN ASH

Similar to *F. americana*, this tree is also a fast-growing native of North America but is not as large; it reaches 20 m (about 65 ft) in height with a similar spread. Its green leaves are divided in 5–9 leaflets and can be hairy, like stalks. This species prefers a moist soil.

GINKGO

biloba

MAIDENHAIR TREE

The sole member of its genus, this important deciduous conifer has been found in fossils that are over 200 million years old. Native apparently to Europe, Asia, Australia and America, it is thought to be extinct now in the wild. Fortunately, it is widely cultivated. This hardy tree, valued for its rich autumn/fall foliage and timber, grows up to 40 m (about 130 ft). Its triangular crown broadens out in maturity. The arching branches develop bright green,

Fraxinus ornus

fan-shaped leaves, similar to the maidenhair fern but much larger, which turn deep golden yellow in autumn/fall. Little yellow flowers sprinkle the mature trees in spring, followed by orange-yellow fruits about the size of a small plum. The female tree is not popular among some gardeners as the fallen seeds have an unpleasant odour. This enduring tree survives both arid and wet climates and withstands urban pollution. The tree needs deep fertile soil and it should be propagated from seed or graft. Ginkgos are widely cultivated in China, where their edible seeds are considered a delicacy.

GLEDITSIA

This genus of deciduous, usually spiny trees are grown for their foliage. They require plenty of sun and a fertile, well-drained soil. Their inconspicuous flowers are often followed by large seed pods, if the weather has been particularly hot. Fully hardy. Propagation is from seed in autumn.

G. triacanthos 'Sunburst'

HONEY LOCUST

This deciduous North American species grows up to 15 m (about 50 ft) and develops a broad crown. It is valued for its attractive fern-like foliage, composed of up to 32 leaflets. The immature foliage is golden yellow, turning to deep green in summer and reverting to golden yellow in autumn/fall. Insignificant pea-like flowers appear in green, downy clusters. These are followed by large, shiny, red-ochre seed pods, slightly curved and up to 45 cm (about 18 in) long. The pods are filled with sweet pulp, explaining the common name. This drought-resistant tree is fully hardy, though saplings may be affected by frost. Plant in rich, well-drained soil in full sun. Propagate by budding at the end of summer. The species itself is viciously thorny.

G. triacanthos var. inermis

This variety of *G. triancanthos* is thornless, as is the cultivar 'Sunburst', and as such is much preferred in gardens.

Fraxinus pennsylvanica *Ginkgo biloba*

Gleditsia triacanthos 'Sunburst'

Gleditsia triacanthos var. *inermis*

HALESIA
carolina
syn. H. tetraptera
SNOWDROP TREE, SILVER-BELL TREE, OPPOSUMWOOD

The *Halesia* genus consists of 6 species of beautiful, spring-flowering deciduous trees native to the USA and China. A wide-spreading tree, *H. carolina* comes from North America and can grow to 8 m (about 24 ft) high and 10 m (about 30 ft) across. The bell-shaped, silver-white flowers appear in hanging clusters in late spring and are followed by narrow, 4-winged fruit. The light green leaves are ovate and pointed. This species prefers a sunny, sheltered position in moist, well-drained, neutral to acidic soil. Plant between autumn/fall and late winter. To propagate, layer the shoots in spring. Seed germination can take up to a year and a half. Halesias were named for the Reverend Hales, the eighteenth-century author of *Vegetable Staticks*.

HOHERIA
populnea
LACEBARK, HOUHERE

Native to New Zealand this slender, fast-growing evergreen reaches 8–15 m (about 24–50 ft) and is one of only two in its genus. The tree is valued for its decorative flowers, foliage and bark, which is papery, pale brown and white, shedding in patches. Its glossy, deep green leaves are elliptical and deeply lobed. Thick white clusters of lightly scented, star-shaped flowers appear in late summer to early autumn/fall. This half-hardy species will survive in cool and warm conditions. Plant in rich, porous soil with full sun or partial shade and water regularly. Propagate from cuttings in summer, seed in autumn/fall.

ILEX
HOLLY

Belonging to the Aquifoliaceae family, the hollies are a large genus of about 300 species from Europe, Asia and America. While some are deciduous, the most widely grown species are evergreen, their distinctive glossy leaves, almost always with spines along the edges, being much admired. They are slow-growing, and are often grown as large shrubs, especially as it is easy to control their size by pruning. They are outstanding hedge plants. The spring flowers are white but insignificant; as male and female flowers are borne on separate plants, it is necessary to have both to obtain the decorative berries which ripen in autumn/fall and last through winter. These are usually red, but can also be black or yellow, and are a traditional Christmas decoration. A moist well-drained site is preferred. While green-leaved types will grow in shade, the variegated clones will give better colour in full sun. Hollies can be planted out in late spring or autumn/fall. Propagate from seed in spring, or by semi-hardwood cuttings in late summer. Prune hard, if necessary, in late summer. The plants can fall prey to holly leaf miner and holly aphid, while holly fungus will kill them.

I. × altaclarensis
BROAD-LEAVED HOLLY

A hybrid between *I. aquifolium* and the Canary Island holly, *I. perado*, and available in several cultivars, this hardy vigorous evergreen is pollution tolerant and does well in a coastal situation. While most forms will eventually grow to about 15 m (about 50 ft), they are most often seen as shrubs about 4–6 m (about 12–18 ft) tall. Among the most popular forms are 'Hodginsii', a vigorous male tree with purple twigs and large glossy leaves, and 'Camelliaefolia', a columnar female tree with shiny, sparsely spined leaves and bright red berries.

I. aquifolium
ENGLISH HOLLY, COMMON HOLLY

Upright in youth, this evergreen species can eventually grow 15–18 m (about 50–60 ft) tall. The wild form has dark green leaves, tiny white flowers and red berries, but there are many garden cultivars which are usually less vigorous than the type and are usually treated as tall shrubs. Choose carefully when buying; some cultivars are male, others female.

I. opaca
AMERICAN HOLLY

This evergreen tree has an erect habit and can reach 14 m (about 45 ft). Its leaves are either spined or smooth, matt green above and a lighter green below. It bears red berries in autumn/fall. Although hardy, it does not enjoy a coastal situation.

JUGLANS
nigra
BLACK WALNUT, CALIFORNIA WALNUT

This species from North America and is valued for its foliage, timber and edible nuts. It grows to some 30 m (about 95 ft) with an open crown and red-tinted foliage. The shiny foliage comprises 15 to 25 leaflets some 15 cm (about 6 in) long. These are followed by greenish yellow male catkins, inconspicuous female flowers and, finally, edible nuts. This tree is fully hardy but saplings require shelter from frosts. Plant in deep, rich, porous

Hoheria populnea

Halesia carolina

Ilex aquifolium

Ilex × altaclarensis

Ilex opaca

soil with full sun. Propagate from seed in autumn/fall. In Latin, *Juglans* means 'Jupiter's acorn', so highly did the Romans value the fruit of the European walnut, *J. regia* which is included in this book under fruit trees.

JUNIPERUS

JUNIPER

This northern hemisphere genus contains over 50 species of slow-growing conifers of extremely diverse colour and habit, ranging in height from 9 to 25 m (about 27 to 80 ft). Adult foliage comprises short, scale-like leaves. Species are fully hardy and drought-resistant, able to survive extremes in temperature. Unusually for conifers, they prefer alkaline soil. They also prefer full sun and dry, sandy soil. Trees should be pruned regularly: as with most conifers, new growth will not sprout from brown wood. Propagate from seed or cuttings, or by grafting. Watch for aphids and leafrollers. The blue, berry-like fruit is used to flavour gin.

J. communis

COMMON JUNIPER

This shrub or tree reaches a height of 3 to 12 m (about 9 to 37 ft) and is slim or cone-shaped. It has brownish red bark and fragrant, yellowish green, needle-like foliage borne in groups of three. The globular fruit are blue-black, turning bluish green before finally maturing to black. These fruit are used for flavouring in cooking. This frost-hardy species prefers cool to cold climates.

J. scopulorum
syn. *J. virginiana scopulorum*
ROCKY MOUNTAIN JUNIPER

This species, which can reach 10 m (about 30 ft), has small blue berries and aromatic grey-green foliage. The leaves were used by the Hopi Indians to treat dandruff. The cultivars are more often planted, the best known being 'Skyrocket'.

J. virginiana
PENCIL CEDAR, EASTERN RED CEDAR

Originating in North America, this conifer is valued for its shade and timber. Triangular at first, the tree spreads in maturity and grows to 33 m (about 105 ft). The grey, needle-like foliage is prickly when young. Blue-black cones bear three seeds The timber is used to make pencils (explaining the common name, 'Pencil cedar') and cigar boxes.

KIGELIA
africana
syn. *K. pinnata*
SAUSAGE TREE

This single-species genus is grown for its flowers, foliage and bizarre

long-stemmed fruit. A small, upright, compact tree, it quickly reaches up to 10 m (about 30 ft). The broad shady crown has feather-like foliage, composed of 7 to 11 leaflets. Deep red, bell-shaped blossoms develop in drooping clusters from autumn/fall until spring. They are followed by inedible sausage-like pods which last almost the entire year. Leathery and brown, they hang from stems over 1 m (about 3 ft) long — possibly the longest stemmed fruit in the world.

KOELREUTERIA
paniculata

CHINA TREE, GOLDEN-RAIN TREE, VARNISH TREE, PRIDE OF INDIA

This deciduous Asian native has a broad convex crown and grows quickly to 10–15 m (about 30–50 ft) tall. Its feathery bipinnate foliage grows up to 45 cm (about 18 in) long and turns from green to deep golden yellow in autumn/fall, particularly in cooler climates. Large decorative clusters of golden yellow flowers develop in summer, followed by pinkish brown seed pods,

swollen with black seeds. This frost-hardy species survives arid inland conditions and enjoys full sun and strong alkaline soil. Propagate from seed in spring; root cuttings in winter. The flowers are used in Chinese medicine.

LABURNUM
× *watereri* 'Vossii'

VOSS'S LABURNUM, HYBRID LABURNUM, GOLDEN CHAIN TREE

Native to Europe and parts of Asia Minor, this deciduous hybrid is valued for its beautiful golden chains of flowers. Elegant and erect, it grows 3–10 m (about 9–30 ft). The compound foliage has 3 oval leaflets, shiny dark green on top, soft and downy underneath. Pendent, pea-like flowers develop in golden clusters on long stems in late spring. A few legume-like pods follow, some containing the highly poisonous seeds. This tree likes cold, damp locations with full sun and will tolerate most soil types. Propagate by budding in summer. Do not plant where animals graze, as all parts of this species are toxic.

Laburnum × *watereri* 'Vossi'

Juniperus communis

Kigelia africana

Koelreuteria paniculata

Juniperus virginiana

Juglans nigra

Liquidambar formosana

Maclura pomifera

Larix decidua

Liriodendron tulipifera

Lophostemon confertus

Liquidambar styraciflua

LARIX
decidua
EUROPEAN LARCH

Native to northern Europe, this enduring deciduous conifer has an attractive symmetrical conical shape, opening out in later years. It can reach enormous heights (but can be much less in cultivation), and develops tiered, drooping branches. These are covered in pale green needle-like foliage in spring, turning to golden brown in autumn/fall. Little upright cones with round scales appear in winter, when all the limbs are bare. This cold-climate tree requires good rainfall, well-drained soil and full sun. It is prized by shipbuilders and is also a valuable source of turpentine.

LIQUIDAMBAR
SWEET GUM

This deciduous genus contains three species, one each from Asia, Asia Minor and North to Central America. All are valued for their splendid autumn/fall foliage, which greatly varies in colour. Conical in shape, the trees grow to varying heights, from 8 to 38 m (about 24 to 122 ft). The leaves are palmate, resembling the maple, with 5 to 7 deeply cut, serrated lobes. Frost-hardy when fully grown, these trees can survive extremes in temperature. They prefer a warm moist location but are not salt-resistant. Nothing will grow near them as they are voracious feeders, sucking what goodness there is from the soil. Plant in rich, deep, porous earth with full sun or partial shade. Propagate from seed in autumn/fall; bud in spring. The timber is used to make furniture.

L. formosana
FORMOSA SWEET GUM, CHINESE LIQUIDAMBAR

This tough, fast-growing native of Taiwan and China has a spreading pyramidal shape and reaches some 38 m (about 122 ft). The leaves have 3 lobes and are hairy underneath. They turn from purple in spring to deep green in summer, before changing to brilliant orange-red and purple in autumn/fall. Male and female flowers bloom separately on the same tree, followed by prickly globes of pendent fruit. This valuable timber tree is also used in the manufacture of perfumes.

L. styraciflua
SWEET GUM, RED GUM, BILSTED

This deciduous native of North and Central America has an erect conical shape that may spread in maturity. It grows quickly: up to 38 m (about 122 ft), depending on conditions. The lustrous foliage, with 5 or 7 lobes, is 10–15 cm (about 4–6 in) wide. Young leaves are pale green, maturing to deep green and turning vivid red-purple and orange-yellow in autumn/fall. The branches develop corky shoots in winter. This frost-hardy tree survives hot weather with regular watering. Select seedling trees in autumn/fall as colour is very variable.

LIRIODENDRON
tulipifera
TULIP TREE, TULIP POPLAR, YELLOW POPLAR

This deciduous North American native is valued for its flowers and rich yellow autumn/fall foliage. The tree quickly attains heights of 15–30 m (about 50–95 ft), in a symmetrical pyramid; branches often do not start until halfway up. Distinctive, 4-lobed leaves have blunted middle teeth, giving the foliage a squarish appearance. In spring the tree bears green, scented flowers shaped like tulips, with orange bands encircling the stamens. These are followed by conical seed heads containing winged seeds. This fully hardy species prefers cool climates and enjoys full sun and neutral to acid soil. It may be transplanted up to a good size and is propagated from seed in autumn/fall, budding in summer. The timber, although not very durable, is much used in the USA.

LOPHOSTEMON
confertus
syn. *Tristania conferta*
BRUSH BOX, BRISBANE BOX

This evergreen Australian species is a fast grower, reaching 45 m (about 145 ft) in its rainforest habitat, but only 15–30 m (about 50–95 ft) in the average garden. The brown bark is shed in strips. It has a domed crown and deep green foliage, lanceolate and woody. Little cream flowers with dense, prominent stamens bloom in spring. It is classed as half-hardy but will survive in a broad range of climates. Plant in rich, well-drained soil with full sun; prune saplings in winter to encourage shape. Propagate from seed in spring, cuttings in summer. There is a handsome cultivar with variegated leaves.

MACLURA
pomifera
OSAGE ORANGE, BOWWOOD

Originating in North America, this species is valued for its deciduous foliage, interesting fruit and yellow timber. It grows quickly to 20 m (about 65 ft) with an open, uneven crown and arching branches. Elliptical, deep green leaves turn yellow in autumn/fall. Small clusters of yellow-green flowers appear in summer followed by large, inedible, aggregate fruits. These spherical leathery pods will only develop if both male and female trees are present. The adult tree is frost-hardy, while the immature specimen is frost-tender. Suitable for hedges, the species requires full sun and hot summer temperatures to survive cold winters. Propagate from seed in autumn/fall, cuttings in summer and root cuttings in late winter.

MAGNOLIA
MAGNOLIA

This genus comprises two groups: deciduous species, native to eastern

Magnolia × soulangiana

Malus floribunda

Asia, and evergreens, native to Central America and southern USA. All are valued for their beautiful large flowers. The species range from 12–25 m (about 37–80 ft), with spreading crowns. Their elliptical leaves are lustrous green on top, pitted with brown underneath. The perfumed flowers with silky petals and densely packed stamen bloom on deciduous trees in spring, sometimes before the foliage; on the evergreens, in summer. Seed-bearing cones follow. Trees prefer full sun or partial shade and rich, well-drained soil (slightly acid for deciduous species). If using poorer soil, fertilize first with manure. Transplant with care: the roots are extremely fragile. Propagate from cuttings in summer, seed in autumn/fall; graft cultivars in winter. The genus was named after eighteenth-century botanist Pierre Magnol.

M. campbellii
PINK TULIP TREE, CHINESE TULIP TREE

This deciduous Chinese native has an erect appearance when immature, broadening out later. It grows quickly to 6–15 m (about 18–50 ft) tall. Scattered branches bear pointed, elliptical leaves up to 30 cm (about 12 in) long, powdery underneath. This species takes 15–20 years to flower. The big, scented blooms, light pink inside and darker pink outside, appear from the end of winter to mid-spring. The tree prefers a cool-temperate climate and open space. Plant in moist, acid soil.

M. grandiflora
BULL BAY, SOUTHERN MAGNOLIA, LAUREL MAGNOLIA

This evergreen species from southern USA varies broadly in size and habit: 6–20 m (about 18–95 ft) high, it may be compact and rounded or spreading and conical. It has thick, woody foliage of shiny mid- to deep green leaves, downy brown underneath. Cup-shaped white blooms with a strong citrus scent appear from mid-summer to early autumn/fall, followed by red-brown cones. This moderately frost-hardy species prefers warm climates and moist soil.

Magnolia heptapeta

M. heptapeta
syn. M. denudata, M. conspicua
YULAN, LILY TREE

Native to China, this deciduous spreading tree or tall shrub grows up to 10 m (about 30 ft). It has dark bark and egg-shaped leaves with a hairy underside. Naked branches bear scented, snow-white, tulip-like flowers in early spring. These are followed by rectangular cones containing orange seeds. This frost-hardy species prefers temperate climates.

M. × soulangiana
SAUCER MAGNOLIA, SOULANGE-BODIN'S MAGNOLIA

This deciduous tree develops slowly, reaching 3–8 m (about 9–24 ft), frequently growing multiple trunks and a rounded crown. Tulip-like blooms precede the foliage in early spring, even on young plants. The flower's interior varies from snow white to light pink; the exterior is a deeper pink. The dull green foliage is up to 15 cm (about 6 in) long. This species prefers a warm climate and requires shelter from hot winds. There are several cultivars, blooms ranging in colour from pure-white to deep red. This hybrid was bred in Paris in 1820 by Étienne Soulange-Bodin, from M. heptapeta and M. liliflora.

M. virginiana
SWEET BAY

This hardy species, a native of the eastern USA, can be deciduous or semi-evergreen and grows into a conical tree of 9 m (about 27 ft). It bears bowl-shaped, creamy white, scented flowers from summer to

Magnolia campbellii

Magnolia virginiana

early autumn/fall. Its glossy deep green leaves are grey-white underneath. It prefers well-composted, moist, well-drained soils in a protected, partially shaded position.

MALUS
CRAB-APPLE, APPLE

Native to the northern hemisphere, this diverse genus contains 25 deciduous shrubs and trees, valued for their flowers, foliage and fruit. They grow 9–12 m (about 27–37 ft) tall with spreading, round crowns. Foliage ranges from bronze, hairy and wide-lobed to deep green, linear and neat, while the spring blossom varies in colour from deep purple to pure white. The acidic fruit also varies widely, from edible kinds that can be eaten cooked, to purely ornamental crab apples. Fully hardy, the trees like full sun and cold weather and tolerate any soil that is not too wet. Prune in winter to encourage symmetry; propagate by budding in summer or grafting in winter. Watch for aphids and fireblight.

Malus 'Aldenhamensis'

Magnolia grandiflora

M. 'Aldenhamensis'
PURPLE CRAB

This small, fully hardy English cultivar grows only 4 m (about 12 ft) tall and is valued for its beautiful autumn/fall foliage. The little leaves have shallow-lobed margins and are purplish red when immature. An abundance of claret-coloured blossoms appear in spring, followed by very attractive purplish red crab-apples in autumn/fall.

M. floribunda
JAPANESE FLOWERING CRAB-APPLE, SHOWY CRAB-APPLE

This expansive, thick-crowned tree grows to 10 m (about 30 ft). Its early spring buds are crimson red, blooming into light pink blossoms. The variable foliage is egg-shaped to rectangular, some types with heavily saw-toothed edges and 3 to 5 lobes. Small, reddish yellow, scented crab-apples appear in autumn/fall. The oldest of the decorative crab-apples, this tree is thought to originate in Japan, and is the parent of many hybrids. It is adaptable to most well-composted soils.

Malus hupehensis

M. hupehensis
syn. M. theifera
HUPEH CRAB

A native of China and Japan, this vigorous tree can grow to 10 m (about 30 ft). Its large, dark green, oval leaves are sharply toothed, and in spring single pink buds open to large white flowers. The fruit, yellow tinged with red, appear in early autumn/fall.

M. 'Red Jade'

This is a weeping specimen growing to 12 m (about 37 ft) high and almost as wide, with deep green oval leaves. Its single white flowers appear in spring and are followed by red crab apples which persist on the tree.

MAYTENUS
boaria

MAYTEN

Originating in Chile, this small, handsome evergreen grows 6–8 m (about 18–24 ft) tall. Lustrous deep green foliage growing on slender stalks is lance shaped and slightly lobed. Inconspicuous starry flowers bloom in late spring. Perfect for small gardens, this frost-hardy tree prefers cool climates, although saplings need protection from winter winds. Plant in full sun or partial shade. Propagate from cuttings in summer, suckers in autumn/fall and spring. Mayten is inclined to be invasive in some countries, such as New Zealand.

MELIA
azedarach

PERSIAN LILAC, BEAD TREE, CHINABERRY, WHITE CEDAR

This expansive Asian native, growing 6–12 m (about 18–37 ft) tall, is valued for its foliage, flowers, fruit and timber. Deep green, bipinnate leaves have numerous leaflets. Scented, star-shaped flowers bloom in spring in bluish purple clusters, resembling lilacs. The green fruit matures to yellow-orange in autumn/fall. This frost-hardy species flourishes in warm coastal areas, tolerates arid conditions and may be

Malus 'Red Jade'

Maytenus boaria

Melia azedarach

planted in any reasonable soil if given full sun. Propagate from seed in autumn/fall. Check for white cedar moth caterpillars in late summer to autumn/fall. The fine timber of this tree is used to make furniture and its fruit, although poisonous to both animals and humans, is used to make medicines. The species does occur in northern Australia, although most Australian plantings are of Iranian origin. It has become invasive in some countries, such as South Africa.

NAGEIA
falcata
syn. Podocarpus falcatus

This grand conifer grows erect up to 15–30 m (about 50–95 ft) in cultivation. It has peeling bark and shiny, slender, dark green foliage. Its large, greenish blue seed pods are globe shaped and hang from a short, thick stem (*Podocarpus* means 'footed stalk'). A frost-hardy species, it prefers a mild climate. It may be grown in moist soils and requires full sun. Propagate from seed.

NOTHOFAGUS
SOUTHERN BEECH

Native to the southern hemisphere, this diverse genus has over 25 deciduous and evergreen species, including some extremely valuable timber trees. Dome-shaped, they range from short and shrubby to tall and columnar, reaching up to 70 m (about 220 ft). The leaves, resembling those of their close relative the northern beech, are egg-shaped to rectangular with heavily lobed edges and are downy when young. Insignificant flowers develop in late spring, followed by seed pods containing 3 triangular beechnuts. These fully to frost-hardy trees grow in cold temperate to subtropical climates. They like full sun or partial shade and deep, rich, neutral to acid soil that is moist but porous. Protect from strong winds; propagate from seed in autumn/fall.

N. moorei
ANTARCTIC BEECH, AUSTRALIAN BEECH

This erect Australian evergreen has a broad crown, thick foliage and brown, peeling bark. Quick growing, it reaches 18–22 m (about 60–70 ft). The sharp elliptical foliage matures from lustrous golden red to dark green. Seed pods and green-white flowers are inconspicuous. It prefers a mild climate and is not very drought resistant.

N. obliqua
ROBLÉ TREE, CHILEAN BEECH

This graceful, deciduous Chilean native grows fast to 20 m (about 65 ft). It has a wide, spreading crown, pendent branches and serrated

Nothofagus obliqua

Nyssa sylvatica

leaves that turn from deep green to orange-red in autumn/fall. Fully hardy, it requires full sun and well-drained soil. It is much used for its timber in England.

N. solandri
BLACK BEECH

This rapidly growing species is native to New Zealand and is valued for its appearance and timber. Up to 25 m (about 80 ft) tall, it has an erect habit with a rounded crown. The rectangular to oval leaves have slightly furled margins. Green individual blooms are followed by typical fruit. It prefers rich, deep, moist soils in a protected, sunny position.

NYSSA
sylvatica
SOUR GUM, PEPPERIDGE, BLACK GUM, TUPELO

Native to North America and Asia, this striking deciduous species is valued for its autumn/fall foliage, its timber and honey. Its shape is a wide-based pyramid, about 16 m (about 53 ft) high. Large shiny leaves are almost diamond shaped and deep green, turning vivid red and yellow in autumn/fall; although away from its native home the colours are not always reliable, in some years it just turns yellow. Little clusters of flowers, while inconspicuous, contribute to some of the finest honey in the world. This species likes very warm, humid conditions and relishes waterlogged, slightly acid soil. Plant in full sun or partial shade and avoid transplanting. Propagate from seed in autumn/fall, cuttings in summer.

Oxydendrum arboreum

Nothofagus solandri

Nothofagus moorei

OXYDENDRUM
arboreum
SORREL TREE

The *Oxydendrum* genus consists of one species, *O. arboreum*, a hardy, deciduous tree native to the southern USA. It grows to 15 m (about 50 ft) and is popular for its long, lanceolate, deep green foliage, which turns a striking scarlet in autumn/fall, and its panicles of white, slim, vase-shaped summer flowers. To obtain the rich autumn/fall colour, plant the tree in an open, sunny to partially shady position sheltered from winds in an acid, moist soil. Propagate from softwood cuttings in summer or early autumn/fall.

Nageia falcata

PARROTIA
persica
PERSIAN WITCH-HAZEL, PARROTIA, IRONWOOD

Originating in Iran, this compact deciduous species is valued for its decorative autumn/fall foliage. It grows to reach some 10 m (about 30 ft), and often has pendent limbs. Upright spirals of wiry crimson stamens appear on leafless branches in early spring, followed by glossy, egg-shaped foliage. The leaves have undulating margins and turn vivid red, yellow and orange in autumn/fall. The tree is fully hardy, though frosts may damage buds, and prefers a cool climate. Plant in a protected location in deep, rich soil: it withstands lime but shows the best leaf colours in a neutral to acid soil. Propagate from seed in autumn/fall, cuttings in summer. The genus was named after famous botanist F. W. Parrot.

PAULOWNIA
tomentosa
syn. *P. imperialis*
ROYAL PAULOWNIA, EMPRESS TREE, PRINCESS TREE, KURRI

This deciduous Chinese genus is valued for its beautiful flowers and large foliage. *P. tomentosa* grows very rapidly to around 6–15 m (about 18–50 ft). The foliage consists of paired green leaves, sometimes divided into 3 lobes. Upright, conical blooms are lilac and strongly scented. The tree can be cut almost to the ground annually to develop branches around 3 m (about 9 ft) tall with huge leaves. The timber is used in Asian countries to make furniture. These trees like cold climates, some species withstanding extremely cold temperatures, although severe frosts may damage buds and saplings. Plant in rich, porous soil and full sun. Prune severely in spring to encourage large leaves. Propagate from seed in autumn/fall and spring; cuttings in winter.

PELTOPHORUM
africanum

Native to all the tropics and subtropics of Africa, this genus contains 15 evergreen or deciduous species valued for their broad shady crowns, flowers and decorative fruit. *P. africanum*, a semi-deciduous species, reaches 13 m (about 40 ft) in height. The compound leaves are fern-like. Golden yellow, scented flowers appear in terminal bunches in summer. Frost-tender, the trees prefer temperatures above 8°C (about 46°F) and grow well in subtropical to tropical climates. Locate in a sheltered, semi-shady position with sandy, porous soil. Pruning is not required; propagate from seed or cuttings in summer.

PHELLODENDRON
amurense
AMUR CORK TREE

This deciduous Asian native grows to 12 m (about 37 ft), spreading widely. Its shiny dark green foliage has a spicy aroma and turns yellow in autumn/fall. Small green flowers appear, male and female on separate trees, followed by small black, spherical fruit. This cool-climate tree is fully hardy (though young shoots may be affected by frost) but enjoys warm summers. Plant in full sun and rich, porous soil. Propagate from cuttings in summer, seed in autumn/fall and root cuttings in late winter. Rather than referring to the production of cork, the common name describes the older tree's corky bark.

PICEA
SPRUCE

This northern hemisphere genus of about 50 species of hardy, evergreen conifers are mostly found in the mountains. Generally of columnar habit, they range in height from prostrate forms to 40 m (about 130 ft). They have short needles that grow from a peg on the stems. The long, pendulous cones have woody brown scales. Planted in deep, moist, well-drained, acid soil in a sunny position, they grow into excellent specimen trees. Propagate from seed or heel cuttings in autumn/fall, and protect the young shoots from frost. Fungus and moulds can also be a problem. The trees are used in the timber industry, and for resin and turpentine production.

P. abies
syn. *P. excelsa*
NORWAY SPRUCE, COMMON SPRUCE

This is a fast-growing tree, to 40 m (about 130 ft), with a narrow crown that broadens in maturity. Instantly recognizable as the European Christmas tree, it has mid-green, short, stiff needles that stand out from the shoots. The mid-brown, cigar-shaped cones, around 18 cm (about 7½ in) long, hang down from the branches. Ripening in autumn/fall, they follow the insignificant early summer flowers. The bark is smooth and orange-brown when young; with age it cracks and darkens to a brownish grey. It is adaptable to most soil types and prefers an open sunny position. There are many cultivars, including dwarf and prostrate forms.

P. omorika
SIBERIAN SPRUCE

A native of the area formerly known as Yugoslavia, this slender, columnar conifer can reach 30 m (about 95 ft); however, it does grow slowly. The drooping branches with curved up ends have flat needles, shiny green above and white underneath. The 4–6 cm (about 2–2½ in) long cones are purple-black, while the bark of an immature tree is orange-brown. Tolerant of pollution and most soils, and free from insect problems, this graceful conifer in one of its smaller cultivars is an excellent choice for a city garden.

Peltophorum africanum

Phellodendron
amurense

Parrotia persica

Paulownia tomentosa

Picea abies

Picea omorika

Pinus nigra

Picea pungens 'Koster'

Pinus palustris

P. pungens 'Koster'

KOSTER BLUE, COLORADO SPRUCE

This North American evergreen tree's glaucous foliage makes it one of the most attractive of all conifers. The leaves are rigid and thorny, maturing from silvery deep blue to green. Spiralled branches support tubular, scaled cones, 10 cm (about 4 in) long. This frost-hardy species likes cooler climates, well-drained soil and full sun. Prune regularly as fresh growth will not bud from deadwood. These trees dislike being moved, so transplant them young. Prone to aphids and mites. Although cutting-grown plants and bluish seedlings are available, a well-grafted plant is preferable. This is one of many cultivars of *P. pungens;* others include 'Aurea', which has golden leaves and 'Caerulea', which has bluish white leaves.

PINUS

PINE

This northern hemisphere genus comprises 80 variable evergreen conifers, between 6 and 60 m (about 18–190 ft) high. Many species are conical when immature, their crowns expanding in later life. The leaves, cylindrical needles up to 45 cm (about 18 in) long, are erect when young and develop in clustered whorls of 2, 3 or 5. Upright yellow-red male catkins and female flowers appear on the same tree. The latter develop into scaled seed-bearing cones, borne singly or in bunches depending upon type. Preferred habitats range from cold high altitudes to subtropical coasts, some fully hardy species growing in

difficult positions such as wind-swept cliffs. All enjoy full sun. Prune young trees' candle-like young shoots if necessary to control shape; propagate from seed or by grafting. Prone to leafroller caterpillars. Pines are grown for their softwood, oil and resin.

P. bungeana

LACE-BARK PINE

This native evergreen tree of China grows to a height of 30 m (about 95 ft) with a spread of 5 m (about 15 ft). It has a conical crown and pale, flaking bark, while the leaves are smooth, rigid, flattened needles. The cones are oval and may be solitary or paired. It prefers an open, sunny position in alkaline soils.

P. densiflora

JAPANESE RED PINE

This Japanese species grows quickly, averaging 15–25 m (about 50–80 ft), with a level crown. It has a contorted trunk and limbs, and shiny green foliage. Its yellow-purple cones are 5 cm (about 2 in) in diameter. Fully hardy, it prefers moderate climates.

P. nigra

BLACK PINE

This variable species from southern Europe is more commonly grown in two forms. *P. nigra maritima* (Corsican pine), a narrowly columnar tree to 30 m (about 95 ft), is tolerant of pollution. Preferring warm summers, it will grow in most soils. It has grey-green twisted needles in pairs and mid-brown pointed cones. It is mainly grown for timber.

Pinus bungeana

P. nigra nigra (Austrian pine) is broad crowned and dense, up to 30 m (about 95 ft) tall, with long dark green needles grouped in whorls. It grows well in exposed situations, especially in chalky soils.

P. palustris

PITCH PINE

This evergreen tree native to the south-eastern USA has bright green, slender, 18 cm (about 7½ in) needles and reddish brown, scaly, spiny cones. It grows to a height of 33 m (about 105 ft). It prefers damp but well-drained soils in an open, sunny position.

P. pinea

STONE PINE, ITALIAN STONE PINE

This attractive species grows 10–18 m (about 30–60 ft) tall and is native to southern Europe and Asia Minor. Its distinctive convex crown spreads from a short, stout trunk. The paired rigid needles are deep green; blue-green when immature. The large, globular cones mature to lustrous brown and produce edible nut-like seeds. Frost-hardy.

Pinus pinea

Pinus densiflora

Pinus strobus

Pinus radiata

P. ponderosa

WESTERN YELLOW PINE, BIG PINE, BULL PINE

A tall conifer, to 30 m (about 95 ft) with a conical crown, this species is native to the western USA. Its yellow-brown bark splits into large plates, and it has 25 cm (about 10 in) long, dark green to grey, sharp needles growing in threes. The distinctive, egg-shaped, dark brown cones, around 10 cm (about 4 in) long, have spines on the scales when ripe. Its close-textured wood is yellow.

P. radiata

syn. *P. insignis*

MONTEREY PINE, RADIATA PINE

The fastest growing pine, this species is commonly grown for its timber as well as its shelter and shade. It grows 25 m (about 80 ft) or more, its conical shape maturing into a broad, flat crown. Silky green needles, grouped in threes, grow up to 15 cm (about 6 in) long. Its long-lasting fruit is yellow and irregularly egg-shaped. This frost-hardy species is easy to grow, given full sun and sufficient water.

P. strobus

EASTERN WHITE PINE, WEYMOUTH PINE

This fast-growing, frost-resistant conifer was introduced to Britain from North America in the eighteenth century and named for Lord Weymouth. It can grow to 35 m (about 110 ft) and has a conical habit with an open crown. The short, blue-green needles grow in fives. Its pointed cones are pale green when immature, ripening to brown and often covered with white resin. Although an excellent timber tree, it is prone to rust disease and does not tolerate pollution.

P. sylvestris

SCOTS PINE, SCOTCH PINE

A native of Europe and Asia, this beautiful evergreen can grow to 30 m (about 95 ft), showing a conical habit which broadens into a flat top with maturity. The grey-green paired needles are stiff and twisted, and the young green cones ripen after 2 years to a brown colour and release winged seeds. The distinctive bark is a warm orange-red on the upper trunk, grey and fissured at the base. The wood is excellent for making furniture and fencing, among other products.

P. thunbergiana

syn. *P. thunbergii*

JAPANESE BLACK PINE

Growing to 40 m (about 130 ft), this native of Japan and Korea changes from a conical to a rounded shape with age. It has dark green, pointed and twisted paired needles, and the brown cones grow to 6 cm (about 2½ in) long. This is a good choice for a coastal position.

PISTACIA

chinensis

CHINESE PISTACHIO

This deciduous species, prized for its autumn/fall foliage, is native to Asia. A fast grower, it averages 5–12 m (about 15–37 ft), sometimes reaching 25 m (about 80 ft). Low and spreading or erect and dome-shaped, it has narrow, fern-like

Pinus thunbergiana

Pinus sylvestris

Pinus ponderosa

leaves comprising 10 or more green leaflets. These turn vivid hues of red, yellow and purple in autumn/fall. Tiny red flowers are followed by red spherical seed pods that ripen to blue. This half-hardy tree prefers moderate climates. It will flourish in most soil types, given full sun, and withstands pruning. Propagate from seed in autumn/fall and winter, cuttings in summer. The European species, *P. vera*, bears the famous pistachio nut.

PITTOSPORUM
eugenioides
TARATA

This evergreen, columnar tree, native to New Zealand, grows to a height of 6 m (about 18 ft) with a spread of 3 m (about 9 ft). It belongs to a genus of evergreen trees and shrubs that are grown for their ornamental foliage and fragrant flowers. Honey-scented, star-shaped, pale yellow flowers are produced in small clusters in spring. The leaves, 10 cm (about 4 in) long, are narrowly oval, wavy edged and a glossy dark green. It is adaptable to most soils but prefers an open, sunny position and is drought and frost resistant. In cold regions, grow species against north- or west-facing walls. Propagate from seed in autumn/fall or spring or from semi-ripe cuttings in summer. The cultivar 'Variegatum' has dark green leaves with white margins. Some species, such as *P. crassifolium* and *P. ralphii*, make good wind-resistant hedges in mild coastal areas.

PLATANUS
PLANE TREE, SYCAMORE

This diverse deciduous genus of wide-crowned species reaches up to 45 m (about 145 ft). The scaly yellow, brown and white trunks are often buttressed or multiple, the lower branches are arching and gnarled. The wide, maple-like foliage consists of 5 lobes and ranges from light green to dark green. Insignificant flowers are followed in autumn/fall by hanging bunches of large, spherical fruit. Trees vary from fully hardy to frost-hardy, growing in climates from cold to warm-temperate. All like full sun. Some species prefer rich, well-drained soil; others like arid conditions. Propagate from cuttings, or from seed in autumn/fall.

P. × acerifolia
syn. *P. × hybrida, P. × hispanica*
LONDON PLANE

This popular hybrid, from Asia's *P. orientalis* and North America's *P. occidentalis*, is robust and fast growing, reaching up to 25 m (about 80 ft) with a wide, spreading crown. Shiny, pale green leaves with 3 to 5 lobes are 25 cm (about 10 in) wide. Little red flowers appear in pendent clusters, followed by paired spherical fruit. Grow in full sun in deep, fertile, well-drained soil. This tree is able to withstand extremes in temperature and substantial pollution. It is a common sight in England, flanking suburban avenues.

P. orientalis
CHINAR, ORIENTAL PLANE

Native to an area stretching from southern Europe to India, this tree is valued for its hardiness, shade and beauty. It grows fast, to 25 m (about 80 ft) or more. Smooth, lustrous light green leaves with 5 to 7 deeply cut teeth are up to 20 cm (about 8 in) wide. Green pendent flower clusters are followed by uneven seed pods hanging in clusters of 2 to 6. Grow in deep, cool, moist, rich soil in an open, sunny position. The species has a strong tendency to sucker and requires frequent pruning.

PODOCARPUS
totara
TOTARA, MAHOGANY PINE

This diverse ornamental genus of evergreen conifers for cool to warm-temperate climates is native to Australia, New Zealand, South America and South Africa. Species vary from low and spreading to slender and erect. *P. totara*, valued for its timber, gradually reaches up to 20 m (about 65 ft) and sometimes more and has a thick, wide convex crown. Its little pointed leaves are deep green-brown, narrow and rigid. Small red cones like berries are 1 cm (about ½ in) in diameter and are borne individually on short stems (*Podocarpus* means 'footed stalk'). This tree is frost-hardy, preferring cool climates, and prefers a position in full sun or partial shade in most soils types. *P. t.* 'Aureus' is much admired for its golden-tinted leaves.

POPULUS
POPLAR, ASPEN, COTTONWOOD

These deciduous trees, native to the northern hemisphere and related to the willows, are valued for their rapid growth, autumn/fall foliage and yellow softwood. Reaching 27–40 m (about 86–130 ft), they are very fast growing. Brightly coloured catkins appear in the leaf axils in late winter to early spring; leaves turn yellow in autumn/fall. These fully hardy trees like warm weather but will not survive in arid conditions. Plant in rich, moisture-retentive soil with full sun. Propagate from cuttings in summer or by grafting. Some species have a strong tendency to sucker, and are unsuitable for small gardens. Some are prone to canker and fungi. Cultivated for over 2000 years, the Lom-bardy poplar lined Roman roads, and was called *arbor populi*, the tree of the people.

P. alba
SILVER POPLAR, WHITE POPLAR,
SILVER-LEAF POPLAR, ABELE

This central European species grows extremely quickly to 15–25 m (about 50–80 ft), with a very attractive conical shape and silky grey bark. The leaves have 3 to 5 deeply cut lobes with wavy edges. Deep green on top, frosty white and downy underneath, they turn a beautiful golden yellow in autumn/fall. This tree likes alkaline soil and suckers very strongly.

P. deltoides
COTTONWOOD, NECKLACE POPLAR

This temperate species grows rapidly to 15–30 m (about 50–95 ft). Lofty with an expansive crown, it is valued for its timber and appearance. The large cordate leaves are bright green, and turn dull yellow in autumn/fall. Pendent yellow and red catkins appear in spring.

Pistacia chinensis

Platanus × acerifolia

Podocarpus totara 'Aureus'

Populus alba

Platanus orientalis   *Populus deltoides*

A Field Trip to the Coromandel Peninsula

New Zealand's pohutukawa (*Metrosideros excelsa*) has the ability to grow where no other tree can—along the coastal cliffs of the hills, bays and beaches of northern New Zealand. The spreading roots of this tree allow it to grow on rock faces and other precipitous sites, totally out of the reach of any competition. To the people of northern New Zealand, a beach without a pohutukawa is considered no beach at all—such is the character that these trees add to the coastal landscape.

The pohutukawa's Latin name is *Metrosideros excelsa*— 'ironwood of excellence'—a reference to the density of the pohutukawa's hard, reddish brown wood. Also known as the New Zealand Christmas tree, the pohutukawa flowers from December to early January, at the height of the summer holiday season. The display of crimson-red flowers brightens the headlands, cliffs and bays with splashes of colour that are visible for many miles. The summer climate here is mild and pleasant, rarely getting too hot or too cold—about 25°C (about 77°F) during the day. This, with bright sunshine, provides perfect conditions both for trees and holiday makers.

Across the wide Hauraki Gulf, 40 km (about 25 miles) east of Auckland, lies the Coromandel Peninsula, home to some of the greatest pohutukawa groves. Short heavy downpours

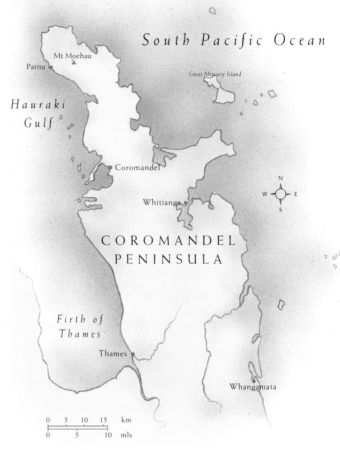

Pohutukawa flowers add colour to coastal areas in summertime.

of rain occur regularly throughout the year, creating lush growth and almost perfect conditions for these trees. From time to time harsh storms lash the coast with salt-laden air. Winds buffet the trees, crashing the odd tree on its side, where generally they regrow with a new crop of branches.

The old miners' road between Thames and Coromandel twists and bends along the coast at the foot of the steep hills and cliffs, only a few metres above the high-tide mark. It runs around many rocky bays with oyster-encrusted rocks and 400- to 800-year old shady pohutukawas at every point.

Once you reach Coromandel—a distance of 54 km (about 34 miles) from Thames—continue up the coast to the base of Mount Moehau. Here, and right along the coastal cliffs and bays, are some of the largest pohutukawas to be found any-where. At times they grow into huge spreading trees with great branches that bend and twist to the ground, where they re-root, encouraging even more growth. In many places the road passes under their spreading branches.

Near the base of Mount Moehau is the small hamlet of Paritu which, together with Fantail Bay just to the north, is one of the best places to view the pohutukawa. Standing slightly out to sea on the granite quarry wharves at Paritu, you can look back at the stony beaches and rocky bays, along which the pohutukawas go right down to the water's edge. Granite rocks covered in lichen add to the beauty of the coast-line. At Christmas, you will see bright red carpets on the ground under the trees, where the stamens have fallen.

The crimson flowers drip with nectar, attracting song-birds such as the tui and bellbird. The introduced starlings also enjoy the nectar; the pollen from the flowers often turns their chests yellow, creating great confusion as to their ident-ity. The road continues on until you reach Fantail Bay, where you look out to sea through the pohutukawas' contorted trunks. Fantails flit and dart about, in and under the canopy, eating insects attracted to the rich nectar in the flowers. Bees swarm to the trees, creating a persistent buzzing sound.

Other animals, plants and insects find a haven in these trees. Epiphytes festoon old pohutukawas, with great clumps of *Collospermum hastatum,* a lily-like plant, growing in the crown along the branches. *Pyrrosia serpens,* a climbing fern, scrambles up the trunks. After dark, Australian brush-tailed possums come out to devour the fresh pohutukawa shoots, killing many trees in the process. Wetas—large tree-climbing insects of the cricket family—also come out at night to eat the leaves, making loud scraping noises.

If you leave the coast road and travel inland, you will see a cousin of the pohutukawa, the northern rata (*Metrosideros robusta*). This is a tree of the inland forests, often germinating as an epiphyte high on the crown of old trees. Where the pohutukawa and rata meet—most often in the steep, hilly country of Coromandel Peninsula—hybrids are produced, sharing characteristics of both trees.

To the Maori people, the pohutukawa has been esteemed from time immemorial. At Cape Reinga, the furthest prom-ontory of land at the northern tip of New Zealand, lies the most sacred pohutukawa tree of all. According to the Maori legend it is from this point that the souls of the dead depart from this world into the life hereafter.

Metrosideros excelsa

Metrosideros

The genus *Metrosideros* consists of 20 or more species of trees and shrubs, some creeping over rocks or up trees with clinging roots. About half the species are found only in New Zealand while most of the others occur on other Pacific Islands, as far east as Hawaii. Few apart from the pohutukawa have become widely cultivated.

The beautiful pohutukawa is generally called the 'New Zealand Christmas tree' in other countries, even in the northern hemisphere where it flowers from about May to July. It is only suited to milder temperate climates.

Although the twisted, contorted shape of the stout trunk and branches is too irregular to be of any great commercial value, the pohutukawa is most highly prized for sea-shore planting. In South Africa, Australia and California it has been found to be one of the most resistant of all small trees to con-tinued exposure to salt spray. Popular for beachfront parks and espla-nades, it will grow at reasonable speed into a low tree with a dense, rounded canopy, even in quite poor soils such as dune sands, as long as the ground is not prone to waterlogging.

Metrosideros excelsa

Many new varieties are being produced; these have been selected for their growth and vigour. However, planted trees seldom rival those on the New Zealand seashores in the abundance of flowers and richness of colour.

P. nigra 'Italica'
syn. P. pyramidalis
LOMBARDY POPLAR

This slender, stately cultivar, said to have been developed by the ancient Romans, grows extremely quickly up to 30 m (about 95 ft). Its rhomboid-oblong leaves mature from reddish brown to lustrous green before turning deep golden in autumn/fall. Red catkins appear on male trees in spring. Fully hardy, it requires deep, damp soil, full sun and an open location.

P. tremuloides
QUAKING ASPEN

A 20 m (about 65 ft) fast growing deciduous tree from North America, grown for its graceful habit and the way the dark green leaves flutter in the slightest breeze. They turn brilliant gold in autumn/fall. Fully hardy, it likes sun and moist soil.

Prunus × amygdalo-persica

Prunus sargentii

Prunus mume

PRUNUS
CHERRY, PEACH, PLUM

This large genus contains over 200 evergreen or deciduous shrubs and trees and thousands of cultivars. They are grown either for their fruit or for their ornamental foliage, flowers and bark. Reaching 5–6 m (about 15–18 ft), their shape is inversely conical. Members of the Rosaceae family, they bear sweetly scented single or double rose-like flowers with 5 petals ranging from white to scarlet. All species are fully hardy and thrive in most well-drained soils. The evergreens like partial shade; prune in spring and propagate from cuttings in summer and autumn/fall. Deciduous types (useful for hedges) prefer full sun; prune after flowering and propagate from seed in autumn/fall or cuttings in winter. Bud or graft cultivars in spring and autumn/fall.

Prunus × blireiana

Prunus cerasifera 'Nigra'

P. × amygdalo-persica
POLLARD ALMOND

This very attractive, squat deciduous hybrid is valued for its flowers. It reaches up to 6 m (about 18 ft) and has deep green lanceolate leaves with finely serrated margins. Broad, deep pink flowers with protruding purplish red stamens appear on leafless branches at the end of winter; inedible green almonds follow. This hybrid withstands arid conditions. Prune while in bloom and guard against peach curly-leaf fungus.

P. × blireiana
DOUBLE-ROSE CHERRY-PLUM

This popular deciduous hybrid grows up to 4 m (about 12 ft). It has a squat appearance with slender arching branches and red-purple elliptical leaves that change to golden brown in autumn/fall. Its red-pink, semi-double flowers, blooming in early spring, are fragrant and very attractive.

P. cerasifera 'Nigra'
PURPLE-LEAF PLUM

This well-known cultivar is admired for its impressive foliage and flowers. It has an attractive dome shape, reaching 5–10 m (about 15–30 ft) tall. Its leaves, a vibrant deep purple, stay bright until they fall. In early spring lots of pretty pink or white flowers bloom, one to each slender stem. These are followed by the cherry-plum fruit, which is edible when cooked. Plant in light to medium, well-drained soil. This tree tolerates arid conditions.

P. incisa
FUJI CHERRY, CUT-LEAVED CHERRY

A small, deciduous tree originating in Japan, this species can reach 10 m (about 30 ft). Its oval, sharply toothed leaves are red when young, darkening to green in summer and then orange-red in autumn/fall. The pink buds, opening to white or pale pink, appear in early spring before the leaves. The form 'Praecox' flowers in early winter.

P. mume
UME, JAPANESE APRICOT

This small deciduous tree from China, Korea and Japan grows to about 6 m (about 18 ft). It bears abundant flowers in late winter or early spring before the leaves appear. The species is white or pink, but double-flowered cultivars in white or light or deep pink are popular. This is the 'plum blossom' which is such a favourite subject with Chinese and Japanese painters because it flowers while snow is still on the ground. It is fast growing, and trees rapidly assume quaintly gnarled trunks and branches. Frost-hardy, it prefers cool-temperate climates.

P. sargentii
SARGENT CHERRY, FLOWERING CHERRY

One of the most spectacular of the flowering cherries, this native of Japan and Korea is a spreading tree to 20 m (about 65 ft) when mature. Its slender leaves are bronze-red when young and open at the same time as the clusters of blush pink flowers. The leaves turn a deep

Populus tremuloides

Populus nigra 'Italica'

green and then, being one of the first trees to change colour, they turn a brilliant red and yellow in early autumn/fall.

P. serrulata
JAPANESE FLOWERING CHERRY

Originating in east Asia, this decidu-ous species is the parent of many cultivars. It grows quickly, up to 10 m (about 30 ft), with a dome shape and spreading habit. Its scaly bark is a glossy reddish brown. The finely toothed glossy leaves turn from deep green to orange and yellow in autumn/fall. Long-stemmed termi-nal clusters of white unscented flowers appear in spring, followed by little spherical fruit, brownish red ripening to black; but the gar-den varieties rarely fruit. It prefers cooler climates. Avoid pruning where possible.

P. serrulata 'Amanogawa'

This erect deciduous flowering cherry grows up to 10 m (about 30 ft) high and 4 m (about 12 ft) wide. Its deep green, sharply elliptical leaves turn reddish orange in au-tumn/fall. Light pink, semi-double perfumed flowers appear at the end of spring.

P. serrulata 'Mount Fuji'
syn. *P. serrulata* 'Kojima',
P. s. 'Shirotae'

Reaching up to 7 m (about 21 ft) high and wide, this small spreading cultivar has a broad crown and slightly arching branches. Green, lacy edged leaves appear in early spring and turn orange-red in au-tumn/fall. Large, scented white flowers, single or semi-double, appear in mid-spring.

P. 'Shirofugen'
JAPANESE CHERRY

This strong-growing, wide-spread-ing garden hybrid reaches 10 m (about 30 ft) high and 15 m (about 50 ft) wide. It has copper-bronze young leaves which turn to red and orange in autumn/fall. The double flowers appear in clusters. They are pink in the bud, open to white in late spring and then fade to dark pink.

Prunus subhirtella 'Pendula'

P. subhirtella 'Pendula'
HIGAN CHERRY, ROSEBUD CHERRY

This deciduous spreading tree has a wide crown and arching branches. It grows 6–12 m (about 18–37 ft) tall and develops sharply elliptical, serrated deep green leaves which turn yellow in autumn/fall. Light pink flowers, predominantly single with 5 petals, appear from winter to early spring before the foliage. These are followed by little spheri-cal brown-red fruit. This cultivar prefers cooler climates. The cultivar 'Autumnalis' is more reliably winter flowering.

P. 'Taihaku'
GREAT WHITE CHERRY

This vigorous, deciduous, spreading tree grows to 8 m (about 24 ft) with a spread of 10 m (about 30 ft). It has very large, single, pure white flowers which are borne in mid-spring and bronze-red, young leaves that mature to dark green.

P. × yedoensis
YOSHINO CHERRY

This Japanese hybrid is an elegant, fully hardy deciduous tree. It grows up to 8 m (about 24 ft) tall and spreads up to 10 m (about 30 ft) wide, with a convex crown and pendent limbs. White or light pink flowers with an almond fragrance open in early spring, preceding the deep green foliage. This tree prefers a cooler climate with full sun and well-drained soil. It is much planted in Washington DC.

Prunus × *yedoensis*

PSEUDOTSUGA
menziesii
syn. *P. douglasii, P. taxifolia*
DOUGLAS FIR

This majestic species, one of North America's most impressive conifers, grows 20–70 m (about 65–220 ft) in an attractive pyramid shape. It spreads to 9 m (about 27 ft). Its deeply grooved, grey-brown bark is set off by the bluish green foliage, which comprises needles 3 cm (about 1½ in) long, arranged in whorls. Immature leaves turn claret red in winter. The woody brown cones hang down and are 7–10 cm (about 3–4 in) long. This fully hardy tree prefers cold climates, though it will survive in warm weather. It grows quickly in fertile soil, especially if it is also cool, deep, moist and well drained. Plant in open spaces in full sun or partial shade; propagate from cold-treated seed or by grafting. The Douglas fir is America's leading Christmas tree. Its valuable timber is known as Oregon pine.

Prunus serrulata 'Mount Fuji'

Prunus serrulata

Prunus serrulata 'Amanogawa'

Prunus 'Taihaku'

Prunus 'Shirofugen'

Pseudotsuga menziesii

Pterocarya fraxinifolia

Pyrus calleryana

Quercus ilex

Pyrus salicifolia 'Pendula'

Quercus alba

PTEROCARYA

fraxinifolia

CAUCASIAN WINGNUT

This rapidly developing deciduous tree, native to the Caucasus and Iran, is a relative of the walnut. It grows up to 35 m (about 110 ft) with a spreading convex crown. Its fern-like, compound foliage consists of up to 20 lance-shaped leaflets. Pendent yellowish green chains of attractive male and female catkins appear in summer. These are followed by drooping clusters of green, winged nuts with red markings. This species prefers warm climates and waterside locations. Prune suckers frequently and propagate from cuttings or suckers in summer; seed in autumn/fall.

PYRUS

PEAR

This genus contains small, deciduous species native to Europe, Asia and Africa. They are valued for their foliage, flowers and edible fruit. Foliage is diverse, from ovate and hairy to linear and smooth, and in many species assumes brilliant colour in autumn/fall. White flowers are followed by plump fruit in various shades of brown, yellow and green. Species range from fully hardy to half-hardy and enjoy well-drained soil with full sun. Propagate from seed in autumn/fall; bud cultivars in summer, graft in winter.

P. calleryana

CHINESE PEAR, BRADFORD PEAR

This fully hardy Asian native grows up to 15 m (about 50 ft). It has shiny elliptical leaves that turn from deep green to red in autumn/fall. An abundance of white blossoms appear in mid- to late spring, followed by little brown fruit. A number of selected cultivars are available.

P. salicifolia 'Pendula'

SILVER PEAR, WEEPING SILVER PEAR, WILLOW-LEAF PEAR

Native to south-eastern Europe and the Caucasus, this fully hardy tree grows to 10 m (about 30 ft), with a domed shape and gracefully arching branches. The tasselled lanceolate foliage, similar to the willow's but silver-grey, emerges soon after the flower buds. Flat-topped clusters of small white flowers appear in abundance in spring, followed by small, yellowish brown fruit. It is frost-hardy but prefers a cool climate.

QUERCUS

OAK

This extremely diverse genus contains some 450 species of evergreen or deciduous trees and shrubs, mostly native to the northern hemisphere. Ranging from small and shrubby to very tall and erect, they grow slowly. Foliage varies from wide, multi-lobed and leathery to lustrous, thin and papery. All species bear acorns inside woody pods, which also differ from species to species: slender and sharp or stubby and flat; sleek-shelled or downy and rough. All species prefer cooler weather and deep, damp, well-drained soil. Some like alkaline soils and full sun; others prefer semi-shade. Propagate from seed in autumn/fall—also a time to guard against oak-leaf miner. The heavily grained timber, moisture- and salt-resistant, is prized by boatbuilders and carpenters.

Q. agrifolia

CALIFORNIAN LIVE OAK

This evergreen species from the western USA can reach a height and spread of 15 m (about 50 ft). Its lustrous dark green leaves are stiff and sharply toothed. It is fully hardy, and enjoys full sun and moist soil.

Q. alba

AMERICAN WHITE OAK

This large deciduous tree can attain a height of 30 m (about 95 ft) and spread to 22 m (about 70 ft). Its shiny, deep green leaves have marked lobes and turn crimson in autumn/fall. It prefers a sunny position.

Q. ilex

HOLM OAK, EVERGREEN OAK, HOLLY OAK

Native to southern Europe, this round-headed, dense evergreen can grow to 28 m (about 90 ft). Its oval leaves are toothed (similar to holly) when young, but become entire with age, and are a lustrous dark green above and white and downy underneath. Frost-hardy, it grows well in an exposed position, particularly on the coast, and makes a good windbreak.

Q. macrocarpa
BUR OAK

This domed, spreading, deciduous species grows slowly to 20 m (about 65 ft). Its large, oblong, lobed leaves are a lustrous deep green, and take on hues of yellow and brown in autumn/fall. The acorn cup is covered with hairy scales.

Q. nigra
WATER OAK

The water oak is a large deciduous tree which has an eventual height of 30 m (about 95 ft). The lustrous bright green leaves persist on the tree well into winter.

Q. palustris
PIN OAK, SPANISH OAK

Originating in North America, this expansive deciduous species is valued for its timber, shade and autumn/fall foliage. A fast grower, it averages 10–24 m (about 30–77 ft) in cultivation, and up to 40 m (about 130 ft) in the wild. Slim, arching branchlets bear glossy green foliage in spring. These heavily serrated oval leaves turn scarlet then glossy brown in autumn/fall and once dead endure until the following spring. Small, slim, globe-shaped acorns are half covered by their cup. This tree's dense root system means transplanting is quite easy, as long as plenty of earth is taken.

Q. robur
ENGLISH OAK, COMMON OAK

As a symbol of Britain, the English oak was widely planted throughout the British empire, in both suitable and unsuitable climates. This fully hardy species grows quickly, ranging widely in height between 10 and 35 m (about 30 and 110 ft), with an expansive crown and large, heavy branches. The leaves, inverted ovals

Quercus macrocarpa

with 6 to 12 serrations and 2 small auxiliary wing teeth, turn from deep green to golden brown in autumn/fall. Egg-shaped acorns are one-third covered by their cup and develop in small bunches on slender stems.

Q. rubra
syn. Q. borealis
RED OAK

This fast-growing, deciduous tree native to North America can reach 30 m (about 95 ft) and becomes large domed with maturity. Its alternate matt green leaves are deeply lobed and turn crimson or reddish brown in autumn/fall. This is not a tree for the city as it needs an open position to reach its potential.

Q. suber
CORK OAK

Valued for its dense soft bark, used to make cork, this moderately frost-hardy evergreen has a broad, spreading crown up to 15 m (about 50 ft) high. The glossy deep green leaves are egg-shaped and serrated

Quercus suber

Quercus robur

with a fleecy underside. Single oval acorns are half covered by their cup.

RHUS
SUMACH, TOXICODENDRON

This genus contains over 150 species of small deciduous trees, shrubs and climbers valued for their vibrant autumn/fall foliage. Species are fully frost-hardy and require full sun. *Toxicodendron* means 'poison tree'—avoid contact with bare skin as they contain a toxic resin.

R. succedanea
syn. Toxicodendron succedaneum
WAX TREE

This popular species grows to 9 m (about 27 ft). Immature foliage has a purple tint, turning shiny deep green before finishing with a splendid autumn/fall display of deep red, yellow and purple. Yellow-green flowers appear in thick terminal clusters from the leaf axils, followed by big drooping bunches of spherical fruit that ripen to brown. These are a source of wax.

Quercis nigra

Quercus rubra

Quercus palustris

Rhus typhina 'Laciniata'

Rothmannia capensis

Robinia pseudoacacia 'Frisia'

Robinia pseudoacacia 'Frisia'

Salix alba

Salix babylonica

R. typhina 'Laciniata'
syn. *R. typhina* 'Dissecta'
STAG'S HORN SUMACH, VELVET SUMACH

This North American species has an expansive crown and grows quickly to 3–6 m (about 9–18 ft). Its compound pinnate foliage has up to 30 light green, tasselled leaflets which turn beautiful shades of red and orange in autumn/fall. Dense clusters of little green-white flowers appear in summer, followed by red seed pods in woolly bunches. This species prefers temperate climates and has a strong tendency to sucker. The leaves are a source of tannin.

ROBINIA
BLACK LOCUST

This deciduous genus contains 20 species of trees and shrubs, native to North America but now common worldwide. They grow up to 25 m (about 80 ft) with a rounded shape and spreading habit. The scented flowers and fruit are typical of the Leguminoseae family, the peas resembling those of the locust tree (hence the common name). The species will survive in a broad range of temperatures and soils but dislikes saturated soil. Plant in full sun and protect the fragile limbs from strong winds. Propagate from seed and suckers in autumn/fall, cultivars by grafting. The genus was named after seventeenth-century herbalist Jean Robin, who first cultivated it.

R. pseudoacacia
BLACK LOCUST, FALSE ACACIA

This erect hardwood timber tree grows 10–15 m (about 30–50 ft) and has a tough grooved trunk and thorny branches. Its fern-like leaves, composed of up to 23 elliptical leaflets, turn yellow in autumn/fall. Pendent clusters of scented, wisteria-like flowers appear in spring, followed by sleek seed pods that endure until the following spring. This species has a strong suckering habit; avoid planting near pathways.

R. pseudoacacia 'Frisia'

This expansive deciduous cultivar is thornless and grows up to 15 m (about 50 ft) high and 10 m (about 30 ft) wide. Its feather-like foliage has rounded leaflets and changes from gold in spring to yellowish orange in autumn/fall. Plant this fully hardy tree in well-drained soil with full sun.

ROTHMANNIA
capensis
WILD GARDENIA, COMMON ROTHMANNIA

This small tree, native to South Africa, is related to *Gardenia*. It can reach a height of 5 m (about 15 ft) and spread of 3 m (about 9 ft) and has glossy green leaves. It is valued for its bell-shaped, scented flowers, in cream to yellow with reddish-brown throat markings, up to 4 cm (about 2 in) long. These are followed by round fruits, 60–70 mm (about 2½ in) in diameter. Half-hardy, it will develop fairly quickly in rich, well-drained, neutral to acid soil, and full sun or partial shade. Frost-tender, it is suited to tropical and subtropical areas. Propagate from seed in spring or semi-ripe cuttings in summer.

SALIX
WILLOW, OSIER

Originating in the northern hemisphere, these 250 deciduous species of trees and shrubs grow to 10–25 m (about 30–80 ft) with convex crowns, rough, twisted trunks and weeping branches. Excellent shade trees, their narrow, tassel-like foliage often drapes along the ground. Pendent male and female catkins usually develop on different trees and may be slender and soft or thick and leathery. Trees vary from fully to frost-hardy and love waterside locations, where eroded banks benefit from their strong suckering habit. They will grow in all except arid soils and require full sun, or partial shade in hot regions. Prune every two years; propagate from cuttings in summer and winter. Watch for caterpillars, gall mites, aphids and canker. The high quality timber has been used in the manufacture of cricket bats, whips and baskets.

S. alba
WHITE WILLOW

This fast-growing though rather short-lived deciduous tree from Europe reaches to about 10 m (about 30 ft) tall, but it is often pollarded to gain long, flexible shoots for basket making. The leaves are lance-shaped and turn yellow rather fitfully in autumn/fall. This is a popular tree for wet ground, holding riverbanks and the like, but its roots are greedy so it is not very popular as a garden tree. Cricket bats are made from the wood of *S. a. caerulea*. Both are fully hardy.

S. babylonica
WEEPING WILLOW, NAPOLEON'S WILLOW

This very attractive, popular tree is native to China and grows up to 15 m (about 50 ft). It has a broad dome and erect branches that support distinctively arching branchlets. The light green lanceolate leaves, brushing the ground, are slender and thinly lobed. This temperate species will grow in most conditions if planted by waterways. The name comes from the unlikely story that these were the trees growing in Babylon under which the Hebrews sat and wept.

Schinus areira

Salix matsudana 'Tortuosa'

Salix 'Chrysocoma'

Sassafras albidum

Schinus terebinthifolia

Sapium sebiferum

Salix caprea

S. caprea
PUSSY WILLOW, GOAT WILLOW,
GREAT WILLOW

Native to Asia, this dense shrub or
tree grows 3–10 m (about 9–30 ft)
tall. The rounded deep green leaves
are 5–10 cm (about 2–4 in) long
with a fleecy grey underside. Decorative grey male catkins with yellow
stamens appear in spring before the
foliage. This species grows well in
brackish marshlands but its very
strong suckering habit can cause
problems in the garden.

S. 'Chrysocoma'
syn. S. alba 'Tristis'
GOLDEN WEEPING WILLOW

This French cultivar, a hybrid between S. alba and S. babylonica,
grows rapidly up to 18 m (about
60 ft) with a spread of some 20 m
(about 65 ft). Its pendent limbs
produce long, thin, arching yellow
branchlets that droop to the ground.
Lance-shaped, yellow-green leaves
turn golden yellow in autumn/fall.
Both male and female flowers develop on the same tree. This fully
hardy tree requires full sun and
moist soil to thrive.

S. matsudana 'Tortuosa'
CORKSCREW WILLOW,
DRAGON CLAW WILLOW

This popular northern Asian tree
resembles S. babylonica, but is
smaller growing to only 15 m
(about 50 ft). Its branchlets and
shiny green leaves are tortuous and
twisted (as the cultivar name implies). Catkins appear at the same
time as the lanceolate, serrated foliage. This fully hardy tree prefers
damp soil and full sun.

SAPIUM
sebiferum
CHINESE TALLOW TREE, WAX TREE

This variable deciduous tree, native
to China and Japan, grows 6–13 m
(about 18–40 ft) tall. Its thick
crown is composed of pointed
leaves, oval to diamond, which turn
a beautiful lustrous crimson or orange-red in autumn/fall. Slender
yellow catkins are followed by
white, waxy fruit, their 3 seeds held
together with wax. This warm-
temperate tree will not survive below 5°C (about 40°F); the foliage is
at its most vivid in hotter areas.
Plant this species in rich, porous
soil in a position with full sun.
Prune if necessary and propagate
from seed in spring, semi-ripe
cuttings in summer. Wax from the
fruit of S. sebiferum is used to make
soap and candles.

SASSAFRAS
albidum
SASSAFRAS

This erect, deciduous North American native reaches up to 6 m
(about 18 ft), widening to 1 m
(about 3 ft) in maturity. The foliage, either egg-shaped or with 3
deep lobes, turns from lustrous deep
green to striking red and yellow in
autumn/fall. Inconspicuous yellow-
green flowers bloom in spring, followed by blue fruit. This fully hardy
species likes full sun or partial shade
and rich, porous, slightly acid soil.
Propagate from seed or suckers in
autumn/fall, or from root cuttings in
winter. Sassafras oil is extracted
from the bark and roots of these
trees.

SCHINUS

This genus consists of about 28
species of evergreen trees and
shrubs, usually grown for their
foliage and as shade trees. Half-
hardy, they prefer a sunny position
with some protection from winds.
Plant in moist, well-drained, well-
composted soil. Propagate from
semi-ripe cuttings in summer or
seed in spring.

S. areira
syn. S. molle
PERUVIAN PEPPER TREE, PEPPER TREE,
PEPPERCORN TREE, MOLLE, PIRUL, MASTIC

Native to South America, this handsome evergreen grows quickly to
15 m (about 50 ft) with a broad
rounded crown and elegant arching
branches. Pendulous, pinnate foliage
is a dark glossy green, comprising up
to 40 slender lance-shaped leaflets.
Little yellow flowers appear in
branched racemes from late winter to
summer, followed by drooping 'necklaces' of small, shiny, reddish pink
berries; these can be used as a substitute for pepper. This species
endures extreme drought but is
only half-hardy. The Incas planted
this tree to shade their royal roads.

S. terebinthifolia
BRAZILIAN PEPPER TREE

This stout, evergreen bushy small
tree is native to tropical America; it
can become a pest in some areas. It
has oval, mid- to deep green leaflets, 3 to 13 on each leaf, and bears
panicles of insignificant greenish
flowers. Dense clusters of round,
orange berries follow the bloom,
but only if male and female plants
have been grown together. This
species grows to a height of 8–15
m (about 24–50 ft) with a spread
of 5 m (about 15 ft).

Sophora microphylla

Sequoiadendron giganteum

Sophora japonica

Sciadopitys verticillata

Sequoia sempervirens

Sophora tetraptera

Schotia brachypetela

SCHOTIA
brachypetela
WEEPING BOER-BEAN, TREE FUCHSIA

Originating in subtropical South
Africa, this erect or compact semi-
evergreen grows 6–12 m (about
18–37 ft) tall. It has fern-like foliage,
which in colder climates is shed
before the tree blossoms in spring.
The shiny, deep crimson flowers have
prominent stamens and develop in
thick clusters. They produce an
abundance of nectar irresistible to
parrots (hence 'parrot tree'). This
half-hardy tree is best suited to hot
climates and, with regular watering,
will grow in most soils. Prune saplings to encourage an erect shape.
Propagate from heat-treated seed;
move small plants with caution.

SCIADOPITYS
verticillata
JAPANESE UMBRELLA PINE, UMBRELLA PINE,
PARASOL PINE

Native to Japan, this fully hardy
evergreen conifer is valued for its
perfect pyramid shape and unusual
foliage. It grows very slowly up to
12 m (about 37 ft) in cultivation,
and up to 40 m (about 130 ft) in the
wild. Its horizontal open spirals of
dark green needles look like the ribs
of an umbrella. Ovate woody cones
with numerous wide, curved scales
mature for two years before dispers-
ing their seeds. This tree prefers
cold mountain locations with damp,
acid soil and will not tolerate lime
or urban smog. Plant in a protected
site in full (but not hot) sun and
water liberally. It will benefit from
yearly mulching with its composted
leaves. Propagate from seed and
transplant when young. The genus
name comes from two Greek words:
skias, 'shade', and pitys, 'fir tree'.

SEQUOIA
sempervirens
CALIFORNIAN REDWOOD, SEQUOIA

This tough evergreen conifer, native
to the western USA, is prized for its
timber. It averages 30 m (about
95 ft); much taller in the wild. It is
either pyramidal or columnar in
shape, with rigid branches.
Whorled foliage comprises 2 rows
of small, light green needles which
are narrow and slightly flattened,
with 2 frosty bands underneath.
Male and female flowers appear on
the same tree followed by rectangular
to obovate green cones, ripening to
deep brown. This tree will survive
in a wide range of climates; extremely cold weather may affect the
foliage but not the plant itself. Suckers should be pruned immediately
and general pruning is tolerated.
Redwoods are extremely long living,
with some specimens estimated to
be about 3500 years old. The genus
boasts the world's tallest tree, at
about 110 m (362 ft).

SEQUOIADENDRON
giganteum
syn. *Sequoia gigantea,*
Wellingtonia gigantea
BIG TREE, MAMMOTH TREE, WELLINGTONIA

This long-living evergreen conifer,
native to America's Sierra Nevada,
has an attractive triangular shape
and the broadest trunk of all known
species. This vigorous tree averages
20–50 m (about 65–160 ft) tall and,
like its redwood relative, grows taller
in the wild. Its bluish green needles
mature to brown and drape along the
ground during the first 50 years of
life, after which it develops no new
lower branches. This is one of the
largest and longest lived of all trees;
one specimen has been recorded as
3000 years old. These trees like
cool climates, full sun and damp
soil. Propagate from seed.

SOPHORA

This diverse and widespread genus
belongs to the Leguminoseae (pea)
family and contains semi-evergreen
and deciduous species. They are
valued for their shape, leaves and
flowers. They vary in height, 5–25
m (about 15–80 ft), and have thick
fern-like foliage with differing
numbers of oval leaflets. The pea-
like flowers hang in thick terminal
clusters during summer, generally
in shades of white and yellow.
Species vary from fully to frost-
hardy and prefer moderate temperatures. Plant in rich porous soil

with full sun. Pruning is tolerated.
Propagate deciduous species from
seed or cuttings in autumn/fall;
semi-evergreens from softwood
cuttings in summer.

S. japonica
PAGODA TREE, SCHOLAR TREE

Native to Japan, China and Korea,
this deciduous species grows 6–
15 m (about 18–50 ft) high and
wide. Its round crown is composed
of deep green foliage with up to 16
oval leaflets. Older trees bear big,
open clusters of little yellowish
white pea-like flowers in late summer, followed by green elliptical
seed pods. This fully hardy species
enjoys hot summers. The leaves of
S. japonica are said to have medicinal qualities.

S. microphylla
WEEPING KOWHAI

Originating in New Zealand, this
short, spreading evergreen grows to
3–5 m (about 9–15 ft) in height,
developing stiff branches with arching branchlets. These are covered
with glossy, feather-like leaves, composed of up to 40 leaflets with downy
undersides. In spring, pea-like, light
yellow flowers appear along pendent stems. This species is basically
frost-hardy but in cool climates
likes a sheltered spot. Plant in rich
soil with good drainage.

S. tetraptera
NORTH ISLAND KOWHAI

This semi-evergreen New Zealand
species varies between 5 and 10 m
(about 15 and 30 ft), a compact
shrub or broad triangular tree. It
has slender, deep green foliage with

up to 40 leaflets. Golden blooms with lacy margins appear in spring, followed by winged seed pods. It is moderately frost-hardy. *S. tetraptera* is the national flower of New Zealand.

SORBUS

This genus, a member of the Rosaceae family, has deciduous and semi-evergreen species native to Europe, North America and temperate Asia. Shrubs or trees, growing 9–27 m (about 27–86 ft), are valued for their foliage, timber and edible fruit. Leaves vary from green to plain deep purplish red, the deciduous species displaying intense autumn/fall colours. Little white 5-petalled flowers appear in spring, followed in summer by enduring pendent bunches of berries. These cool-climate trees range from frost-hardy to frost-tender, preferring full sun or partial shade and rich, moisture-retentive soil. Propagate by grafting in winter, from buds and cuttings in summer or seed in autumn/fall. Susceptible to fireblight. Some species' edible fruit is used to make cider.

S. aria
WHITEBEAM

This European deciduous tree grows quickly up to 15 m (about 50 ft) and spreads to 10 m (about 30 ft). The single, oval, saw-toothed leaves are frosty grey when immature, maturing to deep green with downy white undersides. Sprays of spring blossoms give way to oval fruit, dark red with brown markings.

Sorbus aria

S. aucuparia
ROWAN, MOUNTAIN ASH, QUICKBEAM

Originating in Europe and Asia, this erect broad-crowned tree grows 6–12 m (about 18–37 ft) tall and is valued for its flowers, foliage and edible fruit. These green pinnate leaves comprise up to 15 leaflets and change to yellowish red in autumn/fall. Big dense sprays of white spring blossom are followed by a profusion of elliptical orange-red summer berries, turning golden yellow in autumn/fall. The fruit is used to make Rowan jelly. This deciduous species is suited to most climates and should not be re-planted until of considerable size. The cultivar *S.* 'Beissneri' has attractive greenish gold foliage.

S. cashmiriana

A native of Kashmir, this spreading deciduous tree can attain a height of 9 m (about 27 ft), though it is often smaller. Its mid-green leaves are made up of 17–19 elliptical leaflets, and are grey-green underneath. The pendent clusters of white to pale pink flowers appear in early summer and are followed by 1 cm (about ½ in) wide globular white fruits, which endure into winter.

S. commixta
syn. *S. discolor* of gardens

A strong-growing deciduous native of Japan, this species has an erect habit when young but spreads with maturity. It grows to 10 m (about 30 ft) in height. The lustrous mid-green leaves have 6–7 pairs of oblong leaflets and take on bright red

Sorbus aucuparia

and orange hues in autumn/fall. White flowers in panicles 10 cm (about 4 in) wide appear in spring, and are followed by bright scarlet fruit.

S. hupehensis
CHINESE ROWAN

This small elegant Chinese species reaches up to 12 m (about 37 ft) and is good for small gardens. The bluish green deciduous foliage, with up to 17 slightly serrated leaflets, turns reddish orange in autumn/fall. Open sprays of spring blossom are replaced by big clusters of egg-shaped white fruit, pink in winter.

STUARTIA
syn. *Stewartia*

A member of the Theaceae family, this genus comprises 10 species of hardy, deciduous, flowering trees and shrubs which are grown for their blooms, autumn/fall colours and decorative peeling bark. Originally from Asia and the USA, they vary in height from 5–18 m (about 15–60 ft). Plant in well-drained, neutral to acid soil. They prefer a sunny to partially shaded position with a cool root run, and should not be moved. Propagate from seed in autumn/fall, or softwood heel cuttings in late summer. The genus is named for John Stuart, an eighteenth-century British prime minister.

S. ovata
syn. *S. pentagyna*
MOUNTAIN CAMELLIA

A native of North America, this small tree grows slowly to 5 m

(about 15 ft). Its mid-green, oval leaves are downy underneath, and turn yellow in early autumn/fall. The bowl-like flowers appear in mid-summer and are white with orange-yellow centres.

S. pseudocamellia
syn. *Stewartia pseudocamellia*
JAPANESE STEWARTIA

This deciduous Japanese native is valued for its foliage, flowers and decorative scaly bark. Compact or expansive, it reaches 6–12 m (about 18–37 ft) and has elliptical irregularly lobed leaves that turn attractive shades of yellow, red and purple in autumn/fall. Large, snow white, camellia-like flowers with dense yellow stamens appear in summer, followed by downy seed pods. Fully hardy; prefers moderate temperatures and rich acidic soil. Provide partial shade and protect from stiff winds. Propagate from seed in autumn/fall, cuttings in summer.

STYRAX
japonicus
SNOWBELL TREE

This deciduous spreading tree belongs to a genus consisting of about 130 evergreen and deciduous trees and shrubs which are native mainly to the tropical and warm-temperate zones of the northern hemisphere. It grows to 9 m (about 27 ft) high and wider still. The lustrous light green leaves are oval and tapered, while the white, star-shaped flowers that appear in early summer are particularly striking. The blooms are seen to best advantage if the tree is

Stuartia pseudocamellia

Sorbus hupehensis

Thuja occidentalis

Syringa reticulata

Taxus baccata

Taxodium distichum

Styrax japonicus

turn coppery brown in autumn/fall. Purplish brown female cones develop individually, the smaller male cones in bunches. 'Cypress humps'—protruding, cone-shaped mounds that help the tree breathe in swampy ground—often radiate from the roots. This fully hardy species loves water and does best in saturated soil or even shallow water with full sun. Propagate from seed and cut-tings; prune young trees to encourage symmetry. The valuable timber resists moisture and termites.

TAXUS
baccata
YEW

This long-living evergreen conifer originates in Europe, Africa and Asia. It grows slowly to some 15 m (about 50 ft) and almost double that in the wild, its irregular conical shape becoming level-crowned in maturity. Its slender needles are deep green with a greenish yellow underside and develop in typical whorls. Small pollen-rich bunches of male flowers and green globular female flowers develop on separate trees. Unusually, this conifer has no cones; the female flower develops instead into an individual seed partly enclosed in a fleshy red case. This frost-hardy tree likes full sun and tolerates pruning; it is greatly favoured for hedging and topiary. It propagates simply from seed and cuttings in spring and is prone to scale insects. The Irish yew is a narrowly upright cultivar of Irish origin. Both it and the regular type prefer moist climates.

THUJA
ARBORVITAE

This small genus comprises 5 species of evergreen conifers, native to North America or Asia. They grow up to 70 m (about 220 ft), gradually developing a pyramid shape. They have heavily grooved trunks and flat compound foliage. Woody green seed-bearing cones of varying size mature to brown before releasing their seeds. Trees tolerate pruning and will grow in most soils but prefer moderate climates and full sun. Propagate from seed or simply from cuttings. Several of the species are among the world's most valuable softwood timber trees, used extensively to build houses.

T. occidentalis
AMERICAN ARBORVITAE, WHITE CEDAR, TREE OF LIFE

This fully hardy North American native reaches up to 15 m (about 50 ft), its triangular shape becoming columnar in later life. Its bark is orange-brown and its aromatic foliage develops in flat V-shaped sprays of deep yellow-green scales

planted on raised ground. Grow this hardy species in well-drained but moist, neutral to acid soil in sun or partial shade. Propagate from seed or heel cuttings in summer. To retain the attractive shape of the tree, prune young specimens by removing all the stems apart from the strongest. With mature trees, take out the side and crossing branches to retain an open crown.

SYRINGA
reticulata

Belonging to a genus of deciduous trees and shrubs from the temperate areas of the northern hemisphere, this species can grow to 10 m (about 30 ft) and has a broad yet conical habit. Its bright green leaves are oval and tapered. The large, fragrant flowerheads of tubular, single, white flowers appear from early summer. Fully hardy, this species will thrive in a sunny to partly shaded position with deep, well-drained soil. Lilacs benefit from dead-heading when young, and should be pruned after flowering to retain their shape. Propagate from softwood cuttings, or by layering. As with all lilacs, watch for leaf miner, leaf spot and blight.

TAXODIUM
distichum
SWAMP CYPRESS, BALD CYPRESS

Originating in the southern USA, this deciduous conifer quickly reaches up to 50 m (about 160 ft), erect to broadly triangular with a level crown. Soft green spirals of slender leaves and shorter ovate scales appear on the same tree and

Thujopsis dolabrata

Tilia × petiolaris

Tilia tomentosa

Tilia × europaea

Thuja plicata, young tree

Tilia cordata

with blue-green undersides. Grow in well-drained, alkaline soil in an open, sunny position. Drought and frost resistant. This moderate-climate species is valued for its white softwood and general appearance.

T. plicata
WESTERN RED CEDAR, GIANT ARBORVITAE, WESTERN ARBORVITAE

Native to an area spreading from California to Alaska, USA, this species grows quickly to 15–30 m (about 50–95 ft), and up to 70 m (about 220 ft) in the wild. It has a spread of 5 m (about 15 ft). Triangular to columnar, it has brownish red, scaly bark and upstretched limbs. Sprays of shiny green scales, backed with silver, hang from their extremities. Its very small, erect cones open like flowers to disperse their seeds. It is frost-hardy. Its soft but durable timber is among the most sought after in the world. Propagate from seed or from cuttings between autumn/fall and winter.

THUJOPSIS
dolabrata

HIBA, MOCK THUJA

This handsome Japanese evergreen grows slowly to 6–14 m (about 18–45 ft). Pyramidal or low and spreading, this conifer is valued for its thick foliage: large, flat fans of shiny needles, dark green with frosted white undersides. Its little rounded cones are bluish grey and consist of fleshy scales. This frost-hardy tree prefers cool climates and damp soil. Prune to encourage shape or restrict size. Propagate from cuttings or cold-treated seed.

TILIA
LIME, LINDEN

This genus is made up of over 25 deciduous species native to Asia, Europe and North America grown for their flowers and stately habit. These elegant trees grow fast to 30 m (about 95 ft). They are generally upright with extremely wide, buttressed trunks and noticeable suckers. Their heart-shaped foliage has slightly saw-toothed, furled edges and frosted downy undersides. Five-petalled yellowish green tiny flowers appear in long racemes in spring to summer. The flowers are highly scented and they prove irresistible and sometimes deadly to bees. These fully hardy trees prefer cool weather and rich, porous soil. However, they will grow in most soil types, given regular water and full sun or partial shade. Propagate from seed in autumn/fall; some species and cultivars are propagated by grafting and layering in late summer. The versatile timber—a pale honey colour— is used for woodcarvings, musical instruments, clogs and blinds.

T. cordata
syn. *T. parviflora*
SMALL-LEAVED LIME

A handsome, deciduous tree with a narrow-domed head, this species can reach 30 m (about 95 ft). A European native, it has alternate, small, heart-shaped, dark green leaves that are sharply toothed with tufts of hair on the undersides. The fragrant yellow-white flowers appear in summer in pendent clusters. It prefers cool, deep, moist soils in an open, sunny position. This is a popular tree for lining avenues.

T. × europaea
COMMON LINDEN, COMMON LIME

Native to Europe, this quick-growing tree reaches 18–35 m (about 60–110 ft), erect at first and spreading in old age. The slightly serrated, cordate leaves are deep green on top, light green and smooth underneath. Terminal clusters of scented yellow-white flowers appear in late spring to early summer, followed by little spherical ribbed seed pods. The flowers can be dried and used to make linden tea.

T. × petiolaris
WEEPING SILVER LINDEN, PENDENT SILVER LIME, WEEPING LIME

This weeping tree, native to southern Europe and west Asia, reaches between 18 and 25 m (about 60 and 80 ft) high. It has a triangular shape which expands in old age. The pointed, cordate leaves are 5–10 cm (about 2–4 in) long, deep green on top and silver-felted underneath. Creamy yellow flowers bloom in terminal clusters, followed by bumpy, nut-like seed pods. Propagate from seed in autumn/fall or by layering.

T. tomentosa
SILVER LINDEN

This deciduous tree native to southern Europe can grow to 25 m (about 80 ft) with a spread of 4 m (about 12 ft). The green, heart-shaped leaves have irregularly serrated margins and a whitish undersurface. The fragrant yellowish white flowers occur in terminal clusters. It is adaptable to most soils in an open, sunny position and is frost resistant but drought-tender.

Ulmus glabra

Ulmus americana

Ulmus procera

TRISTANIOPSIS

laurina

syn. *Tristania laurina*

WATER GUM, KANOOKA

From the east coast of Australia, this small erect evergreen grows 5–15 m (about 15–50 ft) and has sleek light brown bark. Its thick rounded crown bears lance-shaped foliage up to 10 cm (about 4 in) long. Leaves are shiny deep green with a pale green verso and may turn red in cooler climates. During summer, terminal clusters of little vivid yellow flowers develop in the leaf axils. Half-hardy, it prefers full shade and damp, rich, well-drained soil. Prune when required and propagate from seed. Suitable for small gardens and hedges, the flowers make for fine honey.

TSUGA

canadensis

CANADIAN HEMLOCK, EASTERN HEMLOCK

This elegant evergreen conifer is native to North America and Asia. It is very changeable in colour and shape, but generally grows from 15 to 25 m (about 50 to 80 ft), often developing multiple upstretched trunks. The bark is dark and heavily grooved and the foliage is deep green, comprising two ranks of flat narrow leaves. These are lightly serrated and often twist to reveal silvery white stripes underneath. Pale brown, egg-shaped cones contain little winged seeds from which the tree is propagated. It is fully hardy. The 'hemlock' in the common name apparently derives from its leaves' resemblance to those of the poisonous plant.

ULMUS

ELM

This genus contains over 15 fully hardy species of deciduous trees and shrubs native to Asia, Europe and North America. The majestic, round-crowned trees have attained heights up to 50 m (about 160 ft). The elliptical foliage varies: from slender, deep green and shiny to broad, mid-green and roughly textured; heavily or finely serrated; with or without prominent parallel

Ulmus parvifolia

Tsuga canadensis

ribs. Inconspicuous flowers with reddish stalks but no petals appear in early spring. Thick clusters of greenish white pods, containing single winged seeds, develop at the ends of branches in summer. Plant these moderate-climate trees in rich, well-drained soil with full sun. Propagate from seed or cuttings or by grafting the numerous suckers. The timber is used to make rustic furniture. Many of England's finest specimens were wiped out by the deadly fungus, Dutch elm disease.

U. americana

AMERICAN WHITE ELM, WHITE ELM

Growing as wide as it does high, to 30 m (about 95 ft), this deciduous native of North America forms a domed crown with drooping, wide-spreading branches. The large, glossy leaves are lanceolate and toothed, and the attractive bark is grey with deep ridges. The flowers are small catkins. It prefers light to medium, well-drained soil in an open, sunny position.

U. glabra

syn. *U. montana*, *U. scabra*

WYCH ELM, SCOTS ELM

Shorter and broader than the English elm, this deciduous, oval-crowned tree grows to 30 m (about 95 ft). A native of northern Europe, it bears small purple flowers before its ovate, double-toothed, mid-green leaves appear. The rough leaves turn golden yellow in autumn/fall. Unlike other elms, it does not develop suckers, relying on winged fruit to reproduce. Its wood is red-brown in colour and is traditionally used for coffins.

U. parvifolia
CHINESE ELM

Native to China, Japan, Korea and Taiwan, this species grows fast to 10–15 m (about 30–50 ft). Its trunk and pendent branches are covered with decorative grey bark variegated with white and yellow-brown. Small, glossy, egg-shaped leaves are slightly serrated and atypically endure well into winter (in warmer climates, until the following spring). This frost-hardy species tolerates most climates but prefers warm weather. Propagate from seed or root cuttings in autumn/fall.

U. procera
ENGLISH ELM

This upright European species reaches up to 30 m (about 95 ft) high and spreads up to 15 m (about 50 ft) wide with a thick, rounded crown. It has dark, furrowed bark and wide, elliptical foliage. Seed pods, each containing one sterile seed, appear before the serrated leaves. These are deep green, textured above and felty beneath, turning yellow in autumn/fall. This fully hardy tree prefers moderate temperatures and is propagated from cuttings in summer or suckers in autumn/fall. With a very strong tendency to sucker, it is not recommended for small gardens.

U. procera 'Louis Van Houtte'
syn. U. glabra 'Lutescens'

This small elm has a thick rounded dome and grows up to 12 m (about 37 ft). Its vivid, light yellow foliage is lightly serrated and turns golden yellow-green in summer. This fully hardy tree requires full sun, well-drained soil and shelter from summer winds. Propagate by grafting on to non-suckering stock.

U. pumila
SIBERIAN ELM

This deciduous, spreading tree can reach 15 m (about 50 ft). Its dark green oval leaves are dentate.

UMBELLULARIA
californica
CALIFORNIA BAY, CALIFORNIA LAUREL, OREGON MYRTLE, PEPPERWOOD

This single-species North American genus is a valuable shade tree that reaches up to 25 m (about 80 ft). Changeable in habit, it varies from compact and dome-shaped in open coastal areas to large, broadly spreading and multi-trunked in damp forests. Its glossy, bright green leaves are lanceolate and aromatic when crushed. Little clusters of insignificant yellow blossoms are followed by small, inedible purple fruit. This frost-hardy species prefers cool climates and moist, shady locations. However, it is able to survive in full sun and even extended periods of drought, once fully established. The spicy leaves of *U. californica* are similar to bay leaves, but stronger, and may be substituted for them in cooking.

ZELKOVA
serrata
JAPANESE ELM

Native to Japan, this expansive deciduous tree rapidly reaches 12–18 m (about 37–60 ft). Erect, with sculpted limbs, it is valued for its shade and timber. The slender cordate foliage, similar to its relative the elm's, is fine-pointed and lightly serrated. Little inconspicuous green flowers, the males in clusters, appear in spring and are followed by enduring leathery fruit. This fully hardy species prefers cool weather, open spaces and some wind protection. Plant in deep, damp, well-drained soil and allow full sun. Propagate from seed in autumn/fall. The timber is highly regarded in Japan.

ZIZIPHUS
jujuba
syn. Zizyphus jujuba
CHINESE DATE, JUJUBE

This tree is native to an area stretching from south-eastern Europe to China. It grows quickly up to 15 m (about 50 ft) and ranges in habit from compact and shrubby to open and spreading. The leaves are rectangular to elliptical with angled teeth. Little creamy flowers develop in clusters in spring, succeeded by the lush, reddish orange fruit. Edible and sweet, they ripen in winter. Plant this frost-tender tree in light porous soil with full sun or partial shade and water frequently. Prune to encourage dense growth and propagate from seed or cuttings. 'Chinese dates' are a delicacy in Middle Eastern countries and are delicious cooked or uncooked.

Zelkova serrata

Ziziphus jujuba

Umbellularia californica

Ulmus pumila

Tristaniopsis laurina

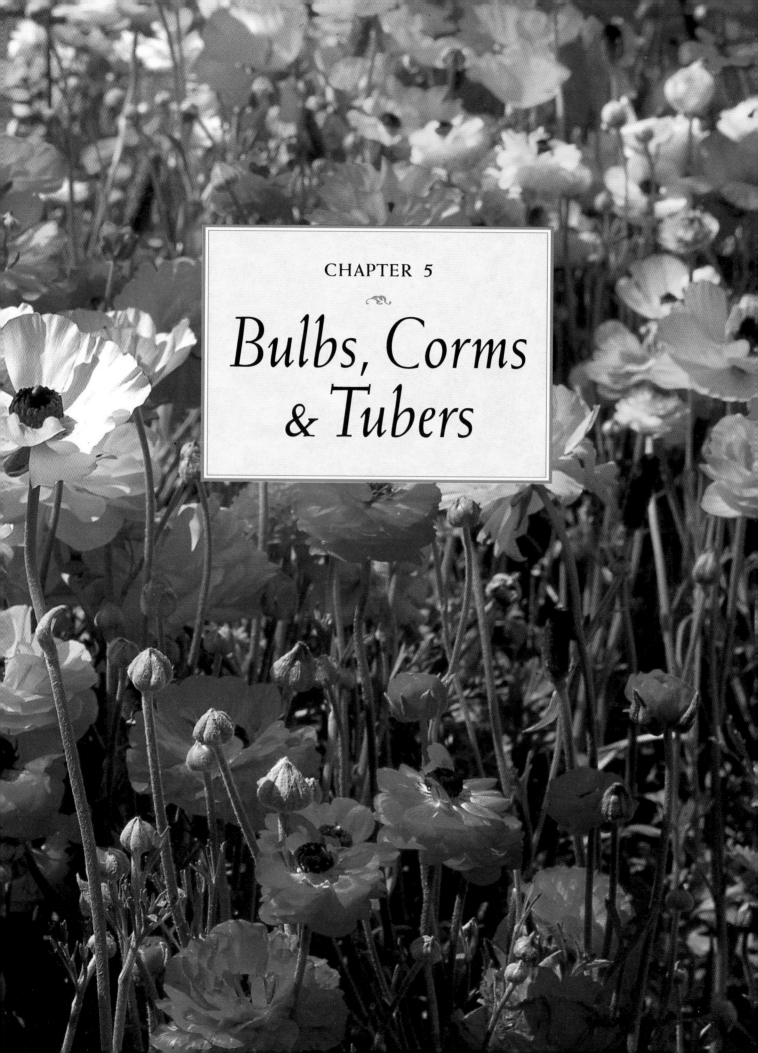

CHAPTER 5

Bulbs, Corms
& Tubers

The history of bulbs and how they came to western Europe to be hybridized into the plants we grow today makes fascinating reading. Most of the bulbs we think of as being indigenous to Europe can be traced back to their native habitat much further east in the mountainous regions of Asia Minor, while others were gathered initially from southern Africa.

In the centuries of European worldwide exploration, bulbs, as well as other exotic plants, were prized by naturalists and form the basis of modern strains of the bulbs marketed today. Narcissus for instance were grown by the ancient Egyptians, tulips came from Turkestan while gladiolus and nerines originated in the mountains of the southwestern Cape of South Africa.

As bulbs have differing flowering times, there is no limit to the type and number which can be included in the garden to provide for almost year-round

colour. The term bulb, horticulturally speaking, includes true bulbs, corms and tubers.

Bulbs

True bulbs, of which the onion is an easily identified example, are made up of a series of scales joined at the base which enclose and protect a central bud. These scales collect and store food for the following year's growth and flowering and it's for this reason that it is necessary to allow the leaves of true bulbs to die down naturally as they continue to manufacture and store food for the following season, well after the flower has finished. This process also makes it possible for true bulbs such as hyacinths, narcissus and tulips to flower successfully in pots or jars as they use this stored energy to produce the current season's flowers. True bulbs reproduce by forming bulbils around the base of the plant and these can be easily removed when bulbs are lifted, even though they may take several years to flower.

Corms

A corm has a swollen base of solid storage tissue. Once flowering is over a new corm develops on top and the original one dies, often producing new corms or pips around the perimeter before it withers completely. Gladiolus and freesias are good examples of a corm.

Tubers

Again a food storage system, a tuber can be formed from stems or roots. 'Eyes' are produced from these swollen areas and form new plants. Dahlias are easily identified as being this type of bulb as is the common potato which will produce eyes if it is stored for a long time.

Creating Effects with Bulbs

Basically bulbs have evolved in the above ways because of environmental factors. They are able to store food for long, dry, dormant periods, then, in very quick time when the climate is

The elegant flower of the tulip has made it one of the most popular bulbs in the world.

right, shoot, flower then gather enough food for the following year. Some northern hemisphere bulbs like crocus and fritillaria wait for the watering they receive as the snow melts to suddenly burst upon the scene. These and many other bulbs are very particular regarding their environment as many temperate climate gardeners have realized when they have omitted to 'refrigerate' their tulip bulbs to chill them before planting. Other bulbs are far more accommodating and will often naturalize in the most unlikely places because the soil, combined with the surrounding ecosystem is to their liking.

Even in small gardens a natural effect can be created, especially under lightly foliaged deciduous trees as the roots of the trees ensure adequate drainage and there's less competition from grass. These woodland companions need to be chosen with consideration to their dormant period. Choose bulbs like trilliums and scillas and many of the narcissus species which are early to shoot and bloom; as their dormancy approaches the overhead canopy is beginning its active growth.

The informality of a woodland bulb display relies to a great extent on the naturalistic way in which the bulbs are planted. Planting in drifts, random scatterings of the bulbs, whereby they are left to grow where they land when thrown by the handful, is the best method of ensuring this. Size of the drift is governed by available space, of course, yet it is the very randomness of the display rather than its size that is the eye-catching element. Often a gardener in cold areas relies on bulb drifts to give a welcome colour display in early spring and is tempted to mix different species and colours, however a more pleasing effect is achieved by having drifts of different colour or species flowering on from one drift to the next rather than a 'hundreds and thousands' look. Bluebells look good in such a design with the blue species in the lighter, more open areas and the white flowering ones grouped closer to say the dark green background of evergreen shrubs.

There are many hardy bulbs which we often associate with 'old' gardens. Long left to their own devices they surprise us each year with their colourful appearance amid the shrubbery. Some of these, like *Amaryllis belladonna*, send up tall, single stems holding clusters of pale pink trumpets at the cusp of the summer–autumn/fall season

The sunny narcissus flowers are ideal for indoor decoration.

while the snowflake with its dainty green-tipped white bells lets us know when spring is almost here.

Planting bulbs among shrubs usually needs careful consideration because we can very easily lose track of where they are while they are dormant, and gardeners everywhere always have the tendency to fill any vacant space with something new which takes their fancy. As discussed earlier, competition from overhanging shrubs also has to be taken into account.

Many of the more delicate bulbs are overpowered by surrounding plants and are ideally suited to rock gardens where individual pockets can be given over to one particular species. Rockeries really need to be placed on an existing slope or where a change of level is being designed into the garden, otherwise dwarf bulbs can be placed in a brick or stone paved outdoor area where they can pop up in unpaved pockets from under a fine gravel scree. Provided drainage has been catered for, these pockets are ideal for dwarf tulips, crocus, freesias, ixias, sparaxis, babianas, lachenalias and other delicate bulbs which would be lost in the general shrubbery.

Raised beds filled with good quality, free-draining soil, are a sure way of providing the bulbs with the freedom from competition and drainage they need. These beds can be made using treated logs, railway sleepers or a couple of rows of old bricks. For a gardener wishing to perfect the hobby

of growing prized, delicate bulbs rather than opting for a general garden display, these beds may well be the answer. Alternatively these raised beds can be filled with free-draining sand and pots of bulbs plunged into them to ensure they don't dry out, then when the flowers appear each individual pot can be taken indoors or placed in a prominent position in the garden or on the patio where the blooms can be appreciated.

Growing Conditions

Generally bulbs prefer well-drained, slightly acidic soil. Most have evolved in areas with prolonged dry periods followed in the growing season by melting snow or good rains. Therefore, most are unable to withstand prolonged periods of waterlogged soil, but there are always exceptions to the rule and the arum lily thrives in moist sites as do the Japanese and flag iris.

Similarly there are very few bulbs which can be grown in really shady areas and still flower well. Again, luckily for the gardener looking to highlight a shady spot with yearly colour there is *Clivia miniata* which produces bright orange flowers each spring, or the more delicate lily of the valley and snowflakes providing that wonderful flowering highlight of white blooms against green foliage so often employed by professional landscapers to such good effect.

Allium christophii

Albuca canadensis

Amaryllis belladonna

Allium moly

Anemone blanda

Allium narcissiflorum

ALBUCA
canadensis

This genus is native to southern
and tropical Africa, even though its
name suggests it is from Canada. *A.
canadensis* grows up to 1 m (about
3 ft) high and the grey-green leaves
grow to 15 cm (about 6 in) long.
The pendulous flowers, which appear in late spring, are about 2.5 cm
(about 1 in) long. The inner petals
appear joined, as if forming a tube;
the outer petals are yellow, with a

green stripe on each petal. This
species is half-hardy. The large
bulbs should be planted in autumn/
fall fairly close to the surface, in full
sun or slight shade. They can be
propagated from offsets or from
seed.

ALLIUM

Garlic and onions belong to this
large genus of over 700 species,
native to Asia, Africa and America.
There are many very attractive ornamental species as well as edible
ones. Many species have a pungent
onion or garlic scent but this is
usually only noticeable when parts
of the plant are bruised or crushed.
Most are frost-hardy and easy to
grow; some are so vigorous they
can become difficult to control.
They vary greatly in size: from 4–
5 cm (about 2 in) high to 1 m
(about 3 ft). Smaller species are
ideal in a rockery. Bulbs should be
planted in autumn/fall in well-
drained soil, 4–10 cm (about 2–
4 in) deep, depending on the size of
the bulb. Flowering time is late
spring to early autumn/fall. Propagation can be from offsets, which
multiply freely, or from seed.

A. christophii
syn. A. albopilosum

This attractive, hardy species grows
up to 60 cm (about 24 in) high.
The broad leaves are green and
shiny on top and white beneath.
The sturdy stem bears a rounded
umbel of flowers up to 30 cm
(about 12 in) wide. The individual
violet flowers borne in spring are
star-shaped. They turn black as the
seeds ripen and are very useful for
dried flower arrangements. Bulbs
should be planted in autumn/fall,
6 cm (about 2½ in) deep in well-
drained soil. *A. christophii* grows
best in full sun. Propagate by dividing offsets.

A. moly
GOLDEN GARLIC

Native to Spain, *A. moly* grows up
to 35 cm (about 14 in). Broad,
grey-green basal leaves surround
stems which each bear an umbel of
up to 40 flowers. The bright yellow,
star-shaped flowers appear in summer. It is very hardy and can be
planted in full sun or partial shade.
Bulbs or seeds should be planted in
autumn/fall in well-drained soil.
Propagate by division of bulbs. The
Spanish once regarded this plant as
a sign of prosperity if they discovered it in their gardens.

A. narcissiflorum

This delightful species grows up to
30 cm (about 12 in) high. Slender,
grey-green leaves surround a stem
bearing an umbel of up to 12 nodding flowers. The purple, bell-

shaped flowers appear in summer.
Plant bulbs and seeds in autumn/fall
in well-drained soil. This hardy
species grows well in full sun.
Propagate by division of bulbs.

AMARYLLIS
belladonna

This outstanding plant is a gardener's dream: half- to frost-hardy, easy
to grow and, as the name *belladonna*
('beautiful lady') implies, very beautiful. Native to South Africa, it is an
autumn/fall flowering bulb. A
sturdy, fast-growing stem up to
50 cm (about 20 in) high is topped
with a glorious display of rosy pink,
lily-like flowers. The strap-like
basal leaves appear after the long
flowering period. Plant large bulbs
in late summer at soil level or just
below, in well-drained soil. A fairly
sunny position is best in cool areas,
but they may need light shade in
very warm areas. Cut down flower
stalks once flowering is finished but
ensure the plant is well watered
through winter. Grown easily from
seed, it often self-sows freely. The
genus *Amaryllis* once contained
many species, including hippeastrums. Now, *A. belladonna* is
considered to be the only true *Amaryllis* and other species have been
reclassified.

ANEMONE
WINDFLOWER

This highly varied genus is mainly
native to southern Europe and the
Middle East. Size and flower colour
vary greatly, as do flowering times;
the planting of tubers can be stag-
gered to provide a succession of
glorious blooms. Most species are
fairly hardy and do well in rich,
well-drained soil in a sunny or
lightly shaded situation. Take care
that the tubers are not upside
down. Flowers usually appear
about 4 months after planting.
Grow from seed planted in summer, being careful to protect the
seedlings from hot sun. Plant new
tubers each year for best results, as
they become weakened after
blooming. *Anemos* is Greek for
'wind', hence the common name.

A. blanda
WOOD ANEMONE

This delicate-looking species is
frost-hardy. Native to Greece, it
grows to 20 cm (about 8 in) with
green, oval, toothed leaves. The
star-shaped flowers which appear
in spring can be white, pink or blue
and are about 3 cm (about 1½ in)
wide. *A. blanda* self-seeds freely
and, given moist, slightly shaded
conditions, should spread into a
beautiful display of flowers.

Anomatheca laxa

Aristea ensifolia

Arum italicum

Anemone nemorosa

Asphodeline lutea

A. coronaria
WIND POPPY

Many hybrids have evolved from this fully hardy species, the most commonly planted anemone native to the Mediterannean region. It grows up to 25 cm (about 10 in) in height and has a spread of 20 cm (about 8 in). The poppy-like flowers are up to 10 cm (about 4 in) wide and can range in colour from red to purple to blue. They have black stamens, 6 petals, and are open, solitary and terminal. *A. coronaria* is usually treated as an annual. 'De Caen' is a single and 'St Brigid' is a popular semi-double, with colours ranging from pink to purple to scarlet to blue. Excellent as a cut flower.

A. nemorosa
WOOD ANEMONE, FAIRY'S WINDFLOWER

This hardy, speading species grows to 20 cm (about 8 in) with a spread of 30 cm (about 12 in). The flowers are white with a rosy pink undersurface, solitary, 4 cm (about 2 in) across and terminal. The leaves are deep green, 3 lobed and deeply toothed. It bears globular clusters of hairy nutlets. Plant in moist soil in a protected, shady position. The flower is said to have originated from the ground where the goddess Venus' tears fell after the death of Adonis. Some European peasants still regard anemones superstitiously as a flower of bad luck.

ANOMATHECA
laxa
syn. *Lapeirousia laxa*
SCARLET FREESIA

This freesia-like native of South Africa grows to 60 cm (about 24 in) with long, narrow basal leaves and produces one-sided spikes bearing up to 12 flowers. The tubular, star-shaped red to scarlet flowers, 3 cm (about 1½ in) wide (although there is a form only half that size), appear in spring. Corms should be planted in autumn/fall in well-drained soil in a sunny or partially shaded situation. Water regularly during summer. If left undisturbed, it should self-seed freely. It can be propagated from offsets or from seed sown in late summer, which may flower the next spring but will usually produce a much better display in the second year. It is half-hardy.

ARISTEA

This genus of evergreen, clump-forming, rhizomatous perennials are grown for their spikes of blue flowers. They prefer a position in the sun in a well-drained soil and are half-hardy. It is best not to move established plants. Propagate from seed in autumn/fall or spring.

A. ecklonii

This profuse flowering perennial rhizome grows 30–60 cm (about 12–24 in) tall. An evergreen, it forms clumps of long, lanceolate green leaves, above which the cup-like blue flowers appear in summer. Rhizomes should be planted in well-drained soil in full sun or partial shade. Half-hardy, they need to be kept moist and do well beside a pond or stream. Propagate from seed in autumn/fall or spring. Very young plants can be divided as long as the rhizomes are not allowed to dry out. Older plants do not transplant well.

A. ensifolia

This elegant, summer-flowering perennial grows up to 1.5 m (about 4½ ft) tall. Iris-like leaves surround a stem with a raceme covered in purple to blue 2 cm (about 1 in) flowers, which close at night. Rhizomes should be planted in well-drained soil in full sun or partial shade. Half-hardy, they need to be kept moist and do well beside a pond or stream. Propagate from seed in autumn/fall or spring. Very young plants can be divided as long as the rhizomes are not allowed to dry out. Older plants do not transplant well.

ARUM
italicum
ITALIAN ARUM, JACK IN THE PULPIT, LORDS AND LADIES

Although many plants are commonly called arums, only a few truly belong to this genus. Frost-hardy, *A. italicum* grows to 30 cm (about 12 in). Broad, arrow-shaped, marbled leaves appear in autumn/fall. The flower is a light green, hooded spathe with a yellow spadix. It appears in early spring and is followed by orange berries which last until late summer. Tubers should be planted in autumn/fall in rich, moist soil in partial shade, with plenty of water during the growing season. Although frost-hardy, they need protection in cold areas. They can be divided once foliage has died, or propagated from seed in autumn/fall.

ASPHODELINE
lutea
ASPHODEL

A native of the Mediterranean, this fragrant, frost-hardy perennial plant grows to 60 cm (about 24 in) in height with a spread of 75 cm (about 30 in). Furrowed, grey-green leaves appear below spear-like stems bearing racemes of yellow, star-shaped flowers, some 3 cm (about 1½ in) long. Plant in full sun in well-drained soil, although it is adaptable to most conditions and positions, and keep moist before the flowering period in spring. Can be propagated by dividing the roots carefully in late winter, or from seed in autumn/fall or spring.

Anemone coronaria

BABIANA
stricta
BABOON FLOWER, BOBBEJAANTJIE

Baboons seem to find the bulbs of this delightful South African plant very tasty and early Dutch settlers often saw them digging up the plants. These half-hardy plants grow to 20 cm (about 8 in). The hairy, slender leaves are strongly ribbed and spikes bearing up to 10 cup-shaped flowers appear above the foliage. The freesia-like flowers, which appear in spring, are blue to violet but there are pale coloured forms of white or cream; some are fragrant. Plant the corms in autumn/fall in sandy soil in a sunny position. They look best planted in large clumps. Provide plenty of water during the growing season. Propagate from offsets or seed in autumn/fall.

BEGONIA
BEGONIA

These immensely popular plants are grown worldwide for their exotic summer blooms and beautiful foliage.

Large-flowered, tuberous begonias are usually called B. × tuberhybrida. They are available with flowers in every colour of the rainbow, as singles or doubles, with many variations of frills and ruffles. They like temperate to warm conditions and are frost tender. The tubers should be planted in spring in partial shade in a rich, moist soil. Sometimes they are planted in pots and started indoors in winter and transferred outside when the weather is warmer. They may need to be staked as the large flowers are heavy. Water should be decreased after flowering, and when the leaves have started to yellow the tuber should be lifted and dried very carefully before storage. Propagate from seed or from stem or leaf cuttings, but this is best done in a greenhouse.

B. × tuberhybrida
'Camellia' and 'Rose' flowered types
TUBEROUS BEGONIA

The most popular of the tuberous begonias, these bear large to enormous, 25 cm (about 10 in) or more, double flowers in every colour but blue. To have the biggest flowers they should be disbudded, sacrificing the small female flowers that grow on either side of the central male. There are many named varieties in an ever-changing selection.

B. × tuberhybrida multiflora

Usually single flowered, these are grown not so much for the individual flowers as for the massed effect. They are available in the same range of colours as the others and are grown in the same way, except that they need no disbudding. Plants can be floppy and will benefit from staking.

B. × tuberhybrida pendula
BASKET BEGONIA

The basket begonias carry their flowers in pendent sprays, which look very good cascading from hanging baskets. The flowers are single or double, and usually smaller than the large-flowered types. They come in the same range of colours and are grown in the same way.

BELAMCANDA
chinensis
LEOPARD LILY, BLACKBERRY LILY

This little known native of China and Japan is a member of the Iridaceae family, along with irises. Growing to 1 m (about 3 ft), the foliage is sword-shaped like that of an iris. Branched spikes of orange-red, spotted flowers appear in summer, giving it the name 'leopard lily'. The flower produces clusters of black, shiny seeds, hence the other name, 'blackberry lily'. Tubers should be planted in spring, just below the soil level in rich, well-drained soil in full sun or partial shade. Water well in summer. They are frost-hardy but need some protection in very cold winters. Propagate by division or from seed.

BRIMEURA
amethystina
syn. Hyacinthus amethystinus

This hyacinth-like, frost-hardy native of Spain grows to 25 cm (about 10 in). Slender, strap-like foliage surrounds stems which bear up to eight delicate, 1 cm (about $^1/_2$ in), bell-shaped flowers ranging in colour from white to blue. Plant bulbs in autumn/fall in rich, well-drained soil in full sun or partial shade. Propagate by division or from seed in autumn/fall.

BRUNSVIGIA

Members of this South African genus are similar in character to the belladonna lily. However, they are far more tender and can be quite difficult to grow. Tall stems bear a dazzling mass of flowers in autumn/fall. The scented flowers radiate from the top of the stem like a candelabra. The bulbs are huge, up to 25 cm (about 10 in). They should be planted in rich, sandy soil in full sun. Water well in the growing season but keep dry when dormant. Propagation is slow. Seedlings can take up to 4 years to flower. Offsets must be fairly large before division and may take years to flower.

Begonia × tuberhybrida

Begonia × tuberhybrida pendula

Belamcanda chinensis

Babiana stricta

Begonia × tuberhybrida multiflora

Brimeura amethystina

B. josephinae
JOSEPHINE'S LILY

The beautiful Josephine's lily grows up to 75 cm (about 30 in). The stout stem bears a mass of bright red, funnel-shaped flowers in autumn/fall. The 5 cm (about 2 in) wide flowers are scented and radiate out from the top of the stem. Strap-like leaves appear after flowering. The large bulbs are very expensive.

B. orientalis
CANDELABRA FLOWER

The sturdy stem grows up to 75 cm (about 30 in) and bears a flowerhead which can be up to 50 cm (about 20 in) wide. The small crimson flowers appear in autumn/fall before the leaves. The foliage often lies flat on the ground and is tender to frost.

BULBINELLA
floribunda
CAT'S-TAIL

This native of South Africa produces 60 cm (about 24 in) flower stalks in late winter to early spring. The stalk is topped with a 10 cm (about 4 in) spike crammed with tiny yellow to orange flowers. Long, narrow basal leaves appear in autumn/fall. The plant disappears completely in summer. Bulbs should be planted in well-drained soil with the top of the bulb at soil level. Quite hardy to frost, it likes a sunny situation and plenty of water during the growing season. Propagate from seed or by division. Excellent as a long-lasting cut flower.

CALADIUM
bicolor
ELEPHANT EARS

This genus of perennials native to the USA have long-stalked, ornamental leaves arising from the tubers. They are frost-tender, to a minimum 18°C (about 64°F), and require a position in partial shade in moist, humus-rich soil. *C. bicolor* grows to a height of 50 cm (about 20 in) and has a spread of 1 m (about 3 ft). It has creamy-white, *Arum*-like flowers. Propagate in spring by dividing the tubers.

CAMASSIA
esculenta
syn. *C. quamash*
QUAMASH

This North American native grows to 90 cm (about 36 in) and produces a densely covered flower spike above an erect stem and slender basal leaves. The blue, star-shaped flowers which appear in summer have 6 petals and measure 2.5 cm (about 1 in). Bulbs should be planted in late autumn/fall in

Bulbinella floribunda

Camassia esculenta

Canna 'Lenape'

Brunsvigia orientalis

Brunsvigia josephinae

loamy, rich, moist soil. Position in partial shade or full sun if the soil is very moist. Frost-hardy, it does well in cool temperatures. Propagate by division or from seed, the latter may take up to five years to produce flowers. North American Indians once ate the large bulbs of quamash.

CANNA
'Lenape'

This genus of showy, robust, rhizamatous perennials are grown for their striking flowers and ornamental foliage. They are frost-tender to a minimum 10–15°C (about 55–59°F) and require a warm, sunny position in humus-rich, moist soil. They are ideal for growing in containers. *C.* 'Lenape' produces bright yellow flowers with a red throat; it grows to a height of 80 cm (about 32 in). Propagate in spring by division or in winter from seed.

Caladium bicolor

Chasmanthe aethiopica

Cardiocrinum giganteum

Chlidanthus fragrans

Clivia nobilis

Chasmanthe floribunda var. *floribunda*

CARDIOCRINUM
giganteum
syn. *Lilium giganteum*
GIANT LILY

A magnificent, summer-flowering plant reaching up to 4 m (about 12 ft). Unfortunately, the giant lily is not for the gardener who needs to see overnight results. A small bulb planted today is unlikely to flower for 5 years. The tall, sturdy stem bears up to twenty 25 cm (about 10 in) flowers, tubular at the base and trumpet-shaped at the top. The cream flowers are striped with maroon-red blotches at the throat and are heavily scented. The large bulbs should be planted in rich, acid soil in partial shade. Water and fertilize well once shoots appear. The main bulb dies after flowering but propagation is possible from offsets (which flower in 3 or 4 years) and seed. A good plan is to buy 3 sizes of bulbs, to ensure some flowers each year.

CHASMANTHE

This genus consists of about 10 species of corms native to tropical Africa and South Africa, grown for their flowers. They are half-hardy to frost-tender. Plant corms in autumn/fall in sun or partial shade and a moist, well-drained soil. Keep moist during the growing season and allow to dry out after flowering. Propagate from offsets or from seeds sown in autumn/fall.

C. aethiopica

This half-hardy South African native shares some characteristics with gladiolus. Ribbed, sword-shaped leaves fan out from the base and the

Clivia miniata

stems rise to 1.5 m (about 4½ ft). Yellow to red, slender, tubular flowers, 2.5 cm (about 1 in) long, are borne fan-like on one side of the stem in late spring and early summer. They are quite tender to frost.

C. floribunda var. floribunda
FLAMES, SUURKANOLPYPIE

Found wild in the south-western Cape area of South Africa, this perennial, branched herb has sword-shaped leaves up to 50 cm (about 20 in) long, and 5 cm (about 2 in) wide. Curved, almost hood-shaped, orange-red flowers, alternately arranged on flat spikes, are borne in late winter and early spring. Must be left undisturbed for several years.

CHIONODOXA
luciliae
syn. *C. gigantea*
GLORY-OF-THE-SNOW

These delicate-looking flowers are seen emerging from the melting snow in Europe and parts of Asia, giving the name *Chionodoxa*, Greek

for snow glory. Ideal for a rock garden in a cool climate, they grow to 15 cm (about 6 in), flowering in early spring. Narrow, basal leaves surround a slender stem which bears up to six, 1 cm (about ½ in), mauve to blue star-shaped flowers with white centres. Bulbs should be planted in cool to cold areas only, in well-drained soil, dressed with a layer of mulch, in autumn/fall. They will spread well of their own accord and can be propagated from seeds or offsets in autumn/fall.

CHLIDANTHUS
fragrans

SEA DAFFODIL, FAIRY LILY, PERUVIAN LILY

This little known South American bulb is frost-tender and ideal for coastal areas. Growing to 25 cm (about 10 in), the bare stem carries up to 5 bright yellow, sweetly scented, trumpet-shaped blooms about 7 cm (about 3 in) long. Basal foliage is like that of a daffodil. Plant the late spring-flowering bulbs in autumn/fall in loose, well-drained soil in a sunny position;

Chionodoxa luciliae

plant in pots in cool areas. Given the right conditions, the bulbs increase rapidly. Propagation is from offsets. This fragrant species is a good cut flower.

CLIVIA
BUSH LILY, FIRE LILY

These South African natives produce a glorious display of funnel-shaped flowers in spring or summer. They are quite easy to grow in all but frost-prone areas. Plant in a sheltered position in rich, well-drained soil. Keep fairly dry in winter and increase watering in spring and summer. Propagate by division after flowering. Seed can also be used but this can be slow to flower. In cooler areas they can be grown in pots; when quite pot bound they flower best.

C. miniata
FIRE LILY, BUSH LILY

This showy species grows up to 45 cm (about 18 in). A cluster of up to 12 funnel-shaped flowers appear in spring. The 8 cm (about 3 in) flowers are orange-red, paler at the throat. The foliage is glossy, thick and strap-like. It does well in a shaded area. Yellow and cream varieties are also available. Hybrids of *C. miniata* are becoming very popular.

C. nobilis
DROOPING CLIVIA, NATAL CLIVIA

This attractive species grows up to 40 cm (about 16 in). The pendulus, tubular flowers, orange and tipped with green, are borne in clusters, up to 30 on each stem. The leaves are glossy and strap-like.

COLCHICUM
AUTUMN CROCUS

This genus of flowering corms is native mainly to Europe and Asia. Masses of crocus-like flowers appear in autumn/fall, followed by the strap-like basal foliage. Frost-hardy, they are very easy to grow. However, they are not suitable for very hot areas. Plant the corms in late summer in well-drained soil in sun or partial shade. Corms will also usually flower without any soil, so they can be kept inside for display and planted after flowering. Propagate from seed or by division in summer. The plants are poisonous, although their active ingredient colchicine is used in the treatment of certain forms of cancer. *C. speciosum* is one of the most striking of the autumn crocuses, producing mauve-purple, goblet-shaped flowers.

C. autumnale

The best known of the species, this grows to 15 cm (about 6 in) and has rosy pink to white, goblet-shaped flowers up to 10 cm (about 4 in) long. Each corm produces masses of flowers and multiplies freely. There is also a double-flowered form.

C. 'Lilac Wonder'

As the name suggests, this hardy cultivar produces large, up to 20 cm (about 8 in) long, lilac flowers. The tulip-like flowers appear in autumn/fall, followed by the strap-like foliage.

CONVALLARIA
majalis
LILY-OF-THE-VALLEY

Renowned for its glorious perfume, this beautiful plant is native to the northern hemisphere, and does best in cool climates. It is low-growing, up to 20 cm (about 8 in), with thick, oval to oblong, dark green leaves. The dainty, white, bell-shaped flowers appear in spring. The rhizomes, or 'pips' as they are commonly known, should be planted in autumn/fall in a partially shaded position in a cool or cold area. Soil should be rich and moist, and a dressing of mulch will give good results. Water well during the growing period. Given the right conditions, *C. majalis* spreads freely, sometimes becoming overcrowded when it will need to be divided.

CRINUM

These natives of South America, Asia, Africa and Australia are valued for their large, lily-like flowers and the ease with which they grow. Up to 20 scented flowers are borne on a tall, thick stem, usually in summer to early autumn/fall. The large bulbs should be planted in rich moist soil with the neck of the bulb above ground level. Partial shade is best, particularly in very hot areas. Propagation is best from seed as dividing the plants is difficult. Flowers usually take a few seasons to develop with either method. They are tender to frost and susceptible to caterpillars, slugs and snails.

C. bulbispermum
ORANGE RIVER LILY

This species reaches up to 1.2 m (about 4 ft). Glossy, oblong leaves are borne on a thick leaf stalk. The sturdy scape rises beside the stem and is topped with a cluster of large, 25 cm (about 10 in), funnel-shaped flowers in white to pink, sometimes striped with dark pink.

C. moorei
MOORE'S CRINUM, BUSH LILY

This popular species grows up to 75 cm (about 30 in). The strong stem bears a cluster of 10 cm (about 4 in) funnel-shaped flowers. The semi-pendent blooms are pale pink with white at the throat. The foliage is glossy and strap-like.

C. × powellii
CAPE LILY

This well-known and easily grown hybrid between *C. bulbispermum* and *C. moorei* grows up to 1 m (about 3 ft). Strap-like foliage is produced on a thick stalk and the bare scape is crowned with up to 10 scented, pink flowers.

CROCOSMIA
MONTBRETIA

These half- to fully hardy South African natives bear attractive displays of flowers in summer. Tall, pleated leaves form a fan of foliage, similar to a gladiolus. A branched spike of brightly coloured flowers sits atop the tall stem. Plant the corms in winter in rich soil with adequate drainage in a position which receives morning sun. Water well through summer. They will multiply freely and should not be divided unless overcrowded. This should be done in spring if necessary.

C. aurea

A 90 cm (about 36 in) stem bears a branching spike of yellow to orange, 7 cm (about 3 in), tubular flowers. The slender leaves are sword-shaped. It likes a shaded position.

C. crocosmiiflora

Growing to 75 cm (about 30 in), the stem bears a branching spike of up to 40 orange-red, gladiolus-like flowers of about 2.5 cm (about 1 in). Bayonet-shaped foliage forms a fan from the base of the plant. This species is frost-hardy but needs a warm situation in cold climates.

Colchicum autumnale

Crinum moorei

Colchicum 'Lilac Wonder'

Crinum × powellii

Crocosmia crocosmiiflora

Crinum bulbispermum

Convallaria majalis

Crocosmia aurea

Crocus, Dutch hybrids

Crocus flavus

Crocosmia masonorum

Cyclamen coum subsp. *coum*

Crocosmia 'Lucifer'

Crocus tomasinianus

Cyclamen coum subsp. *caucasicum*

C. masonorum

A tall species, growing up to 1.2 m (about 4 ft). The branched stem is topped with an arched display of tangerine flowers. The 6-petalled flowers are quite large, up to 7 cm (about 3 in) wide. The narrow, bayonet-shaped foliage is pleated. It is useful as a cut flower.

CROCUS

CROCUS

Heralding the beginning of spring in Europe, crocuses pop up through the snow, the cheerful displays a sign that winter is over. The goblet-shaped flowers vary greatly in colour. The foliage is grass-like, with a silver-white stripe along the centre of the leaf. Fully hardy, they do best in a cool to cold area. In warm areas the corms may flower in the first season but may not flower again. They can be grown in pots in warmer areas, in a cool spot. Corms should be planted in early autumn/fall in moist, well-drained soil in full sun or partial shade. Keep well watered until the foliage begins to

die. They do not spread very fast but clumps can be divided if they are overcrowded. Seed can be planted in autumn/fall, but plants grown from seed usually will not flower for three years.

C., autumn-flowering

A number of the autumn-flowering crocuses flower before their leaves appear in winter or early spring, and are therefore striking when planted among prostrate ground covers. *C. asturicus* produces mauve flowers with pointed petals; *C. longiflorus* syn. *C. odorus* is one of the most fragrant crocuses, producing flowers that are purple-lilac on the outside and pale mauve-blue on the inside, with an orange-yellow centre.

C., Dutch hybrids

The Dutch hybrids are vigorous plants with large flowers up to 15 cm (about 6 in) long. The colour range is varied, white to yellow to purple to blue. There are also some striped varieties. Many of these hybrids derive from *C. vernus*. They

should be planted in autumn/fall in well-drained soil at a depth of about 10 cm (about 4 in).

C. flavus
syn. *C. aureus*

A profusion of 10 cm (about 4 in) goblet-shaped flowers in spring. The scented flowers are orange-yellow, with an orange throat. Increases easily from seed. Grows more readily in a warmer climate than most other yellow species.

C., spring-flowering

The spring-flowering crocuses are fully hardy; they require well-drained soil and a sunny situation or partial sun only in warmer climates. *C. ancyrensis* produces deep yellow, fragrant, long-lasting flowers; *C. susianus* syn. *C. angustifolius* is one of the oldest cultivated crocuses, producing bright yellow flowers with a bronze tinge on the outside.

C. tomasinianus

Grows to 10 cm (about 4 in) with lavender to purple, sometimes white-throated, goblet-shaped flowers. One of the more easily grown species, it does well in a rockery, or naturalized under deciduous trees. There is also a purple-maroon form.

CYCLAMEN

CYCLAMEN

The flower of the cyclamen must be one of the most elegant of all plants. These winter-flowering natives of the Mediterranean region are often used in pots indoors but can also be

grown in the garden. Florist's cyclamen (*C. persicum*) is usually bought already in flower for an indoor display. Keep the pot in good light but out of direct sun in an unheated room. It is rather frost-tender, although the other species are rated frost- to fully hardy. Tubers should be planted in light, fibrous soil, rich in organic matter with excellent drainage in partial shade. Water regularly during growth but allow to dry out during summer. The tubers are best left undisturbed and should grow larger each year, flowering more abundantly each season. Propagate from seed in autumn/fall. Plants should flower in a year. Some cyclamens are susceptible to black rot.

C. coum subsp. caucasicum

This popular, Middle Eastern species grows to 10 cm (about 4 in). The leaves are dark green, round to heart-shaped and marbled with silver. The abundant, dark pink flowers which are stained crimson at the base are 2 cm (about 1 in) long.

C. coum subsp. coum

Profusely blooming species popular for its elegant, pink to crimson flowers. The dark green leaves are round to heart-shaped. It grows to a height of 10 cm (about 4 in). There is also a delightful white form, stained crimson at the base of the petals.

C. hederifolium
syn. *C. neapolitanum*

This autumn/fall-flowering species can produce corms up to 15 cm

(about 6 in) wide. Growing to 10
cm (about 4 in) it has dark green,
marbled, ivy-shaped foliage. The
flowers are white to rose-pink,
darker at the base and some strains
are perfumed.

C. repandum
IVY-LEAVED CYCLAMEN

A native of France and Greece, this
species has striking mid-green
leaves that are cordate and lobed,
often marbled above and always
reddish purple below. The fragrant
white, pink or red flowers with
twisted, reflexed petals appear on
slender stems in spring; the plant
may continue flowering into summer in cool areas. Elegant, to 15 cm
(about 6 in) high, they should be
spaced 20 cm (about 8 in) apart
when planting.

CYPELLA
herbertii

This iris-like cousin of the Tigridia
is native to the cooler parts of South
America. The unusual flowers
bloom only for a day, but new flowers appear through most of the
summer months. The branched
flower stem grows to 90 cm (about
36 in) bearing 7 cm (about 3 in)
triangular blooms. The large,
pointed outside petals are copper to
tan; the much smaller inner petals
are purple and gold. The green
foliage is like that of an iris, sword-
shaped and pleated. This half-hardy
species should be planted in full
sun in light, well-drained soil. Water well through the growing season
and allow to dry out in winter. The
bulbs should be lifted in areas
which have very wet winters. Propagation is from offsets or from seed
planted in winter/spring.

CYRTANTHUS
macowanii
FIRE LILY

This large genus of about 50 species
has brightly coloured, tubular,
curved flowers nodding down from
the top of a hollow stem. The
scented flowers bloom at various
times, depending on the species.
The grass-like foliage usually dies
down over winter. Although some
species have been found growing in
swamps, they are best planted in
rich, well-drained soil in a sunny
situation. The neck of the bulb
should be at ground level. Water
well through the growing season.
The bulbs are best left undisturbed
but may need dividing if overcrowding occurs. *C. macowanii*
grows to 50 cm (about 20 in) and
has brilliant scarlet or coral red
flowers. They do well planted in
pots and make a long-lasting, perfumed cut flower. Propagate from
seed planted in spring.

Eranthis hyemalis

Dracunculus vulgaris

DICHELOSTEMMA

This genus of summer-flowering
bulbs and corms is related to
Brodiaea and some of its species are
also classified under that genus.
Native to the USA, they bear their
dense, terminal clusters of tubular
or star-shaped flowers on slender,
erect (up to 1 m/about 3 ft), leafless
stems. They put out narrow, strap-
like, basal leaves and are hardy if
grown in a sunny, sheltered site.
Plant the corms in late summer in
well-drained soil and water regularly until the flowers die, after
which the corms should be dried
out. Propagate from offsets in au-
tumn/fall or from seed sown in
spring or autumn/fall. These dainty
flowers look their best planted in
groups.

D. ida-maia
syn. *Brodiaea ida-maia*
**CALIFORNIAN FIRECRACKER, FLORAL FIRE-
CRACKER**

The unusual-looking flowers of this
summer-flowering species consist of
a crimson tube with 6 yellow and
green tipped petals. They are produced in clusters of up to 20 at the
top of the slender, 1 m (about 3 ft),
erect stems. The leaves of this half-
hardy bulb are basal and semi-erect.

D. pulchellum
syn. *Brodiaea pulchella*

The slender, leafless stem of this
summer-flowering species is up to
60 cm (about 24 in) in length; it
carries dense clusters of pale lilac to
mauve bell-shaped flowers 1–2 cm
(about ½–1 in) long. The bracts are
a deep purple. The narrow, basal
leaves are semi-erect.

Cyrtanthus macowanii

DRACUNCULUS
vulgaris
syn. *Arum dracunculus*
STINK LILY, DRAGON LILY

This relative of the arum is not a
plant you would want to grow beside your front door. It emits a potent, foul odour which attracts flies
for pollinating. A native of the
Mediterranean region, it grows to
about 90 cm (about 36 in). The
large leaves are red-veined and
deeply divided. In late spring, a
thick stem bears one or more large,
up to 40 cm (about 16 in) spathes,
like that of the arum, green on the
outside and red to purple to black
on the inside, with a purple to black
spadix. Plant the large tubers in
winter in well-drained soil in partial
shade. Water well through the
growing season but allow to dry out
after flowering. In cold areas, protect with a dressing of mulch in
winter, although the plant is rated
frost-hardy. Propagate from seed or
offsets in autumn/fall.

ERANTHIS
hyemalis
syn. *E. cilicicus*
WINTER ACONITE

This delightful, ground-hugging
native of Asia and Europe belongs
to a genus of clump-forming perennials with knobbly tubers grown for
their cup-shaped flowers, which are
surrounded by leaf-like ruffs of
bracts. They flower in late winter to
early spring. Sunny yellow, goblet-
shaped flowers about 3 cm (about
1½ in) wide are perched on a ruff
of green, divided leaves. It grows to
a height of 12 cm (about 5 in) with

Cypella herbertii

Cyclamen hederifolium

a spread of 15 cm (about 6 in).
Plant the tubers in early autumn/fall
in rich, slightly damp soil. The species likes full sun to partial shade
and is fully hardy. It does best in
cooler areas, naturalized under a
deciduous tree or in a rock garden
where it will spread quite rapidly.
Propagate by division any time in
summer or from seed in autumn/
fall.

ERYTHRONIUM
DOG-TOOTH-VIOLET

Native to Asia, Europe and North
America, these little plants bear
delicate, reflexed, star-shaped flowers in spring. The dark green foliage
is often attractively mottled.
Erythronia are fully hardy and do
best in cooler areas. Plant the tubers
in autumn/fall in well-drained soil
which is rich in organic matter.
Keep plants moist in partial to full
shade. They multiply easily and
should be left undisturbed until
overcrowding occurs. Propagate
from offsets in summer or from seed
in autumn/fall.

Freesia, Florist's hybrids

E. dens-canis
DOG'S TOOTH VIOLET

The most widely grown species, reaching to 20 cm (about 8 in), it has beautiful, oval, marbled foliage. The reflexed, star-shaped flowers are white to lilac, about 5 cm (about 2 in) wide. The common name refers to the shape of the corm.

E. 'Pagoda'

This hardy cultivar grows to 30 cm (about 12 in) and has marbled green foliage. The creamy yellow flowers are star-shaped, reflexed and nodding, about 5 cm (about 2 in) across.

EUCOMIS
comosa
syn. E. punctata
PINEAPPLE LILY

This native of South Africa has a spike of flowers which looks very similar to a pineapple; it is even topped with a tuft of pineapple-like leaves. It grows to 70 cm (about 28 in). Dark green, crinkly, strap-like leaves surround the tall, purple spotted scapes. The hundreds of star-shaped flowers, white to green and sometimes spotted with purple, are borne on a spike in autumn/fall. Plant bulbs in spring in full sun in well-drained soil. Half-hardy, it may need to be lifted in very cold winters. Water well through the growing season. Propagate by division in winter or from seed in spring, but it takes a long time to flower. Makes an excellent, long-lasting cut flower.

FREESIA
FREESIA

These South African natives are extensively grown for their brightly coloured and deliciously scented spring flowers. They are rather tender but easily grown in most areas except those that suffer heavy frost. Slender, sword-shaped leaves surround wiry stems which bear spikes of goblet-shaped flowers. The weight of the flowers can be too much for the stems so they may need to be supported by twigs or wire. Plant the corms in autumn/fall in full sun in well-drained soil. They look best in a massed display. Water well through the growing season but allow to dry out once flowering is finished. The clumps are best left undisturbed for three years; they can then be divided in autumn/fall. Seed should be sown in late summer. In cold climates, they grow very well in pots in a cool greenhouse.

F. alba
syn. F. refracta alba

This widely grown species flowers in early spring. The creamy white, goblet-shaped flowers are 5 cm (about 2 in) long and are borne on a spike. Slender, bayonet-shaped leaves surround wiry stems up to 30 cm (about 12 in) long. This highly scented species makes an excellent cut flower.

F., Florist's hybrids

There are many named strains of hybrid freesias available; they come in shades of white, pink, blue, red or yellow, and grow from 15–35 cm (about 6–14 in) in height. Some have semi-double flowers whose weight makes the plant top-heavy enough to need staking. None is difficult to grow, although they need glasshouse culture in frosty climates or if blooms outside of their natural spring season are desired. Some strains are well scented, others almost scentless.

FRITILLARIA
FRITILLARY

These relatives of the lily and tulip are native to Asia, Europe and North America. Fully hardy, they do best in areas with cold winters. They are not easy to grow, but their nodding, bell to goblet-shaped flowers which appear in spring are worth the trouble. Plant bulbs in early autumn/fall in partial shade in well-drained soil rich in organic matter. Water well through the growing season but allow to dry out after flowering. In areas which have high summer rainfall, the bulbs will need to be lifted. Handle the rather soft bulbs gently, and keep them out of the ground for as short a time as possible. Propagate from offsets in summer, but clumps are best left undisturbed for a few years. Seed can be sown in autumn/fall but will take 4 or 5 years to bloom.

F. imperialis
CROWN IMPERIAL

This is the tallest species and also the easiest to grow. The stems reach up to 1 m (about 3 ft) or more and the leaves are borne in whorls along the stem. The flowers are also arranged in a whorl or crown at the top of the scape, and above the flowers is a bunch of leaves. The bell-shaped flowers are 3 cm (about 1½ in) long and can be yellow to orange to red; they have a heavy, rather unpleasant odour.

F. meleagris
SNAKE'S HEAD LILY, LEPER'S LILY

Slender stems reaching to 35 cm (about 14 in) each bear one nodding, goblet-shaped bloom. The maroon, green or white flowers are 2.5 cm (about 1 in) long and are blotched or checkered. A few slender leaves are found along the stem. Does well naturalized under deciduous trees or in a rock garden, provided it has plenty of moisture while growing.

Freesia alba

Fritillaria imperialis

Erythronium 'Pagoda'

Eucomis comosa

Erythronium dens-canis

F. persica

This Mediterranean species can be grown in warmer areas than most other species. It grows to about 1 m (about 3 ft) and bears up to 25 nodding, bell-shaped flowers on a spike. The 2.5 cm (about 1 in) flowers which appear in spring are dark purple to brown to blackish purple. Dozens of narrow, green leaves appear along the stem.

GALANTHUS

SNOWDROPS

These natives of Europe and western Asia flower in late winter and herald the coming of spring. Fully hardy they do best in cold areas. Delightful, white, nodding flowers appear above daffodil-like foliage. Plant bulbs in autumn/fall in rich, moist soil in partial shade. In very cold areas they may be planted in full sun. They are best divided or transplanted immediately after flowering, before the leaves start to die off. They can be grown from seed which will bloom a few years after sowing. Snowdrops do well in a rockery and are an excellent cut flower.

G. ikariae

syn. G. latifolius

Fine stems reaching to 10 cm (about 4 in), each bear one delicate, 2.5 cm (about 1 in), nodding, bell-shaped flower. The outer petals are pure white, the inner petals are green at the throat. The blue-green foliage is narrow and strap-like. It does well in a rock garden.

G. nivalis

This most commonly grown species reaches about 22 cm (about 9 in). The slender, blue-green leaves are strap-shaped. Each fine stem bears one nodding, bell-shaped, 2.5 cm (about 1 in) flower. The outer petals are white and the tubular inner petals green and white. There are many cultivars derived from this species, including a double-flowered one.

GALTONIA

candicans

BERG LILY, SUMMER HYACINTH

This South African native produces delightful bell-shaped flowers for 6 weeks in the middle of summer. The flower spike bears up to 20 white blooms which are sometimes green at the tips. Broad, blue-green, strap-shaped leaves surround stems which can reach up to 2 m (about 6 ft). Plant bulbs in late autumn/fall about 15 cm (about 6 in) deep in well-drained, compost-rich soil in a sunny position. It is half-hardy. Water well through the growing season and allow to dry out after flowering. Propagate from offsets in autumn/fall or from seed which will usually bloom in three years. Protect from slugs and snails.

GLADIOLUS

GLADIOLUS

Gladioli are native to Africa, Europe and the Middle East. They vary greatly in size, colour, flowering time and even the arrangement of the blooms on the flower spike.

Most of the widely cultivated hybrids originate in South Africa. The hybrids are divided into 3 main groups—Large-flowered, Primulinus and Butterfly. The Large-flowered types are those that are usually seen in florist's arrangements, sometimes with ruffled flowers which are arranged alternately either side of the 2 m (about 6 ft) long stem. The Primulinus group have smaller flowers, often blotched, arranged irregularly on a 30 cm (about 12 in) stem. The Butterfly group have blotched, ruffled flowers on 90 cm (about 36 in) stems. Corms should be planted about 12 cm (about 5 in) deep in very well-drained, sandy soil in a sunny position. In cool areas, plant in early spring; in warm areas, plant from autumn/fall until spring for a succession of blooms. The tall stems may need staking. Water well through summer and cut off spent flower stems. Corms will need to be lifted in cold areas and Large-flowered gladioli are best lifted in all areas, especially those with a high winter rainfall. Make sure they are pefectly dry before storing. Can be propagated from offsets although these may take a few years to bloom.

G. alatus

KALKOENTJIE

This small species grows to about 30 cm (about 12 in). Flowers are red to orange and yellow at the base. Good drainage is essential. It is excellent in a rockery.

G., Butterfly hybrids

These resemble the Large-flowered hybrids (see below) but have slightly smaller, ruffled flowers, usually with contrasting blotches in the throat. They come in the same range of colours and are grown in the same way.

G. byzantinus

A Mediterranean species reaching to about 1 m (about 3 ft). The slender stem bears up to 15 pink to magenta blooms.

Gladiolus, Butterfly hybrids

Galanthus ikariae

Fritillaria persica

Gladiolus byzantinus

Galanthus nivalis

Fritillaria meleagris

Galtonia candicans

Gladiolus alatus

Haemanthus coccineus

Gladiolus callianthus

Gloriosa superba

Herbertia drummondii

Habranthus robustus

Gladiolus tristis

Gladiolus carneus

Gladiolus × colvillei

Gladiolus, Large-flowered hybrids

G. callianthus
syn. *Acidanthera bicolor*
PEACOCK FLOWER

This scented species grows to about 90 cm (about 36 in). The mainly white flowers often have a crimson blotch at their base. The 10 cm (about 4 in) long flowers have 6 outer petals and the inner petals appear to form a tube. Half-hardy, it flowers in autumn/fall. Protect from thrips, and water lavishly while in growth.

G. carneus
syn. *G. blandus*
PAINTED LADY

A lovely, spring-flowering plant with arching spikes of white, funnel-shaped flowers stained with purple or yellow blotches. It is half-hardy and easily grown, multiplying vigorously.

G. × colvillei
syn. *G. nanus*

Up to 10, elegant, 7 cm (about 3 in) dark pink, yellow or white blooms on a 45 cm (about 18 in) spike. Usually flowers in late spring.

G., Large-flowered hybrids

These are the familiar gladioli of the flower shops. They grow up to 1.5 m (about 4½ ft) tall with one-sided flower spikes that can carry up to 24 wide open flowers. The individual flowers are normally about 10 cm (about 4 in) wide, although they may be as large as 14 cm (about 5½ in). Every colour but blue is available. Half-hardy, they are best planted in spring and lifted in late autumn/fall to be stored for the winter. Rich soil, sun, and vigilant protection from thrips are needed. Propagate by growing on offsets, which take 3 years to flower.

G. tristis
YELLOW MARSH AFRIKANER

Each 60 cm (about 24 in) slender stem carries up to 6 highly scented, bright yellow flowers, about 7 cm (about 3 in) wide. It prefers a richer soil than the sandy soil favoured by most species. Many spring-flowering hybrids derive from this popular species.

GLORIOSA
superba
GLORY LILY, TIGER'S CLAWS

This is a tropical species from Africa, only suitable for the garden where there is no chance whatever of frost. However, it does grow very well as a pot plant and greenhouse grown flowers are popular with florists. They resemble tigerlilies but are brilliant in red and gold. The plants climb by means of tendrils on the ends of the leaves and need support. Plant the tubers in autumn/fall, taking care as the plant is very poisonous. *G. rothschildiana* is very similar and some authorities consider it merely a variety of *G. superba*.

HABRANTHUS
robustus
PAMPAS LILY

This beautiful plant is a relative of the *Hippeastrum* and comes from the Argentine pampas. A trumpet-shaped flower about 10 cm (about 4 in) long appears on each 30 cm (about 12 in) stem. The flowers, which appear in summer, are rose-pink, often fading to white. The glossy, green basal foliage is strap-like. Tender to frost, it is easily grown in warm to temperate areas. Plant the bulbs in a sunny position in autumn/fall in well-drained soil rich in organic matter. Water well through the growing season. Can be propagated from offsets when dormant or from seed, which will usually flower in the third year.

HAEMANTHUS
coccineus
BLOOD LILY

The half-hardy *Haemanthus* genus, with its brightly coloured flowers, originates in Africa and prefers mild to warm conditions. This autumn/fall-flowering species grows to 35 cm (about 14 in). The two broadly oval, dark green leaves are hairy on the underside, and they lie on the soil. A sturdy, purple-spotted stem bears a cluster of slender, bright red flowers enclosed by scarlet to pink bracts and followed by red berries. Plant bulbs in autumn/fall or spring in partial shade in a compost-rich, well-drained soil. Water and feed well during the growing season, but allow it to get completely dry during its summer dormancy. The plants are best left undisturbed for a few years when they can then be propagated from offsets, or from seed, which takes a few years to flower. The common name has no sinister connotations, it merely refers to the colour of the flowers.

HERBERTIA
drummondii
BLUE TIGER FLOWER

This spring-flowering South American native is a relative of the *Tigridia* and the iris. The foliage is like that of an iris, sword-shaped and pleated. The stems reach to 30 cm (about 12 in) and bear short-lived, triangular flowers about 5 cm (about 2 in) wide. The outer petals are violet-blue and the smaller inner petals are often spotted. It is frost-tender and does best in temperate to warm areas. Plant the corms in autumn/fall in a sunny to

Hyacinthoides hispanica

Hippeastrum 'Red Lion'

Hyacinthus orientalis

Hippeastrum 'Apple Blossom'

Hyacinthoides non-scripta

Hippeastrum advenum

Hermodactylus tuberosus

partially shaded position. The soil should be light and well drained but enriched with compost. Water well through the growing season but allow to dry out after flowering. Propagate by dividing corms in winter or from seed in autumn/fall.

HERMODACTYLUS
tuberosus
syn. *Iris tuberosa*
SNAKE'S HEAD IRIS, WIDOW IRIS

This frost-hardy relative of the iris gets its common names from the appearance and unusual colours (often black and green) of its flowers. Native to the Middle East and Mediterranean region, it grows to 40 cm (about 16 in). The tall, blue-green foliage is slender and squarish. The perfumed, iris-like flowers, yellow-green and purple-black, appear in early spring. Plant the tubers in early autumn/fall in very well-drained soil in a sunny spot. Leave clumps undisturbed for a few years, then divide in spring or summer. Alternatively, grow from seed, but this may be difficult to obtain.

HIPPEASTRUM

BARBADOS LILY

These magnificent plants with their showy, trumpet-shaped flowers are native to tropical South America. They have been widely hybridized and it is these cultivars which are usually grown by the average gardener. Half-hardy, in cold areas they will need to be protected from frost. They can also be grown in a glasshouse or inside as a pot plant. A single bulb in a pot will produce a

display that any florist would be hard pressed to match. Bulbs should be planted in autumn/fall in well-drained soil rich in organic matter, with just the tip of the bulb exposed, in full sun or partial shade. Water and feed well through the growing season and allow the bulb to dry out after the foliage dies down. Clumps are best left undisturbed for a few years when they can then be divided. They can also be grown from seed sown in spring. Protect from snails.

H. advenum
syn. *Rhodolphiala bifurcata*
CHILEAN LILY

Up to 6 dark red, trumpet-shaped flowers about 5 cm (about 2 in) long are borne on a 30 cm (about 12 in) stem. The stem and flowers appear in summer before the blue-green, slender, strap-like foliage appears. There is also a bright red form and a yellow form.

H. 'Apple Blossom'

This is the most popular of all the Dutch-bred hybrid hippeastrums. A sturdy stem reaching up to 45 cm (about 18 in) bears clusters of up to 6 stunning pale pink and white blooms. Trumpet-shaped flowers, up to 20 cm (about 8 in), appear in spring, followed by slender foliage. It is frost-tender.

H. 'Red Lion'

Up to 6 blood-red, trumpet-shaped flowers appear in spring on a thick, 50 cm (about 20 in) stem. The very showy blooms can be 20 cm (about 8 in) long. Slender, blue-green foliage appears after the flowers.

HYACINTHOIDES
syn. *Endymion, Scilla*
BLUEBELLS

The hardy, European bluebells with their attractive, scented flowers are popular with gardeners all over the world. Equally at home in a rock garden, naturalized under deciduous trees or in the flower border, they thrive in moist, partially shaded conditions. Bulbs should be planted in autumn/fall in rich, moist soil. Water well until the flowers start to die. They should multiply freely but are best left undisturbed for a few years, then divided in late summer.

H. hispanica
syn. *Endymion hispanica,*
Scilla campanulata
SPANISH BLUEBELL

The most popular and most easily grown species, it grows to about 30 cm (about 12 in) and flowers in spring. The 2.5 cm (about 1 in) nodding, bell-shaped flowers are lilac to blue. The bright green foliage is strap-like. It multiplies freely.

H. non-scripta
syn. *Endymion non-scripta,*
Scilla non-scripta
ENGLISH BLUEBELL

The English bluebell flowers in early spring and can continue flowering into summer. The very fragrant, nodding, bell-shaped flowers in lavender-blue, pink or white are about 1 cm (about ½ in) long on fine stems reaching to about 30 cm (about 12 in). The slender, strap-like foliage is glossy green.

HYACINTHUS
orientalis
HYACINTH

Popular with gardeners all over the world, the popular named varieties of hyacinth are cultivars of *H. orientalis* which originally comes from the Middle East and Mediterranean region. A spike of flowers is massed on top of a 30 cm (about 12 in) stem. The sweetly perfumed spring flowers vary enormously in colour. 'King of the Blues' is a favourite, but many others are available in white, pale yellow, pink, red or purple.

The glossy green foliage is strap-like. Plant the bulbs in clumps in autumn/fall in rich, well-drained soil in full sun or partial shade. Frost-hardy, hyacinths do best in cool areas, as well as in pots. It is best to buy new bulbs each year, as the flowers are never so magnificent as in that first spring; but, planted in a congenial spot, they will continue to bloom each spring for years.

HYMENOCALLIS

SPIDER LILY, FILMY LILY

The unusual, beautiful, flowers of the spider lily resemble daffodils except for the delicate, spider-like petals surrounding the inner bloom. Mainly native to South America, they are not too fussy about conditions; but are usually frost-tender and do best in temperate or warm areas. Bulbs should be planted in winter, about 15 cm (about 6 in) deep in well-drained soil. A partially shaded position is best. Water very well during growth and never allow

to dry out completely. Offsets form quickly and should be divided in winter.

H. × festalis

This half-hardy to frost-tender plant grows to about 50 cm (about 20 in) and has deliciously scented flowers. The glossy green foliage is slender and strap-like. Each stem bears up to five 10 cm (about 4 in) white flowers. The inner trumpet-shaped cup of petals is surrounded by 6 slender, spider-like petals.

H. littoralis

Pure white, trumpet-shaped flowers surrounded by 6 thread-like petals are borne on 75 cm (about 30 in) stems. The almost strap-like foliage is bright green. This species is frost-tender.

IRIS

IRIS

This wide-ranging genus, named for the Greek goddess of the rain-

bow, is valued all over the world for its beautiful and distinctive flowers. Size, colour and growing conditions vary greatly but the unusual flowers are easily recognized. Each flower has 6 petals: 3 outer petals, called 'falls', droop away from the centre and alternate with the inner petals, called 'standards'. Irises are divided into 2 main groups, rhizomatous (which we have included in the chapter on annuals and perennials) and bulbous. The bulbous irises are divided into 3 groups, which some botanists raise to the status of 3 new genera: *Xiphium*, which includes the Dutch irises of the florist shops as well as the species *I. xiphium, latifolia, lusitania* and *tingitana* from which they have been derived (they are mostly native to Spain, Portugal and North Africa); *Iridodictyum*, which bear small, winter and spring flowers and are mainly native to the Middle East; and *Juno*, also from the Middle East and Central Asia, which are noteworthy for their handsome leaves and spectacular flowers, with diminutive standards but well-developed falls. All are fully hardy, and enjoy a sunny position with ample moisture during growth but very little during their summer dormancy. All are planted in autumn/fall.

IRIDODICTYUM

RETICULATA IRISES

The best known species is *I. reticulata* from Central Asia. It grows to about 10 cm (about 4 in) high in flower, and has flowers in various shades of blue: several named varieties are available, differ-

ing mainly in the precise colour of the flowers. Foliage is short during the late winter/early spring flowering time, becoming longer after bloom. It likes sun and perfectly drained soil and is propagated from seed or by division. Other species in the group, all fully hardy, include: *I. histrio* and *I. histrioides*, both blue; *I. bakeriana*, blue and purple; and *I. danfordiae*, yellow. The whole group does best in cold-winter climates. All species make delightful pot plants.

JUNO

Mainly native to Central Asia, the Junos have a reputation for being difficult to grow, but where winters are cold and summers dry they are easy enough to grow in a sunny, perfectly drained position. Most species have fleshy roots attached permanently to the bulbs and great care must be taken never to damage these. The species all have handsome foliage.

I. bucharica

syn. I. orchioides

This iris grows to about 45 cm (about 18 in). The 6 cm (about 2½ in) scented flowers can be varied in colour. Standards and falls can both be white or yellow, or standards can be white and falls yellow. It requires a rich soil and is slow to increase. Take care not to damage the thick lateral roots when transplanting.

XIPHIUM

These are the best known of the bulbous irises, and best known among them are the Dutch hybrids. They grow to about 80 cm (about 32 in) in flower, with rather straggly grey-green leaves and bear one or two flowers on long stems. Fully hardy and easy to grow, they like rich, well-drained soil and sun. Water freely while they are in growth, and keep them dry in summer. They are propagated by division in autumn/fall. Handle the bulbs gently as they bruise easily. The so-called English and Spanish irises, mainly derived from *I. latifolia*, are similar to Dutch hybrids but flower later in spring.

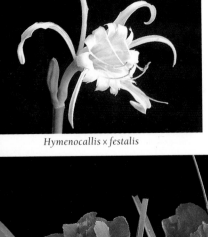

Hymenocallis × festalis

Iris reticulata

Iris 'Symphony' (Dutch hybrid)

Iris 'Professor Blauw' (Dutch hybrid)

Iris bucharica

Hymenocallis littoralis

I., Dutch hybrids

These are familiar flower-shop flowers; florists keep them in bloom just about all year by chilling the bulbs and planting in greenhouses. There are many named varieties, in shades of white, blue, violet, or yellow. The blue 'Professor Blaauw' and yellow and white 'Symphony' are typical. In the garden they flower in mid-spring.

I. latifolia
syn. *I. xiphioides*

Most of the bulbous English irises (so-called because of their great popularity in eighteenth-century England) are derived from this species from Spain. It grows to 75 cm (about 30 in), and the 10 cm (about 4 in) flowers which appear in summer are purple-blue or white. The falls are 'winged' and often have a golden blotch.

I. tingitana

This magnificent species from northern Africa has 15 cm (about 6 in) wide, light blue flowers. It is temperamental in cultivation and is normally represented in gardens by its cultivar 'Wedgwood', a hybrid with a Dutch iris. This grows to 70 cm (about 28 in) tall, and has 12 cm (about 5 in) light blue flowers. It is cultivated the same way as the Dutch hybrids.

IXIA
AFRICAN CORN LILY

The South African corn lily produces masses of delightful, star-shaped flowers on wiry stems in spring. These flowers close in the evening and on cloudy days. The tallest species grows to about 60 cm (about 24 in). The leaves are usually long and slender. They are sensitive to frost but easy to grow in temperate to warm areas. The bulbs should be planted in early autumn/fall in well-drained soil. Blood and bone mixed into the soil before planting will help produce good blooms. A sunny position is ideal except in warm areas where they will need protection from hot sun. Water well through winter and

spring but allow to dry out after flowering. Propagate from offsets in autumn/fall. Seed can be used and this should flower in the third year.

I. maculata
YELLOW IXIA

This is the most commonly grown species. The wiry stems grow to about 45 cm (about 18 in), with 5 cm (about 2 in) flowers clustered along the top, with brown centres, and orange to yellow petals, sometimes with pinkish red undersides; garden forms come in white, yellow, pink, orange or red.

I. paniculata
syn. *Morphixia paniculata*
BUTT IXIA

The slender stems grow to about 60 cm (about 24 in) and are topped with spikes of buff to pale pink blooms. The 5 cm (about 2 in) flowers, star-shaped and tubular at the base, appear in late spring.

I. viridiflora
GREEN IXIA

The exquisite, jewel-like flowers make this a popular species. The 5 cm (about 2 in) flowers are borne on a spike atop the 60 cm (about 24 in) stem. The star-shaped flowers are turquoise with a purple-black centre.

IXIOLIRION
tataricum
syn. *I. montanum, I. pallasii*
TARTAR LILY

Popular in Europe and America, this native of the Middle East and

central Asia flowers in spring. The slender stem reaches to about 45 cm (about 18 in) and bears clusters of up to six tubular, star-shaped, violet to blue flowers. The foliage is slender and grass-like. Plant bulbs in autumn/fall in full sun in well-drained soil. A protective layer of mulch will be needed in cool areas. Plant in a pot in areas with severe frost. Water well during growth and allow to dry out after flowering. Propagate from offsets or seed in autumn/fall.

LACHENALIA
CAPE COWSLIP, SOLDIER BOYS, YIOOLTJIE

Massed in clumps or planted in window boxes, these South African natives make a striking display. Spikes of pendulous, tubular flowers stand erect above narrow, sometimes marbled, strap-like foliage. Plant bulbs in autumn/fall in well-

drained soil enriched with organic matter. They like a sunny position and lots of water until the foliage begins to die off. They need to be kept dry when dormant and may need to be lifted in areas with a high summer rainfall. They are sensitive to frost and can be planted in pots or window boxes in cool areas. They spread quite freely and can be divided in autumn/fall.

L. aloides var. aloides
syn. *L. tricolour*
CAPE COWSLIP

This species grows to about 30 cm (about 12 in). Flowers appear on a spike in winter to spring above strap-like foliage. The nodding, tubular flowers flare out at the tips, and are usually golden yellow and green at the tips. The base of the petals is sometimes red to orange. There are various forms and many hybrids derived from this species.

Ixia maculata

Iris tingitana 'Wedgwood'

Lachenalia aloides var. *aloides*

Iris latifolia

Ixiolirion tataricum

Ixia viridiflora

Ixia paniculata

Lilium, Asiatic hybrid

Leucojum aestivum

Lilium 'Bright Star' (Aurelian)

Leucojum autumnale

Lachenalia bulbifera

Leucocoryne ixioides odorata

Lilium 'Royal Gold' (Trumpet)

L. bulbifera
syn. *L. pendula*
RED LACHENALIA

This species grows to about 25 cm (about 10 in), with a spike of flowers appearing in winter to spring. The pendulous, tubular flowers are pink to red to yellow and the flared tips are violet to purple. The green foliage is strap-like.

LEUCOCORYNE
ixioides odorata
GLORY OF THE SUN

This native of Chile is a bit of a gamble for the gardener. One year you may get a magnificent display of blooms and the next spring it may refuse to flower at all. Flowers are borne in clusters on wiry stems up to 45 cm (about 18 in) tall. The 5 cm (about 2 in), sweetly scented flowers are reflexed and star-shaped, white in the centre, graduating to blue at the tips with prominent yellow anthers. The foliage is long and slender. Plant bulbs in autumn/fall in full sun in light, well-drained soil with plenty

of water in winter and spring and allow to dry out over summer. Half-hardy, it does best in temperate areas. Propagate from seed or offsets in autumn/fall, but this is difficult.

LEUCOJUM
SNOWFLAKE

A genus of spring- and autumn-flowering bulbs resembling the snowdrop, these delightful flowers are native to North Africa and the southern Mediterranean. The pendent, bell-shaped flowers consist of 6 evenly sized petals, borne singly or in twos and threes at the top of a thin stem which can grow up to 60 cm (about 24 in). The mid-green to deep green leaves are narrow and strap like. The bulbs multiply freely, and large clumps of nodding blooms make a glorious display. Some of the species prefer partial shade in moist soil, while others thrive in a sunny position with well-drained soil. The bulbs should be planted in late summer or early autumn/fall and only lifted for dividing when they produce few flowers and many leaves. Propagate

from offsets in spring or early autumn/fall or from seed sown in autumn/fall.

L. aestivum
SUMMER SNOWFLAKE, GIANT SNOWFLAKE

These dainty, spring-flowering bulbs are native to Europe and Asia. The fragrant flowers are white with a green spot near the tip of each petal and are borne in clusters atop 50 cm (about 20 in) stems. The blue-green leaves are long and slender. Frost-hardy, the small bulbs should be planted in autumn/fall in a sunny position, but need protection from hot sun in warm areas. Under a deciduous tree is ideal. The soil should be rich, moist and well-drained. Propagate from seed or the freely forming offsets in autumn/fall or spring, but clumps are best left undisturbed for a few years.

L. autumnale
AUTUMN SNOWFLAKE

This species has delicate white flowers, flushed with pink, which appear singly or in twos and threes at the top of a thin, 25 cm (about 10 in) high stem. Its erect, pencil-thin basal leaves, which usually follow the flowers, add to the plant's dainty air. As the common name implies, the flowers appear in late summer or early autumn/fall. The bulbs should be planted 4 cm (about 2 in) deep in well-drained soil in a sunny position.

LILIUM
LILY

Many plants are commonly called lilies but the 'true' lilies are the

many species and hybrids of the magnificent *Lilium* genus. The elegant flowers possess a breathtaking beauty often accompanied by a glorious perfume. The flowers have 6 petals arranged in a variety of ways, and 6 stamens. The scaly bulbs should be planted in autumn/fall, but in cold areas they are best planted in spring. The soil should be rich with excellent drainage and the bulbs planted fairly deep as they like a cool root run. A dressing of mulch in spring helps keep the roots cool. A partially shaded position is best as the flowers need protection from hot afternoon sun. Tall species may need staking. Dead flowers should be removed but leaves and stems should not be cut back until autumn/fall. Clumps are best left undisturbed for a few years; they can then be lifted and divided. In recent years, many hybrids, easier to grow than most true lilies, have been created, and have become very popular. The most important groups are the Asiatic or Mid-Century hybrids, the Trumpet hybrids, the Aurelians which have trumpet or bowl shaped flowers, and the spectacular Oriental hybrids. They need lime-free soil, although *L. candidum* prefers an alkaline soil and *L. regale* and *L. lancifolium* will put up with a little lime.

Asiatic hybrids

Raised from *L. lancifolium, bulbiferum, croceum* and other Asiatic species. These are summer flowering and mostly grow to about 1 m (about 3 ft) tall. Most have upward-facing, flat flowers in shades from white through yellow and pink to orange and russet-red. They have no scent. Fully hardy, they do best in a sunny position and are first-rate cut flowers, much grown in greenhouses by florists for out-of-season bloom. Propagate by division. Bulbs can be left in the ground if they have good drainage. There are many named varieties: the yellow 'Connecticut King' and orange 'Enchantment' are popular.

Trumpet hybrids

Deriving from *L. regale*, the trumpet hybrids flower in late summer. They can reach 2 m (about 6 ft) and carry as many as 30 outward facing trumpets in shades from white through pink to yellow, usually with purple shadings on the outside. They are usually fragrant and are easily grown in light shade and lime free, well-drained soil.

Aurelian hybrids
syn. *L. aurelianense*

The name comes from the Latin name for Orléans in France where the earliest varieties were bred. They derive from crosses between the

Chinese *L. henryi* and trumpet lilies and resemble the Trumpet hybrids except the flowers may be flat or bowl shaped. Some cultivars are well scented, others scentless. They are fully hardy.

Oriental hybrids

Most glamorous of all lilies, the Oriental hybrids grow to 2 m (about 6 ft) tall and bear many bowl-shaped flowers as much as 25 cm (about 10 in) wide in shades from white to crimson. They are powerfully scented and very desirable (and expensive) cut flowers. Derived from crosses of *U. auratum*, *speciosum* and *ribellum*, they like a temperate climate, light shade and perfectly drained very acid soil. They are subject to virus and care needs to be taken to obtain clean stock. There are many cultivars.

SPECIES

L. auratum
GOLDEN-RAYED LILY OF JAPAN

This magnificent species grows up to 2 m (about 6 ft). Each stem bears up to eight open-faced blooms, about 20 cm (about 8 in) wide. The flowers are white, red spotted, and have a yellow or red stripe along each petal.

L. candidum
MADONNA LILY

This beautifully scented species is thought to be the oldest lily in cultivation. It grows to 2.3 m (about 7 ft) and bears up to 20 trumpet-shaped blooms in summer. The pure white flowers can be 15 cm (about 6 in) wide and slightly reflexed. It is sometimes tricky to grow, being very subject to virus. Cool climates and mildly alkaline soils suit it best. Plant with the nose of the bulb almost at ground level.

L. formosanum

This is an elegant lily which grows to 2 m (about 6 ft). The flowers which appear in late summer are trumpet-shaped and reflexed. The petals are pure white on the inside and pink to purple-brown on the outside. It is easily grown from seed. Mature bulbs are prone to viruses and often do not give a good display of blooms, so they should be replaced every few years. It is half-hardy.

L. henryi

This lily from Central China grows to about 2 m (about 6 ft), with each stem bearing as many as 40 reflexed flowers in pale apricot. The bulbs can be as much as 20 cm (about 8 in) in diameter, an indication of the great vigour of the species. It tolerates lime and is resistant to viruses. Fully hardy, it is the chief parent of the Aurelian hybrids.

L. lancifolium
syn. *L. tigrinum*
TIGER LILY

One of the most popular species and also one of the oldest in cultivation, the tiger lily grows to about 1.5 m (about 4½ ft). It produces masses of bright orange, trumpet-shaped, sharply reflexed flowers. The 18 cm (about 7½ in) blooms are spotted with purple and are usually pendent. The tiger lily can harbour viruses without showing any ill effects and for this reason is best grown away from other lilies. It is much grown in its native China for the edible bulbs.

L. longiflorum
EASTER LILY, ST JOSEPH LILY, BERMUDA LILY, CHRISTMAS LILY

A lovely, pure white lily which grows to 1.2 m (about 4 ft). Up to 8 slender, trumpet-shaped flowers are borne on each stem. The fragrant blooms, 20 cm (about 8 in) long, appear in summer. It is half-hardy, and one of the best lilies for warm-winter climates.

L. martagon
TURK'S CAP LILY

Native to Europe, this species flowers in summer and bears many reflexed flowers in mauve-pink or white, with a strong fragrance. Fully hardy, it does best in cool climates. The name, 'Child of Mars', dates from a time when even gardening was governed by astrology.

Lilium auratum

Lilium henryi

Lilium martagon

Lilium 'Wildfire' (Oriental hybrid)

Lilium lancifolium   *Lilium candidum*

Lilium longiflorum

Lilium formosanum (white form)

A Field Trip to Darling and Malmesbury

South-western Cape Province, in the southern tip of Africa, is known to botanists worldwide as the 'Cape Floral Kingdom'. Unlike the rest of sub-Saharan Africa this region has a Mediterranean climate—cold, wet winters and hot, dry summers. It is also geologically and topographically diverse—a coastal plain of largely sand or limestone and, further inland, a gently undulating landscape made up of shale and clay. Rising abruptly from this are the rugged parallel ranks of the Cape Fold Mountains, whose jagged and forbidding slopes dominate the skyline. The soil here is deficient in nutrients due to the acid sandstone formation of the mountains. *Gladiolus* is one of many genera of plants that have adapted and thrive in this region of contrast.

Gladiolus species are bewildering in their variety and have been beloved by colonists from the earliest days of European settlement. A number of species common in the vicinity of Cape Town have acquired picturesque names, and one of the best loved of these is the kalkoentjie or little turkey (*Gladiolus alatus*). This delightful little plant derives its name from the appearance of the flowers, which resemble a brilliantly hued turkey head, resplendent with wattles. The flowers are predominantly bright reddish orange, but the lower two petals are yellowish green with orange tips. Other similar species,

In springtime the meadows near Cape Town are a beautiful sight.

also sharing the common name of kalkoentjie, are variously coloured in greens and browns and all have a delightful scent, but none has quite the impact of *G. alatus*. You cannot see a colony of these plants without feeling a little cheerier for the experience.

G. alatus is a small plant, usually 15–25 cm (about 6–10 in) tall, with four strap-shaped leaves. The spike bears up to six flowers 3–5 cm (about 1–2 in) in diameter. The dorsal petal is the largest and forms a shallow hood arching forward, while broad lateral petals curve back like wings. The three stamens, arched together in front of the flower, are pollinated by long-tonged bees of the Anthophoridae family.

Although it is widespread in the south-western Cape, one of the best places for a field trip to see the kalkoentjie is only half an hour's drive from Cape Town. And the best time to see them in bloom is spring, particularly September. As the flowers of a number of showy plants, particularly the annual daisies and the bulbs *Oxalis* and *Romulea*, close in the late afternoon and only open again in the warmth and light of mid-morning, you need not rush off early in the morning to start your trip.

With your back to the splendid massif of Table Mountain, which guards Table Bay and Cape Town harbour, drive towards Malmesbury on the N7 national road. Soon you will see the narrow flats of the west coast and, inland, the gently rolling country of the Swartland. In winter much of this flat, sandy land near the coast is inundated with water. Snowy white arums (*Zantedeschia aethiopica*), thrusting their heads out of clumps of dark, arrow-shaped leaves, are a common sight along drainage lines and roadside ditches.

Clay soil on the rising ground in this area supports a natural vegetation dominated by a grey, small-leaved shrublet which is covered by a confetti of small white flowers in winter, followed by a similar scattering of fluffy white seeds. This is known as the renosterbos or rhinoceros bush (*Elytropappus rhinocerotis*), and as the name suggests, it was once a favourite food of the (now rare) rhinoceros. During spring, annuals

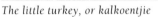

The little turkey, or kalkoentjie   *Gladiolus dalenii*   *Gladiolus priorii*

and bulbous plants emerge in abundance, and along the road verges and in patches of undisturbed veld a haze of colour greets your eyes. Some introduced Australian mimosas, the Sydney golden wattle (*Acacia longifolia*) and the golden wattle (*A. cyclopis*), create a magnificent sea of fragrant, yellow blossom in spring but, unfortunately, also form impenetrable woodlands, almost suffocating all other plant growth.

Continue along the N7 towards Malmesbury for 35 km (about 22 miles), and when you reach the turnoff to Atlantis and Mamre stop the car and breathe in the beauty around you. On either side of the road, bordering a small stream, are meadows as resplendent with flowers as an oriental rug. Tall orange bugle lilies (*Watsonia meriana*) stand at attention in serried ranks along the road. Beyond them in the meadows, *Gladiolus alatus* forms orange patches among the velvet blue of bobbejaantjie or little baboon (*Babiana angustifolia*), and the glistening pink of the large sundew (*Drosera cistiflora*). Some 35 km (about 22 miles) to the north-west, a blood red form of *D. cistiflora* grows near the village of Darling, which holds a justifiably famous wildflower show each spring. A host of smaller species are scattered about with profligate generosity, including various sorrels (*Oxalis*) of different colours, the brick red form of the small iris (*Moraea tricolor*), the quaintly formed orchids, *Holothrix villosa* and *Satyrium odorum*, and the heavenly scented *Gladiolus tenellus*—this one is a favourite with the local children, who gather it for their posies.

Further north in Namaqualand, also well known for its spectacular displays of spring flowers, you will see another orange-flowered kalkoentjie (*Gladiolus equitans*). This species is not nearly as common as *G. alatus*, and is a larger plant with much broader leaves. Also, the green kalkoentjie (*G. orchidiflorus*), a taller and more slender species with lovely dove-grey flowers marked with maroon, is common here.

Seeing the kalkoentjie or little turkey in its natural environment, surrounded by other equally colourful flora, is a pleasure you are unlikely to forget.

Gladiolus

The genus *Gladiolus*, which includes many popular commercially cultivated plants, boasts some 220 species. While some *Gladiolus* species are native to western Asia and southern Europe, the great majority are African, with an overwhelming concentration of species in South Africa, where also are found all the largest and brightest flowered species, with the little turkey (*G. alatus*) a fine example. They belong to the 'Cape bulbs', a tremendously diverse and colourful assortment of bulbs from the southern tip of Africa. These have contributed more to the gene pool of garden and florists' bulbs than the plants of any other region. Many (including *Gladiolus*) are members of the iris family, Iridaceae, which are not true bulbs but, for the most part, are corms.

Gladiolus flowers are often regarded as too large and gaudy. If you share this view of the traditional large hybrid varieties, you may be surprised at the graceful forms of many of the wild species and some of the 'old-fashioned' hybrids, which have flowers that are more delicately coloured and loosely arranged.

Gladiolus alatus

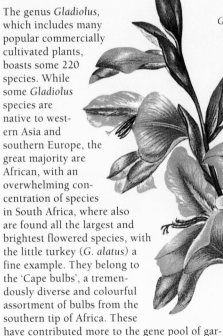
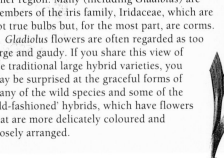

L. pardalinum

LEOPARD LILY, PANTHER LILY

This native of California can grow
to 3 m (about 9 ft) high. Its long,
narrow leaves are produced in
whorls, and between 6 and 10
recurved flowers, sometimes fragrant, appear in summer. The petals
are red at the tips and orange-yellow at the throat, where they are
marked with maroon spots. This
hardy lily prefers a sunny position
with a little shade in summer.

L. regale

REGAL LILY

Growing up to 2.3 m (about 7 ft),
this easily grown lily from western
China bears from 3 to 20 fragrant
blooms on each stem. The trumpet-
shaped flowers, up to 15 cm (about
6 in) long, appear in summer. The
inside of the petals is white with a
yellow base, the outside is carmine.
There is also a pure white form. The
leaves are green and lanceolate.
Plant in well-drained soil in an
open, sunny position.

L. speciosum

This popular, fragrant species grows
up to 1.5 m (about 4½ ft). The
'Turk's cap' (reflexed) flowers are
pendent, up to 10 cm (about 4 in)
long. There are many forms, varying
from white to crimson, some spotted. It flowers late summer to early
autumn/fall. It is half-hardy.

LITTONIA

modesta

CLIMBING LILY, CLIMBING BELL

In summer this native of South
Africa produces masses of blooms
on a climbing stem. It reaches to
about 2 m (about 6 ft), climbing up
stakes or other plants by means of
leaf tendrils which wind around the
supports. The 3 cm (about 1½ in)
yellow-orange flowers are produced
at the leaf axils and are bell-shaped
and nodding. Plant the tubers in
late winter to early spring in rich
soil with good drainage. Frost-
tender, it needs a sunny position.
Water well through spring and

summer but allow to dry out when
dormant. Propagate by division in
late winter or from seed in spring.

LYCORIS

SPIDER LILY, SURPRISE LILY

The spider-like flowers of these
natives of China and Japan appear
in late summer to early autumn/fall.
The 50 cm (about 20 in) flower
stems appear before the foliage.
Each scape carries 4 or 5 blooms.
The flowers are trumpet-shaped but
the petals are very slender and
sharply reflexed. It has slender,
strap-like leaves. Plant the bulbs in a
sunny position in rich, well-drained
soil. They like plenty of water during growth but need warm, dry
conditions when dormant. They are
half- to moderately hardy. Clumps
are best left undisturbed for a few
years; they can then be divided
when dormant at the end of summer. This genus is named for Marc
Antony's actress mistress.

L. aurea

GOLDEN SPIDER LILY

This lily grows to 40 cm (about 16
in) and bears a cluster of 4 or 5 tea-
rose yellow flowers. The 7 cm
(about 3 in) flowers have narrow,
sharply recurved petals and prominent stamens. The slender leaves are
strap-like.

L. radiata

RED SPIDER LILY

This is the most common species.
The 40 cm (about 16 in) stems bear
clusters of 4 or 5 red blooms. The
10 cm (about 4 in) flowers have

slender, sharply reflexed petals,
with prominent red stamens.

L. squamigera

This species, a native of Japan,
grows up to 70 cm (about 28 in) in
height. It is hardy but requires protection from cold winds. It has
strap-like leaves, 2.5 cm (about 1
in) wide. Appearing in late summer
or early autumn/fall, the inflorescence is made up of between 6 and
8 scented, funnel-shaped flowers,
pink in colour and with a yellow
throat. The petals can be up to 10
cm (about 4 in) long and are
reflexed at the tips.

MORAEA

spathulata

syn. M. spathacea

LARGE YELLOW TULIP

These beautiful, iris-like plants
belong to a genus of about 50 species, only a few of which are in
cultivation. The flowers are often
short lived, usually only lasting a
couple of days. They vary greatly in
size, flowering time and colour. *M.
spathulata* is a half-hardy species
that grows to 1.2 m (about 4 ft). It
has bayonet-shaped foliage. The
bright yellow, iris-like flowers,
around 8 cm (about 3 in) wide,
appear in spring. Plant in full sun in
a fairly rich soil with good drainage.
They need plenty of water during
growth but must be kept dry when
dormant. Propagate from offsets
when dormant or from seed.

MUSCARI

GRAPE HYACINTH

The popular grape hyacinths are
natives of the Mediterranean region.
A short spike bears grape-like clusters
of bright blue or white flowers in
early spring. Fully to half-hardy, they
do best in cool areas. They look best
planted in clumps and need a rich,
well-drained soil. Plant the bulbs in
autumn/fall in a sunny position, but
protect from hot sun in warm areas.
The slender, strap-like leaves appear
soon after planting, as the summer
dormancy period is very short. The
clumps should spread freely and are

Lycoris radiata

Lycoris aurea

Lilium speciosum

Lilium regale

Littonia modesta

Moraea spathulata

Muscari plumosum 'Comosum'

Muscari armeniacum 'Blue Spike'

Narcissus (Unnamed) (Div. 3)

Narcissus 'Tahiti' (Div. 4)

best left undisturbed for a few years. Divide the bulbs if they become overcrowded. They can also be grown from seed.

M. armeniacum
GRAPE HYACINTH

Growing to about 5 cm (about 2 in), this is one of the best loved of spring bulbs. The flowers may be blue or white, and there are several named cultivars of which 'Heavenly Blue' is the best known.

M. armeniacum 'Blue Spike'

This fairly new species grows to 20 cm (about 8 in). The flower spikes bear clusters of rounded, bell-shaped double blooms. The flowers are blue, sometimes rimmed with white. The foliage is slender and strap-like.

M. plumosum 'Comosum'
syn. *Leopoldia plumosa*
FEATHERED HYACINTH

This unusual plant grows to 30 cm (about 12 in). It has strap-shaped leaves and curious flowers whose petals are so elongated that the inflorescence looks like a plume of lavender feathers. Frost-hardy, it is as easily grown as other *Muscari* but multiplies less quickly.

NARCISSUS
DAFFODIL, JONQUIL, NARCISSUS

The sunny yellow spring flowers of the daffodil are popular all over the world. They are easy to grow, multiply freely and bloom year after year. Native to the northern hemisphere, the genus is extremely varied, but all flowers have 6 petals which surround a cup or corona. They are grouped into 12 'divisions' or classes, the most important of which are: the Trumpet narcissi (Div. 1) which have trumpets as long as the outer petals or perianth, the Large-cupped narcissi (Div. 2), with trumpets from one-third to two-thirds as long; Small-cupped narcissi (Div. 3), with trumpets less than one-third the length of the petals; and Double-flowered narcissi (Div. 4) with double flowers, either one or several per stem. Divs 5 to 9 cover hybrids of important species such as *N. tazetta, triandrus,*

Narcissus 'Fortune' (Div. 2)

cyclamineus, jonquilla and *poeticus.* Div. 10 covers the wild species. Div. 11 covers the split-cupped hybrids. Div. 12 consists of miscellaneous species. Colour ranges from white to yellow, although individual varieties may have white, yellow, red, orange or pink trumpets and each group is further subdivided according to colours. They are usually fully hardy and grow best in cool areas. Bulbs are usually planted in autumn/fall, 10–15 cm (about 4–6 in) deep in rich, well-drained soil. Full sun is fine in cool areas, but they will need some shade in warmer areas. Water well during growth and allow to dry out once the leaves die down. Remove spent flowers. Clumps will multiply freely and should be left undisturbed for a few years. Lift and divide them in autumn/fall. The common names daffodil, jonquil and narcissus are rather loosely applied, usage varying widely from place to place.

N., Trumpet hybrids (Div. 1)

These are the best known of all daffodils with their large flowers

and long trumpets. There are innumerable named cultivars, which may be all yellow, white with yellow trumpets, all white, or white with pale pink trumpets. They are the first of the big daffodils to flower. The all-gold 'King Alfred', raised in 1890, is the classic cultivar but its name has been very loosely applied, and some authorities consider the original variety may be extinct.

N., Large-cupped daffodils (Div. 2)

Flowering a week or two later than the trumpets, this is a large class with many named varieties. The popular pink-cupped cultivars with their white perianths mostly belong here but there are many others, in various combinations of white or yellow perianths with cups in white, yellow, orange or red.

N., Small-cupped daffodils (Div. 3)

These resemble the first two groups except for their smaller cups, and like them come in many named cultivars. They flower at the same time as the Div. 2 types.

Muscari armeniacum

Narcissus 'Ptolemy' (Div. 1)

N., Double-flowered daffodils (Div. 4)
DOUBLE NARCISSI

These can have either a solitary large flower or several smaller ones, and either the whole flower can be double, with extra petals with segments of the corona intermixed; or the corona is doubled, like a pompom set against the outer perianth. Some of the most ancient cultivars are double flowered, but as a group they are less popular than the others. They tend to be late flowering and must not suffer drought when the buds are developing or they will not open properly.

Narcissus tazetta (Div. 8)

Narcissus 'Pink Pageant' (Div.11)

Narcissus jonquilla (Div. 7)

Narcissus poeticus (Div. 9)

Narcissus 'Tête-à-Tête' (Div. 6)

Narcissus cyclamineus (Div. 6)

Narcissus 'Silver Chimes' (Div. 5)

Narcissus bulbocodium (Div. 10)

N. triandrus hybrids (Div. 5)

The type species *N. triandrus* is native to Spain, however it is not usually cultivated. This division is represented by garden forms which have pendent, nodding flowers, a straight-edged cup and slightly reflexed petals. The blooms appear in spring, and there are usually several per stem. The forms vary in height from 15–45 cm (about 6–18 in). 'Hawera' grows to 20 cm (about 8 in) and thrives in the sun. With its light yellow flowers it makes a good pot plant. 'Silver Chimes' is creamy white and delicately scented. The popular 'Thalia' has pale yellow petals and a white cup with 3 or more blooms per stem.

N. cyclamineus hybrids (Div. 6)

These hybrids grow to 38 cm (about 15 in). Their trumpet-shaped cups are longer than those of *N. triandrus*, and their petals are narrow and strongly reflexed. They flower in early to mid-spring. Good examples are: 'February Gold', an early bloomer that naturalizes well and has single, lasting flowers with yel-low petals and slightly darker yellow trumpets; 'Dove Wings', a mid-spring bloomer with small flowers comprising white petals and a long, primrose-yellow trumpet; and 'Tête-à-Tête', profusely and early flowering with lasting blooms consisting of golden-yellow petals and an orange, frilled corona.

N. jonquilla hybrids (Div. 7)

Possessing the characteristics of the wild jonquil of southern Europe and northern Africa, this group of narcissi are scented, with the cups shorter than the flat petals. Spring-flowering, there are often 2 blooms on a stem, which grows to 40 cm (about 16 in), while the leaves are dark green. 'Suzy' flowers in mid-spring and has 2 or more fragrant blooms on its sturdy stem, the flowers having golden petals and a deep orange cup. 'Stratosphere' has 3 blooms with a cup of a deeper golden yellow than its petals. 'Trevithian' flowers early in spring and produces up to 3 large, rounded blooms of a primrose yellow colour.

N. tazetta hybrids (Div. 8)

These narcissi have many-flowered stems and grow up to 40 cm (about 16 in). The cup is small and straight sided, with broad, often frilled petals. The sweetly scented blooms appear from late autumn/fall to spring. The leaves are dark green. This class can be further subdivided into those similar to *N. tazetta* and which are generally too frost-tender to be grown outdoors but often flourish in indoor pots, and those resulting from a cross between *N. tazetta* and *N. poeticus* and referred to as poetaz narcissi. 'Grand Soleil d'Or' is a late autumn/fall- to early spring-flowering half-hardy bulb. Growing to 35 cm (about 14 in), the petals are a rich yellow and the cup orange. 'Paper White' is best grown indoors; in winter to mid-spring it produces 10 or more strongly scented blooms with white petals per stem. 'Minnow' is a frost-hardy, mid-spring bloomer with 4 fragrant flowers per stem; the cups are lemon yellow and the petals a lighter yellow. It grows to 17 cm (about 7 in).

N. poeticus hybrids (Div. 9)

This is a late-spring to early-summer flowering division. The plants grow to 40 cm (about 17 in) and produce one, occasionally two, blooms per stem. The petals are white and the small cup often has a frilled red or orange rim. 'Actaea' produces fragrant flowers in late spring with a flat yellow cup rimmed with orange. 'Cantabile' is completely white. 'Pheasant's Eye', has a red cup and white petals.

N., Wild species (Div. 10)

This division covers the wild species, which flower from early autumn/fall to early summer. They usually bear single flowers; some are trumpet shaped, others funnel shaped. A well-known example of the funnel-shaped narcissi is *N. bulbocodium*.

N., Split-cupped hybrids (Div. 11)

Characterized by having a cup or corona that is split along at least a third of its length, these narcissi are also referred to as Collar, Papillon, Orchid or Split-corona daffodils. The edges of the split cup bend back towards the petals, and are sometimes frilled. They all flower in spring. 'Baccarat' is yellow; 'Ahoy', 'Cassata' and 'Pink Pageant' have soft yellow cups and broad white petals; and 'Orangery' and 'Pick Up' have orange cups and white petals.

NECTAROSCORDUM
siculum subsp. *bulgaricum*
syn. N. dioscoridis,
Allium bulgaricum

The genus name means 'nectar-bearing onion', and this is a relative of the *Allium* (onion) genus. In spring it bears elegant, pendent, bell-shaped flowers; pale pink tinged with purple and green. The upright foliage dies off quickly. A frost-hardy plant, it likes most soil and semi-shade. Keep drier in summer. Propagate from offsets in summer. It makes a lovely cut flower.

NERINE
GUERNSEY LILY

Although the common name might suggest otherwise, these are native to South Africa. They were originally found in Guernsey, but these were the result of bulbs washed up onto the island after a shipwreck. The pretty, spider-like flowers are borne in clusters at the top of tall stems, usually in autumn/fall. The foliage is strap-like. The bulbs should be planted in sandy soil with good drainage in a sunny position. Water well during growth but allow to dry out over the summer dormancy period. They are not suitable for areas with high summer rainfall or severe frosts. They can be propagated from seed or offsets, but the plants do not like being disturbed and may take a couple of years to flower. They are good plants for pots, and can be brought inside when in flower. Half-hardy, they need a warm, sheltered spot in cool climates.

N. *bowdenii*
PINK SPIDER LILY, LARGE PINK NERINE

A sturdy stem of 60 cm (about 24 in) bears up to 12 pink blooms. The flowers are trumpet-shaped but the narrow petals are split and reflexed. They have a crimson rib running along their centre and the edges are frilled. There is also a white form.

N. *filifolia*
SPIDER LILY, GRASS-LEAVED NERINE

This plant grows to 25 cm (about 10 in) and bears a 10 cm (about 4 in) cluster of rosy pink blooms. The flowers are trumpet-shaped with slender, reflexed petals. The foliage is grass-like and almost evergreen.

N. *flexuosa* 'Alba'

A sturdy stem up to 60 cm (about 24 in) bears a cluster of up to 15 white flowers. The trumpet-shaped flowers have narrow, reflexed petals. The foliage is narrow and strap-like and appears before the flowers.

N. *sarniensis*
GUERNSEY LILY, RED NERINE

This delightful species grows up to 60 cm (about 24 in). The sturdy stem bears up to 20 bright red, 7 cm (about 3 in) blooms. The trumpet-shaped flowers have sharply reflexed petals and prominent stamens. The strap-shaped leaves usually appear after flowering.

NOMOCHARIS
pardanthina
syn. N. mairei

These elegant, fully hardy plants come from the Himalayas, western China and Burma and are related to liliums. A slender stem grows to about 1 m (about 3 ft) and bears whorls of leaves and up to 12 blooms in summer. The 10 cm (about 4 in) wide, nodding flowers are white to rose and spotted with crimson. Plant the bulbs in a partially shaded area in rich, well-drained soil. It does best in cool, moist conditions and acid soil, and can be propagated by division or from seed, although seed may take many years to flower. It is not easy to propagate, and expensive to buy, but it is a glorious plant where conditions suit.

NOTHOLIRION
thomsonianum
FALSE LILY

This frost-hardy native of the Himalayas closely resembles a lilium. Blooming in spring, the main bulb dies after flowering, although it first produces a number of offspring. A tall spike up to 1 m (about 3 ft) emerges from a rosette of basal leaves and bears up to 40 nodding, funnel-shaped blooms in pink to lilac. Bulbs should be planted in autumn/fall in rich, well-drained soil. It likes cool, but not too cold, moist conditions, Water well except when dormant. Propagate from seed or offsets in autumn/fall, but offsets may take a few years to flower.

Nectaroscordum s. subsp. *bulgaricum*

Nerine filifolia

Nerine bowdenii

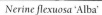
Nerine flexuosa 'Alba'

Notholirion thomsonianum

Nerine sarniensis

Ornithogalum arabicum

Rhodohypoxis baurii

Polianthes tuberosa

Ornithogalum thyrsoides

Ornithogalum umbellatum

Oxalis adenophylla

Ranunculus asiaticus

should be lifted in winter. They multiply quite freely and clumps should be divided every one to two years to prevent overcrowding. Also grow them from seed sown in autumn/fall or spring.

O. arabicum

Flowering in early summer, this Mediterranean species carries as many as 15 scented, open, white flowers with black ovaries in their centres. Their basal leaves are strap like. Reaching a height of 45 cm (about 18 in), these plants prefer a sunny, sheltered position. They are often grown as pot plants where their climatic needs can be more easily tended to.

O. thyrsoides
CHINCHERINCHEE

This frost-tender species from South Africa grows to 45 cm (about 18 in). A cluster of up to 20 star- to cup-shaped, white flowers is borne on a spike. The basal leaves are strap shaped. The cut flowers last for weeks, even out of water. The flowers absorb dye and bunches of chincherinchees are sold in a myriad of colours.

O. umbellatum
COMMON STAR OF BETHLEHEM

The leaves of this hardy, clump-forming perennial are mid-green with a central white stripe. The loose clusters of white flowers with green striping appear at the top of the 30 cm (about 12 in), erect stems in early summer. The flowers open only in sunshine. This species can become invasive.

OXALIS
adenophylla

Belonging to a large genus of semi-evergreen shrubs and bulbous, rhizomatous and fibrous-rooted perennials as well as half-hardy annuals, this species comes from South America and has a fibrous tuber. Growing to 7 cm (about 3 in) high, it forms a dense mat of grey-green foliage. The leaves are compound, consisting of up to 12 palmate leaflets. Suitable for a rockery, the open purple-pink flowers with a darker centre appear in late spring to early summer. Plant in spring or autumn/fall in a sunny or partially shaded, well-drained site in any garden soil, though the plants will benefit from leaf mulch. Propagate by division after they have flowered.

POLIANTHES
tuberosa
TUBEROSE

This native of Mexico produces a mass of sweetly scented blooms in summer or early autumn/fall. A tall stem up to 1 m (about 3 ft) is

ORNITHOGALUM

This large genus of spring- to summer-flowering plants is native to Asia, Africa and Europe. Clusters of star- to cup-shaped flowers are borne along the top of tall stems. They are easy to grow. Half- to fully hardy. Plant bulbs in autumn/fall or spring in well-drained soil. They like full sun but will need partial shade in warm areas. Keep the plants moist until the leaves begin to die off. They need to be kept dry when dormant. Frost-tender species

topped with a spike bearing clusters of tubular, star-shaped, creamy white flowers. A double variety, 'The Pearl', is more widely available than the single. The slender leaves are strap shaped. The tubers should be planted in spring when there is no chance of frost, in a sheltered, sunny position. This frost-tender plant needs a rich soil with good drainage. Water well once leaves appear and allow to dry out when the leaves start to die off. The tubers only bloom once, so they should be lifted in autumn/fall and the offsets stored for planting in spring. Tuberoses are first-rate cut flowers.

PUSCHKINIA
scilloides
syn. P. libanotica, P. sicula
STRIPED SQUILL, LEBANON SQUILL

Belonging to the Liliaceae family, this genus of small bulbs is related to Scilla. Native to the northern regions of the Middle East, the hardy, clump-forming plants are often grown in rockeries and at the front of a border, or indoors in pots. Reaching a height of 10–20 cm (about 4–8 in), these spring-flowering bulbs have 2 semi-erect, mid-green, basal, strap-like leaves and a slim spike of up to 6 pale blue, star-shaped flowers with a darker line down the petals. The small flowers are similar in appearance to hyacinths, and like them have a strong scent. Plant several together, in autumn/fall, in a sunny to partially shaded site in well-drained soil to which peat or compost has been added. They can be propagated from offsets in late summer, or from seed in autumn/fall. Slugs can sometimes be a problem, but otherwise these plants are trouble free and easy to grow.

RANUNCULUS
asiaticus
PERSIAN BUTTERCUP

This frost-hardy native of the Mediterranean region is parent to many hybrids and cultivars popular all over the world. Masses of single or double flowers are borne on 35 cm (about 14 in) stems in spring. The gorgeous blooms are available in many colours, yellow, orange, red, pink, white and more. The stems are slender, erect and flowering, and the leaves are dark green, segmented and long petioled. The corms should be planted in autumn/fall in a sunny position in well-drained soil enriched with organic matter. Water well through the growing season and allow to dry out after flowering. The rhizomes are usually lifted after flowering and should be stored in a cool dry place. Propagation is by division or from seed sown in spring.

Sprekelia formosissima

Sternbergia lutea

Scilla peruviana

Sparaxis tricolor

RHODOHYPOXIS
baurii
RED STAR

This charming dwarf plant comes from the mountains of South Africa and is frost-hardy, although it appreciates a warm spot in cold areas. It produces masses of star-shaped flowers in late spring to early summer. The small stems grow to about 10 cm (about 4 in) and each bears one 6-petalled, red, pink or white flower. The hairy foilage is grasslike. The bulb-like tubers should be planted in early spring in rich, acidic, well-drained soil. It needs plenty of water during the growing season but must be kept dry in winter. Plant in full sun, but protect from direct hot afternoon sunlight. Propagate by division or from seed in spring. It is excellent for rockeries.

SAUROMATUM
venosum
syn. S. guttatum
MONARCH-OF-THE-EAST, VOODOO LILY

One of the Araceae family, this perennial tuber flowers in the spring, even without earth or moisture. The large, greenish brown spathe appears before the leaves and can become contorted and curved. The long stem, to 45 cm (about 18 in), bears smallish, lobed, bright green leaves in summer. It is frost-tender and so needs a sheltered, partially shaded site in well-drained soil. The tubers must be completely dried off, or lifted, in autumn/fall when they become dormant. Plant out again in spring, and propagate from the offsets.

SCILLA

This fully to half-hardy genus of bulbs belongs to the Liliaceae family. The leaves appear in basal clusters and the flowers in spikes. Bluebells are very much a part of the woodland and garden scene, growing naturalized under trees, or planted in rockeries, at the front of beds and under shrubs. Plant 10 cm (about 4 in) apart in a moist, well-drained soil in a sunny to lightly shaded site in late summer or early autumn/fall. The clumps should be divided in late summer and replanted immediately so the bulbs retain their vigour. Rust can cause problems to the leaves. 'Spring Beauty' is a cultivar with the brightest of blue flowers.

S. peruviana
CUBAN LILY, WILD HYACINTH, SQUILL

This plant, actually native to southwest Europe, has a dense cluster of up to 50 star-shaped flowers which are borne in summer on a 30 cm (about 12 in) stem. The 2 cm (about 1 in) flowers are usually blue, sometimes white or purple. The dark to olive-green foliage is glossy and strap like. Plant bulbs in autumn/fall in well-drained soil. It will need partial shade in warm areas. It is quite hardy to frost, but needs sun in cool climates. Water well during the growing season. Clumps are best left undisturbed for a few years. Propagate by division or from seed in autumn/fall.

S. siberica
SIBERIAN SQUILL, SPRING SQUILL

As the common name implies, this early spring-flowering bluebell is native to Russia. The glossy, basal, strap-shaped leaves are followed, on each bulb, by 3 or 4 spikes, up to 15 cm (about 6 in) high, which bear bright blue, bell-shaped flowers. Their blue is so strong that they should be mass planted on their own for the full effect to be appreciated.

SPARAXIS
tricolor
VELVET FLOWER, HARLEQUIN FLOWER

This frost-tender native of South Africa is easily grown in warm areas. The 30 cm (about 12 in) wiry, drooping stems bear a spike of up to 5 funnel- to star-shaped blooms in spring. The 5 cm (about 2 in) flowers are red to pink or orange. The centre is usually yellow, outlined in black. The flowers close at night and on dull days. The stiff leaves are lance shaped. Plant corms in autumn/fall in a sunny spot in well-drained soil. Water well during the growing season, but allow to dry out when dormant. The corms should be lifted in areas which have wet summers. Propagate from the freely produced offsets or from seed in early autumn/fall.

SPREKELIA
formosissima
JACOBEAN LILY, MALTESE CROSS LILY, AZTEC LILY

This beautiful Mexican native grows to 45 cm (about 18 in) in height with a spread of 12–15 cm (about 5–6 in). In summer it produces bright red, 12 cm (about 5 in) long flowers. The lower 3 petals form an open tube and the upper petals curve upwards and outwards. The green leaves are strap shaped. Plant the bulbs in autumn/fall in sun in cool areas, in partial shade in warm climates. The flowers will need protection from hot sun.They need rich, well-composted, moist, well-drained soil. Water well during the growing season but keep dry when dormant. It is sensitive to severe frosts and should be grown in pots in cold areas. It does not like being disturbed, so clumps should be left for a few years, then divided in autumn/fall. The flower resembles the red cross borne by the Spanish religious order of St Jacob of Calatrava; hence the common name.

STERNBERGIA
lutea
AUTUMN CROCUS, AUTUMN DAFFODIL

The delightful autumn/fall-flowering lily-of-the-field is native to the Mediterranean region. The buttercup-yellow, crocus-like flowers are 5 cm (about 2 in) long and are borne singly on 15 cm (about 6 in) stems. The slender leaves are deep green, semi-erect and strap shaped. Bulbs should be planted in spring in rich, well-drained, alkaline soil in a sunny position. In cool areas they should be grown against a sunny wall. It is only just frost-hardy and needs warm, dry conditions when dormant in summer; it is best grown in pots in areas with wet summers. Clumps should be left undisturbed and only divided (in summer) when they are overcrowded. Makes an excellent plant in a rock garden.

Tritonia crocata

Triteleia laxa 'Queen Fabiola'

Tricyrtis hirta

Tulbaghia violacea

Tristagma uniflora

Tigridia pavonia

TIGRIDIA
pavonia
TIGER FLOWER, JOCKEY'S CAP LILY

This brightly coloured Mexican native blooms in summer. The triangular flowers are short-lived, often lasting for only a day, but a succession of new blooms will keep appearing for weeks. The 13 cm (about 5 in) flowers are usually red with a yellow centre spotted with purple, borne on 60 cm (about 24 in) stems. The foliage is iris-like, sword-shaped and pleated. Plant bulbs in spring in a sunny position in rich, well-drained soil. Water well during the growing season, but allow to dry out when dormant. Lift in cool areas or those with high winter rainfall, as they are half-hardy. Propagate from freely formed offsets or seed sown in spring.

TRICYRTIS
hirta
TOAD LILY

Native to cool, mountainous areas of Asia, the toad lily produces trumpet- to star-shaped flowers in late summer to autumn/fall. The 1 m (about 3 ft) branching stems have hairy, stem-clasping leaves and the flowers are borne at the axils of these upper leaves. The 5 cm (about 2 in) flowers are white, spotted with purple. It is frost-hardy. Plant the bulbs in spring in rich, moist, sandy soil in a partially shaded spot. It can also be propagated from offsets in spring or from seed sown in autumn/fall.

TRISTAGMA
uniflora
syn. Ipheion uniflorum,
Triteleia uniflora
SPRING STARFLOWER

This delightful native of Argentina is very easy to grow and produces masses of star-shaped, pale blue flowers in spring. The 3 cm (about 1¹/₂ in) flowers are borne singly on leafless stems. It grows to about 20 cm (about 8 in). The slender, grey-green foliage has an oniony scent, particularly when it is crushed. The small bulbs should be planted in autumn/fall in full sun or partial shade in well-drained soil. It is frost-hardy and likes plenty of water through winter and spring. It will spread rapidly and the clumps can be divided after a couple of years in autumn/fall. The plant has suffered many name changes over the past 40 years; let us hope the new one, *Tristagma*, will stick.

TRITELEIA
laxa 'Queen Fabiola'
ITHURIEL'S SPEAR, CALIFORNIAN BLUEBELL

This native of California and Oregon, USA, grows to 45 cm (about 18 in). In late spring it produces a scape of up to 30 pink to lilac-blue blooms. The 5 cm (about 2 in) flowers are funnel-shaped; the leaves are slender and grass-like. Plant the corms in a sunny position in well-drained soil. In very warm areas it should be planted in partial shade. Water well during the growing season, less during the summer dormancy period. It is hardy except to severe frost and should be grown in pots in cold areas. Propagate from offsets in autumn/fall.

TRITONIA
crocata
syn. T. hyalina
BLAZING STAR, ROOIKALKOENTJIE

The freesia-like plant is native to South Africa. The wiry stems grow to 50 cm (about 20 in) and bear a spike of pretty, cup-shaped blooms. The 5 cm (about 2 in) flowers which appear in late spring to summer are bright orange to red with yellow throats and purple anthers. The erect green leaves are sword-shaped. Plant the corms in autumn/fall in a sunny position in light, well-drained soil. Water well during the growing season but allow to dry out after flowering. It is half-hardy and needs protection from frost. It multiplies quite freely and can be divided in autumn/fall, or grown from seed. It make a good cut flower.

TULBAGHIA
violacea
SWEET GARLIC, WILD GARLIC

This easily grown South African native is delightful to look at but smells strongly of garlic. A tall 60 cm (about 24 in) stem bears a round cluster of tubular, star-shaped, mauve flowers. The lilac to pink flowers appear in summer to autumn/fall. The masses of evergreen leaves are slender and grass-like. The rhizomes should be planted at the end of winter in rich, moist soil in partial shade. It is half-hardy and could be grown in a pot in cold areas. Clumps are best left undisturbed for a few years. Propagate by division in late winter or by sowing seed in spring. It is good as a border plant or in a rockery. The bulbs are edible.

TULIPA
TULIP

The elegant flower of the tulip has, with good reason, made it one of the most popular bulbs in the world. Tulips originated in the Middle East and Asia and have been cultivated for hundreds of years. The genus contains about 100 species, but the most commonly grown tulips are the highly developed cultivars grouped under *T. gesneriana* which vary in colour, shape and flowering time. There are very many cultivars which were formerly grouped into a large number of classes. Recently the classification has been simplified, the main groups being: Single Early, Double Early, Single late, Double late, and the Parrot tulips. The Single Late tulips are themselves subdivided, and there are also important groups of garden varieties derived from *T. fosteriana, greigii* and *kaufmanniana*. The other species are grouped as 'botanical tulips'. Tulips do best in cool areas but can be grown in pots in warm climates. Nearly all are fully hardy. The bulbs should be planted in late autumn/fall, about 15 cm (about 6 in) deep, in a sunny position in rich, limed, and well-drained soil. Water well during the growing season. Spent flowers can be removed but allow the leaves to die off naturally. It is essential to lift the bulbs in areas with a wet summer, and store in a cool, well ventilated spot. Propagate by division in autumn/fall.

GARDEN TULIPS
T. gesneriana

These are of complex hybrid origin, and grouped into a number of classes, which follow. They are very popular and delightful for cutting, but must have a cold climate. In mild-winter areas they are best treated as annuals, by chilling the bulbs for 3 to 6 weeks in the vegetable drawer of the refrigerator before planting in late autumn/fall. They come in a vast range of colours, everything but true blue; the virus-infected striped varieties are now less popular than they used to be.

SINGLE EARLY TULIPS

These are the first of the garden tulips to flower, and bear their flowers on stems about 40 cm (about 16 in) tall. They are the best varieties for forcing for early bloom in a greenhouse and come in the full range of colours.

DOUBLE EARLY TULIPS

These have mostly arisen as sports of single varieties and flower at the same time. The range of colours is wide, but it is a matter of taste whether you like these multi-petalled flowers. They are long-lasting cut flowers.

SINGLE LATE TULIPS

These are the most widely grown tulips flowering in late spring. They are taller, to 65 cm (about 26 in), than the early varieties and divided as follows:

Darwin tulips

Most popular group, growing about 60 cm (about 24 in) tall with flowers almost rectangular in profile and coming in the full range of colours. There is a sub-group with fringed petals. All are excellent for cutting.

Cottage tulips

These are more egg-shaped than the Darwins, and include the lily-flowered tulips with their pointed petals as well as a group called 'viridiflora' tulips with green markings on the petals. They open wider than the Darwins, to give a more graceful effect. Most are about 60 cm (about 24 in) tall.

Darwin hybrid tulips

Derived from crosses between the Darwins and *T. fosteriana*, these tulips grow to about 60 cm (about 24 in), and despite their rather limited colour range—red, yellow and orange—rival their parents in popularity. The flowers can be very large, though they are not as long lasting as the Darwins. They are more reliable in mild-winter areas.

PARROT TULIPS

Sports of Darwin and Cottage tulips, these are grown for their fantastically fringed and ruffled flowers. They grow to about 50 cm (about 20 in) and are available in the usual colours.

Double early tulip, 'Peach Blossom'

Single late tulips

Single early tulip, 'Kees Nellis'

Cottage tulips

Darwin hybrid tulip, 'Golden Oxford'

Tulipa gesneriana

Parrot tulip, 'Flaming Parrot'

Darwin hybrid tulip, 'Queen of Night'

Double late tulips

Tulipa saxatilis

Tulipa clusiana

Tulipa fosteriana

Tulipa tarda

Tulipa acuminata

Tulipa greigii

Urceolina peruviana

Rembrandt tulips

REMBRANDT TULIPS

Though the great Dutch master is not known to have painted tulips, his name is attached to all the striped tulips. These striped or broken flowers were indeed very popular in Holland in his time, so much so that speculation in tulip bulbs nearly upset the Dutch economy and the government of the day had to step in to stop the 'tulipomania'. Since discovering that the stripes are caused by a virus, they have become less popular and they should be grown apart from other tulips lest the virus spread. Nonetheless, an evenly broken flower in red or pink and white can be very pretty.

DOUBLE LATE TULIPS

These have their admirers, but they are less desirable than the Double Earlies, the many petalled flowers often proving too heavy for the 60 cm (about 24 in) tall stems. They are essentially cut flowers.

SPECIES OR BOTANICAL TULIPS

T. acuminata
HORNED TULIP

A most curious tulip, thought not to be a true species but an ancient cultivar of Turkish origin. It grows about 40 cm (about 16 in) tall, and is distinguished by its curious long, narrow petals in red and yellow.

T. clusiana
syn. *T. aitchisonii*
LADY TULIP

This tulip has 25 cm (about 10 in) stems which bear one or two cup-shaped blooms which eventually open out almost flat. The flowers are white, the outside petals and inside base stained dark pink. It flowers in mid-spring.

T. fosteriana

This low-growing, mid-season tulip from Central Asia is rarely grown, but it has a number of garden varieties much admired for their enormous, 25 cm (about 10 in) wide flowers. They are almost all red.

T. greigii

This early to mid-season species has given rise to a popular group of hybrids, which mostly grow about 30 cm (about 12 in) tall, with wide-open flowers in the usual tulip colours, often with contrasting edges to the petals. The foliage is variegated with red-brown or purple on a green background.

T. kaufmanniana
WATER LILY TULIP

This early flowering species is admired for the elegant form of its pale yellow flowers, strongly marked with red on the outside. There are several named varieties in shades of red, pink and yellow. They mostly grow about 25 cm (about 10 in) tall.

T. saxatilis
syn. *T. bakeri*
ROCK TULIP

A species originating in Crete, it does well in warmer climates. The 45 cm (about 18 in) stems bear up to 3 goblet-shaped flowers which eventually open out almost flat. The purple-pink flowers have bright yellow centres. It flowers in early spring.

T. tarda
syn. *T. dasystemon of gardens*

This small tulip grows to 15 cm (about 6 in). Each stem bears up to 6 white flowers with yellow centres. The pointed petals sometimes have a red or greenish tinge. It flowers in early spring.

URCEOLINA
peruviana
syn. *U. miniata*
LITTLE URN PLANT

This easily grown native of the Peruvian Andes has red, nodding, urn-shaped flowers with protruding yellow anthers. The 38 cm (about 15 in) slender stems each bear up to 6 blooms in spring, before the glossy, strap-like leaves. Plant bulbs in late autumn/fall in a sunny position in well-drained soil. Water well during the growing season. It is not hardy to severe frosts and could be planted in a pot in cold areas. Clumps may be left undisturbed for a few years. Propagate from offsets in autumn/fall. The name comes from the Latin, *urceolian*, meaning 'small pitcher'.

VALLOTA
speciosa
syn. *Cyrtanthus purpureus*
SCARBOROUGH LILY

This beautiful plant, with its showy red flowers, is originally from South Africa. The stout, 30 cm (about 12 in) stem bears up to 5 orange-red, trumpet-shaped blooms. The flowers appear in summer to autumn/fall and are about 10 cm (about 4 in) wide. The thick, green leaves are strap-shaped. It is half-hardy. Plant the bulbs in late winter in rich, well-drained soil, and in partial shade in very warm areas. Water well through the growing season but allow to dry out over winter. Remove spent flowerheads. The small offsets can be removed from the parent bulb and planted out in late winter. It makes a glorious display as an indoor pot plant.

VELTHEIMIA
VELDT LILY, FOREST LILY

These unusual natives of South Africa produce a dense spike of pendent, tubular flowers in winter or spring. Bulbs should be planted in autumn/fall in moist, rich, well-drained soil in partial shade. Reduce watering when flowering is finished. They are frost-tender and should be grown in pots in cold areas. Propagate from offsets in autumn/fall.

V. bracteata
syn. *V. viridifolia*
FOREST LILY

Found in the wild in the eastern Cape area of South Africa, *V. bracteata* has wavy, glossy green leaves growing in a rosette. Rocket-like inflorescences on strong, erect peduncles are produced in spring and early summer. The drooping, tubular flowers are pink, red or pale yellow. It thrives in semi-shade beneath trees or shrubs, and also makes a good potted specimen. Plant in rich, well-drained soil and water occasionally.

V. capensis
syn. *V. glauca*

A strong stem growing up to 45 cm (about 18 in) bears a dense spike of pendent, tubular, 2.5 cm (about 1 in) blooms. The rosy pink to red flowers are sometimes tipped with green. The glossy, dark green leaves have wavy edges.

WATSONIA

These beautiful natives of South Africa produce fragrant flowers in spring and summer. They appear quite similar to the gladiolus and have lance-shaped leaves and a tall flowering spike. The corms should be planted in autumn/fall in light, well-drained soil in a sunny spot. They like plenty of water during the growing season. They are half-hardy. Clumps are best left undisturbed and they should spread freely. They can be propagated from seed or by division when clumps become overcrowded.

W. beatricis
BEATRICE WATSONIA

This evergreen species grows to 1.2 m (about 4 ft). The flower spike bears 8 cm (about 3 in) long, tubular, star-shaped flowers which are salmon pink. The green foliage is sword-shaped. Hardier than other species, it can withstand some frost. There is some doubt about whether this plant, common in nurseries under this name, is the true wild species, which is now correctly known as *W. pillansii*.

W. borbonica subsp. borbonica
syn. *W. pyramidata*
PINK WATSONIA

This delightful species grows to 1.5 m (about 4½ ft). The stem bears a spike of lilac to pink, 5 cm (about 2 in), funnel-shaped flowers. The slender green leaves are sword-shaped. It flowers in spring.

ZEPHYRANTHES
STORM LILY, RAIN LILY

These charming natives of central and southern America often appear quite suddenly after summer rain. The widely trumpet-shaped flowers are borne singly on short stems. They are easy to grow and should be planted in late autumn/fall to early winter in a sunny position. Soil should be rich with excellent drainage. Give plenty of water during the growing season but reduce this after flowering. They are frost- to half-hardy, but should be grown in pots in very cold areas. Clumps are best left undisturbed for a few years. Propagate from offsets in autumn/fall or from seed sown in spring. They are excellent in rockeries or borders.

Z. candida
syn. *Argyropsis candida*
FLOWER OF THE WEST WIND

This vigorous species grows to 15 cm (about 6 in). The starry, cup-shaped, white flowers are 5 cm (about 2 in) wide and are borne singly on the slender stems. The grass-like foliage is evergreen and hardy.

Z. grandiflora
syn. *Z. carinata, Z. rosea*
PINK STORM LILY

This popular species grows to 25 cm (about 10 in). The 10 cm (about 4 in) flowers are dusky pink. The slender leaves are strap-shaped. There are many forms, some with smaller flowers.

Vallota speciosa

Veltheimia capensis

Watsonia beatricis

Zephyranthes grandiflora

Veltheimia bracteata

Zephyranthes candida

Watsonia borbonica subsp. *borbonica*

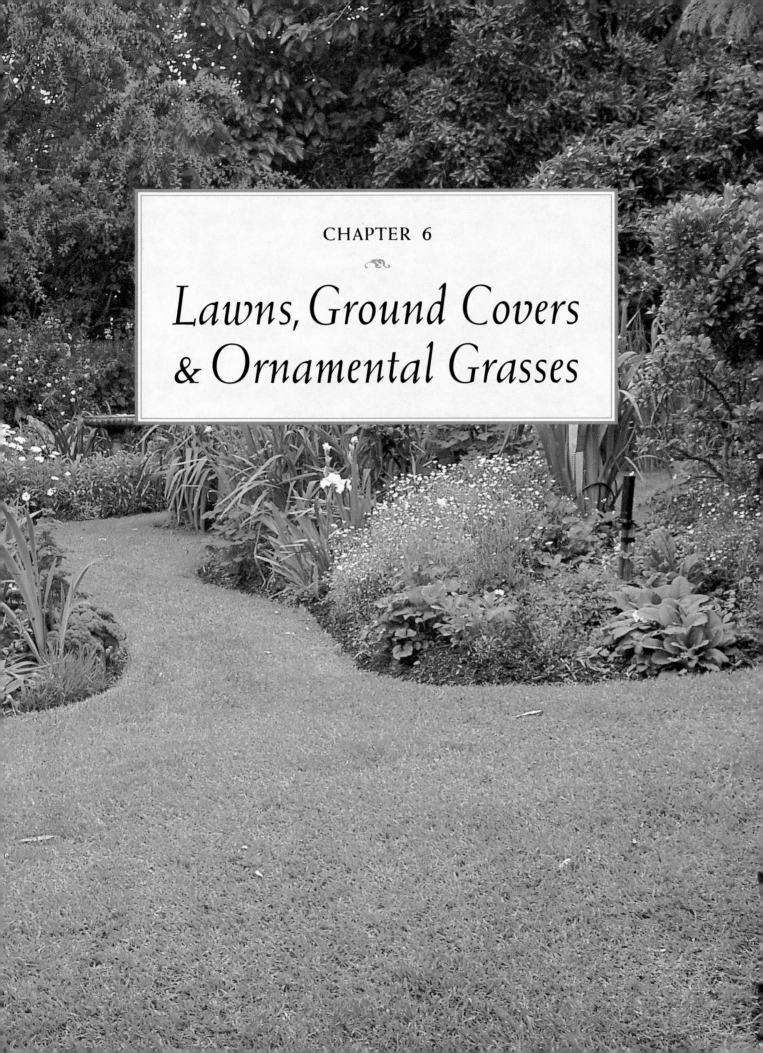

CHAPTER 6

Lawns, Ground Covers & Ornamental Grasses

The soil is the mother of the garden, and a gardener treats it with all due respect; but bare earth, mud when it rains and dust when it does not, makes a most unsuitable floor for a garden. We can, of course, lay paving or gravel, but they are hard, expensive, and reflective of heat and glare. The universal favourite for flooring the main part of a garden is lawn. It is soft and quiet underfoot, it doesn't reflect glare, and its greenness is the most flattering backdrop imaginable for plants and flowers.

No one species will give a perfect, year-round sward—the finest lawns are the result of careful blending. Every area has its favourite lawn grass species, and these are the ones you should choose. We do suggest that if you choose the finest, slow-growing types you'll have less work to do in the long run, even if they are more trouble to establish than the faster growing meadow and pasture grasses.

Looking After a Lawn

Nonetheless the meadow grasses can become an acceptable lawn if they are regularly shorn, and that brings us to the least loved of all gardening tasks—mowing. No one enjoys it, and many shortcuts are devised by the lazy in the hope of having to take the mower out less frequently. Most common is cutting too short or leaving it to grow too long. Alas, none works. All weaken the grass and encourage the weeds: and so the time saved is spent (with interest) on weeding. A weedy lawn actually needs mowing more frequently than a clean one—the weeds grow faster than the grass so that unacceptable shagginess sets in sooner.

It's best to encourage a good, dense growing turf, by watering as needed, fertilizing at least once a year (in spring) and cutting short enough for neatness but not so short as to scalp the grass. With most fine grasses, 2 or 3 cm (about 1 in) is short enough, and it is desirable not to let the grass get more than about twice as long as that so it won't be unduly shocked when it is cut. When you come to mow, you'll be grateful for

having kept the lines of the lawn simple—getting the mower around wriggly edges and island flowerbeds is time consuming and frustrating. Whether you choose a rotary mower or a reel-cut type is up to you; the reel does give a more velvety finish (and is the only way to get that smart striped effect, caused by the way it 'lays' the grass like the pile of a carpet) but it is more trouble to maintain. Untidy edges will spoil the effect of the most immaculate mowing; allow time for trimming them, either with shears or a powered edging clipper. And don't be careless about safety. Turn the mower off whenever you leave it unattended, even for a minute; keep your hands and feet well away from the blades; and usher small children safely out of harm's way.

It can be tempting to allow the clippings to lie, to rot down and return the nourishment they contain; but this doesn't really work. They'll just make half-rooted 'thatch' and clog up the crowns of the grass plants. Off to the compost heap with them!

In nature, grass tends to grow in the spring and then brown off with summer's heat, to return green with the

A well-manicured lawn can provide a flattering backdrop to flowers and foliage plants.

spring; but in gardens we want spring green all year. Except in the moistest of climates, this means watering. It is amazingly easy to do this wastefully—just sprinkle lightly until the lawn looks refreshed and repeat when it looks tired again. This will be pretty soon; light watering encourages the grass roots to linger near the surface. It is much better to water infrequently—even in the hottest, driest climates, this means no more than every ten days or so—but do it thoroughly so the water penetrates right into the soil and the roots go down deep after it.

The constant removal of foliage from the grass strips it of nutrients, and these ought to be made up to it by occasional fertilizing. This is easy; just buy a ready-made lawn fertilizer, sprinkle it on, and water heavily at once to wash it into the soil—if you don't it can burn the leaves. You can apply it at the manufacturer's suggested rate in one go, but it is more effective to divide the quantity in half and give two doses a fortnight apart.

If you started out with clean soil and keep the grass flourishing, weeds should cause little headache. If any get in, just dig them out (an old kitchen knife is a useful implement here) or spot treat them with glyphosate. The lawn should soon grow over the resulting bare patch, especially if you assist it with water and fertilizer.

Meadow Gardens

There is, however, one currently fashionable style of lawn to which all these rules don't apply, and that is the flowering meadow. Here, the grass is deliberately inter-planted with 'weeds'—primroses, small bulbs, cornflowers, Flanders and Californian poppies, daisies and the like—the aim being to create an effect like the carpets of flowers you see in old tapestries. Very pretty and romantic it can be too. Here, you don't want the grass to flourish so much it smothers the flowers, so you start with rather poor soil, apply fertilizer with a sparing hand, water very judiciously, and mow only a few times a year.

Precisely when depends on your chosen flowers: but as a guide, you'll probably mow in late winter to give the spring flowers a setting of short grass; again when they have shed their seeds and died down; and perhaps again in autumn/fall. Always keep the mower as high as it will go.

Miscanthus sinensis is ideal for perennial borders, water gardens and screens.

Ground Covers

It is a short step from the flowering meadow to leaving out the grass and carpeting the ground entirely with low-growing, easy-care plants, known, naturally enough, as ground covers.

You can use annuals as temporary ground cover—nasturtiums are excellent—but the best ground covers are spreading, evergreen perennials or dense, low-growing shrubs. Flowers are a feature of many, but far more important is the ability to make a carpet dense enough to smother weeds without growing too tall—ankle height is about right. Then a good ground cover needs to be presentable all year; to need little in the way of trimming or spraying; and to be easy to propagate to cut down on cost. It is possible to weave patterns with several species, but the stronger will tend to crowd out the weaker—and simplicity usually looks better anyway. Ground covers cannot be walked on.

Prepare your bed as thoroughly as for any other plant, plant at the appropriate season, and mulch at once; the last thing you want is weeds getting in between the young plants. If you like, you can plant some low-growing annuals between your permanent plants—and they will remind you to water and fertilize. Ground covers may be low, low maintenance when they are established, but when young they need care!

Ornamental Grasses

You can supplement the flowers in your meadow with grasses chosen for their ornamental foliage and flowers rather than their ability to stand cropping into lawn: but you will need to place them with care as many are quite tall. They can be placed anywhere in the garden that you want their airy grace, and it is currently fashionable to include them in plantings with more orthodox annuals and perennials. The important thing is to choose species that stay in sedate clumps; those that run about will turn themselves into weeds as soon as your back is turned. Most retain their form as they die off for the winter, and their golden and brown tints can be a lovely feature of the autumn/fall and winter garden—but if they might be a fire hazard, by all means cut them down when they dry off. (You can use them in dried flower arrangements indoors.)

Agrostis tenuis

Asarum caudatum

Asarum canadense

Festuca elatior

LAWNS AND GROUND COVERS

AGROSTIS

tenuis

COLONIAL BENT, BROWN TOP, BENT GRASS, NEW ZEALAND BENT

Regarded highly for its tolerance of the cold, this attractive and durable annual grass is widely grown in New Zealand, the cooler Australian states and in parts of North America. Although frost-resistant, it is drought-tender. Left unmown, this New Zealand native grows to 40 cm (about 16 in) in height. A recommended mowing height is 20 mm (about ¾ in). A prodigious spreader, it has a creeping stem, with bright green, narrow leaves. It prefers moist soil that drains well, in a sunny, open location, although it will grow in light shade. Compared with other bent grasses, this more erect species needs less care. Propagate from seed. Watch out for diseases such as brown patch and dollar spot.

ASARUM

This genus consists of over 70 rhizomatous perennials, both evergreen and deciduous, which are commonly called wild ginger. Originating in temperate areas of the northern hemisphere, these fully hardy tufted plants make very good ground covers. The leaves are either kidney shaped or cordate, and the small tubular flowers that arise to 4 cm (about 2 in) are often hidden below the leaves. These plants prefer a shady site in moist, well-drained soil and can be planted out any time between autumn/fall and spring. They spread rapidly, and every few years the clumps should be divided in spring. They can also be propagated from seed.

A. canadense

This evergreen species has kidney-shaped, and often pointed, downy leaves 5–20 cm (about 2–8 in) across. Originally from North America, its bell-shaped flowers are a purple-brown colour and appear late in spring or early summer.

A. caudatum

An evergreen rhizome, this species produces small, cordate, deep green leaves, which grow to 8 cm (about 3 in) high and 10 cm (about 4 in) across. In spring or early summer, small, bell-like, red-brown flowers appear.

BOUTELOUA

gracilis

syn. B. oligostachya

MOSQUITO GRASS, SIGNAL-ARM GRASS, BLUE GRAMA

A semi-evergreen grass, this is a native of the grasslands of America and belongs to the Gramineae family. The narrow green leaves are clump forming, and grow to 25 cm (about 10 in) high. The narrow flower spike appears in summer, rising above the leaves to 50 cm (about 20 in). The flowerhead is carried almost horizontal to the stem—hence the common name signal-arm grass—and the bisexual brown florets hang downwards. This grass will thrive in any well-drained soil in a sunny situation and can be propagated in spring either by division or from seed.

FESTUCA

FESCUE

A native of Asia and temperate Europe, this genus provides good grassed areas requiring little maintenance and are ideal for playing fields, street-side plantings and parks in cold through to moderate climates. They grow deep roots and forms tufts, with short rhizomes and bright green leaves 6 mm (about ¼ in) wide. The turfs have a loose texture, wear well and tolerate semi-shade. They also withstand drought and frost well. A mowing height of 5 cm (about 2 in) is recommended for these lawns. Disease and pests rarely affect the fescues.

F. elatior
TALL FESCUE

This is a species with a tendency to clump, making it more suited to coarser lawns such as those grown for playing fields. It is also good for controlling erosion. Its leaves are tough and it will grow in compacted soil. As it does not send out runners, sow thickly to ensure a close turf. Lightly fertilize each month through summer, only once or twice in autumn/fall and spring. Sow seeds in autumn/fall.

F. rubra
RED FESCUE, CREEPING FESCUE

Excellent for a lawn, this rhizomatous grass forms both thick and loose clumps, and is similar to *F. ovina* (sheep's fescue). Its grey-green and bristle-like leaves grow to 25 cm (about 10 in). The spikelets, which can reach 60 cm (about 24 in) high, come in shades of red or purple and bear panicles of long narrow flowers in summer.

F. rubra 'Commutata'
NEW ZEALAND FESCUE, CHEWINGS FESCUE

A tuft-forming grass, this species is often sown with bent grasses, with which it shares common needs and preferences. Established on steep slopes and left ungroomed it makes for an appealing cover. Propagate this species from seed.

FRAGARIA
chiloensis

Belonging to the family Rosaceae, and taking its name from the Latin word for fragrance, this genus has 15 species of evergreen perennials. *F. chiloensis* grows wild in coastal areas of North and South America. Spreading by means of runners, it grows in dense tufts with the lower leaves forming rosettes. It reaches a height of 30 cm (about 12 in) with a spread of 45 cm (about 18 in). The 5 cm (about 2 in) long, obovate, trifoliate leaves are a lustrous deep green, and hairy underneath. The summer flowers have 5 petals and are followed by round red fruit. Plant in any well-drained soil in a sunny or partially shaded site from autumn/fall to spring. Propagate in spring from seed or runners.

LOLIUM
perenne
PERENNIAL RYE GRASS

This perennial grass grows in clumps up to 50 cm (about 20 in) high and 30 cm (about 12 in) in

Festuca rubra

Lolium perenne

Fragaria chiloensis

spread. The linear leaves are glossy, smooth and dark green. The yellowy green flowers, which appear in late spring and summer, are narrow, spike-like blooms 15 cm (about 6 in) long. It has smooth, whippy stems that tend to lie down under the lawn mower, springing back up later. This fast-sprouting species from Europe thrives in most well-drained soils, in open, sunny locations. Propagate from seed. It is a very coarse grass needing frequent mowing and is best for rough areas rather than for fine lawn.

MENTHA
requienii
CORSICAN MINT

This species belongs to a genus of hardy to half-hardy, perennial, evergreen and semi-evergreen plants that are cultivated for their aromatic foliage. Along with well-known species used as kitchen herbs there are in the genus numerous ornamental species which, as well as being suitable for a shrub border or rockery, make excellent

ground covers. Many of them, however, are vigorous to the point of invasiveness. This semi-evergreen, creeping perennial grows to 1 cm (about ½ in) high and has small, round, pale green leaves with a peppermint aroma, and light purple, short flowers which appear in summer. Thriving in any moist, well-drained soil, it is unlike most of the genus in that it needs a shaded site. It should be planted out in early spring, which is also the best time to divide this species. It will tolerate light foot traffic and looks good planted between stepping stones. It is frost-hardy.

OPHIOPOGON
japonicus
MONDO GRASS

This evergreen perennial is grown for its neat tufts of leathery, glossy, deep green, grass-like leaves. Spreading by stolons the tufts develop into mats,which makes this Japanese native popular with landscape gardeners as a ground cover. Growing to a height of 20 cm

Ophiopogon japonicus

(about 8 in) and spreading at least three times as wide, the leaves are topped by white or pale purple insignificant flowers in summer. These are followed by dark, blue-black berries. Because the species is half-hardy, it needs a sheltered site, preferably in shade, with fertile and moist but well-drained soil. Plant out in spring or early autumn/fall; established plants may also be divided at this time. This species can also be grown from seed. The plants will benefit from an annual mulch.

Thymus serpyllum

POA
pratensis
KENTUCKY BLUE GRASS, MEADOW GRASS

Although producing an appealing blue-green lawn, this native of central Europe will not take the heavy traffic of playgrounds or playing fields and does not survive dry conditions. It does well in cooler climates but is slightly frost-tender. This perennial has smooth, erect stems and small, flat, pointed leaves. If left ungroomed, it will grow to 15 cm (about 6 in) in height and spread. In spring and mid-summer, it bears spikelets in spreading panicles. Establish in light, sandy soil that drains well. Although it tolerates shade, a sunny, open location is best. It needs ample watering. Propagate from seed or by division. It is vulnerable to attack by rust and other diseases, including fusarium blight brought on by a hot summer.

THYMUS
THYME

This genus consists of over 300 evergreen species of herbaceous perennials and sub-shrubs, ranging from prostrate plants to 20 cm (about 8 in) high. Chosen for their aromatic leaves, these natives of southern Europe and Asia are frequently featured in rockeries, grown between stepping stones, or for a display on banks. Some species are also used in cooking. The flowers are often tubular and vary from white through pink to mauve. For thick, dense plants, the flowerheads should be removed after flowering. These hardy to frost-tender plants should be planted out from early autumn/fall through to early spring in a sunny site with well-drained soil. Propagate by division in spring or late summer.

T. pseudolanuginosus
syn. *T. lanuginosus* of gardens

This species is fully hardy and evergreen. Growing to a height of up to 5 cm (about 2 in) and mat forming, it is a useful ground cover. Its small grey leaves are elliptical, with straggly white hairs. The aromatic leaves grow on short, hairy stems. Tubu-

Poa pratensis

lar, two-lipped pink-mauve flowers appear in summer.

T. serpyllum
WILD THYME, MOTHER-OF-THYME, CREEPING THYME

A smaller plant than garden thyme, this native of Europe grows to a height and spread of 10 cm (about 4 in), to form a useful ground cover. Its creeping stem is woody and branching, and the scented, bright green leaves are elliptical to lanceolate. The bluish purple flowers are small and tubular with two lips, and are borne in spring and summer in dense terminal whorls. This species prefers alkaline soil, and full sun intensifies the aroma of the leaves. Propagate from cuttings or by root division. It will take moderate foot traffic, but needs replanting every few years to maintain a dense cover.

ORNAMENTAL GRASSES

ARUNDO
donax
GIANT REED

This giant perennial grass is one of the most striking of summer foliage plants. Growing to a height of 6 m (about 18 ft) and spread of 1 m (about 3 ft), it is an excellent ornamental plant for large gardens. In mild areas it can grow very vigorously and will need confining. Floppy, blue-green leaves are borne on thick stems, and dense panicles of creamy spikelets appear in summer. It is half-hardy and prefers a sunny situation and moist soil. In winter, when the foliage becomes untidy, it should be cut to the ground, creating luxurious new spring and summer growth. *A. donax* 'Versicolor' is a popular variegated cultivar.

BRIZA
media
QUAKING GRASS

An evergreen, tuft-forming perennial grass that grows to 30–60 cm (about 12–24 in) high, with a spread of 8–10 cm (about 3–4 in). It has mid-green leaves and in sum-

Thymus pseudolanuginosus

Butomus umbellatus

Carex elata 'Aurea'

mer bears open branched flower clusters of about 30 hanging, brownish purple spikelets. They make very good dried flower decorations and are excellent for dyeing. Fully hardy, plant in full sun in well-drained, poor soil. Propagate from seed in spring or autumn/fall, or by division in spring.

BUTOMUS
umbellatus
FLOWERING RUSH

This elegant, marginal water plant is the only member of its genus. Related to the lilies, it is a rush-like, deciduous perennial and has razor-sharp, narrow, twisted, mid-green leaves and tall stalks of rose-pink flowers in summer. Fully hardy, it grows to a height of 1 m (about 3 ft) and spread of 45 cm (about 18 in). Plant in a warm, sunny area in a shallow pool or boggy soil. Propagate from seed in spring or late summer, or by division in spring. The plant's name translates as: 'a plant that cuts the mouth of oxen when grazing'.

Arundo donax

CALAMAGROSTIS
× *acutiflora*

A member of the Gramineae family, this clump-forming grass has a strong upright habit, with its leaves growing to 1 m (about 3 ft). Its wispy flowerheads are long and thin and light brown in colour. They rise on hollow stems above the leaves, reaching a height of 1.5 m (about 4½ ft). The flowers persist on the stems into winter. This plant is suitable for a position at the back of a bed. Plant out in spring in any moist, well-drained soil, in sun or in partial shade. Divide the clumps in spring, or propagate seed in either spring or autumn/fall.

CAREX
SEDGE

This large genus contains over 1500 temperate perennials with grass-like foliage. Predominately clump-forming and evergreen, they make resilient decorative potted plants. Many species have sharp, pendent leaves and catkin-type flowers. Male and female blooms may appear on the same head or on the same stem. Plant in full sun or partial shade and only water when surface roots seem dry. Propagate by division in spring.

C. elata 'Aurea'
syn. *C. stricta* 'Aurea'
GOLDEN SEDGE

This evergreen, tuft-forming perennial sedge is useful for growing in damp places and beside ponds. It has golden-yellow leaves, and blackish brown flower spikes that are borne in summer. It reaches a height of 40 cm (about 16 in) and spread of 15 cm (about 6 in). Fully hardy, it grows best in a sunny situation in fertile, wet soil.

C. morrowii

Native to Japan, this evergreen perennial sedge can grow to 30 cm (about 12 in) high with a spread of 45 cm (about 18 in). Clump forming, it has strongly arching, narrow, deep green leaves and insignificant flowers in summer. The cultivars are more often grown. 'Variegata' has white-striped, rich green leaves.

COIX
lacryma-jobi
JOB'S TEARS

This tuft-forming annual grass is native to east Asia and grows to a height of 50 cm–1 m (about 20–36 in) with a spread of 10–15 cm (about 4–6 in). It has insignificant spikelets, broad green leaves and hard, beady, green fruits that change in autumn/fall to a shiny, greyish mauve colour. Half-hardy, it prefers a sunny situation and well-drained soil. Propagate from seed in spring or autumn/fall. The fruits are used to make bead necklaces.

CORTADERIA
selloana
syn. *C. argentea*
PAMPAS GRASS

Native to Argentina and Brazil, this perennial, clump-forming, stately grass grows to a height of 3 m (about 9 ft) and spread of 1.5 m (about 4½ ft). Its stems are tall and reed-like and the leaves are long and slender, growing outwards from the base. In summer, erect, silvery, plume-like panicles appear above the leaves. Pink varieties are also available. Propagate from seed or by division. It can be invasive, and in some areas is considered a noxious weed.

DESCHAMPSIA
caespitosa
TUFTED HAIR GRASS

This evergreen perennial wild grass is particularly useful for the natural-look garden or in a woodland setting. A member of the Gramineae family, it can reach a height of 1 m (about 3 ft) and spread to 30 cm (about 12 in). Fully hardy, this elegant grass has narrow, dark green leaves which form tufts. The summer flowers are held in delicate panicles of light brown; they persist well into winter. These flowers and their stems make excellent dried flowers. They thrive in any moist, well-drained soil in a sunny or partly shaded site. As with all grasses, the clumps can be divided in spring, or seed sown in either

spring or autumn/fall. There are many cultivars with attractive, different-coloured flowerheads.

FESTUCA

This is a genus of evergreen, tuft-forming perennial grasses with rounded flower stems and basal, alternate, long, narrow leaves. They bear panicles with flowerheads comprised of spikelets with one or more florets. These grasses are fully hardy and will do best in full sun in any well-drained soil.

F. amethystina

A native of the Alps and southern Europe, this fescue takes its name from the deep purple panicles of flowers that appear in late spring and early summer. It grows to 25 cm (about 10 in) high with a similar spread. A dense evergreen, its slender leaves are blue-green and rough edged. It will thrive in full sun in well-drained soil and looks good planted on a bank.

F. glauca
BLUE FESCUE

This decorative perennial grass grows in clumps to a height and spread of 10 cm (about 4 in). The leaves are narrow, and their colour ranges from silvery white to blue-grey. Insignificant flowers bloom in summer. Closely spaced and left untrimmed, it is suitable for use as an edging to flowerbeds and as a ground cover. This is a very easily grown species which thrives in most soils. Propagate by division of clumps in spring.

Cortaderia selloana

Deschampsia caespitosa

Coix lacryma-jobi

Calamagrostis × *acutiflora*

Briza media

Festuca glauca

Festuca amethystina

Carex morrowii 'Variegata'

HELICTOTRICHON
sempervirens
syn. *Avena candida, A. sempervirens*
BLUE OAT GRASS

This evergreen perennial grass deserves to be given prominence in a garden planting. Out of a genus of over 90, this native of south-western Europe is the species that is most commonly grown. It has silver-blue leaves which arch and grow to 1 m (about 3 ft). The oat-like summer flowers are produced in drooping panicles on stems that can reach a height of 1.2 m (about 4 ft). A hardy plant, it can be grown in any well-drained soil provided it is in a sunny position. Divide clumps any time between late autumn/fall and spring. This grass looks good when contrasted with purple and pink low-growing plants.

IMPERATA
cylindrica 'Rubra'
JAPANESE BLOOD GRASS

One of the Gramineae family, this stunning grass has erect, sword-like,

mid-green leaves that grow to 35 cm (about 14 in). They appear in mid- to late summer and their ends very soon turn the colour of blood, hence their common name. Then by autumn/fall the whole plant has turned this vibrant colour. This is an excellent plant for providing colour contrast. Half-hardy, it will need protection in winter. Its preferred siting would be in moist, well-drained soil with some shade. It can be divided in spring, and seed should be sown in either spring or autumn/fall.

MILIUM
effusum 'Aureum'
BOWLES' GOLDEN GRASS, MILLET GRASS

An evergreen, tuft-forming perennial grass grown for its yellow foliage and flowers. Good for growing in perennial borders, water gardens, or as a ground cover, and effective when planted under white variegated shrubs. Its flat leaves are golden-yellow in spring and fade to yellowish green in summer. Panicles

of greenish yellow spikelets are produced in summer and these can be cut and used for dried arrangements. It grows to a height of 1 m (about 3 ft) and spread of 30 cm (about 12 in). Fully hardy, it grows best in the shade in a well-drained, rich, moist soil. Propagate from seed in spring or autumn/fall, or by division in spring. It also self-seeds readily. The Bowles in question in the common name was a very influential English gardener of the Edwardian period. He was fond of plants with unusual leaves.

MISCANTHUS
sinensis 'Variegatus'
JAPANESE SILVER GRASS

This large, herbaceous perennial grass grows to a height of 2 m (about 6 ft) with a spread of 50 cm (about 18 in). One of the most popular ornamental grasses, it is grown for its overall plant form and is good for perennial borders, water gardens, naturalized areas, screens and specimen planting. Clump-forming, it has linear leaves with silvery white stripes and margins. Long-lasting beige, red tinged flower heads are borne in autumn/fall—they are good for drying and dyeing. Frost-hardy, it requires a sunny situation and well-drained moist soil. Divide every 5–7 years to keep the plants growing vigorously. Propagate by division in spring.

MOLINIA
caerulea

A native of acid heathlands in Europe, and south-west and northern Asia, this tuft-forming, deciduous perennial grass forms large tussocks growing up to 45 cm (about 18 in) when in flower. It has broad, flat, mid-green leaves and in summer bears panicles of purplish spikelets. It is fully hardy and grows best on acid soils in full sun, tolerating any fertile, neutral soil. It has swollen stem bases which at times have been used as pipe cleaners and toothpicks. It is one of the most attractive garden grasses, especially in its finest variegated forms. Propagate by division in spring.

Imperata cylindrica 'Rubra'

PENNISETUM

This genus of tuft-forming, herbaceous, perennial grasses belongs to the Poaceae family. They have narrow green basal leaves and rounded flower stems. Dead foliage may be cut back on herbaceous perennials when dormant. Propagate species from seed in spring or autumn/fall or by division in spring.

P. alopecuroides
syn. *P. compressum*
SWAMP FOXTAIL, FOUNTAIN GRASS

This herbaceous perennial grass, a native of Argentina, has narrow, mid-green leaves which can attain a height of 1 m (about 3 ft). Forming a dense clump, this species lives for longer than most in the genus, but will need protection against frost. In late summer feathery panicles of purple-brown, bristle-like flowers appear, slightly taller than the leaves. Enduring well into winter, these flowering stems make good dried flowers. 'Hameln' is a shorter form, to 50 cm (about 20 in) high, and its flowers appear in early summer. Both make good specimen plants.

P. setaceum
syn. *P. ruppellii*
AFRICAN FOUNTAIN GRASS

Native to tropical Africa, this species belongs to the same genus as many cereal and fodder plants. Arching, coppery spikes with bearded bristles form brush-like flower clusters on this herbaceous perennial grass. Appearing in summer, they last into winter. This half-hardy species grows into tufts comprising very rough stems and long, narrow leaf

Pennisetum alopecuroides

Molinia caerulea 'Variegata'

Miscanthus sinensis 'Variegatus'

Pennisetum setaceum

Helictotrichon sempervirens

blades. It grows to 1 m (about 3 ft) with a spread of 50 cm (about 20 in). Plant in moist soil in full sun. It is not suitable as a lawn grass, but makes an attractive tall ground cover (perhaps with some spring bulbs intermixed) or a feature plant in a flower border.

PHALARIS
arundinacea var. *picta*
GARDENER'S GARTERS, REEDY GRASS

This clump-forming perennial grass is easily grown, bearing reed-like leaves with white stripes and, in summer, terminal panicles of purplish or pale green spikelets on stout, upstanding stems. Indigenous to North America and Europe, it can grow to 1.5 m (about 4½ ft) but is generally kept lower in a garden. This fully hardy evergreen likes well-drained soil and semi-shade. It can prove invasive. Propagate by division of the clumps.

PLEIOBLASTUS
pygmaeus
syn. *Arundinaria pygmaea, Sasa pygmaea*
DWARF BAMBOO

This spreading, rhizomatous bamboo can be used to help control erosion. Left uncut, the dark green foliage (variegated in most of the commonly available strains) of this frost-hardy evergreen will grow to 50 cm (about 20 in) and spread indefinitely. Cut back almost to the ground in early spring to ensure a lush crop of fresh new leaves.

SASA

This genus consists of over 150 species of rhizomatous, woody grasses. They are found in eastern Asia, especially Japan. They are usually not very tall. Propagate from seed in autumn/fall or by division in spring.

S. palmata
This spreading, evergreen bamboo grows to a height of 2 m (about 6 ft) with an indefinite spread. Its flowers are insignificant but the wide, rich green leaves make it an excellent foliage plant, adding grace and contrast to borders and rock gardens. *S. palmata* does best in a sheltered, not too dry situation in sun or shade. Its hollow stems are streaked with purple and bear one branch at each node.

S. veitchii
syn. *S. albomarginata*

This fully hardy bamboo grows to a height of 1.5 m (about 5 ft) and spreads indefinitely. Its 25 cm (about 10 in) long leaves turn white at the edges. Its stems, which branch from each node, are generally purple with a whitish powder beneath the node. Grow in well-drained soil in full sun.

SCIRPUS
lacustris subsp. *tabernaemontani* 'Zebrinus'
syn. *S. tabernaemontani* **'Zebrinus'**

This is an evergreen sedge with white-banded, leafless stems. In summer, it carries brown spikelets. Growing 1.5 m (about 4½ ft) high, this fully hardy perennial spreads widely. It likes full sun, wet soil and is not deterred even by brackish water; however, it is invasive and will need regular division.

SINARUNDINARIA
nitida
syn. *Arundinaria nitida*

Classified as belonging to two separate genera and families—Bambuseae and Gramineae—this is an evergreen bamboo which can grow to 4 m (about 12 ft). Originating in China, it is very similar to *S. murielae* but its mid-green leaves are smaller. Its canes are purple and a number of branches grow out from the nodes. The insignificant flowers appear only rarely. Frost-hardy and clump forming, this species is particularly effective as a screen or hedge; to achieve this, individual plants should be grown 1.5 m (about 4½ ft) apart. It also looks good mass planted in a large garden. Plant out in late spring or early summer in moist, well-drained soil in a sunny or a partially shaded position that will provide shelter from winds. Propagate by division in late spring.

STIPA

This widely distributed genus consists of 300 species of perennial tufted and hardy annual grasses. The perennials are noted for their tall flowering spikes with large feathery panicles. The leaves are narrow and straight edged. The larger growing species, with flower spikes that can reach over 2 m (about 6 ft), are often grown as specimen plants, sited where they can be seen to best advantage but will not overwhelm other plantings. To propagate, sow seed or divide the plants any time in late spring.

S. gigantea
GOLDEN OATS

Native to Spain, this evergreen perennial is best grown as a specimen plant. It is a long-living species with narrow green leaves which can reach 75 cm (about 30 in). In summer the upright stems bear bristle-like, silver-purple flowers that appear in large, open panicles up to 22 cm (about 9 in) long. These persist into winter, turning a deep golden colour. Cut the flower stems in mid-summer for drying. A clump-forming species, it prefers a light soil in a sunny position.

S. pennata
WILD OATS

Golden anthers hang from the long-awned, silver spikelets that form delicate, airy panicles on this perennial grass in summer through to winter. The leaves are narrow and 50 cm (about 20 in) or more in length. A frost-hardy species which likes well-drained soil and full sun, it reaches a height of 2.5 m (about 7½ ft).

Sasa palmata

Phalaris arundinacea var. picta

Stipa gigantea

Sinarundinaria nitida

Stipa pennata

Pleioblastus pygmaeus

Sasa veitchii

CHAPTER 7

Vegetables
& Herbs

There's nothing to quite match the flavour of home-grown vegetables or herbs. They can be picked at the moment of perfection and eaten or preserved within hours to the benefit of both the family's health and budget. What's more, vegetables like spinach and rhubarb, or herbs, are always bunched for sale and we often have to buy more than is immediately needed for a meal. Home grown, these are readily available by the sprig or leaves can be cut as required.

To be grown successfully, vegetables do need to be chosen with consideration to climate. Vegetables such as beans, tomatoes and the ground vine crops like cucumbers and squash are frost-sensitive and therefore need to be planted out when the prospect of frost is over. They like temperatures of around 20°C (about 68°F) to set fruit. On the other hand, many of the root crops (those with the edible parts underground), like spinach

and peas, grow well in temperatures of between 12 and 18°C (about 53–64°F) and are not as susceptible to frost. Then there are the cabbages, cauliflowers and brussel sprouts, all members of the same family, which revel in cool temperatures and are quite frost-hardy.

All vegetables must have ample sunlight, and this factor, more than any other, can dictate the positioning of a vegetable garden. Other points to consider include competition from tree or shrub roots, prevailing winds and drainage, although this last factor is usually able to be rectified by raising the beds or by underground piping.

The size of the garden also needs careful thought. Depending on space available and the time you are prepared to spend in the garden, any number of beds can be made, but it's a good idea to begin small. Beds are easily extended or new ones made. A bed of up to 1.2 m (about 3½ ft) wide is easily cultivated from both sides. Length can be determined by available space, but 2 m (about 6 ft) gives ample room for the compact and quick growers. Others, like the vine crops, take up a lot more

garden space and need the use of a bed the whole season to complete their cycle. The perennial plants such as rhubarb and asparagus, as well as many of the herbs which occupy the same space for many years, need a bed of their own or to be grouped at one end of a highly cultivated bed so that they are not interfered with when the rest of the garden is being prepared for the new season's crop.

Consider too the choice of vegetables you plan to grow. Yield per plant is a very important factor when space is limited. For instance beans take up relatively little space and their yield is tremendous over a season. Salad vegetables and the leaf crops too are worth considering before, say, a plot given over to potatoes which don't really spoil when left on the greengrocer's shelf.

One very practical way to overcome limited space is to build a trellis towards the back of a garden to hold climbing beans, peas, even cucumbers. Sited correctly, this trellis will not shade the lower growing vegetables and it can act as a windbreak to a row of corn or some tomatoes.

The herb garden—a source of health and wonderful fragrance.

Pots too can be used. They need not be restricted to growing herbs; they are also ideal for such long-cropping vegetables as capsicums, tomatoes, eggplant or the 'bush' varieties of cucumbers or pumpkins. Placed on a sunny patio they can be easily observed and given immediate attention if this is required.

Planting

Some seeds, like the quick growing radish or beans, melons and carrots, can be sown directly into their permanent garden positions. Finer seeds are better planted into seedbeds or frames where germination and early growth can be closely monitored. A seedbed needs to have soil of a fine consistency, perfect drainage and to be placed where it receives adequate sunlight and warmth and is well protected from any drying winds. The surface should be flat so that fine seeds are not washed away. Shallow grooves can be made with a length of dowel or similar, then the seeds carefully dropped into these miniature farrows and covered with a light soil layer. Water with a fine mist or spray, ensuring the surface is neither too wet nor allowed to dry out.

Gardeners in colder areas can sow seeds in frames in protected areas while it is still too early to plant outdoors. These plants are then transplanted into their permanent positions when all possibility of frost is over. When the weather warms up then it may be possible to sow another batch or two in a well-prepared, outdoor seedbed in the successive weeks. By making these regular small sowings the household won't be inundated by a glut of vegetables all maturing at the one time.

Many gardeners prefer to buy their seedlings at the nursery. Transplanting should be done in the cool of the evening. Using a garden knife or small trowel, and holding the plants by their leaves, loosen them gently from the seedbed or punnet and place a bunch of them on a board—covering them with a cloth or damp kitchen paper towel will prevent them drying out. Use a piece of dowel to make a row of holes sufficiently deep so the tiny roots will not be bent or broken, then gently prise the seedlings apart and place single plants in the prepared holes, pushing the soil firmly around them with two fingers. Water each plant to ensure any air pockets are filled with soil. The seed-

Nothing can beat the flavour of home-grown vegetables.

lings do benefit from being given some protection in the form of a leafy branch, cut down milk carton or similar until they have time to become accustomed to their new surroundings.

Planting the same vegetables in the same position each year is not good garden practice as the plants of the same family are often prone to similar diseases and this only accentuates the problem. And, although chemicals can be used, one of the benefits of growing vegetables is that you can decide which, and indeed if any, chemicals to use. Plants of the same family also take up similar nutrients and it was for this reason that crop rotation was first introduced. Today these nutrients can be replaced by commercial fertilizers.

Different crops require different types of fertilizers, the green plants grown for their leaves need a high nitrogen content, while plants grown for their fruit need a more balanced diet. When a garden is as intensively used as it is for vegetable growing it pays to supplement the use of chemical fertilizers with organic material to ensure its continued good health. Organic fertilizers such as compost can be dug into the soil at the changeover of the seasons. Straw or similar material used as a mulch during the growing season is usually sufficiently decomposed to be dug into the garden at the end of summer. You'll be amazed at the difference in soil texture and general health of the soil when this is done.

Vegetables need to be grown quickly to promote maximum quality in both leaf and fruiting types. To ensure this rapid, uninterrupted development it is necessary to keep soil adequately moist at all times. It follows then that sandy soil, which dries out more rapidly than heavy soil, needs to be watered more frequently. Many of the vine crops and tomatoes are prone to leaf diseases if leaves are subject to continued moisture, so in beds where these types of vegetables are to be grown a trickle hose or a depression running the length of the bed and filled with water each morning could be used instead of sprinklers which spray moisture indiscriminately over foliage and ground alike.

Close planting and mulching are two ways to ensure moisture is conserved. Close planting may produce less vigorous plants or a marginally less prolific crop, but the home gardener can progressively use, and so thin out, rows as plants mature. Mulching saves the gardener time and energy in other ways as well. It helps with soil temperature control at both extremes and stops heavy rain washing away soil from around the fibrous roots that are often very near the surface of many of the annual vegetables. Mulching also limits weed growth. Many gardeners today rely solely on mulched or 'no dig' beds for successful vegetable growing.

Do try gardening with vegetables and herbs as it really is the most satisfying of the stress reducing hobbies and you'll glow with pleasure at the bountiful results of your leisure!

Allium ascalonicum

VEGETABLES

ALLIUM

This is a large genus consisting of more than 700 species of perennials and biennials that grow in temperate climates around the world and range in size from 10–150 cm (about 4–60 in). Some species are edible, including the onions, garlic and chives. The most ornamental species, which are brightly coloured with beautiful flowers, are found in the northern hemisphere. Common to the genus is the oniony smell emitted when the leaves are bruised or pinched. The onion species may need the protection of a cloche if the soil is cold. Both the onion and ornamental species have the same pest and disease enemies such as onion fly, stem eelworm, rust and onion white rot. The name derives from the Celtic, *all*, meaning hot.

A. ascalonicum
SHALLOT

A carefully thinned bed of shallots will self-perpetuate by dropping seeds or generating new clusters of bulbs. Like all onions, shallots like a light, fertile, weed-free soil. They are usually propagated by dividing the clumps of bulbs.

A. cepa
ONION, SPRING ONION, SCALLION

Onions need a cool climate and a sunny, open position in a well-drained bed of soil. Sow the seeds or immature onions in mid-spring in holes 1 cm (about ½ in) deep and 30 cm (about 12 in) apart, and water moderately. Harvest in late summer when the leaves have begun to yellow. The onion was a popular vegetable among the Greeks and Romans but never eaten by the Egyptians who regarded it as sacred. The spring onion is an immature onion which has not yet made a bulb. It likes the same conditions as other onions. In a warm climate seeds can be sown at any time of the year.

A. cepa var. aggregatum
TREE ONION

Otherwise known as golden shallots or the Egyptian onion, these have a more delicate taste than spring onions and can be used instead of chives. Propagate from the small bulbs that grow among the flowers or by division.

A. porrum
LEEK

Easier to grow than the onion and more suited to cold climates, the leek likes a sunny spot and a moist light soil. Sow seeds in spring or summer or plant seedlings 20 cm (about 8 in) apart with 30 cm (about 12 in) between rows, filling each hole gently with water. Keep clear of weeds and, once the base of the leek is at least 2 cm (about 1 in) thick, harvest as needed.

APIUM
graveolens var. dulce
CELERY

Native to the Mediterranean, this leafy vegetable is a boon to any salad, but a challenge for the home gardener to grow well. It needs a well-prepared, loamy soil that can

Allium cepa var. *aggregatum*

Allium cepa

drain water but still hold the desired amount. It also commands a lot of space and regular doses of liquid fertilizer. Prior to some hard work put in by Italian gardeners some 400 years ago, celery was nothing more than a bitter-tasting weed, and even now its stalks need to be blanched to remove bitterness. This is done by shoring the soil up around them to exclude the light when they reach a height of 30 cm (about 12 in). You can also bundle the plant up in black plastic, and self-blanching varieties are available. Water diligently if the summer is dry. Septoria leaf spot is a serious celery problem.

A. graveolens var. rapaceum
CELERIAC

Easier to grow than celery and with a longer growing season, this is similar to the turnip (often called turnip-rooted celery) but with a celery flavour. Keep well watered even when cool, and harvest the roots when about 10 cm (about 4 in) across. The leaves are edible but inferior to regular celery.

ASPARAGUS
officinalis
ASPARAGUS

A frost-hardy perennial of the lily family this vegetable seems to have been cultivated and eaten all over the world as far back as the ancient Egyptians. Sow seeds in spring or set young plants in winter in 25 cm (about 10 in) deep trenches in a sunny part of the garden. Give asparagus a good 30 cm (about 12 in) between each plant so that its fleshy roots can wander freely. The soil should be well-drained and rich with compost or manure. Do not harvest the young shoots (spears) until the third spring, and always stop in time to allow sufficient shoots to mature to keep the plants going. The red berries should be picked before they go to seed and the plants should be mulched every summer.

BETA
vulgaris
BEETROOT

A relatively easy vegetable to grow, it is fast growing and should be given space and an open position. It needs a deep, fertile soil that has been previously cultivated. Sow seeds in autumn/fall in 2 cm (about 1 in) holes 20 cm (about 8 in) apart. When the first leaves appear weed out the weaker seedlings. Keep the soil moist and pull out the beetroot by hand. In warm climates it can be harvested almost all year round, but in cold climates bulbs will need to be picked and then stored over winter. It is susceptible to boron deficiency and white fly. It was once valued by the Romans and Greeks for its leaves rather than the root itself.

Asparagus officinalis

Apium graveolens var. *dulce*

Beta vulgaris

Apium graveolens var. *rapaceum*

Allium porrum

B. vulgaris var. *cicla*
SILVERBEET, SWISS CHARD

Similar to spinach, but better in warm climates, it has the same requirements as beetroot. It is easy to grow and will tolerate shade or sun. Sow in mid-spring and summer. Snails and slugs are the only real problem. Harvest the leaves, a few at a time, as needed.

BRASSICA

There are 30 species of this annual or biennial vegetable, some grown for cooking, oilseed and mustard, others for animal fodder. It is native to the Mediterranean and parts of Asia. Most of the *Brassica* species love a lime-rich, moist, well-drained soil. Seedlings should be raised in seedbeds and then carefully replanted 6 to 8 weeks later in a sheltered spot in soil that has been prepared previously for an earlier crop. Brassicas are more prone to pests and diseases than other vegetables so ensure all soil is weed-free and not wet. Club root is a common disease in these vegetables, and crop rotation should be practised.

B. campestris var. *rutabaga*
SWEDE, RUTABAGA

Similar to turnips but larger and sweeter, swedes are frost-hardy and prefer a fertile soil. Sow seeds in late spring to early summer in 2 cm (about 1 in) deep holes 45 cm (about 18 in) apart. Harvest in mid-autumn/fall. Watch for slugs and snails.

B. oleracea *gonglyoides*
KOHLRABI

With characteristics of both the turnip and cabbage, this is a versatile vegetable with a slightly nutty flavour that can be eaten raw or cooked. Sow seeds in holes 1 cm (about ½ in) deep and spaced 20 cm (about 8 in) by 80 cm (about 32 in) apart. Weed very lightly as root disturbance will slow growth.

B. oleracea var. *acephala*
KALE

A variety of flat-leafed or curly-leafed, headless cabbage that is prolific in northern Europe because of its tolerance to cold. Plant out the seedlings in 2 cm (about 1 in) holes 45 cm (about 18 in) apart. Sow the flat-leafed variety from seed as they do not tolerate transplanting. In Scotland its broth is a traditional Highland dish.

B. oleracea var. *botrytis*
WHITE CAULIFLOWER

Mark Twain scathingly labelled the cauliflower 'a cabbage with a college education', but time has proved this to be a very popular vegetable with a long history. It prefers a humus-rich soil for large compact head production. Plant seedlings 60 cm (about 24 in) apart and across. Do this with care as they hate being transplanted. Keep the soil moist and with the right amounts of boron, magnesium and potassium.

B. oleracea var. *bullata*
SAVOY CABBAGE

This variety is extremely frost-hardy and will thrive in very cold conditions. It is larger and stronger in flavour than European cabbage, with dark, wrinkled leaves.

B. oleracea var. *capitata*
EUROPEAN CABBAGE

There are many varieties of this very popular cabbage and they range in their seasonal tolerance. This ensures that these cabbages can be grown worldwide in many different climatic zones. Water regularly and mulch well, keeping the soil

Brassica oleracea gonglyoides

Brassica oleracea var. acephala

Beta vulgaris var. cicla

Brassica oleracea var. botrytis

well drained. Space seedlings between 30–50 cm (about 12–20 in) apart, depending on variety. The Greeks regarded the cabbage, native to southern Europe, as a cure for hangover which may be true considering its high nutritional value. Red cabbage, with its purple leaves, is a slow-maturing cabbage that needs a long growing season. However, its solid, chewy flesh makes it the best of all the cabbage species for pickling and frying.

B. oleracea var. cymosa
BROCCOLI

Broccoli has the same soil needs as other *Brassica* species. Sow seeds in late spring. Plant seedlings in late summer 50 cm (about 20 in) apart in 60 cm (about 24 in) rows, water well and mulch to save weeding work. It is ideally grown in raised beds. Keep clear of weeds and do not allow to flower as it will stop growing. Harvest 10 or 11 weeks after planting. Grubs and water-logging are two major problems.

B. oleracea var. gemmifera
BRUSSELS SPROUTS

Timing is crucial when planting Brussels sprouts since they need to mature in the coldest part of the year in order to form compact hearts. In warm climates sow or plant in summer. In cold climates sow or plant in mid-spring. In autumn/fall remove any yellowing leaves and make sure the soil stays firm around the stem of the plant.

B. pekinensis
WOM BUK, CHINESE CABBAGE

Resembling lettuce more than cabbage, this fast-growing species is native to China and was only introduced to Europe in the nineteenth century. Sow seeds 10 cm (about 4 in) apart with 40 cm (about 16 in) between rows. This species is easy to grow as long as it is kept moist. Tie the leaves together after they begin to form their heart shape. Harvest the whole plant as you would a regular cabbage.

Brassica oleracea var. *capitata*

Brassica oleracea var. *cymosa*

Brassica oleracea var. *bullata*

Brassica pekinensis

Brassica oleracea var. *gemmifera*

Capsicum annuum (Chilli pepper)

Capsicum annuum (Bell pepper)

B. sinensis
BOK CHOY, CHINESE CABBAGE

This species looks like silverbeet and is also known as Chinese mustard. These run to seed quickly so sow them in small groups every 10 days. Harvest the entire plant or take a few leaves as needed after 6 to 8 weeks.

CAPSICUM

Closely related to the tomato, and like it native to Central America and a lover of hot, humid summers. The genus contains both ornamental species, grown for their brightly coloured fruit—they are far too hot to eat—and edible types, which divide into the sweet or bell peppers. They can be cooked as a vegetable and eaten raw in salads. The chilli peppers are used fresh or dry to add a sharp, hot flavour to cooking.

GROSSUM GROUP

C. annuum
SWEET BELL PEPPER, CAPSICUM

Extremely high in vitamin C and available in lots of different hybrids. Sow the seeds in containers in a compost-rich soil and then leave in a greenhouse for 8 weeks until late spring. This plant is quite frost-tender and, once planted outside, seedlings may need to be covered with cloches to keep warm. Keep plants well watered. Capsicums contain more vitamin C and vitamin A if they are left to mature until they turn a deep red colour, but they are good eating when green. Red spiders and mites are common pests.

LONGUM GROUP

C. annuum
CHILLI PEPPER, CAPSICUM

A much smaller fruit than the sweet bell pepper and a more profuse grower, this plant needs the same conditions as the green capsicum and can be sun dried and stored in jars. Wash your hands after handling, as the 'hot' substance capsicain is present in all parts of the plant.

Brassica rapa

Brassica sinensis

B. rapa
TURNIP

The turnip was a staple food of the northern European working classes until the potato upstaged it. It is suited more to the cooler regions of the world. In order to produce a quick crop, grow turnips in fertile soil in rows approximately 35 cm (about 14 in) apart. Keep the young plants moist at all times during the growing period. Harvest the turnips when they are a little bigger than a golf ball.

CICHORIUM

This genus of perennials from the Mediterranean and the Middle East is distantly related to the lettuce. The 2 species in gardens, however, have little in common except their family relation—they are grown and used in the kitchen quite differently.

C. endivia
ENDIVE, CURLY ENDIVE

This is a relative of chicory, grown for its leaves. As with most salad vegetables, it needs a humus-rich soil which is kept moist so that it won't run to seed. Sow the seeds 30–35 cm (about 12–14 in) apart in a shaded position in late summer. Use liquid fertilizer every now and then as the plants are growing. The leaves are usually eaten green as a bitter salad; they rather resemble lettuce but are more sharply flavoured. Snails and slugs can be a problem.

C. intybus
CHICORY

The plants are usually grown from spring-sown seed, allowed to grow through the summer and then lifted a few at a time during winter to be replanted in boxes of moist earth in a dark warm place. The resulting shoots (chicons) will be almost pure white and sweet in flavour; they are ready to harvest when they are 25 cm (about 10 in) long; about 3 or 4 weeks from transplanting. The

whole procedure succeeds best in a cool climate; in warm winter areas chicory is a gourmet luxury. Chicory root is used to make caffeine-free coffee and can also be eaten raw or grated. It is a common weed along highways with its bright blue flowers.

COLOCASIA
esculenta
TARO

Widely grown throughout the tropical regions for the edible tubers, it has large, heart-shaped, mid- to dark green leaves often with prominent veins. It likes a well-drained acid soil and will flourish in tropical, hot, wet conditions. Keep the soil around the base of the plant firm to support the slender stem. Propagate from young suckers or sections of tuber. Harvest 8 months after planting. Young shoots can be cooked and eaten like asparagus.

CUCUMIS
sativus cultivars
APPLE CUCUMBER, LONG GREEN CUCUMBER

The cucumber, a native of India, was as popular with Roman emperors as it is today. In cold climates sow seeds in containers and then transfer the seedlings to a greenhouse or cloche. In warm climates sow into high-compost soil in the garden in late spring and cover with a light layer of soil. Ensure seedlings are free of weeds and that the ground is moist and not hot as this

will destroy cucumber vines. The vines have to be trained on a frame or outdoor trellis in warm climates, to keep the fruit away from the soil. Harvest in summer, removing the small cucumbers to encourage further production. Apple cucumber cultivars are compact and can be grown hydroponically, however they are quite vulnerable to downy mildew. Long green cucumbers are more resistant to mildew; pick them when they are a deep green colour. Both vining and compact (bush) cultivars are available.

Cucumis sativus cultivar

Cichorium intybus

Colocasia esculenta

Cichorium endivia

Cynara scolymus

Summer squash

Pumpkin

Courgette

CUCURBITA

This is an ancient vegetable genus that dates back to 7000 BC in Central America and 1000 BC in North America. So hybridized are the species that applying Latin names can be quite arbitrary. There are squashes, pumpkins, marrow, zucchinis, trombones, butternuts and many others. Most species of this genus are easy to raise and have the same need of a warm, rich soil. In warm climates sow from early spring to late summer. In cold climates sow indoors in early summer. To prepare the garden for seedlings dig holes 30 cm (about 12 in) square, 90 cm (about 36 in) apart for bush varieties and 1.2 m (about 3½ ft) apart for the trailing varieties of pumpkin. Fill with a good fertilizer mix. Plant out seedlings in spring, watering well beforehand. Watch for slugs and keep well irrigated as they are water hungry. Harvest in autumn/fall. The genus has been grown and interbred in gardens for so long that its botany is rather confused; most types are usually given as forms of *C. pepo*, but some authorities loudly disagree. The issue has been sidestepped by simply listing them under the common names used in gardens. However, the common name may also vary from country to country.

Courgette, zucchini, vegetable marrow

Marrow used to be eaten when fully ripe and about the size of a large cucumber; but in recent years the fashion has been to eat them when very small when they are called courgettes (UK) or zucchini. There are varieties selected to be at their best when immature (i.e. as zucchini) and others that are best when mature; but you can in fact eat all of them at either stage. They need fertile soil, sun and lots of moisture so they will grow quickly. Plant seedlings 50 cm (about 20 in) apart and feed with liquid manure as the first fruit forms. Remove any damaged or sick leaves and fruit.

Pumpkin

Food for pigs in much of Europe but a delicious vegetable for the table elsewhere. The pumpkin is a sprawling vine which ripens its fruit in autumn/fall. They will keep all winter if left until cold withers the vine before harvesting, but they can be taken earlier as soon as they are ripe. There are many varieties ranging greatly in size and weight. They like rich soil, warmth, and water while growing. There is an overlap between pumpkin and winter squash in Commonwealth and American terminology—but they are grown and eaten in much the same way.

Summer squash

This is a trailing vine that likes rich, well-drained soil in full sun. Grown during the warm weather, summer squash are eaten while young. Watch for powdery mildew.

Vegetable spaghetti

This delightful marrow cultivar is easy to grow and features bright yellow fruit whose flesh looks much like spaghetti when boiled.

Winter squash

More hardy than summer squash, this vegetable needs little attention as long as the soil is rich and there is plenty of sunlight. Winter squash are allowed to mature on the vine and eaten in winter.

CYNARA
scolymus
GLOBE ARTICHOKE

Native to the Mediterranean, the globe artichoke is one of many vegetables once considered to be an aphrodisiac. It has delicate, grey-green leaves and is easy to grow in most soils and positions. Make sure it has enough space (one or two plants are enough in a small garden) and a rich soil. Plant suckers 90 cm (about 36 in) apart in early spring. Remove yellowing leaves and stems in autumn/fall. Cut the plump flower buds from the plants in spring and summer before the flowers begin to open. *C. cardunculus*, the cardoon, has magnificent deep purple flowerheads and grey-green leaves. It is the stem of this species that is the edible part, while the flowerheads can be dried for decoration.

DAUCUS
carota
CARROT

This famous root vegetable is native to Afghanistan and was introduced to Europe 600 years ago. Sow in deep, warm, aerated soil that is loamy, in rows 25 cm (about 10 in) apart, making sure the earth is firmly compacted around the seeds. Keep the earth moist around the seedlings and thin the rows out when they are 2 cm (about 1 in) high. The carrot gives a high yield even in a small garden and can be stored easily in bins or boxes between layers of sand. Once they are big enough to pick, avoid leaving them in the ground during wet weather as the root will split. The carrot is vulnerable to carrot-fly, greenfly and aphids.

HELIANTHUS
tuberosus
JERUSALEM ARTICHOKE

A relative of the sunflower, this plant has nothing whatsoever to do with Jerusalem, and is in fact a native of North America. It is grown for its pleasant flavoured tubers. This is a very enthusiastic plant which in some conditions may need controlling. It will grow in any soil as long as it is well watered and should be placed in a sunny corner. Plant divisions of the tuber 15 cm (about 6 in) deep and 30 cm (about 12 in) apart in late winter. Hoe when necessary during the year and harvest when the tops have died, usually the following autumn/fall. Dig out all the tubers otherwise they will sprout up and take over the garden.

HIBISCUS
esculentus
OKRA, GUMBO

Sometimes known as *Abelmoschus esculentus*, this attractive plant with pale yellow flowers with a red heart is similar to the ornamental hibiscus. The edible part of the plant is the starchy seed pod which is used for general flavouring as well as in Indian curries and Cajun cooking. It does best in warm climates. Sow 3 or 4 seeds together in early summer in aerated, fertilized soil. Ensure there are 40 cm (about 16 in) between each clump of seeds and that rows are 70 cm (about 28 in) apart. Thin seedlings out and weed soil throughout the year. Pick the pods after the flowers have opened (late

summer through to autumn/fall) or when they are 10 cm (about 4 in) long. Do not leave mature pods on the plants. Watch for aphids and caterpillars.

IPOMOEA
batatas
SWEET POTATO

This native of Central America and the Pacific islands comes in both a white-fleshed or, more recently, orange-fleshed variety. Plant cuttings in rows 1 m (about 3 ft) apart in soil that has been fertilized and dug thoroughly. In a frost-free climate sweet potato can be planted at any time, but it is not recommended for planting in cool climates. Keep the young plants clear of weeds until the vines are big enough to cover the ground. Keep the soil moist while the tubers grow. Harvesting depends on the variety of sweet potato and ranges from 16 weeks to 40 weeks after planting. After digging them out let the tubers dry in the sun for half a

day before storage. Watch for potato moth, potato scab and aphids.

LACTUCA
sativa
LETTUCE

From the Latin, *lac*, meaning milk, referring to its milky white sap, this biennial originated in the Middle East and the Mediterranean. Praised through history for its healthy or sleep-inducing properties, lettuce is a salad plant with a very delicate root system. It grows up to 1 m (about 3 ft) high. Sow lettuce seeds in spring or summer in the open ground or sow in seed boxes for later transplanting. Ensure that the seed is right for the climate as there are many kinds of lettuce to suit different climates. The soil must be humus-rich and evenly moist. Thin the seedlings gradually until they are 30 cm (about 12 in) apart. Sudden changes in temperature can leave the lettuce open to disease. Ensure they do not flower. Water regularly over summer, avoiding

excessive water on leaves. Winter growers will need little water. Watch for slugs, grey mould and greenfly. Popular types include the common iceberg with globular heads like pale green cabbages, cos lettuce with more open darker heads, and mignonette with ruffled pink-tinted leaves. All come in an array of cultivars.

Hibiscus esculentus

Daucus carota

Ipomoea batatas

Helianthus tuberosus

Lactuca sativa (mignonette type)

Lycopersicon esculentum

Phaeolus vulgaris

Phaesolus coccineus

Nasturtium officinale

Pastinaca sativa

Pisum sativum

L. sativa var. *asparagina*
CELTUCE

A native of the Far East, this vegetable features an edible stem similar to a celery stalk and edible bright green, curled leaves. Sow seeds in late summer and autumn/fall. Ensure that the soil is rich in organic manure. Water the plants to keep them tender and hoe well. They will be ready to harvest 10 weeks after sowing.

LYCOPERSICON
esculentum
TOMATO

This native of South America was regarded with suspicion for centuries because of its infamous relative, the deadly nightshade. Its basic needs are sunshine, moist, well-drained soil and a frost-free area. In cold climates use a cloche to keep the soil warm. In open ground plant seedlings in rows 1 m (about 3 ft) apart and keep 30–60 cm (about 12–24 in) between each plant. Seedlings can be grown in windowsill pots and then gently planted out when 12 cm (about 5 in) high. It is essential that tomatoes are supported by stakes as they grow and are sheltered from strong winds. Prune secondary shoots and keep soil moist, mulching if necessary. Pick tomatoes when they are ripe. Beware of slugs and birds eating the ripe fruit.

NASTURTIUM
officinale
WATERCRESS

An aquatic plant, watercress will flourish in a damp, shaded corner of the garden as well as in a pond. Plant from cuttings 10 square cm (about 4 square in) apart in early autumn/fall. Make sure the soil has been thoroughly and deeply fertilized. Water thoroughly and constantly and prune the shoots to keep growth thick. Cut back any flowers that appear.

PASTINACA
sativa
syn. *Peucadeneum officinale, P. sativum*
PARSNIP

A hardy root vegetable which is related to the carrot, parsnip is nutritious and sweet and able to be grown year round in warm climates and mid-spring in cold climates. It needs a sunny position and deep, fertile soil. The roots tend to divide in stony soil so ensure that the soil is stone free before sowing. Water well in dry weather and thin out the weak seedlings. Hoe or mulch to keep weeds off. Harvest when the leaves start to yellow. Watch for slugs, canker, celery fly or greenfly.

PHAESOLUS
BEANS

This genus, native to the warm-temperate to tropical regions of the Americas, contains more than 20 species of mostly twining climbers. Beans are grown for their edible pods and seeds. Frost-tender, they grow best in enriched, well-drained soil. They are also suitable for planting in tubs and flowerbeds.

P. coccineus
SCARLET RUNNER BEANS

This vigorous climber comes in different varieties and can grow up to 3.5 m (about 10½ ft) high. It needs a rich, deep, slightly acid soil in a sheltered position. Sow seeds in late spring in double rows 5 cm (about 2 in) deep and 30 cm (about 12 in) apart. Water well in dry weather. Pick the bean pods when they reach 12–17 cm (about 5–7 in) long. Watch for slugs. The plants are perennial and can be kept for several years, though they bear most heavily in their first year.

P. vulgaris
FRENCH BEANS

The annual French beans, known as kidney beans, string beans or haricot beans, come in dwarf or climbing varieties that need staking. They prefer a warm, rich soil in a sunny, sheltered spot. Mulch with straw to keep off weeds and to keep the soil moist. Harvest 10 to 12 weeks after sowing, picking every 2 to 3 days. Watch for slugs. There are many varieties available, with strings and without.

PISUM
sativum
PEA, BUSH AND CLIMBING VARIETIES

There is an enormous range of peas, from the bush type which is good for humid climates; tall climbing plants which need trellising to the newer snap pea that can be eaten when immature or fully developed. Peas need a sunny, well-drained, rich, previously manured soil bed that contains some lime and dolomite for a good yield. Plant seedlings 5 cm (about 2 in) apart in rows 10 cm (about 4 in) apart. When the seedlings are 8 cm (about 3 in) high stake them with short twigs. The tall varieties will need wire or plastic netting to support them as they grow. Keep weeds down and water when dry. Pick the pods from the lower stems. Watch for mildew, mites and blight.

P. sativum var. *macrocarpum*
SNOW PEA, MANGETOUT PEA

This variety prefers a temperate climate and a moist sandy soil. Sow 5 cm (about 2 in) deep when the garden is likely to be frost-free. Use a trellis for climbing varieties. Pick the pods when they are still immature. The pod as well as the peas are eaten.

PSALLIOTA
campestris
syn. Agaricus campestris
MUSHROOM

This common fungus is happy to grow indoors or outdoors, under houses or in sheds, as long as it is dark, dry and the temperature is constant, ideally between 10–13°C (about 50–55°F). The mushroom lives on different sorts of compost, and home gardeners can either buy a mushroom kit or prepare their own compost full of well-rotted manure. Plant mushroom spawn in lumps 2 cm (about 1 in) deep and 25 cm (about 10 in) apart. Keep moist and humid at this stage. After 2 weeks cover the compost with a layer of soil (this is called casing) which must be pre-sterilized to avoid the lethal fungus diseases that prey on mushrooms. Do not firm it down, keep it moist but not soaking. Mushrooms will appear 3 weeks after casing. Pick them by twisting out, not pulling.

RAPHANUS
sativus
RADISH

Eaten by Egyptian slaves, the ancient Chinese and much favoured by the modern Japanese, the well-travelled radish has a winter variety, usually cooked, and a summer variety which is used in salads. The summer radish is easily and quickly grown in a rich, moist soil out of full sun. Sow directly into rows 30 cm (about 12 in) apart and thin out seedlings so that the roots aren't competing. In hot weather keep well watered. Harvest 4 weeks after sowing in warm climates. In cooler climates wait for a further 3 weeks. Don't leave in the ground too long as they turn woody. Keep birds away from the young leaves.

RHEUM
rhabarbarum
RHUBARB

There are numerous varieties of this plant that can supply the home gardener with edible stems for a good 4 to 10 years. It is best grown from roots in a fertile, phosphorous-rich soil. Choose a cool position and plant the roots firmly with 90 cm (about 36 in) between each row and each plant. Leave it to get established in the first year and start harvesting in the second and third years, making sure not to pull off too many sticks as this will weaken further production. Ensure that all flowers are removed and feed with fertilizer after harvesting. Eat only the stalks as the leaves are poisonous. Watch for brown rot.

RUMEX
scutatus
SORREL

This is a low-growing perennial with pale green, oval-shaped leaves and yellow-red flowers. French sorrel used to be eaten in the same way as spinach, but sorrel's tart flavour is more suitable for sauces, salads or in soups. Sow in spring or plant from divisions, leaving 30 cm (about 12 in) between each plant. Remove flowers to encourage new growth. Do not eat too much sorrel as it contains oxalic acid which is toxic in large amounts.

SOLANUM

A Central and South American genus of great horticultural importance. *Solanum* includes the egg-plant and the potato, and used to include the tomato too, though it is now usually given a genus of its own *Lycopersicon*. There are several ornamental species and many tropical weeds, but they should be approached with caution as it is the exception rather than the rule for them to be edible.

S. melongena
AUBERGINE, EGGPLANT

This tropical vegetable native to Asia has large, purple fruit. It is a relative of the potato and tomato, and needs warm conditions and low level humidity. Cloches should be used in cold climates to protect young plants. Plant seedlings in spring in well-drained soil which is frost-free. The rows should be 1 m (about 3 ft) apart with 60 cm (about 24 in) between each seedling. Feed young plants with liquid fertilizer but stop as soon as fruit develops. Prune away any secondary shoots to increase fruit size. Harvest the fruit if it gives slightly when squeezed. Watch for verticillium wilt.

S. tuberosum
POTATO

Native to South America and one of the most widely eaten vegetables, the potato was preceded to the Western world by the sweet potato. It was grown as a delicacy until the nineteenth century but can now be bought in all sorts of varieties. Potatoes can be scatter grown throughout the garden. Prepare the soil with well-rotted manure or compost. Plant tubers when the soil is frost-free, usually late summer in cool climates or late winter in hot climates. If planting in rows keep them 30 cm (about 12 in) apart and cover with 8 cm (about 3 in) of soil.

For best results plant in sloped mounds for good drainage. Protect shoots from frost with straw or soil. Do not expose potatoes to the light as they will turn green and toxic. (They can be restored by putting them in the dark for a couple of weeks.) Harvest in dry conditions with a fork when foliage turns yellow. Watch for aphids.

Solanum melongena

Rheum rhabarbarum

Pisum sativum var. macrocarpum

Solanum tuberosum

Rumex scutatus

Psalliota campestris

Raphanus sativus

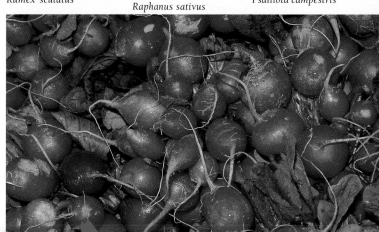

Valerianella locusta

Spinacia oleracea

Zea mays

Taraxacum officinale

Tetragonia tetragonioides

Vicia faba

Tragopogon porrifolius

SPINACIA
oleracea
ENGLISH SPINACH

Native to the Middle-East and partial to cool climates, spinach can be a challenge to grow well. It prefers well-drained soil and a cool position in the garden, so find a spot in part-shade and dig in generous amounts of manure. Sow in autumn/fall or in spring in cool climates, spacing plants 10 cm (about 4 in) apart. Keep the soil free of weeds and well watered so that the plant will not run to seed. Harvest the first leaves 8 weeks after sowing and then as needed. Watch for chewing insects and downy mildew.

TARAXACUM
officinale
DANDELION

Regarded highly in Europe, but as an uninteresting weed in Australia, these plants feature toothed leaves, large yellow flowers and round seed heads. The roots, flowers and leaves are all edible. Grow scattered in the lawn or any corner of the garden. For a good, juicy plant ensure the soil is rich and moist. Sow in early summer 30 cm (about 12 in) apart. Cut off the flowers when plants have matured and harvest the roots in autumn/fall.

TETRAGONIA
tetragonioides
syn. T. expansa
NEW ZEALAND SPINACH

Sir Joseph Banks brought this plant back to England from New Zea-

land, but it became more popular in the USA and Europe. Unlike true spinach, it prefers warm summers and a humus-rich soil. Soften the seeds overnight and sow them in groups of 3 in spring, making sure to leave 90 cm (about 36 in) between each group. Thin the weaker seedlings out and keep weeds away from the remaining young plants. Water regularly and harvest the leaves as they are needed.

TRAGOPOGON
porrifolius
SALSIFY

Also known as the oyster plant, this plant belongs to the daisy family and is valued for its edible, white tap roots. It prefers a light soil free from stones. It grows best in temperate climates. Sow the large seeds in lots of 3 in spring. Keep 20 cm (about 8 in) between each group and 30 cm (about 12 in) between each row. Mulch with compost to keep weeds down and water to maintain moisture. Harvest the root from autumn/fall onwards. It can be baked, roasted, boiled or made into soup. It is fairly pest and disease free.

VALERIANELLA
locusta
CORN SALAD

Rampant in corn fields in cool to cold climates and a hardy grower, this is a good substitute for lettuce in winter. Sow the seeds in late summer and early autumn/fall in a sunny spot in the garden. Place seeds 25 cm (about 10 in) apart.

Make sure the soil is lightly raked and forked. Ideally it should be situated where another crop was previously grown. Keep the soil moist and harvest the leaves as they are needed. Watch for slugs. There are two types, not always labelled distinctly by seedsmen: one forms loose hearts like a small lettuce, the other just makes clumps of loose leaves. Both are equally good eating.

VICIA
faba
BROAD BEANS

A good source of protein, the broad bean is native to the Mediterranean and Far East. It prefers a temperate climate and a sunny position in rich, well-drained soil, preferably where no beans were previously grown. Ensure good bean production by digging in organic fertilizer some weeks before sowing. Sow seeds in mid-autumn/fall in double rows 20 cm (about 8 in) apart and leave 10 cm (about 4 in) between each plant. In cold climates sowing can be left until early spring. Shelter seedlings from the wind with stakes.

Make sure that the soil is not too wet as this may encourage root rot. Beans are ready to be picked 2 or 3 months after planting. Do not wait until the pods are too large or they will be tough and unappetizing. Broad beans are vulnerable to aphids.

ZEA
mays
SWEET CORN, MAIZE, MEALY

With its origins in ancient Mexico, sweet corn has had an uphill battle to win a place on the dinner table in Europe, where it has been seen more as fodder than human fare. Corn needs an open, spacious position and is a dramatic addition to the home garden. It likes a nitrogen and lime-rich soil and needs hot weather to grow well. Sow in early summer in short rows 60 cm (about 24 in) apart. Weed gently and water thoroughly in really dry weather. Tie the stems to stakes as they grow taller and be sure to keep the soil firm around the plant base. Harvest when the corn kernels are yellow by twisting the cobs firmly from the stem.

HERBS

ALLIUM

See genus entry under Vegetables, page 320.

A. sativum
GARLIC

There are two main types of garlic. The mauve flowered variety known as 'Giant Russian' (*A. giganteum*) or 'Jumbo' is very much larger and milder than the more potent, small or common garlic (*A. sativum*), which has dainty white flowers. Individual cloves are planted 5 cm (about 2 in) deep in autumn/fall in warmer areas or in spring where there is frost-risk. Good drainage, a rich organic soil and a sunny position are its requirements. Garlic will take up to 5 or 6 months to mature. Tall flower stalks should be removed for better flavour. Harvest when the leaves have turned yellow and fallen over. Handle gently to avoid bruising and allow to dry off and harden thoroughly before storage. Garlic planted near roses enhances their perfume and helps to keep aphids away. For at least 5000 years garlic has been used for culinary, medicinal and strength-giving purposes as well as a plague preventative and charm against vampires and witchcraft.

A. schoenoprasum
CHIVES

Chives are grown for their narrow, cylindrical leaves which are used for flavouring and garnishing savoury dishes. It is a hardy, perennial plant which grows up to 25 cm (about 10 in) high in small, neat clumps. It bears numerous balls of mauve flowers in late spring and summer which are edible and can be added to salads. Chives do best in a fertile, well-drained soil in full sun or part-shade and should be kept well watered. They are easily grown by seed or division of small bulbs. Bulbs should be spaced about 10 cm (about 4 in) apart because they will quickly multiply and develop into clumps. Lift and divide the clumps every 2 or 3 years to invigorate the tufts. Chives make an attractive edging for the herb garden and can be grown in window boxes, troughs and flower pots. Frequent cutting stimulates fresh, bushy growth and tenderer leaves.

ALOYSIA
triphylla
syn. *Lippia citriodora*
LEMON VERBENA

This wonderfully fragrant perennial shrub from South America is valued for its delicious, lemon scented leaves. It grows up to 3 m (about 9 ft) and is partly deciduous in winter. Very small, white or lilac flowers are borne at the ends of the stems in late summer and autumn/fall. Half-hardy, it is best positioned in full sun in a warm, sheltered position. It prefers a well-drained, fertile soil and needs regular watering in summer. Propagate from soft tip cuttings in spring or semi-hardwood cuttings in summer. Lemon verbena is commercially cultivated for its fragrant oil used in the cosmetics industry. The leaves are also used to flavour tea. Dried leaves retain their scent exceptionally well and are an excellent potpourri ingredient.

ANDROPOGON
nardus
syn. *Cymbopogon citratus*
LEMON GRASS

This aromatic, grass-like plant has very long, grey-green leaves reaching to 2 m (about 6 ft). From the tropics, it does best in warm climates where it will multiply readily and quickly form large clumps, so allow plenty of space for spreading. A rich soil, good drainage, full sun and plenty of water are its requirements. It is frost-tender. Propagate by division. The fleshy white part at the base of the plant is used in South-East Asian cooking and is best when fresh. The leaves are used fresh or dried to make a herbal tea.

ANETHUM
graveolens
DILL

This deliciously aromatic annual grows to about 1.5 m (about 4½ ft) high with pretty, feathery, thread-like leaves. Yellow flowers are borne on umbels in summer followed by the pungent dill seeds. Fully hardy, dill requires a humus-rich, well-drained soil and a sunny position. The seed is best sown in spring where it is to grow, as seedlings are difficult to transplant. Both the leaves and seeds are used as flavourings. Since earliest times the seeds have been used to aid digestion.

ANGELICA
archangelica
ANGELICA

A fast-growing, robust biennial, angelica grows to 2 m (about 6 ft) high and will live longer if emerging flowerheads are removed before the seed develops. It has handsome, deeply divided, bright green leaves and umbels of small, green or white flowers in late summer. It is frost-hardy. Soil should preferably be rich, moist and well-drained. It does best in filtered sunlight with protection from strong winds. Propagate from seed in late summer. The roots, leaves, stalks and seeds of angelica are all used in cooking and for flavouring. The young stems are crystallized for confectionery decoration. The seeds, stems and roots are used to flavour liqueurs such as chartreuse, Benedictine and vermouth.

Allium schoenoprasum

Anethum graveolens

Angelica archangelica

Aloysia triphylla

Andropogon nardus

Allium sativum

ARTEMISIA
dracunculus
TARRAGON

Essential in French cuisine, tarragon is grown for its narrow, aromatic leaves which have a delicate, peppery aniseed flavour. Half-hardy, it grows up to 1 m (about 3 ft) high in the warmer months then dies back to a perennial root-stock over winter. Full sun and a fertile, well-drained soil are its requirements. As it produces no seed,

Coriandrum sativum

propagate by division in early spring. The tarragon seed sometimes offered is the flavourless *A. dracunculoides* known as Russian tarragon. Tarragon loses most of its flavour during drying. Before the plant dies down for a winter's rest, gather the leaves and make tarragon vinegar and butter.

BORAGO
officinalis
BORAGE

This decorative, annual herb is grown for its cucumber flavoured leaves and pretty, lilac, star-shaped flowers. It grows to around 75 cm (about 30 in) high and bears clusters of nodding flowers in spring and summer. Fully hardy, it requires full sun to part-shade, good drainage and a light, porous soil. Propagate from seed in spring. Protect from snails. The fresh young leaves are used raw in salads and cool drinks or cooked with vegetables. The edible, blue flowers have been used to decorate salads from the early seventeenth century. Flowers may also be crystallized for cake decoration. It used to be said that eating borage flowers gave you courage.

CARUM
carvi
CARAWAY

Since ancient Egyptian times, caraway has been cultivated for its condiment and medicinal properties. It is an attractive biennial plant growing to 60 cm (about 24 in) high

with finely cut, lacy leaves rather like its relative the parsley. In its second year small, white flowers are produced in umbels, followed in late summer by a crop of seeds. Fully hardy, it will grow well in a light, moist, but well-drained soil in full sun. Propagate from seed in early autumn/fall in mild winter areas or in spring. The small black seeds are used to flavour cakes, breads, sauces and pickles. Their flavour is best when dried. Caraway has also been used as an ingredient of love potions, to prevent pigeons from straying and as protection from witches.

CHAMAEMELUM
nobile
CHAMOMILE

This is a delightfully aromatic, mat-forming perennial which grows to 30 cm (about 12 in) tall and has fine, bright green leaves and masses of small, white daisies in spring, summer and autumn/fall. Non-flowering varieties are used in chamomile lawns. Fully hardy, it grows best in full sun in a moist, but well-drained fertile soil. It creeps along the ground by runners which take root as they spread. Propagate by division or from seed in spring. Dried chamomile flowers can be used in potpourri, sleep pillows, hair rinses and facials. Renowned as a herbal tea, chamomile has been credited with the power to treat dyspepsia, flatulent colic, fever, stomach cramps, wounds, swelling and also callouses.

CORIANDRUM
sativum
CORIANDER

This herb is grown mainly for its seed and aromatic leaves, although in Thai cuisine the whole of the coriander plant, including the roots, is used. Coriander is a fast-growing annual reaching to 75 cm (about 30 in) high with parsley-like leaves and umbels of tiny, white flowers in summer. The flowers are followed by small, round, aromatic seeds. Fully hardy, it requires a light, well-drained soil and full sun. Propagate from seed in early spring. Fresh leaves will provide an exotic tang in Asian dishes. The dried seeds are used in curry powders, chutneys, confectionery, cakes and sauces.

CUMINUM
cyminum
CUMIN

Cumin is grown commercially in India, China, Japan and the Middle East for its powerfully flavoured seeds. It is a small annual which grows to 30 cm (about 12 in) high with finely divided leaves and small, white flowers in summer, followed by aromatic seeds. It is frost-tender and grows best in warm climates. Grow in a light, well-drained soil in a sunny position. Propagate from seed sown in spring in a warm situation. The dried seed is an important ingredient in curry powders. Both the Dutch and Germans flavour cheese with it, and it is used in many Mexican and Middle Eastern dishes.

Artemisia dracunculus

Carum carvi

Chamaemelum nobile

Borago officinalis

CURCUMA
domestica
syn. C. longa
TURMERIC

A tropical member of the ginger family, turmeric is grown for its bright orange, underground stems or rhizomes. This perennial herb can grow to 1 m (about 3 ft) in hot areas. It forms clumps of lance-shaped leaves and dense clusters of pale yellow flowers in summer. Frost-tender, it prefers the warmth of tropical regions but can be successfully grown in warm-temperate areas. In cooler areas, grow in a glasshouse. It requires a rich, moist, well-drained soil and lots of sun. Propagate by division. Turmeric has been used in the East since antiquity. The dried root provides colour and pungent fragrance to chutneys, pickles and curry powders; it is harvested when the foliage begins to dry off in autumn/fall. It is used as a substitute for saffron (*Crocus sativas*) the world's most expensive spice and one very rarely grown in home gardens.

ELETTARIA
cardamomum
CARDAMOM

An important and pungent oriental spice, cardamom seeds come from a perennial shrub which originated in southern India. It grows to 3 m (about 9 ft) tall and has large, dark green, lance-shaped leaves. The flowering stems spread horizontally near the ground and bear small, yellow flowers during spring. These are followed by grey-green, oblong pods which contain dark reddish brown seeds. Frost-tender, cardamom is for tropical and warm regions only where it requires a rich, moist soil and a shaded position. In cooler areas, grow in a glasshouse. The seed pods are gathered before they ripen and are then dried before storage. Seeds should be left in the pods until required for use. Propagate by division. Cardamom is used in curry powders, pastries, baked apples and fruit salads.

FOENICULUM
vulgare
FENNEL

Common fennel is a tall, graceful perennial which grows to 2 m (about 6 ft) with thick, glossy stems, masses of feathery foliage and flat clusters of yellow flowers on tall, erect stems during summer. The flowers are followed by aromatic, brown seeds. Bronze fennel is similar but has rich bronzy green leaves and grows to around 1.5 m (about 4½ ft) high. Half-hardy, in cool climates it will die back to the roots over winter and is sometimes grown as an annual. It prefers full sun to

Foeniculum vulgare var. *dulce*

Hyssopus officinalis

part-shade, a rich, alkaline, well-drained soil and regular watering during dry periods. Propagate from seed in mid- to late spring. Both the leaves and seeds have a pleasant aniseed flavour and are used for flavouring fish and other savoury dishes. The seeds are also used in breads and biscuits.

F. vulgare var. dulce
FLORENCE FENNEL, FINOCCHIO

Florence fennel is distinct from common fennel in having a pronounced swelling at the base of the leaves where the stems overlap. It is an annual and needs to be grown from seed each year. Culture conditions are similar to common fennel. The crisp, white bulb, with the texture of celery, is cooked as a vegetable or grated raw for salads.

GLYCYRRHIZA
glabra
LIQUORICE

This perennial, native to southern Europe, is grown commercially for the juice of its sweet roots, used in the production of liquorice. The plant has large, mid-green leaves

Foeniculum vulgare

and bears pea-like, bluish purple and white flowers on short upright spikes in late summer. It grows to a height and spread of 1 m (about 3 ft). Fully hardy, it requires a sunny position and a deep, rich, moist but well-drained soil. Propagate from seed in autumn/fall or spring, or by division in spring.

HYSSOPUS
officinalis
HYSSOP

This bushy perennial grows to 60 cm (about 24 in) and has narrow, pointed, dark green leaves. Spikes of rich blue flowers, that are attractive to bees and butterflies, are borne in late summer. White and pink flowering forms are also available. Fully hardy, hyssop is evergreen in mild climates; in cool areas it dies down for the winter. It prefers a light, well-drained, alkaline soil and full sun. Propagate from seed, cuttings or by division in spring. The slightly bitter leaves are used in small quantities with fatty meats and fish. A tea made from the leaves is taken for respiratory complaints and to aid digestion.

Elettaria cardamomum

Curcuma domestica

Mentha × piperita

Mentha 'Citrata'

Levisticum officinale

Lavandula angustifolia

Melissa officinalis

Laurus nobilis

Juniperus communis

JUNIPERUS
communis
JUNIPER

An evergreen, bushy shrub or small tree, juniper grows to 3 m (about 9 ft). There are a number of ornamental forms in varying shapes, sizes and foliage colour. It has sharply pointed, needle-like leaves, small, yellow flowers and bears fleshy, green berries that take up to 3 years to ripen to black. To ensure berry production grow both male and female plants. Fully hardy, juniper requires excellent drainage and a sunny position. In warm climates provide a cool, moist root run. Propagate from semi-hardwood cuttings in late summer or early autumn/fall. The berries have a resinous flavour and are used to flavour gin. A few berries make an excellent addition to stews and stuffings for poultry.

LAURUS
nobilis
BAY

This medium-sized, evergreen tree which reaches 7 m (about 21 ft) is slow growing and can be kept in a pot for a number of years. It withstands clipping and makes an excellent topiary subject. Half-hardy, it can be grown in a tub and brought indoors where winters are frosty. In warm areas grow in a humus-rich, well-drained, sunny position. Protect from both dry winds and scorching sun in hot areas. Propagate from cuttings. Watch for scale insects. Bay leaves are best used fresh in cooking to flavour marinades, soups, sauces, stews and meat dishes. Dried leaves may be used in cooking, though they lose flavour quickly; they add scent to potpourri.

LAVANDULA
angustifolia
syn. L. officinalis
LAVENDER

This beautiful, small, rounded shrub, native to southern Europe, is valued for its perfumed, lavender flowers and aromatic grey-green foliage. Fully hardy, it thrives in cool-temperate areas in a light, rather alkaline, well-drained soil. Grow in an open, sunny position to avoid fungal disease. Propagate from cuttings in autumn/fall or spring. The best quality essential oil is extracted from this plant, but many other species and varieties of lavender can be grown for their fragrant flowers. Dried lavender flowers are used in potpourri mixtures, lavender bags and moth repellent sachets. The herb can be used sparingly in cooking, but it is an acquired taste.

LEVISTICUM
officinale
LOVAGE

From southern Europe, this robust, coarse-growing perennial reaches 2 m (about 6 ft) tall and looks and tastes like a large celery. It has deeply lobed, dark green leaves, umbels of small, yellow flowers in summer and brown seeds which ripen in late summer or early autumn/fall. Fully hardy, it prefers a fairly cool climate and does best in full sun or part-shade in a rich, moist soil. Propagate by root division in spring or from seed in late summer. The stems are cooked and eaten and tender young leaves can be added to salads and savoury dishes. Levisticum americanum and Ligusticum scoticum are also called lovage.

MELISSA
officinalis
LEMON BALM

A native of southern Europe, this hardy perennial, 60 cm (about 24 in) high, is grown for its fresh, lemony scented and flavoured leaves. Small, white flowers that appear in late summer attract pollinating bees into the garden. Lemon balm will thrive in a rich, moist soil in full sun or part-shade. It is very hardy and spreads rapidly. It will die down in winter but shoot again in spring. Propagate from cuttings or by root division. The lemon-scented leaves are valued as a calming herbal tea. They will give a light, lemon flavour to fruit salads, jellies, iced tea and summer drinks, and can be used as an emergency substitute for lemon in cooking.

MENTHA
MINT

This is a large genus of herbs, some evergreen and some deciduous, from just about all the continents. They vary in size from tiny creeping ground covers to bushy plants about 40 cm (about 16 in) high, and in flavour from refreshing to so strong they must be used with circumspection. As a rule, they are frost-hardy, like sunshine and rich soil and need lots of moisture (poor drainage matters not at all) and are invasive growers, spreading rapidly by runners. To keep them from taking over, try growing them in large pots, watering regularly and repotting annually.

M. 'Citrata'
EAU DE COLOGNE MINT

Of garden origin and thought to be a variety of peppermint, this mint is too strong and bitter to use in cooking. It is grown for the delicious fragrance of its dark green leaves; perhaps the sweetest and most flower-like of any scented-leafed plant. It has purplish stems and mauve flowers in early summer. Like all the tribe it is a rampant spreader by underground runners.

M. × piperita
PEPPERMINT

This spreading perennial, grown for its aromatic foliage and culinary uses, grows to a height and spread of 60 cm (about 24 in). Spreading by means of underground stems, it forms a carpet of oval, toothed, mid-green and reddish green leaves. Purple flowers appear in spring. Plant this fully hardy herb in sun or shade in moist, well-drained soil. Propagate by division in spring or autumn/fall.

M. spicata
SPEARMINT

This fast-growing perennial, reaching 60 cm (about 24 ft), is the most popular mint used in cooking. It has crinkly, dark green leaves and as it has a tendency to put down roots all over the garden is often best grown in a separate bed or container. Fully hardy, it thrives in a sunny or partially shaded position in a moist, but well-drained soil. Plants should be cut back regularly to encourage fresh growth. Propagate by root division. This is the mint used in mint sauce, mint jelly and to flavour new potatoes and green peas. Fresh sprigs are used as a garnish in fruit drinks or desserts.

MONARDA
didyma
BERGAMOT, BEE BALM

Native to North America, this herb was used by the American Indians and early colonists as a tea. With its spidery flowers in white, pink or red borne in late summer, bergamot is one of the showiest of the culinary herbs. The showiest variety is 'Cambridge Scarlet'. It is a hardy perennial growing to 1 m (about 3 ft) tall with dark green, slightly toothed leaves that when crushed or brushed against emit an exotic, citrus-like scent. It prefers part-shade and a rich, moist soil with a cool root run in hot climates. Cut plants back periodically to keep compact. Propagate by division in spring. The young leaves may be used in salads, but mainly it is used as a soothing tea. Add a few leaves to China or Indian tea for an Earl Grey flavour.

NEPETA
cataria
CATNIP, CATMINT

A native of Europe, catnip is a hardy perennial with branching, upright stems growing up to 1 m (about 3 ft). It has aromatic, grey-green leaves and whorls of white flowers from late spring through to autumn/fall. Provide a light, rich soil in sun or part-shade and moderate water for best results. Cut back each year to prevent the plant from becoming straggly. Propagate by root division or from seed in spring. Cats are attracted to this plant and will lie in it or play in it and sometimes dig it up. Fortunately, their interest is only in the spring growth; once the plants start to flower they lose interest. Its tea is said to be relaxing.

OCIMUM
basilicum
BASIL

A favourite with cooks, basil is one of the most widely used herbs in Mediterranean cooking. It is a tender, annual plant growing to 30 cm (about 12 in) with light green, oval leaves that have a delicious, warm, spicy fragrance. Small white flowers are carried in whorls towards the ends of the stems in late summer. Full sun and a moderately rich, moist, but well-drained soil are its requirements. Grow in a warm protected position. There are a number of varieties of basil including a compact small-leaf type; a crinkled, lettuce leaf variety and the beautiful 'Dark Opal' with rich purple stems and leaves. There are perennial varieties also, but their flavour is inferior. Regularly pinch back all basil plants to encourage bushy growth and to prevent them going to seed quickly. Propagate from seed sown when there is no frost. Watch for chewing insects or snails. Fresh leaves are best; freeze it for the winter; it loses flavour when dried.

ORIGANUM

Native to the Mediterranean region and parts of Europe and India, these frost-tender perennials are often grown as annuals in cooler climates. They like sun and rich, well-drained soil. Trim regularly and propagate from seed in spring or by root division.

O. hortensis
syn. *Majorana hortensis*
SWEET MARJORAM

A highly aromatic plant up to 60 cm (about 24 in) high, marjoram is grown for its sweet and spicy, small, grey-green leaves. The flowers consist of tiny, white, knot-like clusters from which the plant gets another common name, knotted marjoram. Leaves are used fresh or dried for savoury foods and are said to aid digestion. Marjoram has a special affinity with tomatoes and goes well with many meats.

O. vulgare
OREGANO, WILD MARJORAM

A close relative of marjoram, oregano has a sharper, more pungent flavour. It has a sprawling habit and grows to 60 cm (about 24 in) high with dark green, oval leaves and small, white or pink flowers in summer. The leaves, fresh or dried, are used in many Mediterranean-inspired dishes. In Italy oregano is used in pizza toppings and pasta dishes.

Ocimum basilicum

Mentha spicata

Nepeta cataria

Monarda didyma

Origanum vulgare

Origanum hortensis

Salvia officinalis

Polygonum odoratum

Salvia elegans

Ruta graveolens

Petroselinum crispum

Rosmarinus officinalis

PETROSELINUM
crispum
PARSLEY

Cultivated for thousands of years for its flavour and health-giving properties, parsley is still one of the most popular herbs grown. It is a biennial plant which grows to 30 cm (about 12 in) high. The most commonly used are the curly-leaved form and the stronger, flat-leaved Italian variety. Parsley does best in full sun or light shade in warm climates. It likes a moist, well-drained position and regular feeding. For best flavour, harvest the leaves before the plant flowers. Propagate from seed. To speed up germination soak the seeds in warm water overnight before planting.

POLYGONUM
odoratum
VIETNAMESE MINT

A native of Indochina, this half-hardy, fast-growing perennial, 60 cm (about 24 in) high, has long, dark green leaves with a distinct hot, spicy taste. Pink flowers in slender spikes appear in late summer and autumn/fall. Vietnamese mint prefers partial shade, a rich soil and plenty of moisture. It can die back in winter frosts but will reshoot in spring. Propagate from cuttings or by division. The leaves are used as a garnish in many Vietnamese dishes including salads and soups. It is also used in other South-East Asian cooking.

ROSMARINUS
officinalis
ROSEMARY

A beautiful, aromatic shrub, rosemary has been cultivated for centuries for flavouring food and for medicine. It will grow to 1 m (about 3 ft) high, has resinous, narrow, needle-like leaves and small flowers in shades of mauve-blue, off and on all year. Half-hardy rosemary can be grown outdoors in warm climates, but should be taken in for winter where temperatures fall much below zero. In the garden it will flourish in a light, well-drained soil in a sheltered position with plenty of sun. It will withstand salt-laden air. Propagate from cuttings or by layering. Rosemary leaves can be used fresh or dried to flavour meat dishes, chicken, fish and vegetables. Dried branches can be used in wreath-making and leaves in potpourri.

RUTA
graveolens
RUE

One of the bitter herbs used for warding off insects and disease, rue is also one of the most decorative herbs with its very pretty, grey-green, lacy leaves. It is a hardy perennial growing 60 cm (about 24 in) high with clusters of small yellow-green flowers in summer. Grow in a slightly alkaline, well-drained soil in full sun. Protect from strong winds and severe frost in cold climates. Trim after flowering. Propagate by division in spring or from stem cuttings in late summer. The leaves and flowers are used in small posies. Rue has been used in the past for medicinal purposes, but can be dangerous if taken in large doses and during pregnancy.

SALVIA

This mainly northern hemisphere genus includes an enormous number of species. Almost all are aromatic and many are grown just for their brightly coloured flowers (see chapter 'Annuals & Perennials'). The following are the most important kitchen species.

S. elegans
syn. S. rutilans
PINEAPPLE SAGE

This half-hardy shrub reaches 1 m (about 3 ft) and is grown for its light green foliage which has a distinct pineapple scent and flavour. Its whorls of red flowers are borne in late summer and autumn/fall. This species is frost-tender so winter protection is needed in cool climates. It likes full sun and a moist, well-drained soil. Propagate from cuttings. Leaves are used in fruit salads, summer drinks and tea.

S. officinalis
SAGE

Sage is a decorative, frost-hardy perennial plant which grows to 60 cm (about 24 in) high, with downy, grey-green, oval leaves and mauve-blue flowers on tall spikes during summer. There are several forms of sage, those with plum-red leaves, greenish-purple variegated leaves, tricoloured leaves and golden variegated leaves. All are attractive and edible. Grow in an open, sunny, well-drained position. In hot areas plants are best in light shade. Trim frequently, but never into hard wood, to keep shapely. Propagate from cuttings. Sage is highly valued for its medicinal qualities and has been used for centuries for curing all manner of ailments and is reputed to give longevity to those who use it.

SATUREJA

Native to the Mediterranean, savory was much loved by the Ancient Greeks and Romans for the refreshing flavour. Among many of its uses savory is added to dishes featuring mildly flavoured meats like chicken and pork.

S. hortensis
SUMMER SAVORY

This bushy annual grows 40 cm (about 16 in) high and has narrow, dark green leaves and pale lavender flowers in late summer. Grow in a humus-rich, well-drained soil in full sun and provide plenty of water. Propagate from seed in spring where it is to grow. The leaves have a sweet, spicy flavour with a hint of thyme and are traditionally used as a flavouring for bean dishes. Use also to flavour vinegar, salad dressings and butter.

S. montana
WINTER SAVORY

A low, spreading perennial which grows to 30 cm (about 12 in), winter savory has dark green, pointed leaves and tiny white flowers with pink markings in summer. Winter savory prefers a light, well-drained, alkaline soil and less moisture than summer savory. It may need winter protection in cold climates. It benefits from regular cutting back to stimulate fresh growth and prevent legginess. Propagate by division or from cuttings. It makes a good edging or border plant and is often grown to attract bees. The leaves, sharper and more peppery than summer savory, are used to flavour meat casseroles and roasts.

SYMPHYTUM
officinale
COMFREY

This robust, clump-forming perennial grows to 1 m (about 3 ft) with large, lance-shaped leaves and clusters of pretty, mauve, pendent flowers in late spring and summer. Grow in part-shade and a humus-rich, well-drained soil. It may die down to the roots in cold areas. Propagate by root division. It is an excellent companion plant in the garden, where it keeps the surrounding soil rich and moist. Wilted leaves are used as a mulch and when added to the compost heap will help activate decomposition. In the Middle Ages, comfrey's chief claim to fame was its ability to aid in knitting fractured and broken bones. It is mildly poisonous if eaten in sufficient quantities.

THYMUS
THYME

No herb garden should be without at least one variety of thyme. There are many species and varieties, all are perennials with tiny, aromatic leaves and small flower spikes that appear at the end of the stems during summer. Thyme likes a light, well-drained soil and full sun if possible. It is generally hardy once established but may need winter protection in very cold areas. Keep well trimmed for compact growth. Propagate by division or layer stems. Historically thyme has been associated with courage, strength, happiness and well-being.

T. × citriodorus
LEMON-SCENTED THYME

This delightful, rounded shrub grows 30 cm (about 12 in) high and has tiny, oval, lemon-scented leaves and pale lilac flowers. Leaves are used fresh or dry in poultry stuffings or to add lemon flavour to fish, meat and vegetables.

T. vulgaris
COMMON THYME

This is the most popular culinary thyme, producing the strongest aromatic leaves. It grows to 30 cm (about 12 in) high. The tiny, mid-green leaves are used in vinegars, butters and to flavour a variety of meat or vegetable dishes. Thyme tea is used to aid digestion, sore throats and coughs.

ZINGIBER
officinale
GINGER

Originating in southern Asia, this tender, perennial plant is grown for its spicy, tuberous roots. It can reach up to 2 m (about 6 ft) high in hot areas, has long, lance-shaped leaves and bears spikes of white flowers with purple streaks in summer. Ginger prefers the warmth of tropical regions but can be successfully grown outdoors in warm, frost-free, temperate areas. A humus-rich, well-drained soil and light shade are its requirements. Propagate from small pieces of root cuttings. The fresh root is peeled and finely chopped or grated and used to flavour many Asian dishes, curries and chutneys. Dried and powdered ginger is used in sweet dishes and cakes. It is often recommended as a therapeutic infusion for colds and travel sickness, and was once thought to safeguard against marauding tigers.

Zingiber officinale

Thymus × citriodorus

Saturnja hortensis

Symphytum officinale

Saturveja montana

Thymus vulgaris

CHAPTER 8

*Fruit Trees, Nut Trees
& Other Fruits*

Scholars have been arguing for centuries over the identity of the most famous fruit tree of all, the one that caused so much trouble for Adam and Eve. Tradition says it was an apple; some learned people say no, it was an apricot; still others point out that it was called the Tree of Knowledge, a species rarely met with now.

Let us leave them to it and content ourselves with the thought that the author of *Genesis* knew what he was about when he described the chief attraction of the garden of Eden as its fruit trees, with no mention of lawns, flowers or other frivolities.

There are few things so delightful as picking your own fruit, and if it comes from a tree you planted yourself the pleasure is all the greater. The delight won't be just at harvest time either: fruit trees tend to be comely in habit and often beautiful in flower. And few are large, so they take up little space.

Choosing a Fruit Tree

They can be classed into two broad groups: the tropical fruits, members of several plant families, mainly evergreen, and often rather stately growers; and the temperate fruits, deciduous and almost all cousins of the rose. The citrus are a kind of link between the two; evergreen and with members that like hot climates and others that don't mind it coolish. Which to choose? Your own favourite, that goes without saying; but you need to take your climate into account. There is no joy in pining after mangoes if you suffer frost or cherries if you can't provide them with the cold winters they need. Then, there is no point in growing just any sort of variety. Just about all types of fruit have been bred and improved by gardeners for centuries, and come in a bewildering number of varieties. Some of the tropical types (citrus too) can be easily grown from seed, but seedling trees almost always turn out inferior. Insist on a top-quality named cultivar, and check that it is suited to your purpose. (Apples, for

instance, come in 'dessert' and 'cooking' varieties, and so do mangoes, cherries and bananas.) It sometimes happens that the very choicest varieties are rather weak growers and therefore not popular with orchardists; but why grow an ordinary pear that you can buy at the greengrocer's when you could have the incomparable 'Doyenne du Comice'?

The named varieties are almost always grafted, and you may be offered the same one on several different understocks. Usually this is because by choice of a more or less vigorous stock you can tailor the final size of the tree, but sometimes one stock will be better than another in different soils. If in doubt, ask your supplier for advice, bearing in mind that bigger isn't necessarily better—you may prefer to have two smaller trees instead of one large one. That way you might have both a dessert and a cooking apple, or have an early-ripening variety and one that ripens later to spread your crop. (You can indeed buy ultra-dwarf strains of such fruit as apples and peaches, which are great if your gardening is confined

Malus domestica 'Red Delicious', an excellent dessert apple.

to containers on an apartment balcony: but their crop is proportionately tiny too.)

With some of the temperate fruits, notably apples, pears and sweet cherries, you need two trees in any case, as they are not 'self-fertile'—the flowers must receive the pollen of a different variety or there will be no fruit. Not that pollinating insects respect fences; the spouse tree could be in the garden of a co-operative neighbour. Or you might graft a branch of a compatible variety onto your main tree, being careful not to accidentally prune it off later.

Then, before you make your final choice, check with your local Department or Ministry of Agriculture whether your favourites are subject to pests or diseases which you are required by law to spray against. Alas, the number of enemies of fruit is legion (indeed, in different countries there are different enemies), and neglected backyard fruit trees can be a potent source of infestation not only to the neighbours' trees but to commercial orchards—which is why the law takes an interest. The Agriculture people can give you all the details, but take heart—the job isn't as burdensome as all that, and there will be some fruit that you can grow that doesn't suffer unduly from problems.

Growing Fruit Trees

Almost all fruit trees need sun and fertile soil, and are best if they don't suffer undue drought while the fruit is ripening. They benefit too from some fertilizer in spring, but there is no need to grow them in mulched beds like vegetables; they can be grown in association with flowers and shrubs, in any way that suits your garden design. Careful and regular pruning will control the size of the tree and increase its fruitfulness, but you only have to come across some ancient apple tree, untouched by the shears for years yet groaning with fruit, to realize that pruning is optional. Most warm climate fruits need little pruning in any case. A specialised form of pruning is training the tree espalier, that is flat against a wall. The idea was originally that the warmth reflected from the masonry encourages the fruit to ripen earlier. It is a lot of work, as you will need to prune each year, but worth doing if you are short on space or want to grow a variety which is on the borderline of hardiness in your climate. (Peaches and figs, for instance, are

'Valencia' *is the best known variety of* Citrus sinensis, *the sweet orange.*

almost always grown against walls in Britain, and mangoes and loquats are trained similarly elsewhere.) Choose a tree grafted on a 'dwarfing' rootstock or it will be too vigorous.

All the above applies to nut trees too; after all they are just fruit trees, but we eat a different part of the fruit—the seeds rather than the fleshy covering. They aren't so popular, perhaps because we tend to regard nuts as an occasional luxury, but they are well worth growing, and the crop keeps without having to be preserved. As a group, they are less subject to pests and need less care generally.

Not all fruit grows on trees. There are those that grow on vines, of which the grape is the supreme example, others being the kiwifruit or Chinese gooseberry and the granadilla, sometimes called the passionfruit and a great favourite in warm climates. All are great for covering fences and pergolas, and all are handsome plants. However selection of varieties is just as important as ever, especially with grapes; not only are varieties specially designed for wine, for

eating fresh or for making raisins, they have very marked likes and dislikes about climate. All the vine fruit need regular pruning to keep them under control, but no more than any other vigorous climber does.

Then there are the bush fruits, fruit shrubs rather than fruit trees. They can be the answer if you are short on space (although most like cool climates) and they are well worth growing, as their fruit tends to be soft and easily damaged on the way to market. Grow your own, and you can have the very best. This is particularly true of strawberries, everyone's favourite—and everyone can grow them, for this is a creeping perennial, to be tucked in at the front of any convenient bed or even in containers.

When is a fruit not a fruit? When it is a vegetable. The tomato is a fruit, but the plant is an annual to be grown in the vegetable patch rather than the orchard; and the fruit a savoury one, for main course dishes rather than dessert. The same is true of zucchini, capsicums, squashes, even melons. Everyone calls them vegetables, and so shall we.

Annona squamosa

Ceratonia siliqua

FRUIT TREES AND NUT TREES

ANNONA
squamosa
CUSTARD APPLE, SUGAR APPLE

There are many varieties of the custard apple, a popular fruit that originated in the tropical regions of Africa, Asia and the Americas. Its flowers are pale green and pleasantly scented. The large fruit has a custard-like texture and is delicious when eaten fresh. This is a semi-deciduous tree growing to 5 m (about 15 ft). Plant in a warm, sheltered position as the fruit yield may be damaged by low temperatures and the tree itself is frost-tender. Propagate by grafting.

ARAUCARIA
bidwillii
BUNYA BUNYA

From a genus of conifers native only to the South Pacific region, this 25 m (about 80 ft) tall tree has a short, stout trunk and massive, scaly branches that make it too large for a small city garden. The fruit grows high up, is the size of a pineapple and has the appearance of a fat, green pine cone. Keep young trees moist at the base and clear of weeds and grass. This is a slow-growing, frost-hardy tree which will fruit only after 10 or more years. Australian Aborigines considered its dark red seeds to be a delicacy. Propagate from seed (germination takes 12 months). Eat the nuts fresh, roasted or boiled or they may be ground into flour for cakes.

CARICA
papaya
PAWPAW

This is an evergreen, frost-tender tree, native to South and Central America, which grows to 8 m (about 24 ft) high and is topped with a cluster of large, deep-lobed leaves that drop away as the soft stem grows up. Plant where it will receive lots of warmth and shelter in a well-drained, moist, organic soil.

The large fruit, which weighs up to 2 kg (about 4½ lb), will reduce in size after 4 years of harvesting. Before picking the fruit let it ripen as long as possible on the branch. Propagate from seed and plant the seedlings in summer, watering regularly. Watch for powdery mildew, fruit rot (especially if the tree is in a warm-temperate climate and exposed position) and fruit bugs.

CARYA
illinoinensis
PECAN

A native of the USA, and from the same family as the walnut, the pecan tree's large size may make it impractical for the average garden. The nuts have a smooth, brown shell and a large kernel. Moderately frost-hardy, these trees prefer a dry-summer climate and because of their large taproot need deep, well-drained soil. The fruit will fall early if there is insufficient water or nutrition. Prune the young tree to encourage it to grow to a single, upright stem. Once they are collected, nuts should dry out for several weeks before they are stored. Watch for elephant beetle, bark weevil or pecan scab.

CASTANEA
sativa
SPANISH CHESTNUT, SWEET CHESTNUT

This fully hardy, deciduous Mediterranean native is valued for its timber, shade and edible fruit which is delicious roasted. It grows slowly to 15 m (about 50 ft), with dark green foliage and an open crown. The leaves, which turn brown in autumn/fall, are egg-shaped and heavily serrated, 12–20 cm (about 5–8 in) long, with a hairy underside. Creamy golden, malodorous flowers bloom in early to mid-spring. In late summer to early spring, glossy brown chestnuts develop inside spiny, spherical pods. This species enjoys warm summers and a rich, well-drained, acid soil, otherwise it can be prone to root rot. Propagate mainly from seed in autumn/fall. It is prone to chestnut blight and has a tendency to sucker. The tree is very long lived and some English specimens were reputedly planted by the Romans.

CERATONIA
siliqua
CAROB

Native to the eastern Mediterranean, this evergreen tree or shrub can grow to 13 m (about 40 ft) but can be pruned to a more suitable garden size. It has glossy, green leaves and long, brown, bean-like pods 25 cm (about 10 in) long. It

Carya illinoinensis

Castanea sativa

Araucaria bidwillii

Carica papaya

prefers full sun but can tolerate light shade. It requires hot summers to perform well. Fertilizing is usually not necessary and the tree is remarkably resistant to summer drought. The carob pods are ready to be picked in autumn/fall when they are dark brown. When eaten fresh they are sweet and chewy. Roasting and powdering them for use as a chocolate substitute can be arduous but rewarding, and the branches can be used as emergency fodder for stock in times of drought. Do not plant the tree too close to the house as many people find the odour of the flowers objectionable.

CITRUS

Native to South-East Asia, it is thought citrus fruit trees were introduced to the Middle East and Europe in the time of the Romans. They are half-hardy to frost-tender and do best in a warm, humid climate with mild winters. The attractive white flowers in spring and fruit in winter make them a valued tree. A nitrogen-rich, well-drained soil and a sunny position are their requirements. Water and fertilize well. They are attacked by a number of pests including scale insects, aphids, holy cross bug, fruit-fly and fungus. Although citrus are more reliable when grown from seed than most fruit trees, they are almost always budded to ensure the perpetuation of the desired variety. Understocks vary with type, but the most common is *Poncirus trifoliata* which gives greater resistance to cold and to certain viruses.

C. aurantifolia
LIME

Known as the West Indian or key lime, this is a small, slender, thorny evergreen which reaches 3 m (about 9 ft) high and wide. Native to Malaysia this tree can only be grown in tropical and subtropical areas as it is frost-tender. In cooler areas grow in a glasshouse. It makes a perfect tub tree when put in a sheltered, sunny spot and will produce lots of fruit. The fruit is best in cool drinks and is acidic and strongly flavoured. Propagate by grafting or budding. Watch out for citrus scab and brown scale.

C. aurantium
SOUR ORANGE, SEVILLE ORANGE

These half-hardy small trees originated in China and are grown as ornamental shrubs or providers of fruit for marmalade and jelly. The heavy-fruiting 'Seville' and 'Chinotto' orange trees with their glossy, dark-green leaves and small growth habit are excellent in containers or as border growers. The dwarf variety 'Bouquet de Fleurs' is

a more fragrant, ornamental shrub, smooth-stemmed and showy. Propagate from seed. Watch for the fungus disease melanose (dark brown spots on the wood and fruit) and citrus scab.

C. limon
LEMON

Native to Pakistan and India, this only just half-hardy tree or shrub is an attractive evergreen that grows to 4 m (about 12 ft) high and 3 m (about 9 ft) wide. The most common cultivar is 'Eureka' which is a smooth-stemmed tree with an all-year-round display of fruit and flowers if grown in frost-free climates. 'Meyer' is smaller than most lemons with a less acidic flavour, and is rather hardier than other lemons. Plant in well-drained soil and fertilize regularly with nitrogen. Propagate by budding. The lemon is less prone to disease than other citrus trees, but be careful of the fungus, melanose (dark brown spots), which must be pruned off once it appears on the wood.

Citrus medica

Citrus paradisi

Citrus aurantifolia

C. medica
CITRON

The fruit is like a lemon, but has a rougher, highly fragrant skin. Young foliage has a purplish tinge as do the flowers. Propagate by budding. Use for marmalade and candied peel as it has little juice. The tree is about as hardy as a sour orange.

C. paradisi
GRAPEFRUIT

Native to the West Indies where it was called forbidden fruit, grapefruit is relatively large for a citrus

Citrus aurantium

tree at 5 m (about 15 ft) high. The fruit is prominently displayed on the tree's outer section, hanging in golden yellow clusters that should be left until fully ripe before being picked. The tree is half-hardy. If it is grown in a cool climate the fruit takes up to 18 months to ripen. The Australian 'Wheeny' variety can be grown in a temperate climate but other varieties such as 'Marsh Seedless', 'Thompson' and 'Ruby' need very warm summers in order to ripen. Propagate by budding. Watch for stem pit virus, spread by the black citrus aphid.

Citrus limon

C. reticulata

MANDARIN, TANGERINE

This is the largest citrus group and has a wide range of climate tolerance among its varieties: the hardiest can take an occasional light frost. It grows to 3 m (about 9 ft) high and is a good fruit tree for the suburban garden. The fruit is similar to oranges, but smaller and looser skinned. It is slow-growing and hardy, with heavily perfumed flowers. Prune to remove dead wood. Propagate by budding. As with most citruses, watch for citrus scab and melanose fungus.

C. sinensis

SWEET ORANGE

The sweet orange travelled the trade routes as far back as the mid-fifteenth century and was introduced to the Western world by Arab traders. A large, half-hardy evergreen, it is grown commercially in subtropical climates. It can be grown in cooler climates if it is grafted *Poncirus trifoliata* rootstock

which helps it tolerate cold winters and also gives it greater resistance to certain virus diseases. Propagate by budding. Humidity encourages fungal diseases. Orange blossom is traditionally worn by brides in their hair. 'Valencia' is the best known variety of sweet orange, much grown commercially.

C. sinensis 'Washington Navel'

NAVEL ORANGE

This small, slow-growing tree grows best away from humid-summer coastal areas as this climate does not suit it. It has a distinctive, button-like growth on its seedless fruit, which many consider superior in mildness and sweetness to 'Valencia'. It is a mutation of the sweet orange.

C. × tangelo

TANGELO

An evergreen tree growing up to 4 m (about 12 ft) high and 3 m (about 9 ft) wide, it is derived from a cross between mandarin and

grapefruit. Tangelo is renowned for its juicing properties and as a superb dessert fruit with its tart, yet sweet, flavour. Plant in well-drained soil in a warm spot sheltered from frost. As with all citrus trees, regular watering is essential, especially when the tree is fruiting. Apply nitrogen fertilizer from early spring until mid-summer. Propagate by budding. Watch for citrus scab and fungi.

CORYLUS
avellana

HAZELNUT, FILBERT

A hardy, deciduous, small tree that grows up to 4 m (about 12 ft) high and wide. It will grow in a wide range of climates, is frost-hardy and prefers mild summers. The tree should be placed in full light where it is sheltered from strong winds. It produces the best crop of nuts, which grow in clusters and ripen in autumn/fall, in fertile, well-drained soil. Propagate by layering or from cuttings. The hazelnut has long

been steeped in mystic lore; parts of the plant were supposedly used for rituals in ancient times. In modern days it is eaten as a dessert and much used in the making of sweets and chocolates.

CYDONIA
oblonga

QUINCE

Native to the Middle East, this is a moderately frost-hardy, deciduous tree growing 3–4 m (about 9–12 ft) high and 3 m (about 9 ft) wide. Its soft green leaves turn an attractive golden yellow before falling and it is not fussy about soil, making it an ideal ornamental for potting or for borders. Its highly aromatic fruit can be left on the tree for a few weeks after it ripens without harm. Pick with care as it bruises easily. Prune minor branches or shoots which have produced fruit. Propagate from cuttings. It is vulnerable to fruit-fly and the fungus quince fleck. Quinces cannot be eaten raw and are best cooked for jellies or sauces. Quinces are thought to be the 'golden apples' that feature in Greek mythology.

CYPHOMANDRA
betacea

TAMARILLO, TREE TOMATO

This is an evergreen shrub or small, shrubby tree from South America with large, green leaves and, depending on the variety, dark red or yellow-orange fruit. Train it up against a wire fence or stake it to protect from the wind, as it is very

Corylus avellana

Citrus sinensis 'Washington Navel'

Citrus reticulata

Cydonia oblonga

Citrus × tangelo

Citrus sinensis

inclined to top-heaviness. This is a shallow-rooted plant which prefers a subtropical or temperate climate and moist, but not wet soil. It grows to 3 m (about 9 ft) in height. Prune lightly after fruiting and take cuttings at 1 m (about 3 ft) high to encourage more shoots. Propagate from cuttings and plan to replace the trees after 5 years or so as they are short lived. The fruit will mature throughout the year and can be used for jam or on ice-cream.

DIOSPYROS
kaki

PERSIMMON

This attractive, deciduous tree is common in Japan and China and grows to 5 m (about 15 ft) high and wide. The leaves are dark green and glossy, changing colour in autumn/fall to a handsome russet and gold. The tree can be kept in a large container and even if pruned will continue to fruit happily. The fruit is golden orange and is either astringent (in which case it should be eaten when quite ripe), or non-astringent (eat while still firm and crunchy or dry for future use, as is done in Japan). The tree is vulnerable to root rot so plant in well-drained soil. Beware of mealy bug, cinnamon fungus and collar rot. No pruning is needed.

ERIOBOTRYA
japonica

LOQUAT

In its natural state this subtropical tree will grow to 7 m (about 21 ft) high but in domesticity can be kept quite small by regular post-harvest pruning. Large, dark green leaves have a silver-grey underside and the scented, creamy coloured flowers form in multiple clusters. It prefers a temperate to subtropical climate. Its fruit is pear-shaped, small and sweet. Prune the more fragile shoots after the first fruiting; this will improve future harvests and make the tree more compact. Fruit-fly and birds can be a problem. Remove the bitter seeds and stew for jam or eat the fruit raw in salads. The tree can be propagated easily from seed, but grafted, named varieties give superior fruit.

FEIJOA
sellowiana

FEIJOA, PINEAPPLE GUAVA

Native to Brazil and Argentina, this evergreen grows to 3–4 m (about 9–12 ft) high and wide, and features green foliage and, in early summer, attractive red and white flowers. It is reasonably frost-hardy and makes a good windbreak or can be pruned to make a tall hedge. Don't let the soil dry out and water

well while fruiting. The fruit is large and pale green, with a similar taste to pineapple and should not be stored for too long before consumption. Plant in pairs of different varieties to ensure pollination. 'Unique' is a good cultivar for the domestic garden, being self-fertile. Its worst enemy is fruit-fly.

FICUS
carica

FIG

Originally from the Mediterranean and Asia, this deciduous tree varies in height from 3–9 m (about 9–27 ft). It flourishes in deep, lime-rich soils and a mild, dry climate and ideally should bear fruit twice a year. A distinguishing feature of this plant is the way the flower is formed and held within the fruit itself. May be trained as a wall plant. The yield is greater when its root range is limited, or containerized. Propagate from cuttings. Figs have few natural enemies although wasps and birds might find the near-ripe fruit very tempting. There are several named varieties, varying in their tolerance of cold and whether their fruit are best eaten fresh or dried. 'Brown Turkey' is usually thought the most luscious. Little pruning is needed, though old trees may be pruned hard to rejuvenate them.

Diospyros kaki

Cyphomandra betacea

Ficus carica

Feijoa sellowiana

Eriobotrya japonica

Juglans regia

Malus domestica 'Golden Delicious'

FORTUNELLA

japonica

KUMQUAT

This small, evergreen, ornamental
shrub made the journey from the
Orient to the West in the nineteenth century. It is excellent in a
large tub and its glossy, green foliage and small, golden fruit can also
be a highlight in a flower border.
There is a pretty variety with variegated leaves also. Half-hardy, it
will survive fairly open spaces on
patios and courtyards. Propagate
from seed. Kumquats are used in
marmalades and liqueurs.

JUGLANS

regia

WALNUT

A forest tree, this species grows
10–25 m (about 30–80 ft) high and
20 m (about 65 ft) wide. It can take
several years before the tree starts to
bear any nuts so patience is required. The variety 'Wilson's Wonder' fruits young, although its nuts
are not thought to be of the very
highest quality. A silver-grey trunk
ends in a canopy of arching
branches, making this a good
source of shade in a spacious garden. Prune early to form a central
branch and a well-spaced system of
boughs. It is cold- and wind-hardy,
although young trees may be damaged by harsh frost. Ensure that the
soil is deep, loamy and well
drained. Water well to increase nut
production and pick the nuts from
the ground after they have fallen.
Large birds can be a problem as well
as the erinose mite and nut-boring
beetles.

MALUS

A member of the Rose family, this
genus contains the crab apple and
the garden apple (*M. domestica*);
there are many species and varieties
of both. The genus is extremely
hardy, tolerating subtropical to
subarctic conditions, though they

Malus 'Bramley's Seedling'

do best in temperate climates with
cold winters. Well-drained soil is
essential for growth. They prefer
deep, humus-rich, sandy loams in
full light, although shade is tolerated. Plant in early spring in colder
climates and autumn/fall in warmer
areas. Pruning consists basically of
thinning out branches to allow
plenty of air and light around the
fruit, though the fruiting apples are
subjected to various detailed systems. Once established, it is rarely
necessary to do more than shorten
(in summer) the current season's
over-long shoots. Thrips, mites,
aphids moth larvae and fruit-fly are
just some among quite a few unwel-
come guests. Apple trees are not
fertile to their own pollen, so it is
necessary to grow two or more
varieties to have a crop. The size of
the tree depends on the understock,
and in most gardens trees grafted on
a 'dwarfing' stock will be best.

Fortunella japonica

M. baccata 'Dolgo'

This deciduous tree grows to 5 m (about 15 m) and has finely serrated, ovate leaves. It has white flowers and bears deep red fruit. Plant in a sunny position.

M. 'Bramley's Seedling'

This well-known cooking apple bears its large green fruit, occasionally flushed red, between October and March. Its flowers, which appear in early spring, can be damaged by frost. This variety grows to a rather large size for the average garden.

M. 'Discovery'

This tasty dessert apple from England appears in late summer. It is a small, deciduous tree that grows to a height of 2–4 m (about 6–12 ft).

M. domestica 'Delicious'

'Golden Delicious' is a hardy, prolific tree with juicy golden fruit and 'Red Delicious' is an excellent dessert apple. Neither keeps very well after being picked.

M. domestica 'Granny Smith'

This Australian-bred apple was a lucky seedling in the garden of a woman called Granny Smith. The pale green fruit keeps well and is excellent for cooking or eating fresh. It is vulnerable to apple scab (black spot).

M. domestica 'Gravenstein'

A medium to large aromatic apple native to Germany which is striped red and yellow. This is a large tree which should be placed with care in

Malus 'Discovery'

the home garden. Partly self-fertile, it is the best choice where only one apple tree is grown, though fruit will be more abundant if it has a mate.

M. domestica 'Jonathan'

This American-raised cultivar is very popular in that country and also in Australia and New Zealand for its sweet bland flavour and bright red colour. It is sometimes a rather weak-growing tree.

Malus domestica 'Jonathan'

Malus domestica 'Granny Smith'

Malus domestica 'Gravenstein'

Malus 'Gorgeous'

Malus pumila

Morus nigra

Malus 'John Downie'

Mespilus germanica

M. 'Golden Hornet'
FLOWERING CRAB

An attractive erect tree with an open habit, this species can grow to 5 m (about 15 ft). Its oval leaves are mid-green, and in spring it is covered with single white flowers around 2 cm (about 1 in) wide. The bright yellow fruit which follow remain on the tree well into autumn/fall, after the foliage has dropped.

M. 'Gorgeous'

The 'Gorgeous' crab apple was developed in New Zealand and has showy white flowers that are followed by glossy, dark red fruit in autumn/fall. They are first rate for making crab apple jelly as well as being highly ornamental.

M. 'James Grieve'

This tasty eating apple is available in late summer. Yellow and red, it is frost-hardy but prone to disease and

easily bruised. Its blossom appears in spring.

M. 'John Downie'

This large English crab apple grows to 5 m (about 15 ft). It yields an abundant crop of red fruit in autumn/fall. The spring flowers are white, and it is a rather smaller tree than 'Gorgeous'.

M. pumila
CRAB APPLE

This tree grows to 4–5 m (about 12–15 ft) high and its branches spread to 2 m (about 6 ft). Its lance-shaped leaves have serrated margins. Pink and white flowers are produced in spring. The small, attractive fruit of the crab apple tree is ideal for stewing and has for generations been used to make jellies and jams.

MESPILUS
germanica
MEDLAR

A deciduous tree native to the Balkans that grows from 3–5 m (about 9–15 ft) in height. It has handsome foliage that turns a lovely red in autumn/fall. Its showy spring flowers are white and are followed by odd looking, small, brown fruit that resemble acorns. A hardy tree requiring full sun, it is not popular or well known as a fruit-bearer and may be planted solely for display. If grown for its fruit, harvest only when the medlar comes away easily

from the stalk and leave to ripen until the flesh is brown and soft. Medlar may be either cooked and used in pies or eaten raw, once the pips are removed, though the fruit must be almost rotten-ripe before being palatable. Pick them when the leaves fall and store them for after-ripening.

MORUS
nigra
BLACK MULBERRY

From the same family as the fig tree, the deciduous mulberry has a 5–10 m (about 15–30 ft) tall trunk and wide-spreading branches. This slow-growing species is native to Iran and is valued for its ornamental, heart-shaped leaves and black fruit. The flowers are unisexual catkins and spikes. This tree commands a lot of space in the garden but can be grown in tubs or trained *espalier* as long as it has been pruned and shaped from early growth. It loves a temperate climate and the fruit will ripen in early summer, becoming easy prey for passing birds. It is adaptable to most soils in an open, sunny position and is drought and frost resistant. Propagate from seedlings. The white mulberry (*M. alba*) is more suitable for warm-winter climates however, fruit is not quite as good. Its leaves are fed to silkworms. Do not plant either *M. nigra* or *M. alba* where the fruit can fall on paving, as it will stain it.

Malus 'Golden Hornet'

OLEA
europaea subsp. *europaea*
OLIVE

This is a hardy, evergreen tree that grows to 7 m (about 21 ft) high and originates in the eastern Mediterranean where it is grown mostly for its oil but also for eating, either green or ripe but always pickled. It has glossy, narrow, green leaves, small yellow-white flowers and attractive spreading branches. It prefers warm summers and cool winters. It should be potted and grown in a greenhouse for protection in colder climates and tolerates most soils as long as they are well-drained. Water thoroughly in summer to ensure good fruiting. Fruit will not appear for at least 8 years but the tree is ornamental in its own right, developing an interesting gnarled trunk as it ages. There are several named varieties, some being better for eating, others for oil. 'Virgin' olive oil is that from the first pressing of the fruit, and is the best quality.

PERSEA
americana
syn. *P. gratissima*
AVOCADO

Native to Central America and reaching a height of 8 m (about 24 ft) and 6 m (about 18 ft) wide this large, evergreen tree has glossy, dark green leaves and tiny spring flowers. It prefers warmth and shelter in the garden (young trees are frost-tender) and may be grown indoors providing it is exposed to 4 hours of sunlight each day. Water regularly and ensure the soil is salt-free and aerated. Avocados are not self-pollinating and it is best to plant more than one. Pollinate the flowers by hand if only one tree is growing. Thrips, fruit-fly and red scale are the main invading insects and root rot is common. The best-known varieties are 'Fuerte', with large, green-skinned fruit in summer and early autumn/fall; and 'Hass', which bears dark-skinned fruit in winter and spring. Gardeners with room for both can have avocados virtually all year round. Other, newer varieties are also becoming available.

PINUS
pinea
PINE NUT, ITALIAN STONE PINE

This tall pine tree is a native of Italy and one of the most popular nut bearers there, the pine nuts (pignons or pignolias) being much used in cooking. They are very rich in protein. The tree is easily grown in a subtropical or temperate climate. The pines contain an average of 100 nuts and should be picked when slightly green and left to open in a warm, dry spot. When the pine opens out, the nuts can be shaken out. Propagate from seed or cuttings. Eat them raw or roasted.

PISTACIA
vera
PISTACHIO

Belonging to the same family as the mango and cashew, this tree is valued as an ornamental garden tree as well as a nut bearer. It features red-gold leaves in autumn/fall, and red male and white female flowers on separate trees; at least one of each is needed for a crop of nuts although bisexual, grafted trees are sometimes available and grafted trees of known sex are always to be preferred to seedlings. It prefers hot, dry summers and mild to cold winters. Loamy, organic soil is best for quick growth of the tree. The pistachio's long, deep roots make it drought tolerant but it should be well watered to ensure a good crop. *Pistacia chinensis*, the Chinese pistachio, is grown solely for its dazzling autumn/fall colours, its fruit being too small to be worth eating.

PRUNUS

This genus contains over 400 species of deciduous and evergreen

Pistacia vera

Olea europaea subsp. *europaea*

shrubs or trees grown for their fruits or nuts and as ornamentals. Most species are half- to fully hardy and prefer a well-drained soil. Propagate from seed in summer, from cuttings, or by grafting or budding. Prune regularly.

P. armeniaca
APRICOT

This deciduous tree grows to 6 m (about 18 ft) high and 5 m (about 15 ft) wide. Dwarf varieties are now available which may be grown in pots. Apricot trees flourish in warm-summer areas with well-drained, alkaline soil. A wet spring will mean a smaller crop. Prune for the first 4 years to a vase shape with 6 or 7 main branches. Light brown apple moth, fruit-fly, and fungal diseases can be a threat. In areas with spring frost, the tree is best given the shelter of a warm wall.

Prunus armeniaca

Pinus pinea

Persea americana

P. avium
SWEET CHERRY

This tree grows to 10 m (about 30 ft) tall and has white blossoms. Dwarf hybrids that grow to only a few metres high are available and these will live and fruit happily in tubs. It is suited to fan training against a high wall or fence. Otherwise, prune gradually to an open vase shape with 10 or so main branches. Do not prune in winter or during wet weather as cherry wood is prone to fungus. While cherries are ripening, cover the tree with plastic netting to keep birds away. Watch for root weevil and moth larvae. Cherries are not self-fertile (except for the new variety 'Stella'), so two trees will be necessary. They need a cold winter to fruit. The Japanese flowering cherry (P. serrulata) bears no fruit.

P. cerasus
SOUR CHERRY

This species is suitable for the domestic garden, being smaller, more compact and naturally self-fertilizing. The fruit ripens in late summer, but is acidic and needs to be cooked or preserved. Like the sweet cherry, it needs cold winters.

P. domestica and P. salicifolia
PLUM

The plums are of mixed origin but the European varieties are usually assigned to P. domestica and the Japanese (many of which were bred in the USA) to P. salicifolia. The main distinction is that the European plums are lovers of cooler climates than the Japanese. Both types come in many named varieties, but whereas just about all the Japanese plums are dessert fruit, the European plums include varieties best suited to cooking (jam making, pies, etc.) or drying for prunes. Damsons are European plums with rather small but very sweet fruit; greengages are similar but green-yellow even when ripe. Plum blossoms are quite lovely and some species of trees are grown purely for their display of beautiful red leaves.

Plum trees are generally very easy to grow and will tolerate different soil types; these species prefer a potash-rich mixture which is well watered. They like a temperate climate with dry summers and should be planted in a sunny sheltered position. Prune regularly in summer to slow growth and pick the plums only when fully ripe. Use netting to protect the trees from birds. Aphids, scales and mites can be a problem, as can brown rot, bacterial spot and plum mosaic virus.

P. dulcis
syn. P. amygdalus
ALMOND

A deciduous tree from South-East Asia that grows to 6 m (about 18 ft) high and 5 m (about 15 ft) wide. This is a stone fruit which is closely related to the peach. However the flesh of the fruit is inedible while the kernel is sweet. Pink blossoms grow in clusters of 5 and 6. Ideally, this tree should be grown in a dry-summer climate in a well-drained, salt-free soil. Young trees are frost-tender. As with other stone fruit, weed the base area well and feed the young tree nitrogen. Prune to an open vase shape encouraging 3 or 4 main branches. It is prone to shot-hole disease which appears on the fruit as purple spots, spoiling the nut inside. Almonds are not self-fertile and two varieties that blossom at the same time are needed to produce fruit.

P. persica
PEACH

This deciduous tree grows to 5 m (about 15 ft) high and wide, and is the most commonly grown of the stone fruit. Most feature pink-tinged blossoms, yellowish red-skinned fruit and should be grown in a warm climate. Cultivated dwarf varieties are perfect for placing in tubs or among flower beds and shrubberies. Peach trees must be planted in well-drained soil as waterlogging can be fatal. Plant where the tree, including the interior branches, will receive the most light and shelter from frosts. If new shoots aren't pruned the tree will overbear and the fruit will be small and of poor quality. Pick the peaches when they just start to soften. Propagate from seed. Peaches are susceptible to a number of diseases including peach leaf curl and brown rot. They are officially self-fertile, but crops will be better if two varieties are grown. The trees are not long lived, 25 years or so.

P. persica var. nectarina
NECTARINE

The nectarine is almost identical to the peach in habit and flowers but needs more attention as it is less hardy than the peach. Its fruit is usually smaller and smooth skinned. There are several named varieties; seedlings often give rise to normal peaches.

PSIDIUM
cattleianum
CHERRY GUAVA, STRAWBERRY GUAVA

Native to tropical Central and South America, this medium-sized, hardy evergreen is related to the feijoa. It is fast growing with a smooth trunk and large, white flowers. Its pear-shaped fruit has dark red flesh which is high in vitamin C. It prefers a warm, frost-free climate, plenty of water for good fruit production and some shelter from the wind when it is young. The tree should be pruned to encourage prolific flowering, with old wood and lower branches being removed. Propagate from cuttings, or by grafting or budding. It is susceptible to fruit-fly. Guavas are excellent for juicing, or for using in jams and jellies.

Prunus cerasus

Prunus domestica

Prunus avium

Prunus persica var. nectarina

Prunus persica

Prunus dulcis

PUNICA
granatum
POMEGRANATE

This very attractive, compact but very thorny tree is from the Middle East where about 20 named varieties, varying in flavour from acid to very sweet, are grown. It is valued not only for its sweet fruit but for its large, red blooms which appear in late spring and early summer. It grows to 5 m (about 15 ft) and its glossy leaves, showy scarlet flowers and orange fruit make it popular as an ornamental, long-living shrub. Pomegranate requires hot summer conditions to produce good crops. Prune lightly in winter to encourage new growth. Pomegranates start to bear fruit after 5 to 6 years; the fruit should be harvested when it becomes an orange-brown colour. Do not leave it too long on the tree as it tends to split. Propagate from cuttings or rooted suckers. Watch out for fungal rot. Use the fruit kernels in salads or desserts and eat the pulp fresh. A warm summer is needed for the fruit to ripen, and the double-flowered varieties (red, pink or white) are mostly sterile. There is also available a miniature variety, P. granatum 'Nana', which only grows to approximately1 m (about 3 ft) with small, decorative flowers and fruit.

PYRUS
PEAR

Thousands of years of cultivation have produced many different shapes, sizes and fruit of pear trees, some more suitable for the domestic garden than others. Usually a large tree, it is thought to have originated in the Mediterranean. It flourishes in a moist, mild climate. Plant in a warm, protected spot where it will receive maximum sunlight. In a small garden, train it to grow on a lattice or wire frame. Alternatively, pear trees grafted onto quince stock are good for home gardens. It can stand a reasonable amount of water and responds well to loamy soil with the occasional boost of nitrogen-rich fertilizers. Cross-pollination is needed for productive fruiting. The main enemies of the pear are scale, mites, blossom blight and stony pit.

P. communis 'Beurre Bosc'

This is popular worldwide for its large, soft, sweet pears that are ideal for baking. It is prone to the pear scab fungus.

P. communis 'William's Bon Chrétien'
BARTLETT PEAR

This is a sweet, musky flavoured, medium-sized pear which bears the name of an English schoolteacher but is thought by some to have been cultivated by the Ancient Romans. It is the most widely grown Bartlett pear cultivar for canning. 'Red Bartlett' is the red-skinned cultivar.

P. pyrifolia
NASHI PEAR

Native to China but also much cultivated in Japan, this tree is an excellent, compact, fruit bearer. Plant among garden shrubs where its white blossoms and glossy, green leaves can be seen to advantage. It has two types, the Japanese nashi, which is more apple-shaped with green or brown skin, and the Chinese nashi, which is more traditionally pear-shaped. The nashi pear is easier to grow than the European pear in mild-winter areas, and more suited to domestic use. Grow on a trellis and prune excess shoots. It is more disease hardy than the European pear, and not so dependent on cross-pollination for fruit, although crops will be better if the tree does have a mate; a European pear will be perfectly adequate.

SAMBUCUS
nigra 'Aurea'

This bushy, deciduous shrub is grown for the creamy white, star-shaped, fragrant flowers it bears in early summer, followed by round, black berries. The yellow leaves are each composed of five yellow leaflets. It prefers a rich, well-drained soil and plenty of sun. Fully hardy, it grows to a height and spread of 6 m (about 18 ft). Propagate from suckers or from cuttings taken in late autumn/fall. Remove old flowerheads before they set seed.

THEOBROMA
cacao
CACAO TREE, COCOA TREE

This widely cultivated tree grows quickly to 8 m (about 24 ft), with a thick convex crown that spreads in maturity. The pink, yellow or white flowers are followed by angular seed pods.

Theobroma cacao

Pyrus pyrifolia

Sambucus nigra 'Aurea'

Pyrus communis 'Buerre Bosc'

Pyrus communis 'William's Bon Chrétien'

Psidium cattleianum

Punica granatum

OTHER FRUITS

ACTINIDIA
chinensis
syn. *A. deliciosa*
KIWIFRUIT, CHINESE GOOSEBERRY

This deciduous vine is native to the Yangtze Valley in China and is now grown in warm areas around the world. It should be planted on a sturdy trellis or pergola (as it grows quickly and quite wildly) in deep

Arachis hypogaea

soil which is high in nitrogen. It prefers a sheltered spot away from the winds, early frosts and hot sun that can damage the fruit. Prune regularly in summer and winter to ensure large, good quality fruit. Water abundantly in summer. The first fruit will appear after 4 to 5 years. Kiwifruit's main enemies are light brown apple moth larvae, fruit-fly, root rot and the leaf-roller caterpillar. You must have a male and a female (named varieties are superior) to produce fruit; grafted plants carrying both sexes are often available. Prune in the same manner as grapes.

ANANAS
comosus
syn. *A. sativas*
PINEAPPLE

Cultivated by Central American Indians for centuries, the pineapple was praised by early European visitors as the finest of all fruit and shipped back to the Old World. To offer the expensive exotic to a guest

Actinidia chinensis

Ananas comosus

was a great compliment; hence the use of pineapple motifs in architecture to symbolize hospitality. A member of the bromeliad family, the plant makes a bushy, 1 m (about 3 ft) tall clump of sword-shaped leaves from which the flower stems arise, the clustered flowers developing into a single aggregate fruit. The leaves are viciously edged with tiny thorns, but recently smooth-leaved cultivars have been developed. Suited only to gardens in the tropics and subtropics, it needs a greenhouse in temperate and cool climates to provide the constant warmth it needs to fruit. Sunshine, regular watering, and the richest possible soil are essential. Named varieties are occasionally available, but the easiest way to acquire a plant is to make a cutting from the shoot atop a choice fruit. It will, if happy, fruit in about two years. Once established, faster and heavier crops will come from plants propagated from side shoots, which should be done every few years as old plants do not fruit pro-

Cucumis melo (rock melon)

Citrullus lanatus

lifically. There is a cultivar with variegated leaves, grown mainly for ornamental purposes, as its fruit is rather small.

ARACHIS
hypogaea
PEANUT

This is an herbaceous annual with bright green, clover-like leaves and small, pea-shaped, yellow flowers that blossom in summer. Native to Brazil, it grows to a height of 30 cm (about 12 in) with a spread of 40 cm (about 16 in). It can be planted to good effect in flower borders or in containers, but is frost-tender so grow only where it will enjoy a long hot summer. They need a long growing season with consistently warm soil, although in mild-summer areas the nuts will not ripen. The peanuts themselves are actually seeds that grow underground, so make sure that the soil (which should be slightly acid) is loose enough for the peanut to grow productively. If the soil is too damp the peanuts will rot, therefore keep well drained and well composted. Peanut plants should be ready to pull up when the foliage turns yellow in autumn/fall. Cure nuts for a few weeks before eating.

CITRULLUS
lanatus
syn. *C. vulgaris*
WATERMELON

This is a large, heat-loving vine with crinkled leaves similar to rather large ivy leaves. Sow seeds in spring in rich, well-drained soil in a sunny position. (Mostly it grows rampantly, and without much encouragement, from compost heaps in the back garden.) Watch for cucumber beetles. The rind can be pickled and of course the sugary, red-pink flesh inside is delicious, but the longer and hotter the summer the better the crop will be.

CUCUMIS
MELON

Native to Africa where there are 40 species, most melons grow on vines and are grouped according to the characteristics of their fruit. They need a long, hot growing season to produce sweet fruit, and in a cooler climate the vines should be encouraged to grow over concrete or rocks, or trained over black plastic in order for heat to circulate around the plant. Plant in humus-rich soil and water generously but not too much. A dry climate is preferable, as humid conditions can affect the quality of the fruit and make the plant more prone to the fungus, anthracnose. Hand pollinate if growing melons on a small scale. Propagate from seed.

CANTALUPENSIS GROUP
C. melo
CANTALOUPE, ROCK MELON

This is a compact plant with oval-shaped or round fruit with netted rinds and orange flesh.

INDORUS GROUP
C. melo
HONEYDEW MELON

A small, bushy plant with a harder rind than most melons, making it suitable for long storage. The skin is usually smooth and the flesh is pale green or yellow.

RETICULATUS GROUP
C. melo
NETTED MELON

This melon has net markings on the rind, orange flesh and is widely grown in the USA.

FRAGARIA
STRAWBERRY

This small, frost-hardy perennial grows no more than 20 cm (about 8 in) high and 40 cm (about 16 in) wide. These plants are capable of growing all over the world in all sorts of climates, including the Arctic. The strawberry itself is a false fruit made up of tiny pips. Modern, more robust strawberry plants can produce fruit for 6 months if grown properly; some will bear fruit year round in a warm climate. Plant in tubs, pots, garden beds or even boxes that have been lined with straw, potting mix and fertilizer. Ensure the soil is free draining and acidic. The plants will grow in sun or partial shade and need protection from wind, and in cold climates should be grown in slits in sheets of plastic. Propagate from runners and replant with fresh, virus-free stock every few years. Snails, strawberry aphids and birds are a nuisance. There are many named varieties of the garden strawberry, varying in their preferred climates and especially in flavour. Each area has its own favourites.

F. alpina
ALPINE STRAWBERRY

The fruit from this variety is small and hardy and tastes very tangy. Alpine strawberries make a good ground cover under trees or near walls and are less susceptible to attack by birds. The fruit can be red or yellow, and plants usually don't make runners. They are propagated from seed.

F. ananassae
GARDEN STRAWBERRY

The name means 'pineapple flavoured', a curious description for the garden strawberry which arose from crossing American species.

HUMULUS
lupulus
HOP, COMMON HOP, BINE

Native to southern Britain, this perennial climber is often found wild in hedgerows. Fully hardy, its twisting stems have prickles with barbs which allow the plant to climb, always in a clockwise direction, to 6 m (about 18 ft). Its mid-green, palmate leaves have 3–5 roughly toothed lobes, and are up to 15 cm (about 6 in) wide. The small, green-yellow male and female flowers are carried on separate plants: the male ones are held in panicles, while the female ones are cone shaped and covered with scales. Appearing in late summer, it is the female flowers that develop into hops, and it is for this essential part of the brewing industries that

the plant has been cultivated for centuries. It will thrive in well-drained soil in either sun or partial shade, and can be propagated in spring from cuttings.

PASSIFLORA

This genus contains over 400 species of evergreen or semi-evergreen tendril-climbing vines, primarily, though not exclusively, native to tropical America. They are grown as ornamentals or for their pulpy fruit. Flowers range from pale pink to purple-red and fruits from pale yellow through to purple-black, depending on the species. Plant in rich, well-drained soil in full sun and provide support. Propagate from seed or cuttings. Most species are frost-tender and are susceptible to nematodes.

P. edulis
PASSIONFRUIT

This species of passionfruit vine is a common sight in gardens in temperate climates and is valued for its glossy, bright green leaves, purple-white flowers and flavoursome fruit. Train on a pergola or trellis and prune into shape to prevent tangling, which encourages insect infestation. It is hardy and likes a well-drained, sandy soil and occasional doses of nitrogen fertilizer. The fruit will grow quickly and should be picked when its skin has turned purple and is still smooth. This species is self-fertile. Propagate from seed or better still by grafting a selected, named variety; seedlings

can be unreliable. The Spanish conquistadors regarded the flower of the passionfruit as a symbol of the crucifixion.

P. mollissima
syn. *Tacsonia mollissima*
BANANA PASSIONFRUIT

This attractive, fast-growing vine does well in cool climates and features pink flowers and long, golden yellow fruit. Train against a trellis or

Humulus lupulus 'Aureus'

Fragaria ananassae

Passiflora edulis

Fragaria alpina

Rubus 'Boysen'

Passiflora mollissima

Ribes nigrum

Physalis peruviana

Ribes grossularia

Ribes sativum

fence, or over a supporting tree where the fruit and flowers can be seen to advantage. Drought-hardy and generous in its crop, it often fruits in the first year. The fruit is not as sweet as the ordinary passionfruit but can still be used for cakes and fruit salads. Banana passionfruit spreads like a weed in South Africa and is best not cultivated there.

PHYSALIS
peruviana
CAPE GOOSEBERRY

This edible species of _Physalis_ is an attractive bush with grey-green leaves and gold berries. It is frost-tender so it is best grown in the shelter of another bush or tree. Hot weather usually means that the fruit will be sweet, while a cooler, temperate climate can lead to sour-tasting berries. Propagate from cuttings. Use for chutney or jam or in fruit salads.

RIBES

A member of the Grossulariaceae family, this genus contains about 150 species of deciduous fruit-bearing shrubs. They grow to a height of 1–2 m (about 3–6 ft) and spread of 1–1.5 m (about 3–4½ ft). Frost-hardy, they are unsuited to warm-winter climates. Most species prefer deep, rich, well-drained, slightly acidic soil. Plant in sun or partial shade, and water well during summer. Prune annually to shape as required by the species. Diseases, insects and birds can be a problem.

R. grossularia
GOOSEBERRY

The thorny-stemmed gooseberry bush grows to 1 m (about 3 ft) high. It can tolerate quite poor soil as long as it is salt-free and grows best in cool, moist positions in sun or partial shade. The thorny stems should be kept in mind when placing it in a small garden. Shape as a

short-stemmed bush or tie the shoots against a fan-shaped wire support. Pick the fruit while it is still hard if using for cooking, but wait until it is soft if eating it fresh. Propagate from cuttings. Botrytis, birds, caterpillars and mildew are problems; only mildew-resistant varieties should be grown.

R. nigrum
BLACKCURRANT

This very popular garden shrub reaches up to 2 m (about 6 ft) and produces green-white flowers and sweet, black fruit high in vitamin C. Frost-hardy, it prefers a rich, loamy soil which can hold water. Plant it deep in the soil and enrich wood growth with potash and nitrogen-rich fertilizer. Weeds must be controlled and preferably eradicated before planting the blackcurrant bush. Prune old shoots to encourage new growth. The fruit should be picked when the upper berries are starting to fall from the cluster.

Propagate from cuttings. Watch for currant borer moth, mites and leaf spot.

R. sativum
REDCURRANT

This is very similar to the blackcurrant and prefers the same conditions. Its beautiful, glossy, red berries ripen earlier and are less likely to fall prematurely. They are usually used in cooking. White currants are a form of the red, and are grown in exactly the same way.

RUBUS

This genus includes a large number of the berry fruits, including raspberries and blackberries. The plants produce long, trailing shoots known as canes which bear fruit in their second season and then die. These plants need supporting frames to keep the fruit away from the ground, and to keep the plants under control—any shoot that lies on the ground will take root. In a small garden the plants can be trained against a wall or trellis. Cool climates are best and an acidic, well-drained soil that holds water well. Make sure that the ground is well clear of weeds before planting. Propagate from pieces of root or root suckers.

R. 'Boysen'
BOYSENBERRY

Like all bramble berries this is a rampant grower with long canes that are either thorny or smooth, the thornless variety being much easier to manage. It prefers a warm-temperate climate and depending on the fertility of the soil it may need vigorous pruning. The large, purple-red berries take 6 weeks to ripen, when they can be quite black. The best variety is 'Thornless', the merits of which are indicated by its name.

R. fruticosus
BRAMBLE, BLACKBERRY

This British native rambler is found growing wild in woods, hedgerows and also as a weed in the garden. The cultivated blackberry's stems will grow to 3 m (about 9 ft) with a similar spread and will need support. The prickly, arching stems bear deep green leaves with 3–5 leaflets which are felt like on the undersides. The white or pink flowers, up to 4 cm (about 2 in) across, appear during summer and are followed by the purple blackberries.

R. idaeus
RASPBERRY

R. idaeus from Europe (especially it is said from Mt Ida in Greece where Zeus was born) is the main parent of the garden raspberries. The modern cultivars all make tall lax bushes with delicious red fruit, much used for jam but also eaten fresh. There are both summer and autumn/fall fruiting varieties; be sure to buy certified virus-free stocks and control aphids, which spread virus diseases.

R. 'Logan'
syn. R. Logan baccus
LOGANBERRY

This is a hybrid between a blackberry and a garden raspberry, said to have originated in the garden of Judge Logan in California in 1881. It has a crimson, tart fruit highly suitable for cooking. The plant is raspberry-like in growth.

SECHIUM
edule
CHOKO, CHAYOTE

Native to South America and from the same family as the melon and cucumber, this is strictly a perennial fruit that grows on a strong, bright green vine. It requires sun, and plenty of space to grow as its tendrils will grip onto and climb almost anything. In a temperate climate chokos are frost-tender. Propagate from a shooting choko fruit in spring. The large, hairy green fruit can be boiled, baked or stewed but not overcooked or it will be tasteless.

VACCINIUM
corymbosum
BLUEBERRY

A fast-growing, deciduous shrub with lovely, small white flowers and handsome autumn/fall colours. It

looks best when planted as a thick hedge so that the flowers and berries form a mass of white or blue, depending on the season. It does well in cold climates and prefers a well-drained but constantly moist, loamy, acidic soil. It is self-fertile. The cooler the climate the tastier the fruit will be. Propagate from cuttings. The blueberry is harder to reproduce than other berry fruit.

VITIS
vinifera
GRAPE

V. vinifera is native to Europe and the Mediterranean and has been cultivated since remote antiquity. A vigorous, frost-hardy, deciduous vine, it has given rise to a multitude of varieties with either black or white (pale green or yellow) fruit, some being designed for wine, others for eating fresh or dried. They need cool winters and low summer humidity or mildew will be a major worry. Train on a pergola or fence where it is sunny, and in deep soil so that the vine can dig its roots down. Pruning depends on grape type and upon the way the vine is being grown. For pergola vines, train on a single trunk until it reaches the horizontal beams, then allow it to spread out. Birds are a problem, so cover the vines with bird netting or put paper bags around the grape clusters. Cut the grapes with sharp scissors when fully ripe. Grapes need annual pruning after the leaves have fallen to control the vine's growth and encourage heavy fruiting. They are traditionally propagated by cuttings but where there is the slightest chance of phylloxera, an insect that feeds on the roots, being present they are best grafted on resistant understocks.

Vitis vinifera

Vaccinium corymbosum

Sechium edule

Rubus idaeus

Rubus 'Logan'

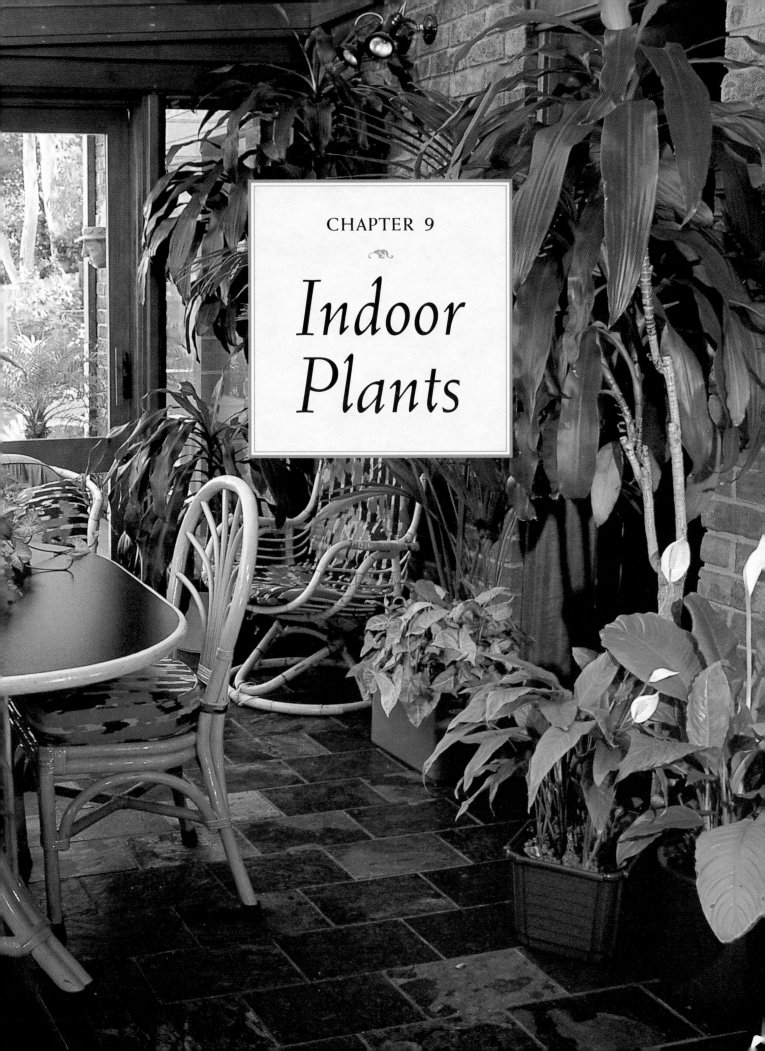

CHAPTER 9

Indoor Plants

*Y*ou'd be forgiven for thinking that in an art as ancient as gardening, there was nothing new; yet house plants are quite a recent idea. True, the Victorians grew fuchsias on their window sills and ferns in miniature greenhouses called Wardian cases; but the idea of using growing plants as major features in interior design—and growing a large range of species too—had to wait for several things to happen.

First, modern architecture had to increase the size of our windows, so that rooms would be bright enough for plants to flourish. Then, electric light had to supersede gas, whose fumes will kill off just about anything except aspidistras and parlour palms. Even now, if you cook with gas you may well find plants don't flourish in your kitchen. Finally, central heating had to make our houses consistently warm enough for tropical plants, for tropical forests are among the few natural environments where decorative plants grow in gloom comparable to the interior of a building.

The Importance of Light

We humans can adjust our eyes to an extraordinary range of brightness; but then we don't need light to photosynthesize. Plants do; and the first rule in growing any plant in the house is to give it adequate light. We almost always place our furniture in the best lit places in the room—and why not, rooms are designed for our own comfort first of all—but that often means that the corners where plants fit the decor best are the darkest in the room. The brightest place is in front of or just next to a window, but if you habitually keep your curtains drawn during the day for privacy, your room can be dim no matter how large your windows. There are plants that can take very low levels of light, but the range is limited, and pretty well confined to plants with plain green leaves. (Variegated leaves are almost always short on chlorophyll, and flowering takes a lot of energy which the plant can only derive from light.) It is a matter of cutting your cloth according to your measure, but remember that a flourishing plant, no matter how plain, is an asset to a room; a struggling one, all weak, pale and drawn, isn't. You can overcome the forces of darkness by placing the plant under a lamp, but it will have to be fitted with a special bulb (a 'grow-light' or fluorescent bulb, to be bought at most plant nurseries) that maximizes the frequencies of light that plants use—ordinary lights are of little use. Alternatively, have two plants and rotate them weekly or fortnightly between the garden or greenhouse.

Humidity

The next requirement is adequate humidity, and here there can be real conflict between our ideas of comfort and those of our plants, many of which would be happiest in a Turkish bath rather than the average living room. If

It's very important to provide adequate light for indoor plants.

you have a well-lit bathroom or kitchen they can be good places for plants, but you can assist by growing several plants together—they will help humidify the air for each other—and by standing your pots on saucers filled with pebbles which you keep constantly moist (on, not in; you don't want the roots standing in water).

Air-conditioning and central heating can dry the air out to desert-like levels. It is often said that house plants dislike air-conditioning, but this isn't strictly true. If they are standing on wet pebbles, they should be fine—and you'll be more comfortable too, and the piano will stay in better tune, for their presence. But you must keep your rooms at a reasonably even temperature. If you save energy by setting your system to come on and adjust the temperature by 10°C (about 18°F) in the half-hour before you come home, your plants will resent it. Happily, the 18–21°C (about 64–70°F) that most people find comfortable will suit most plants too, and if it falls by a couple of degrees during the night they'll appreciate it.

*The peace lily (*Spathiphyllum *'Mauna Loa'), one of the most popular indoor plants.*

Watering

More house plants drown than die of thirst—water with care. Just about all should be allowed to dry out a little between waterings: but if you can't be so hard-hearted, pot them in terracotta pots, whose porosity makes it harder to over-water than impervious plastic. It looks better too. You can then use the best method of testing: tap the pot and if it rings, the plant needs water; if you hear a dull thud, it doesn't. This doesn't work with plastic! Alternatively, try one of the various self-watering pots, which allow the plants to draw just the water they need from a reservoir in the bottom. Or try concentrating on spathiphyllums, which are among the very few house plants that like constant damp feet!

Temporary Plants

It is all very well to say that happiness comes from concentrating on the easy plants, but you would be less than human if you were not to fall sometimes for one of the difficult but spectacular flowering types like cyclamen, gloxinias or poinsettias. They aren't impossible—just difficult, needing warmer or cooler conditions than usual, high humidity and great care in watering—but they

really aren't happy in the average room. Unless you have a greenhouse or sheltered, totally frost-free place in the garden to use as a convalescent home, resign yourself to their being temporary delights. They'll still last longer than a bunch of cut flowers.

Fertilizing and Repotting

Sooner or later, if a plant flourishes the question of fertilizing or repotting will arise. The advent of slow-release fertilizers has made fertilizing easy. Just buy one formulated for indoor plants, and apply it in spring as growth begins (it's astonishing how, even indoors, plants remain aware of the seasons) according to the directions on the packet. As always, don't overdo the dosage. Fertilizer will usually allow you to at least put off the decision about repotting: but if you feel the plant's shoes really are getting too tight, do the job in spring, handle the plant gently, and don't go up to a pot more than a size bigger than the old one. If you like, you can tease off some of the old soil from the roots to allow more fresh soil, which should be the best, premium grade potting mix you can buy. Naturally, you won't be tempted to put your plant in a container, no matter how beautiful, which has no drainage holes. If you can't

resist, put some pebbles in the bottom, and use it purely as a decorative mask for the holey-bottomed one in which the plant is actually growing.

Pests

Alas, pests sometimes follow house plants indoors. The worst are mildew and root rot (almost always a result of over-watering), red spider and mealy bug. All can be controlled by spraying with insecticides and fungicides, but who would be crazy enough to spray such poisons indoors, quite apart from the mess? If you can't take the plant outside to spray, you can use a systemic insecticide which is stirred into the soil. Fungi are more difficult, and if a plant really is severely infested, it might be wise to consider disposing of it, soil and all. (Wash the pot out with bleach and you can re-use it.)

A final word—dust. This settles invisibly on house plants and robs the leaves of light. Wipe it off regularly with a damp cloth, and, better yet, stand your plants out in the summer rain every so often. If you can bear to forego their company, a few weeks outside in the shadiest place in the garden each summer will do them a power of good; but bring them back in the instant you sense autumn/fall in the air.

Anthurium scherzerianum

Aspidistra elatior

Alocasia macrorrhiza

Aphelandra squarrosa 'Louisae'

ALOCASIA
macrorrhiza
GIANT ELEPHANT'S EAR, CUNJEVOL, GIANT TARO

This is a member of a genus of plants from Sri Lanka and tropical South-East Asia which are grown for their spectacular foliage of large leaves with highlighted veins on long stalks. This species has 1 m (about 3 ft) long stalks which carry the broad, arrowhead-shaped, glossy green leaves which grow to 1 m (about 3 ft) in length. It produces insignificant but fragrant flowers on a spadix enclosed in a leaf-like, yellowish-green spathe. It can be grown outdoors only in warmer climates as it is frost-tender, and does best indoors in cool climates. If potted, grow in a rich, peaty mixture. Outdoors, grow in well-drained soil in a shady position with

high humidity. Water heavily and feed regularly with diluted fertilizer. May be propagated from suckers which root easily or by division of rhizomes or stem cuttings planted in spring.

ANTHURIUM
scherzerianum
FLAMINGO FLOWER

Grown for its attractive flowers and foliage, this tropical plant from Columbia grows to 60–80 cm (about 24–32 in), often in a greenhouse or indoors, but given the right conditions will grow outdoors. Anthuriums have long-stalked, heart-shaped leaves and long-lasting, graceful, glossy, bright red or pink spathes with yellow or red spadices. Indoors, they need bright light, high humidity and constant warmth and moisture to flower. *A.*

scherzerianum has red flowers and curled orange to yellow spadices. Plant outdoors in a humid position, in well-drained, peaty soil in full or part-shade out of the wind. Water well, keeping the soil moist but not soggy. The temperature must not fall below 15°C (about 59°F). Propagate from rhizomes in early spring. Potted plants need dividing and repotting every few years. *A. andraenum* and its hybrids are larger and warmer growing.

APHELANDRA
squarrosa 'Louisae'
ZEBRA PLANT

Native to South America, this popular indoor plant takes its common name from its large, glossy, dark green leaves, heavily striped by white veins. It grows to 1 m (about 3 ft). It is sometimes called 'Saffron spike' due to the bright yellow flower bracts which surround the tiny white flowers and which appear in spring. Needs bright light, but not direct sunlight, and warm, reasonably humid conditions, especially when flowering. For high humidity stand the pot on a tray of pebbles and water. It is best in a rich, porous soil and can be grown in relatively small pots as it prefers to be slightly pot-bound. Keep well watered in the warmer months and less in winter, but never let soil ball dry out, and fertilize regularly. As it tends to become leggy, prune back after flowering, leaving one or two pairs of leaves. Propagate by cutting off side shoots that have roots. Leaf-drop can be caused by dry roots, low or sudden

drops in temperature, or by direct sun. Browning of leaf tips or brown leaf spots may be caused by low humidity.

ASPIDISTRA
elatior
CAST-IRON PLANT

This is a species of evergreen perennials from Japan, China and the Himalayas, and was one of the most famous house plants of the Victorian era. The tough, long, narrow, dark green leaves are pointed at the tips and arch elegantly on a clump of 15 cm (about 6 in) stems to a length of 60 cm (about 24 in). There is also a handsome variegated form. The cream to dark purple, bell-shaped flowers grow at soil level and are screened from view by the leaves; it is something of an event to see them, as indoor plants seldom flower. It is known, for good reason, as the 'cast-iron plant' as its ability to withstand neglect makes it one of the toughest and most adaptable house plants. It can be kept in bright to very low light, but direct sunlight burns the leaves. Water lightly when soil is dry and do not stand the pot in water. Feed occasionally and regularly wipe leaves with a damp cloth to maintain the gloss. When the plant becomes very crowded, divide the root crown and repot in late winter to early spring.

BEGONIA
BEGONIA

Begonias are native to all tropical regions except Australia and there are over 1500 known species. They are prized for their beautifully coloured foliage and attractive flowers, making an ideal indoor plant with a number of varieties readily available. This diverse group includes rhizomatous, fibrous-rooted and tuberous plants. They all have waxy leaves and a succulent form. They do well in indoor potting mix with either peat moss, leafmould or decomposed cow manure added to increase acidity. Grow in bright to moderate light, with fresh air, above average humidity and temperatures of 16–30°C (about 60–85°F). Humidity can be maintained by standing the pot on a tray of pebbles and water. Keep soil moist but not soggy. Fertilize in the spring growing season. Pinch back young plants to stop them becoming gangly and to encourage flowers. Most begonias can be propagated from stem and leaf cuttings in spring, by division of rhizomes or from seed. Begonias are susceptible to grey mould, powdery mildew and botrytis from late spring to early autumn/fall if conditions are too damp.

B. auriculata
CATHEDRAL WINDOWS

This evergreen rhizomatous begonia grows to 30–35 cm (about 12–14 in) high and the spreading trunk to a width of 40 cm (about 16 in). The green and red leaves are thick and ear-shaped. It has tall spikes of pink flowers.

B. x cheimantha 'Gloire de Lorraine'
CHRISTMAS BEGONIA, LORRAINE BEGONIA

The single, white to pale pink flowers appear in winter on this round-leafed plant. The leaves are bright green and it grows to a height of 30 cm (about 12 in).

B. 'Cleopatra'

This is a popular, easy-to-grow plant with 5 cm (about 2 in) wide, star-shaped leaves. The yellow-green leaves have brown markings with a reddish underside. Clusters of pale pink flowers bloom in early spring.

B. masoniana
IRON CROSS BEGONIA

This plant's name is derived from the bold, brown, iron cross mark on the bright green, puckered leaves. This evergreen, rhizomatous plant grows to a height of 45–60 cm (about 18–24 in) and a spread of 30–45 cm (about 12–18 in). The single, pinkish white flowers are insignificant.

B. rex 'Merry Christmas'
syn. B. ruhrtal

Rex are the most common foliage begonias and are available in many cultivars. This evergreen, creeping, rhizomatous variety has a band of emerald green with a rose-red centre and silver highlights on the leaf. The leaves are 15–20 cm (about 6–8 in) long with the plant growing to 25–30 cm (about 10–12 in) high.

BILLBERGIA
VASE PLANT

This genus, comprising about 50 species and many garden varieties, was originally from the jungles of the American tropics where most grew on rocks or suspended in trees. With their exotic foliage of long, thin, stiff leaves, often edged with small teeth, and showy flowers, they are easy to grow and make an ideal indoor plant. The flower displays appear at many times of the year. The rosette of leaves form a cup and it is by filling this cup that the plant should be watered. A porous, fast-draining soil mix is required, but they will grow sitting in a pot of stones. The plant multiplies quickly and can be propagated by division. Scale and mealy bug can be a problem, and brown leaves

may be due to too much sun. Ensure the pot is heavy enough as the weight of the foliage may cause the plant to fall over.

B. leptopoda

The striking grey-green leaves are heavily powdered with silver and framed by small spines or teeth. Dark blue flowers enclosed in salmon-pink bracts appear in winter. A height of 30 cm (about 12 in) is reached. This is one of a number of similar species, all spectacular.

B. nutans
QUEEN'S TEARS, FRIENDSHIP PLANT

Almost hardy, this species can be grown out of doors in shady places where it will only have to endure the occasional light frost. Indoors it likes a rich potting mix and good light. The leaves are long and narrow, plain olive green, and the pendent clusters of flowers appear in spring. They are a unique combination of pale green and navy blue, but it is the pink bracts that grow along the flower stems that catch the eye.

B. pyramidalis var. concolor

A showy, erect spike of pyramid-shaped, rose-red and purple-tipped flowers appears from late summer to mid-winter. Broad, apple-green leaves form rosettes, sometimes with silver banding. It grows to 30–50 cm (about 12–20 in).

Begonia 'Cleopatra'

Begonia rex 'Merry Christmas'

Billbergia nutans

Begonia x c. 'Gloire de Lorraine'

Begonia masoniana

Billbergia pyramidalis var. *concolor*

Begonia auriculata

Billbergia leptopoda

Costus speciosus

Calathea makoyana

Codiaeum variegatum

Cordyline terminalis 'Imperialis'

Calathea zebrina

Callisia navicularis

CALATHEA
PEACOCK PLANT

Native to South America and the West Indies, this large genus of plants are grown for their decorative foliage. The long-stalked, mostly upright leaves are usually large with beautiful colourings in shades of green, white, pink, purple and maroon, with contrasting markings. Many leaves have purple undersides. Calatheas require moderate to bright light, but never full sun, and high humidity achieved by misting frequently or standing the pot on a tray of pebbles and water. Clean the leaves with a damp cloth. Do not allow to dry out completely and feed with half-strength fertilizer every 4 to 5 weeks, when conditions are warm and growth is active. A standard potting mix, with sand added to the mix for good drainage, is needed. Repot annually as they exhaust the soil and do not like to be overcrowded. Propagate by division in early spring. These plants are occasionally bothered by aphids, mealy bugs, red spider mites and thrips.

C. makoyana
PEACOCK PLANT

This dwarf species has oval, pale yellow-green leaves with a feathery design of darker green markings. The underside has the same markings in purple.

C. zebrina
ZEBRA PLANT

The large, velvety, floppy leaves on short stems are deep green, marked by parallel stripes or bars of pale chartreuse. The undersides are purplish red. In winter the leaves turn yellow and can be removed to reveal clusters of chocolate brown bracts which are the spring flowers.

CALLISIA
navicularis
syn. Tradescantia navicularis

Grown for its decorative foliage, this low-growing perennial reaches 5–8 cm (about 2–3 in) high and has creeping shoots which root where they touch the soil. Two rows of oval, keeled, reddish green leaves enclose the stem. In summer to autumn/fall clusters of small, stalkless, 3-petalled, pink to purple flowers appear in the leaf axils. Grow in well-drained, moist, fertile soil in full light but not direct sunlight. If grown outdoors it is frost-tender to a minimum of 10–15°C (about 50°–59°F). Propagate from tip cuttings inserted into light compost in mid-spring or summer.

CODIAEUM
variegatum
CROTON

Originally from Malaysia and Polynesia, this tropical, well-known indoor plant is grown for its brilliantly coloured foliage. The glossy, leathery leaves come in a range of shapes and are variegated in red, yellow, pink and orange, with only the new leaves in green. The small flowers are insignificant. It reaches a height of 1–2 m (about 3–6 ft). Grow outdoors only in warm climates in half- to full shade with a minimum temperature of 10–13°C (about 50–55°F). If grown indoors it requires bright light, a moist atmosphere and rich, well-drained soil. Water well during the warm season but allow to dry out between waterings when the temperature is low. To encourage branching, remove tips from very young plants. Repot in spring in a peaty compost. Propagate from stem cuttings in spring or summer. Mealy bug or soft scale can be a problem.

CORDYLINE
terminalis 'Imperialis'
TI TREE, TI PLANT, HAPPY PLANT

From Polynesia, this is the only species of Cordyline not native to Australia and New Zealand. Most plants are started from 'logs', which are small sections of mature branches imported from Hawaii. It resembles a palm with lance-shaped leaves on cane-like stems. The ti tree needs plenty of room indoors to grow to its full height of 2–4 m (about 6–12 ft). It prefers filtered sunlight and needs higher temperatures and humidity than others of the genus. To increase humidity, stand the plant on a tray of pebbles and water, but do not mist the leaves. It can be allowed to dry out in winter, but keep moist during the growing season from spring to autumn/fall. Problems arise from aphids, mealy bugs, scale and thrips. Fluoride in the water or perlite in the potting mix can cause browning of the leaves.

COSTUS
SPIRAL FLAG, SPIRAL GINGER

This genus of clump-forming perennials comprises 150 species scattered throughout the tropics, particularly Asia and South America. They have attractive flowers carried in heads whose bracts are arranged rather like a pine cone. Preferring temperatures above 18°C (about 64°F), they are suitable for planting outdoors only in tropical or subtropical regions, but they make a showy indoor plant. Grow in humus-rich soil in a well-lit position, but not direct sunlight, and a humid atmosphere. It requires an abundance of water. Propagate by division or from seed in spring. Plants grown indoors may be bothered by red spider mite. C. speciosus bear white, sometimes pinkish, flowers with yellow centres.

CRYPTANTHUS
zonatus
ZEBRA PLANT, EARTH STAR

Cryptanthus have earned the name 'earth star' because of the unusual shape of the low-growing rosettes. C. zonatus is a native of Brazil, growing to 10–15 cm (about 4–

6 in) high. The attractive foliage resembles a zebra skin with sepia-green leaves that are wavy edged and banded crosswise with ivory and tannish brown markings. In summer, a cluster of tubular, white flowers appears in each rosette. It is very easy to grow indoors. Grow in a standard potting mix with some sphagnum moss or peat added. Water regularly, maintain humidity and give the plants moderate to bright light. Propagate from offsets which are liberally produced in late spring to summer.

CTENANTHE
lubbersiana
BAMBURANTA

Originally from Brazil, this splendidly marked, foliage plant is an erect, leafy perennial. It produces insignificant flowers. The most commonly grown Ctenanthe, this variegated species grows to 75 cm (about 30 in) or more. The lance-shaped, green leaves are patterned in irregularly shaded bands of pale yellow-green with pale green undersides. The attractive leaves grow on tall, branching stems. Small, white flowers on one-sided spikes are produced intermittently. Grow in a standard potting mix; add coarse sand to aid drainage. A humid atmosphere is important, so mist foliage occasionally. Keep evenly moist and do not allow to dry out completely. Propagate by division or from basal offsets in spring, but do not repot too often as it likes to be crowded. Give bright to moderate light but direct sunlight may cause the leaves to curl. Low humidity may result in poor growth.

CYCLAMEN
persicum
FLORIST'S CYCLAMEN

From the woodlands of the Middle East, this is the most common species grown indoors and is readily available. From the heart-shaped leaves, which are often marbled light and dark green with silver markings, rise waxy flowers in shades of white and pink, sometimes ruffled or edged with a contrasting tone. There is profuse flowering over a long period in winter. Needs high humidity so stand on a tray of pebbles. To continue flowering it must be kept cool at night. Thoroughly water, avoiding getting water in among the bases of the leaves for fear of rot, then let the surface become just dry. In summer leave in the pot but do not water. Repot in autumn/fall in potting mix with a sprinkling of lime and blood and bone; resume watering. Often flowers are not as good after the second year. Susceptible to black root rot.

Cyperus involucratus

Dieffenbachia 'Amoena'

CYPERUS
involucratus
syn. *C. flabelliformis*

Grass-like plants, *Cyperus* come from tropical and subtropical areas. *C. involucratus* grows to about 1 m (about 3 ft) and sends up triangular, hollow stalks crowned by a whorl of leaf-like bracts. The green flower spikes appear in summer. Grow in rich compost and water well by standing the pot in a dish of water. Direct sunlight is tolerated. Repot when the plant fills the container. If the tips brown, the atmosphere may be too dry. A lack of new stems may be due to too little light.

DIEFFENBACHIA
DUMB CANE

These decorative foliage plants from tropical America reach ceiling height when mature. The large, variegated leaves are oval-shaped. Popular indoor plants, they are easy to maintain, provided humidity is maintained by mist spraying, and extremes of temperatures are minimized by keeping them away from windows in winter. Bright to moderate light suits them. Allow the surface soil to become dry in between thorough waterings as root rot may occur if over watered. Propagate in spring or summer from cuttings or stems laid horizontally in compost, but be careful to wash

Cyclamen persicum

Cryptanthus zonatus

your hands. The common name is due to the poisonous sap which causes the mouth and tongue to swell, rendering speech impossible.

D. 'Amoena'
syn. *D. seguine* 'Amoena'

This robust plant of up to 2 m (about 6 ft) has large, sword-like, deep green leaves marked with cream-white bars and blotches along the lateral veins. It has insignificant, greenish white flowers and flourishes in poor light.

Ctenanthe lubbersiana

Drosera capensis

Episcia cupreata

Episcia 'Pink Brocade'

Epipremnum aureum

Dizygotheca elegantissima

Dieffenbachia s. 'Rudolph Roehrs'

D. seguine 'Rudolph Roehrs'
syn. D. seguine 'Roehrsii'

This evergreen perennial grows to a height of 1 m (about 3 ft) or more with a similar spread. It has broadly lance-shaped, finely blotched leaves that grow to 40 cm (about 16 in) in length and are chartreus coloured with mid-ribs and edges in green.

DIZYGOTHECA
elegantissima
syn. Aralia elegantissima
FALSE ARALIA, FINGER ARALIA

An elegant, erect plant from the New Hebrides which can grow to 2 m (about 6 ft) indoors. When young, the leaves are bronze-green changing to a lustrous, dark green with maturity. Between 7 and 10 thin, finger-like leaflets with saw-toothed edges grow from slender, mottled green stems. Grow in an all-purpose soil mix in bright, indirect light with no direct sun. Water well during growing period, and at other times only when the top soil is dry—it is extremely sensitive to the level of moisture in the soil,

developing leaf drop if it is too high. Difficult to propagate, it prefers to be pot-bound; repot every 2–3 years in spring. Susceptible to whitefly, red spider mite and mealy bug. It can be grown outdoors in warm, frost-free climates, where it grows to a 6 m (about 18 ft) tree with coarse adult foliage—very different from the way it looks indoors.

DROSERA
capensis
CAPE SUNDEW

This insect-eating plant grows to 15 cm (about 6 in) with small rosettes of narrow leaves covered in sensitive, red, glandular hairs which secrete fluid. It attracts insects which get stuck to the leaves and are digested by enzyme secretions. In summer there are many small, purple flowers on leafless stems. Frost-tender and delicate to grow, it should be planted in a pot, preferably in a greenhouse, in a mixture of peat and sphagnum moss, standing the pot on a saucer of water. If

grown outdoors plant in the sun in a similar mixture; do not let the soil dry out. Water only with rainwater as it is very sensitive to the impurities found in tapwater. Propagate from seed or by division of rhizomes in spring.

EPIPREMNUM
aureum
syn. Scindapsus aureus
POTHOS, DEVIL'S IVY

This evergreen root climber is sometimes mistaken for a philodendron. It is a fast-growing plant which can be kept in water for months or planted in good, rich, moisture-retentive soil. The apple-green, heart-shaped leaves are marbled with creamy white or gold. It needs bright, indirect light and a humid and draught-free location. Water regularly during spring and summer, less in winter. Pinch out shoot tips to encourage branching. Propagate in late spring from leaf-bud or stem cuttings, which are kept in barely moist soil in a dark position until they have rooted. Poor light may cause a lack of variegation.

EPISCIA

From the jungles of tropical America and the West Indies, this relative of the African violet makes an ideal plant for hanging baskets. The attractive, ornamental leaves cascade from runners down the sides of the pot or basket with, given the right conditions, long-lasting, colourful flowers. Plant in African violet mix or porous, peaty, indoor plant mix in bright light (no

direct sun). They require constant warmth and humidity, so are well suited to a sunny bathroom or glassed area. Keep moist at all times, but take care not to over water as it leads to rotting. Pinch back stems after flowering to encourage branching, and repot every year in spring. Propagate in summer by laying runners in compost, from stem cuttings or by division. Lack of flowers may be due to poor light.

E. cupreata
FLAME VIOLET

This evergreen creeper, native to America, prefers rich, moist soils in a protected, shaded position. It grows to a height of 2 m (about 6 ft). The attractive, felted, bronze leaves have silver veins. This plant intermittently produces tubular, scarlet flowers with yellow centres.

E. 'Pink Brocade'

The runners bear deep, copper-green leaves variegated in silver and pink. Small pink flowers appear in summer but not freely.

FICUS

A genus of great variety, with some of the most reliable and adaptable house plants, grown for their foliage and tropical effect. Their leathery leaves allow them to tolerate a dry atmosphere. They need bright light, but will tolerate low light and an average room temperature and a winter temperature of at least 13°C (about 55°F). Water moderately, keeping moist in the warmer months, and very little when the temperature is low. Over watering may lead to leaf drop. Sponge leaves with a damp cloth. Propagate from stem or leaf-bud cuttings and repot when roots fill the pot, but remember, figs like to be slightly cramped. They are generally pest free, but red spider mite may cause problems.

F. benjamina
WEEPING FIG

This evergreen species can reach 20 m (about 65 ft) high in its native India. It is one of the most popular of all indoor plants with its tree-shaped, weeping habit and attractive, pendulous branches. The slender, elliptical leaves are light green when young, up to 13 cm (about 5 in) long, and turn a glossy green as they mature.

F. elastica 'Decora'
INDIA RUBBER TREE, RUBBER PLANT

One of the most foolproof of all indoor plants, this strong-growing *Ficus* has broad, leathery, glossy, deep green leaves 20–30 cm (about 8–12 in) long. New leaves are encased in rosy pink sheaths that wither and drop, the emerging leaves having a pinkish bronze hue. They can grow to 3 m (about 9 ft) or more and tolerate less light than most plants of this size.

F. lyrata
FIDDLE-LEAF FIG

A handsome indoor plant, particularly when young, it has huge, lustrous, dark green leaves shaped like a fiddle. The leaves are 30 cm (about 12 in) or more long and are prominently veined. It may grow to 3 m (about 9 ft) indoors and will tolerate low light. Older specimens often appear scraggy and need pruning to make the plant bushy.

GESNERIA
cuneifolia
FLORAL FIRE CRACKER

The genus *Gesneria* is native to the islands of the Caribbean and are ideal for growing in terrariums. The dark green leaves with light green underside are spoon-shaped and serrated, and can grow to a length of 15 cm (about 6 in). Bright orange, tubular flowers appear from leaf axils in summer. They like a well-drained, leaf-rich soil, bright light and high humidity. Propagate in spring from leaf cuttings.

GRAPTOPHYLLUM
pictum
CARICATURE PLANT

This evergreen shrub grows to over 1 m (about 3 ft) tall and has oval, pointed, green leaves with yellow variegation in the centre. In spring and summer red to purple tubular flowers appear on terminal spikes. Plant in well-drained, fertile soil in part-shade. It can be grown outdoors in subtropical climates. Give plenty of water when growing in the warmer months and less in cooler weather. It requires temperatures above 16°C (about 61°F). To promote branching, tip prune young plants and cut back hard after flowering. Propagate from semi-ripe cuttings in spring or summer.

GUZMANIA

The plants in this genus of bromeliads are known for their formation of rosettes of smooth leaves and attractive flowers. The long-lasting bracts in red, green or yellow surround a spike of white flowers. Grow in a pot of open, rubble-filled compost. Water moderately during the growing season, less at other times, but always keep the leaf vases filled with water. Propagate in spring or summer from suckers on the parent stem; the original plant usually dies after flowering. *G. lingulata* is the most common of the genus, with basal rosettes of broadly strap-shaped, apple-green leaves growing to a height of 30–45 cm (about 12–18 in). The much showier orange-red bracts surround the clusters of tubular, white to yellow flowers.

HEDERA
COMMON ENGLISH IVY

There are several species of ivy, but the most famous and the only one to thrive indoors is *H. helix*, which is available in many named varieties.

As a trailing plant it makes an excellent hanging basket, but it can also be trained to climb almost any kind of support. It comes in a wide array of leaf shapes and colours. Use an all-purpose potting soil and place in a cool, bright spot. It will tolerate some direct weak sun, and likes extra humidity by misting or placing on a tray of pebbles and water. Keep moist, but not soggy, and do not let the soil dry out completely. In spring, prune to encourage bushy growth. Propagate from stem cuttings or rooted runners. Spider mites, scale, thrips and aphids might be a problem. If the plant is not doing well place outdoors.

H. helix 'Cripsii'
VARIEGATED IVY

There are many cultivars of ivy with variegated leaves, suitable for growing indoors. 'Cripsii' has attractive marblings of dark grey-green with cream; 'Glacier' and 'Gloire de Marengo' are similar in colour. 'Goldheart' is perhaps the best of the green-and-gold cultivars.

Gesneria cuneifolia

Guzmania lingulata

Graptophyllum pictum

Ficus elastica 'Decora'

Hedera helix 'Crispii'

Ficus lyrata

A Field Trip to Fortin de las Flores

The little town of Fortin de las Flores is about a one-day drive east from Mexico City. Set in lush tropical jungle, Fortin is a mecca for bromeliad lovers in general, and more particularly a major native habitat for the epiphytic bromeliad, *Tillandsia ionantha*. This is one of the 'air plants', so-called because they do not use roots to obtain nutrients and appear to survive on nothing but air. The trip to Fortin takes you comfortably along the toll roads that radiate from Mexico City to outlying areas. You will pass through a wide variety of landscapes—green valleys, desert vegetation, mountain country, tropical jungle and pine forests—in abrupt and striking succession.

The toll road following highway F190 and then F150 takes you through the states of Puebla and Veracruz in the heart of Mexico, a region rich in churches and pyramids as well as orchids and bromeliads. On the way you will have the rewarding experience of seeing four of the country's most famous mountains (Popocatepetl, Ixtaccihuatl, Malinche and Orizaba), all snow-capped and in stark contrast to the surrounding jungle.

This route also takes you through the city of Puebla, one of Mexico's oldest and yet most progressive centres. Continuing on past the Tehuacan turn-off, the road climbs the Sierra Madre Oriental mountain range, at an altitude of 2200 m (about 7200 ft), and there are spectacular views of the valley of Acultzingo. At the peak you can find broad leaf air plants of the genus *Tillandsia* thriving in the moist and cloudy

Mexican landscapes vary from desert to jungle to mountainsides.

atmosphere. Soon however, you will quickly descend to an oak forest which is home to the succulents *Echeveria nuda* and coral-beads (*Sedum stahlii*).

If you have time, a side trip to the Tehuacan Valley provides an ideal opportunity for cactus lovers. In areas uncleared by farming you can find many huge cacti colonies of the genera *Opuntia*, *Stenocereus*, *Ferocactus* and *Mammillaria*, and also various *Agave* species. It is also home to some of the drier-growing air plants, including the ball moss (*Tillandsia recurvata*) and several related species.

On the road to Fortin is the home of Dr Alfred Lau, an evangelist and leading world cacti expert whose interests extend to the conservation of orchids, bromeliads, passion flower vines and other tropical plants. A visit to his garden is a must. There you can wander through 1.2 ha (3 acres) of landscaped garden, featuring epiphytes landscaped on to citrus and other trees. A nearby motel, the Posada Loma, is the usual stopping point for bromeliad enthusiasts, as it too has an excellent garden.

The town of Fortin de las Flores is a beehive of people, bars, open-style shops, livestock, and even a resort hotel. The town is surrounded by jungle, and trails run into it from the edges of town. It is possible to walk these trails, starting at the edge of the tropical fruit orchards or roadsides, to study the rich variety of flora, bird life and, occasionally, animals. It is a delight to sit quietly and watch the humming birds feeding from the flowers and you may even catch sight of the elusive toucan or bands of spider monkeys.

In the jungle around Fortin the blushing bride (*Tillandsia ionantha*) can be found growing on the trees both above and in front of you. Fallen branches make the best studies as recently fallen branches will still have plants intact and alive. Usually no more than 5 cm (about 2 in) across, *T. ionantha* grows either singly or in clumps, forming a rosette of fleshy pointed leaves frosted with silver scales. Its common name, blushing bride, refers to the way the leaves turn red when the plant is in bloom, in contrast to the blue of its flowers.

Tillandsias growing on tree trunks in the jungle.

Tillandsia ionantha

Ball moss (*T. recurvata*) grows here too, with other air plants. This small, clumping plant with small blue flowers grows in ball formations on trees, power lines and house roofs. Another air plant that grows in association with *T. ionantha* is Spanish moss (*T. usneoides*), which has long, grey strands and small, scented, green flowers. Its habit of tangling around tree branches makes it popular as bird nest material.

Be careful when examining the larger air plants. They hold quantities of water between their leaves, and a plant tipped on to the ground is likely to reveal cockroaches, salamanders, frogs, spiders and other insects that could sting and bite. As well, watch out for paper wasp nests in the trees as even a slight tap on these can disturb the wasps.

A short trip north on highway F139 will bring you to the town of Huatusco, where *T. ionantha* was first recorded in 1898. The jungle in this area is also home to many beautiful broad leaf air plants including *T. deppeana, T. multicaulis* and *T. lieboldiana,* which has bright red bracts and blue tubular flowers which attract pollinating birds and butterflies. If you study the moss-covered branches you will also find many different orchids, cacti and ferns, as well as various *Columnea* and *Anthurium* species. On the floor of the jungle grow giant *Spathiphyllum* species, including elephant ears, which are used as rain hats by the Indian children. Fruit salad plant (*Monstera deliciosa*) is common in all its trailing and compact forms. The colour-changing chameleon and brightly coloured iguana are among the many lizards seen scuttling across the roads and walking tracks. The jaguar and ocelot, both magnificent cats, can occasionally be spotted in the area.

The best time to visit this area is during the earlier months of the year, when the average temperature is around 18°C (about 64°F), and before the rainy season which lasts from June to September.

The whole region covered in this field trip is botanically very rich, but for those who love bromeliads, particularly the epiphytic ones, the jungle around Fortin is the botanic equivalent of heaven.

Tillandsia

Tillandsias are members of the Bromeliaceae family. With 1500 or more species divided among about 60 genera, the family is almost entirely confined to the Americas, the majority South American.

Tillandsia is the largest bromeliad genus, and it is best represented in Mexico and the adjacent countries. Its over 400 species include the most extreme epiphytes, or 'air plants', which appear literally to subsist on nothing but air. Most tillandsias have leaves clothed in minute silvery scales which behave like sponges, soaking up water from rain or mist and absorbing it into the plant's tissues. The scales also trap dust and fine organic debris, from which the plants derive their nutrient minerals; rainwater also contributes essential nitrogen, converted to soluble form by tropical thunderstorms. Successful cultivation of tillandsias requires high humidity combined with high light levels.

Many new forms of *T. ionantha* are emerging, especially from countries in which they are grown for the commercial horticultural market. Popular for its unusual appearance and its adaptability, *T. ionantha* is exported in huge quantities from Mexico and other Central American countries to satisfy a growing world market.

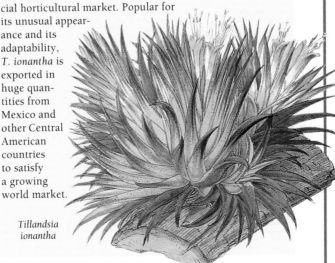

Tillandsia ionantha

Hoya carnosa

Hedera helix 'Pittsburgh'

Hoya bella

Hemigraphis alternata

Nematanthus gregarius

Monstera deliciosa

Maranta leuconeura

H. helix 'Pittsburgh'

syn. H. helix 'Hahn's Self-branching'

A dense, branching plant, this cultivar has closely set, small, deep green leaves.

HEMIGRAPHIS
alternata
RED IVY

This creeping or trailing plant has wonderful foliage of ivy-like, heart-shaped or oblong, deeply puckered, metallic, purplish grey leaves with wine-red undersides and stems. The white summer flowers hardly show at all. Grow in an all-purpose potting mix in bright light, but not direct sunlight. They like average room temperature and humidity. Keep moist and water frequently in the growing season, less in winter. Cut back the spindly stems and pinch off the growing tips to encourage a bushy shape. Propagate from stem cuttings in spring or summer. It is rarely bothered by pests.

HOYA

Twining and/or root climbers with waxy foliage, native to Malaysia, China, India and tropical Australia. They all bear clusters of scented, star-shaped flowers in summer. If the plant is supported on a frame and also slightly pot-bound it is more likely to flower, but may not do so for several years. Plant in any potting soil that drains well, in bright to very bright light, with moderate temperatures and humidity. Allow the soil surface to become quite dry between waterings. As the new flowers come from the same spurs as the old ones it is best not to prune or pick. Propagate from semi-ripe cuttings in summer. Be careful where you place the plant as sticky honeydew drips from the flowers.

H. bella
BEAUTIFUL HONEY PLANT

From India, this shrubby species has pendulous stems and bright green, narrow, lance-shaped leaves. It looks best when grown in a hanging pot or basket where the summer flowers can be easily admired. The star-shaped white flowers, with red or purplish pink centres, hang in flattened clusters.

H. carnosa
WAX PLANT

Native to Queensland, Australia, this twining plant can be grown against a small framework. From summer to autumn/fall, it has dark green, glossy, oval leaves and scented, star-shaped flowers, white to pink in colour and with dark pink centres.

MARANTA
leuconeura var. kerchoviana
RABBIT TRACKS, PRAYER PLANT

Maranta is a genus from tropical America, containing plants grown for their strongly patterned, coloured foliage. Variety *kerchoviana* has oval, light green leaves with brown blotches on either side of the central vein. The insignificant white to mauve flowers appear intermittently. *Maranta* in general are called 'prayer plants' because they fold their leaves into a vertical or upright position, as in prayer, to funnel the condensing dew down to the roots. Grow in humus-rich, well-drained soil, using a shallow container, in moderate to low light. They need even, warm temperature and high humidity, but avoid mist spraying as the leaves are easily marked. Keep continually moist. Propagate from stem cuttings or by division in spring or summer. Dry soil or low humidity may cause browning of leaf tips.

MONSTERA
deliciosa
FRUIT SALAD PLANT, SWISS-CHEESE PLANT

A close relative of *Philodendron* and a native of the West Indies and tropical America, the huge, broad, glossy, perforated and deeply-cut leaves of *M. deliciosa* grow from woody stems with aerial roots. Mature plants bear thick, cream spathes, followed by sweet-smelling, cone-like, edible fruits, that take about a year to ripen, and usually only outdoors. They are easy to grow and adjust to all but the coldest indoor conditions. Plant in an all-purpose mix in large containers with a stout support for the aerial roots. Some roots can be planted back into the container to help support the plant. Requires bright, indirect light and a high degree of humidity. Water when soil is dry to touch, and feed monthly with a soluble plant food during warm conditions. As *M. deliciosa* prefer to be pot-bound, repot every 2–3 years in spring. Prune tops off tall plants to limit growth. The lower leaves will drop, but serious leaf drop may result if the plant is moved or there is a sudden environmental change.

NEMATANTHUS
gregarius
syn. N. radicans, Hypocyrta radicans
CLOG PLANT

A relatively easy to grow, trailing plant, it has closely set, glossy, dark green leaves. The dark yellow or orange flowers look puffy and bloom throughout the year, especially if it is slightly pot-bound. It prefers an African violet potting soil

Nidularium fulgens

Neoregelia carolinae 'Tricolor'

Pedilanthus tithymaloides

mix, and bright light with some cool morning sun. Keep the soil moist and the atmosphere humid by placing on a tray of pebbles and water, or mist frequently. It can be grown outdoors in partial shade but is frost-tender. Mealy bug, red spider mite, whitefly and scale may cause problems.

NEOREGELIA

About 50 species and many varieties comprise this spectacular genus of bromeliads. They produce some of the largest rosettes of colourful, thick, shiny leaves, designed to attract fertilizing insects to the tiny flowers blooming deep within the vase. They need bright light with some direct sunlight to maintain colour, and a humid atmosphere. Water regularly and keep the rosette centres full at all times. Propagate from offsets in spring or summer.

N. carolinae
HEART OF FLAME, BLUSHING BROMELIAD

A spreading rosette of 40–60 cm (about 16–24 in) across, composed of light olive-green, strap-shaped, saw-toothed leaves. Just before flowering, which can be at any time of the year, the youngest, inner leaves turn crimson. The cluster of small, inconspicuous, blue-purple flowers is surrounded by crimson-red bracts. The cultivar 'Tricolor', with cream-striped leaves, is seen more often than the species itself.

N. marmorata

This native of America prefers well-composted, moist, well-drained soils in a protected, partially shaded position. Spreading to 50–60 cm (about 20–24 in), the rosettes of red-tipped, pale green leaves are mottled in reddish brown. White flowers bloom deep in the vase in spring to summer. Propagate from offset division in spring or summer.

NEPENTHES
PITCHER PLANT

These insectivorous plants have adapted leaves which form pendulous, coloured pitchers with lids. Insects are attracted to these and

Peperomia caperata

drown in the liquid in the pitcher before being absorbed into the plant as food. In rainforests, plants climb via tendrils on the leaf ends. They are suitable for hanging baskets in a garden where the minimum temperature is 18°C (about 64°F), or for a greenhouse in a temperate climate. Grow as an indoor plant in moist, fertile soil with peat and moss added, in filtered sun and a very humid atmosphere. Propagate from stem cuttings in spring or summer, or from seed in spring.

NIDULARIUM
fulgens
BIRD'S NEST BROMELIAD

Sometimes called 'friendship plants' and resembling the genus *Neoregelia*, *N. fulgens* has dense rosettes of strap-shaped, saw-toothed, glossy, yellow-green foliage with dark green spots. A rosette of scarlet bracts surrounds the white and violet flowers, which appear mainly in summer. The plant is happy in any open, fibrous mix. Position in an area of bright light for good foliage and colour. Water regularly, keeping the rosettes full at all times. Propagate from offsets in spring or summer.

PEDILANTHUS
tithymaloides
ZIGZAG PLANT, DEVIL'S BACKBONE, JACOB'S LADDER

Popular as a greenhouse plant in Britain in the nineteenth century, this slow-growing succulent from the West Indies, usually grows to about 45 cm (about 18 in). The fleshy, erect stems change direction

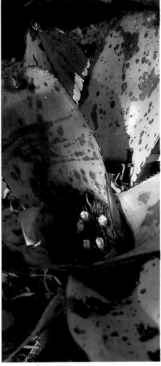

Neoregelia marmorata

at each node, hence the name 'zigzag plant'. Leaves are mid-green and sprout from the stems in two rows, resembling ribs on a backbone. (Variegated cultivars are popular.) Showy red bracts shaped like a bird's head, encase small, scarlet flowers, but such flowers are rarely produced indoors. Water sparingly, allowing the soil surface to dry out between waterings. The plant needs very bright light with some direct sun and a dry atmosphere, so it is well suited to wintering in heated rooms. Propagate from seed or summer cuttings, hardened thoroughly. The stems, when cut, secrete poisonous, milky sap. Mildew may be caused by a humid atmosphere.

PEPEROMIA
RADIATOR PLANT

Most of these small plants come from the tropical rainforests of Central and South America. Ideal in terrariums or dish gardens, they have diverse and beautifully marked and shaped leaves. They produce

Nepenthes, hybrid

long-stemmed spikes of flowers. Well suited to the average home environment, peperomias like bright light (but not direct sun), especially near a window, with high humidity in summer. Keep moist in warm weather, and be sure to water the plants from below as the leaves mark easily; in winter it is best to allow the plants to dry out between waterings. Use a half-strength, soluble fertilizer once a month in spring and summer. Peperomias are easily propagated from leaf or stem cuttings in spring or summer. Repot annually. Watch carefully for mealy bugs, red spider mites and whitefly, which may pester these plants.

P. caperata
EMERALD RIPPLE

From the pinkish stems of this species grow oval, deeply corrugated and veined, dark green leaves. Tight clusters of white flower spikes appear irregularly. It grows to a height of 15 cm (about 6 in) with a similar spread. Propagate from seed or by leaf cuttings.

Pisonia umbellifera 'Variegata'

Philodendron selloum

Peperomia obtusifolia 'Royal Gold'

Philodendron bipennifolium

Philodendron oxycardium

Peperomia 'Sweetheart'

P. obtusifolia
BABY RUBBER PLANT

This is a bushy perennial with fleshy leaves and occasional spikes of minute flowers. The plain green species is a handsome plant growing about 30 cm (about 12 in) tall. More common are the variegated cultivars with the leaves marbled in grey-green and cream or gold. Good light but not direct sun is needed. Cut back if the plants grow straggly and propagate from cuttings.

P. 'Sweetheart'

Typical of the hybrid peperomias, that appear from time to time, 'Sweetheart' is named for its heart-shaped leaves. *P. marmorata*, the silver-heart peperomia, resembles it except that the leaves have silver markings. Both are a shade larger than *P. caperata*.

PHILODENDRON
PHILODENDRON

Shrubs or climbers native to the tropical forests of Central and South America, these are adaptable, strong plants with handsome leaves and a long life expectancy, making them successful and popular indoors. Arum-like flowers are produced on mature plants in optimum conditions. Grow in bright light with a warm, moist atmosphere, as high humidity improves growth. Water when the surface soil dries out and sponge any dust from the leaves. They need support by tying the aerial roots to a stout pole or moss-covered netting. Remove young stem tips to encourage branching. Philodendrons like to be crowded, so do not plant in too large a pot. Most will drop their lower leaves. Propagate from stem or leaf-bud cuttings in summer. They are free from pests and diseases.

P. bipennifolium
syn. P. panduriforme
FIDDLE-LEAF PHILODENDRON

This climber attaches itself to suitable supports by means of aerial roots. A decorative plant, it is unusual for the guitar-like shape of the lobed, bright green leaves. It likes medium light, and in a large pot will grow 2–3 m (about 6–9 ft) tall. Cut back if necessary.

P. oxycardium
syn. P. scandens
SWEETHEART VINE, MONEY PLANT

A rapid climber with glossy, heart-shaped, rich green leaves. It may either grow up a column or trail down. The aerial roots on the trailing stems will attach to anything. This is the most common and popular of the genus.

P. selloum

Officially a climber, but in effect a clumpy perennial with a short stem from which the huge, deeply lobed leaves are carried on stalks 60 cm (about 24 in) or more long. It is a magnificent specimen plant, though as a full-grown specimen it can reach 1.5 m (about 4½ ft) high and wide, a bit big for all but the largest rooms. Several cultivars are available, some smaller than usual, others with variegated leaves, and there are several even larger hybrids of which 'Sao Paolo' is most notable. The flowers are insignificant.

PISONIA
umbellifera 'Variegata'
BIRDCATCHER TREE, MAP PLANT

Known in its native New Zealand as 'Para para', this plant is also found in Australia and neighbouring Norfolk and Lord Howe Islands. The 30–40 cm (about 12–16 in), oval leaves are beautifully patterned in tones of pale to dark green and creamy white, resembling a map (hence the common name). The small, greenish flowers rarely appear indoors. The fruit that forms when grown in its native habitat gave it the other common name of 'birdcatcher tree'. Grow in a standard indoor mix in warm temperature and bright light, but keep out of direct sun, wind or warm draughts. Water freely and regularly during the growing season, but in winter allow to dry out between waterings. Mist the plant, and wipe the leaves with milk and water when dull. To encourage bushing, pinch out the growing tips while the plant is young. Propagate from semi-ripe cuttings in summer.

POLYSCIAS
filicifolia
FERN-LEAF ARALIA, MING ARALIA

P. filicifolia, from tropical Asia and Polynesia, is an unusual house plant with large, 30 cm (about 12 in) long leaves divided into bright green, serrated leaflets. They are not easy to grow as they are fussy plants. Grow in a container of standard peaty mix with sand and a little charcoal added. It needs bright light (but not direct sunlight) and warm temperature—keep away from glass windows in cool climates. Keep humidity high by misting or standing on a tray of pebbles and water, and keep out of draughts. Water freely in summer; keep drier at other times. Feed monthly with half-strength, soluble fertilizer during the warm months. *P. filicifolia* is at its best when the plants are young as the stems tend to grow straggly. These, however, can be cut back in spring. It prefers to be pot-bound so repot only when roots emerge from the pot hole. Propagate from stem-tip or stem-section cuttings in summer. Watch for two-spotted mites and scale.

PROTASPARAGUS
syn. *Asparagus*
ASPARAGUS FERN

These climbers are grown for their foliage. They are related to the asparagus of the kitchen table, but their shoots are too skinny to eat. They need a fertile, well-drained soil. Propagate in spring by division or from seed.

P. densiflorus 'Sprengeri'

This is a sprawling, trailing perennial which grows from small tubers. Its stems grow about 80 cm (about 32 in) long and, being well clad with bright green leaves, they look charming trailing from a hanging basket, despite the occasional sharp thorns. In early spring it bears abundant tiny, white, heavily scented, flowers, usually followed by red berries. Remove spent stems for neatness. Requires good light and regular watering.

P. setaceus
syn. *Asparagus plumosus*

A slender, climbing perennial with leaves divided many times into tiny segments, giving an ultra-ferny appearance. It is very easy to grow, provided it is never allowed to quite dry out and receives good light. Old leaves need to be removed for neatness, and over-long stems can be cut to the base in early spring to encourage new growth. Handle with care as the plant has some hooked and razor-sharp thorns.

SAINTPAULIA
AFRICAN VIOLET

A native of East Africa, saintpaulias were originally collected in the late nineteenth century by Baron von Saint Paul. The several thousand varieties are some of the most popular flowering indoor plants because of their attractive foliage, compact nature, long flowering periods and wide range of flower colours. Although African violets have a reputation for being difficult to grow, given the right conditions this is generally not the case. They do demand certain soil, however, so it is easiest to plant in commercial African violet mix. Constant temperature, moderate humidity and maximum, bright, indirect light will ensure prolonged flowering. In winter this may need to be supplemented with artificial light. Use room temperature water, allowing the surface soil to dry out a little between waterings. Avoid splashing the foliage. Feed once a month in the warm season with half-strength, soluble fertilizer. If the plant is overleafy, flowers may not appear, so remove some of the leaves. African violets prefer to be slightly pot-bound to bloom well, but repot when very leafy and no longer flowering well. They are easy to propagate from leaf cuttings stuck in a layer of pebbles on top of a moist sand and peat mixture, so that leaves do not rot. African violets are vulnerable to attack by cyclamen mite, mealy bug or powdery mildew.

S. ionantha

Ionantha means 'with violet-like flowers' in Greek, and this species has clusters of tubular, 5-lobed, violet-blue flowers of semi-succulent texture, growing on the stems above the leaves. The mid-green leaves, with reddish green undersides, are scalloped, fleshy and usually have a hairy surface. There are thousands of cultivars available, now far removed from the species. The flowers can be single or double, usually 2–5 cm (about 1–2 in) across, and come in shades from white through mauve and blue to purple, and pale and deep pink to crimson. Some cultivars are particoloured and others have ruffled, scalloped or variegated leaves. Named cultivars are available, but they change constantly and most growers simply offer a selection by colour and flower type. Fully grown plants are normally 25 cm (about 10 in) wide.

S. miniature and trailing types

These African violets are derived from crosses of *S. ionantha* and other lesser known *Saintpaulia* species. They can be compact ro-

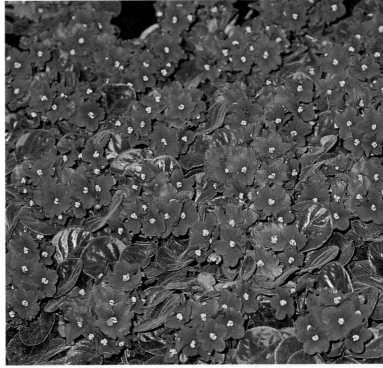

Saintpaulia ionantha

Protasparagus densiflorus 'Sprengeri'

Polyscias filicifolia

Saintpaulia (miniature)

settes, no more than 8 cm (about 3 in) across with leaves and flowers in proportion—effectively miniatures of the *S. ionantha* cultivars and available in the same range of colours—or trailing types, which may develop stems as much as 10 cm (about 4 in) long. The leaves and flowers are equally tiny; some flowers are bell shaped rather than flat. These miniature types have the reputation of being easier to grow than the large ones, but their tiny pots dry out quickly and they do need regular watering.

Protasparagus setaceus

SANSEVIERIA

BOWSTRING HEMP,
MOTHER-IN-LAW'S TONGUE

Native to India, and to southern and tropical Africa, these popular and resilient indoor plants are grown for their stiff, fleshy, patterned 30–60 cm (about 12–24 in) tall leaves. Stems of greenish white flowers appear in late spring if conditions have been warm enough during the previous year. The flowers have a slight fragrance. Grow in standard, indoor potting soil with a deep layer of pot rubble for drainage. For good growth, place in bright light with average house temperature and humidity. Sansevierias look their best, however, when the humidity is high, so mist occasionally. Water enough to moisten the soil but allow to dry between waterings in warm weather and, in cool weather, only enough to prevent the soil drying out completely. Over watering may cause rotting at the base of the leaves and roots. Feed monthly in spring and summer with half-strength, soluble plant food. Repot only when the plant fills the pot. Propagate from leaf cuttings or by division in spring or summer. In Africa the fibres are a source of hemp.

S. trifasciata

From the central rosette emerge stiff, lance-shaped leaves, 60–120 cm (about 24–48 in) long, and 4 cm (about 2 in) or more wide. The dark green leaves are banded with grey-green and yellow. The plant sometimes has racemes of tubular, green flowers but rarely when grown indoors.

S. trifasciata 'Hahnii'

This plant has rosettes of banded, grey and green leaves, and is smaller than the other two sansevierias mentioned.

S. trifasciata 'Laurentii'

The narrow upright leaves resemble *S. trifasciata* but they have broad, yellow margins. It sometimes has pale green flowers. Propagate by division.

SCHEFFLERA

syn. *Brassaia, Heptapleurum*

These attractive, subtropical and tropical trees can grow to 2–4 m (about 6–12 ft) indoors and much taller outdoors. The glossy foliage is split into leaflets. They are easy to grow (but rarely flower) indoors. Plant in a standard indoor potting soil, in bright light but no direct sunlight, with average to warm temperatures. Keep humidity high by misting or placing on a tray of pebbles and water. Water freely when in full growth, less at other times, allowing the top of the soil to dry out between waterings. Feed every 6 to 8 weeks in warmer weather, with soluble plant food. Propagate by taking 10 cm (about 4 in) long stem cuttings from just below the node in early spring. Falling leaves may be due to low temperature or too little water. Usually pest free, but occasionally there are problems with red spider mites, mealy bugs and aphids.

S. actinophylla

QUEENSLAND UMBRELLA TREE

The most common indoor species, its glossy foliage resembles segments of an umbrella. Long green stalks are crested by light green leaves divided into 5 to 16 leaflets, the whole being as much as 50 cm (about 20 in) wide. In summer spikes of small red flowers arise from the top of the tree, but this rarely happens indoors where it usually grows to about 2 m (about 6 ft) tall. If the plant gets too big, cut it back in spring.

S. arboricola

MINIATURE UMBRELLA TREE

This plant resembles *S. actinophylla*, but the leaves are only about 12 cm (about 5 in) wide, and it grows into a bushy shrub approximately 80 cm (about 32 in) tall and wide. It can be cut back if it grows straggly. (Outdoors in tropical climates it becomes a 10 m [about 30 ft] tree.) Variegated-leaved cultivars are available. The insignificant flowers and brown-orange fruit are rarely seen indoors.

S. digitata

This is the only species in the genus native to New Zealand. It has rich green leaves that are shaped like a hand and divided into 5 to 10 oval leaflets. In spring there are tiny greenish flowers followed in autumn/fall by small, globular, dark violet fruit, but this happens rarely indoors.

SERISSA

foetida

From South-East Asia, this evergreen shrub has small, oval, deep green leaves that have an unpleasant smell if they are bruised. From spring to autumn/fall 4- or 5-lobed, funnel-shaped, white flowers appear. Cultivars with double flowers or variegated leaves are available also. It is a most attractive garden shrub for frost-free areas; indoors it needs high humidity and good light. Water moderately when growing and less at other times. After flowering, the shape can be retained by trimming. Propagate from semi-ripe cuttings in summer.

SPATHIPHYLLUM

Most species of this genus come from tropical America, but some are native to Malaysia. They are lush, with dark green, oval leaves that stand erect or arch slightly, and beautiful white, cream or green flowers, resembling arum lilies, that bloom reliably indoors. Grow in loose and fibrous, porous potting soil in filtered light away from the sun. To re-create tropical conditions, increase the humidity by placing the plant on a tray of pebbles and water or mist regularly; sponge any dust from the leaves. Water regularly, keeping the soil moist but not soggy, and allow it to dry out a little in winter. Feed every 4 to 6 weeks with half-strength, soluble fertilizer in spring and summer. Propagate by division in spring or summer. Generally pest free, yellowing of foliage may be caused by too much light.

Schefflera actinophylla

Serissa foetida

Schefflera arboricola

Schefflera digitata

Sansevieria trifasciata 'Laurentii'

Sansevieria trifasciata

Sansevieria trifasciata 'Hahnii'

S. 'Mauna Loa'
PEACE LILY

The leathery, lance-shaped, glossy, mid-green leaves reach lengths of 45–60 cm (about 18–24 in). Oval, white, papery spathes, surrounding white spadices, are borne intermittently, turning green with age. It is the best known of a fairly large number of large-flowered cultivars; others are 'Clevelandii', which is shorter, and 'Aztec'.

S. wallisii
WHITE SAILS

This is a dwarf species with clusters of glossy green, lance-shaped leaves on reed-like stems growing to 30 cm (about 12 in). A white spathe encloses tiny, creamy white spadices of fragrant flowers tightly packed around an upright spike. The colour changes to green with age.

SYNGONIUM
podophyllum
syn. *Nephthytis triphylla*
ARROWHEAD VINE

This plant closely resembles its relative, the climbing *Philodendron*, with its handsome climbing or trailing foliage. It has an unusual feature of changing leaf shape with maturity. The young, arrowhead-shaped leaves on the end of erect stalks become, with age, lobed with 7 to 9 glossy leaflets growing to 30 cm (about 12 in) long. There are several varieties with variegated leaves in cream or pink. Grow in an all-purpose potting soil in a warm moist environment. This species tolerates fairly low to bright light, but no direct sunlight. Water thoroughly, allowing the surface to dry out between waterings. Feed when conditions are warm, every 4 to 6 weeks with half-strength, liquid fertilizer. Propagate from stem cuttings in spring or summer. To encourage branching and more young leaves, pinch off long stems.

TILLANDSIA

This genus contains over 350 species of mainly epiphytic plants. Commonly called 'air plants', these bromeliads are grown for their unusual flowers. The flowers are usually carried on spikes, heads or panicles and range in colour from white to purple and green to red. Plant in well-drained sphagnum moss or they may be grown on slabs of bark or driftwood. They are often positioned high up in hanging baskets in order to catch the rising heat. Mist regularly and water moderately in summer and sparingly at other times. Propagate from offsets or by division in spring to summer.

T. cyanea
PINK QUILL

Dense rosettes of grass-like, arching leaves are usually deep green and often reddish brown when new. In summer to autumn/fall the spectacular, paddle-shaped flowerheads rise on tall stems from among the foliage. They consist of overlapping pink or red bracts with deep violet-blue flowers emerging. This variety needs maximum humidity and is best grown in a compost of tree fern fibre, peat and sand.

T. lindenii

The thin, smooth, pointed, arching leaves with red-brown lines grow in a typical rosette. In autumn/fall a large flower spike of crimson or pink-tinted bracts overlaps dense clusters of pansy-shaped, deep blue or purple-blue flowers arising just above the leaves.

TOLMIEA
menziesii

PICK-A-BACK PLANT, PIGGYBACK PLANT,
MOTHER-OF-THOUSANDS, YOUTH-ON-AGE

Native to the west coast of the USA, this popular house plant is suitable for both pots and hanging baskets. Bright green, hairy leaves that are ivy shaped with toothed edges, send out new plantlets at the junction of the leaf and stalk. There is also a form with variegated leaves. In spring there are spikes of nodding, tubular to bell-shaped, rich brown and green flowers. Hot, dry air can harm these plants so grow in a cool area in bright to moderate light in an all-purpose potting mix. Keep soil moist but not soggy, and water sparingly in winter. Feed every two months in the warmer season with half-strength, soluble fertilizer. Propagate by planting leaf cuttings or plantlets in spring or summer. Frequent attacks by spider mite create brown or brittle leaves, requiring immediate treatment.

Tillandsia lindenii

Syngonium podophyllum

Spathiphyllum 'Mauna Loa'

Tolmiea menziesii

Spathiphyllum wallisii

Tillandsia cyanea

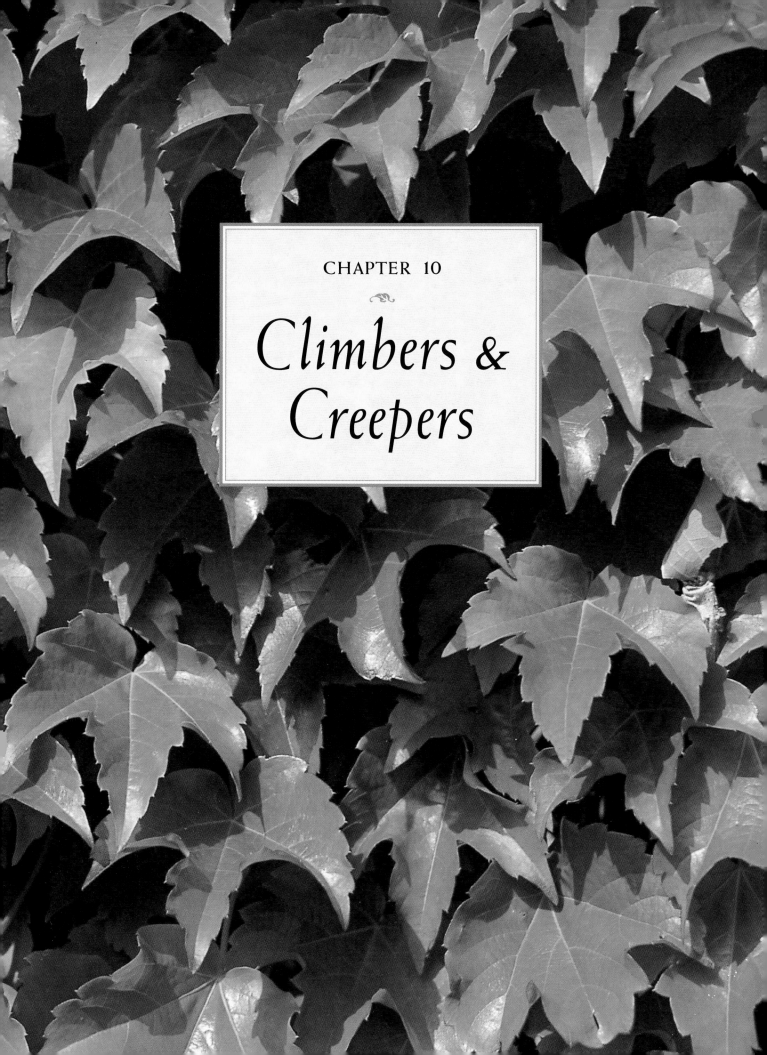

CHAPTER 10

Climbers & Creepers

*T*here's nothing as welcoming as a vine-covered arch over a front gate or a delicate rambler twining its way in and around window shutters to display its perfumed flowers to perfection. In these and other subtle ways climbers play an important role in the overall garden landscape.

By their very nature climbers set out to reach the high spots where there's less competition for light. Some are suited to providing a focal point in a small garden or in a tight spot as they need very little ground or wall space; other more adventurous types will sprawl over a garden shed, camouflaging it in no time. Climbers come mainly from temperate or tropical forests where competition has forced them to evolve various means of ensuring their lax stems reach the light that is essential for manufacturing food. These modifications allow some vines to twine around a host while others have thorns or hooks, tendrils, sucker discs even aerial roots to reach out for an anchorage on supporting plants.

The most common climbing mechanism is simply for a vine to twine; *Pandorea jasminoides*, *Phaseolus caracalla* and the delicate *Sollya heterophylla* are among the most accommodating. All they need is a post or open support such as lattice or a wire frame. Plants with thread-like tendrils such as sweet peas or the wonderful range of clematis need fine supports to allow the slender, modified leaf parts to grip. Those with sucker pads, like parthenocissus, are ideal for solid masonry walls although their position should be chosen with care as the pads will leave unsightly marks on the masonry should they ever need to be removed. *Hydrangea petiolaris*, the climbing hydrangea, and the temperate garden climber *Campsis grandiflora* are two vines which rely on their aerial roots to grip onto a solid surface, as does the true ivy, *Hedera helix*. Be warned though, true ivy is fine contained on walls but its brush-like roots can very soon help in a takeover bid for the complete garden if allowed ground space. The scramblers, like roses and some tropical plants such as bougainvillea, have thorns or hooks by which to hoist their branches even

higher—in a garden with the correct support and a little time spent on training they are docile and most rewarding to grow.

Once these characteristics are known and understood, climbers can be chosen to suit any existing garden situation or be coupled with a new structure to add a wonderful softening effect.

Arbours, Pergolas and Balcony Gardens

Arbours and pergolas are generally firm, solid structures built to last and can take strong growing twiners such as wisteria and the ornamental grapes. Both of these are deciduous, providing shade in summer and allowing the sun to penetrate during the colder months. However, pergolas can be 'double planted' with less vigorous plants to give a combined show. For instance, a delicate, soft look can be achieved by highlighting the single, yellow flowers of the rose 'Mermaid' against the small, starry, white flowers of the dainty potato vine. As well, these delicate twiners can be used on a growing frame such as an established flowering fruit tree and

A climbing rose—the perfect complement to a timber pergola.

when the blossoms synchronize there are few more beautiful sights that a gardener could look forward to.

One of the joys of sitting under a pergola is being able to enjoy the flowers of the covering vine. Those with pendulous sprays such as *Akebia quinata* and *Thunbergia grandiflora* as well as the superb wisterias will certainly delight. However, some other vines will provide a carpet of fallen petals but the flowers remain hidden to all but those looking out from balconies or windows above. For this reason many vines are best grown on a vertical surface such as a trellis or lattice or strands of wire stretched between two vertical posts to form a screen or fence. Here the complete surface area of the plant provides a breathtaking display while taking up very little actual garden space. Aspect needs to be taken into account when growing climbers in this way. In cold areas tender plants can be damaged if frozen tissue is thawed rapidly against a wall receiving early morning sun, while in warmer areas both the last rays of the sun and reflected heat from nearby paved areas can scorch new summer growth on plants which have been trained against a wall.

Often the very reason for choosing to plant a vine against a wall is because it takes up very little space, yet this also could mean the root run is limited. Take care here with soil preparation and fertilizing to provide the best possible conditions for what is to be a feature plant. Often in these conditions, protected by eaves or next to a concrete slab, the climber is best planted away from the house then trained back against it. Then again in cases like this you could consider using a decorative tub filled with a good quality potting mix. Tubs can be used to grow cascading plants like the colourful nasturtiums or dwarf sweet peas with some branches allowed to tumble over the edge while others are trained upwards to camouflage the lower twiggy sections of the main vine.

Many balcony gardens rely solely on tub culture to produce stunning effects with cascading vines and shady canopies. The risk of these tubs overheating and drying out can be greatly reduced by 'mulching' the surface area and sides of the pots with a growing veil. In these often exposed situations care should be taken never to allow the pots to dry out or its contents to become overheated—one cunning method to overcome this is

Clematis montana 'Rubens' provides a spectacular spring display.

to drop a plastic pot containing the plant into a more decorative one so the pot is insulated. Grouping say three or five pots together to generate shade for one another is another way to ensure a successful high-rise or balcony garden.

Soil Preparation and Planting

As most climbers will be permanent, time spent preparing the soil well by digging it over will certainly pay dividends. Like most plants, climbers need good drainage; this is especially important in those pockets against house walls. In these spots it is very often worthwhile to dig deep and wide to unearth any leftover builder's rubble buried just beneath the surface. These positions are often a lot drier than the open garden so be generous with garden compost or animal manure to help with moisture retention.

Pruning

General pruning rules apply equally to climbers as to any other plant. In the very early stage of a climber's growth, finger or tip pruning encourages a single stem to branch out, giving more than one stem to be trained up a trellis—this can become the basis for an informal or stylised espaliered effect say

for a rose growing on stretched wire supports. Then as the climber matures, flowering can be encouraged by pruning; but as in the case of shrubs you have to become aware of the flowering characteristics of your chosen plant. Most will flower at the tips of branches so by pruning at nodes and allowing two or three extra branches to be formed, flowering can be increased. But, it must also be remembered that some vines flower on new or the present season's growth while others take till the next season to produce their blooms, and pruning needs to be carried out keeping this in mind. Of course rambling type roses, for instance, flower on long new canes, and in general these can be cut well back after flowering. However, many of the climbing roses form a permanent mainframe of branches which adhere to horizontal trellising, then each year flowering side shoots appear and in turn these are pruned back to make way for further flowers. Even though they are thorny, roses trained in this way are very easily managed and are very long lived.

If a vine is tied onto a support be sure to check the ties regularly, particularly in the growing season, as they can very easily injure the plant if they become too tight. Vines may take that little bit more of a gardener's time but it is very satisfying to see the end results.

Araujia hortorum

Antigonon leptopus

Akebia quinata

Actinidia chinensis

ACTINIDIA
chinensis
syn. *A. deliciosa*
CHINESE GOOSEBERRY, KIWI FRUIT

Native to China, this deciduous
vine, strong-growing to 9 m (about
27 ft), is valued for its fragrant
creamy flowers in spring and summer, and delicious brown, hairy
fruit which ripen in autumn/fall.
The vine is attractive, with large
velvety leaves and red, hairy stems.
It is extremely vigorous and requires a strong trellis, pergola, wall
or fence to support it. Plant both
male and female vines, or a grafted
bisexual vine, to produce a fruit
crop. It is frost-hardy, but needs
warm summers to ripen the fruit.
Grow in deep, well-drained, humus-rich soil, in a warm, fairly
frost-free position sheltered from
hot drying winds. Prune early in
winter before new growth begins.
A. kolomitka is similar in habit but
grown for its pink and white variegated leaves rather than its fruit.

AKEBIA
quinata
FIVE-LEAF AKEBIA, CHOCOLATE VINE

Deciduous (or semi-evergreen in
warm areas), this decorative, twining climber from China is grown for
its attractive habit, leaves and flowers. The grey-green leaves are divided into 5 leaflets and fragrant,
purple-mauve, drooping flowers
appear in late spring. Male and
female plants are needed for the
female plants to produce interesting
sausage-shaped, edible fruit in mild
climates. Fully hardy, the plant
likes full sun, good drainage and

Allamanda cathartica

plenty of water during summer. It
will grow to 10 m (about 30 ft) or
more and requires a strong support.
Prune after flowering and cut down
to the base every 3 or 4 years to
remove tangled growth. Propagate
from cuttings or by layering in
spring.

ALLAMANDA
cathartica
GOLDEN TRUMPET VINE

Native to South America, this vigorous, evergreen climber, fast-growing
to 5 m (about 15 ft), bears large,
yellow, trumpet-shaped flowers up to
12 cm (about 5 in) across in summer.
It has whorls of lance-shaped leaves
and makes a luxuriant cover for
walls and strong fences in frost-free
areas. It is frost-tender. Grow in full
sun or partial shade in humus-rich
soil and water well during the growing period. Regular tip pruning
improves its appearance. Propagate
from softwood cuttings in spring
and summer, and watch for two-

spotted mite. It will take heavy
pruning and can be grown in a large
container.

AMPELOPSIS
brevipedunculata var.
maximowiczii
syn. *A. heterophylla,*
Vitis heterophylla
TURQUOISE-BERRY VINE

This vigorous, deciduous climber
will twine with the aid of tendrils
5 m (about 15 ft) or more. It has
grape-like, lobed leaves, small
greenish flowers in summer, and in
autumn/fall bunches of berries like
miniature grapes that ripen from pale
green to turquoise, bright blue and
violet. Grow in a sunny or partially
shaded position in a moisture-retentive, but well-drained soil. It is fully
hardy. It grows rapidly and needs
strong support and plenty of room to
spread. Cut back hard to the main
branches when berries have finished.
Propagate from cuttings in summer or
by layering in autumn/fall.

Ampelopsis brevipedunculata var.
maximowiczii

ANTIGONON
leptopus
CORAL VINE, CHAIN OF LOVE

A dainty, fast-growing, showy
creeper that climbs by tendrils and
may grow to 7 m (about 21 ft) or
more. It bears masses of deep pink,
heart-shaped flowers from early
summer to autumn/fall and is easily
grown in warm, frost-free areas. In
cool areas it can be grown as a summer-flowering annual. The plant
does best in a sunny situation in
well-drained, fertile soil. Keep well
watered during spring and summer.
It is ideal for trellises, pergolas and
arbours where a light cover is desirable. Remove spent flowerheads and
cut out old twiggy growth in early
spring. Propagate from seed sown in
spring or from cuttings in late spring.

ARAUJIA
hortorum
syn. *A. sericofera*
CRUEL PLANT, KAPOK VINE

An evergreen twining vine growing
to 7 m (about 21 ft) with broad,
heart-shaped, scented, white
flowers in late summer and green,
pointed seed pods which contain
numerous silky seeds. It is half-hardy,
and thrives in a rich, well-drained soil
in a sunny position. A native of Peru,
this species has become a weed in
warm climates, particularly in South
Africa. The seeds, thought to be
poisonous to poultry and dogs, germinate readily and should be removed and disposed of carefully to
prevent the plant from becoming
invasive.

ARISTOLOCHIA

BIRTHWORT, DUTCHMAN'S PIPE

This large genus of over 500 species comprises evergreen and deciduous, tender and hardy climbing and herbaceous perennials, native to many different climatic regions. The climbers are most often cultivated, chosen for their cordate leaves and unusually shaped flowers, which have a globe-shaped swelling at the base and a hood above. Insects are attracted into the mouth of the flowers by a strong scent, and pollen is scattered over their bodies. The plants require well-drained, humus-rich soil in a sunny position with some shade in summer, and support for their climbing habit. In spring, prune the previous year's growth to 2 to 3 nodes. Propagate from seed in spring or from semi-hardwood cuttings in summer. Watch out for two-spotted mite and whitefly.

A. durior

syn. *A. macrophylla, A. sipho*
DUTCHMAN'S PIPE

A native of North America, this deciduous species is hardy and will climb to at least 7 m (about 21 ft). Fast growing, it needs support for its climbing stems. Its mid-green cordate leaves are large and attractive, and the brown, yellow and green flowers, up to 3 cm (about 1½ in) long, appear in early summer. Initially tubular, the 3-lobed flower opens to a mouth that is purple-brown in colour.

A. elegans

CALICO FLOWER

This creeper, fast-growing to 6 m (about 18 ft), is native to Brazil and needs high humidity and protection from frost. It has fleshy, heart-shaped leaves and in summer, bears strangely shaped, maroon flowers with white, thread-like markings. Plant in humus-rich, well-drained soil in a partially shaded position. An interesting plant for verandah columns or a pergola. Propagate from semi-ripe cuttings in late summer, or seed in spring. It can be grown as an annual in cool climates.

ASARINA

erubescens

CLIMBING SNAPDRAGON

This dainty, semi-evergreen climber has velvety, heart-shaped leaves and bears pink, tubular flowers resembling snapdragons in late spring and early summer. It has twining stems up to 3 m (about 9 ft) tall and adapts well to hanging baskets and window boxes. Moderately frost-hardy, it requires full sun, good drainage and regular watering in summer. Easily propagated from seed in spring.

Aristolochia elegans

BEAUMONTIA

grandiflora

HERALD'S TRUMPET

This beautiful, large, woody, evergreen climber growing to 8 m (about 24 ft) needs strong support for its thick twining stems. It is valued for its large, fragrant, white, trumpet flowers, which appear in late spring and summer, and handsome, deep green leaves. Frost-tender, it is best suited to subtropical areas, but it can also be grown in a protected position in warm-temperate districts. Soil should be deep and fertile with good drainage. It requires full sun and regular watering in summer. Prune immediately after flowering. Propagate from cuttings in late summer.

BIGNONIA

capreolata

syn. *Doxantha capreolata*
CROSS VINE, TRUMPET FLOWER

This genus consists of the one species, a climber that is evergreen in all but the coldest regions where it may lose its leaves in winter. Climbing by tendrils, it can reach a height of 10 m (about 30 ft). The leaves are made up of 2 slender, oblong leaflets, together with a tendril. The summer clusters of trumpet-shaped flowers are orange to red, followed in autumn/fall by pod-like fruit up to 15 cm (about 6 in) long. Plant in a sunny site in well-drained, humus-rich soil for a good display of blooms. If pruning is necessary, this should be done in spring. Propagate from semi-hardwood or hardwood cuttings in summer or autumn/fall or by layering in winter.

BOMAREA

caldasii

syn. *B. kalbreyeri*
CLIMBING ALSTROEMERIA

This attractive, evergreen, twining climber to 3 m (about 9 ft) bears large clusters of bright orange, pendulous bell flowers in summer. Grow in well-drained, humus-rich soil and water regularly in summer. Half-hardy, it is ideal for a warm, environment in a sunny or partially shaded position. It needs strong

Bomarea caldasii

Asarina erubescens

Bougainvillea glabra

support and will form an attractive dense screen on a fence or trellis. Cut back hard after flowering to encourage fresh growth. Propagate by division of underground stems in early spring.

BOUGAINVILLEA

BOUGAINVILLEA

Native to South America, bougainvilleas are valued for their glorious, flamboyant flowers and their ability to cover a large area. There is a large range of different kinds and colours to choose from, but all do best in warm to hot climates in full sun. They are evergreen in the tropics, but may be deciduous in cooler climates. The flowering period is early spring and can extend well into autumn/fall. The true flowers are insignificant, but the surrounding bracts are brilliantly coloured, often changing colour or shade as they age. Only water when needed and do not over fertilize, particularly with nitrogen as this will produce luxuriant leaf growth but very little in the way of

Beaumontia grandiflora

Bougainvillea 'Hawaiian Gold'

Bougainvillea 'Scarlett O'Hara'

colourful bracts. Bougainvilleas need strong support for vigorous growth, but can be controlled by pruning after flowering, when rampant plants can be ruthlessly cut back without harm. Flowers appear on the new wood. Propagate from semi-hardwood cuttings any time in summer. With regular heavy pruning, they can be grown in large containers.

B. glabra

This is the parent of several varieties. A vigorous shrubby vine growing to 10 m (about 30 ft), with masses of bright purple floral bracts in spring and summer.

B. 'Hawaiian Gold'

A rather frost-tender, evergreen cultivar that will reach up to 7 m (about 21 ft). Floral bracts are a magnificent shade of orange-gold.

B. 'Scarlett O'Hara'

A fast-growing, free-flowering cultivar growing to 8 m (about 24 ft), with spectacular sprays of rosy crimson bracts in summer.

Campsis grandiflora

Celastrus scandens

Celastrus orbiculatus

Cissus antarctica

Campsis × tagliabuana

B. spectabilis

A strong and fast-growing species from Brazil, this plant is mainly evergreen and can grow to 7 m (about 21 ft). It can also be grown in a pot where, with hard pruning, its height can be kept to a manageable 3 m (about 9 ft). Its dark green leaves are oval with fine hairs and the showy bracts, which appear in summer in large panicles, are a deep red. There are several cultivars available.

CAMPSIS

TRUMPET CREEPER, TRUMPET VINE

This genus contains two species of deciduous root climbers that used to be part of the *Bignonia* and *Tecoma* genera, but are now differentiated because of the leaf shape—the leaves have between 7 and 11 leaflets, arranged oppositely in pairs. Originally from the temperate regions of the northern hemisphere, the plants are grown for their orange-scarlet, trumpet-like flowers which appear in summer. While frost-hardy they require a sunny

site, preferably with some shelter, with well-drained soil. They will need to be watered in summer. They can be propagated in winter from root or hardwood stem cuttings or by layering, and in summer from semi-hardwood cuttings. Established plants should be pruned hard in late winter or early spring, removing the previous season's flowering wood to within 5 cm (about 2 in) of the ground.

C. grandiflora
syn. *C. chinensis,
Bignonia grandiflora*
CHINESE TRUMPET CREEPER

This vigorous, woody-stemmed climber from China will reach up to 10 m (about 30 ft) with the aid of aerial rootlets clinging to a support. Deciduous and fast-growing, it produces eye-catching clusters of trumpet-shaped scarlet to orange flowers, up to 10 cm (about 4 in) long, in late summer and autumn/fall. Only just frost-hardy, it requires full sun in a well-drained, humus-rich soil. Water generously during the growing season. Prune in

spring and propagate from semi-ripe cuttings taken in summer, or from layers or suckers.

C. radicans
syn. *Bignonia radicans,
Tecoma radicans*
TRUMPET HONEYSUCKLE, TRUMPET VINE

Originating in North America, this species will grow to 13 m (about 40 ft) in a sunny site. It prefers light to medium, well-drained soils with a plentiful water supply. Its pale green pinnate leaves are roughly toothed and felt like underneath, and the terminal clusters of orange-scarlet, trumpet-like flowers, up to 8 cm (about 3 in) long, appear in late summer or early autumn/fall.

C. × tagliabuana

This hybrid between *C. grandiflora* and *C. radicans* will grow to 10 m (about 30 ft). Its leaves are light green, and it is best known in its cultivar 'Madame Galen', which bears prolific clusters of salmon red, pendent, trumpet-shaped flowers up to 8 cm (about 3 in) long in late summer or early autumn/fall. Propagate from semi-ripe cuttings in summer or by layering in winter.

CELASTRUS

This genus consists of 30 species of deciduous shrubs and woody climbers which are grown mainly for their unusual and striking fruits. Native to Asia and North America, the climbers can reach 10–14 m (about 30–45 ft) in height. The most commonly grown species carry the male and female flowers on separate plants, so one of each sex must be grown to produce the brilliantly coloured fruits. They are an excellent choice to cover an old tree stump or grow over a wall as they will need support. Plant in well-drained soil in full sun or partial shade any time from autumn/fall to spring. Plants will benefit from a spring pruning of old wood and a general tidy-up, and from an occasional feed. Propagate from seed or by layering in spring, or from cuttings in summer and autumn/fall.

C. orbiculatus
syn. *C. articulatus*
ORIENTAL BITTERSWEET

From China, this deciduous, vine-like climber is valued for its brilliantly coloured red and gold, pea-like berries which are retained through winter. Grow in humus-rich, moisture-retentive soil in sun or partial shade and provide good, roomy support for the twining stems as they can reach 6 m (about 18 ft) or more. It is fully hardy. Pruning is only necessary to maintain shape, and is best done in late winter. Propagate from root cuttings or layering in autumn/fall, or from seed sown in spring.

C. scandens
AMERICAN BITTERSWEET, STAFF TREE

Native to North America and growing to 10 m (about 30 ft), this twining, frost-hardy climber has alternate oval leaves up to 10 cm (about 4 in) long. The insignificant, star-shaped, green-yellow flowers have 5 petals and appear in summer in small clusters. These are followed by bunches of pea-like fruits which split into three, revealing orange insides and bright red seeds. The fruit can persist on the plants well into winter. It is necessary to grow one specimen of each sex or a self-fertile plant otherwise the fruits, which are the main attraction of this climber, will not appear.

CISSUS

antarctica

KANGAROO VINE

This vigorous inhabitant of Australian rainforests is grown for its handsome, rich green, oval leaves and its ability to cover large areas. When given support, it will climb by tendrils up to 5 m (about 15 ft) or more in the garden. Without support it will effectively scramble over rocky slopes and banks. This plant grows well in partial shade or full shade in humus-rich, well-drained soil with some water retention. It is frost-tender and in cool areas can be grown as a house plant, as it will accept reasonably dark situations. Regular pruning improves its appearance. Propagate from stem cuttings or fresh seed. In warm areas it can be used as a ground cover, although it tends to climb any tree or shrub within reach.

CLEMATIS

VIRGIN'S BOWER, TRAVELLER'S JOY

The generally woody climbers of this romantic genus are from moist temperate regions of the world, but nearly all the popular, larger-flowered garden plants have come from Japan and China. They climb by twisting their tendrils about a support and are a lovely choice for training on verandah posts, arbours, bowers and trellises. Showy, bell-shaped or flattish flowers with 4 to 6 petals are followed by masses of fluffy seed heads, often lasting well into winter, which inspired the common names. The most important requirement for successful cultivation is a well-drained, humus-rich, permanently cool soil with good moisture retention. The plants like to climb up to the sun with their roots in the shade. Prune old, twiggy growth in spring and propagate from cuttings or by layering in summer. In some areas where clematis is a problem, plants are often grafted.

Clematis 'Duchess of Edinburgh'

Clematis 'Lasurstern'

Clematis recta var. mandshurica

C. armandii

A vigorous evergreen climber from China, this clematis can grow to 8 m (about 24 ft) and spread twice as wide. Its lustrous deep green, trifoliate leaves have ovate-lanceolate leaflets with marked veining. The fragrant white flowers of this early-flowering species are saucer shaped, around 6 cm (about 2½ in) wide, and appear in spring. Although frost-hardy this species will need a protected site, preferably facing the sun.

C. 'Duchess of Edinburgh'

This early, large-flowered clematis grows to a height of 2–3 m (about 6–9 ft). It produces double white flowers with yellow anthers and green outer petals in summer. Frost-hardy. Be aware that it may sometimes be weak growing.

C. 'Jackmanii'

Produced in 1862, this is still the most popular large-flowered cultivar. It will climb up to 3 m (about 9 ft), and produces spectacular purple flowers, 15 cm (about 6 in) across, in summer and autumn/fall. It is deciduous and fully hardy.

C. 'Lasurstern'

A beautiful, large-flowered cultivar with semi-double, lavender-blue flowers in late spring and early summer. It will reach up to 3 m (about 9 ft) and is fully hardy.

C. montana

This vigorous, deciduous species from the Himalayas will reach up to 10 m (about 30 ft) or more. It bears prolific, sweetly perfumed, pure white flowers with yellow anthers in clusters in late spring. Fast-growing and fully hardy, it is ideal for covering a small shed or wall. It was introduced to England in 1831 by Lady Amherst, wife of the Governor-General of India. *C. m.* 'Rubens' is a popular pink form. Prune hard after flowering.

C. recta var. mandshurica

A native of Europe, this perennial creeper grows to 1 m (about 3 ft). The white flowers occur in stiff, upright, terminal umbels, while the fruit are dark brown, smooth, compressed seeds with long, yellowish tails. Plant in a protected, partially shaded position in moist, rich soil.

C. tangutica

LEMON PEEL CLEMATIS

This long-flowering species from China grows up to 6 m (about 18 ft). It bears curious, nodding, lantern-shaped flowers, with clear yellow 'thick-skinned' petals, in summer and early autumn/fall. The flowers are followed by decorative silky seed heads. Grow in humus-rich soil in a protected, partially shaded position. It is frost resistant but drought-tender.

C. viticella

VIRGIN'S BOWER

A deciduous species from southern Europe which is a sub-shrub with a bushy habit, this climber can reach 4 m (about 12 ft). Its dark green pinnate leaves have ovate, sometimes lobed, leaflets and the nodding, bell-shaped violet or purple flowers appear in late summer and autumn/fall. The plant dies back in

Clematis tangutica

Clematis 'Jackmanii'

winter and should be pruned to within 60 cm (about 24 in) of the ground. This species is the parent of many beautiful hybrids, including 'Abundance', light pink-purple; 'Alba Luxurians', white with a mauve tinge and dark anthers; 'Kermesina', deep crimson-purple; and 'Mme Julia Correvon', burgundy red twisted petals.

CLITORIA

ternatea

BUTTERFLY PEA

A lovely evergreen twining up to 4 m (about 12 ft), with slender stems and fresh green leaves divided into 3 or 5 oval leaflets. Large, dark blue, pea-like flowers with yellow centres bloom in summer, followed by flat pods. There is also a double-flowered form. It is frost-tender, growing best in full sun in warm, sheltered sites in humus-rich, well-drained soil. Provide good support for twining stems and thin out growth with annual spring pruning. Propagate from cuttings in summer or from seed.

Clematis montana

Clitoria ternatea

Clytostoma callistegioides

Combretum bracteosum

Distictis buccinatoria

Dolichos lablab

Ficus pumila

CLYTOSTOMA
callistegioides
VIOLET TRUMPET VINE

This evergreen creeper native to
tropical South America is grown for
its showy, trumpet-shaped flowers.
Fast-growing and densely foliaged, it
climbs to 4 m (about 12 ft) by means
of tendrils and needs good support.
In late spring and summer the pale
lavender flowers with purple streaks
are carried atop long, drooping
stems, making it ideal for training
over fences and tall tree stumps in
warm areas. Half-hardy, it prefers a
sunny position, humus-rich soil,
good drainage and regular watering
in summer. It is frost-tender. Thin
out less vigorous canes after flowering. Propagate from cuttings taken
in summer.

COMBRETUM
bracteosum
HICCUP NUT

This climbing, evergreen shrub is
native to South Africa, growing to a
height and spread of over 3 m
(about 9 ft). It has smooth, dull
green leaves which are paler underneath, and in summer, bears a profusion of orange-red flowers with
rounded heads. The nutty fruit that
follows is said to either cause or cure
hiccups. Frost-tender, it does best in
full sun, in a rich, well-drained,
composted soil, with frequent watering in summer. It is ideal as a wall
climber or cascading down a bank.

DISTICTIS
buccinatoria
syn. *Phaedranthus buccinatorius*
MEXICAN BLOOD FLOWER, CHERERE

A native of Mexico, this half-hardy,
evergreen, woody climber reaching
5 m (about 15 ft) bears large clusters of trumpet flowers in bright
shades of red in early spring and
summer. This vigorous vine clings
with tendrils to surfaces such as
rough brick and stone. It grows best
in sun or semi-shade in fertile, well-
drained soil and needs regular watering in summer. Prune in spring.
Propagate from softwood cuttings in
early summer.

DOLICHOS
lablab
syn. *Lablab purpureus*
HYACINTH BEAN

This deciduous, twining plant with
a spread of about 6 m (about 18 ft)
is often grown as an annual for
quick cover to hide unattractive
fences, walls and sheds. Frost-
tender, it will die down in winter. It
is easily grown in full sun in any
well-drained soil. Pink to mauve pea-
like flowers appear from early summer to autumn/fall, followed by many
large seed pods which can make the
plant unsightly. The plant can be
removed and easily replaced by sowing the seed in late winter; in other
words, growing it as an annual. In
some parts of the world it is grown as
a forage or green manure crop.

ECCREMOCARPUS
scaber
CHILEAN GLORY FLOWER

This native of Chile and Peru is a
lightweight, sub-shrubby tendril
climber grown for its attractive
flowers, blooming over a long season from summer into autumn/fall.
It is evergreen, with dainty leaves and
racemes of small, orange-red, tubular
flowers, followed by fruit pods containing winged seeds. Grows sparsely
to a height of 2–3 m (about 6–9 ft).
Half-hardy, it can be grown as an
annual in areas prone to frost. It
grows best in full sun in a light, well-
drained soil. Keep moist during the
growing season and support with
small sticks until attached to the main
trellis. Propagate from seed in early
spring.

FICUS
pumila
CREEPING FIG

From Japan and China, this decorative creeper is a useful evergreen
climber for covering walls or fences.
It clings by aerial roots along the
stems and, although often slow to get
started, it later grows very vigorously.
It has small, bright green, heart-
shaped juvenile leaves and a neat
habit. Young growth is an attractive
bronze. Remove any mature woody
branches that stand out from the
support to retain juvenile leaves. Half-
hardy, it is best grown in full sun or
semi-shade in a well-drained, fertile
soil. Propagate from semi-hardwood
cuttings. A tiny-leaved form, *F. p.*
'Minima', is less rampant.

GELSEMIUM
sempervirens
CAROLINA JASMINE

A well-behaved, evergreen twiner
with glossy green leaves and
fragrant, yellow trumpet flowers,
which appear for many months in

spring and again in autumn/fall. Half-hardy, it likes a sunny, warm, sheltered position and a fertile, well-drained soil. It grows quickly but tidily to 3 m (about 9 ft) and can be trained on fences, walls, or a pergola near the house, where the perfume can be enjoyed. All parts of the plant are poisonous and should be kept away from children. Thin out older growth after flowering. Propagate from semi-hardwood cuttings in summer.

HARDENBERGIA
violacea
syn. H. monophylla
PURPLE CORAL PEA, FALSE SARSAPARILLA

Used as a ground cover for scrambling over banks or as a climber when given support, this beautiful twining plant from Australia can grow under adverse conditions. It will withstand dry conditions, some frost and will grow in most soils with good drainage. Semi-shade or a fairly sunny position is preferred. Lovely sprays of purple pea flowers are borne in spring. Propagate from presoaked seed. H. comptoniana is similar, with slightly larger, pale flowers. It has a pink form also.

HEDERA
IVY

Useful for enhancing many a situation, ivies have long been well-loved, hardy evergreen creepers. Their firmly clasping habit was once considered a lucky love charm. They can be used for ground cover, clothing walls and fences, covering tree stumps and arches, growing up pillars and posts, edging borders and masonry work, trailing from containers and as indoor specimens. In sun or shade they are adaptable to a wide variety of conditions, soils and climates. Regular pruning is recommended so that the attractive, lobed juvenile leaves are retained and no flowers are produced. If the mature growth (which produces tiny green flowers in autumn/fall, followed by black berries) is struck as cuttings, the resultant plants remain as shrubs. This is called 'arborescent ivy'. Propagate from cuttings or rooted stems. The charming fashion of ivy topiary has been revived and wire topiary frames are now available in many garden centres. As the ivy grows over the shape the sideshoots are regularly clipped to produce a dense cover.

H. canariensis 'Variegata'

A handsome, popular ivy with broad, leathery leaves, dark green in the middle shading to silver-grey and bordered with cream or white. Some leaves are completely white or cream. This slightly frost-tender ivy is particularly showy and looks good covering large areas of walls or fences.

H. helix
ENGLISH IVY, COMMON IVY

This fully hardy species will produce a dense, dark green cover. It is often used as a ground cover in shade where grass has difficulty thriving, and is also excellent for climbing up walls and hiding paling fences. There are innumerable named varieties with unusually shaped and/or variegated leaves. They are often grown as house plants.

HIBBERTIA
scandens
GUINEA FLOWER, GUINEA GOLD VINE

A native of Australia, this soft twining climber or trailing plant can grow up to 4 m (about 12 ft) high or be trained along the ground as an effective ground cover. It has broad, dark green leaves and large, showy buttercup yellow flowers from spring through the warmer months. Any moderately fertile, well-drained soil is suitable. It will grow in full sun or semi-shade and is a good choice for sandy, coastal gardens, as it tolerates salt spray. Half-hardy, it is ideal for warm climates. Lightly prune to shape in spring and propagate from semi-ripe tip cuttings in late summer.

HYDRANGEA
petiolaris
syn. H. anomala subsp. petiolaris
CLIMBING HYDRANGEA

This deciduous, self-clinging climber grows up to 15 m (about 50 ft) or more and bears beautiful, flattened heads of small white flowers in summer. It has oval, finely toothed leaves, and is fully hardy. Plant in humus-rich, well-drained moist soil in full sun, with some protection from hot afternoon sun, and water regularly in summer. Propagate from semi-hardwood cuttings in summer. Prune after flowering, trimming close to the support.

Hedera canariensis 'Variegata'

Hydrangea petiolaris

Hibbertia scandens

Hedera helix

Gelsemium sempervirens

Hardenbergia violacea

IPOMOEA
MORNING GLORIES

Care should be taken when choosing these ornamental climbers, as some rampant species can become extremely invasive in warm districts. Native to tropical and warm-temperate regions, most species have a twining habit and masses of funnel-shaped flowers which are at their best in the early morning. Half-hardy to frost-tender, they are best suited to warm coastal districts or tropical areas. Any moderately fertile, well-drained soil is suitable and they prefer a sunny position. These plants are useful for covering sheds, fences, trellises and banks. They may also be grown in pots. Propagate in spring from seed which has been gently filed and presoaked to aid germination, or from cuttings.

I. alba
syn. *Calonyction aculeatum*
MOON FLOWER

From tropical America, this fast-growing, soft-stemmed, perennial

vine grows up to 7 m (about 21 ft) and is cultivated for its large, white, fragrant flowers, 15 cm (about 6 in) across, which open at night during summer. It is frost-tender, but is easily grown as an annual in cool areas.

I. nil
syn. *I. imperialis*

This soft-stemmed, twining perennial is short lived and so is best treated as an annual. Half-hardy, it grows to 4 m (about 12 ft). Its stems are covered with hairs, and the leaves are cordate. The large, trumpet-shaped flowers appear from summer through to early autumn/fall, in a variety of shades. 'Scarlett O'Hara' is a cultivar with dark crimson blooms.

I. quamoclit
syn. *Quamoclit pennata*
CYPRESS VINE

An annual climbing vine that is half-hardy, this species can grow to 4 m (about 12 ft) when planted in a warm, sheltered site. Of tropical

origin, its bright green leaves are ovate and finely dissected. The narrow, orange and scarlet tubular flowers are produced from summer to early autumn/fall.

I. tricolor
syn. *I. violacea, I. rubrocaerulea*
MORNING GLORY

This Mexican climbing perennial is half-hardy and is more often grown as an annual. It can reach a height of 3 m (about 9 ft), with a spread of 1.5 m (about 4½ ft). The cord-like, twining stems hold cordate, light green leaves. The large blue to mauve flowers open in the morning—hence the common name—and gradually fade during the day. They are funnel shaped, widening to a trumpet as they open, and can reach 12 cm (about 5 in) across. They appear continually throughout summer and into early autumn/fall. This species will need a sheltered, sunny site.

JASMINUM
JASMINE

These mostly woody stemmed, climbing plants are valued for their showy, fragrant flowers. Most like a sunny or lightly shaded position with a moderately fertile, well-drained soil. They must have adequate water during spring and summer. Some species are easily propagated by layering, others can be raised from semi-ripe cuttings in summer. The flowers of some species are used in making essential oils for perfume.

J. officinale
COMMON JASMINE, POET'S JASMINE

Introduced to Europe from the East during the Tudor period, this vigorous, deciduous or semi-evergreen climber can reach up to 9 m (about 27 ft) high. Sweetly fragrant, white flowers are borne in terminal clusters throughout summer and autumn/fall. It is moderately frost-hardy. Elizabethan poets referred to its common use on arbours, and it also provides beautiful covering for pergolas, arches, bowers or trellises.

J. polyanthum

This vigorous, scrambling, woody-stemmed evergreen climber from China is fast-growing but tender and easy to grow in mild climates only. In cool areas it makes a pretty pot plant. Very fragrant, white flowers with pink buds are produced in spring. It has dark green leaves composed of 5–7 leaflets. It grows to 6 m (about 18 ft) and requires a good pruning after flowering to keep tidy and under control.

KADSURA
japonica

Valued for its bright red berries in autumn/fall, this evergreen, twining climber grows up to 3 m (about 9 ft) tall. It has attractive, rich green, oval leaves and lightly perfumed, small, cream flowers in summer. Fully hardy, this plant does best in semi-shade in a well-drained soil. Male and female flowers grow on separate plants, so both are needed to produce berries. Propagate from cuttings in summer.

KENNEDIA
rubicunda
RUNNING POSTMAN

Endemic to Australia, these climbing or scrambling plants were named after John Kennedy, a London nurseryman. They are widely cultivated for their showy, pea-like flowers which attract birds. Half-hardy to frost-tender, they thrive in a light, well-drained soil and a sunny situation, but will tolerate light shade. *K. rubicunda* is an extremely vigorous species that grows up to 5 m (about 15 ft) and should be kept well away from nearby shrubs and trees, as it will quickly climb over anything in reach. It bears showy, dark red pea flowers in small sprays in spring and early summer. In spring or after flowering, invasive growth can be cut back reasonably hard without harming the plant, but keep well watered until new growth is established. Propagate from presoaked seed any time in spring.

LAPAGERIA
rosea
CHILEAN BELLFLOWER

Native to Chile (where it is the national flower) this beautiful evergreen climber can reach 5 m (about 15 ft) on support. The oval leaves are bright glossy green. Waxy, pinkish red, bell-like flowers, faintly spotted within, are borne for a long period through summer and autumn/fall. Half-hardy, it needs a warm, sheltered spot in cool climates. Grow in humus-rich, well-drained soil in partial shade, and keep fairly dry in winter. Propagate

Ipomoea alba

Jasminum officinale

Jasminum polyanthum

Kennedia rubicunda

Lapageria rosea

from presoaked seed in spring or layers in autumn/fall. Watch for two-spotted mite and thrips.

LATHYRUS

SWEET PEA, EVERLASTING PEA

This genus takes its name from the Greek for 'pea'. It has over 130 species of annuals, sub-shrubs and perennials, most of which are climbers. Originating in the temperate regions of the northern hemisphere and also found in Africa and South America, the climbers vary in height from 1–3 m (about 3–9 ft), and have pinnate leaves (one of which becomes a twining tendril). The racemes of flowers appear between spring and summer. Easily recognized by their wing-shaped petals, the flowers are excellent for cutting. They are followed by long, slender seed pods. Sweet peas require well-drained soil that has been enriched with humus, and need plenty of sunlight with a cool root run. For all but the lower-growing species, support should be provided. Dead-head annually and pick the seed pods to prolong the flowering period. Tip-pruning will encourage bushiness, and the perennials' growth should be cut back in late autumn/fall. Propagate the annuals from seed in either early spring or autumn/fall, and the perennial species by division in spring or from seed in autumn/fall. These beautiful plants are subject to various diseases such as mildew, mould and rust, while slugs and aphids can be a problem.

L. latifolius

PERRENIAL PEA, EVERLASTING PEA

This perennial, tendril climber from Chile grows to about 2 m (about 6 ft) high. It has dull green foliage and dense heads of pink, rose or white, scentless pea flowers in spring and summer. The stem is vigorous and twining, while the fruit are long pods. Fully hardy, it is easily grown in a humus-rich, well-drained soil. It needs the support of a sunny fence or trellis. The plant responds to regular feeding and watering when the buds are forming. Propagate from seed or cuttings or by division in spring.

Lonicera hildebrandiana

L. odoratus

SWEET PEA

This delicately scented climbing annual originated in southern Italy and can climb to 3 m (about 9 ft) high, given good support. Relatively fast growing, it has ovate, mid-green leaves which are borne in pairs, with a climbing tendril. The racemes of soft-coloured flowers— pinks, whites, blues and purples, up to 15 per raceme—appear in summer.

LONICERA

HONEYSUCKLE, WOODBINE

Grown for their masses of perfumed flowers, these are perhaps the most romantic climbers of all. They are perfect for covering arches, arbours and bowers, where they will provide a sweet summer evening fragrance. Grow in a well-drained, moisture-retentive soil in sun or semi-shade.

L. caprifolium

HONEYSUCKLE, WOODBINE

A deciduous, twining climber growing up to 5 m (about 15 ft) with light green, oval, pointed leaves that are joined at the base. Highly scented, yellow flowers, tinted with pink on the outside appear in summer and autumn/fall. It is frost-hardy. There are many named cultivars with brightly coloured flowers.

L. × heckrottii

This deciduous hybrid is a semi-climber, or can be grown as a shrub. Its pointed leaves are 6 cm (about 2½ in) long, grey underneath, and

its yellow flowers are tinged with pink. Appearing in summer, they are 4 cm (about 2 in) long and arranged in whorls.

L. hildebrandiana

GIANT HONEYSUCKLE, BURMESE HONEYSUCKLE

This deciduous climber from Burma reaching up to 20 m (about 65 ft) bears large, creamy flowers in summer that turn orange with age; they are only faintly scented. It needs strong support and is frost-tender.

Lathryus latifolius

Lonicera × heckrottii

Lonicera caprifolium

Mandevilla laxa

Mandevilla × amabilis 'Alice du Pont'

Mandevilla splendens

Macfadyena unguis-cati

Lonicera japonica 'Aurea-reticulata'

Manettia inflata

Lonicera japonica

L. japonica
JAPANESE HONEYSUCKLE

This vigorous climber from east Asia, growing to 10 m (about 30 ft), has glossy, dark green leaves. Pairs of fragrant, white flowers ageing yellow, or sometimes purple-tinged, appear in late summer to autumn/fall. This species is only just frost-hardy, but can become an invasive weed.

L. japonica 'Aurea-reticulata'

This less vigorous, slow-growing cultivar is suited to mild climates and does well in shade. Its leaves have attractive gold veins, but it bears only a few flowers.

MACFADYENA
unguis-cati
syn. *Doxantha unguis-cati*
CAT'S CLAW CREEPER

A beautiful, evergreen vine grown for its large, bright yellow flowers in the shape of a flattened trumpet up to 10 cm (about 4 in) across. These are borne in profusion in late spring. It clings by tiny, 3-pronged tendrils, like little claws, and climbs to a mature height of up to 10 m (about 30 ft). An excellent climber for covering a high fence or garden shed, it likes a sunny, well-drained position and is frost tender. Prune back hard after flowering to keep in check. Propagate from semi-ripe cuttings in late summer.

MANDEVILLA

Native to tropical America, these woody-stemmed climbers are grown for their profusion of showy trumpet-shaped flowers, which are sometimes fragrant. They do best in warm, frost-free climates with partial shade in summer. Soil should be deep, rich and well-drained. Provide ample water on hot days. Propagate from semi-ripe cuttings in summer. In cool areas they grow very well in frost-free greenhouses.

M. × amabilis 'Alice du Pont'
syn. *Dipladenia* × *amabilis* 'Alice du Pont'

A twining climber growing up to 4 m (about 12 ft) with handsome, oval, glossy leaves and clusters of large, deep pink, scentless, trumpet flowers over a long period in summer. It is frost-tender and needs a warm protected position with light shade.

M. laxa
syn. *M. suaveolens*
CHILEAN JASMINE

From Argentina, this fast-growing, woody vine reaches 6 m (about 18 ft) or more and is deciduous in cool areas. It is half-hardy. In summer it produces heavily perfumed, white trumpet flowers in profusion —these make good cut flowers. The plants can be pruned heavily in early spring to keep it tidy and en-courage new growth.

M. splendens
syn. *Dipladenia splendens*

One of the showiest species of its genus, this evergreen twisting climber is native to Brazil and climbs to 3 m (about 9 ft). Its lus-trous green leaves are wide and ellip-tical to rectangular, reaching a length of 20 cm (about 8 in). At the end of spring to the beginning of summer, attractive, deep reddish pink, trumpet-shaped flowers with yellow middles appear. This species prefers temperatures above 10°C (about 50°F).

MANETTIA
inflata
syn. *M. bicolor*
BRAZILIAN FIRECRACKER

This evergreen, light, twining climber reaches 2 m (about 6 ft) and produces small, decorative, tubular flowers, bright red and tipped with gold, in spring and summer. Origi-nally from South America, this plant does best in a warm climate. Soil should preferably be rich, slightly acidic, with good drainage. Provide regular water and some shade in summer. This climber is pretty for training up a pillar, over a trellis or trailing from a hanging basket. Propagate this species from softwood cuttings in late spring. It can be grown as an indoor plant, in which case it should be given plenty of bright light.

Mucuna bennettii

Pandorea jasminoides

Passiflora caerulea

MUCUNA
bennettii

The leaves of this strong, fast-growing tropical climber are divided into 3 oval leaflets, and in summer have large, pendant clusters of pea-like, orange-scarlet flowers. It will only grow in summer in moist, but well-drained, humus-rich soil in partial shade. Frost-tender, it needs abundant water during growth, less at other times. The vigorous growth requires a well-supported, large area for climbing. Crowded stems may be thinned out in spring. Propagate from seed in spring or by layering in late summer.

PANDOREA

Named after Pandora of Greek mythology, this is a small genus of beautiful twining climbers native to Malaysia and Australia. They are grown for their spectacular, long-lasting displays of tubular bell flowers and make excellent pergola or trellis subjects. Frost-tender, they are ideal for warm-temperate or tropical areas; where the temperature reaches freezing, *P. pandorana* may survive if given a warm, sheltered spot. The soil should be well-drained and enriched with humus. Most require abundant moisture and a sunny position protected from strong winds. Propagate from fresh seed in spring or semi-ripe cuttings in summer.

P. jasminoides
syn. *Tecoma jasminoides*
BOWER CLIMBER

This very attractive climber from Australia grows up to 5 m (about 15 ft) and has lush, deep green, glossy leaflets. Showy, pale pink trumpet flowers with a deep carmine throat are borne from late spring to autumn/fall in warm climates. A pure white flowering form is also in cultivation, and there is a form with variegated leaves is available.

P. pandorana
syn. *Tecoma australis*
WONGA-WONGA VINE

Also from Australia, this robust, woody climber up to 6 m (about

Parthenocissus tricuspidata

Pandorea pandorana

18 ft) bears masses of very showy, tubular flowers in spring and summer. The flowers are usually creamy white with reddish throats, but a number of cultivars are available, one with pure white flowers and another with gold and brown flowers. This is a very good climber for covering arches, and pergolas and for disguising unattractive sites such as wire mesh fences.

PARTHENOCISSUS

These charming climbing plants from North America and Asia have deciduous, attractively cut leaves, some with magnificent autumn/fall colouring. The genus name is from the Greek *parthenos*, meaning 'virgin', and *kissos*, 'creeper'. They climb by tendrils with tiny disc-shaped suckers and are the perfect climbers for growing on buildings and walls. They are fully hardy and they will grow best in humus-rich, well-drained soil in filtered sunlight with protection from hot winds. Propagate from hardwood cuttings in late winter or early spring.

Parthenocissus quinquefolia

P. quinquefolia
syn. *Ampelopsis quinquefolia*, *Vitis quinquefolia*
VIRGINIA CREEPER

A high climber growing 15 m (about 50 ft) or more. The handsome leaves divided into 5 leaflets make an attractive green wall cover in summer and turn a brilliant red in autumn/fall.

P. tricuspidata
syn. *Ampelopsis veitchii*
BOSTON IVY, JAPANESE IVY

Ideal for covering large walls, this ivy will reach up to 20 m (about 65 ft). The 3-lobed leaves, 20 cm (about 8 in) across, turn spectacular shades of red and purple in autumn/fall.

PASSIFLORA
PASSION FLOWER

Native chiefly to tropical South America, these showy, tendril climbers are treasured for their ornamental blossoms and their delicious fruit, notably the well-known passionfruit. Half-hardy to

Passiflora coccinea

frost-tender, they are best suited to warm areas. A humus-rich, well-drained soil and a sunny aspect are preferred. Water regularly in summer and provide good support. Prune congested or overgrown plants in spring. Propagate from seed or semi-ripe cuttings or by layering in summer.

P. caerulea
BLUE PASSION FLOWER

In summer this half-hardy, fast-growing evergreen or semi-evergreen climber to 10 m (about 30 ft) produces beautiful flowers with pale pink petals, banded with blue or purple. There are followed by edible but not especially delicious egg-shaped, yellow fruit.

P. coccinea
RED PASSION FLOWER

A robust, evergreen climber to 4 m (about 12 ft) grown for the brilliant, large, scarlet flowers borne in summer and autumn/fall, set among large, dark green, crinkly leaves. It is frost-tender and also needs protection from hot winds.

Rosa 'Albertine'

Rosa banksiae lutea

Phaseolus caracalla

PHASEOLUS

caracalla

syn. *Vigna caracalla*

SNAIL CREEPER

A decorative, evergreen, twining climber with soft green foliage composed of 3 leaflets and curiously twisted, pea-like flowers in shades of purple, white and yellow. The flowers have a delightful perfume and are produced from mid-summer to early autumn/fall. Frost-tender, it is best suited to warm-temperate and tropical areas, where it will grow rapidly to 3 m (about 9 ft), scrambling over everything in reach. Grow in full sun in humus-rich, well-drained soil and protect from drying winds. Prune tangled growth in spring. Propagate from seed sown in spring.

POLYGONUM

aubertii

syn. *Fallopia aubertii*

RUSSIAN VINE, MILE-A-MINUTE PLANT

This deciduous, fully hardy, twining climber certainly lives up to its common name. A vigorous and

Pyrostegia venusta

rampant grower, it can reach 12 m (about 37 ft) and needs to be kept in check with hard pruning. Its leaves are broad and cordate, and its panicles of small, white to green flowers, maturing to pink, are borne in summer. Small white fruit follow in autumn/fall. Plant in a sunny to partially shaded site with moist but well-drained soil. Unlike other species in the genus, it can tolerate an alkaline soil. Propagate from semi-hardwood cuttings in summer.

PYROSTEGIA

venusta

FLAME VINE, GOLDEN SHOWER

From South America, this magnificent creeper will reach great heights of 10 m (about 30 ft) or more in warm climates. This climber is grown chiefly for its brilliant display of orange-gold flowers in autumn/fall, winter or spring, depending on the climate. Frost-tender, it will thrive in most well-drained soils but will only flower well in full sun. Water well in summer and grow on a strong pergola or arch where the

Rosa 'Albéric Barbier'

flowers can droop down freely. After flowering prune out old shoots and spent flowers. Propagate from semi-hardwood cuttings in summer or autumn/fall.

ROSA

ROSE

Climbing roses vary greatly in their habit from short-stemmed, rambling or pillar roses to tall vigorous climbers capable of reaching up to 10 m (30 ft) high. They beautifully decorate fences, walls, trellises, pergolas, arches, pillars and columns, and are ideal for small gardens where there is not enough room for a conventional rose bed. Species growing to around 4 m (about 12 ft) are useful for covering walls and fences; those short-stemmed roses held close to the foliage are best for growing on pillars; and miniature climbers look pretty cascading down retaining walls and tall containers. Most roses are fully hardy and require humus-rich soil, full sun and ample water. Give climbers room to develop and

tie back canes as they grow. Some of the pillar roses need only light pruning, but old vigorous climbers may need more severe cutting back. Always remove spent blooms to prolong flowering. Aphids, blackspot and mildew can cause problems.

R. 'Albéric Barbier'

A vigorous, fully hardy rambler growing to 5 m (about 15 ft). Yellow buds open to full double, creamy white blooms in spring. The fragrant flowers are carried in large trusses; foliage is dark and glossy.

R. 'Albertine'

A beautiful, vigorous rambler to 6 m (about 18 ft), good for growing over a pergola. Fragrant, double, ruffled, coppery-pink blooms are borne in large trusses in spring. It is fully hardy but a little prone to mildew.

R. banksiae lutea

This extremely vigorous, thornless climber will reach up to 10 m (30 ft). Clusters of small, white or yellow, double flowers are borne in spring. Light green foliage is small and pointed. As flowers are borne on permanent spurs produced on older wood, remove only dead wood when pruning.

R. 'Climbing Cécile Brünner'

BUTTONHOLE ROSE, SWEETHEART ROSE

A sport of the dwarf polyantha 'Cécile Brünner' which grows to only 1 m (about 3 ft), this climbing variety can reach 10 m (about 30 ft). A vigorous grower, it needs sun to flourish. Its small flowers are tinged with pink.

Rosa 'Mermaid'

R. 'Climbing Lady Hillingdon'

A climbing tea rose with rather stiff growth to 4 m (about 12 ft). The large, double, apricot-yellow blooms with pointed petals are borne freely throughout the warmer months. It is frost-hardy, but appreciates a sunny wall in cold districts.

R. 'Golden Showers'

An upright climber, growing to 2.5 m (about 7½ ft), this rose can also be grown as a shrub if pruned properly. The double flowers are fragrant and golden yellow. Opening flat, they are carried in great quantities during summer and autumn/fall. Watch out for black spot.

R. 'Handel'

Ideal for a wall, fence or pillar, this frost-hardy, free-flowering 3 m (about 9 ft) climber bears semi-double, ivory-cream flowers edged and flushed deep pink. They are borne in clusters from spring to autumn/fall. Watch for mildew.

R. 'Madame Alfred Carrière'

This is the most popular white climber among the old garden roses (it is classed as a Noisette); and bears scented, medium-sized, double flowers, white with faint touches of pink, all season. It grows to about 6 m (about 18 ft).

R. 'Mermaid'

This extremely vigorous climber, reaching 8 m (about 24 ft), is for large areas only. Its stiff, thorny canes are rather awkward to train and tie. It makes an impressive climber for walls, as its flowers are large, prolific and continuous from spring to autumn/fall. The single flowers are yellow with prominent stamens. The glossy foliage is oval and dark green. It is frost-hardy, but appreciates a sunny wall in cold districts.

R. 'New Dawn'
syn. R. 'Everblooming Dr Van Fleet'

A vigorous and very hardy climber up to 6 m (about 18 ft), this rose looks good grown in a hedge or up a wall or tree. It has glossy, dark green leaves, and its small double flowers are cup shaped and a delicate pale silvery pink. Heavily scented, the clusters of flowers bloom in great profusion throughout summer and into autumn/fall.

Rosa 'Climbing Cécile Brünner'

Rosa 'Golden Showers'

Rosa 'Handel'

Rosa 'New Dawn'

Rosa 'Madame Alfred Carrière'

Rosa 'Climbing Lady Hillingdon'

R. 'Zéphirine Drouhin'

A fully hardy, semi-climbing bourbon rose growing to 2.5 m (about 7½ ft), noted for its lack of thorns and recurrent, fragrant blooms. The long, pointed buds open to semi-double, deep pink blooms from spring to autumn/fall.

SCHIZOPHRAGMA
hydrangeoides
JAPANESE HYDRANGEA

From Japan and Korea, this vigorous, deciduous, woody-stemmed climber clings by aerial roots for support. It will grow to 9 m (about 27 ft) or more and makes a spectacular cover for pergolas and large walls. The large, flattened flowerheads, 30 cm (about 12 in) across, are composed of very small white flowers surrounded by ornamental, white bracts, and are borne in summer. It has attractive, deep green, toothed leaves 12 cm (about 5 in) long on long, red stalks. Grow in a humus-rich, moist, but well-drained soil in full sun. It is frost hardy. Train young plants on the support until established, and remove spent blooms. Propagate from semi-ripe cuttings in summer.

SOLANDRA
maxima
CUP OF GOLD, HAWAIIAN LILY, GOLDEN CHALICE VINE

A giant Mexican climber valued for its huge flowers and ability to cover very large areas. It is a rampant, woody vine growing to 10 m (about 30 ft) or more requiring plenty of space and a sturdy support. The yellow flowers, up to 25 cm (about 10 in) across, with a near purple stripe down the centre of each petal, are produced in spring and summer. Frost-tender, it requires fertile soil, good drainage and full sun. It will tolerate wind, drought and salt spray, making it an excellent plant for seaside gardens. Prune in summer to keep the plant in bounds and promote more flowers. Propagate from semi-ripe cuttings in summer.

SOLANUM

With a worldwide distribution, this very large genus of annuals, perennials, shrubs, trees and climbers includes potatoes, tomatoes and other food plants, as well as a few medicinal and poisonous plants. The climbers are valued for their ornamental flowers, foliage and fruit. They are fast-growing and require fastening to support. They do best in a warm, sunny position in fertile, well-drained soil. Cut back congested growth in spring. Propagate from seed.

S. jasminoides
POTATO VINE

From South America, this quick-growing, semi-evergreen climber reaches 5 m (about 15 ft) and bears showy clusters of pale blue flowers in summer and autumn/fall, followed by small, purple berries. It is half-hardy; in cool areas it can be potted up in autumn/fall to spend the winter under glass. The cultivar 'Album' has masses of star-shaped, white flowers.

S. seaforthianum

A showy vine growing to 6 m (about 18 ft) and bearing large clusters of violet-blue flowers with yellow stamens in summer, followed by small, scarlet berries. It is frost-tender.

STEPHANOTIS
floribunda
WAX FLOWER

This evergreen climber can grow to a height and spread of 3 m (about 9 ft). It is grown for its pleasant fragrance and its attractive foliage of paired, waxy, deep green leaves. The pendulous, tubular, white flowers have widely flared lobes, and appear in clusters of about 4 blooms from spring to autumn/fall. The flowers are very popular as bridal decorations. Plant in well-drained soil in partial shade. This climber is frost-tender, but may be grown indoors and forced into flower throughout the year. Propagate by layering.

Solandra maxima

Solanum jasminoides

Solanum seaforthianum

Stephanotis floribunda

Thunbergia alata

Thunbergia grandiflora

Trachelospermum jasminoides

Strongylodon macrobotrys

Tecomanthe speciosa

STRONGYLODON
macrobotrys

JADE VINE

A large, twining climber up to 20 m (about 65 ft), valued for the spectacular, long, pendulous sprays of blue-green flowers, almost 50 cm (about 20 in) long, borne throughout summer. Native to the Philippines, this species is frost-tender, suitable only to subtropical and warm-temperate areas. Plant in humus-rich, moist, but well-drained soil, with partial shade in summer. Grow over a pergola or large arch where there is freedom for the long racemes of flowers to hang down. Propagate from seed or cuttings.

TECOMANTHE
speciosa

This vigorous twisting climber grows to 10 m (about 30 ft). Its compound leaves consist of up to 5 leaflets. In autumn/fall, lush cream, green-tinged flowers are borne. This frost-tender species requires temperatures above 10°C (about

50°F), peaty soil with good drainage and protection from the summer sun. Water liberally during the growth period and stake stems. Prune closely packed stems in spring. Propagate from seed in spring or semi-ripe cuttings in summer.

THUNBERGIA

CLOCK VINE

This genus contains 200 species of annual twisting climbers and perennial evergreen clump-forming shrubs. These species are native to Africa, Asia and Malagasy. Their leaves, which are entire, have up to 5 lobes. The cylindrical blooms are borne individually from the leaf axils or in trusses. The species range from half-hardy to frost-tender and prefer temperatures above 10°C (about 50°F). They will grow in any reasonably rich soil with adequate drainage. Full sun is preferred, except during the summer months when partial shade and liberal water should be provided. Support stems and prune densely

packed foliage during early spring. Propagate from seed in spring and semi-ripe cuttings in summer. This genus was named after the eighteenth-century Swedish botanist Dr Carl Peter Thunberg who worked in Africa.

T. alata

BLACK-EYED SUSAN

Native to the tropics of Africa, this vigorous annual or perennial twisting climber grows quickly to 3 m (about 9 ft). Its deep green, cordate leaves grow to 8 cm (about 3 in) long. It bears masses of 4 cm (about 2 in) wide orange flowers with black throats all summer. It is perennial in frost-free areas.

T. grandiflora

BLUE TRUMPET VINE, SKY FLOWER

Originally from India, this quick-growing, vigorous climber to 5 m (about 15 ft) is grown for its drooping clusters of large, sky-blue trumpet flowers, borne in summer and autumn/fall. It has large-toothed, heart-shaped leaves up to 20 cm (about 8 in) long and looks best

when grown on a trellis, fence or pergola. It is frost-tender, and requires humus-rich, well-drained soil, lots of water and protection from dry summer winds. Propagate from semi-hardwood cuttings in summer.

TRACHELOSPERMUM
jasminoides

STAR JASMINE

Valued for its perfumed, star-shaped flowers, this attractive, evergreen, twining climber from China grows up to 7 m (about 21 ft) high. It has lance-shaped leaves, and hanging clusters of white flowers are produced in summer. Frost-hardy, this plant does best in a sunny position in well-drained, fertile soil. Although it is slow-growing during the early stages, it will flourish once established and is excellent for training on pillars, pergolas and arches. It can also be used as a ground cover. Prune congested or straggly branches in autumn/fall. Propagate from semi-ripe cuttings in summer or autumn/fall.

TROPAEOLUM
speciosum
FLAME NASTURTIUM

A herbaceous, perennial climber with slender stems reaching up to 3 m (about 9 ft). It has a tuberous rhizome and attractive, bright green foliage composed of 6 oval leaflets. Scarlet flowers in summer are followed by blue fruit. Grow in partial shade in a humus-rich, moist, but well-drained soil. Native to China, this species is frost-hardy. Propagate from seed or by division of tubers.

VITIS

This genus consists of deciduous woody-stemmed, tendril climbers. They are grown for their foliage (on trellises and the like as ornamentals) and fruits (grapes). Grow in humus-rich, moisture-retentive, but well-drained soil in full sun or partial shade. Propagate from hardwood cuttings taken in late autumn/fall or winter.

V. coignetiae
CRIMSON GLORY VINE

A rapid-growing climber reaching 15 m (about 50 ft), with green, slightly lobed leaves which change to deep crimson, orange and scarlet in autumn/fall. Clusters of small, black berries with a glaucous bloom are borne in late summer. Its tendrils coil around supports and need plenty of room to spread. Frost-hardy, the leaf colour is best in cool climates. Prune in winter when the plants are completely dormant.

V. vinifera 'Purpurea'
TEINTURIER GRAPE

This ornamental variety of the fruit-bearing grape is a deciduous tendril climber that can reach 7 m (about 21 ft). Its ovate leaves have between 3 and 5 serrated lobes and are claret-red, with white hairs when young. They age to a deep purple colour. In summer, 7 cm (about 3 in) long panicles of small green flowers appear, followed by greenish purple fruit.

WISTERIA
WISTERIA

The deciduous wisteria is one of the most popular plants for pergolas, where the large, drooping sprays of perfumed flowers are best displayed. Providing welcome summer shade, the soft, light green, luxuriant foliage is particularly attractive. Wisterias like a sunny position and a humus-rich, well-drained soil. Although they take some time to establish, they become large, vigorous plants and need strong support for healthy future growth. Prune after flowering and again in late winter; only prune in winter if really necessary to control size. Propagate from cuttings or by layering in late summer. With regular pruning, and some support in the early years, wisteria can be grown as a large, free-standing shrub or standard.

W. floribunda
JAPANESE WISTERIA

This vigorous, woody-stemmed climber up to 10 m (about 30 ft) bears pendulous, purple-blue flowers of around 50 cm (about 20 in) or more long. The flowers are fragrant and are often produced after the leaves in spring. This climber is fully hardy.

W. floribunda 'Alba'

A beautiful, white flowering climber with drooping sprays up to 60 cm (about 24 in) long. It is fully hardy.

W. floribunda 'Violacea Plena'

Fragrant, double purple flowers are borne in early summer on this fully hardy climber.

W. sinensis
syn. *W. chinensis*
CHINESE WISTERIA

Native to China, this vigorous, fully hardy, woody-stemmed climber will reach up to 30 m (about 95 ft) high. The sprays of slightly fragrant, lavender-blue flowers up to 30 cm (about 12 in) long appear in spring on bare branches before the leaves, creating a magnificent sight.

W. venusta
syn. *W. brachybotrytis* f. *alba*
SILKY WISTERIA

Originally from Japan, this deciduous, woody-stemmed climber can reach 9 m (about 27 ft). Its deep green leaves, around 35 cm (about 14 in) long, are pinnate with 9 to 13 leaflets. The scented flowers hang in 15 cm (about 6 in) long racemes, and are white with a yellow mark on the base of the petals. They appear in early summer, but can spot flower again during autumn/fall.

Wisteria sinensis

Wisteria floribunda 'Alba'

Wisteria f. 'Violacea Plena'

Vitis coignetiae

Wisteria floribunda

Wisteria venusta

Seasonal Calendars

❧

Keys

The following lists are keys to the Seasonal Calendars that follow. If you wish to find out how to care for a particular plant in a particular month, for example, *Helleborus niger* in December, you simply locate it in the keys below (Perennials, hardy, winter flowering), find that group in the Seasonal Calendars (page 404) and you will discover that this plant needs to be protected with glass or cloches. For ease of reference, each plant is also listed in the Index to Plants, with page numbers referring to where it occurs in the text and where it occurs in these keys.

ANNUALS & PERENNIALS

The cultivation of annual and perennial plants is rewarding as a large variety of flowering plants can be grown to appear throughout the year. To grow the more unusual flowers from seed requires patience, as germination can be erratic, and constant attention, as seedlings need an even light source and must never be allowed to dry out. In other words, their best chance of healthy development requires daily care.

Perennials, on the other hand, are not called hardy for nothing. Different perennials can be found for cold, mountainous climates, for salt-spray coastal gardens and for excessively dry, wet or shady positions. Simple maintenance practices such as removing spent flowers, checking under leaves for pests and a tidy up during winter are all they need. Regular mulching and fertilizing during the growing and flowering seasons helps maintain their vigour, and before long there will be excess plants to give away to friends.

Annuals, half-hardy

Ageratum houstonianum
Amaranthus caudatus
Amaranthus tricolor 'Joseph's Coat'
Begonia, Semperflorens group
Browallia americana

Calceolaria × herbeohybrida
Callistephus chinensis
Celosia cristata
Cleome hassleriana
Cosmos bipinnatus
Cosmos sulphureus
Dimorphotheca pluvialis
Dimorphotheca sinuata
Dorotheanthus bellidiformis
Euphorbia marginata
Eustoma grandiflora
Exacum affine
Gomphrena globosa
Helichrysum bracteatum
Hunnemannia fumariifolia
Impatiens balsamina
Impatiens, New Guinea hybrids
Impatiens walleriana
Kochia scoparia f. trichophylla
Lobelia erinus 'Cambridge Blue'
Mina lobata
Moluccella laevis
Nicotiana alata
Nicotiana × sanderae
Nierembergia hippomanica var. violacea
Pelargonium × zonale
Petunia 'Bonanza'
Petunia 'Cascade'
Portulaca grandiflora
Rhodochiton astrosanguineum
Salpiglossis sinuata
Salvia farinacea 'Blue Bedder'
Salvia splendens
Schizanthus pinnatus
Senecio elegans
Silene coeli-rosa
Tithonia rotundifolia 'Torch'
Torenia fournieri
Tropaeolum peregrinum

Xeranthemum annum
Zinnia angustifolia
Zinnia elegans
Zinnia haageana 'Old Mexico'

Annuals, hardy

Agrostemma githago
Brachycome iberidifolia
Calendula officinalis
Centaurea cyanus
Centaurea moschata
Chrysanthemum carinatum
Clarkia amoena
Cobaea scandens
Coleus blumei
Coleus thyroideus
Consolida ambigua
Convolvulus tricolor
Coreopsis tinctoria
Dahlia, dwarf or bedding
Dianthus, annual or marguerite carnations
Dianthus chinensis
Eschscholzia californica
Felicia bergeriana
Gaillardia pulchella
Gazania 'Daybreak'
Gazania, sunshine hybrids
Gilia capitata
Gypsophila elegans
Gypsophila paniculata 'Bristol Fairy'
Helianthus annuus
Iberis amara
Iberis umbellata
Lathyrus odoratus
Lavatera trimestris
Limonium sinuatum
Linaria macroccana 'Fairy Bouquet'
Linum grandiflorum 'Rubrum'
Lobularia maritima
Lupinus hartwegii
Lupinus texensis
Malcolmia maritima
Myosotis 'Blue Ball'
Nemesia strumosa
Nemophila insignis
Nigella damascena
Oxypetalum caeruleum
Papaver nudicaule
Papaver rhoeas
Papaver somniferum
Pelargonium crispum

Phacelia campanularia
Phlox drummondii
Reseda odorata
Ricinus communis
Rudbeckia hirta
Sanvitalia procumbens
Scabiosa atropurpurea
Scabiosa caucasia
Tagetes erecta
Tagetes patula
Tropaeolum majus
Viola cornuta
Viola tricolor
Viola × wittrockiana

Biennials

Alcea rosea
Anchusa capensis 'Blue Angel'
Bellis perennis
Campanula medium
Cheiranthus cheiri
Dianthus barbatus
Digitalis purpurea
Echium vulgare
Echium wildprettii
Erysimum hieraciifolium
Euphorbia characias subsp. wulfenii
Lunaria annua
Matthiola incana
Myosotis alpestris
Oenothera biennis
Viola × wittrockiana

Perennials, frost-tender

Alpinia purpurata
Alpinia zerumbet
Begonia metallica
Begonia 'Orange Rubra'
Canna × generalis
Catharanthus roseus
Diascia barberae
Felicia amelloides

Perennials, hardy, winter flowering

Arctotis × hybrida
Coreopsis verticillata
Helleborus foetidus
Helleborus lividus subsp. corsicus
Helleborus niger

Helleborus orientalis
Iris japonica
Iris unguicularis
Primula obconica
Primula × polyantha
Viola odorata
Viola sororia 'Freckles'

Perennials, hardy, spring–early summer flowering

Acaena 'Blue Haze'
Acanthus spinosus
Achillea filipendulina 'Gold Plate'
Achillea millefolium
Achillea 'Moonshine'
Achillea tomentosa
Adonis aestivalis
Aethionema armenum
Ajuga reptans
Anthemis tinctoria
Antirrhinum majus
Aquilegia, McKana hybrids
Aqilegia vulgaris hybrids
Arctotis × hybrida
Argyranthemum frutescens
Armeria maritima
Aster alpinus
Astilbe × arendsii
Aurinia saxatilis
Bellis perennis
Bergenia cordifolia
Bergenia hybrids
Bergenia stracheyi
Brunnera macrophylla
Campanula carpatica
Campanula portenschlagiana
Campanula poscharskyana
Campanula takesimana
Centaurea dealbata
Centaurea hypoleuca
   'John Coutts'
Cetranthus ruber
Cephalaria gigantea
Cerastium tomentosum
Convolvulus cneorum
Convolvulus sabatius
Coreopsis verticillata
Corydalis flexuosa
Corydalis lutea
Cosmos atrosanguineus
Dahlia, cactus dahlias
Dahlia, collarette dahlias
Dahlia, decorative dahlias
Dahlia, pompon dahlias
Dahlia, waterlily or Nymphaea
   dahlias
Delphinium belladonna
Delphinium grandiflorum
Dianella tasmanica
Dianthus × allwoodii
Dianthus caryophyllus cultivars
Dianthus, border carnations
Dianthus, perpetual-flowering

carnations
Dianthus deltoides
Dianthus plumarius
Dicentra formosa
Dicentra spectabilis
Dictamnus albus
Dietes grandiflora
Dietes iridiodes
Diplarrhena moraea
Dodecatheon meadia
Duchesnea indica
Epimedium grandiflorum
Epimedium perralderanum
Epimedium pinnatum
   subsp. colchicum
Epimedium rubrum
Epimedium × warleyense
Erinus alpinus
Euphorbia polychroma
Gaillardia aristata
Gaura lindheimeri
Gazania krebsiana
Geranium incanum
Geranium phaeum
Geranium sanguineum
Gerbera jamesonii
Geum × borisii
Geum 'Mrs Bradshaw'
Globularia cordifolia
Helianthemum nummularium
Helipterum anthemoides
Hemerocallis hybrids
Heuchera × brizoides
Hosta sieboldiana
Hypericum cerastoides
Iberis sempervirens
Iris, bearded hybrids
Iris ensata
Iris, Louisiana hybrids
Iris missouriensis
Iris ochroleuca
Iris, Pacific Coast hybrids
Iris pallida 'Variegata'
Iris pseudacorus
Iris pseudacorus 'Variegata'
Iris spuria hybrids
Kniphofia hybrids
Lamium maculatum
Libertia grandiflora
Lotus berthelotti
Lupinus, Russell hybrids
Lysichiton camtschatcensis
Matthiola 'Mammoth Column'
Meconopsis betonicifolia
Meconopsis cambrica
Mertensia virginica
Myosotidium hortensia
Myosotis colensoi
Nertera granadensis
Oenothera missouriensis
Ourisia macrophylla
Pachysandra terminalis
Paeonia 'Bowl of Beauty'
Paeonia mlokosewitschii
Paeonia officinalis

Papaver orientale
Paradisea liliastrum
Patersonia glabrata
Pelargonium cucullatum
Pelargonium × domesticum
Pelargonium 'Orange Ricard'
Pelargonium peltatum
Pelargonium tomentosum
Peltiphyllum peltatum
Penstemon heterophyllus 'True Blue'
Phlox stolonifera
Podophyllum peltatum
Polygonatum × hybridum
Pratia angulata
Pratia pedunculata
Primula denticulata
Primula florindae
Primula japonica
Primula malacoides
Primula vialli
Primula vulgaris
Pulsatilla vulgaris
Ramonda myconi
Ranunculus aconitifolius
Sarracenia flava
Scaevola aemula
Scaevola 'Mauve Clusters'
Sedum rosea
Silene vulgaris subsp. maritima
Sisyrinchium graminoides
Smilacina racemosa
Soleirolia soleirolii
Tanacetum coccineum 'Brenda'
Tellima grandiflora
Thalictrum aquilegiifolium
Tiarella cordifolia
Tradescantia virginiana
Trillium grandiflorum
Trollius europaeus
Veronica gentianoides
Veronica prostrata
Vinca major
Vinca minor
Viola hederacea
Viola reichenbachiana
Viola riviana Purpurea group
Yucca whipplei
Zantedeschia aethiopica

Perennials, hardy, late summer–autumn flowering

Acaena microphylla
Acanthus mollis
Aconitum napellus
Actaea alba
Agapanthus 'Blue Baby'
Agapanthus campanulatus
Agapanthus praecox subsp. orientalis
Alchemilla mollis
Alstroemeria aurea
Alstroemeria, Ligtu hybrids
Anagallis linifolia
Anaphalis margariticea

Anchusa azurea
Anemone × hybrida
Antirrhinum majus
Argemone mexicana
Artemisia arborescens
Artemisia lactiflora
Artemisia 'Powys Castle'
Artemisia stelleriana
Aruncus dioicus
Aster frikartii 'Mönch'
Aster novae-angliae 'Barr's Pink'
Aster novae-angliae
   'Harrington's Pink'
Aster novi-belgii 'Mulberry'
Astilbe chinensis 'Pumila'
Astrantia major
Baptisia australis
Calceolaria integrifolia
Calocephalus brownii
Campanula isophylla
Campanula lactiflora
Campanula persicifolia
Catananche caerula
Ceratostigma plumbaginoides
Chelone obliqua
Cimicifuga racemosa
Codonopsis clematidea
Crambe maritima
Crepis incana
Cyperus papyrus
Delphinium elatum hybrids
Dendranthema grandiflora
Dichorisandra thyrsiflora
Dierama pulcherrimum
Digitalis × mertonensis
Doryanthes excelsa
Echinacea purpurea
Echinops ritro
Epilobium angustifolium
Eremurus, Shelford hybrids
Erigeron glaucus
Erigeron karvinskianus
Eryngium × oliverianum
Eryngium tripartitum
Eryngium variifolium
Eupatorium purpureum
Filipendulina vulgaris
Galega officinalis
Galeobdolon argentatum
Geranium 'Johnson's Blue'
Glechoma hederacea
Gunnera manicata
Hedychium coronarium
Hedychium gardnerianum
Helenium 'Moorheim Beauty'
Helianthus salicifolius
Helichrysum hookeri
Heliconia humilis
Heliconia psittacorum
Heliopsis 'Light of Loddon'
Hemerocallis fulva
Hesperis matronalis
Heuchera 'Palace Purple'
Heuchera sanguinea
Hibiscus moscheutos

Hosta lancifolia
Hosta tokudama
Houttuynia cordata 'Chamaeleon'
Hypericum calycinum
Impatiens sodenii
Incarvillea delavayi
Inula oculis-christi
Kirengeshoma palmata
Kniphofia uvaria
Leonotis leonurus
Leucanthemum × superbum
Liatris spicata
Ligularia dentata 'Desdemona'
Ligularia tussilaginea
     'Aureomaculata'
Limonium latifolium
Linum narbonense
Linum perenne
Liriope muscari
Lobelia cardinalis
Lobelia 'Vedrariensis'
Lychnis coronaria
Lychnis × haagena
Lysimachia punctata
Macleaya cordata
Malva moschata
Mazus radicans
Mimulus cardinalis
Mimulus moschatus
Mirabilis jalapa
Myosotis scorpioides
Neomarica caerulea
Nepeta × faassenii
Oenothera speciosa
Osteospermum ecklonis
Osteospermum jucundum
Penstemon barbatus
Penstemon × gloxinoides
Penstemon pinifolius
Perovskia atriplicifolia
Phlomis russeliana
Phlox paniculata
Phormium cookianum 'Tricolor'
Phormium hybrids
Phormium tenax 'Purpureum'
Physostegia virginiana
Platycodon grandiflorus
Plectostachys serphyllifolia
Polemonium caeruleum
Polygonum affine
Potentilla 'Monsieur Rouillard'
Potentilla nepalensis
Raoulia australis
Rheum palmatum 'Atrosanguineum'
Rodgersia aesculifolia
Rodgersia pinnata
Rodgersia podophylla
Romneya coulteri
Roscoea cauteloides
Rudbeckia fulgida 'Goldsturm'
Salvia aurea
Salvia elegans
Salvia nemorosa
Salvia uliginosa
Sanguisorba canadensis

Schizostylis coccinea 'Grandiflora'
Sedum spectabile
Sedum spurium
Sempervivum arachnoideum
Sempervivum tectorum
Senecio cruentus
Sidalcea 'Rose Queen'
Sisyrinchium striatum
Solanum pseudocapsicum
Solidago 'Golden Wings'
Solidago species and hybrids
X Solidaster luteus
Stachys byzantina
Stokesia laevis
Telekia speciosa
Thalia dealbata
Thalictrum delavayi
Thunbergia alata
X Venidio-arctotis cultivars
Veratrum nigrum
Verbascum nigrum
Verbascum olympican
Verbena × hybrida
Verbena venosa
Veronica austriaca subsp. teucrium
Veronica spicata
Viola hederacea
Yucca filamentosa
Yucca gloriosa
Zantedeschia rehmannii
Zauschneria californica
Zingiber zerumbet

Alpines

Aquilegia caerulea
Arabis caucasica 'Plena'
Aubrieta deltoidea
Erodium pelargoniflorum
Gentiana acaulis
Gentiana asclepiaea
Gentiana lutea
Gentiana sino-ornata
Papaver alpinum
Parochetus communis
Phlox subulata
Saponaria ocymoides
Saxifraga caespitosa
Saxifraga paniculata
Saxifraga stolonifera

Water garden plants

Acorus calamus
Caltha palustris
Nelumbo nucifera
Nymphaea alba
Nymphaea 'Aurora'
Nymphaea candida
Nymphaea × helvola
Nymphaea, Laydeckeri hybrids
Nymphaea marliacea 'Carnea'
Nymphaea nouchali var. caerulea
Nymphaea odorata
Pontederia cordata

SHRUBS

The cultivation of shrubs will only be successful if they are correctly located. A sun-loving shrub will never flower brilliantly in a dark, damp corner; instead, it will sulk for years and produce only one or two flowers.

Always provide adequate water during dry spells as water stress often leaves shrubs vulnerable to insect attack. Using plenty of mulch around plants will help to conserve water. Conversely, planting in water-logged soils may result in shrubs suffering root rot or fungal diseases, so an even balance needs to be found.

Regular, controlled pruning after flowering will result in healthy, well-formed shrubs. Deciduous shrubs should *not* be cut back when the leaves drop off as the next season's flowers may be inadvertently removed as well. If you don't have the time for regular pruning plant the same shrub in groups of three or five, as this will look much better than one straggly individual. Also, lightly fertilize every few months rather than in one big hit; avoid heaping animal manures up around plants' main stems.

Wander through a botanic garden to see shrubs growing in their prime. At the same time you can discover which shrubs might be suitable for your garden.

Hardy, deciduous

Acer palmatum 'Dissectum
     Atropurpureum'
Acer palmatum 'Dissectum Viridis'
Aesculus parviflora
Amelanchier alnifolia
Aronia arbutifolia 'Brilliant'
Caesalpinia gilliesii
Callicarpa species
Calycanthus floridus
Calycanthus occidentalis
Carmichaelia odorata
Caryopteris × clandonensis
Ceanothus 'Gloire de Versailles'
Chimonanthus praecox
Clethra alnifolia
Corylopsis pauciflora
Corylopsis spicata
Cotinus coggyria
Daphne genkwa
Deutzia × rosea
Deutzia scabra
Dipelta floribunda

Edgeworthia papyrifera
Euonymus alatus
Euonymus europaeus
Exochorda racemosa
Hamamelis × intermedia
Hamamelis mollis
Hamamelis vernalis
Hamamelis virginiana
Indigofera decora
Itea virginica
Kerria japonica
Kolkwitzia amabilis
Lonicera × purpusii
Lonicera tatarica
Magnolia quinquepeta
Magnolia stellata
Malus sargentii
Myrica pensylvanica
Paeonia lutea
Paeonia suffruticosa
Physocarpus opulifolius
Potentilla fruticosa 'Tangerine'
Prunus glandulosa 'Rosea Plena'
Prunus 'Shimidsu Sakura'
Punica granatum var. nana
Rhus aromatica
Ribes sanguineum
Salix purpurea
Sambucus canadensis
Sophora japonica
Spartium junceum
Staphylea colchica
Symphoricarpos orbiculatus
Symphoricarpos rivularis
Tamarix gallica
Tamarix parviflora
Viburnum × bodnantense
Viburnum × carlecephalum
Viburnum carlesii
Viburnum dentatum
Viburnum farreri
Viburnum lantana
Viburnum opulus 'Nanum'
Viburnum opulus 'Sterile'
Viburnum plicatum 'Mariesii'
Viburnum prunifolium
Viburnum trilobum
Vitex agnus-castus

Frost-hardy, evergreen

Abelia × grandiflora
Abelia schumannii
Abutilon megapotamicum
     'Variegatum'
Agapetes serpens
Andromeda polifolia
Arbutus unedo 'Compacta'
Arctostaphylos manzanita
Arctostaphylos uva-ursi
Artemisia ludoviciana
Aucuba japonica
Azara microphylla
Baccharis pilularis 'Twin Peaks'
Banksia ericifolia

Banksia integrifolia
Boronia heterophylla
Brugmansia × candida
Bursaria spinosa
Buxus microphylla
    var. japonica
Buxus sempervirens
Callistemon citrinus
Cantua buxifolia
Cestrum elegans
Cestrum 'Newellii'
Chaenomeles speciosa
Chamaecyparis obtusa
Clianthus puniceus
Coleonema pulchrum
Cordyline banksii
Corokia cotoneaster
Corokia × virgata
Coronilla glauca
Corynabutilon vitifolium
Crinodendron hookerianum
Daboecia cantabrica
Daphne × burkwoodii
Daphne cneorum
Daphne odora
Daphne tangutica
Desfontainea spinosa
Dodonaea viscosa
Drejerella guttata
Dryandra species
Elaeagnus pungens
Elaeagnus pungens 'Maculata'
Enkianthus campanulatus
Epacris impressa
Eremophila glabra
Eremophila maculata
Eriogonum umbellatum
Escallonia × exoniensis
Escallonia rubra
Euonymus fortunei
Euonymus japonicus
    'Aureomarginatus'
X Fatshedera lizei
Fatsia japonica
Fothergilla major
Francoa appendiculata
Fremontodendron californicum
Gaultheria procumbens
Gaultheria shallon
Grevillea 'Boongala Spinebill'
Grevillea lavandulacea
Grevillea 'Robyn Gordon'
Grewia occidentalis
Griselinia littoralis
Halimium lasianthum
Ilex × altaclarensis 'Wilsonii'
Ilex aquifolium
Ilex cornuta
Ilex crenata
Ilex glabra
Ilex 'Golden King'
Itea ilicifolia
Juniperus chinensis
Juniperus conferta
Juniperus horizontalis

Juniperus sabina
Juniperus sabina 'Tamariscifolia'
Kalmia latifolia
Leptospermum laevigatum
Leptospermum scoparium
    'Red Damask'
Leucadendron salignum
Leucothoe fontanesiana
Ligustrum japonicum
Ligustrum lucidum
Ligustrum ovalifolium 'Aureum'
Ligustrum quihoui
Ligustrum sinense
Lonicera fragrantissima
Lonicera nitida
Mahonia aquifolium
Mahonia lomariifolia
Mahonia repens
Melaleuca nesophylla
Myrica californica
Myrtus communis
Nandina domestica
Nandina domestica 'Nana'
Olearia macrodonta
Olearia phlogopappa
Osmanthus delavayi
Osmanthus heterophyllus
    'Variegatus'
Pachystegia insignis
Parahebe catarracte
Parahebe lyallii
Parahebe perfoliata
Paxistima canbyi
Pernettya macronata
Phlomis fruticosa
Photinia × fraseri
Photinia glabra
Photinia serrulata
Pieris formosa
Pieris forrestii
Pieris japonica
Pimelia prostrata
Pinus mugo
Pittosporum crassifolium
Pittosporum tobira
Platycladus orientalis
Polygala chamaebuxus
Polygala × dalmaisiana
Prostanthera rotundifolia
Prunus laurocerasus
Pseudowintera colorata
Raphiolepis × delacourii
Raphiolepis indica
Rhamnus alaternus
Rhamnus californicus
Ruscus aculeatus
Santolina chamaecyparissus
Santolina virens
Sarcococca hookeriana
Sarcococca ruscifolia
Skimmia japonica
Taxus cuspidata
Teucrium chamaedrys
Teucrium fruticans
Thuja occidentalis 'Rheingold'

Vaccinium macrocarpon
Viburnum × burkwoodii
Viburnum davidii
Viburnum tinus
Westringia fruticosa

Partly to fully frost-tender

Abutilon × hybridum
Acacia acinacea
Acacia boormannii
Acacia pravissima
Alogyne huegelii
Anisodontea
    hypomandarum
Ardisia crispa
Ardisia japonica
Baeckea virgata
Bauhinia galpinii
Begonia fuchsioides
Bougainvillea species
Bouvardia hybrids
Bouvardia longiflora
Brachyglottis greyi
Brachyglottis monroi
Brugmansia sanguinea
Brugmansia suaveolens
Brunfelsia pauciflora
Burchella babulina
Caesalpinia pulcherrima
Calliandra tweedii
Callistemon viminalis
Carissa macrocarpa
Carpentaria californica
Cassia artemisioides
Ceanothus impressus
Ceanothus thyrsiflorus
Cestrum aurantiacum
Cestrum nocturnum
Chorizema cordatum
Clerodendron thomsoniae
Clerodendron trichotomum
Clerodendron ugandense
Coprosma × kirkii
Coprosma repens
Correa alba
Correa 'Dusky Bells'
Correa pulchella
Cuphea ignea
Dahlia excelsa
Deutzia 'Rosalin'
Duranta repens
Escallonia 'Apple Blossom'
Eupatorium megalophyllum
Euphorbia fulgens
Euphorbia milii
Euphorbia pulcherrima
Euryops pectinatus
Gamolepsis chrysanthemoides
Gardenia augusta 'Florida'
Gardenia thunbergia
Garrya elliptica
Gordonia axillaris
Grevillea rosmarinifolia

Hakea laurina
Hakea sericea
Heliotropium arborescens
Hovea lanceolata
Hymenolepis parviflora
Hypoestes aristata
Justicia carnea
Kunzea baxteri
Lagerstroemia indica
Lagerstroemia indica hybrids
Lantana camara
Lantana montevidensis
Leptospermum petersonii
Leucospermum cordifolium
Loropetalum chinense
Malvaviscus arboreus
Melaleuca hypericifolia
Melaleuca incana
Melastoma affine
Melianthus major
Michelia figo
Mimulus aurantiacus
Myoporum parvifolium
Myrtus ugni
Nerium oleander
Nerium oleander 'Album'
Nerium oleander 'Punctatum'
Nerium oleander 'Splendens
    Variegatum'
Ochna serrulata
Olearia arborescens
Osmanthus fragrans
Pentas lanceolata
Pittosporum tenuifolium
Plumbago auriculata
Protea cynaroides
Protea neriifolia
Rondeletia amoena
Russelia juncea
Salvia africana-lutea
Senecio petasitis
Senna corymbosa
Sparmannia africana
Streptosolen jamesonii
Sutherlandia frutescens
Tecoma stans
Tecomaria capensis
Telopea speciosissima
Ternstroemia gymnanthera
Tetrapanax papyriferus
Thevetia peruviana
Tibouchina urvilleana

Berberis

Berberis darwinii
Berberis ottawensis 'Superba'
Berberis thunbergii

Buddleja

Buddleja alternifolia
Buddleja davidii
Buddleja globosa
Buddleja salviifolia

Calluna

Calluna vulgaris

Camellia

Camellia granthamiana
Camellia japonica
Camellia japonica
    'Adolphe Audusson'
Camellia japonica 'Desire'
Camellia japonica 'Elegans'
Camellia japonica
    'Kingyo-Tsubaki'
Camellia japonica 'Lady Vansittart'
Camellia japonica 'Yamato Nishiki'
Camellia lutchuensis
Camellia reticulata
Camellia sasanqua
Camellia sasanqua 'Hiryu'
Camellia sasanqua 'Yuletide'
Camellia sinensis
Camellia × williamsii
Camellia × williamsii 'Donation'

Choisya

Choisya ternata

Cistus

Cistus 'Brilliancy'
Cistus ladanifer
Cistus salviifolius

Cornus

Cornus alba
Cornus nuttallii

Cotoneaster

Cotoneaster apiculatus
Cotoneaster dammeri
Cotoneaster horizontalis
Cotoneaster lacteus
Cotoneaster microphyllus
Cotoneaster multiflorus
Cotoneaster salicifolius

Cytisus

Cytisus × praecox
Cytisus scoparius

Erica

Erica carnea
Erica cinerea
Erica × darleyensis
Erica erigena 'W.T. Racklift'
Erica mammosa
Erica mediterranea
Erica tetralix
Erica vagans

Forsythia

Forsythia × intermedia
Forsythia × intermedia
    'Beatrix Farrand'
Forsythia suspensa

Fuchsia

Fuchsia 'Gartenmeister Bonstedt'
Fuchsia magellanica cultivars
Fuchsia magellanica var. gracilis
Fuchsia magellanica
    var. gracilis 'Alba'
Fuchsia procumbens

Genista

Genista aetnensis
Genista lydia
Genista monosperma
Genista pilosa 'Vancouver Gold'
Genista tinctoria

Hebe

Hebe × andersonii 'Variegata'
Hebe × franciscana 'Blue Gem'
Hebe hulkeana
Hebe speciosa

Helichrysum

Helichrysum selago

Hibiscus

Hibiscus mutabilis
Hibiscus rosa-sinensis
Hibiscus rosa-sinensis
    'Apple Blossom'
Hibiscus rosa-sinensis 'Cooperi'
Hibiscus rosa-sinensis 'Madonna'
Hibiscus rosa-sinensis 'Sabrina'
Hibiscus syriacus
Hibiscus syriacus 'Ardens'
Hibiscus syriacus 'Blue Bird'

Hydrangea

Hydrangea aspera var. aspera
Hydrangea macrophylla
Hydrangea macrophylla 'Blue Wave'
Hydrangea paniculata 'Grandiflora'
Hydrangea quercifolia

Hypericum

Hypericum patulum
Hypericum 'Rowallane'

Jasminum

Jasminum mesnyi
Jasminum nudiflorum

Lavandula

Lavandula angustifolia
Lavandula dentata
Lavandula stoechas

Philadelphus

Philadelphus coronarius
Philadelphus 'Lemoinei'
Philadelphus lewisii
Philadelphus mexicanus
Philadelphus 'Virginal'

Phygelius

Phygelius species

Pyracantha

Pyracantha angustifolia
Pyracantha cocchinea
Pyracantha crenulata
Pyracantha hybrids

Rhododendron

Rhododendron arboreum
Rhododendron augustinii
Rhododendron auriculatum
Rhododendron 'Chrysomanicum'
Rhododendron ciliicalyx
Rhododendron 'Fragrantissimum'
Rhododendron × gandavense
Rhododendron gumpo azaleas
Rhododendron Hardy hybrids
Rhododendron indica azaleas
Rhododendron jasminiflorum
Rhododendron javanicum
Rhododendron kurume azaleas
Rhododendron lochae
Rhododendron luteum hybrids
Rhododendron maccabeanum
Rhododendron ponticum
Rhododendron trichostomum
Rhododendron yakushimanum

Rosa

Alba roses
Bourbon roses
Centifolia or Provence roses
Cluster-flowered bush roses
Damask roses
Ground cover roses
Hybrid Perpetual roses
Large-flowered bush roses
Miniature roses
Modern garden roses
Modern shrub roses
Moss roses
Old garden roses
Patio roses
Polyantha roses
Portland roses
Rosa chinensis and varieties

Rosa foetida
Rosa gallica and varieties
Rosa glauca
Rosa moyesii
Rosa pimpinellifolia
Rosa rugosa
Rosa virginiana
Tea roses
Wild roses

Spiraea

Spiraea 'Anthony Waterer'
Spiraea cantoniensis
Spiraea thunbergii
Spiraea vanhouttei

Syringa

Syringa laciniata
Syringa 'Maréchal Foch'
Syringa meyeri
Syringa × persica
Syringa 'Souvenir de Louis Spaëth'
Syringa vulgaris

Weigela

Weigela florida
Weigela florida 'Eva Ratke'
Weigela florida 'Variegata'

TREES

Choosing the right tree for a location requires careful consideration—the tiny seedling tree you admire in a pot may grow to overwhelm a small garden or cause major problems to building foundations and underground pipes. Always check the mature height of a tree before purchase and allow plenty of room for it to fully develop. Visit an arboretum to see trees growing at their best when choosing one for your garden.

At planting time dig a hole at least three times the root volume and add compost and a complete fertilizer. To help the tree get off to a good start, cut off any coiled or damaged roots, plant firmly and leave a slight depression around the main stem to allow rainwater to collect. Although many trees are drought-tolerant, they still require a good supply of water. As the tree grows, avoid root disturbance at all times and remove any crossing or rubbing branches. Fertilize to the dripline of trees during rainy weather.

When pruning mature trees always cut flush to a branch or trunk, leaving no stubs—these look unsightly and give insect pests and diseases an easy entry to the tree. Seasonal checks for insect pests may be necessary. Small holes or sawdust on the trunk indicate the presence of borers.

Ornamentals

Acacia baileyana
Acacia dealbata
Acer beurgeranium
Acer ginnala
Acer griseum
Acer japonicum
Acer macrophyllum
Acer negundo 'Aureo-variegatum'
Acer palmatum
Acer platanoides
Acer platanoides 'Crimson King'
Acer pseudoplatanus
Acer rubrum
Acer saccharinum
Aesculus californica
Aesculus × carnea
Ailanthus glandulosa
Alberta magna
Albitzia julibrissin
Albitzia lophantha
Alectryon excelsa
Alnus cordata
Alnus glutinosa
Alnus jorullensis
Amelanchier lamarckii
Angophora costata
Aralia elata
Arbutus menziesii
Arbutus unedo
Banksia serrata
Bauhina variegata 'Candida'
Beaucarnea recurvata
Betula nigra
Betula papyrifera
Betula pendula
Betula pendula 'Dalecarlica'
Bolusanthus speciosus
Butea monosperma
Callicoma serratifolia
Calodendrum capense
Carpinus betulus
Carpinus caroliniana
Cassia fistula
Cassia javanica
Cassia multijuga
Castanea sativa
Castanospermum australe
Casuarina glauca
Catalpa bignonioides
Cedrela sinensis
Celtis occidentalis
Cercidiphyllum japonicum
Cercis canadensis

Cercis siliquastrum
Chionanthus virginicus
Chorisia speciosa
Citharexylum quadrangulare
Citharexylum spinosum
Cladastris lutea
Clusia rosea
Cordyline australis
Cornus capitata
Cornus controversa
Cornus florida
Cornus kousa
Cornus mas
Corylus avellana 'Contorta'
Corynocarpos laevigata
Crataegus coccinea 'Plena'
Crataegus laevigata 'Paul's Scarlet'
Crataegus × lavallei
Crataegus phaeonopyrum
Crataegus pubescens
Cussonia spicata
Dais cotinifolia
Davidia involucrata
Diospyros kaki
Dombeya tiliacea
Elaeocarpus reticulatus
Embothrium coccineum
Erythrina crista-galli
Eucalyptus globulus
Eucalyptus gunnii
Eucalyptus pauciflora
Eucryphia cordifolia
Eucryphia × nymansensis
Fagus grandifolia
Fagus sylvatica
Fagus sylvatica 'Pendula'
Fagus sylvatica f. purpurea
Franklinia alatamaha
Fraxinus americana
Fraxinus ornus
Fraxinus oxycarpa 'Raywood'
Fraxinus pennsylvanica
Gleditsia triacanthos 'Sunburst'
Gleditsia triacanthos var. inermis
Halesia carolina
Hoheria populnea
Ilex × altaclarensis
Ilex aquifolium
Ilex opaca
Juglans nigra
Kigelia africana
Koelreuteria paniculata
Laburnum × watereri 'Vossii'
Liquidambar formosana
Liquidambar styraciflua
Liriodendron tulipifera
Lophostemon confertus
Maclura pomifera
Magnolia campbellii
Magnolia grandiflora
Magnolia heptapeta
Magnolia × soulangiana
Magnolia virginiana
Maytenus boaria
Melia azedarach

Nothofagus moorei
Nothofagus obliqua
Nothofagus solandri
Nyssa sylvatica
Oxydendrum arboreum
Parrotia persica
Paulownia tomentosa
Peltophorum africanum
Phellodendron amurense
Pistacia chinensis
Pittosporum eugenioides
Platanus × acerifolia
Platanus orientalis
Populus alba
Populus deltoides
Populus nigra 'Italica'
Populus tremuloides
Pterocarya fraxinifolia
Quercus agrifolia
Quercus alba
Quercus ilex
Quercus macrocarpa
Quercus nigra
Quercus palustris
Quercus robur
Quercus rubra
Quercus suber
Rhus succedanea
Rhus typhina 'Laciniata'
Robinia pseudoacacia
Robinia pseudoacacia 'Frisia'
Rothmannia capensis
Salix alba
Salix babylonica
Salix caprea
Salix 'Chrysocoma'
Salix matsudana 'Tortuosa'
Sapium sebiferum
Sassafras albidum
Schinus areira
Schinus terebinthifolia
Schotia brachypetela
Sophora japonica
Sophora microphylla
Sophora tetraptera
Sorbus aria
Sorbus aucuparia
Sorbus cashmiriana
Sorbus commixta
Sorbus hupehensis
Stuartia ovata
Stuartia pseudocamellia
Styrax japonicus
Syringa reticulata
Tilia cordata
Tilia × europaea
Tilia × petiolaris
Tilia tomentosa
Tristaniopsis laurina
Ulmus americana
Ulmus glabra
Ulmus parvifolia
Ulmus procera
Ulmus procera 'Louis Van Houtte'
Ulmus pumila

Umbellularia californica
Zelkova serrata
Ziziphus jujuba

Conifers

Abies cephalonica
Abies concolor
Abies procera 'Glauca'
Agathis australis
Agathis robusta
Araucaria araucana
Araucaria bidwillii
Athrotaxis selaginoides
Calocedrus decurrens
Cedrus atlantica
Cedrus deodara
Cephalotaxus harringtonia
Chamaecyparis lawsoniana
Chamaecyparis pisifera
Cryptomeria japonica
Cryptomeria japonica 'Elegans'
× Cupressocyparis leylandii
Cupressus arizonica
Cupressus macrocarpa
Cupressus sempervirens
    'Swane's Golden'
Cupressus torulosa
Ginkgo biloba
Juniperus communis
Juniperus scopulorum
Juniperus virginiana
Larix decidua
Nageia falcata
Picea abies
Picea omorika
Picea pungens 'Koster'
Pinus bungeana
Pinus densiflora
Pinus nigra
Pinus palustris
Pinus pinea
Pinus ponderosa
Pinus radiata
Pinus strobus
Pinus sylvestris
Pinus thunbergiana
Podocarpus totara
Pseudotsuga menziesii
Sciadopitys verticillata
Sequoia sempervirens
Sequoiadendron giganteum
Taxodium distichum
Taxus baccata
Thuja occidentalis
Thuja plicata
Thujopsis dolabrata
Tsuga canadensis

Malus

Malus 'Aldenhamensis'
Malus floribunda
Malus hupehensis
Malus 'Red Jade'

Pyrus

Pyrus calleryana
Pyrus salicifolia 'Pendula'

Prunus

Prunus × *amygdalo-persica*
Prunus × *blireiana*
Prunus cerasifera 'Nigra'
Prunus incisa
Prunus mume
Prunus sargentii
Prunus serrulata
Prunus serrulata 'Amanogawa'
Prunus serrulata 'Mount Fuji'
Prunus 'Shirofugen'
Prunus subhirtella 'Pendula'
Prunus 'Tahaiku'
Prunus × *yedoensis*

BULBS, CORMS & TUBERS

Bulbs are one of the easiest groups of plants to grow, as they are adaptable to a wide range of climates and growing conditions. Select firm, healthy bulbs when buying and check around the surface or under the outer papery casing for any sign of insects or grubs. Soft, damp spots or grey mould may indicate damage from a fungus. Many bulbs in or near flowering time are now available in pots.

If you live in a warm climate and wish to grow cold-climate bulbs, you may have to give the bulbs an artificial winter in the refrigerator crisper for six weeks before planting. In a cold climate, lift frost-tender bulbs over winter, grow them in pots and plant them out in spring when the danger of frost has passed.

Certain bulbs are known as 'garden escapees'. Freesias in lawns or on roadsides in spring are popular with everyone, however, other bulbs appearing in prime country pasture cause heartache to farmers. Check with a reputable dealer if in doubt about the suitability of any bulb.

Winter–early spring flowering

Anemone coronaria
Bulbinella floribunda
Chasmanthe floribunda
    var. *floribunda*

Crocus, Dutch hybrids
Crocus tomasinianus
Eranthis hyemalis
Freesia alba
Freesia, Florist's hybrids
Galanthus ikariae
Galanthus nivalis
Hermodactylus tuberosus
Hyacinthoides non-scripta
Iris, Iriodictyum irises
Iris, Juno irises
Lachenalia aloides var. *aloides*
Lachenalia bulbifera
Veltheimia capensis

Spring flowering

Albuca canadensis
Allium christophii
Anemone blanda
Anemone nemorosa
Anomatheca laxa
Asphodeline lutea
Babiana stricta
Brimeura amethystina
Chasmanthe aethiopica
Chasmanthe luciliae
Chlidanthus fragrans
Clivia miniata
Convallaria majalis
Crocus flavus
Crocus, spring flowering
Cyrtanthus macowanii
Dracunculus vulgaris
Erythronium dens-canis
Erythronium 'Pagoda'
Fritillaria imperialis
Fritillaria meleagris
Fritillaria persica
Gladiolus alatus
Gladiolus, Butterfly hybrids
Gladiolus byzantinus
Gladiolus carneus
Gladiolus × *colvillei*
Gladiolus tristis
Herbertia drummondii
Hyacinthoides hispanica
Hymenocallis × *festalis*
Hymenocallis littoralis
Iris bucharica
Iris, Xiphium irises
Iris, Dutch hybrids
Iris tingitana
Ixia maculata
Ixia paniculata
Ixia viridiflora
Leucocoryne ixioides odorata
Leucojum aestivum
Moraea spathulata
Muscari armeniacum
Muscari armeniacum 'Blue Spike'
Muscari plumosum 'Comosum'
Narcissus cyclamineus hybrids
Narcissus, Double-flowered
    daffodils

Narcissus jonquilla hybrids
Narcissus, Large-cupped daffodils
Narcissus poeticus hybrids
Narcissus, Small-cupped daffodils
Narcissus, Split-cupped hybrids
Narcissus tazetta hybrids
Narcissus triandrus hybrids
Narcissus, Trumpet hybrids
Narcissus, Wild species
Nectaroscordum siculum subsp.
    bulgaricum
Notholirion thomsonianum
Ornithogalum thyrsoides
Oxalis adenophylla
Puschkinia scilloides
Ranunculus asiaticus
Rhodohypoxis baurii
Sauromatum venosum
Scilla siberica
Sparaxis tricolor
Tristagma uniflora
Triteleia laxa 'Queen's Fabiola'
Tritonia crocata
Tulipa acuminata
Tulipa clusiana
Tulipa, Cottage tulips
Tulipa, Darwin hybrid tulips
Tulipa, Darwin tulips
Tulipa, Double early tulips
Tulipa, Double late tulips
Tulipa fosteriana
Tulipa gesneriana
Tulipa greigeii
Tulipa kaufmanniana
Tulipa, Parrot tulips
Tulipa, Rembrandt tulips
Tulipa saxatilis
Tulipa, Single early tulips
Tulipa, Single late tulips
Tulipa tarda
Urceolina peruviana
Veltheimia bracteata
Watsonia borbonica
    subsp. *borbonica*

Summer flowering

Allium moly
Allium narcissiflorum
Aristea ecklonii
Aristea ensifolia
Belamcanda chinensis
Camassia esculenta
Cardiocrinum giganteum
Clivia nobilis
Crinum bulbispermum
Crinum moorei
Crinum × *powellii*
Crocosmia aurea
Crocosmia crocosmiiflora
Crocosmia masonorum
Cypella herbertii
Dichelostemma ida-maia
Dichelostemma pulchellum
Galtonia candicans

Gladiolus, Large-flowered
    hybrids
Habranthus robustus
Iris latifolia
Lilium, Asiatic hybrids
Lilium auratum
Lilium, Aurelian hybrids
Lilium candidum
Lilium formosanum
Lilium henryi
Lilium lancifolium
Lilium longiflorum
Lilium martagon
Lilium, Oriental hybrids
Lilium pardalinum
Lilium regale
Lilium speciosum
Lilium, Trumpet hybrids
Littonia modesta
Lycoris aurea
Lycoris radiata
Lycoris squamigera
Nomocharis pardanthina
Ornithogalum arabicum
Ornithogalum umbellatum
Polianthes tuberosa
Scilla peruviana
Sprekelia formosissima
Tigridia pavonia
Tricyrtis hirta
Tulbaghia violacea
Vallota speciosa
Watsonia beatricis
Zephyranthes candida
Zephyranthes grandiflora

Autumn flowering

Amaryllis belladonna
Brunsvigia josephinae
Brunsvigia orientalis
Clivia nobilis
Colchicum autumnale
Colchicum 'Lilac Wonder'
Crocus, Autumn flowering
Gladiolus callianthus
Haemanthus coccineus
Leucojum autumnale
Nerine bowdenii
Nerine filifolia
Nerine flexuosa 'Alba'
Nerine sarniensis
Sternbergia lutea

Indoor

Arum italicum
Begonia × *tuberhybrida*
Begonia × *tuberhybrida multiflora*
Begonia × *tuberhybrida pendula*
Caladium bicolor
Canna 'Lenape'
Cyclamen coum subsp. *caucasicum*
Cyclamen coum subsp. *coum*
Cyclamen hederifolium

Cyclamen repandum
Eucomis comosa
Gloriosa superba
Hippeastrum advenum
Hippeastrum 'Apple Blossom'
Hippeastrum 'Red Lion'
Hyacinthus orientalis

LAWNS, GROUND COVERS & ORNAMENTAL GRASSES

Cultivating the perfect lawn is the aim of every gardener; it can even develop into an obsession. The key to success is a fine, even, well-drained surface that is free from weeds. The chosen grass or ground cover must be suitable for the climate and be able to withstand its intended use. Softer grasses or ground covers are suitable for occasional foot traffic, while tough grasses are more able to withstand sport, children and dogs. Pests and diseases will take hold in lawns if an unsuitable type has been chosen.

Regular watering is essential to keep a nice green surface but is fairly wasteful of a valuable resource. A brown lawn will quickly recover after adequate rain. Light, frequent applications of fertilizer during the growing season will gain the best results.

Always weed and mow on a regular basis, never mowing the lawn to lower than 20 to 30 millimetres in height. Ground cover lawns may just need the occasional once over with a whipper-snipper or hedge shears if the area is small.

Ornamental grasses, sedges and bamboos grow best in garden conditions that are not overly fertile. Add some moisture-retaining compost to the soil and give them plenty of space to develop. However, some form of barrier may be necessary to stop the spread of vigorous species. Few pests worry them.

Propagation is from seed or by division of clumps in spring. When dividing clumps or cultivating soil near them, be sure to wear protective clothing as the sharp leaf blades and fine hairs can irritate the skin.

Lawns & ground covers

Agrostis tenuis
Asarum canadense
Asarum caudatum
Bouteloua gracilis
Festuca elatior
Festuca rubra
Festuca rubra 'Commutata'
Fragaria chiloensis
Lolium perenne
Mentha requienii
Ophiopogon japonicus
Poa pratensis
Thymus pseudolanuginosus
Thymus serpyllum

Ornamental grasses, sedges & bamboos

Arundo donax
Briza media
Butomus umbellatus
Calamagrostis × *acutiflora*
Carex elata 'Aurea'
Carex morrowii
Coix lacryma-jobi
Cortaderia selloana
Deschampsia caespitosa
Festuca amethystina
Festuca glauca
Helictotrichon sempervirens
Imperata cylindrica 'Rubra'
Milium effusum 'Aureum'
Miscanthus sinensis 'Variegatus'
Molinia caerulea
Pennisetum alopecuroides
Pennisetum setaceum
Phalaris arundinacea var. *picta*
Pleioblastus pygmaeus
Sasa palmata
Sasa veitchii
Scirpus lacustris subsp.
    tabernaemontani 'Zebrinus'
Sinarundinaria nitida
Stipa gigantea
Stipa pennata

VEGETABLES & HERBS

It was not practicable to include vegetables in the Seasonal Calendars in this book. For detailed information refer to books specifically dealing with vegetables.

Herbs are ideally suited to cultivation in cool-temperate climates where summers may be hot but not humid. They can tolerate a range of growing conditions within a garden, from dry, gravelly, limy positions in full sun to cool, moist, partly shaded positions.

Herbs don't need a special garden of their own although this is often more convenient. Prepare the garden position by adding plenty of compost and a light application of fertilizer, or else grow in pots with a good-quality potting mix and some slow-release fertilizer.

Annual herbs grown from seed need to be sown regularly to ensure a constant supply for the kitchen. They tend to bolt to seed when fluctuations of temperature occur. Perennial herbs should be tip pruned regularly for compact growth, checked occasionally for invasions of leaf-eating insects or snails and tidied up in late winter before spring growth starts.

Cuttings strike readily during spring and summer, or herbs can be divided during the cooler months. Frost-tender herbs may need to be moved to a sheltered position during winter in cold climates. Otherwise, their demands are few.

Herbs make good companion plants and mix happily with flowers, vegetables and fruit or they can be used as a ground cover among shrubs.

Herbs

Allium sativum
Allium schoenoprasum
Aloysia triphylla
Andropogon nardus
Anethum graveolens
Angelica archangelica
Artemisia dracunculus
Borago officinalis
Carum carvi
Chamaemelum nobile
Coriandrum sativum
Cuminum cyminum
Curcuma domestica
Elettaria cardamomum
Foeniculum vulgare
Foeniculum vulgare var. *dulce*
Glycyrrhiza glabra
Hyssopus officinalis
Juniperus communis
Laurus nobilis
Lavandula angustifolia
Levisticum officinale
Melissa officinalis
Mentha 'Citrata'
Mentha × *piperita*
Mentha spicata
Monarda didyma
Nepeta cataria
Ocimum basilicum
Origanum hortensis

Origanum vulgare
Petroselinum crispum
Polygonum odoratum
Rosmarinus officinalis
Ruta graveolens
Salvia elegans
Salvia officinalis
Satureja hortensis
Satureja montana
Symphytum officinale
Thymus × *citriodorus*
Thymus vulgaris
Zingiber officinale

FRUIT TREES, NUT TREES & OTHER FRUITS

The basic requirement for fruit and nut trees is a good, deep, fertile soil that is well drained. Have your soil tested in a laboratory to see if it is deficient in certain elements; this will save a lot of problems later on after planting. As well, check with a reputable dealer for varieties suitable for your area and for the pollination requirements.

Remember to always choose virus-free or organically grown trees. Prune to allow light and air into the tree and to encourage continuous cropping. Keep the area around trees free of weeds and mulch and fertilize regularly.

Pest and disease problems may be numerous, so always seek expert advice on the safest way of dealing with them. Plant companion plants that are beneficial for insect control and fruit and nut production. Do not attempt to grow cool-temperate fruits in warm climates. If you follow these simple procedures you will soon be able to enjoy the 'fruits' of your labour.

Tropical to subtropical

Annona squamosa
Arachis hypogaea
Araucaria bidwillii
Carica papaya
Citrullus lanatus
Cyphomandra betacea
Persea americana
Psidium cattleianum
Theobroma cacao

Cool-temperate

Castanea sativa
Fragaria alpina

Fragaria ananassae
Humulus lupulus
Juglans regia
Malus baccata 'Dolgo'
Malus 'Bramley's Seedling'
Malus 'Discovery'
Malus domestica 'Delicious'
Malus domestica
   'Granny Smith'
Malus domestica 'Gravenstein'
Malus domestica 'Jonathan'
Malus 'Golden Hornet'
Malus 'Gorgeous'
Malus 'James Grieve'
Malus 'John Downie'
Malus pumila
Mespilus germanica
Morus nigra
Pyrus communis 'Beurre Bosc'
Pyrus communis
   'William's Bon Chretien'
Pyrus pyrifolia
Ribes grossularia
Ribes nigrum
Ribes sativum
Rubus 'Boysen'
Rubus fruticosus
Rubus idaeus
Rubus 'Logan'
Sambucus nigra 'Aurea'
Vaccinium corymbosum

Warm-temperate

Actinidia chinensis
Ananus comosus
Carya illinoinensis
Ceratonia siliqua
Cucumis melo
Diospyros kaki
Eriobotrya japonica
Feijoa sellowiana
Ficus carica
Fortunella japonica
Olea europaea subsp. europaea
Passiflora edulis
Passiflora mollissima
Physalis peruviana
Pinus pinea
Pistacea vera
Punica granatum
Sechium edule
Vitis vinifera

Citrus

Citrus aurantifolia
Citrus aurantium
Citrus limon
Citrus medica
Citrus paradisi
Citrus reticulata
Citrus sinensis
Citrus 'Washington's Navel'
Citrus × tangelo

Prunus

Prunus armeniaca
Prunus avium
Prunus cerasus
Prunus domestica
Prunus dulcis
Prunus persica
Prunus persica var. nectarina
Prunus salicifolia

INDOOR PLANTS

Cultivation of indoor plants is simple if they are given positions with reasonable light and warmth, kept evenly moist (but slightly drier in winter), and have regular weak doses of liquid fertilizer. Check regularly for pests such as mealy bug, scale insects and mites on the stems and undersides of leaves, as these bugs thrive in warm, enclosed conditions. Also, take plants outside occasionally to wash the dust from the leaves, never allowing them to sit in the sun as they will quickly burn.

If you live in a warm climate, don't be tempted to plant indoor plants in the garden if they have become too big—they may grow even bigger outside and cause real problems.

Propagation is fairly easy, particularly from stem or leaf cuttings during the warmer months. Clump-forming types can be divided once they have outgrown their pots. Seasonal flowering plants such as cyclamen are best discarded after they flower, as they rarely perform as well the next year.

Indoor foliage plants

Alocasia macorrhiza
Aspidistra elatior
Calathea makoyana
Calathea zebrina
Callisia navicularis
Codiaeum variegatum
Cordyline terminalis 'Imperialis'
Cryptanthus zonatus
Ctenanthe lubbersiana
Cyperus involucratus
Dieffenbachia 'Amoena'
Dieffenbachia seguine
   'Rudolph Roehrs'
Dizygotheca elegantissima
Epipremnum aureum
Ficus benjamina
Ficus elastica 'Decora'

Ficus lyrata
Hedera helix 'Cripsii'
Hedera helix 'Pittsburgh'
Hemigraphis alternata
Maranta leuconeura
   var. kerchoviana
Monstera deliciosa
Neoregelia carolinae
Neoregelia marmorata
Nepenthes species
Nidularium fulgens
Pedilanthus tithymaloides
Peperomia caperata
Peperomia obtusifolia
Peperomia 'Sweetheart'
Philodendron bipennifolium
Philodendron oxycardium
Philodendron selloum
Pisonia umbellifera 'Variegata'
Polyscias filicifolia
Protasparagus densiflorus
   'Sprengeri'
Protasparagus setaceus
Sansevieria trifasciata
Sansevieria trifasciata 'Hahnii'
Sansevieria trifasciata 'Laurentii'
Schefflera actinophylla
Schefflera arboricola
Schefflera digitata
Syngonium podophyllum
Tolmiea menziesii

Indoor flowering and foliage plants

Anthurium scherzerianum
Aphelandra squarrosa 'Louisae'
Begonia × cheimantha
   'Gloire de Lorraine'
Begonia 'Cleopatra'
Begonia masoniana
Begonia rex 'Merry Christmas'
Billbergia leptopoda
Billbergia nutans
Billbergia pyramidalis var. concolor
Billbergia saundersii
Drosera capensis
Episcia cupreata
Episcia 'Pink Brocade'
Graptophyllum pictum
Guzmania lingulata
Nematanthus gregarius
Serissa foetida
Spathiphyllum 'Mauna Loa'
Spathiphyllum wallisii
Tillandsia cyanea
Tillandsia lindenii

Indoor flowering plants

Costus species
Cyclamen persicum
Gesneria cuneifolia
Hoya bella
Hoya carnosa

Saintpaulia ionantha
Saintpaulia, miniature
   and trailing types

CLIMBERS & CREEPERS

Climbers and creepers are adaptable to a wide range of climates, and even exotic-looking subtropical ones may adapt to cold, frosty areas. They will look ragged, tattered or even leafless over winter, but will spring back into growth once the weather warms up.

Be prepared to work hard with climbers and creepers, pruning, training and tying them up to shape them the way you want; even self-clinging types will wander if they are not controlled. Be careful not to leave training for too long, as brittle stems will break.

Carefully prepare the soil before planting climbers and creepers by digging in plenty of compost and a complete fertilizer to ensure healthy results. Adequate water during the growing season and mulching are also essential practices. Check the Seasonal Calendars for information on propagation and pest and disease problems.

Hardy

Actinidia chinensis
Akebia quinata
Ampelopsis brevipedunculata
   var. maximowiczii
Aristolochia durior
Bignonia capreolata
Campsis grandiflora
Campsis radicans
Campsis × tagliabuana
Celastrus orbiculatus
Celastrus scandens
Clematis armandii
Clematis 'Duchess of Edinburgh'
Clematis 'Jackmanii'
Clematis 'Lasurstern'
Clematis montana
Clematis recta var. mandshurica
Clematis tangutica
Clematis viticella
Eccremocarpus scaber
Hedera canariensis 'Variegata'
Hedera helix
Hydrangea petiolaris
Jasminum officinale

Kadsura japonica
Lathyrus latifolius
Lathyrus odoratus
Lonicera caprifolium
Lonicera × heckrottii
Lonicera japonica
Lonicera japonica 'Aurea-reticulata'
Parthenocissus quinquefolia
Parthenocissus tricuspidata
Polygonum aubertii
Rosa 'Albéric Barbier'
Rosa 'Albertine'
Rosa banksiae lutea
Rosa 'Climbing Cécile Brünner'
Rosa 'Climbing Lady Hillingdon'
Rosa 'Golden Showers'
Rosa 'Handel'
Rosa 'Madame Alfred Carrière'
Rosa 'Mermaid'
Rosa 'New Dawn'
Rosa 'Zépherine Drouhin'
Schizophragma hydrangeoides

Vitis coignetiae
Vitis vinifera 'Purpurea'
Wisteria floribunda
Wisteria floribunda 'Alba'
Wisteria floribunda
 'Violacea Plena'
Wisteria sinensis
Wisteria venusta

Conservatory

Allamanda cathartica
Araujia hortorum
Beaumontia grandiflora
Bomarea caldasii
Bougainvillea glabra
Bougainvillea 'Hawaiian Gold'
Bougainvillea 'Scarlett O'Hara'
Bougainvillea spectabilis
Cissus antarctica
Clitoria ternatea
Combretum bracteosum

Distictis buccinatoria
Jasminum polyanthum
Kennedia rubicunda
Lonicera hildebrandiana
Macfadyena unguis-cati
Mandevilla laxa
Mandevilla splendens
Manettia inflata
Mucuna bennettii
Pandorea jasminoides
Pandorea pandorana
Passiflora caerulea
Passiflora coccinea
Phaseolus caracalla
Pyrostegia venusta
Solanum jasminoides
Solanum seaforthianum
Stephanotis floribunda
Strongylodon macrobotrys
Tecomanthe speciosa
Thunbergia alata
Thunbergia grandiflora

Annuals

Antigonon leptopus
Aristolochia elegans
Asarina erubescens
Clytostoma callistegioides
Dolichos lablab
Eccremocarpus scaber
Ficus pumila
Gelsemium sempervirens
Hardenbergia violacea
Hibbertia scandens
Ipomoea alba
Ipomoea nil
Ipomoea quamoclit
Ipomoea tricolor
Lapageria rosea
Mandevilla × amabilis
 'Alice du Pont'
Solandra maxima
Tropaeolum speciosum

Seasonal Calendars

	W	I N T E	R
PLANT	**DECEMBER**	**JANUARY**	**FEBRUARY**
ANNUALS & PERENNIALS			
Annuals, half-hardy	Order seed catalogues and place orders early	Sow seeds of pelargoniums at 10°C (50°F) • Clean old pots and seed trays with hot water and bleach ready for spring sowing	Start sowing varieties that need a long growing season such as *Lobelia* and *Impatiens*, provided the minimum temperature is 15°C (59°F) • Sow seed thinly to avoid damping-off disease
Annuals, hardy	Winter-flowering pansies in bloom during mild weather	Deadhead winter-flowering pansies to encourage new flowers	Sow seed of summer-flowering plants in small pots or modular trays in a cold frame or unheated greenhouse
Biennials	Firm roots if loosened by wind or frost	Firm roots if loosened by wind or frost	Firm roots if loosened by wind or frost
Perennials, frost-tender	Water overwintering plants sparingly	Water sparingly • Check regularly for pests and diseases	Prune back overwintered plants • Repot and water well to encourage new growth • Pot up cuttings rooted last summer
Perennials, hardy, winter flowering	Protect buds of *Helleborus niger* and *Iris unguicularis* with glass or cloches	Pick flowers for indoors when the buds are just opening	Remove dead flowerheads
Perennials, hardy, spring–early summer flowering	Pot up some early-flowering perennials to bloom indoors	Feed plants with a slow-release fertilizer	Feed plants with a slow-release fertilizer
Perennials, hardy, late summer–autumn flowering	Cut back dead foliage to ground level • Continue dividing large clumps during mild spells	Cut back dead foliage to ground level • Continue dividing large clumps during mild spells	Take root cuttings of *Acanthus*, *Anchusa* and *Romneya*
Alpines	Alpines with fleshy or woolly leaves dislike winter wet; cover them with cloches or panes of glass • Sow seed of alpines that need a cold period in order to germinate • Cover seed with coarse grit and stand in a cold frame	Alpines with fleshy or woolly leaves dislike winter wet; cover them with cloches or panes of glass • Sow seed of alpines that need a cold period in order to germinate • Cover seed with coarse grit and stand in a cold frame	Build new rock gardens and alpine beds ready for spring planting
Water garden plants	Cut back dead foliage of bog garden and marginal plants • Don't cut hollow stems below water level	Cut back dead foliage of bog garden and marginal plants • Don't cut hollow stems below water level	Winter dormancy

Seasonal Calendars

S P R I N G			
MARCH	**APRIL**	**MAY**	**PLANT**
			ANNUALS & PERENNIALS
Continue sowing seed in a warm environment • Alternatively, buy ready-germinated seedlings or young plantlets • Water seedlings from below to avoid damping-off disease • Ventilate greenhouse whenever weather allows to prevent fungal diseases	Continue sowing seed in a warm environment • Prick out seedlings when they are large enough to handle • Clean greenhouse glass so seedlings get maximum light • Hang yellow 'sticky traps' to monitor pests • Ventilate frequently	Continue sowing seed, selecting varieties with a short growing season • If pests are a problem under glass introduce a biological predator • Start hardening off • Delay planting out until at least the end of the month when frost is past • Containers can be planted up under cover if space allows	*Annuals, half-hardy*
Continue sowing seed under cover in cold, wet areas; otherwise, sow outdoors directly where plants are to flower • Thin out autumn-sown seedlings • Pinch out tops of sweet peas when plants are 10 cm (about 4 in) high	Sow seed outdoors directly where plants are to flower • Harden off seedlings sown under cover and plant out • Pinch out tops of *Lathyrus* (sweet peas) • To provide cut flowers, sow a few rows of seed in an out-of-the-way corner	Sow seed outdoors directly where plants are to flower • Sow seed of winter-flowering pansies in gentle heat	*Annuals, hardy*
Flowering begins • Feed *Cheiranthus* (wallflowers) and other spring bedding plants if the leaves are pale using a liquid fertilizer	Spring bedding plants in flower • Plant out summer-flowering biennials such as *Digitalis* (foxglove) • Thin out plants sown in situ to 30–45 cm (about 12–18 in) apart	Spring bedding finishes flowering • Pull up and compost plants •Plant out summer-flowering bienniels such as *Digitalis* (foxglove) • *Myosotis* can be left until it self-seeds • Revitalize ground with compost and fertilizer ready for summer bedding	*Biennials*
Take cuttings from new shoots of overwintered plants • Buy and pot up young plantlets	Take cuttings from new shoots of overwintered plants • Buy and pot up young plantlets • Clean greenhouse glass so plants get maximum light	Begin hardening off plants grown under cover ready for planting at the end of the month when frost is past • Pinch out tips of cuttings to encourage bushy growth	*Perennials, frost-tender*
Leave dead flowerheads on *Helleborus orientalis* so it can self-seed	——	——	*Perennials, hardy, winter flowering*
Flowering begins • Feed plants with a general fertilizer if not done last month • Mulch borders with compost or well-rotted manure • Finish dividing clumps of established summer-flowering plants	Stake tall-growing plants early using canes and string or special grow-through plant supports • Protect plants from slugs, especially *Delphinium* and *Hosta*	Take basal cuttings of many perennials such as *Achillea, Anthemis, Delphinium* and *Lupinus*. Thin out shoots of densely growing clumps if they weren't divided earlier	*Perennials, hardy, spring–early summer flowering*
Buy and plant new stock • Mulch borders with compost or well-rotted manure and fertilizer • Hoe lightly to keep down weeds	Lift, divide and replant established clumps of plants such as *Aster* and *Schizostylis*	Feed with a slow-release fertilizer • Support tall-growing plants using canes and string or grow-through plant supports • Water new plants during dry spells	*Perennials, hardy, late summer–autumn flowering*
Weed rock gardens and alpine beds thoroughly • Spread a fresh top-dressing of coarse grit • Best time for new planting • Sow seed of quick germinating alpines	Plant up troughs and containers now, ensuring good drainage • Add colour with dwarf bulbs, available in pots • Apply a slow-release fertilizer to beds and rock gardens • Take basal cuttings of cushion-forming plants such as *Saxifraga*	Cut back straggly plants of *Aubrieta* and *Arabis* after flowering • Continue weeding • Prick out or pot up seedlings and grow on for planting out next spring	*Alpines*
Feed bog garden plants with slow-release fertilizer • Use specially formulated aquatic plant fertilizer for plants growing in a pond	Feed plants if not done earlier • Lift, divide and replant large established clumps of marginal and bog garden plants	Buy and plant new marginal and aquatic plants • Deep water aquatics should be gradually lowered to their final position over a couple of weeks	*Water garden plants*

Seasonal Calendars

PLANT	SUMMER		
	JUNE	JULY	AUGUST
ANNUALS & PERENNIALS			
Annuals, half-hardy	All plants can now go outside after hardening off • Water regularly, paying particular attention to containers and hanging baskets • Spare plants can be potted up and kept in reserve to fill gaps later	Water plants thoroughly during dry spells and liquid feed once a week • Use a high-potash fertilizer to boost flowering • Remove dead heads every couple of days	Inspect plants for pests, especially aphids, and spray if necessary in early evening and still weather to minimize danger to beneficial insects • Keep watering and liquid feeding plants, especially in containers, but switch to a high-nitrogen fertilizer
Annuals, hardy	Flowering commences of autumn-sown plants • Thin out seedlings of direct-sown plants to 10 cm (about 4 in) apart and water well before-hand to minimize root disturbance • Make final sowings of quick maturing plants such as *Tropaeolum* (nasturtiums)	Flowering of direct-sown plants commences • Deadhead *Lathyrus* (sweet peas) frequently or flowering can stop if plants set seed	Collect ripe seeds when the heads are brown • Store seed in paper bags or envelopes • Some plants like *Nigella* have ornamental heads that are useful for flower arranging • Plants can also be allowed to self-seed for an informal effect
Biennials	Regularly water biennials trans-planted last month • Pull up and compost plants if not done earlier • Leave *Lunaria* to develop ornamental pods for drying	In a seed bed, sow seed of spring-flowering biennials for next year, such as *Cheiranthus* (wallflower) and *Myosotis* (forget-me-not)	Water seedlings and thin out overcrowded clumps
Perennials, frost-tender	All plants can now go outside after hardening off • If buying plants, they may need the same treatment if growth is soft • Pot up cuttings rooted in early spring • Tender perennials are ideal for borders and containers in a sunny position	Continue planting out • Young plants raised from cuttings earlier should now be large enough to go outside • Water plants regularly during dry spells and deadhead often to encourage more blooms • Container-grown plants benefit from a weekly liquid feed	Water plants regularly during dry spells and deadhead often to encourage more blooms
Perennials, hardy, winter flowering	Cut back old flowerheads and tattered leaves of any plants that look straggly	—	—
Perennials, hardy, spring–early summer flowering	Cut back foliage on plants such as *Geranium* and *Papaver orientale* that have finished flowering to encourage a neat mound of new foliage and a possible extra flush of flowers • Tall plants like *Delphinium* should just have the top of the flowered stem re-moved • Continue protecting suscept-ible plants against slugs and snails	Flowered stems of *Euphorbia* can be completely cut off at ground level • Wear gloves to protect from milky sap, which can irritate the skin • Collect ripe seed and sow immedi-ately in pots or trays in a cold frame	Bearded hybrid irises) that have formed established clumps can be divided immediately after flowering • Discard old pieces of rhizome and replant young pieces • First trim leaves by half to prevent wind rocking • Water during dry spells until established
Perennials, hardy, late summer–autumn flowering	Continue staking and supporting tall-growing plants	Apply a dressing of general fertilizer • Mulch the ground to conserve water	Flowering begins
Alpines	Plants that are bare in the centre can be rejuvenated by making up an equal mix of potting compost, grit and garden soil and working it well into the centre	Many plants can be rejuvenated by division • Replant the younger, outer pieces and discard the old centre • Take tip cuttings of many plants	Continue taking cuttings • Water new plants during dry weather

Seasonal Calendars

A U T U M N			
SEPTEMBER	**OCTOBER**	**NOVEMBER**	**PLANT**
			ANNUALS & PERENNIALS
Pull up and compost plants that have finished flowering • Fill gaps with any spare potted plants that have been kept in reserve, or buy pot-grown ones from nurseries • Keep feeding, watering and deadheading plants for a long display	Healthy plants of *Impatiens* and *Begonia semperflorens* can be potted for use as indoor pot plants for another few weeks • Compost any plants killed by frost • Clean and store containers for use next year, or plant them with bulbs and biennials	Order seed catalogues	*Annuals, half-hardy*
Pull up and compost plants that have finished flowering • On well-drained soil, sow seed now for next year • For pot plants next spring, sow annuals like *Calendula* and *Clarkia*	Plant out winter-flowering *Viola* (pansies)	Deadhead *Viola* (pansies) to encourage more flowers • Firm in if roots are loosened by frost	*Annuals, hardy*
Tranplant spring-flowering biennials as soon as space becomes available, digging in compost and fertilizer first to improve ground • Early planting will give better flowers • Pinch out tips to encourage bushy growth • Avoid planting *Cheiranthus* if club root is a problem	Continue transplanting biennials into their flowering position, completing by the end of the month • Early planting will give better flowers • Water well during dry spells	Firm in plants if roots become loosened by frost or wind	*Biennials*
Most plants propagate readily from cuttings taken now • Take 10 cm (about 4 in) cuttings, using a sharp knife to cut just below a leaf joint • Remove the lower leaves, put cutting in compost and cover with polythene • Leave geraniums uncovered as they are prone to rot	Move plants under cover to a greenhouse or conservatory before the first frosts • Some plants like *Felicia* can survive in an unheated structure, but most need a frost-free environment to survive • Rooted cuttings in small pots can be kept on a windowsill indoors	Water plants sparingly so the compost is only just moist • Prevent diseases such as botrytis by ensuring good ventilation, spacing plants well apart and removing dead leaves immediately	*Perennials, frost-tender*
Pot up plants such as *Helleborus niger* for indoor pot plants • Buy and plant new stock, which will establish well in autumn	Pot up plants such as *Helleborus niger* for indoor pot plants • Buy and plant new stock, which will establish well in autumn	——	*Perennials, hardy, winter flowering*
Lift, divide and replant early-flowering perennials • Buy and plant new stock	Dead leaves and stems can be cut back from now until early spring, but if left it provides ideal shelter for beneficial insects such as ladybirds • Protect any slightly delicate plants with straw or dry bracken	Dead leaves and stems can be cut back from now until early spring, but if left it provides ideal shelter for beneficial insects such as ladybirds • Protect any slightly delicate plants with straw or dry bracken	*Perennials, hardy, spring– early summer flowering*
Flowering time	If frost threatens, cut remaining flowers for a vase	Cut back dead leaves and stems from now until early spring • Protect any slightly delicate plants with straw or dry bracken	*Perennials, hardy, late summer–autumn flowering*
——	——	Alpines with fleshy or woolly leaves dislike winter wet; cover them with cloches or panes of glass	*Alpines*

PLANT	DECEMBER	JANUARY	FEBRUARY
W	**I**	**N**	**T**	**E**	**R**

PLANT	DECEMBER	JANUARY	FEBRUARY
SHRUBS			
Shrubs, hardy, deciduous	Continue planting during mild spells when soil conditions allow • Don't plant when the ground is frozen or waterlogged • Check new plants and firm in if roots are loosened by frost or wind	Check new plants and firm in if roots are loosened by frost or wind • Weed and tidy borders so long as soil isn't too wet • Prune overgrown hedges	Prune overgrown deciduous hedges before birds start nesting • Shape so the base is wider than the top
Shrubs, frost-hardy, evergreen	Firm in new plants if loosened by frost or wind	—	Thin out overgrown plants such as *Prunus laurocerasus* by removing entire branches where they join the main stem or at ground level
Shrubs, partly to fully frost-tender	If severe frosts threaten, cover susceptible outside evergreens with fleece or polythene • Remove as soon as possible or it could cause fungal diseases	Tender shrubs in containers under cover are best watered sparingly • Prevent fungal diseases by spacing plants well apart, removing dead leaves and flowers and ventilating whenever weather permits	Tender shrubs in containers under cover are best watered sparingly • Prevent fungal diseases by spacing plants well apart, removing dead leaves and flowers and ventilating whenever weather permits
Berberis	Plant new stock during mild spells • Evergreen species provide good winter interest	Plant new stock during mild spells • Evergreen species provide good winter interest	Prune deciduous species by thinning out older branches and shortening long shoots
Buddleja	Winter dormancy	Winter dormancy	Prune last year's growth to 2 to 3 buds • Old shrubs can be hard pruned
Calluna	—	—	—
Camellia	Select camellias while in flower • Sun may damage flowers in morning if wet with dew	Prepare planting site • Dig in plenty of compost • Add cocopeat • Ensure soil is well drained to deter root rot	Prune while blooming to remove dead, diseased or straggling branches
Choisya	Knock snow off bushes to prevent damage • Move pot-grown plants to a sheltered spot	Knock snow off bushes to prevent damage • Move pot-grown plants to a sheltered spot	Knock snow off bushes to prevent damage • Move pot-grown plants to a sheltered spot
Cistus	Protect from very cold winds	Protect from very cold winds	Protect from very cold winds
Cornus	Stems of many varieties provide good winter colour	Stems of many varieties provide good winter colour	Hard prune all stems to 30 cm (about 12 in) from the ground • Weed and mulch ground underneath
Cotoneaster	*C. horizontalis* is deciduous in cold climates	*C. horizontalis* is deciduous in cold climates	*C. horizontalis* is deciduous in cold climates
Cytisus	Winter dormancy	Winter dormancy	Winter dormancy
Erica	*E. carnea* in flower	*E. carnea* in flower	*E. carnea* in flower

SPRING

MARCH	APRIL	MAY	PLANT
			SHRUBS
Mulch established plants in borders with compost, manure or chipped bark • Mushroom compost isn't suitable for ericaceous plants as it contains some lime • Feed with a slow-release fertilizer • Make sure the ground is weed free before mulching • Finish planting bare-rooted shrubs	Mulch and feed plants if not done last month • Hoe the borders often to catch weeds as they germinate • Dig up dead shrubs, but check first by scraping off some bark to see if the stem is still green and alive • Prune deciduous shrubs with colourful foliage by cutting last year's growth by half • Pot on cuttings taken last summer	Keep on top of weeding, especially around new plants • Dig out the roots of perennial weeds and burn them as they'll thrive on a compost heap • On grafted plants, rub out any shoots growing below the graft union • Water autumn-planted shrubs during long dry spells	*Shrubs, hardy, deciduous*
Camellias begin to flower • Plants should be sited away from early morning sun, which can damage blooms	Lime-hating plants benefit from a feed with sequestered iron, especially if they show signs of magnesium deficiency (yellowing between leaf veins) • Take conifer cuttings from wide shoots 7.5–10 cm (about 3–4 in) long	Prune wall-trained shrubs by cutting back outward-growing shoots to 2 to 3 buds • Water autumn-planted shrubs during long dry spells • Lightly trim evergreen hedges, but watch out for birds' nests	*Shrubs, frost-hardy, evergreen*
Water container-grown plants more frequently as growth begins • Remove protection from plants outside when weather improves	Plant evergreens that are susceptible to frost damage so they will be well established before next winter, including plants such as *Ceanothus* and *Choisya* • Container-grown plants benefit from top-dressing with fresh potting compost, but remove top few centimetres of old compost first • Add controlled-release fertilizer	Finish planting evergreens if possible • Water well during dry spells right through the summer • Prune out shoot tips scorched by frost • Tender shrubs can be moved outside for the summer • This is a good month to buy and plant tender shrubs as there should be a good range available	*Shrubs, partly to fully frost-tender*
Plant new stock	Water autumn- and spring-planted stock during dry spells	Water autumn- and spring-planted stock during dry spells	*Berberis*
Complete pruning • Weed, mulch and feed	Give plenty of space when planting	*B. alternifolia* in flower	*Buddleja*
Plant new stock suitable for acid soils or special beds only • Water well during dry spells	Plant new stock suitable for acid soils or special beds only • Water well during dry spells	Plant new stock suitable for acid soils or special beds only • Complete planting as soon as possible	*Calluna*
Test soil pH if growth is unsatisfactory	Prune long or straggly growth • Lightly fertilize with azalea/camellia food	Mulch around plants as weather warms up	*Camellia*
Fertilize and mulch	Prune out frost-damaged shoots, cutting back to healthy growth	Thin out overgrown plants	*Choisya*
Ensure perfect drainage when planting • Dig in compost and slow-release fertilizer	Flowering • Prune lightly after flowering	Take cuttings • Apply light application of fertilizer	*Cistus*
Prune as soon as possible if not done last month	Feed variegated cultivars with a high-potash fertilizer to boost leaf colour	Variegated cultivars in full leaf	*Cornus*
Lightly prune • Fertilize with complete fertilizer	When planting ensure soil is well drained	Mulch plants to conserve water	*Cotoneaster*
Plant new stock in a sunny position, ensuring soil is well drained • Cut back summer-flowering varieties if necessary	Old, leggy plants are best dug up and replaced with fresh new stock • Sow seed of *Cytisus* species • Pot up cuttings rooted last summer	*C.* x *praecox* and cultivars in flower • Cut back immediately after flowering if necessary	*Cytisus*
Dig in plenty of compost and complete fetilizer before planting • Established plants can be propagated by layering	Sow seed; keep moist until germination	Fertilize and mulch	*Erica*

	S U M M E R		
PLANT	**JUNE**	**JULY**	**AUGUST**
ANNUALS & PERENNIALS (continued)			
Water garden plants	Remove any dead leaves and flowers before they rot and contaminate pond water • In the bog garden, pot up any self-sown seedlings	If aphids attack *Nymphaea* (water lilies) and marginal plants, weigh the leaves under water so pond creatures can eat the pests • Don't use chemicals as they'll poison the water	As for July • Thin out water lily leaves if growth is too dense—they should cover a third to a half of the water's surface
SHRUBS			
Shrubs, hardy, deciduous	Prune overgrown shrubs that have just flowered by taking out a third of the oldest branches at or near ground level • Take out dead and damaged growth as well • Propagate shrubs by softwood cuttings	Propagate by half-ripe cuttings • Trim dead flowers from *Santolina* and similar shrubs	Start preparing ground for autumn planting • Remove weeds, dig soil and incorporate plenty of well-rotted manure or compost under bare-rooted shrubs for autumn delivery • Continue taking half-ripe cuttings
Shrubs, frost-hardy, evergreen	Prune overgrown shrubs that have just flowered by taking out a third of the oldest branches at or near ground level • Water container-grown plants regularly	Propagate shrubs by half-ripe cuttings	Continue taking half-ripe cuttings • Finish trimming hedges
Shrubs, partly to fully frost-tender	Water container-grown plants regularly • Don't let them dry out	Water container-grown plants regularly • Don't let them dry out	Water container-grown plants regularly • Don't let them dry out • Train cuttings of *Fuchsia* up as standards
Berberis	Prune overgrown evergreen varieties by thinning out branches at ground level and shortening long growths	Finish pruning evergreen varieties	Take cuttings 7.5–10 cm (about 3–4 in) long
Buddleja	—	*B. davidii* and *B. globosa* in flower • Deadhead regularly to encourage new flowers	Ensure adequate water during dry spells, although all are drought-tolerant
Calluna	—	Take cuttings of side shoots 2.5–5 cm (about 1–2 in) long • Flowering begins	Take cuttings of side shoots 2.5–5 cm (about 1-2 in) long • Flowering begins
Camellia	Sunburn may cause brown patches on leaves; move plants to a cooler location	Check for aphids, thrips and mealy bug • Cut out variegated leaves	Check for aphids, thrips and mealy bug • Cut out variegated leaves
Choisya	*C. ternata* in flower	*C. ternata* in flower	—
Cistus	Apply gravel mulch to imitate natural habitat	Ensure adequate water during dry spells, although *Cistus* is drought-tolerant	*Cistus* resents humid weather • Ensure soil is well drained • Allow free air movement around plants
Cornus	—	—	—
Cotoneaster	Take cuttings from semi-ripe wood • Flowering now	*Cotoneaster* is drought-tolerant	Ensure adequate water while lightly fertilizing
Cytisus	Pot up seedlings from spring-sown seed	Propagate named varieties by cuttings 7.5–10 cm (about 3–4 in) long	Propagate named varieties by cuttings 7.5–10 cm (about 3–4 in) long
Erica	—	Take cuttings of side shoots 2.5–5 cm (about 1–2 in) long	Take cuttings of side shoots 2.5–5 cm (about 1–2 in) long

A U T U M N

SEPTEMBER	OCTOBER	NOVEMBER	PLANT
			ANNUALS & PERENNIALS (continued)
Cut back dead stems and leaves • Hollow stems shouldn't be cut below water level • Trim back overgrown oxygenating plants • Net the pond to keep it clear of leaves	Finish cutting back and tidying plants	Winter dormancy	*Water garden plants*
			SHRUBS
Buy and plant new shrubs • Autumn is the ideal time to plant as the soil is warm and moist to encourage good root growth, so plants will be well established in time for an explosion of growth next spring • Saves summer watering too	Continue planting • This is the best month to move established plants if necessary • Collect berries, remove and clean seeds and sow immediately • Take hardwood cuttings • Rooted cuttings taken last year can now be lifted and potted	Bare-rooted shrubs now available • Soak the roots in a bucket of water for an hour before planting • Continue taking hardwood cuttings	*Shrubs, hardy, deciduous*
Finish planting new stock by the end of the month if possible	Pot-grown shrubs usually need some frost protection as the root ball is above ground • Put containers close together, against a wall, and wrap the pots with sacking or bubble polythene	Evergreens in exposed sites can be scorched by cold winds; protect with windbreak netting if necessary	*Shrubs, frost-hardy, evergreen*
Move fully tender shrubs into a heated greenhouse or conservatory by the end of the month in colder areas	Move partly tender shrubs in containers under cover • All fully tender shrubs should be under cover before the first frosts	Water containers sparingly • Cover outdoor shrubs with fleece or polythene during severe frosts	*Shrubs, partly to fully frost-tender*
Take cuttings 7.5–10 cm (about 3–4 in) long • Plant new stock	Continue planting	Sow seed outside in a nursery bed • Seedlings usually exhibit variation	*Berberis*
Prune old flowers • Apply compost around plants	Prune tall stems by half to prevent wind rocking	Prune tall stems by half to prevent wind rocking	*Buddleja*
Trim back tall-growing varieties to promote bushy growth • Finish taking cuttings	Plant new stock in lime-free soil	Clip off dead flower stems close to foliage	*Calluna*
Lightly fertilize; water well before and after • Apply compost mulch around plants; keep away from the main stem	——	*C. sasanqua* begins flowering • Only suitable outdoors in mild areas	*Camellia*
——	Move pot-grown plants to a sheltered spot	Knock snow off plants to avoid damage	*Choisya*
——	——	——	*Cistus*
Plant new stock	Plant new stock	Plant new stock • Leaves fall to reveal colourful stems of many varieties	*Cornus*
Red fruits appear • Cut branches for indoor decoration	Collect and sow seed; keep moist until germination	Keep seed moist	*Cotoneaster*
Propagate named varieties by cuttings 7.5–10 cm (about 3–4 in) long	Plant new stock	——	*Cytisus*
Take cuttings of side shoots 2.5–5 cm (about 1–2 in) long • Plant new stock • *E. carnea* and *E. x darleyensis* tolerate alkaline (limy) soils • Other species need lime-free soil	——	Flowering begins	*Erica*

| | W I N T E R | | |
PLANT	DECEMBER	JANUARY	FEBRUARY
SHRUBS (continued)			
Forsythia	Winter dormancy	Winter dormancy	Cut stems for a vase to force indoors
Fuchsia	Protect outdoor plants with straw or bracken against severe frosts	Protect outdoor plants with straw or bracken against severe frosts	Protect outdoor plants with straw or bracken against severe frosts
Genista	—	—	—
Hebe	Protect large-leaved species with fleece during severe frosts	Protect large-leaved species with fleece during severe frosts	Protect large-leaved species with fleece during severe frosts
Helichrysum	—	—	—
Hibiscus	—	—	—
Hydrangea	Frost may cause some damage in cold districts; wait until spring to prune	Frost may cause some damage in cold districts; wait until spring to prune	Frost may cause some damage in cold districts; wait until spring to prune
Hypericum	—	—	Cut back *H. patulum* to ground level
Jasminum	*J. nudiflorum* in flower	*J. nudiflorum* in flower	Prune flowered shoots on *J. nudiflorum* to 2 to 3 buds
Lavandula	—	—	Winter dormancy
Philadelphus	Winter dormancy	Winter dormancy	Protect plants during severe frosts
Phygelius	Protect plants during severe frosts	Protect plants during severe frosts	—
Pyracantha	—	—	—
Rhododendron	—	—	Flowering in warmer districts
Rosa	Firm in plants loosened by wind	Firm in plants loosened by wind	Firm in plants loosened by wind
Spiraea	—	—	—
Syringa	—	—	—
Weigela	—	—	—

S P R I N G			
MARCH	**APRIL**	**MAY**	**PLANT**
			SHRUBS *(continued)*
Flowering begins	In flower	Prune hard immediately after flowering • Thin out branches on mature shrubs	*Forsythia*
Remove coverings if weather permits • Pot on cuttings taken last year • Take 5 cm (about 2 in) tip cuttings of non-flowering shoots	Prune old stems of hardy species back to ground level • Feed and mulch	Feed with a high-potash fertilizer to boost flowering	*Fuchsia*
Sow seed • Plant new stock	Pot up cuttings rooted last year	In flower • Pot up young plants raised from seed in spring	*Genista*
——	Pot up cuttings • Plant new stock	Cut back frost-damaged shoots to healthy growth	*Hebe*
Plant new stock of hardy species	Cut back *H. selago*	Plant new stock	*Helichrysum*
Plant *H. syriacus* in full sun and well-drained soil	Plant *H. syriacus* in full sun and well-drained soil • Water new plants well	——	*Hibiscus*
Plant new stock in light shade and moisture-retentive soil	Prune dead tips back to new shoots • Mulch with leafmould	Liquid fertilize as buds develop • Take cuttings	*Hydrangea*
Thin out stems of *H. patulum* 'Hidcote' • Plant new stock	——	Take cuttings 5 cm (about 2 in) long from basal shoots of smaller species	*Hypericum*
Feed and mulch after pruning	Thin out *J. nudiflorum* if overgrown	Thin out *J. nudiflorum* if overgrown	*Jasminum*
Plant out new stock	Prune to boost bushy growth, but don't cut into old stems	Feed and mulch	*Lavandula*
Feed and mulch	——	In flower	*Philadelphus*
——	Hard prune border plants to 30 cm (about 12 in) • Tie in wall-trained plants	Feed and mulch	*Phygelius*
Feed and mulch	On wall-trained plants, cut back outward-growing shoots to 2 to 3 buds • Tie in remaining shoots	In flower	*Pyracantha*
Main flowering period • Apply compost or well-rotted animal manure and a complete plant food for rhododendrons • Water well before planting	Most varieties in flower	Deadhead if possible • Prune lightly after flowering • If growth is poor, check soil pH • Use a systemic insecticide regularly to combat insect damage on leaves	*Rhododendron*
Main pruning time for cluster-flowered and large-flowered bush roses	Feed and mulch • If necessary, start preventative sprays against fungal diseases	Continue spraying if necessary • Mulch thickly with straw or old cow manure; keep mulch away from plant stems • Lightly apply fertilizer every 6 weeks	*Rosa*
Hard prune *Spiraea rivularis*	——	Fertilize and mulch well	*Spiraea*
Feed and mulch	Flowering begins	In flower	*Syringa*
Feed and mulch	——	Tip prune young plants regularly	*Weigela*

| | S U M M E R | | |
PLANT	JUNE	JULY	AUGUST
SHRUBS (continued)			
Forsythia	Finish pruning as soon as possible	——	——
Fuchsia	Feed with a high-potash fertilizer to boost flowering	Take softwood cuttings	Take softwood cuttings
Genista	Thin out shoots on overgrown plants after flowering • Pinch out shoot tips on young plants	——	Take heel cuttings 5–10 cm (about 2–4 in) long
Hebe	Ensure adequate water during dry spells, although most are drought-tolerant	Check for damage by scale insects or leaf miner	Downy mildew may occur in humid weather; spray with a fungicide
Helichrysum	Take cuttings	Take cuttings	——
Hibiscus	Check for insect pests but spray only when necessary	Take heel cuttings	Flowering begins
Hydrangea	Protect from hot, dry winds as foliage and flowers may burn	——	Powdery mildew may occur in humid weather; spray with a fungicide • Take cuttings
Hypericum	Take cuttings 5 cm (about 2 in) long from basal shoots of smaller species	Rust can be a problem • Spray with a systemic fungicide, but replace with other plants if the problem persists	Propagate larger species by heel cuttings 10 cm (about 4 in) long
Jasminum	Mulch and feed	——	Take semi-ripe cuttings 7.5–10 cm (about 3–4 in) long
Lavandula	In flower • Harvest flowers for drying	Propagate by heel cuttings	Trim off dead flowers with shears
Philadelphus	In flower	Thin out older branches to encourage growth from base	Take semi-ripe cuttings
Phygelius	——	In flower	Remove tops of flowered stems to encourage more blooms
Pyracantha	In flower	Tie in stems of wall-trained plants	Continue tying in wall-trained plants
Rhododendron	Apply compost or leaf litter around plants • Supply adequate water • Do not dig around plants as root system may be damaged	Protect plants from hot afternoon sun • Propagation may be carried out by layering	Remove unsprayed plants badly damaged by insect attack • Check for mildew during humid weather; spray with a fungicide
Rosa	Continue spraying if necessary • Mulch thickly with straw or old cow manure; keep mulch away from plant stems • Lightly apply fertilizer every 6 weeks	Spray rust spores with sulphur; remove affected leaves • Prune back sucker growth from base rootstocks • Propagate by budding	Continue deadheading • Prune out flowered stems of ramblers
Spiraea	Provide adequate water during dry spells • Take softwood cuttings	Take semi-ripe cuttings	Take semi-ripe cuttings
Syringa	——	——	——
Weigela	Take softwood cuttings • Prune after flowering	Ensure adequate water during dry spells • Mulch • Lightly fertilize	——

A U T U M N

SEPTEMBER	OCTOBER	NOVEMBER	PLANT
			SHRUBS *(continued)*
Propagate by layering • Plants often layer themselves and these can be potted up	Take hardwood cuttings • Plant new stock	Continue planting	*Forsythia*
Towards end of month, pot up tender species ready to move under cover	Protect the crowns of outdoor species from frost with straw or bracken • Leave dead stems on for extra protection • Move tender species to a frost-free place	Protect the crowns of outdoor species from frost with straw or bracken • Leave dead stems on for extra protection • Move tender species to a frost-free place	*Fuchsia*
Take heel cuttings 5–10 cm (about 2–4 in) long	Plant new stock in well-drained soil	Plant new stock in well-drained soil	*Genista*
Plant new stock of hardy species	Plant new stock of hardy species	—	*Hebe*
—	Pot up *H. selago* and move to a frost-free place	Water tender plants under cover sparingly	*Helichrysum*
Plant new stock in a sunny site • In colder areas, choose a sheltered spot	Long shoots can be shortened after flowering	—	*Hibiscus*
Plant new stock in moisture-retentive soil enriched with organic matter	Finish autumn planting	—	*Hydrangea*
Propagate larger species by heel cuttings 10 cm (about 4 in) long	Plant new stock	Propagate *H. patulum* by division	*Hypericum*
Take semi-ripe cuttings 7.5–10 cm (about 3–4 in) long • Plants can also be propagated by layering	Plant new stock	—	*Jasminum*
Finish gathering leaves for drying	—	—	*Lavandula*
—	Winter dormancy	Winter dormancy	*Philadelphus*
Tie in tall shoots	Cut tall stems back by half	—	*Phygelius*
Autumn berry	Autumn berry	—	*Pyracantha*
Water well to boost flowering	Plant new stock	—	*Rhododendron*
Pick up and burn diseased leaves to avoid spores overwintering	Cut stems of cluster-flowered and large-flowered bush roses by half	Cut stems of cluster-flowered and large-flowered bush roses by half	*Rosa*
—	Winter dormancy	Winter dormancy	*Spiraea*
—	Thin out main stems of large plants	Thin out main stems of large plants	*Syringa*
—	Winter dormancy	Winter dormancy	*Weigela*

W I N T E R

PLANT	DECEMBER	JANUARY	FEBRUARY
TREES			
Ornamentals	Continue planting during mild spells when ground conditions allow • *Arbutus* species in flower	Remove damaged or dead branches • Check tips frequently in case they are rubbing the bark	Remove damaged or dead branches • Check tips frequently in case they are rubbing the bark
Conifers	Protect plants by planting during mild spells when ground conditions allow	Protect plants by planting during mild spells when ground conditions allow	Protect plants by planting during mild spells when ground conditions allow
Malus	Continue winter pruning, completing by the end of the month if possible • Check stored fruit for signs of rot	Check and firm in recently planted trees if roots have been loosened	Feed with slow-release fertilizer and mulch with well-rotted manure
Pyrus	Continue winter pruning, completing by the end of the month	Check and firm in recently planted trees if roots have been loosened	Feed with slow-release fertilizer and mulch with well-rotted manure
Prunus	—	Check and firm in recently planted trees if roots have been loosened • If not using organic control (see February) against peach leaf curl, begin preventative sprays or copper fungicide	Feed with slow-release fertilizer and mulch with well-rotted manure • Protect peaches and nectarines against peach leaf curl organically by covering with polythene so the spores can't be spread by rain
BULBS, CORMS & TUBERS			
Winter–early spring flowering	—	Flowers appear in mild areas	*Eranthis* and *Galanthus* in flower
Spring flowering	Finish planting tulips as soon as possible	Take care not to damage dormant bulbs when forking over borders	—

S P R I N G			
MARCH	**APRIL**	**MAY**	**PLANT**
			TREES
Plant bare-rooted stock by the end of the month • Mulch established trees and feed with slow-release fertilizer	Mulch and feed if not done last month • Container-grown stock can still be planted, but will need watering right through to autumn • Plant pot-grown *Eucalyptus* as young plants so they develop good roots • *Aesculus, Cercis* and *Sorbus* in flower	Mulch and feed if not done last month • *Aesculus, Cercis* and *Crataegus, Malus* and late *Prunus* varieties in flower	*Ornamentals*
Plant new stock into well-prepared ground so long as it can be watered right through to autumn	Weed, mulch and feed established plants, but don't cultivate soil deeply as the roots are shallow • Take cuttings of side shoots 7.5–10 cm (about 3–4 in) long	Weed around rock garden conifers and apply a fresh gravel mulch	*Conifers*
Apply a feed of potash • Spray against scab when flower buds are still closed, then again once they begin to show colour • Begin spraying against mildew • Control suckers with a systemic insecticide • Do not spray when in flower or pollinating insects will be killed • If gardening organically, keep trees in good condition with plenty of fertilizer and water and they'll be less prone to disease	Clear weeds from the ground underneath • Continue preventative spraying	Put up codling moth traps to catch the male moths • One trap should protect up to 5 trees • Ensure plenty of water after flowering to boost fruit size	*Malus*
Apply a feed of potash • Spray against scab when flower buds are still closed, then again once they begin to show colour • Begin spraying against mildew • Control suckers with a systemic insecticide • Do not spray when in flower or pollinating insects will be killed • If gardening organically, keep trees in good condition with plenty of fertilizer and water and they'll be less prone to disease • Trees previously attacked by pear midge can be sprayed with permethrin when buds are still closed	Clear weeds from the ground underneath • Continue preventative spraying	Ensure plenty of water after flowering to boost fruit size	*Pyrus*
Plums, cherries and peaches flower now, so protect wall-trained plants from frost using fleece or polythene	Plums, cherries and peaches flower now, so protect wall-trained plants from frost using fleece or polythene • Prune fan-trained trees by removing outward-growing shoots • Thin out overcrowded or crossing shoots • Tie in the remaining shoots	Ensure plenty of water after flowering to boost fruit size • Rub out shoots that appear from below the graft union	*Prunus*
			BULBS, CORMS & TUBERS
Eranthis and *Galanthus* finish flowering • Buy and plant them 'in the green' for the best results • Lift and divide established clumps • *Anemone coronaria, Crocus* species and early *Iris* in flower	Finish planting and transplanting *Eranthis* and *Galanthus* • Leave dead heads on bulb species so they self-seed	If necessary, clear leaves when they have become completely yellow	*Winter–early spring flowering*
Main flowering season begins	Deadhead large bulbs as soon as flowering finishes • Feed with potash and allow the leaves to die back naturally • Water during dry weather • If bulbs need to be moved, heel in a trench to die back	Deadhead large bulbs as soon as flowering finishes • Feed with potash and allow the leaves to die back naturally • Water during dry weather • Watch out for pests and diseases such as eelworm and viruses • Throw out infected bulbs (don't compost them)	*Spring flowering*

| PLANT | S U M M E R | | |
	JUNE	JULY	AUGUST
TREES			
Ornamentals	Water autumn- and spring-planted trees during dry spells • *Laburnum* and *Liriodendron* in flower	Mature trees of *Castanea* and *Catalpa* in flower	Prepare planting site for new trees by digging in plenty of well-rotted compost and slow-release fertilizer • *Koelreuteria* in flower
Conifers	Sooty mould can appear as a result of honeydew secreted by aphids • Spray with insecticide if necessary	Conifer hedges can now be pruned • X *Cupressocyparis leylandii* should be cut back to 45 cm (about 18 in) below the eventual desired height	Prepare planting site for new trees by digging in plenty of well-rotted compost and slow-release fertilizer
Malus	The 'June drop' naturally thins out fruits, but if a heavy crop remains, thin out further to improve fruit size and quality	—	Prepare planting site for new trees by digging in plenty of well-rotted compost and slow-release fertilizer • Summer prune cordon-trained trees by cutting side shoots to 7.5 cm (about 3 in) • Shoots pruned this way last year should have new side shoots cut back to 2.5 cm (about 1 in) • Do the same for shoots growing from main branches of espalier and fan-trained trees
Pyrus	The 'June drop' naturally thins out fruits, but if a heavy crop remains, thin out further to improve fruit size and quality	—	Prepare planting site for new trees by digging in plenty of well-rotted compost and slow-release fertilizer • Summer prune cordon-trained trees by cutting side shoots to 7.5 cm (about 3 in) • Shoots pruned this way last year should have new side shoots cut back to 2.5 cm (about 1 in) • Do the same for shoots growing from main branches of espalier and fan-trained trees
Pyrus	—	—	Prepare planting site for new trees by digging in plenty of well-rotted compost and slow-release fertilizer • Fan-trained trees should have new shoots from the main stems shortened to 10 cm (about 4 in), and last year's side shoots cut to 5 cm (about 2 in) • Prune bush cherries and plums after harvest by taking out dead and damaged branches and thinning remaining ones
BULBS, CORMS & TUBERS			
Winter– early spring flowering	—	—	Plant bulbs as soon as possible
Spring flowering	Deadhead large bulbs as soon as flowering finishes • Feed with potash and allow the leaves to die back naturally • Water during dry weather • If bulbs need to be moved, heel in a trench to die back • Watch out for pests and diseases such as eelworm and viruses • Throw out infected bulbs (don't compost them)	Order bulb catalogues • Lift and store bulbs heeled in trenches earlier	Plant *Narcissus*

A U T U M N

SEPTEMBER	OCTOBER	NOVEMBER	PLANT
			TREES
			Ornamentals
Plant new stock once soil is moist • Stake and tie securely against wind rocking loosening roots • Ornamental fruit begins to colour up on *Crataegus* and *Sorbus* • *Sophora japonica* in flower	Plant new stock once soil is moist • Stake and tie securely against wind rocking loosening roots • Clear fallen leaves from grass and plants underneath; they can be left to rot down on bare soil • Leave windfall fruit on the ground for birds to eat • Clean up seed from ornamental fruits and sow immediately • Peak time for ornamental fruits and autumn leaf colour	Plant new stock once soil is moist • Stake and tie securely against wind rocking loosening roots • Clear fallen leaves from grass and plants underneath; they can be left to rot down on bare soil • Bare-rooted stock should now be available	
Plant new stock • In exposed sites, put up a windbreak of netting to protect against wind and frost damage	Plant new stock • In exposed sites, put up a windbreak of netting to protect against wind and frost damage	Fastigiate trees can be loosely wrapped with netting or wire to protect against snow damage	*Conifers*
Harvest and store fruit • Plant new stock in well-prepared ground	Winter pruning can begin once trees are dormant • Avoid pruning in freezing conditions • Fix grease bands around tree trunks to catch winter moths • Rake up and burn any diseased leaves to avoid the spores overwintering	Winter pruning can begin once trees are dormant • Avoid pruning in freezing conditions • Fix grease bands around tree trunks to catch winter moths • Rake up and burn any diseased leaves to avoid the spores overwintering	*Malus*
Harvest and store fruit • Plant new stock in well-prepared ground	Harvest and store fruit • Plant new stock in well-prepared ground	Harvest and store fruit • Plant new stock in well-prepared ground	*Pyrus*
Plant new stock in well-prepared ground	Trees sprayed earlier this year against peach leaf curl should be sprayed again at leaf fall	—	*Prunus*
			BULBS, CORMS & TUBERS
Complete planting	—	—	*Winter– early spring flowering*
Plant *Narcissus* by the end of the month • Most other spring bulbs can be planted now, except tulips • Plant dwarf bulbs such as *Chionodoxa* and *Scilla siberica*	Finish planting spring bulbs, but start planting tulips now • Late planting minimizes disease risk • Improve drainage on heavy soil • In containers, remove summer bedding and plant bulbs, layering them for the best effect • Plant dwarf bulbs such as *Chionodoxa* and *Scilla siberica*	Finish planting tulips	*Spring flowering*

PLANT	W I N T E R		
	DECEMBER	JANUARY	FEBRUARY
BULBS, CORMS & TUBERS *(continued)*			
Summer flowering	Finish planting tulips as soon as possible	Check stored bulbs and tubers; destroy any showing signs of rot	Pot lily bulbs in a cold frame or greenhouse for an early start
Autumn flowering	Remove any remaining dead flowers	——	——
Indoor	Check hyacinths being forced in the dark and move into light when shoots are 2.5–5 cm (about 1–2 in) high	Water potted bulbs often but take care not to waterlog the compost • Feed weekly with a liquid feed	Potted bulbs that have flowered can be deadheaded then allowed to die back • Feed and water regularly but sparingly until leaves are yellow
LAWNS, GROUND COVERS & ORNAMENTAL GRASSES			
Lawns & ground covers	Aerate the ground to improve drainage in waterlogged areas	Aerate the ground to improve drainage in waterlogged areas	Prepare ground for a new lawn by digging, clearing weeds, raking and levelling the ground • Dig out lawn weeds by hand, or wait until spring to use a weedkiller
Ornamental grasses, sedges & bamboos	Leave flowers for winter decoration in cold districts	Leave flowers for winter decoration in cold districts	Leave flowers for winter decoration in cold districts
HERBS			
	Protect slightly tender herbs like bay with fleece if severe frosts threaten • Water containers sparingly	Potted mint and chives can be forced under cover • Sow parsley in gentle heat	Sow borage, dill and parsley in gentle heat • Begin watering containers under cover • Prepare ground outside for spring planting
FRUIT TREES, NUT TREES & OTHER FRUITS *(see also under Trees)*			
Tropical to subtropical	Protect plants from cold winds	Protect plants from cold winds	Protect plants from cold winds
Cool-temperate	Soak bare-rooted plants well before planting out; do not plant below graft level • Protect young plants from severe frost with fleece • Prune established plants to maintain high yields	Protect young plants from severe frost with fleece • Prune established plants to maintain high yields • Prune to open structure to allow light to reach ripening fruit	Protect young plants from severe frost with fleece • Prune established plants to maintain high yields • Prune to open structure to allow light to reach ripening fruit

S P R I N G			
MARCH	APRIL	MAY	PLANT
			BULBS, CORMS & TUBERS *(continued)*
Plant lily bulbs outside	Protect emerging lily shoots from slugs • Plant new lily bulbs • Tender bulbs including *Gladiolus* can now be planted outside • Add grit to the soil if drainage is poor	Protect emerging lily shoots from slugs • Plant new lily bulbs • Tender bulbs including *Gladiolus* can now be planted outside • Add grit to the soil if drainage is poor • Finish planting as soon as possible	*Summer flowering*
——	*Colchicum* and other autumn-flowering bulbs in leaf • Feed with high-potash fertilizer	*Colchicum* and other autumn-flowering bulbs in leaf • Feed with high-potash fertilizer • Allow leaves to yellow and die back naturally for a good crop of flowers	*Autumn flowering*
Hyacinthus bulbs in pots that have died back can be planted out in the garden • Tubers of begonias can be potted for summer pot plants • Buy and pot slightly tender bulbs such as *Eucomis* and *Arum* for the cold greenhouse	Decrease and stop feeding and watering as foliage turns yellow • Put bulbs such as *Cyclamen* and *Hippeastrum* to rest for the summer	Decrease and stop feeding and watering as foliage turns yellow • Put bulbs such as *Cyclamen* and *Hippeastrum* to rest for the summer	*Indoor*
			LAWNS, GROUND COVERS & ORNAMENTAL GRASSES
Prepare ground for a new lawn by digging, clearing weeds, raking and levelling the ground • Dig out lawn weeds by hand, or wait until spring to use a weedkiller • Firm the ground thoroughly after it has been left to settle for a week or two • Sow lawn seed and lay turf as soon as conditions allow • Start cutting lawn with the blades set high when the grass is dry	Finish sowing or turfing new lawns • Rake out the layer of dead grass in an established lawn, using a lawn rake or powered scarifier • Feed with a high-nitrogen fertilizer • Top-dress any bare patches with lawn seed and compost	Roll new lawns when the grass is 5 cm (about 2 in) high to encourage basal growth • A few days later, cut it with the blades as high as possible • Repair any bumps or hollows in established lawns • Apply weedkiller or mosskiller if necessary	*Lawns & ground covers*
Clumps may be divided and planted out • Sow annual grasses	Cut out dead or overcrowded stems • Cut back vigorous creeping grasses	Cut out dead or overcrowded stems • Cut back vigorous creeping grasses	*Ornamental grasses, sedges & bamboos*
			HERBS
Sow borage, coriander, dill, fennel, parsley, rue and sweet marjoram in gentle heat • Sow hardy annual herbs outside under cloches	Propagate sage and thyme by layering • Sow basil in gentle heat • Sow annuals outside • Pot up seedlings sown earlier • Divide mint and chives • Buy and plant pot-grown herbs • Plant mint in a sunken container as it is invasive • Move containers outside • Mulch and feed established plants	Take softwood cuttings of herbs including rosemary and thyme • Water and feed containers regularly • Trim established herbs to maintain shape	
			FRUIT TREES, NUT TREES & OTHER FRUITS *(see also under Trees)*
Provide adequate water during dry spells • Mulch well	Ensure good pollination of flowers	Apply mulch • Suppress weeds	*Tropical to subtropical*
Plant out container-grown fruit/nuts • Spread a balanced fertilizer just beyond where branches grow • Check weekly for signs of pest or disease problems	Mulch established plants with compost and manure • Check for leaf discolouration as a nutrient deficiency may be present • Protect buds and developing fruit from birds	Spread a balanced fertilizer just beyond where branches grow • Check weekly for signs of pest or disease problems • Protect buds and developing fruit from birds	*Cool-temperate*

	S U M M E R		
PLANT	**JUNE**	**JULY**	**AUGUST**
BULBS, CORMS & TUBERS (continued)			
Summer flowering	Inspect lilies for lily beetles and hand pick them • Finish planting bulbs and tubers	Keep checking for lily beetle	Remove dead flower stems • Feed with potash and water regularly until leaves have yellowed and died back
Autumn flowering	Order bulbs from mail-order catalogues	Plant bulbs such as *Colchicum*, *Crocus* and *Nerine* • *Cyclamen* are best bought as pot-grown plants rather than dry tubers	Finish planting as soon as possible
Indoor	——	——	*Cyclamen* and *Hippeastrum* can be repotted and started into growth • Water sparingly at first until growth is well under way
LAWNS, GROUND COVERS & ORNAMENTAL GRASSES			
Lawns & ground covers	Water new lawns with a sprinkler during dry spells • Mow regularly as growth increases • Feed tired lawns with a liquid fertilizer • Mow long grass containing bulbs once their leaves have yellowed	Rake the lawn before mowing to bring up the runners of perennial weeds • Raise the height of the cut during long dry spells • Unless you have a 'bowling green' lawn, don't bother watering during a drought as it will recover when rain arrives	If the lawn wasn't fed earlier this year, apply a fertilizer that is low in nitrogen • Rake with a lawn rake or scarifier to remove thatch • Prepare ground for new lawns
Ornamental grasses, sedges & bamboos	Cut out dead or overcrowded stems • Cut back vigorous creeping grasses	If planting out, restrict growth around bamboos by inserting a barrier	If planting out, restrict growth around bamboos by inserting a barrier • Sow annual grasses
HERBS			
	Continue sowing seed outside for a continual supply later • Continue taking softwood cuttings • Plant out basil • Keep on top of weeds • Water new herbs planted this spring	Start harvesting herbs for drying • Trim lavender after flowering • Water and feed plants regularly	Take half-ripe cuttings of herbs such as rosemary, lavender and bay • Trim leggy plants to maintain shape • Continue harvesting herbs for drying
FRUIT TREES, NUT TREES & OTHER FRUITS (see also under Trees)			
Tropical to subtropical	Establish plants during or after good summer rain • Add plenty of compost and a complete fertilizer to soil	Fertilize established plants • Buy virus-free stock or from an organic grower	Check for seasonal pests • Identify common problems and treat with safe methods
Cool-temperate	Practise fruit thinning so that branches are able to support the crop • Mulch well to inhibit summer weeds	Summer prune where appropriate to encourage fruit • Bud graft tree fruits on to suitable rootstocks • Take softwood cuttings of *Vaccinium*	Bud graft tree fruits on to suitable rootstocks • Take softwood cuttings of *Vaccinium* • Check for branches rubbing against stakes
Warm-temperate	Use netting to protect developing fruit from birds • Mulch well with compost to inhibit summer weeds	Fertilize regularly with appropriate fertilizer • Water well during dry spells • Summer prune where appropriate to encourage regular crops of high yields	Check for pests and diseases regularly • Allow good air circulation to discourage mildew

A U T U M N

SEPTEMBER	OCTOBER	NOVEMBER	PLANT
			BULBS, CORMS & TUBERS *(continued)*
Remove dead flower stems • Feed with potash and water regularly until leaves have yellowed and died back	Lift tender bulbs and tubers like *Gladiolus* before the first hard frost and store for the winter • Dry bulbs first • Store tubers in trays of damp compost	Lift tender bulbs and tubers like *Gladiolus* before the first hard frost and store for the winter • Dry bulbs first • Store tubers in trays of damp compost • Protect slightly tender bulbs with a thick mulch of straw or bark in cooler areas	*Summer flowering*
Flowering begins	In flower	Don't feed as leaves are produced in spring	*Autumn flowering*
Plant prepared hyacinths to force for Christmas flowers • Other spring bulbs can be planted in a cold frame or greenhouse	Check bulbs being forced and water very sparingly if necessary • Move into light when shoots are 2.5–5 cm (about 1–2 in) high	Moved forced bulbs as necessary	*Indoor*
			LAWNS, GROUND COVERS & ORNAMENTAL GRASSES
Carry out any repairs such as seeding bare patches • Best time of year to sow or turf new lawns • Improve a tired lawn by top-dressing with a mixture of sieved garden soil, compost and sharp sand • Work a 2 cm (about 1 in) layer well into the grass with the back of a rake	Finish seeding by the end of the month • Water newly seeded ground during dry spells	Continue laying turf when weather conditions allow • Aerate any areas where water lies on the surface for any length of time	*Lawns & ground covers*
If planting out, restrict growth around bamboos by inserting a barrier • Sow annual grasses	Remove flowerheads if grass presents a weed problem	Collect seed when fully ripe for sowing	*Ornamental grasses, sedges & bamboos*
			HERBS
Finish taking cuttings this month • Sow parsley for a winter–early spring crop	Move containers under cover • Have material ready to protect herbs like bay in case of hard frosts • Cut back foliage of perennial herbs such as mint once the stems have died back • Put cloches over outside plants of parsley so harvest can continue through winter	Dig over new ground for planting next spring • Pot up mint, chives and tarragon for forcing under cover • Continue cutting back and tidying up plants outside	
			FRUIT TREES, NUT TREES & OTHER FRUITS *(see also under Trees)*
Prune to allow light into the tree or shape for good fruiting	Mulch • Fertilize lightly	Mulch • Fertilize lightly	*Tropical to subtropical*
Prepare ground for planting bare-rooted trees and soft fruit canes • Dig in compost or well-rotted manure • Check soil pH	Check pollination requirements of new plants • Provide stakes or trellis support where appropriate • Take hardwood cuttings from established plants	Check pollination requirements of new plants • Take hardwood cuttings from established plants	*Cool-temperate*
Prepare ground for planting container-grown specimens • Dig in compost or well-rotted manure • Avoid over-rich soil • Check pollination requirements	Provide sturdy trellis or stake where necessary • Take hardwood cuttings from established plants • Remove spent annual summer fruit plants and add to compost	Check pollination requirements • Take hardwood cuttings from established plants • Remove spent annual summer fruit plants and add to compost	*Warm-temperate*

| PLANT | W I N T E R | | |
	DECEMBER	JANUARY	FEBRUARY
FRUIT TREES, NUT TREES & OTHER FRUITS *(see also under Trees) (continued)*			
Warm-temperate	Prune young trees to shape, selecting three main branches to form a framework • Cut back current season's fruited shoots	Cut back current season's fruited shoots • Remove crossing or rubbing branches or dead wood • Protect young plants from cold winds or frost	Remove crossing or rubbing branches or dead wood • Protect young plants from cold winds or frost
Citrus	Choose citrus species by cold tolerance • Some are frost-tender	Cold winds and frost can cause foliage to curl up	Fertilize and mulch
Prunus	Buy virus-free stock from an organic grower	Buy virus-free stock from an organic grower	Water young plants well until established but not excessively • Check for blossom diseases on established trees
CLIMBERS & CREEPERS			
Hardy	Carry out repairs and maintenance to supports and structures while plants are dormant	Prune young *Wisteria* side shoots to within 7.5 cm (about 3 in) of last year's growth • Apply potash to shy-flowering plants • Complete repairs and maintenance before birds start to nest	Thin out branches on *Jasminum officinale* but don't shorten shoots • Cut *Clematis viticella* to 45 cm (about 18 in) • Cut back *Parthenocissus* if necessary
Convervatory	Water plants very sparingly, keeping compost just moist	Water plants very sparingly, keeping compost just moist	Cut back overgrown summer-flowering plants, including *Allamanda* and *Bougainvillea* • Plant or pot up *Bougainvillea* • Thin out overgrown *Passiflora*
Annuals	Order seed from mail-order catalogues	Clean pots and trays ready for sowing next month	*Eccremocarpus* can be treated as an annual; sow seed, which need light to germinate

S · P · R · I · N · G			
MARCH	APRIL	MAY	PLANT
			FRUIT TREES, NUT TREES & OTHER FRUITS *(see also under Trees)* (continued)
Plant out annual fruits of *Cucumis*, *Physalis* and *Sechium* • Fertilize established plants to encourage fruit • Mulch heavily as weather warms up with compost or manure	Fertilize established plants to encourage fruit • Lightly prune *Ficus* and *Fortunella* to shape • Take softwood cuttings where appropriate	Check for any sign of aphids or scale insects and take necessary action • Lightly prune *Ficus* and *Fortunella* to shape • Take softwood cuttings where appropriate	*Warm-temperate*
Choose a sheltered position for planting • Prepare site with compost and a complete fertilizer • Ensure good drainage	Mulch and fertilize • Keep away from main trunk	Keep trunk free from weeds	*Citrus*
Check for blossom diseases on established trees	Check for blossom diseases on established trees	Mulch and fertilize	*Prunus*
			CLIMBERS & CREEPERS
Prune climbing roses • Prune large-flowered hybrid *Clematis* • Plant new deciduous climbers, with rootball 30 cm (about 12 in) from walls or fences • Feed and mulch all plants	Plant evergreen climbers • Cut back *Eccremocarpus* if overgrown or frost damaged • Plant out climbers grown from layers last year • Trim overgrown *Hedera* (ivy), but watch for birds' nests	Tie in *Clematis* and other twining plants regularly to avoid tangled growth • Cut back *Clematis montana* after flowering if overgrown • Water new plants during dry spells	*Hardy*
Plant new stock in pots using John Innes No. 3 potting compost • Start watering established plants regularly as growth intensifies • Sow seed of plants including *Araujia* and *Bomarea*	Water plants regularly • Add a weekly liquid feed throughout the summer • Cut back leggy plants of *Cissus*	Take tip cuttings of *Allamanda* • Cut back *Jasminum polyanthum* after flowering	*Convervatory*
Sow plants such as *Asarina*, *Dolichos* and *Ipomoea* in gentle heat indoors • Prepare ground outside for planting in April/May	Continue sowing annual climbers • Pot on and stake seedlings sown earlier	Sow annual climbers outside directly in soil • Harden off pot-grown plants	*Annuals*

	S U M M E R		
PLANT	**JUNE**	**JULY**	**AUGUST**
FRUIT TREES, NUT TREES & OTHER FRUITS (see also under Trees) (continued)			
Citrus	Check for pests • If the leaves are discoloured, check for signs of deficiency in the soil	Cut off any sections damaged by leaf miner or spray weekly with an insecticide in the cool of the day	Mulch and fertilize
Prunus	Provide adequate water during dry spells	Clear summer weeds away from trees	Clear summer weeds away from trees
CLIMBERS & CREEPERS			
Hardy	Tie in *Clematis* and other twining plants regularly to avoid tangled growth • Cut back *Clematis montana* after flowering if overgrown • Water new plants during dry spells • Keep *Lonicera* well watered to avoid powdery mildew attack • Watch out for aphids and two-spotted mite and spray if the infestation is bad • Look for ready-rooted layers on plants such as *Jasminum* and pot up while still attached to the main plant	Order roses for autumn delivery • Propagate by layering; air layering may be necessary for shoots away from the ground • *Wisteria* side shoots produced this year should be cut back to 5 to 6 buds	Prune rambler roses after flowering
Conservatory	Monitor pests using yellow sticky traps • Introduce a biological predator or spray, but not both or the useful predators will be killed	Take cuttings of *Bougainvillea* and *Cissus* with bottom heat • Take heel cuttings of *Jasminum* and stem cuttings of *Passiflora*	Continue taking cuttings of most plants
Annuals	Plant out pot-grown plants after hardening off • *Tropaeolum speciosum* can still be sown outside	Water and feed plants regularly • Don't allow roots to dry out • Use a high-potash feed	Continue feeding and watering regularly • Switch to a high-nitrogen feed

A U T U M N			
SEPTEMBER	OCTOBER	NOVEMBER	PLANT
			FRUIT TREES, NUT TREES & OTHER FRUITS *(see also under Trees) (continued)*
Mulch and fertilize	Ensure adequate water at all times	Ensure adequate water at all times	*Citrus*
Prepare planting site for new trees several months in advance	Dig in compost and a complete fertilizer • Ensure soil is well drained	Check with a reputable dealer for trees suitable for your area	*Prunus*
			CLIMBERS & CREEPERS
Detach rooted layers from parent plants and stand in a cold frame or sheltered spot over winter	Best planting time for deciduous climbers • Put up supports before planting	Cut back dead stems of herbaceous climbers such as *Lathyrus* • Clear ivy from old walls and woodwork	*Hardy*
Stop feeding plants until spring • Remove all dead and fallen leaves very frequently during winter to avoid fungal diseases	Water infrequently • *Stephanotis* needs high winter temperatures and may be best moved to the house	Water plants very sparingly, keeping compost just moist	*Conservatory*
Collect ripe seed and save for planting next spring	Clear away foliage once it has been killed by frost	Clear away foliage once it has been killed by frost	*Annuals*

Glossary

× (multiplication sign) A sign placed in front of the name of plants with Latin names to show that they are not true wild species but are of hybrid origin, whether natural or artificial; as in Camellia × williamsii or × Brassolaeliocattleya Sylvia Fry.

+ (plus sign) Though grafts do not usually hybridize, it does happen on very rare occasions, and the resulting plant is designated with the + sign, as with + Laburnocytisus adamii, a freak that occurred in a Paris nursery last century when a purple broom was grafted to laburnum stock to create a standard broom.

Acid (of soils) Containing relatively little lime, to give a pH reaction of less than 7, the sort of soil needed to grow such plants as azaleas, camellias, rhododendrons and the like, and in which hydrangeas flower blue. A very acid soil is described as 'sour'.

Aerial root A root that springs from the stem of a plant above ground. The aerial roots of ivy are short and used by the plant to cling to its support. In such plants as monsteras, philodendrons or some of the tropical figs they eventually reach the ground; before they do they draw moisture from the air.

Air-layering A method of propagation applicable to a wide range of trees and shrubs which involves wounding the stem and then packing the wound with damp sphagnum moss. This is all held in place with string and polythene. When roots show, the new plant can be severed and transplanted.

Alkaline (of soils) Containing a great deal of calcium (lime) to give a pH reaction of more than 7. It is the sort of soil preferred by such plants as bearded irises and the cabbage tribe, and in which hydrangeas flower pink. Some gardeners refer to alkaline soils as 'sweet'.

Alternate (of leaves) Springing, one by one, from first one side of the stem and then the other. Whether the leaves are alternate or opposite is an important aid in plant identification.

Annual A plant that lives for only a year—often less—or which is customarily treated as such in gardens.

Anther The part of the stamen that actually produces the pollen, usually carried on a thin stalk called the filament. Lilium auratum has the largest anthers of any flower.

Apex The growing tip of a shoot, or the very end of a leaf, which may take a variety of shapes.

Arbour A structure, usually free-standing, designed to be covered with climbing plants to provide shade. The term is more or less interchangeable with pergola.

Areole The swelling on the stem of a cactus which bears the spines. It is actually the vestigial remains of a shoot.

Axil The 'armpit' of a leaf, where it joins the stem, and where there is usually a growth bud to be found.

Bedding plant A plant, usually low growing, suitable for a mass planting display of flowers or foliage. Most are annuals or short-lived perennials.

Berry In normal use, a small juicy fruit which is eaten entire and unpeeled; to the botanist, a fleshy fruit containing several seeds which does not open when ripe—including citrus fruits and the tomato.

Biennial A plant which flowers and dies in its second year after germination, producing only roots and leaves in the first. Parsley is the best known example.

Bifoliate (of cattleyas and their hybrids) Plants which have two leaves per pseudo-bulb.

Bipinnate (of leaves) Twice pinnate, as in many ferns and such tropical trees as the jacaranda.

Blade The flat part of a leaf, where most photosynthesis occurs.

Bloom A general term for a flower, much used in flower show schedules. Also, a waxy or powdery coating on the skins of leaves or fruits, as on a grape.

Bole The lowest part of the trunk of a tree, from the ground to the lowest branches.

Bract A leaf-like organ, usually associated with a flower or cluster of flowers, but not part of the flower itself. Bracts are smaller and a different shape to ordinary leaves, as in roses; or they may be brightly coloured and resemble petals, as in bougainvilleas and poinsettias.

Bud An immature, unopened flower. Also, an embryo shoot, usually small and pointed, found normally in the axils of the leaves or at the ends of shoots, but also occurring on rootstocks, tubers and the like. It is usually protected by small, waxy scales.

Budding A form of grafting, where the scion consists of a piece of bark carrying a single growth bud, inserted into the bark of the understock. It is used especially for the propagation of roses and fruit trees.

Bulb An underground (usually) organ, consisting of a reduced stem (the base plate) surrounded by modified leaves that store food for the plant's dormancy. The onion is the classic example.

Bulbil A small bulb, carried in the axil of a leaf, as in certain lilies. It offers a convenient means of propagation.

Bulblet A small bulb developing from the base of a mature one and used for propagation. The term 'offset' is sometimes used.

Cactus The most significant family of succulent plants, all perennial and native to the Americas.

Calyx The outermost part of a flower, which encloses and protects the rest while in bud. It is made up of sepals, usually small, green and leaf like, but sometimes coloured and the showiest part of the flower, as in clematis and anemones.

Capsule A fruit which when ripe dries and opens to release the seeds, such as the fruits of lilies and petunias.

Carpel The female organ of the flower, also known as the pistil. A flower may have several or only one.

Catkin The type of flower cluster, usually pendulous, found on such plants as willows or alders. The individual flowers, usually one sex only, are tiny and generally have no petals, being pollinated by the wind.

Caudex The thickened base of the stem of certain plants such as some ferns and Dioscorea elephantipes.

Cladode A flattened stem rather like a leaf and performing the same functions, as in the butcher's broom (Ruscus aculeatus). Similar organs in acacias are called phyllodes.

Climber A plant with stems too long and flexible to be self supporting and which raises itself to the light by climbing into and over other plants. It may attach itself to its support by twining around it, as jasmine or honey-suckle do; by means of tendrils (grapes, peas); by short aerial roots (ivy); or by suckers (Virginia creeper). The latter two need no trellis and are termed self-clinging climbers. Some climbers attach themselves only loosely to their supports and need to be tied in place. The term 'vine', while applicable only to the grape, is often used for any climbing plant, especially in the USA.

Cloche A miniature, portable greenhouse placed over crops in the open ground to protect them from cold or encourage early development. Traditionally made from two or four pieces of glass in a wire frame, but can be simply a wire frame clad in transparent polythene.

Clone A group of plants propagated asexually (that is, by cuttings, grafting, division, etc.) from a single individual and thus genetically all identical, such as roses and fruit trees.

Common names The names by which plants are commonly known, as distinct from their Latin or scientific ones (which, unlike common names, are universally recognized). Sometimes the two coincide and, as a plant can have several common names, it is usual for books to list the plants they describe under their scientific names. The American nursery industry has for some years been attempting to standardize common names, by no means an easy task.

Composite The botanist's term for a daisy, from the way the 'flowers' are in fact made up of many small flowers.

Compost The most effective of all fertilizers, it is made from organic matter such as leaves, grass clippings and manure which has been allowed to rot for a few weeks or months until it has turned black and crumbly; in orchid growing, the soil-free medium, which may or may not contain compost from the compost heap, in which the plants are grown.

Compound (of leaves) Subdivided into several leaflets, as in a rose or palm leaf. Leaves not so subdivided are called 'simple'.

Cone The structure that encloses the primitive flowers and then the seeds of conifers (pines, cypresses, etc.) and cycads. It is made up of overlapping scales, which become woody when the seeds ripen.

Conifer A member of a primitive order of flowering plants (the Gymnospermae), characterized by their cones and usually needle-like leaves. They are all shrubs or trees, usually evergreen, and the hardiest trees in cold climates; they supply the bulk of the world's timber. Pines, cypresses, sequoias and junipers are examples.

Cordate (of leaves) Heart shaped, as in the European lime (*Tilia cordata*).

Corm A bulb-like organ, usually growing underground but without the scales (fleshy modified leaves) of a bulb, and often simply called a bulb by gardeners, such as gladiolus and freesias. When a corm flowers the old corm dies and the plant creates a new one on top of it; bulbs are usually more or less permanent structures.

Cormlet A small corm that grows from around the base of a corm, usually in fair numbers and used for propagation.

Corolla The whole collection of petals that forms the eye-catching part of most flowers. The petals can be separate, as in the rose, or fused together in a bell or trumpet, as in rhododendrons or campanulas.

Corona The cup or trumpet-shaped out-growth in the centre of the flower of narcissi and its relatives, such as *Hymenocallis festalis*. It is formed from the bases of the stamens.

Creeper A plant that makes long shoots that grow along the ground, usually rooting as it goes, such as *Convolvulus sabaticus*. The distinction between a climber and a creeper is not clear cut—many creepers will climb if given the chance, and some climbers will creep if there is nothing to climb on, such as ivy and Virginia creeper.

Crown The more or less permanent base of a herbaceous plant from which the leaves and flower stems grow upwards and the roots downwards; the upper part of a tree, consisting of the branches and top section of the trunk; the corona of a narcissus or narcissus-like plant.

Cultivar A variety of plant which has arisen as the result of cultivation, that is, not naturally, usually by means of hybridization. It may be propagated by any suitable means, and the rules of botany state that it must not be named in Latin but should be given in Roman type with single quotes, for example 'Queen Elizabeth', 'Model of Perfection'. Cultivars that arose before these rulings and were given Latin names are treated similarly, giving rise to such names as *Acer palmatum* 'Dissectum Atropurpureum'.

Cutting A piece of stem or root cut from a plant and used for propagation. According to the state of maturity of the stem from which it is taken, a cutting may be classed as a softwood, semi-mature or hardwood cutting.

Dead-head To remove dead flowers, with the twofold aim of tidying up the plant and preventing it wasting energy in unwanted seed.

Deciduous (of trees and shrubs) Losing all the leaves each year, growing a fresh set later. Typically the leaves fall in autumn/fall, sometimes assuming brilliant colours before they do so, and new leaves grow in spring. Many tropical trees drop at any time of the year in anticipation of a prolonged dry season. A tree that doesn't drop all its leaves is called semi-deciduous.

Die-back The death of the tips of shoots or branches, sometimes followed by the death of the entire shoot. It can be caused by frost or by disease.

Diffuse Growing into many branches, usually used of shrubs to suggest an open, rangy habit of growth rather than a compact one.

Division The simplest method of propagation, whereby a clump of plants is dug up and broken up into several pieces which are then replanted.

Dorsal Situated on the back of an organ.

Double (of flowers) Having more than the 'natural' number of petals. The extra petals are formed from stamens, and where these are completely transformed the flower is apt to be sterile. A flower with only a few extra petals and enough stamens for fertility is described as 'semi-double'.

Elliptic (of leaves) More or less oval in shape.

Entire (of leaves) Having smooth margins, that is, without lobes or serrations, such as an aspidistra or privet leaf.

Epiphyte A plant that grows on, and usually in the branches of, another, but does not steal nourishment from its host, many orchids are examples.

Espalier The technique of training a tree or shrub, most typically a fruit tree such as a peach or a fig, to grow flat against a wall or trellis. It was originally designed to encourage earlier ripening by holding the fruit close to the reflected warmth of the wall, but can also be used for decorative effect.

Evergreen Any plant that retains foliage all year. Evergreen trees and shrubs do drop old leaves, though not until after the new ones have been formed and usually only a few at a time.

F1 hybrid A hybrid strain created by pollinating two very carefully selected parents. The resulting seedlings usually show great vigour and uniformity and many strains of annuals and vegetables are F1 hybrids. It is useless to save seeds from these, as the original cross must be made afresh every time seed is wanted.

Fall The American (and antique English) term for autumn; the lower three petals of an iris, which project out and down (the upright ones are called 'standards').

Family A group of genera which are considered to be closely related. The cacti (family Cactaceae) are one such; the rose family (Rosaceae) includes not only the rose but such fruits as the peach, blackberry, strawberry and apple.

Fan palm A palm with roughly circular (palmate) leaves, so called because they can be used to make fans. A palm with pinnate leaves is called a 'feather palm'.

Fertilizer Anything added to the soil to maintain or increase its fertility. Fertilizers may be organic, that is, derived from once-living matter, as are manure, compost, and blood and bone; or inorganic (artificial), such as sulphate of ammonia or superphosphate, which are prepared in chemical factories.

Fibrous root A fine, young root, usually one of very many. These are the roots that take up moisture and nourishment from the soil.

Filament The stalk of a stamen, which carries the anther.

Floret A single, small flower in a head or cluster of many, as in a delphinium or cluster-flowered rose.

Flower The organ of reproduction, basic in determining to what genus and species the plant belongs. They are normally composed of three parts: the calyx, the corolla, and the sexual organs proper, the male stamens and the female carpels. Not all may be present in any given flower (clematis, for instance have no petals), and they may be, as in orchids or cannas, modified into the most fantastic forms.

Flowerhead A cluster of flowers, which may be so compact as to look like a single flower, as in a daisy.

Frame A miniature greenhouse, designed mainly for propagation. The traditional style is an enclosed bed with wood to a height of about 40 cm (about 16 in) with an old window across the top. A hot frame is heated, a cold one not.

Frond The leaves of a fern. Fronds carrying spore-bearing organs (sori) are called 'fertile' fronds; if not, they are called 'sterile' fronds. In some species the two types are of different appearance. The term frond is also used for the leaves of feather palms; the Latin *frondosa* when applied to many plants means 'leafy'.

Fruit The part of the plant which carries the seed or seeds, and which arises after the flower is pollinated. It may or may not be edible.

Fungus A very large group of evolutionary primitive plants, of which the most relevant to gardeners are mushrooms and the many parasitic fungi that cause most plant diseases.

Genus A group of species which have sufficient in common to be classed as closely related; the name is always Latin. For example, roses are members of the genus *Rosa*, and both the smoking and ornamental tobaccos are of the genus *Nicotiana*.

Glabrous (of leaves and stems) Smooth and non-hairy; a hairy plant is described as 'hispid'.

Glasshouse A structure, traditionally roofed and clad with glass but now often with polythene sheeting, designed to trap the sun's heat and thus allow warmth loving plants to be grown in cool climates. Supplementary heating may be provided.

Glaucous (of leaves) Bluish grey, a more accurate description for the many conifers sold as having 'blue' leaves.

Grafting A method of propagation which involves the uniting of a piece of stem of a desirable plant, the 'scion', to that of a less desirable one, the 'stock' or 'understock', to give a stronger root system than the scion would have naturally. Many different techniques for grafting have been employed.

Greenhouse Originally a lavishly windowed structure where evergreen plants were placed to keep them from winter cold; but now synonymous with 'glasshouse'.

Green manure A crop of annual plants grown to be dug into the soil at maturity to improve or restore its fertility, for instance legumes such as clover, alfalfa or lupins.

Grex A group of hybrid plants of the same parentage; the term is used mainly in the context of orchid breeding. Grex names are given without quotes, such as Vanda Nellie Morley.

Ground cover An extensive planting of a single species of low-growing plants, intended to carpet the ground with foliage and suppress weeds. Also, a plant suitable for such use.

Habit The complete picture of the way a plant grows; a species may be described as being of 'compact', 'weeping' or 'upright' habit, for instance.

Hanging basket A container designed to be suspended in order to show trailing plants such as ivy, Christmas cactus or fuchsias to their best advantage.

Heel A sliver of old wood retained at the base of a cutting. It is traditional in taking cuttings of carnations and roses.

Herb In botany, any plant that does not have permanent woody stems, such as petunias and zinnias. In gardening, a plant whose leaves or shoots are added to food to enhance its flavour or used in the preparation of medicines.

Herbaceous A perennial plant which dies down to the ground each year; a herbaceous border is a planting composed entirely of such plants, for example delphiniums and chrysanthemums.

Humus The final product of rotting organic matter, whether of plant or animal origin.

Hybrid A plant originating from the cross-pollination, either in the wild or as the result of match-making by the gardener, of two different species. If hybrids are crossed, the resulting plants may carry the genes of several species. Hybrids between plants of different genera are rare, though quite common among orchids.

Inflorescence The structure that carries the flowers. It may take any one of a number of forms—a spike (as in gladioli), a raceme (as in delphiniums), a panicle (as in lilacs), an umbel (as in onions); gardeners often refer simply to a 'cluster'. Inflorescences are described as 'terminal' when they grow at the ends of shoots, or axillary, when they arise in the axils of the leaves.

Insectivorous plant The strict term for carnivorous plants; they trap and digest insects to supply them with extra nitrogen, which is difficult to obtain from the swampy soils where they usually grow.

Irregular (of flowers) Having the petals arranged in some way other than radial symmetry, though almost always bilaterally symmetrical, such as on orchids and violets. The scientific term is 'zygomorphic'.

Labellum The lowest of the three petals of an orchid, usually larger or more elaborately shaped and coloured than the others. Also called a 'lip'.

Lanceolate (of leaves) Long and narrow; lance or sword shaped, such as gladiolus and iris leaves.

Lateral A side shoot, growing from the axil of a leaf of the main stem. In many fruit trees it is these shoots that bear the flowers and ultimately the fruit.

Lax Of rather floppy habit, for instance *Philadelphus mexicanus*, the opposite of upright or stiff.

Layering A method of propagation by which a branch of a plant is bent down to the ground where it takes root; the rooted section can then be severed from its parent and transplanted. It is most useful for plants that can be slow or reluctant to root from cuttings; some plants will layer themselves naturally.

Leaflet One of the several leaves in which a compound leaf such as a rose leaf is divided. A leaf has a bud in its axil; a leaflet does not.

Legume A member of the large pea family, which includes peas, beans, clover, lupins, wisteria, acacias, the various brooms, and some trees such as the cassias. They all share the ability to draw nitrogen straight from the air, by courtesy of bacteria that live in nodules on their roots.

Lime A compound of calcium added to soil to make it more alkaline, and also to improve the structure of clay soil; a tropical fruit of the genus *Citrus*; deciduous trees of the genus *Tilia*, also known as lindens.

Linear (of leaves) Very long and narrow, so that they look as though they could be drawn with a single line, such as the leaves of chives.

Lip See *Labellum*

Lithophytic (of orchids and some primitive plants) Growing on the naked surfaces of rocks and deriving nourishment from any litter they can accumulate around their roots.

Lobe One of the divisions in which a scalloped leaf, such as a maple or ivy leaf, is not quite divided; similarly in the corollas of flowers with united petals such as campanulas.

Manure The dung of animals, used as fertilizer. Like all materials of organic origin it adds humus to the soil.

Marginal plant One which in the wild grows in the swampy margins of ponds or lakes, and which can be cultivated in similar positions around a garden pond, such as *Iris ensata*. Most don't mind having their roots submerged for at least part of the year.

Midrib The main central vein of a leaf; the central stalk to which the leaflets of a pinnate leaf are attached.

Monocarpic A plant which flowers only once in its life and then dies, for example *Agave americana* and the fishtail palm (*Caryota urens*).

Monopodial (of orchids) One that does not naturally form a clump of shoots growing from a creeping rhizome, for example the vandas. (Clump-forming orchids such as cattleyas and cymbidiums are described as 'sympodial'.)

Moss A large group of species of primitive non-flowering plants which need moist soil to grow. Most are of very diminutive stature; some are cultivated as ground cover.

Mulch A blanket spread over the bare surface of soil to block the loss of moisture and to discourage the growth of weeds. Most mulches are of such organic matter as manure, compost, straw, bark chips, etc. which eventually rot and add humus to the soil, thus enhancing its fertility. Inorganic materials are also used.

Nectar The sweet, sugary liquid secreted by glands at the base of the petals of some flowers. Bees gather it and concentrate it into honey.

Neutral (of soils) Neither acid nor alkaline, that is having a pH of 7.

Node The point on a stem where a leaf and its axillary bud grows. It is the place to cut when pruning, and also where the base of a cutting should be cut.

Obovate (of leaves) More or less oval in shape.

Offset A shoot arising from the base of a plant which can be detached and used for propagation.

Opposite (of leaves) Arising in pairs, one on either side of the stem. See also *Alternate*.

Organic matter Material derived from things that were once alive, such as manure and compost, and which breaks down to form humus. The addition of organic matter improves the structure and fertility of any soil.

Ovary The lowest part of a carpel where the embryo seeds are. Ovaries found above the calyx are called 'superior', while those found below the calyx are called 'inferior'.

Ovate, ovoid (of leaves and petals) Oval in shape.

Palm Members of the family Palmae or Arecaceae, that is, trees characterized by a normally unbranched trunk topped by a bunch of large leaves and a distinct preference for warm climates.

Palmate (of leaves) Divided into lobes or leaf-lets that spread out from the end of the leaf stalk like the fingers of a hand, as in a maple leaf.

Panicle A type of inflorescence, strictly a compound raceme, as typified by that of the lilac.

Parasite A plant which grows upon another, stealing moisture and nourishment from its host. Mistletoe is an example; more common and less welcome are the parasitic fungi that cause plant diseases.

Pendent Hanging, the way the flower sprays of the wisteria do.

Perennial A plant that lives for three years or more. In botany, the term includes trees and shrubs, while in horticulture it is normally limited to plants that do not produce permanent woody stems, such as irises, peonies or ginger lilies.

Persistent A structure that stays on the plant after it serves its purpose, instead of falling off. The sepals of the rose which stay on the ripening rose hip are an example.

Petal The colourful part of most flowers. Petals are in fact modified leaves, and there are some flowers that have green petals, for example the green zinnia 'Envy'.

Petiole The stalk of a leaf.

pH The scale on which the acidity or alkalinity of soil is measured. It ranges from 1, an acid of fear-some strength, to 14, an alkali of equal ferocity, with 7 being the neutral point. Most garden soils fall somewhere between about pH 5.5 to about 8.6.

Phyllode See *Cladode*

Pinch out The operation of removing the tip of a growing shoot, usually with the fingers, to encourage lateral shoots to grow and make the plant bushier.

Pinna, pinnule Another term for the leaflet of a pinnate or bipinnate leaf.

Pinnate A leaf divided into leaflets arranged on either side of the leaf stalk, as in a rose leaf or those of many palms and ferns.

Pollen The tiny grains of plant substance containing DNA which unite with the embryo seeds contained in the ovary to create the fruit and hence a new generation of flowering plants—a process termed pollination. The transfer is usually carried out by insects, but can also be carried out by nectar-eating birds and sometimes by the wind.

Prostrate A plant of low-growing, ground-hugging habit, such as the prostrate junipers.

Pruning The art of cutting off parts of a plant to encourage more of the sort of growth the gardener desires, or to maintain a compact habit of growth.

Pseudo-bulb The fleshy, bulb-like stem found on many orchids.

Raceme A type of inflorescence, where the flowers are arranged on a long, usually upright stem, each flower having a separate flower stalk as in delphiniums.

Revert To return to normal, as when a variegated plant starts producing plain green leaves. **Rhizomatous** A plant that grows from rhizomes.

Rhizome A creeping stem, growing either at ground level, or just below, and swollen with starch and nutrients to nourish the shoots and roots that grow from it. The rhizomes are the edible part of the ginger plant.

Root The underground parts of a plant which anchor the plant and draw up water and nourishment from the soil.

Rootstock The understock of a grafted plant; the base of a perennial where the roots grow.

Rosette A group of leaves radiating from the same point on a short stem, to give an effect like a green flower, as in sempervivums.

Runner A horizontally growing stem that roots at each node where it touches the ground, as in strawberries and violets.

Scape A leafless flower stem that arises directly from the base of the plant, especially common in bulbs. Narcissi and agapanthus are examples.

Scarify To break or soften the hard coat on the seeds of certain plants, especially legumes such as sweet peas and wattles, to allow water to penetrate and thus speed up germination. It can be done by rubbing carefully with fine sandpaper or soaking the seed for a little while in hot water.

Scientific name The internationally recognized Latin name of a plant which often gives a potted description of the plant or commemorates some person connected with it. The name consists of two parts, the genus name and the species name. The system was first devised by the Swedish botanist Linnaeus in 1753.

Seed The organ of propagation of flowering plants. Seeds are not immortal, and it is not worth saving left-over seeds of vegetables and flowers for the following year; the percentage that will germinate decreases markedly.

Seed head A general term for a dry, inedible fruit that contains seeds.

Seed leaf The leaves contained in the seed which are the first to appear when a seedling germinates; they are different from those that follow. Plants are classified according to whether there are one or two.

Self sow, self seed A plant's habit of shedding seeds around itself which germinate without the gardener's assistance.

Sepal One of the parts of the calyx, usually green, leaf like and sometimes coloured and showy, as in hellebores and clematis. In many one-seed-leaf plants the sepals are almost indistinguishable from the petals, as in lilies and tulips.

Series (also **strain**) A group of plants raised from seed and thus not genetically identical but sufficiently alike to be treated as a garden variety, for example most cultivars of annuals and vegetables.

Sessile Having no stalk, as the flowers of most camellias for example.

Sheath An organ, usually vaguely leaf like, that encloses another, such as a shoot or cluster of flower buds. The sheath that encloses the buds of an agapanthus is an example.

Shoot Any aerial part of a plant that bears leaves.

Shrub A plant with several permanent woody stems that arise from ground level. A tree has only one, but in gardening the distinction is not quite clear cut—many plants such as the larger cotoneasters or bottlebrushes can be treated equally well as large shrubs or small, multi-stemmed trees.

Spadix A fleshy flower stalk which bears many tiny flowers—a speciality of the arum family.

Species A population of wild plants which are sufficiently alike to carry the same name, and which will freely breed with one another to give rise to offspring like themselves. The honour of naming a species goes to the scientist who discovers or describes it.

Sphagnum A type of rather luxuriant growing moss, normally an inhabitant of boggy ground and much used when dried as an ingredient in potting mixes, especially for orchids. Live plants often grow from spores in the dried material, and are welcomed by orchid growers as a sign that conditions are right.

Spike A type of inflorescence where the flowers are borne on a long, usually upright stem. Unlike a raceme, a spike has no separate flower stalks, as in gladioli.

Spikelet The basic unit of the flowers of grasses, consisting of one or more petal-less flowers and an accompanying bract or two.

Spore The equivalent of a seed in non-flowering plants such as ferns and fungi. Much tinier than seeds, they are produced in great numbers and blow about on the wind.

Spreading A plant which grows much wider than it does tall, perhaps with mainly horizontal branches, perhaps by rooting in the ground and making an ever-expanding clump.

Spur A hollow projection from a petal, often containing nectar; the short flowering shoots on such plants as apples, pears or hoyas, which normally continue to flower and fruit for several years.

Stalk, stem The two terms are almost interchangeable, but in horticulture a stem usually has leaves growing from its sides while a stalk does not.

Standard The big petal that stands up at the back of a pea flower; a tree or shrub with a single, rather tall stem before the branches begin. Many trees grow thus naturally; shrubs like roses or fuchsias have to be trained to the form artificially. A half-standard has a shorter stem than usual.

Sterile Incapable of bearing seeds or pollen or both (flowers) or spores (the fronds of ferns).

A plant may produce perfectly normal flowers but not mature fertile seed due to some aberration in its genetic make-up, something which often occurs in hybrids; or the reproductive parts of the flower may have been transformed into the extra petals of a double flower.

Stigma The business part of a carpel, where the pollen lands and is captured.

Stipule Leafy outgrowths that grow at the base of a leaf stalk, as in roses, and on the leaves of sucker shoots.

Stratify A technique used to break the dormancy of seeds of such plants as roses and apples, which need a period of cold before they can germinate. In its simplest form, it involves bundling them up in damp sphagnum moss and putting them in a refrigerator for a few weeks.

Striate (of leaves) Ridged or fluted down the length, as in *Sisyrinchium striatum*.

Sub-shrub A perennial with more or less permanent but not woody stems, such as geraniums or *Phlomis fruticosa*.

Subspecies A group of plants within a species, different from the norm but not sufficiently so to rank them as a species in their own right.

Succulent A plant which has evolved swollen water-filled organs, either stems or leaves, which help it to survive in arid climates. Cacti are the extreme example, but other plants show succulence to a lesser degree, as most orchids do in their pseudo-bulbs.

Sucker A shoot or stem that arises from the roots of a tree or shrub or, undesirably, from the understock of a grafted specimen.

Synonym (usually abbreviated to 'syn.') A scientific name which, though no longer valid, still lingers in use, for example *Cyrtostachys renda* syn. *C. lakka*.

Taproot The main root of a plant, which plunges straight down to anchor it; the swollen taproots of carrots are the most familiar. Most trees have them too, and resent their being damaged.

Tendril A string-like structure which some climbing plants wrap around a branch or trellis to support themselves. Peas have them, as do grapes.

Terminal (of inflorescences and flowers) Appearing at the end of a shoot, as with roses, marigolds and poinsettias.

Terrestrial (of orchids) Growing in the ground, the way most plants do, rather than perched in trees.

Throat The inside part of a trumpet- or tube-shaped flower, often carrying, as in foxgloves and gloxinias, a different pattern or colour to guide insects.

Tooth, teeth The serrations on the edges of a leaf or leaflet, as in rose leaves.

Topiary The art of clipping suitable trees or shrubs such as yew, privet or box into artificial shapes, such as pyramids, globes, peacocks, etc.

Tree A woody plant, often very tall and large but not always, with only one main stem and very rarely more. See also *Shrub*.

Tri- In compound words, indicating three, as trifoliate, tripinnate, etc.

Tuber A fat, starchy underground organ designed to store food for a plant during its dormancy. Many tubers, such as those of the potato, provide food for humans too.

Umbel A type of inflorescence where several flower stalks arise from one point, as in onions, agapanthus and parsley.

Upright A growth habit whereby main branches grow more or less vertically.

Variegated Variegated plants have patterns of other colours as well as green on their leaves, and usually grow less strongly than their plain leaved counterparts as they have less chlorophyll. They are usually the result of cultivation and are sometimes caused by viruses though some species, notably *Coleus blumei*, are variegated naturally.

Variety Strictly speaking, a group of plants arising in the wild which though not sufficiently different from the norm of their species to be of great interest to botanists (they may only differ in flower colour, for instance) are different enough to be of interest to gardeners. A variety is designated as, for instance, *Acacia longifolia* var. *sophorae*, the var. being short for *varietas*. Varieties created by gardeners are supposed to be called cultivars and not given Latin names.

Ventral Situated on the front of an organ.

Virus A disease in plants which is incurable and may be fatal. However, some viruses are relatively benign, such as the one that makes tulips 'break' into stripes.

Whorl Usually of leaves, an arrangement where three or more arise at the same node, as in rhododendrons. Flowers can grow in whorls around the stalk also, as in *Primula malacoides*.

Wood, woody A stem which may not be big enough to use as timber but which contains hardened cells and is more or less permanent. It is characteristic of trees and shrubs, but some climbers, such as the grape, are also woody.

General Index

Index to Plants